THE WORKS
OF
ROBERT INGERSOLL

Complete in
Six Omnibus Editions

No 3

Consisting of

Volume Five

"There can be but little liberty on earth
while men worship a tyrant in heaven."

Volume Six

"Arguments cannot be answered with insults.
Kindness is strength; anger blows out the lamp of the mind. In the
examination of a great and important question, everyone should be
serene, slow-pulsed and calm."

This Edition published by Gannet games, 2017.
ISBN 13:   978 - 1983438462
ISBN 10:   1983438464

CONTENTS

VOLUME FIVE

VOLUME SIX

VOLUME FIVE

Robert Ingersoll, 1877

PREFACE

Several people, having read the sermons of Mr. Talmage in which he reviews some of my lectures, have advised me not to pay the slightest attention to the Brooklyn divine. They think that no new arguments have been brought forward, and they have even gone so far as to say that some of the best of the old ones have been left out.

After thinking the matter over, I became satisfied that my friends were mistaken, that they had been carried away by the general current of modern thought, and were not in a frame of mind to feel the force of the arguments of Mr. Talmage, or to clearly see the candor that characterizes his utterances.

At the first reading, the logic of these sermons does not impress you. The style is of a character calculated to throw the searcher after facts and arguments off his guard. The imagination of the preacher is so lurid; he is so free from the ordinary forms of expression; his statements are so much stranger than truth, and his conclusions so utterly independent of his premises, that the reader is too astonished to be convinced. Not until I had read with great care the six discourses delivered for my benefit had I any clear and well-defined idea of the logical force of Mr. Talmage. I had but little conception of his candor, was almost totally ignorant of his power to render the simple complex and the plain obscure by the mutilation of metaphor and the incoherence of inspired declamation. Neither did I know the generous accuracy with which he states the position of an opponent, and the fairness he exhibits in a religious discussion.

He has without doubt studied the Bible as closely and critically as he has the works of Buckle and Darwin, and he seems to have paid as much attention to scientific subjects as most theologians. His theory of light and his views upon geology are strikingly original, and his astronomical theories are certainly as profound as practical. If his statements can be relied upon, he has successfully refuted the teachings of Humboldt and Haeckel, and exploded the blunders of Spencer and Tyndall. Besides all this, he has the courage of his convictions—he does not quail before a fact, and he does not strike his colors even to a demonstration. He cares nothing for human experience. He cannot be put down with statistics, nor driven from his position by the certainties of science. He cares neither for the persistence of force, nor the indestructibility of matter.

He believes in the Bible, and he has the bravery to defend his belief. In this, he proudly stands almost alone. He knows that the salvation of the world depends upon a belief in his creed. He knows that what are called "the sciences" are of no importance in the other world. He clearly sees that it is better to live and die ignorant here, if you can wear a crown of glory hereafter. He knows it is useless to be perfectly familiar with all the sciences in this world, and then in the next "lift up your eyes, being in torment." He knows, too, that God will not punish any man for denying

1

a fact in science. A man can deny the rotundity of the earth, the attraction of gravitation, the form of the earths orbit, or the nebular hypothesis, with perfect impunity. He is not bound to be correct upon any philosophical subject. He is at liberty to deny and ridicule the rule of three, conic sections, and even the multiplication table. God permits every human being to be mistaken upon every subject but one. No man can lose his soul by denying physical facts. Jehovah does not take the slightest pride in his geology, or in his astronomy, or in mathematics, or in any school of philosophy—he is jealous only of his reputation as the author of the Bible. You may deny everything else in the universe except that book. This being so, Mr. Talmage takes the safe side, and insists that the Bible is inspired. He knows that at the day of judgment, not a scientific question will be asked. He knows that the Haeckels and Huxleys will, on that terrible day, regret that they ever learned to read. He knows that there is no "saving grace" in any department of human knowledge; that mathematics and all the exact sciences and all the philosophies will be worse than useless. He knows that inventors, discoverers, thinkers and investigators, have no claim upon the mercy of Jehovah; that the educated will envy the ignorant, and that the writers and thinkers will curse their books.

He knows that man cannot be saved through what he knows—but only by means of what he believes. Theology is not a science. If it were, God would forgive his children for being mistaken about it. If it could be proved like geology, or astronomy, there would be no merit in believing it. From a belief in the Bible, Mr. Talmage is not to be driven by uninspired evidence. He knows that his logic is liable to lead him astray, and that his reason cannot be depended upon. He believes that scientific men are no authority in matters concerning which nothing can be known, and he does not wish to put his soul in peril, by examining by the light of reason, the evidences of the supernatural.

He is perfectly consistent with his creed. What happens to us here is of no consequence compared with eternal joy or pain. The ambitions, honors, glories and triumphs of this world, compared with eternal things, are less than naught.

Better a cross here and a crown there, than a feast here and a fire there.

Lazarus was far more fortunate than Dives. The purple and fine linen of this short life are as nothing compared with the robes of the redeemed.

Mr. Talmage knows that philosophy is unsafe—that the sciences are sirens luring souls to eternal wreck. He knows that the deluded searchers after facts are planting thorns in their own pillows—that the geologists are digging pits for themselves, and that the astronomers are robbing their souls of the heaven they explore. He knows that thought, capacity, and intellectual courage are dangerous, and this belief gives him a feeling of personal security.

The Bible is adapted to the world as it is. Most people are ignorant, and but few have the capacity to comprehend philosophical and scientific subjects, and if salvation depended upon understanding even one of the sciences, nearly everybody would be lost. Mr. Talmage sees that it was exceedingly merciful in God to base salvation on belief instead of on brain. Millions can believe, while only a few can understand. Even the effort to understand is a kind of treason born of pride and ingratitude. This being so, it is far safer, far better, to be credulous than critical. You are offered an infinite reward for believing the Bible. If you examine it you may find it impossible for you to believe it. Consequently, examination is dangerous. Mr. Talmage knows that it is not necessary to understand the Bible in order to believe it. You must believe it first. Then, if on reading it you find anything that appears false, absurd, or impossible, you may be sure that it is only an appearance, and that the real fault is in yourself. It is certain that persons wholly incapable of reasoning are absolutely safe, and that to be born brainless is to be saved in advance.

Mr. Talmage takes the ground,—and certainly from his point of view nothing can be more reasonable—that thought should be avoided, after one has "experienced religion" and has been the subject of "regeneration." Every sinner should listen to sermons, read religious books, and keep thinking, until he becomes a Christian. Then he should stop. After that, thinking is not the road to heaven. The real point and the real difficulty is to stop thinking just at the right time. Young Christians, who have no idea of what they are doing, often go on thinking after joining the church, and in this way heresy is born, and heresy is often the father of infidelity. If Christians would follow the advice and example of Mr. Talmage all disagreements about doctrine would be avoided. In this way the church could secure absolute intellectual peace and all the disputes, heart-burnings, jealousies and hatreds born of thought, discussion and reasoning, would be impossible.

In the estimation of Mr. Talmage, the man who doubts and examines is not fit for the society of angels. There are no disputes, no discussions in heaven. The angels do not think; they believe, they enjoy. The highest form of religion is repression. We should conquer the passions and destroy desire. We should control the mind and stop thinking. In this way we "offer ourselves a "living sacrifice, holy, acceptable unto God." When desire dies, when thought ceases, we shall be pure.—This is heaven.

Robert G. Ingersoll.

Washington, D. C, April; 1882.

3

INGERSOLL'S
INTERVIEWS ON TALMAGE.

Polonius. My lord, I will use them according to their desert.
Hamlet. God's bodikins, man, much better: use every man after his desert, and who should 'scape whipping? Use them after your own honor and dignity: the less they deserve, the more merit is in your bounty.

Question. Have you read the sermon of Mr. Talmage, in which he exposes your misrepresentations?
Answer. I have read such reports as appeared in some of the New York papers.

Question. What do you think of what he has to say?
Answer. Some time ago I gave it as my opinion of Mr. Talmage that, while he was a man of most excellent judgment, he was somewhat deficient in imagination. I find that he has the disease that seems to afflict most theologians, and that is, a kind of intellectual toadyism, that uses the names of supposed great men instead of arguments. It is perfectly astonishing to the average preacher that any one should have the temerity to differ, on the subject of theology, with Andrew Jackson, Daniel Webster, and other gentlemen eminent for piety during their lives, but who, as a rule, expressed their theological opinions a few minutes before dissolution. These ministers are perfectly delighted to have some great politician, some judge, soldier, or president, certify to the truth of the Bible and to the moral character of Jesus Christ. Mr. Talmage insists that if a witness is false in one particular, his entire testimony must be thrown away. Daniel Webster was in favor of the Fugitive Slave Law, and thought it the duty of the North to capture the poor slave-mother. He was willing to stand between a human being and his freedom. He was willing to assist in compelling persons to work without any pay except such marks of the lash as they might receive. Yet this man is brought forward as a witness for the truth of the gospel. If he was false in his testimony as to liberty, what is his affidavit worth as to the value of Christianity? Andrew Jackson was a brave man, a good general, a patriot second to none, an excellent judge of horses, and a brave duelist. I admit that in his old age he relied considerably upon the atonement. I think Jackson was really a very great man, and probably no President impressed himself more deeply upon the American people than the hero of New Orleans, but as a theologian he was, in my judgment, a most decided failure, and his opinion as to the authenticity of the Scriptures is of no earthly value. It was a subject upon which he knew probably as little as Mr. Talmage does about modern infidelity. Thousands of people will quote Jackson in favor of

5

religion, about which he knew nothing, and yet have no confidence in his political opinions, although he devoted the best part of his life to politics.

No man should quote the words of another, in place of an argument, unless he is willing to accept all the opinions of that man. Lord Bacon denied the Copernican system of astronomy, and, according to Mr. Talmage, having made that mistake, his opinions upon other subjects are equally worthless. Mr. Wesley believed in ghosts, witches, and personal devils, yet upon many subjects I have no doubt his opinions were correct. The truth is, that nearly everybody is right about some things and wrong about most things; and if a man's testimony is not to be taken until he is right on every subject, witnesses will be extremely scarce.

Personally, I care nothing about names. It makes no difference to me what the supposed great men of the past have said, except as what they have said contains an argument; and that argument is worth to me the force it naturally has upon my mind. Christians forget that in the realm of reason there are no serfs and no monarchs. When you submit to an argument, you do not submit to the man who made it. Christianity demands a certain obedience, a certain blind, unreasoning faith, and parades before the eyes of the ignorant, with great pomp and pride, the names of kings, soldiers, and statesmen who have admitted the truth of the Bible. Mr. Talmage introduces as a witness the Rev. Theodore Parker. This same Theodore Parker denounced the Presbyterian creed as the most infamous of all creeds, and said that the worst heathen god, wearing a necklace of live snakes, was a representation of mercy when compared with the God of John Calvin. Now, if this witness is false in any particular, of course he cannot be believed, according to Mr. Talmage, upon any subject, and yet Mr. Talmage introduces him upon the stand as a good witness.

Although I care but little for names, still I will suggest that, in all probability, Humboldt knew more upon this subject than all the pastors in the world. I certainly would have as much confidence in the opinion of Goethe as in that of William H. Seward; and as between Seward and Lincoln, I should take Lincoln; and when you come to Presidents, for my part, if I were compelled to pin my faith on the sleeve of anybody, I should take Jefferson's coat in preference to Jackson's. I believe that Haeckel is, to say the least, the equal of any theologian we have in this country, and the late John W. Draper certainly knew as much upon these great questions as the average parson. I believe that Darwin has investigated some of these things, that Tyndall and Huxley have turned their minds somewhat in the same direction, that Helmholtz has a few opinions, and that, in fact, thousands of able, intelligent and honest men differ almost entirely with Webster and Jackson.

So far as I am concerned, I think more of reasons than of reputations, more of principles than of persons, more of nature than of names, more of facts, than of faiths.

It is the same with books as with persons. Probably there is not a book in the world entirely destitute of truth, and not one entirely exempt from error. The Bible is like other books. There are mistakes in it, side by side with truths,—passages inculcating murder, and others exalting mercy; laws devilish and tyrannical, and others filled with wisdom and justice. It is foolish to say that if you accept a part, you must accept the whole. You must accept that which commends itself to your heart and brain. There never was a doctrine that a witness, or a book, should be thrown entirely away, because false in one particular. If in any particular the book, or the man, tells the truth, to that extent the truth should be accepted.

Truth is made no worse by the one who tells it, and a lie gets no real benefit from the reputation of its author.

Question. What do you think of the statement that a general belief in your teachings would fill all the penitentiaries, and that in twenty years there would be a hell in this world worse than the one expected in the other?

Answer. My creed is this:

1. Happiness is the only good.

2. The way to be happy, is to make others happy. Other things being equal, that man is happiest who is nearest just—who is truthful, merciful and intelligent—in other words, the one who lives in accordance with the conditions of life.

3. The time to be happy is now, and the place to be happy, is here.

4. Reason is the lamp of the mind—the only torch of progress; and instead of blowing that out and depending upon darkness and dogma, it is far better to increase that sacred light.

5. Every man should be the intellectual proprietor of himself, honest with himself, and intellectually hospitable; and upon every brain reason should be enthroned as king.

6. Every man must bear the consequences, at least of his own actions. If he puts his hands in the fire, his hands must smart, and not the hands of another. In other words: each man must eat the fruit of the tree he plants.

I can not conceive that the teaching of these doctrines would fill penitentiaries, or crowd the gallows. The doctrine of forgiveness—the idea that somebody else can suffer in place of the guilty—the notion that just at the last the whole account can be settled—these ideas, doctrines, and notions are calculated to fill penitentiaries. Nothing breeds extravagance like the credit system.

Most criminals of the present day are orthodox believers, and the gallows seems to be the last round of the ladder reaching from earth to heaven. The Rev. Dr. Sunderland, of this city, in his sermon on the assassination of Garfield, takes the ground that God permitted the murder for the purpose of opening the eyes of the people to the evil effects of infidelity. According to this minister, God, in order to show his hatred of infidelity, "inspired," or allowed, one Christian to assassinate another.

Religion and morality do not necessarily go together. Mr. Talmage will insist to-day that morality is not sufficient to save any man from eternal punishment. As a matter of fact, religion has often been the enemy of morality. The moralist has been denounced by the theologians. He

7

sustains the same relation to Christianity that the moderate drinker does to the total abstinence society. The total-abstinence people say that the example of the moderate drinker is far worse upon the young than that of the drunkard—that the drunkard is a warning, while the moderate drinker is a perpetual temptation. So Christians say of moralists. According to them, the moralist sets a worse example than the criminal. The moralist not only insists that a man can be a good citizen, a kind husband, an affectionate father, without religion, but demonstrates the truth of his doctrine by his own life; whereas the criminal admits that in and of himself he is nothing, and can do nothing, but that he needs assistance from the church and its ministers.

The worst criminals of the modern world have been Christians—I mean by that, believers in Christianity—and the most monstrous crimes of the modern world have been committed by the most zealous believers. There is nothing in orthodox religion, apart from the morality it teaches, to prevent the commission of crime. On the other hand, the perpetual proffer of forgiveness is a direct premium upon what Christians are pleased to call the commission of sin.

Christianity has produced no greater character than Epictetus, no greater sovereign than Marcus Aurelius. The wickedness of the past was a good deal like that of the present. As a rule, kings have been wicked in direct proportion to their power—their power having been lessened, their crimes have decreased. As a matter of fact, paganism, of itself, did not produce any great men; neither has Christianity. Millions of influences determine individual character, and the religion of the country in which a man happens to be born may determine many of his opinions, without influencing, to any great extent, his real character.

There have been brave, honest, and intelligent men in and out of every church.

Question. Mr. Talmage says that you insist that, according to the Bible, the universe was made out of nothing, and he denounces your statement as a gross misrepresentation. What have you stated upon that subject?

Answer. What I said was substantially this: We are told in the first chapter of Genesis, that "in the beginning God created the heaven and the earth." If this means anything, it means that God produced—caused to exist, called into being—the heaven and the earth. It will not do to say that God formed the heaven and the earth of previously existing matter. Moses conveys, and intended to convey, the idea that the matter of which the universe is composed was created.

This has always been my position. I did not suppose that nothing was used as the raw material; but if the Mosaic account means anything, it means that whereas there was nothing, God caused something to exist—created what we know as matter. I can not conceive of something being made, created, without anything to make anything with. I have no more confidence in fiat worlds than I have in fiat money. Mr. Talmage tells us that God did not make the universe out of nothing, but out of "omnipotence." Exactly how God changed "omnipotence" into matter is not stated. If there was nothing in the universe, omnipotence could do

8

you no good. The weakest man in the world can lift as much nothing as God.

Mr. Talmage seems to think that to create something from nothing is simply a question of strength—that it requires infinite muscle—that it is only a question of biceps. Of course, omnipotence is an attribute, not an entity, not a raw material; and the idea that something can be made out of omnipotence—using that as the raw material—is infinitely absurd. It would have been equally logical to say that God made the universe out of his omniscience, or his omnipresence, or his unchangeableness, or out of his honesty, his holiness, or his incapacity to do evil. I confess my utter inability to understand, or even to suspect, what the reverend gentleman means, when he says that God created the universe out of his "omnipotence."

I admit that the Bible does not tell when God created the universe. It is simply said that he did this "in the beginning." We are left, however, to infer that "the beginning" was Monday morning, and that on the first Monday God created the matter in an exceedingly chaotic state; that on Tuesday he made a firmament to divide the waters from the waters; that on Wednesday he gathered the waters together in seas and allowed the dry land to appear. We are also told that on that day the earth brought forth grass and herb yielding seed after his kind, and the tree yielding fruit, whose seed was in itself, after his kind. This was before the creation of the sun, but Mr. Talmage takes the ground that there are many other sources of light; that "there may have been volcanoes in active operation on other planets." I have my doubts, however, about the light of volcanoes being sufficient to produce or sustain vegetable life, and think it a little doubtful about trees growing only by "volcanic glare." Neither do I think one could depend upon "three thousand miles of liquid granite" for the production of grass and trees, nor upon "light that rocks might emit in the process of crystallization." I doubt whether trees would succeed simply with the assistance of the "Aurora Borealis or the Aurora Australis." There are other sources of light, not mentioned by Mr. Talmage—lightning-bugs, phosphorescent beetles, and fox-fire. I should think that it would be humiliating, in this age, for an orthodox preacher to insist that vegetation could exist upon this planet without the light of the sun—that trees could grow, blossom and bear fruit, having no light but the flames of volcanoes, or that emitted by liquid granite, or thrown off by the crystallization of rocks.

There is another thing, also, that should not be forgotten, and that is, that there is an even balance forever kept between the totals of animal and vegetable life—that certain forms of animal life go with certain forms of vegetable life. Mr. Haeckel has shown that "in the first epoch, algae and skull-less vertebrates were found together; in the second, ferns and fishes; in the third, pines and reptiles; in the fourth, foliaceous forests and mammals." Vegetable and animal life sustain a necessary relation; they exist together; they act and interact, and each depends upon the other. The real point of difference between Mr. Talmage and myself is this: He says that God made the universe out of his "omnipotence," and I say that, although I know nothing whatever upon the subject, my opinion is, that the universe has existed from eternity—that it

9

continually changes in form, but that it never was created or called into being by any power. I think that all that is, is all the God there is.

Question. Mr. Talmage charges you with having misrepresented the Bible story of the deluge. Has he correctly stated your position?

Answer. Mr. Talmage takes the ground that the flood was only partial, and was, after all, not much of a flood. The Bible tells us that God said he would "destroy all flesh wherein is the breath of life from under heaven, and that everything that is in the earth shall die;" that God also said: "I will destroy man, whom I have created, from the face of the earth; both man and beast and the creeping thing and the fowls of the air, and every living substance that I have made will I destroy from off the face of the earth."

I did not suppose that there was any miracle in the Bible larger than the credulity of Mr. Talmage. The flood story, however, seems to be a little more than he can bear. He is like the witness who stated that he had read *Gulliver's Travels,* the *Stories of Munchausen,* and the *Flying Wife,* including *Robinson Crusoe,* and believed them all; but that Wirt's *Life of Patrick Henry* was a little more than he could stand. It is strange that a man who believes that God created the universe out of "omnipotence" should believe that he had not enough omnipotence left to drown a world the size of this. Mr. Talmage seeks to make the story of the flood reasonable. The moment it is reasonable, it ceases to be miraculous. Certainly God cannot afford to reward a man with eternal joy for believing a reasonable story. Faith is only necessary when the story is unreasonable, and if the flood only gets small enough, I can believe it myself. I ask for evidence, and Mr. Talmage seeks to make the story so little that it can be believed without evidence. He tells us that it was a kind of "local option" flood—a little wet for that part of the country.

Why was it necessary to save the birds? They certainly could have gotten out of the way of a real small flood. Of the birds, Noah took fourteen of each species. He was commanded to take of the fowls of the air by sevens—seven of each sex—and, as there are at least 12,500 species, Noah collected an aviary of about 175,000 birds, provided the flood was general. If it was local, there are no means of determining the number. But why, if the flood was local, should he have taken any of the fowls of the air into his ark?

All they had to do was to fly away, or "roost high;" and it would have been just as easy for God to have implanted in them, for the moment, the instinct of getting out of the way as the instinct of hunting the ark. It would have been quite a saving of room and provisions, and would have materially lessened the labor and anxiety of Noah and his sons. Besides, if it had been a partial flood, and great enough to cover the highest mountains in that country, the highest mountain being about seventeen thousand feet, the flood would have been covered with a sheet of ice several thousand feet in thickness. If a column of water could have been thrown seventeen thousand feet high and kept stationary, several thousand feet of the upper end would have frozen. If, however, the deluge was general, then the atmosphere would have been forced out the same on all sides, and the climate remained substantially normal.

Nothing can be more absurd than to attempt to explain the flood by calling it partial.

Mr. Talmage also says that the window ran clear round the ark, and that if I had only known as much Hebrew as a man could put on his little finger, I would have known that the window went clear round. To this I reply that, if his position is correct, then the original translators of King James' edition did not know as much Hebrew as they could have put on their little fingers; and yet I am obliged to believe their translation or be eternally damned. If the window went clear round, the inspired writer should have said so, and the learned translators should have given us the truth. No one pretends that there was more than one door, and yet the same language is used about the door, except this—that the exact size of the window is given, and the only peculiarity mentioned as to the door is that it shut from the outside. For any one to see that Mr. Talmage is wrong on the window question, it is only necessary to read the story of the deluge.

Mr. Talmage also endeavors to decrease the depth of the flood. If the flood did not cover the highest hills, many people might have been saved. He also insists that all the water did not come from the rains, but that "the fountains of the great deep were broken "up." What are "the fountains of the great deep"? How would their being "broken up" increase the depth of the water? He seems to imagine that these "fountains" were in some way imprisoned—anxious to get to the surface, and that, at that time, an opportunity was given for water to run up hill, or in some mysterious way to rise above its level. According to the account, the ark was at the mercy of the waves for at least seven months. If this flood was only partial, it seems a little curious that the water did not seek its level in less than seven months. With anything like a fair chance, by that time most of it would have found its way to the sea again.

There is in the literature of ignorance no more perfectly absurd and cruel story than that of the deluge.

I am very sorry that Mr. Talmage should disagree with some of the great commentators. Dr. Scott tells us that, in all probability, the angels assisted in getting the animals into the ark. Dr. Henry insists that the waters in the bowels of the earth, at God's command, sprung up and flooded the earth. Dr. Clark tells us that it would have been much easier for God to have destroyed all the people and made some new ones, but that he did not want to waste anything. Dr. Henry also tells us that the lions, while in the ark, ate straw like oxen. Nothing could be more amusing than to see a few lions eating good, dry straw. This commentator assures us that the waters rose so high that the loftiest mountains were overflowed fifteen cubits, so that salvation was not hoped for from any hills or mountains. He tells us that some of the people got on top of the ark, and hoped to shift for themselves, but that, in all probability, they were washed off by the rain. When we consider that the rain must have fallen at the rate of about eight hundred feet a day, I am inclined to think that they were washed off.

Mr. Talmage has clearly misrepresented the Bible. He is not prepared to believe the story as it is told. The seeds of infidelity seem to be

11

germinating in his mind. His position no doubt will be a great relief to most of his hearers. After this, their credulity will not be strained. They can say that there was probably quite a storm, some rain, to an extent that rendered it necessary for Noah and his family—his dogs, cats, and chickens—to get in a boat. This would not be unreasonable. The same thing happens almost every year on the shores of great rivers, and consequently the story of the flood is an exceedingly reasonable one.

Mr. Talmage also endeavors to account for the miraculous collection of the animals in the ark by the universal instinct to get out of the rain. There are at least two objections to this: 1. The animals went into the ark before the rain commenced; 2. I have never noticed any great desire on the part of ducks, geese, and loons to get out of the water. Mr. Talmage must have been misled by a line from an old nursery book that says: "And the little fishes got under the bridge to keep out of the rain." He tells us that Noah described what he saw. He is the first theologian who claims that Genesis was written by Noah, or that Noah wrote any account of the flood. Most Christians insist that the account of the flood was written by Moses, and that he was inspired to write it. Of course, it will not do for me to say that Mr. Talmage has misrepresented the facts.

Question. You are also charged with misrepresentation in your statement as to where the ark at last rested. It is claimed by Mr. Talmage that there is nothing in the Bible to show that the ark rested on the highest mountains.

Answer. Of course I have no knowledge as to where the ark really came to anchor, but after it struck bottom, we are told that a dove was sent out, and that the dove found no place whereon to rest her foot. If the ark touched ground in the low country, surely the mountains were out of water, and an ordinary mountain furnishes, as a rule, space enough for a dove's foot. We must infer that the ark rested on the only land then above water, or near enough above water to strike the keel of Noah's boat. Mount Ararat is about seventeen thousand feet high; so I take it that the top of that mountain was where Noah ran aground— otherwise, the account means nothing.

Here Mr. Talmage again shows his tendency to belittle the miracles of the Bible. I am astonished that he should doubt the power of God to keep an ark on a mountain seventeen thousand feet high. He could have changed the climate for that occasion. He could have made all the rocks and glaciers produce wheat and corn in abundance. Certainly God, who could overwhelm a world with a flood, had the power to change every law and fact in nature.

I am surprised that Mr. Talmage is not willing to believe the story as it is told. What right has he to question the statements of an inspired writer? Why should he set up his judgment against the Websters and Jacksons? Is it not infinitely impudent in him to contrast his penny-dip with the sun of inspiration? What right has he to any opinion upon the subject? He must take the Bible as it reads. He should remember that the greater the miracle the greater should be his faith.

Question. You do not seem to have any great opinion of the chemical, geological, and agricultural views expressed by Mr. Talmage?

Answer. You must remember that Mr. Talmage has a certain thing to defend. He takes the Bible as actually true, and with the Bible as his standard, he compares and measures all sciences. He does not study geology to find whether the Mosaic account is true, but he reads the Mosaic account for the purpose of showing that geology can not be depended upon. His idea that "one day is as a thousand years with God," and that therefore the "days" mentioned in the Mosaic account are not days of twenty-four hours, but long periods, is contradicted by the Bible itself. The great reason given for keeping the Sabbath day is, that "God rested on the seventh day and was refreshed." Now, it does not say that he rested on the "seventh period," or the "seventh good—while," or the "seventh long-time," but on the "seventh day." In imitation of this example we are also to rest—not on the seventh good-while, but on the seventh day. Nothing delights the average minister more than to find that a passage of Scripture is capable of several interpretations. Nothing in the inspired book is so dangerous as accuracy. If the holy writer uses general terms, an ingenious theologian can harmonize a seemingly preposterous statement with the most obdurate fact. An "inspired" book should contain neither statistics nor dates—as few names as possible, and not one word about geology or astronomy. Mr. Talmage is doing the best he can to uphold the fables of the Jews. They are the foundation of his faith. He believes in the water of the past and the fire of the future—in the God of flood and flame—the eternal torturer of his helpless children.

It is exceedingly unfortunate that Mr. Talmage does not appreciate the importance of good manners, that he does not rightly estimate the convincing power of kindness and good nature. It is unfortunate that a Christian, believing in universal forgiveness, should exhibit so much of the spirit of detraction, that he should run so easily and naturally into epithets, and that he should mistake vituperation for logic. Thousands of people, knowing but little of the mysteries of Christianity—never having studied theology,—may become prejudiced against the church, and doubt the divine origin of a religion whose defenders seem to rely, at least to a great degree, upon malignant personalities. Mr. Talmage should remember that in a discussion of this kind, he is supposed to represent a being of infinite wisdom and goodness. Surely, the representative of the infinite can afford to be candid, can afford to be kind. When he contemplates the condition of a fellow-being destitute of religion, a fellow-being now traveling the thorny path to eternal fire, he should be filled with pity instead of hate. Instead of deforming his mouth with scorn, his eyes should be filled with tears. He should take into consideration the vast difference between an infidel and a minister of the gospel,—knowing, as he does, that a crown of glory has been prepared for the minister, and that flames are waiting for the soul of the unbeliever. He should bear with philosophic fortitude the apparent success of the skeptic, for a few days in this brief life, since he knows that in a little while the question will be eternally settled in his favor, and that the humiliation of a day is as nothing compared with the victory of eternity. In this world, the skeptic appears to have the best of the argument; logic seems to be on the side of blasphemy; common sense apparently goes hand in hand with infidelity, and the few things we are absolutely certain of, seem inconsistent with the Christian creeds. This, however, as Mr. Talmage well knows, is but apparent. God has arranged the world in this way for the purpose of testing the Christian's faith. Beyond all these facts, beyond logic, beyond reason, Mr. Talmage, by the light of faith, clearly sees the eternal truth. This clearness of vision should give him the serenity of candor and the kindness born of absolute knowledge. He, being a child of the light, should not expect the perfect from the children of darkness. He should not judge Humboldt and Wesley by the same standard. He should remember that Wesley was especially set apart and illuminated by divine wisdom, while Humboldt was left to grope in the shadows of nature. He should also remember that ministers are not like other people. They have been "called." They have been "chosen" by infinite wisdom. They have been "set apart," and they have bread to eat that we know not of. While other people are forced to pursue the difficult paths of investigation, they fly with the wings of faith.

Mr. Talmage is perfectly aware of the advantages he enjoys, and yet he deems it dangerous to be fair. This, in my judgment, is his mistake. If he cannot easily point out the absurdities and contradictions in infidel lectures, surely God would never have selected him for that task. We cannot believe that imperfect instruments would be chosen by infinite wisdom. Certain lambs have been entrusted to the care of Mr. Talmage, the shepherd. Certainly God would not select a shepherd unable to cope with an average wolf. Such a shepherd is only the appearance of protection. When the wolf is not there, he is a useless expense, and when the wolf comes, he goes. I cannot believe that God would select a shepherd of that kind. Neither can the shepherd justify his selection by abusing the wolf when out of sight. The fear ought to be on the other side. A divinely appointed shepherd ought to be able to convince his sheep that a wolf is a dangerous animal, and ought to be able to give his reasons. It may be that the shepherd has a certain interest in exaggerating the cruelty and ferocity of the wolf, and even the number of the wolves. Should it turn out that the wolves exist only in the imagination of the shepherd, the sheep might refuse to pay the salary of their protector. It will, however, be hard to calculate the extent to which the sheep will lose confidence in a shepherd who has not even the courage to state the facts about the wolf. But what must be the result when the sheep find that the supposed wolf is, in fact, their friend, and that he is endeavoring to rescue them from the exactions of the pretended shepherd, who creates, by falsehood, the fear on which he lives?

SECOND INTERVIEW.

Por. Why, man, what's the matter? Don't tear your hair.
Sir Hugh. I have been beaten in a discussion, overwhelmed and humiliated.
Por. Why didn't you call your adversary a fool?
Sir Hugh. My God! I forgot it!

Question. I want to ask you a few questions about the second sermon of Mr. Talmage; have you read it, and what do you think of it?

Answer. The text taken by the reverend gentleman is an insult, and was probably intended as such: "The fool hath said in his heart, there is no God." Mr. Talmage seeks to apply this text to any one who denies that the Jehovah of the Jews was and is the infinite and eternal Creator of all. He is perfectly satisfied that any man who differs with him on this question is a "fool," and he has the Christian forbearance and kindness to say so. I presume he is honest in this opinion, and no doubt regards Bruno, Spinoza and Humboldt as driveling imbeciles. He entertains the same opinion of some of the greatest, wisest and best of Greece and Rome.

No man is fitted to reason upon this question who has not the intelligence to see the difficulties in all theories. No man has yet evolved a theory that satisfactorily accounts for all that is. No matter what his opinion may be, he is beset by a thousand difficulties, and innumerable things insist upon an explanation. The best that any man can do is to take that theory which to his mind presents the fewest difficulties. Mr. Talmage has been educated in a certain way—has a brain of a certain quantity, quality and form—and accepts, in spite it may be, of himself, a certain theory. Others, formed differently, having lived under different circumstances, cannot accept the Talmagian view, and thereupon he denounces them as fools. In this he follows the example of David the murderer; of David, who advised one of his children to assassinate another; of David, whose last words were those of hate and crime. Mr. Talmage insists that it takes no especial brain to reason out a "design" in Nature, and in a moment afterward says that "when the world slew Jesus, it showed what it would do with the eternal God, if once it could get its hands on Him." Why should a God of infinite wisdom create people who would gladly murder their Creator? Was there any particular "design" in that? Does the existence of such people conclusively prove the existence of a good Designer? It seems to me—and I take it that my thought is natural, as I have only been born once—that an infinitely wise and good God would naturally create good people, and if he has not, certainly the fault is his. The God of Mr. Talmage knew, when he created Guiteau, that he would assassinate Garfield. Why did he create him? Did he want Garfield assassinated? Will somebody be kind enough to show the "design" in this transaction? Is it possible to see "design" in earthquakes, in volcanoes, in pestilence, in famine, in ruthless and relentless war? Can we find "design" in the fact that every animal lives

15

upon some other—that every drop of every sea is a battlefield where the strong devour the weak? Over the precipice of cruelty rolls a perpetual Niagara of blood. Is there "design" in this? Why should a good God people a world with men capable of burning their fellow-men—and capable of burning the greatest and best? Why does a good God permit these things? It is said of Christ that he was infinitely kind and generous, infinitely merciful, because when on earth he cured the sick, the lame and blind. Has he not as much power now as he had then? If he was and is the God of all worlds, why does he not now give back to the widow her son? Why does he withhold light from the eyes of the blind? And why does one who had the power miraculously to feed thousands, allow millions to die for want of food? Did Christ only have pity when he was part human? Are we indebted for his kindness to the flesh that clothed his spirit? Where is he now? Where has he been through all the centuries of slavery and crime? If this universe was "designed," then all that happens was "designed." If a man constructs an engine, the boiler of which explodes, we say either that he did not know the strength of his materials, or that he was reckless of human life. If an infinite being should construct a weak or imperfect machine, he must be held accountable for all that happens. He cannot be permitted to say that he did not know the strength of the materials. He is directly and absolutely responsible. So, if this world was designed by a being of infinite power and wisdom, he is responsible for the result of that design. My position is this: I do not know. But there are so many objections to the personal-God theory, that it is impossible for me to accept it. I prefer to say that the universe is all the God there is. I prefer to make no being responsible. I prefer to say: If the naked are clothed, man must clothe them; if the hungry are fed, man must feed them. I prefer to rely upon human endeavor, upon human intelligence, upon the heart and brain of man. There is no evidence that God has ever interfered in the affairs of man. The hand of earth is stretched uselessly toward heaven. From the clouds there comes no help. In vain the shipwrecked cry to God. In vain the imprisoned ask for liberty and light—the world moves on, and the heavens are deaf and dumb and blind. The frost freezes, the fire burns, slander smites, the wrong triumphs, the good suffer, and prayer dies upon the lips of faith.

Question. Mr. Talmage charges you with being "the champion blasphemer of America"—what do you understand blasphemy to be?

Answer. Blasphemy is an epithet bestowed by superstition upon common sense. Whoever investigates a religion as he would any department of science, is called a blasphemer. Whoever contradicts a priest, whoever has the impudence to use his own reason, whoever is brave enough to express his honest thought, is a blasphemer in the eyes of the religionist. When a missionary speaks slightingly of the wooden god of a savage, the savage regards him as a blasphemer. To laugh at the pretensions of Mohammed in Constantinople is blasphemy. To say in St. Petersburg that Mohammed was a prophet of God is also blasphemy. There was a time when to acknowledge the divinity of Christ in Jerusalem was blasphemy. To deny his divinity is now blasphemy in

New York. Blasphemy is to a considerable extent a geographical question. It depends not only on what you say, but where you are when you say it. Blasphemy is what the old calls the new,—what last year's leaf says to this year's bud. The founder of every religion was a blasphemer. The Jews so regarded Christ, and the Athenians had the same opinion of Socrates. Catholics have always looked upon Protestants as blasphemers, and Protestants have always held the same generous opinion of Catholics. To deny that Mary is the Mother of God is blasphemy. To say that she is the Mother of God is blasphemy. Some savages think that a dried snakeskin stuffed with leaves is sacred, and he who thinks otherwise is a blasphemer. It was once blasphemy to laugh at Diana, of the Ephesians. Many people think that it is blasphemous to tell your real opinion of the Jewish Jehovah. Others imagine that words can be printed upon paper, and the paper bound into a book covered with sheepskin, and that the book is sacred, and that to question its sacredness is blasphemy. Blasphemy is also a crime against God, but nothing can be more absurd than a crime against God. If God is infinite, you cannot injure him. You cannot commit a crime against any being that you cannot injure. Of course, the infinite cannot be injured. Man is a conditioned being. By changing his conditions, his surroundings, you can injure him; but if God is infinite, he is conditionless. If he is conditionless, he cannot by any possibility be injured. You can neither increase, nor decrease, the well-being of the infinite. Consequently, a crime against God is a demonstrated impossibility. The cry of blasphemy means only that the argument of the blasphemer cannot be answered. The sleight-of-hand performer, when some one tries to raise the curtain behind which he operates, cries "blasphemer!" The priest, finding that he has been attacked by common sense,—by a fact,—resorts to the same cry. Blasphemy is the black flag of theology, and it means: No argument and no quarter! It is an appeal to prejudice, to passions, to ignorance. It is the last resort of a defeated priest. Blasphemy marks the point where argument stops and slander begins. In old times, it was the signal for throwing stones, for gathering fagots and for tearing flesh; now it means falsehood and calumny.

Question. Then you think that there is no such thing as the crime of blasphemy, and that no such offence can be committed?

Answer. Any one who knowingly speaks in favor of injustice is a blasphemer. Whoever wishes to destroy liberty of thought,—the honest expression of ideas,—is a blasphemer. Whoever is willing to malign his neighbor, simply because he differs with him upon a subject about which neither of them knows anything for certain, is a blasphemer. If a crime can be committed against God, he commits it who imputes to God the commission of crime. The man who says that God ordered the assassination of women and babes, that he gave maidens to satisfy the lust of soldiers, that he enslaved his own children,—that man is a blasphemer. In my judgment, it would be far better to deny the existence of God entirely. It seems to me that every man ought to give his honest opinion. No man should suppose that any infinite God requires him to tell as truth that which he knows nothing about.

Mr. Talmage, in order to make a point against infidelity, states from his pulpit that I am in favor of poisoning the minds of children by the circulation of immoral books. The statement is entirely false. He ought to have known that I withdrew from the Liberal League upon the very question whether the law should be repealed or modified. I favored a modification of that law, so that books and papers could not be thrown from the mails simply because they were "infidel."

I was and am in favor of the destruction of every immoral book in the world. I was and am in favor, not only of the law against the circulation of such filth, but want it executed to the letter in every State of this Union. Long before he made that statement, I had introduced a resolution to that effect, and supported the resolution in a speech. Notwithstanding these facts, hundreds of clergymen have made haste to tell the exact opposite of the truth. This they have done in the name of Christianity, under the pretence of pleasing their God. In my judgment, it is far better to tell your honest opinions, even upon the subject of theology, than to knowingly tell a falsehood about a fellow-man. Mr. Talmage may have been ignorant of the truth. He may have been misled by other ministers, and for his benefit I make this explanation. I wanted the laws modified so that bigotry could not interfere with the literature of intelligence; but I did not want, in any way, to shield the writers or publishers of immoral books. Upon this subject I used, at the last meeting of the Liberal League that I attended, the following language:

"But there is a distinction wide as the Mississippi, yes, wider than the Atlantic, wider than all oceans, between the literature of immorality and the literature of free thought. One is a crawling, slimy lizard, and the other an angel with wings of light. Let us draw this distinction. Let us understand ourselves. Do not make the wholesale statement that all these laws ought to be repealed. They ought not to be repealed. Some of them are good, and the law against sending instruments of vice through the mails is good. The law against sending obscene pictures and books is good. The law against sending bogus diplomas through the mails, to allow a lot of ignorant hyenas to prey upon the sick people of the world, is a good law. The law against rascals who are getting up bogus lotteries, and sending their circulars in the mails is a good law. You know, as well as I, that there are certain books not fit to go through the mails. You know that. You know there are certain pictures not fit to be transmitted, not fit to be delivered to any human being. When these books and pictures come into the control of the United States, I say, burn them up! And when any man has been indicted who has been trying to make money by pandering to the lowest passions in the human breast, then I say, prosecute him! let the law take its course."

I can hardly convince myself that when Mr. Talmage made the charge, he was acquainted with the facts. It seems incredible that any man, pretending to be governed by the law of common honesty, could make a charge like this knowing it to be untrue. Under no circumstances, would I charge Mr. Talmage with being an infamous man, unless the evidence was complete and overwhelming. Even then, I should hesitate long before making the charge. The side I take on theological questions does not render a resort to slander or calumny a necessity. If Mr. Talmage is an honorable man, he will take back the statement he has made. Even if there is a God, I hardly think that he will reward one of his children for maligning another; and to one who has told falsehoods about "infidels," that having been his only virtue, I doubt whether he will say: "Well done good and faithful "servant."

Question. What have you to say to the charge that you are endeavoring to "assassinate God," and that you are "far worse than the man who attempts to kill his father, or his mother, or his sister, "or his brother"?

Answer. Well, I think that is about as reasonable as anything he says. No one wishes, so far as I know, to assassinate God. The idea of assassinating an infinite being is of course infinitely absurd. One would think Mr. Talmage had lost his reason! And yet this man stands at the head of the Presbyterian clergy. It is for this reason that I answer him. He is the only Presbyterian minister in the United States, so far as I know, able to draw an audience. He is, without doubt, the leader of that denomination. He is orthodox and conservative. He believes implicitly in the "Five Points" of Calvin, and says nothing simply for the purpose of attracting attention. He believes that God damns a man for his own glory; that he sends babes to hell to establish his mercy, and that he filled the world with disease and crime simply to demonstrate his wisdom. He believes that billions of years before the earth was, God had made up his mind as to the exact number that he would eternally damn, and had counted his saints. This doctrine he calls "glad tidings of great joy." He really believes that every man who is true to himself is waging war against God; that every infidel is a rebel; that every Freethinker is a traitor, and that only those are good subjects who have joined the Presbyterian Church, know the Shorter Catechism by heart, and subscribe liberally toward lifting the mortgage on the Brooklyn Tabernacle. All the rest are endeavoring to assassinate God, plotting the murder of the Holy Ghost, and applauding the Jews for the crucifixion of Christ. If Mr. Talmage is correct in his views as to the power and wisdom of God, I imagine that his enemies at last will be overthrown, that the assassins and murderers will not succeed, and that the Infinite, with Mr. Talmage s assistance, will finally triumph. If there is an infinite God, certainly he ought to have made man grand enough to have and express an opinion of his own. Is it possible that God can be gratified with the applause of moral cowards? Does he seek to enhance his glory by receiving the adulation of cringing slaves? Is God satisfied with the adoration of the frightened?

Question. You notice that Mr. Talmage finds nearly all the inventions of modern times mentioned in the Bible?

Answer. Yes; Mr. Talmage has made an exceedingly important discovery. I admit that I am somewhat amazed at the wisdom of the ancients. This discovery has been made just in the nick of time. Millions of people were losing their respect for the Old Testament. They were beginning to think that there was some discrepancy between the prophecies of Ezekiel and Daniel and the latest developments in physical science. Thousands of preachers were telling their flocks that the Bible is not a scientific book; that Joshua was not an inspired astronomer, that God never enlightened Moses about geology, and that Ezekiel did not understand the entire art of cookery. These admissions caused some young people to suspect that the Bible, after all, was not inspired; that the prophets of antiquity did not know as much as the discoverers of today. The Bible was falling into disrepute. Mr. Talmage has rushed to the rescue. He shows, and shows conclusively as anything can be shown from the Bible, that Job understood all the laws of light thousands of years before Newton lived; that he anticipated the discoveries of Descartes, Huxley and Tyndall; that he was familiar with the telegraph and telephone; that Morse, Bell and Edison simply put his discoveries in successful operation; that Nahum was, in fact, a master-mechanic; that he understood perfectly the modern railway and described it so accurately that Trevethick, Foster and Stephenson had no difficulty in constructing a locomotive. He also has discovered that Job was well acquainted with the trade winds, and understood the mysterious currents, tides and pulses of the sea; that Lieutenant Maury was a plagiarist; that Humboldt was simply a biblical student. He finds that Isaiah and Solomon were far in advance of Galileo, Morse, Meyer and Watt. This is a discovery wholly unexpected to me. If Mr. Talmage is right, I am satisfied the Bible is an inspired book. If it shall turn out that Joshua was superior to Laplace, that Moses knew more about geology than Humboldt, that Job as a scientist was the superior of Kepler, that Isaiah knew more than Copernicus, and that even the minor prophets excelled the inventors and discoverers of our time—then I will admit that infidelity must become speechess forever. Until I read this sermon, I had never even suspected that the inventions of modern times were known to the ancient Jews. I never supposed that Nahum knew the least thing about railroads, or that Job would have known a telegraph if he had seen it. I never supposed that Joshua comprehended the three laws of Kepler. Of course I have not read the Old Testament with as much care as some other people have, and when I did read it, I was not looking for inventions and discoveries. I had been told so often that the Bible was no authority upon scientific questions, that I was lulled into a state of lethargy. What is amazing to me is, that so many men did read it without getting the slightest hint of the smallest invention. To think that the Jews read that book for hundreds and hundreds of years, and yet went to their graves without the slightest notion of astronomy, or geology, of railroads, telegraphs, or steamboats! And then to think that the early fathers made it the study of their lives and died without inventing anything! I am astonished that Mr. Talmage himself does not figure in the records of the Patent Office. I cannot account for this, except upon the supposition that he is too honest to infringe on the patents of the patriarchs. After this, I shall read the Old Testament with more care.

Question. Do you see that Mr. Talmage endeavors to convict you of great ignorance in not knowing that the word translated "rib" should have been translated "side," and that Eve, after all, was not made out of a rib, but out of Adam's side?

Answer. I may have been misled by taking the Bible as it is translated. The Bible account is simply this: "And the Lord God caused a deep sleep to fall upon Adam, and he slept. And he took one of his ribs and closed up the flesh instead thereof; and the rib which the Lord God had taken from man made he a woman, and brought her unto the man. And Adam said: This is now bone of my bones, and flesh of my flesh: she shall be called woman, because she was taken out of man." If Mr. Talmage is right, then the account should be as follows: "And the Lord God caused a deep sleep to fall upon Adam, and he slept; and he took one of his sides, and closed up the flesh instead thereof; and the side which the Lord God had taken from man made he a woman, and brought her unto the man. And Adam said: This is now side of my side, and flesh of my flesh." I do not see that the story is made any better by using the word "side" instead of "rib." It would be just as hard for God to make a woman out of a man's side as out of a rib. Mr. Talmage ought not to question the power of God to make a woman out of a bone, and he must recollect that the less the material the greater the miracle.

There are two accounts of the creation of man, in Genesis, the first being in the twenty-first verse of the first chapter and the second being in the twenty-first and twenty-second verses of the second chapter.

According to the second account, "God formed man of the dust of the ground, and breathed into his nostrils the breath of life." And after this, "God planted a garden eastward in Eden and put the man" in this garden. After this, "He made every tree to grow that was good for food and pleasant to the sight," and, in addition, "the tree of life in the midst of the garden," beside "the tree of the knowledge of good and evil." And he "put the man in the garden to dress it and keep it, telling him that he might eat of everything he saw except of the tree of the knowledge of good and evil."

After this, God having noticed that it "was not good for man to be alone, formed out of the ground every beast of the field, every fowl of the air, and brought them to Adam to see what he would call them, and Adam gave names to all cattle, and to the fowl of the air, and to every beast of the field. But for Adam there was not found an helpmeet for him."

We are not told how Adam learned the language, or how he understood what God said. I can hardly believe that any man can be created with the knowledge of a language. Education cannot be ready made and stuffed into a brain. Each person must learn a language for himself. Yet in this account we find a language ready made for man's use. And not only man was enabled to speak, but a serpent also has the power of speech, and the woman holds a conversation with this animal and with her husband; and yet no account is given of how any language was learned. God is described as walking in the garden in the cool of the day, speaking like a man—holding conversations with the man and woman, and occasionally addressing the serpent.

In the nursery rhymes of the world there is nothing more childish than this "inspired" account of the creation of man and woman.

The early fathers of the church held that woman was inferior to man, because man was not made for woman, but woman for man; because

Adam was made first and Eve afterward. They had not the gallantry of Robert Burns, who accounted for the beauty of woman from the fact that God practiced on man first, and then gave woman the benefit of his experience. Think, in this age of the world, of a well-educated, intelligent gentleman telling his little child that about six thousand years ago a mysterious being called God made the world out of his "omnipotence;" then made a man out of some dust which he is supposed to have molded into form; that he put this man in a garden for the purpose of keeping the trees trimmed; that after a little while he noticed that the man seemed lonesome, not particularly happy, almost homesick; that then it occurred to this God, that it would be a good thing for the man to have some company, somebody to help him trim the trees, to talk to him and cheer him up on rainy days; that, thereupon, this God caused a deep sleep to fall on the man, took a knife, or a long, sharp piece of "omnipotence," and took out one of the man's sides, or a rib, and of that made a woman; that then this man and woman got along real well till a snake got into the garden and induced the woman to eat of the tree of the knowledge of good and evil; that the woman got the man to take a bite; that afterwards both of them were detected by God, who was walking around in the cool of the evening, and thereupon they were turned out of the garden, lest they should put forth their hands and eat of the tree of life, and live forever.

This foolish story has been regarded as the sacred, inspired truth; as an account substantially written by God himself; and thousands and millions of people have supposed it necessary to believe this childish falsehood, in order to save their souls. Nothing more laughable can be found in the fairy tales and folk-lore of savages. Yet this is defended by the leading Presbyterian divine, and those who fail to believe in the truth of this story are called "brazen "faced fools," "deicides," and "blasphemers."

By this story woman in all Christian countries was degraded. She was considered too impure to preach the gospel, too impure to distribute the sacramental bread, too impure to hand about the sacred wine, too impure to step within the "holy of holies," in the Catholic Churches, too impure to be touched by a priest. Unmarried men were considered purer than husbands and fathers. Nuns were regarded as superior to mothers, a monastery holier than a home, a nunnery nearer sacred than the cradle. And through all these years it has been thought better to love God than to love man, better to love God than to love your wife and children, better to worship an imaginary deity than to help your fellow-men.

I regard the rights of men and women equal. In Love's fair realm, husband and wife are king and queen, sceptered and crowned alike, and seated on the self-same throne.

Question. Do you still insist that the Old Testament upholds polygamy? Mr. Talmage denies this charge, and shows how terribly God punished those who were not satisfied with one wife.

Answer. I see nothing in what Mr. Talmage has said calculated to change my opinion. It has been admitted by thousands of theologians

and basest motives. Infidels who outwardly live honest and virtuous lives, are inwardly vicious, virulent and vile. After all, morality is only a veneering. God is not deceived with the varnish of good works. We know that the natural man is totally depraved, and that until he has been regenerated by the spirit of God, he is utterly incapable of a good action. The generosity of the unbeliever is, in fact, avarice. His honesty is only a form of larceny. His love is only hatred. No matter how sincerely he may love his wife,—how devoted he may be to his children,—no matter how ready he may be to sacrifice even his life for the good of mankind, God, looking into his very heart, finds it only a den of hissing snakes, a lair of wild, ferocious beasts, a cage of unclean birds.

The idea that God will save a man simply because he is honest and generous, is almost too preposterous for serious refutation. No man should rely upon his own goodness. He should plead the virtue of another. God, in his infinite justice, damns a good man on his own merits, and saves a bad man on the merits of another. The repentant murderer will be an angel of light, while his honest and unoffending victim will be a fiend in hell.

A little while ago, a ship, disabled, was blown about the Atlantic for eighty days. Everything had been eaten. Nothing remained but bare decks and hunger. The crew consisted of Captain Kruger and nine others. For nine days, nothing had been eaten. The captain, taking a revolver in his hand, said: "Mates, someone must die for the rest. I am willing to sacrifice myself for you." One of his comrades grasped his hand, and implored him to wait one more day. The next morning, a sail was seen upon the horizon, and the dying men were rescued.

To an ordinary man,—to one guided by the light of reason,—it is perfectly clear that Captain Kruger was about to do an infinitely generous action. Yet Mr. Talmage will tell us that if that captain was not a Christian, and if he had sent the bullet crashing through his brain in order that his comrades might eat his body, and live to reach their wives and homes,—his soul, from that ship, would have gone, by dark and tortuous ways, down to the prison of eternal pain.

Is it possible that Christ would eternally damn a man for doing exactly what Christ would have done, had he been infinitely generous, under the same circumstances? Is not self-denial in a man as praiseworthy as in a God? Should a God be worshiped, and a man be damned, for the same action?

According to Mr. Talmage, every soldier who fought for our country in the Revolutionary war, who was not a Christian, is now in hell. Every soldier, not a Christian, who carried the flag of his country to victory— either upon the land or sea, in the war of 1812, is now in hell. Every soldier, not a Christian, who fought for the preservation of this Union,— to break the chains of slavery—to free four millions of people—to keep the whip from the naked back—every man who did this—every one who died at Andersonville and Libby, dreaming that his death would help make the lives of others worth living, is now a lost and wretched soul. These men are now in the prison of God,—a prison in which the cruelties of Libby and Andersonville would be regarded as mercies,—in which famine would be a joy.

THIRD INTERVIEW.

Sinner. *Is God infinite in wisdom and power?*
Parson. *He is.*
Sinner. *Does he at all times know just what ought to be done?*
Parson. *He does.*
Sinner. *Does he always do just what ought to be done?*
Parson. *He does.*
Sinner. *Why do you pray to him?*
Parson. *Because he is unchangeable.*

Question. I want to ask you a few questions about Mr. Talmage's third sermon. What do you think of it?

Answer. I often ask myself the questions: Is there anything in the occupation of a minister,—anything in his surroundings, that makes him incapable of treating an opponent fairly, or decently? Is there anything in the doctrine of universal forgiveness that compels a man to speak of one who differs with him only in terms of disrespect and hatred? Is it necessary for those who profess to love the whole world, to hate the few they come in actual contact with?

Mr. Talmage, no doubt, professes to love all mankind,—Jew and Gentile, Christian and Pagan. No doubt, he believes in the missionary effort, and thinks we should do all in our power to save the soul of the most benighted savage; and yet he shows anything but affection for the "heathen" at home. He loves the ones he never saw,—is real anxious for their welfare,—but for the ones he knows, he exhibits only scorn and hatred. In one breath, he tells us that Christ loves us, and in the next, that we are "wolves and dogs." We are informed that Christ forgave even his murderers, but that now he hates an honest unbeliever with all his heart. He can forgive the ones who drove the nails into his hands and feet,—the one who thrust the spear through his quivering flesh,—but he cannot forgive the man who entertains an honest doubt about the "scheme of salvation."

He regards the man who thinks, as a "mouth-maker at heaven." Is it possible that Christ is less forgiving in heaven than he was in Jerusalem? Did he excuse murderers then, and does he damn thinkers now? Once he pitied even thieves; does he now abhor an intellectually honest man?

Question. Mr. Talmage seems to think that you have no right to give your opinion about the Bible. Do you think that laymen have the same right as ministers to examine the Scriptures?

Answer. If God only made a revelation for preachers, of course we will have to depend on the preachers for information. But the preachers have made the mistake of showing the revelation. They ask us, the laymen, to read it, and certainly there is no use of reading it, unless we are permitted to think for ourselves while we read. If after reading the

Bible we believe it to be true, we will say so, if we are honest. If we do not believe it, we will say so, if we are honest.

But why should God be so particular about our believing the stories in his book? Why should God object to having his book examined? We do not have to call upon legislators, or courts, to protect Shakespeare from the derision of mankind. Was not God able to write a book that would command the love and admiration of the world? If the God of Mr. Talmage is infinite, he knew exactly how the stories of the Old Testament would strike a gentleman of the nineteenth century. He knew that many would have their doubts,—that thousands of them—and I may say most of them,—would refuse to believe that a miracle had ever been performed.

Now, it seems to me that he should either have left the stories out, or furnished evidence enough to convince the world. According to Mr. Talmage, thousands of people are pouring over the Niagara of unbelief into the gulf of eternal pain. Why does not God furnish more evidence? Just in proportion as man has developed intellectually, he has demanded additional testimony. That which satisfies a barbarian, excites only the laughter of a civilized man. Certainly God should furnish evidence in harmony with the spirit of the age. If God wrote his Bible for the average man, he should have written it in such a way that it would have carried conviction to the brain and heart of the average man; and he should have made no man in such a way that he could not, by any possibility, believe it. There certainly should be a harmony between the Bible and the human brain. If I do not believe the Bible, whose fault is it? Mr. Talmage insists that his God wrote the Bible for me and made me. If this is true, the book and the man should agree. There is no sense in God writing a book for me and then making me in such a way that I cannot believe his book.

Question. But Mr. Talmage says the reason why you hate the Bible is, that your soul is poisoned; that the Bible "throws you into a rage precisely as pure water brings on a paroxysm of hydrophobia."

Answer. Is it because the mind of the infidel is poisoned, that he refuses to believe that an infinite God commanded the murder of mothers, maidens and babes? Is it because their minds are impure, that they refuse to believe that a good God established the institution of human slavery, or that he protected it when established? Is it because their minds are vile, that they refuse to believe that an infinite God established or protected polygamy? Is it a sure sign of an impure mind, when a man insists that God never waged wars of extermination against his helpless children? Does it show that a man has been entirely given over to the devil, because he refuses to believe that God ordered a father to sacrifice his son? Does it show that a heart is entirely without mercy, simply because a man denies the justice of eternal pain?

I denounce many parts of the Old Testament because they are infinitely repugnant to my sense of justice,—because they are bloody, brutal and infamous,—because they uphold crime and destroy human liberty. It is impossible for me to imagine a greater monster than the God of the Old Testament. He is unworthy of my worship. He commands only my detestation, my execration, and my passionate hatred. The God who commanded the murder of children is an infamous fiend. The God who believed in polygamy, is worthy only of contempt. The God who established slavery should be hated by every free man. The Jehovah of the Jews was simply a barbarian, and the Old Testament is mostly the barbarous record of a barbarous people.

If the Jehovah of the Jews is the real God, I do not wish to be his friend. From him I neither ask, nor expect, nor would I be willing to receive, even an eternity of joy. According to the Old Testament, he established a government,—a political state,—and yet, no civilized country today would re-enact these laws of God.

Question. What do you think of the explanation given by Mr. Talmage of the stopping of the sun and moon in the time of Joshua, in order that a battle might be completed?

Answer. Of course, if there is an infinite God, he could have stopped the sun and moon. No one pretends to prescribe limits to the power of the infinite. Even admitting that such a being existed, the question whether he did stop the sun and moon, or not, still remains. According to the account, these planets were stopped, in order that Joshua might continue the pursuit of a routed enemy. I take it for granted that a being of infinite wisdom would not waste any force,—that he would not throw away any "omnipotence," and that, under ordinary circumstances, he would husband his resources. I find that this spirit exists, at least in embryo, in Mr. Talmage. He proceeds to explain this miracle. He does not assert that the earth was stopped on its axis, but suggests "refraction" as a way out of the difficulty. Now, while the stopping of the earth on its axis accounts for the sun remaining in the same relative position, it does not account for the stoppage of the moon. The moon has a motion of its own, and even if the earth had been stopped in its rotary motion, the moon would have gone on. The Bible tells us that the moon was stopped. One would suppose that the sun would have given sufficient light for all practical purposes. Will Mr. Talmage be kind enough to explain the stoppage of the moon? Everyone knows that the moon is somewhat obscure when the sun is in the midst of the heavens. The moon when compared with the sun at such a time, is much like one of the discourses of Mr. Talmage side by side with a chapter from Humboldt;—it is useless.

In the same chapter in which the account of the stoppage of the sun and moon is given, we find that God cast down from heaven great hailstones on Joshua's enemies. Did he get out of hailstones? Had he no "omnipotence" left? Was it necessary for him to stop the sun and moon and depend entirely upon the efforts of Joshua? Would not the force employed in stopping the rotary motion of the earth have been sufficient to destroy the enemy? Would not a millionth part of the force necessary to stop the moon, have pierced the enemy's centre, and rolled up both his flanks? A resort to lightning would have been, in my judgment, much more economical and rather more effective. If he had simply opened the earth, and swallowed them, as he did Korah and his company, it would have been a vast saving of "omnipotent" muscle. Yet, the foremost orthodox minister of the Presbyterian Church,—the one who calls all unbelievers "wolves and dogs," and "brazen "fools," in his effort to account for this miracle, is driven to the subterfuge of an "optical illusion." We are seriously informed that "God probably "changed the nature of the air," and performed this feat of legerdemain through the instrumentality of "refraction." It seems to me it would have been fully as easy to have changed the nature of the air breathed by the enemy, so that it would not have supported life. He could have accomplished this by changing only a little air, in that vicinity; whereas, according to the Talmagian view, he changed the atmosphere of the world. Or, a small "local flood" might have done the work. The optical illusion and refraction view, ingenious as it may appear, was not original with Mr. Talmage. The Rev. Henry M. Morey, of South Bend, Indiana, used, upon this subject, the following language; "The phenomenon was simply optical. The rotary motion of the earth was not disturbed, but the light of the sun was prolonged by the same laws of refraction and reflection by which the sun now appears to be above the horizon when it is really below. The medium through which the sun's rays passed, might have been miraculously influenced so as to have caused the sun to linger above the horizon long after its usual time for disappearance."

I pronounce the opinion of Mr. Morey to be the ripest product of Christian scholarship. According to the Morey-Talmage view, the sun lingered somewhat above the horizon. But this is inconsistent with the Bible account. We are not told in the Scriptures that the sun "lingered above the horizon," but that it "stood "still in the midst of heaven for about a whole day." The trouble about the optical-illusion view is, that it makes the day too long. If the air was miraculously changed, so that it refracted the rays of the sun, while the earth turned over as usual for about a whole day, then, at the end of that time, the sun must have been again visible in the east. It would then naturally shine twelve hours more, so that this miraculous day must have been at least thirty-six hours in length. There were first twelve hours of natural light, then twelve hours of refracted and reflected light, and then twelve hours more of natural light. This makes the day too long. So, I say to Mr. Talmage, as I said to Mr. Morey: If you will depend a little less on refraction, and a little more on reflection, you will see that the whole story is a barbaric myth and foolish fable.

For my part, I do not see why God should be pleased to have me believe a story of this character. I can hardly think that there is great joy in heaven over another falsehood swallowed. I can imagine that a man may deny this story, and still be an excellent citizen, a good father, an obliging neighbor, and in all respects a just and truthful man. I can also imagine that a man may believe this story, and yet assassinate a President of the United States.

I am afraid that Mr. Talmage is beginning to be touched, in spite of himself, with some new ideas. He tells us that worlds are born and that worlds die. This is not exactly the Bible view. You would think that he imagined that a world was naturally produced,—that the aggregation of atoms was natural, and that disintegration came to worlds, as to men, through old age. Yet this is not the Bible view. According to the Bible, these worlds were not born,—they were created out of "nothing," or out of "omnipotence," which is much the same. According to the Bible, it took this infinite God six days to make this atom called earth; and according to the account, he did not work nights,—he worked from the mornings to the evenings,—and I suppose rested nights, as he has since that time on Sundays.

Admitting that the battle which Joshua fought was exceedingly important—which I do not think—is it not a little strange that this God, in all subsequent battles of the world's history, of which we know anything, has maintained the strictest neutrality? The earth turned as usual at Yorktown, and at Gettysburg the moon pursued her usual course; and so far as I know, neither at Waterloo nor at Sedan were there any peculiar freaks of "refraction" or "reflection."

Question. Mr. Talmage tells us that there was in the early part of this century a dark day, when workmen went home from their fields, and legislatures and courts adjourned, and that the darkness of that day has not yet been explained. What is your opinion about that?

Answer. My opinion is, that if at that time we had been at war with England, and a battle had been commenced in the morning, and in the afternoon the American forces had been driven from their position and were hard pressed by the enemy, and if the day had become suddenly dark, and so dark that the Americans were thereby enabled to escape, thousands of theologians of the caliber of Mr. Talmage would have honestly believed that there had been an interposition of divine Providence. No battle was fought that day, and consequently, even the ministers are looking for natural causes. In olden times, when the heavens were visited by comets, war, pestilence and famine were predicted. If wars came, the prediction was remembered; if nothing happened, it was forgotten. When eclipses visited the sun and moon, the barbarian fell upon his knees, and accounted for the phenomena by the wickedness of his neighbor. Mr. Talmage tells us that his father was terrified by the meteoric shower that visited our earth in 1833. The terror of the father may account for the credulity of the son. Astronomers will be surprised to read the declaration of Mr. Talmage that the meteoric shower has never been explained. Meteors visit the earth every year of its life, and in a certain portion of the orbit they are always expected, and they always come. Mr. Newcomb has written a work on astronomy that all ministers ought to read.

Question. Mr. Talmage also charges you with "making light of holy things," and seems to be astonished that you should ridicule the anointing oil of Aaron?

Answer. I find that the God who had no time to say anything on the subject of slavery, and who found no room upon the tables of stone to say a word against polygamy, and in favor of the rights of woman, wife and mother, took time to give a recipe for making hair oil. And in order that the priests might have the exclusive right to manufacture this oil, decreed the penalty of death on all who should infringe. I admit that I am incapable of seeing the beauty of this symbol. Neither could I ever see the necessity of Masons putting oil on the corner-stone of a building. Of course, I do not know the exact chemical effect that oil has on stone, and I see no harm in laughing at such a ceremony. If the oil does good, the laughter will do no harm; and if the oil will do no harm, the laughter will do no good. Personally, I am willing that Masons should put oil on all stones; but, if Masons should insist that I must believe in the efficacy of the ceremony, or be eternally damned, I would have about the same feeling toward the Masons that I now have toward Mr. Talmage. I presume that at one time the putting of oil on a corner-stone had some meaning; but that it ever did any good, no sensible man will insist. It is a custom to break a bottle of champagne over the bow of a newly-launched ship, but I have never considered this ceremony important to the commercial interests of the world.

I have the same opinion about putting oil on stones, as about putting water on heads. For my part, I see no good in the rite of baptism. Still, it may do no harm, unless people are immersed during cold weather. Neither have I the slightest objection to the baptism of anybody; but if people tell me that I must be baptized or suffer eternal agony, then I deny it. If they say that baptism does any earthly good, I deny it. No one objects to any harmless ceremony; but the moment it is insisted that a ceremony is necessary, the reason of which no man can see, then the practice of the ceremony becomes hurtful, for the reason that it is maintained only at the expense of intelligence and manhood.

It is hurtful for people to imagine that they can please God by any ceremony whatever. If there is any God, there is only one way to please him, and that is, by a conscientious discharge of your obligations to your fellow-men. Millions of people imagine that they can please God by wearing certain kinds of cloth. Think of a God who can be pleased with a coat of a certain cut! Others, to earn a smile of heaven, shave their heads, or trim their beards, or perforate their ears or lips or noses. Others maim and mutilate their bodies. Others think to please God by simply shutting their eyes, by swinging censers, by lighting candles, by repeating poor Latin, by making a sign of the cross with holy water, by ringing bells, by going without meat, by eating fish, by getting hungry, by counting beads, by making themselves miserable Sundays, by looking solemn, by refusing to marry, by hearing sermons; and others imagine that they can please God by calumniating unbelievers.

There is an old story of an Irishman who, when dying, sent for a priest. The reputation of the dying man was so perfectly miserable, that the priest refused to administer the rite of extreme unction. The priest therefore asked him if he could recollect any decent action that he had ever done. The dying man said that he could not. "Very well," said the priest, "then you will have to be damned." In a moment, the pinched and pale face brightened, and he said to the priest: "I have thought of one good "action." "What is it?" asked the priest. And the dying man said, "Once I killed a gauger."

I suppose that in the next world some ministers, driven to extremes, may reply: "Once I told a lie "about an infidel."

Question. You see that Mr. Talmage still sticks to the whale and Jonah story. What do you think of his argument, or of his explanation, rather, of that miracle?

Answer. The edge of his orthodoxy seems to be crumbling. He tells us that "there is in the mouth of the common whale a cavity large enough for a man to live in without descent into his stomach,"—and yet Christ says, that Jonah was in the whale's belly, not in his mouth. But why should Mr. Talmage say that? We are told in the sacred account that "God prepared a great fish" for the sole purpose of having Jonah swallowed. The size of the present whale has nothing to do with the story. No matter whether the throat of the whale of to-day is large or small,—that has nothing to do with it. The simple story is, that God prepared a fish and had Jonah swallowed. And yet Mr. Talmage throws out the suggestion that probably this whale held Jonah in his mouth for three days and nights. I admit that Jonah's chance for air would have been a little better in his mouth, and his chance for water a little worse. Probably the whale that swallowed Jonah was the same fish spoken of by Procopius,—both accounts being entitled, in my judgment, to equal credence. I am a little surprised that Mr. Talmage forgot to mention the fish spoken of by Munchausen—an equally reliable author,—and who has given, not simply the bald fact that a fish swallowed a ship, but was good enough to furnish the details. Mr. Talmage should remember that out of Jonah's biography grew the habit of calling any remarkable lie, "a fish story." There is one thing that Mr. Talmage should not forget; and that is, that miracles should not be explained. Miracles are told simply to be believed, not to be understood.

Somebody suggested to Mr. Talmage that, in all probability, a person in the stomach of a whale would be digested in less than three days. Mr. Talmage, again showing his lack of confidence in God, refusing to believe that God could change the nature of gastric juice,—having no opportunity to rely upon "refraction or reflection," frankly admits that Jonah had to save himself by keeping on the constant go and jump. This gastric-juice theory of Mr. Talmage is an abandonment of his mouth hypothesis. I do not wonder that Mr. Talmage thought of the mouth theory. Possibly, the two theories had better be united—so that we may say that Jonah, when he got tired of the activity necessary to avoid the gastric juice, could have strolled into the mouth for a rest. What a picture! Jonah sitting on the edge of the lower jaw, wiping the perspiration and the gastric juice from his anxious face, and vainly looking through the open mouth for signs of land!

In this story of Jonah, we are told that "the Lord spake unto the fish." In what language? It must be remembered that this fish was only a few hours old. He had been prepared during the storm, for the sole purpose of swallowing Jonah. He was a fish of exceedingly limited experience. He had no hereditary knowledge, because he did not spring from ancestors; consequently, he had no instincts. Would such a fish understand any language? It may be contended that the fish, having been made for the occasion, was given a sufficient knowledge of language to understand an ordinary commandment; but, if Mr. Talmage is right, I think an order to the fish would have been entirely unnecessary. When we take into

34

consideration that a thing the size of a man had been promenading up and down the stomach of this fish for three days and three nights, successfully baffling the efforts of gastric juice, we can readily believe that the fish was as anxious to have Jonah go, as Jonah was to leave.

But the whale part is, after all, not the most wonderful portion of the book of Jonah. According to this wonderful account, "the word of the Lord came "to Jonah," telling him to "go and cry against the city of Nineveh;" but Jonah, instead of going, endeavored to evade the Lord by taking ship for Tarshish. As soon as the Lord heard of this, he "sent out a great wind into the sea," and frightened the sailors to that extent that after assuring themselves, by casting lots, that Jonah was the man, they threw him into the sea. After escaping from the whale, he went to Nineveh, and delivered his pretended message from God. In consequence of his message, Jonah having no credentials from God,—nothing certifying to his official character, the King of Nineveh covered himself with sack-cloth and sat down in some ashes. He then caused a decree to be issued that every man and beast should abstain from food and water; and further, that every man and beast should be covered with sack-cloth. This was done in the hope that Jonah's God would repent, and turn away his fierce anger. When we take into consideration the fact that the people of Nineveh were not Hebrews, and had not the slightest confidence in the God of the Jews—knew no more of, and cared no more for, Jehovah than we now care for Jupiter, or Neptune; the effect produced by the proclamation of Jonah is, to say the least of it, almost incredible.

We are also informed, in this book, that the moment God saw all the people sitting in the ashes, and all the animals covered with sack-cloth, he repented. This failure on the part of God to destroy the unbelievers displeased Jonah exceedingly, and he was very angry. Jonah was much like the modern minister, who seems always to be personally aggrieved if the pestilence and famine prophesied by him do not come. Jonah was displeased to that degree, that he asked God to kill him. Jonah then went out of the city, even after God had repented, made him a booth and sat under it, in the shade, waiting to see what would become of the city. God then "prepared a gourd, and made it to come up over Jonah that it might be a shadow over his head to deliver him from his grief." And then we have this pathetic line: "So Jonah was exceedingly glad of the gourd."

God having prepared a fish, and also prepared a gourd, proposed next morning to prepare a worm. And when the sun rose next day, the worm that God had prepared, "smote the gourd, so that it withered." I can hardly believe that an infinite being prepared a worm to smite a gourd so that it withered, in order to keep the sun from the bald head of a prophet. According to the account, after sunrise, and after the worm had smitten the gourd, "God prepared a vehement east wind." This was not an ordinary wind, but one prepared expressly for that occasion. After the wind had been prepared, "the sun beat upon the head of Jonah, and he fainted, and wished in himself to die." All this was done in order to convince Jonah that a man who would deplore the loss of a gourd, ought not to wish for the destruction of a city.

Is it possible for any intelligent man now to believe that the history of Jonah is literally true? For my part, I cannot see the necessity either of believing it, or of preaching it. It has nothing to do with honesty, with mercy, or with morality. The bad may believe it, and the good may hold it in contempt. I do not see that civilization has the slightest interest in the fish, the gourd, the worm, or the vehement east wind.

Does Mr. Talmage think that it is absolutely necessary to believe all the story? Does he not think it probable that a God of infinite mercy, rather than damn the soul of an honest man to hell forever, would waive, for instance, the worm,—provided he believed in the vehement east wind, the gourd and the fish?

Mr. Talmage, by insisting on the literal truth of the Bible stories, is doing Christianity great harm. Thousands of young men will say: "I can't become a Christian if it is necessary to believe the adventures of Jonah." Mr. Talmage will put into the paths of multitudes of people willing to do right, anxious to make the world a little better than it is,—this stumbling block. He could have explained it, called it an allegory, poetical license, a child of the oriental imagination, a symbol, a parable, a poem, a dream, a legend, a myth, a divine figure, or a great truth wrapped in the rags and shreds and patches of seeming falsehood. His efforts to belittle the miracle, to suggest the mouth instead of the stomach,—to suggest that Jonah took deck passage, or lodged in the forecastle instead of in the cabin or steerage,—to suggest motion as a means of avoiding digestion, is a serious theological blunder, and may cause the loss of many souls.

If Mr. Talmage will consult with other ministers, they will tell him to let this story alone—that he will simply "provoke investigation and discussion"—two things to be avoided. They will tell him that they are not willing their salary should hang on so slender a thread, and will advise him not to bother his gourd about Jonah's. They will also tell him that in this age of the world, arguments cannot be answered by "a vehement east wind."

Some people will think that it would have been just as easy for God to have pulled the gourd up, as to have prepared a worm to bite it.

Question. Mr. Talmage charges that you have said there are indecencies in the Bible. Are you still of that opinion?

Answer. Mr. Talmage endeavors to evade the charge, by saying that "there are things in the Bible not intended to be read, either in the family circle, or in the pulpit, but nevertheless they are to be read." My own judgment is, that an infinite being should not inspire the writing of indecent things. It will not do to say, that the Bible description of sin "warns and saves." There is nothing in the history of Tamar calculated to "warn and save and the same may be said of many other passages in the Old Testament. Most Christians would be glad to know that all such passages are interpolations.

I regret that Shakespeare ever wrote a line that could not be read any where, and by any person. But Shakespeare, great as he was, did not rise entirely above his time. So of most poets. Nearly all have stained their pages with some vulgarity; and I am sorry for it, and hope the time will come when we shall have an edition of all the great writers and poets from which every such passage is eliminated.

It is with the Bible as with most other books. It is a mingling of good and bad. There are many exquisite passages in the Bible,—many good laws,—many wise sayings,—and there are many passages that should never have been written. I do not propose to throw away the good on account of the bad, neither do I propose to accept the bad on account of the good. The Bible need not be taken as an entirety. It is the business of every man who reads it, to discriminate between that which is good and that which is bad. There are also many passages neither good nor bad,—wholly and totally indifferent—conveying 110 information—utterly destitute of ideas,—and as to these passages, my only objection to them is that they waste time and paper.

I am in favor of every passage in the Bible that conveys information. I am in favor of every wise proverb, of every verse coming from human experience and that appeals to the heart of man. I am in favor of every passage that inculcates justice, generosity, purity, and mercy. I am satisfied that much of the historical part is false. Some of it is probably true. Let us have the courage to take the true, and throw the false away. I am satisfied that many of the passages are barbaric, and many of them are good. Let us have the wisdom to accept the good and to reject the barbaric.

No system of religion should go in partnership with barbarism. Neither should any Christian feel it his duty to defend the savagery of the past. The philosophy of Christ must stand independently of the mistakes of the Old Testament. We should do justice whether a woman was made from a rib or from "omnipotence." We should be merciful whether the flood was general, or local. We should be kind and obliging whether Jonah was swallowed by a fish or not. The miraculous has nothing to do with the moral. Intelligence is of more value than inspiration. Brain is better than Bible. Reason is above all religion. I do not believe that any civilized human being clings to the Bible on account of its barbaric passages. I am candid enough to believe that every Christian in the world would think more of the Bible, if it had not upheld slavery, if it had denounced polygamy, if it had cried out against wars of extermination, if it had spared women and babes, if it had upheld everywhere, and at all times, the standard of justice and mercy. But when it is claimed that the book is perfect, that it is inspired, that it is, in fact, the work of an infinitely wise and good God,—then it should be without a defect. There should not be within its lids an impure word; it should not express an impure thought. There should not be one word in favor of injustice, not one word in favor of slavery, not one word in favor of wars of extermination. There must be another revision of the Scriptures. The chaff must be thrown away. The dross must be rejected; and only that be retained which is in exact harmony with the brain and heart of the greatest and the best.

Question. Mr. Talmage charges you with unfairness, because you account for the death of art in Palestine, by the commandment which forbids the making of graven images.

Answer. I have said that that commandment was the death of art, and I say so still. I insist that by reason of that commandment, Palestine produced no painter and no sculptor until after the destruction of Jerusalem. Mr. Talmage, in order to answer that statement, goes on to show that hundreds and thousands of pictures were produced in the Middle Ages. That is a departure in pleading. Will he give us the names of the painters that existed in Palestine from Mount Sinai to the destruction of the temple? Will he give us the names of the sculptors between those times? Mohammed prohibited his followers from making any representation of human or animal life, and as a result, Mohammedans have never produced a painter nor a sculptor, except in the portrayal and chiseling of vegetable forms. They were confined to trees and vines, and flowers. No Mohammedan has portrayed the human face or form. But the commandment of Jehovah went farther than that of Momammed, and prevented portraying the image of anything. The assassination of art was complete.

There is another thing that should not be forgotten.

We are indebted for the encouragement of art, not to the Protestant Church; if indebted to any, it is to the Catholic. The Catholic adorned the cathedral with painting and statue—not the Protestant. The Protestants opposed music and painting, and refused to decorate their temples. But if Mr. Talmage wishes to know to whom we are indebted for art, let him read the mythology of Greece and Rome. The early Christians destroyed paintings and statues. They were the enemies of all beauty. They hated and detested every expression of art. They looked upon the love of statues as a form of idolatry. They looked upon every painting as a remnant of Paganism. They destroyed all upon which they could lay their ignorant hands. Hundred of years afterwards, the world was compelled to search for the fragments that Christian fury had left. The Greeks filled the world with beauty. For every stream and mountain and cataract they had a god or goddess. Their sculptors impersonated every dream and hope, and their mythology feeds, to-day, the imagination of mankind. The Venus de Milo is the impersonation of beauty, in ruin—the sublimest fragment of the ancient world. Our mythology is infinitely unpoetic and barren—our deity an old bachelor from eternity, who once believed in indiscriminate massacre. Upon the throne of our heaven, woman finds no place. Our mythology is destitute of the maternal.

Question. Mr. Talmage denies your statement that the Old Testament humiliates woman. He also denies that the New Testament says anything against woman. How is it?

Answer. Of course, I never considered a book upholding polygamy to be the friend of woman. Eve, according to that book, is the mother of us all, and yet the inspired writer does not tell us how long she lived,—does not even mention her death,—makes not the slightest reference as to what finally became of her. Methuselah lived nine hundred and sixty-nine years, and yet, there is not the slightest mention made of Mrs. Methuselah. Enoch was translated, and his widow is not mentioned. There is not a word about Mrs. Seth, or Mrs. Enos, or Mrs. Cainan, or Mrs. Mahalaleel, or Mrs. Jared. We do not know the name of Mrs. Noah, and I believe not the name of a solitary woman is given from the creation of Eve—with the exception of two of Lamech's wives—until Sarai is mentioned as being the wife of Abram.

If you wish really to know the Bible estimation of woman, turn to the fourth and fifth verses of the twelfth chapter of Leviticus, in which a woman, for the crime of having borne a son, is unfit to touch a hallowed thing, or to come in the holy sanctuary for thirty-three days; but if a woman was the mother of a girl, then she became totally unfit to enter the sanctuary, or pollute with her touch a hallowed thing, for sixty-six days. The pollution was twice as great when she had borne a daughter.

It is a little difficult to see why it is a greater crime to give birth to a daughter than to a son. Surely, a law like that did not tend to the elevation of woman. You will also find in the same chapter that a woman had to offer a pigeon, or a turtle-dove, as a sin offering, in order to expiate the crime of having become a mother. By the Levitical law, a mother was unclean. The priest had to make an atonement for her.

If there is, beneath the stars, a figure of complete and perfect purity, it is a mother holding in her arms her child. The laws respecting women, given by commandment of Jehovah to the Jews, were born of barbarism, and in this day and age should be regarded only with detestation and contempt. The twentieth and twenty-first verses of the nineteenth chapter of Leviticus show that the same punishment was not meted to men and women guilty of the same crime.

The real explanation of what we find in the Old Testament degrading to woman, lies in the fact, that the overflow of Love's mysterious Nile—the sacred source of life—was, by its savage authors, deemed unclean.

Question. But what have you to say about the women of the Bible, mentioned by Mr. Talmage, and held up as examples for all time of all that is sweet and womanly?

Answer. I believe that Esther is his principal heroine. Let us see who she was.

According to the book of Esther, Ahasuerus who was king of Persia, or some such place, ordered Vashti his queen to show herself to the people and the princes, because she was "exceedingly fair to look upon." For some reason—modesty perhaps—she refused to appear. And thereupon the king "sent letters into all his provinces and to every people after their language, that every man should bear rule in his own house;" it being feared that if it should become public that Vashti had disobeyed, all other wives might follow her example. The king also, for the purpose of impressing upon all women the necessity of obeying their husbands, issued a decree that "Vashti should come no more before him," and that he would "give her royal estate unto another." This was done that "all the wives should give to their husbands honor, both to great and small."

After this, "the king appointed officers in all the provinces of his kingdom that they might gather together all the fair young virgins," and bring them to his palace, put them in the custody of his chamberlain, and have them thoroughly washed. Then the king was to look over the lot and take each day the one that pleased him best until he found the one to put in the place of Vashti. A fellow by the name of Mordecai, living in that part of the country, hearing of the opportunity to sell a girl, brought Esther, his uncle's daughter,—she being an orphan, and very beautiful—to see whether she might not be the lucky one.

The remainder of the second chapter of this book, I do not care to repeat. It is sufficient to say that Esther at last was chosen.

The king at this time did not know that Esther was a Jewess. Mordecai her kinsman, however, discovered a plot to assassinate the king, and Esther told the king, and the two plotting gentlemen were hanged on a tree.

After a while, a man by the name of Haman was made Secretary of State, and everybody coming in his presence bowed except Mordecai. Mordecai was probably depending on the influence of Esther. Haman finally became so vexed, that he made up his mind to have all the Jews in the kingdom destroyed. (The number of Jews at that time in Persia must have been immense.) Haman thereupon requested the king to have an order issued to destroy all the Jews, and in consideration of the order, proposed to pay ten thousand talents of silver. And thereupon, letters were written to the governors of the various provinces, sealed with the king's ring, sent by post in all directions, with instructions to kill all the Jews, both young and old—little children and women,—in one day. (One would think that the king copied this order from another part of the Old Testament, or had found an original by Jehovah.) The people immediately made preparations for the killing. Mordecai clothed himself with sack-cloth, and Esther called upon one of the king's chamberlains, and she finally got the history of the affair, as well as a copy of the writing, and thereupon made up her mind to go in and ask the king to save her people.

At that time, Bismarck's idea of government being in full force, any one entering the king's presence without an invitation, was liable to be put to death. And in case any one did go in to see the king, if the king failed to hold out his golden scepter, his life was not spared. Notwithstanding this order, Esther put on her best clothes, and stood in the inner court of the king's house, while the king sat on his royal throne. When the king saw her standing in the court, he held out his scepter, and Esther drew near, and he asked her what she wished; and thereupon she asked that the king and Haman might take dinner with her that day, and it was done. While they were feasting, the king again asked Esther what she wanted; and her second request was, that they would come and dine with her once more. When Haman left the palace that day, he saw Mordecai again at the gate, standing as stiffly as usual, and it filled Haman with indignation. So Haman, taking the advice of his wife, made a gallows fifty cubits high, for the special benefit of Mordecai. The next day, when Haman went to see the king, the king, having the night before refreshed his memory in respect to the service done him by Mordecai, asked Haman what ought to be done for the man whom the king wished to honor. Haman, supposing of course that the king referred to him, said that royal purple ought to be brought forth, such as the king wore, and the horse that the king rode on, and the crown-royal should be set on the man's head;—that one of the most noble princes should lead the horse, and as he went through the streets, proclaim: "Thus shall it be done to the man whom the king delighteth to honor."

Thereupon the king told Haman that Mordecai was the man that the king wished to honor. And Haman was forced to lead this horse, backed by Mordecai, through the streets, shouting: "This shall be done to the man whom the king delighteth to honor." Immediately afterward, he went to the banquet that Esther had prepared, and the king again asked Esther her petition. She then asked for the salvation of her people; stating at the same time, that if her people had been sold into slavery, she would have held her tongue; but since they were about to be killed, she could not keep silent. The king asked her who had done this thing; and Esther replied that it was the wicked Haman.

Thereupon one of the chamberlains, remembering the gallows that had been made for Mordecai, mentioned it, and the king immediately ordered that Haman be hanged thereon; which was done. And Mordecai immediately became Secretary of State. The order against the Jews was then rescinded; and Ahasuerus, willing to do anything that Esther desired, hanged all of Haman's folks. He not only did this, but he immediately issued an order to all the Jews allowing them to kill the other folks. And the Jews got together throughout one hundred and twenty-seven provinces, "and such was their power, that no man could stand against them; and thereupon the Jews smote all their enemies with the stroke of the sword, and with slaughter and destruction, and did whatever they pleased to those who hated them." And in the palace of the king, the Jews slew and destroyed five hundred men, besides ten sons of Haman; and in the rest of the provinces, they slew seventy-five thousand people. And after this work of slaughter, the Jews had a day of gladness and feasting.

One can see from this, what a beautiful Bible character Esther was—how filled with all that is womanly, gentle, kind and tender!

This story is one of the most unreasonable, as well as one of the most heartless and revengeful, in the whole Bible. Ahasuerus was a monster, and Esther equally infamous; and yet, this woman is held up for the admiration of mankind by a Brooklyn pastor. There is this peculiarity about the book of Esther: the name of God is not mentioned in it, and the deity is not referred to, directly or indirectly;—yet it is claimed to be an inspired book. If Jehovah wrote it, he certainly cannot be charged with egotism.

I most cheerfully admit that the book of Ruth is quite a pleasant story, and the affection of Ruth for her mother-in-law exceedingly touching, but I am of opinion that Ruth did many things that would be regarded as somewhat indiscreet, even in the city of Brooklyn.

All I can find about Hannah is, that she made a little coat for her boy Samuel, and brought it to him from year to year. Where he got his vest and pantaloons we are not told. But this fact seems hardly enough to make her name immortal.

So also Mr. Talmage refers us to the wonderful woman Abigail. The story about Abigail, told in plain English, is this: David sent some of his followers to Nabal, Abigail's husband, and demanded food. Nabal, who knew nothing about David, and cared less, refused. Abigail heard about it, and took food to David and his servants. She was very much struck, apparently, with David and David with her. A few days afterward Nabal died—supposed to have been killed by the Lord—but probably poisoned; and thereupon David took Abigail to wife. The whole matter should have been investigated by the grand jury.

We are also referred to Dorcas, who no doubt was a good woman—made clothes for the poor and gave alms, as millions have done since then. It seems that this woman died. Peter was sent for, and thereupon raised her from the dead, and she is never mentioned any more. Is it not a little strange that a woman who had been actually raised from the dead, should have so completely passed out of the memory of her time, that when she died the second time, she was entirely unnoticed?

Is it not astonishing that so little is in the New Testament concerning the mother of Christ? My own opinion is, that she was an excellent woman, and the wife of Joseph; and that Joseph was the actual father of Christ. I think there can be no reasonable doubt that such was the opinion of the authors of the original gospels. Upon any other hypothesis, it is impossible to account for their having given the genealogy of Joseph to prove that Christ was of the blood of David. The idea that he was the Son of God, or in any way miraculously produced, was an afterthought, and is hardly entitled now to serious consideration. The gospels were written so long after the death of Christ, that very little was known of him, and substantially nothing of his parents. How is it that not one word is said about the death of Mary—not one word about the death of Joseph? How did it happen that Christ did not visit his mother after his resurrection? The first time he speaks to his mother is when he was twelve years old. His mother having told him that she and his father had been seeking him, he replied: "How is it that ye sought me: wist ye not that I must be about my Father s business?"

The second time was at the marriage feast in Cana, when he said to her: "Woman, what have I to do "with thee?" And the third time was at the cross, when "Jesus, seeing his mother standing by the disciple whom he loved, said to her: Woman, behold thy son;" and to the disciple: "Behold thy mother." And this is all.

The best thing about the Catholic Church is the deification of Mary,—and yet this is denounced by Protestantism as idolatry. There is something in the human heart that prompts man to tell his faults more freely to the mother than to the father. The cruelty of Jehovah is softened by the mercy of Mary.

Is it not strange that none of the disciples of Christ said anything about their parents,—that we know absolutely nothing of them? Is there any evidence that they showed any particular respect even for the mother of Christ?

Mary Magdalen is, in many respects, the tenderest and most loving character in the New Testament. According to the account, her love for Christ knew no abatement,—no change—true even in the hopeless shadow of the cross. Neither did it die with his death. She waited at the sepulcher; she hasted in the early morning to his tomb, and yet the only comfort Christ gave to this true and loving soul lies in these strangely cold and heartless words: "Touch me not."

There is nothing tending to show that the women spoken of in the Bible were superior to the ones we know. There are to-day millions of women making coats for their sons,—hundreds of thousands of women, true not simply to innocent people, falsely accused, but to criminals. Many a loving heart is as true to the gallows as Mary was to the cross. There are hundreds of thousands of women accepting poverty and want and dishonor, for the love they bear unworthy men; hundreds and thousands, hundreds and thousands, working day and night, with strained eyes and tired hands, for husbands and children,—clothed in rags, housed in huts and hovels, hoping day after day for the angel of death. There are thousands of women in Christian England, working in iron, laboring in the fields and toiling in mines. There are hundreds and thousands in Europe, everywhere, doing the work of men—deformed by toil, and who would become simply wild and ferocious beasts, except for the love they bear for home and child.

You need not go back four thousand years for heroines. The world is filled with them to-day. They do not belong to any nation, nor to any religion, nor exclusively to any race. Wherever woman is found, they are found.

There is no description of any women in the Bible that equal thousands and thousands of women known to-day. The women mentioned by Mr. Talmage fall almost infinitely below, not simply those in real life, but the creations of the imagination found in the world of fiction. They will not compare with the women born of Shakespeare's brain. You will find none like Isabella, in whose spotless life, love and reason blended into perfect truth; nor Juliet, within whose heart passion and purity met, like white and red within the bosom of a rose; nor Cordelia, who chose to suffer loss rather than show her wealth of love with those who gilded dross with golden words in hope of gain; nor Miranda, who told her love as freely as a flower gives its bosom to the kisses of the sun; nor Imogene, who asked: "What is it to be false?" nor Hermione, who bore with perfect faith and hope the cross of shame, and who at last forgave with all her heart; nor Desdemona, her innocence so perfect and her love so pure, that she was incapable of suspecting that another could suspect, and sought with dying words to hide her lover's crime.

If we wish to find what the Bible thinks of woman, all that is necessary to do is to read it. We will find that everywhere she is spoken of simply as property,—as belonging absolutely to the man. We will find that whenever a man got tired of his wife, all he had to do was to give her a writing of divorcement, and that then the mother of his children became a houseless and a homeless wanderer. We will find that men were allowed to have as many wives as they could get, either by courtship, purchase, or conquest. The Jewish people in the olden time were in many respects like their barbarian neighbors.

If we read the New Testament, we will find in the epistle of Paul to Timothy, the following gallant passages:

"Let the woman learn in silence, with all subjection."

"But I suffer not a woman to teach, nor to usurp authority over the man, but to be in silence."

And for these kind, gentle and civilized remarks, the apostle Paul gives the following reasons:

"For Adam was first formed, then Eve."

"And Adam was not deceived, but the woman being deceived was in the transgression."

Certainly women ought to feel under great obligation to the apostle Paul.

In the fifth chapter of the same epistle, Paul, advising Timothy as to what kind of people he should admit into his society or church, uses the following language:

"Let not a widow be taken into the number under threescore years old, having been the wife of one man."

"But the younger widows refuse, for when they have begun to wax wanton against Christ, they will marry."

This same Paul did not seem to think polygamy wrong, except in a bishop. He tells Timothy that:

"A bishop must be blameless, the husband of one wife."

He also lays down the rule that a deacon should be the husband of one wife, leaving us to infer that the other members might have as many as they could get.

In the second epistle to Timothy, Paul speaks of "grandmother Lois," who was referred to in such extravagant language by Mr. Talmage, and nothing is said touching her character in the least. All her virtues live in the imagination, and in the imagination alone.

Paul, also, in his epistle to the Ephesians, says:

"Wives, submit yourselves unto your own husbands, as unto the Lord. For the husband is the head of the wife, even as Christ is the head of the church."

"Therefore, as the church is subject unto Christ, so let the wives be to their own husbands, in everything."

You will find, too, that in the seventh chapter of First Corinthians, Paul laments that all men are not bachelors like himself, and in the second verse of that chapter he gives the only reason for which he was willing that men and women should marry. He advised all the unmarried, and all widows, to remain as he was. In the ninth verse of this same chapter is a slander too vulgar for repetition,—an estimate of woman and of woman's love so low and vile, that every woman should hold the inspired author in infinite abhorrence.

Paul sums up the whole matter, however, by telling those who have wives or husbands, to stay with them—as necessary evils only to be tolerated—but sincerely regrets that anybody was ever married; and finally says that:

"They that have wives should be as though they had none;" because, in his opinion: "He that is unmarried careth for the things that belong to the Lord, how he may please the Lord; but he that is married careth for the things that are of the world, how he may please his wife."

"There is this difference also," he tells us, "between a wife and a virgin. The unmarried woman careth for the things of the Lord, that she may be holy both in body and in spirit; but she that is married careth for the things of the world, how she may please her husband."

Of course, it is contended that these things have tended to the elevation of woman.

The idea that it is better to love the Lord than to love your wife, or your husband, is infinitely absurd. Nobody ever did love the Lord,—nobody can—until he becomes acquainted with him.

Saint Paul also tells us that "Man is the image and glory of God; but woman is the glory of man;" and for the purpose of sustaining this position, says:

"For the man is not of the woman, but the woman of the man; neither was the man created for the woman, but the woman for the man."

Of course, we can all see that man could have gotten along well enough without woman, but woman, by no possibility, could have gotten along without man. And yet, this is called "inspired;" and this apostle Paul is supposed to have known more than all the people now upon the earth. No wonder Paul at last was constrained to say: "We are fools for Christ's sake."

Question. How do you account for the present condition of woman in what is known as "the civilized world," unless the Bible has bettered her condition?

Answer. We must remember that thousands of things enter into the problem of civilization. Soil, climate, and geographical position, united with countless other influences, have resulted in the civilization of our time. If we want to find what the influence of the Bible has been, we must ascertain the condition of Europe when the Bible was considered as absolutely true, and when it wielded its greatest influence.

Christianity as a form of religion had actual possession of Europe during the Middle Ages. At that time, it exerted its greatest power. Then it had the opportunity of breaking the shackles from the limbs of woman. Christianity found the Roman matron a free woman. Polygamy was never known in Rome; and although divorces were allowed by law, the Roman state had been founded for more than five hundred years before either a husband or a wife asked for a divorce. From the foundation of Christianity,—I mean from the time it became the force in the Roman state,—woman, as such, went down in the scale of civilization. The scepter was taken from her hands, and she became once more the slave and serf of man. The men also were made slaves, and woman has regained her liberty by the same means that man has regained his,—by wresting authority from the hands of the church. While the church had power, the wife and mother was not considered as good as the begging nun; the husband and father was far below the vermin-covered monk; homes were of no value compared with the cathedral; for God had to have a house, no matter how many of his children were wanderers. During all the years in which woman has struggled for equal liberty with man, she has been met with the Bible doctrine that she is the inferior of the man; that Adam was made first, and Eve afterwards; that man was not made for woman, but that woman was made for man.

I find that in this day and generation, the meanest men have the lowest estimate of woman; that the greater the man is, the grander he is, the more he thinks of mother, wife and daughter. I also find that just in the proportion that he has lost confidence in the polygamy of Jehovah and in the advice and philosophy of Saint Paul, he believes in the rights and liberties of woman. As a matter of fact, men have risen from a perusal of the Bible, and murdered their wives. They have risen from reading its pages, and inflicted cruel and even mortal blows upon their children. Men have risen from reading the Bible and torn the flesh of others with red-hot pincers. They have laid down the sacred volume long enough to pour molten lead into the ears of others. They have stopped reading the sacred Scriptures for a sufficient time to incarcerate their fellow-men, to load them with chains, and then they have gone back to their reading, allowing their victims to die in darkness and despair. Men have stopped reading the Old Testament long enough to drive a stake into the ground and collect a few fagots and burn an honest man. Even ministers have denied themselves the privilege of reading the sacred book long enough to tell falsehoods about their fellow-men. There is no crime that Bible readers and Bible believers and Bible worshipers and Bible defenders have not committed. There is no meanness of which some Bible reader, believer, and defender, has not been guilty. Bible believers and Bible defenders have filled the world with calumnies and slanders. Bible believers and Bible defenders have not only whipped their wives, but they have murdered them; they have murdered their children. I do not say that reading the Bible will necessarily make men dishonest, but I do say, that reading the Bible will not prevent their committing crimes. I do not say that believing the Bible will necessarily make men commit burglary, but I do say that a belief in the Bible has caused men to persecute each other, to imprison each other, and to burn each other.

Only a little while ago, a British clergyman murdered his wife. Only a little while ago, an American Protestant clergyman whipped his boy to death because the boy refused to say a prayer.

The Rev. Mr. Crowley not only believed the Bible, but was licensed to expound it. He had been "called" to the ministry, and upon his head had been laid the holy hands; and yet, he deliberately starved orphans, and while looking upon their sunken eyes and hollow cheeks, sung pious hymns and quoted with great unction: "Suffer little children to come unto me."

As a matter of fact, in the last twenty years, more money has been stolen by Christian cashiers, Christian presidents, Christian directors, Christian trustees and Christian statesmen, than by all other convicts in all the penitentiaries in all the Christian world.

The assassin of Henry the Fourth was a Bible reader and a Bible believer. The instigators of the massacre of St. Bartholomew were believers in your sacred Scriptures. The men who invested their money in the slave-trade believed themselves filled with the Holy Ghost, and read with rapture the Psalms of David and the Sermon on the Mount. The murderers of Scotch Presbyterians were believers in Revelation, and the Presbyterians, when they murdered others, were also believers. Nearly every man who expiates a crime upon the gallows is a believer in the Bible. For a thousand years, the daggers of assassination and the swords of war were blest by priests—by the believers in the sacred Scriptures. The assassin of President Garfield is a believer in the Bible, a hater of infidelity, a believer in personal inspiration, and he expects in a few weeks to join the winged and redeemed in heaven.

If a man would follow, to-day, the teachings of the Old Testament, he would be a criminal. If he would follow strictly the teachings of the New, he would be insane.

FOURTH INTERVIEW.

Son. *There is no devil.*
Mother. *I know there is.*
Son. *How do you know?*
Mother. *Because they make pictures that look just like him.*
Son. *But, mother—*
Mother. *Don't "mother" me! You are trying to disgrace your parents.*

Question. I want to ask you a few questions about Mr. Talmage's fourth sermon against you, entitled: "The Meanness of Infidelity," in which he compares you to Jehoiakim, who had the temerity to throw some of the writings of the weeping Jeremiah into the fire?

Answer. So far as I am concerned, I really regret that a second edition of Jeremiah's roll was gotten out. It would have been far better for us all, if it had been left in ashes. There was nothing but curses and prophecies of evil, in the sacred roll that Jehoiakim burned. The Bible tells us that Jehovah became exceedingly wroth because of the destruction of this roll, and pronounced a curse upon Jehoiakim and upon Palestine. I presume it was on account of the burning of that roll that the king of Babylon destroyed the chosen people of God. It was on account of that sacrilege that the Lord said of Jehoiakim: "He shall have none to sit upon the "throne of David; and his dead body shall be cast "out in the day to the heat, and in the night to the frost." Anyone can see how much a dead body would suffer under such circumstances. Imagine an infinitely wise, good and powerful God taking vengeance on the corpse of a barbarian king! What joy there must have been in heaven as the angels watched the alternate melting and freezing of the dead body of Jehoiakim!

Jeremiah was probably the most accomplished croaker of all time. Nothing satisfied him. He was a prophetic pessimist,—an ancient Bourbon. He was only happy when predicting war, pestilence and famine. No wonder Jehoiakim despised him, and hated all he wrote.

One can easily see the character of Jeremiah from the following occurrence: When the Babylonians had succeeded in taking Jerusalem, and in sacking the city, Jeremiah was unfortunately taken prisoner; but Captain Nebuzaradan came to Jeremiah, and told him that he would let him go, because he had prophesied against his own country. He was regarded as a friend by the enemy.

There was, at that time, as now, the old fight between the church and the civil power. Whenever a king failed to do what the priests wanted, they immediately prophesied overthrow, disaster, and defeat. Whenever the kings would hearken to their voice, and would see to it that the priests had plenty to eat and drink and wear, then they all declared that Jehovah would love that king, would let him live out all his days, and allow his son to reign in his stead. It was simply the old conflict that is still being waged, and it will be carried on until universal civilization does away with priestcraft and superstition.

The priests in the days of Jeremiah were the same as now. They sought to rule the State. They pretended that, at their request, Jehovah would withhold or send the rain; that the seasons were within their power; that they with bitter words could blight the fields and curse the land with want and death. They gloried then, as now, in the exhibition of God's wrath.

In prosperity, the priests were forgotten. Success scorned them; Famine flattered them; Health laughed at them; Pestilence prayed to them; Disaster was their only friend.

These old prophets prophesied nothing but evil, and consequently, when anything bad happened, they claimed it as a fulfillment, and pointed with pride to the fact that they had, weeks or months, or years before, foretold something of that kind. They were really the originators of the phrase, "I told you so!"

There was a good old Methodist class-leader that lived down near a place called Liverpool, on the Illinois river. In the spring of 1861 the old man, telling his experience, among other things said, that he had lived there by the river for more than thirty years, and he did not believe that a year had passed that there were not hundreds of people during the hunting season shooting ducks on Sunday; that he had told his wife thousands of times that no good would come of it; that evil would come of it; "And now," said the old man, raising his voice with the importance of the announcement, "war is upon us!"

Question. Do you wish, as Mr. Talmage says, to destroy the Bible—to have all the copies burned to ashes? What do you wish to have done with the Bible?

Answer. I want the Bible treated exactly as we treat other books— preserve the good and throw away the foolish and the hurtful. I am fighting the doctrine of inspiration. As long as it is believed that the Bible is inspired, that book is the master—no mind is free. With that belief, intellectual liberty is impossible. With that belief, you can investigate only at the risk of losing your soul. The Catholics have a pope. Protestants laugh at them, and yet the pope is capable of intellectual advancement. In addition to this, the pope is mortal, and the church cannot be afflicted with the same idiot forever. The Protestants have a book for their pope. The book cannot advance. Year after year, and century after century, the book remains as ignorant as ever. It is only made better by those who believe in its inspiration giving better meanings to the words than their ancestors did. In this way it may be said that the Bible grows a little better.

Why should we have a book for a master? That which otherwise might be a blessing, remains a curse. If every copy of the Bible were destroyed, all that is good in that book would be reproduced in a single day. Leave every copy of the Bible as it is, and have every human being believe in its inspiration, and intellectual liberty would cease to exist. The whole race, from that moment, would go back toward the night of intellectual death.

The Bible would do more harm if more people really believed it, and acted in accordance with its teachings. Now and then a Freeman puts the knife to the heart of his child. Now and then an assassin relies upon some sacred passage; but, as a rule, few men believe the Bible to be absolutely true.

There are about fifteen hundred million people in the world. There are not two million who have read the Bible through. There are not two hundred million who ever saw the Bible. There are not five hundred million who ever heard that such a book exists.

Christianity is claimed to be a religion for all mankind. It was founded more than eighteen centuries ago; and yet, not one human being in three has ever heard of it. As a matter of fact, for more than fourteen centuries and-a-half after the crucifixion of Christ, this hemisphere was absolutely unknown. There was not a Christian in the world who knew there was such a continent as ours, and all the inhabitants of this, the New World, were deprived of the gospel for fourteen centuries and-a-half, and knew nothing of its blessings until they were informed by Spanish murderers and marauders. Even in the United States, Christianity is not keeping pace with the increase of population. When we take into consideration that it is aided by the momentum of eighteen centuries, is it not wonderful that it is not today holding its own? The reason of this is, that we are beginning to understand the Scriptures. We are beginning to see, and to see clearly, that they are simply of human origin, and that the Bible bears the marks of the barbarians who wrote it. The best educated among the clergy admit that we know but little as to the origin of the gospels; that we do not positively know the author of one of them; that it is really a matter of doubt as to who wrote the five books attributed to Moses. They admit now, that Isaiah was written by more than one person; that Solomon's Song was not written by that king; that Job is, in all probability, not a Jewish book; that Ecclesiastes must have been written by a Freethinker, and by one who had his doubts about the immortality of the soul. The best biblical students of the so-called orthodox world now admit that several stories were united to make the gospel of Saint Luke; that Hebrews is a selection from many fragments, and that no human being, not afflicted with *delirium tremens,* can understand the book of Revelation.

I am not the only one engaged in the work of destruction. Every Protestant who expresses a doubt as to the genuineness of a passage, is destroying the Bible. The gentlemen who have endeavored to treat hell as a question of syntax, and to prove that eternal punishment depends upon grammar, are helping to bring the Scriptures into contempt. Hundreds of years ago, the Catholics told the Protestant world that it was dangerous to give the Bible to the people. The Catholics were right; the Protestants were wrong. To read is to think. To think is to investigate. To investigate is, finally, to deny. That book should have been read only by priests. Every copy should have been under the lock and key of bishop, cardinal and pope. The common people should have received the Bible from the lips of the ministers. The world should have been kept in ignorance. In that way, and in that way only, could the pulpit have maintained its power. He who teaches a child the alphabet sows the seeds of heresy. I have lived to see the schoolhouse in many a village larger than the church. Every man who finds a fact, is the enemy of theology. Every man who expresses an honest thought is a soldier in the army of intellectual liberty.

Question. Mr. Talmage thinks that you laugh too much,—that you exhibit too much mirth, and that no one should smile at sacred things?

Answer. The church has always feared ridicule. The minister despises laughter. He who builds upon ignorance and awe, fears intelligence and mirth. The theologians always begin by saying: "Let us be "solemn." They know that credulity and awe are twins. They also know that while Reason is the pilot of the soul, Humor carries the lamp. Whoever has the sense of humor fully developed, cannot, by any possibility, be an orthodox theologian. He would be his own laughing stock. The most absurd stories, the most laughable miracles, read in a solemn, stately way, sound to the ears of ignorance and awe like truth. It has been the object of the church for eighteen hundred years to prevent laughter.

A smile is the dawn of a doubt.

Ministers are always talking about death, and coffins, and dust, and worms,—the cross in this life, and the fires of another. They have been the enemies of human happiness. They hate to hear even the laughter of children. There seems to have been a bond of sympathy between divinity and dyspepsia, between theology and indigestion. There is a certain pious hatred of pleasure, and those who have been "born again" are expected to despise "the transitory joys of this fleeting life." In this, they follow the example of their prophets, of whom they proudly say: "They never smiled."

Whoever laughs at a holy falsehood, is called a "scoffer." Whoever gives vent to his natural feelings is regarded as a "blasphemer," and whoever examines the Bible as he examines other books, and relies upon his reason to interpret it, is denounced as a "reprobate."

Let us respect the truth, let us laugh at miracles, and above all, let us be candid with each other.

Question. Mr. Talmage charges that you have, in your lectures, satirized your early home; that you have described with bitterness the Sundays that were forced upon you in your youth; and that in various ways you have denounced your father as a "tyrant," or a "bigot," or a "fool"?

Answer. I have described the manner in which Sunday was kept when I was a boy. My father for many years regarded the Sabbath as a sacred day. We kept Sunday as most other Christians did. I think that my father made a mistake about that day. I have no doubt he was honest about it, and really believed that it was pleasing to God for him to keep the Sabbath as he did.

I think that Sunday should not be a day of gloom, of silence and despair, or a day in which to hear that the chances are largely in favor of your being eternally damned. That day, in my opinion, should be one of joy; a day to get acquainted with your wife and children; a day to visit the woods, or the sea, or the murmuring stream; a day to gather flowers, to visit the graves of your dead, to read old poems, old letters, old books; a day to rekindle the fires of friendship and love.

Mr. Talmage says that my father was a Christian, and he then proceeds to malign his memory. It seems to me that a living Christian should at least tell the truth about one who sleeps the silent sleep of death.

I have said nothing, in any of my lectures, about my father, or about my mother, or about any of my relatives. I have not the egotism to bring them forward. They have nothing to do with the subject in hand. That my father was mistaken upon the subject of religion, I have no doubt. He was a good, a brave and honest man. I loved him living, and I love him dead. I never said to him an unkind word, and in my heart there never was of him an unkind thought. He was grand enough to say to me, that I had the same right to my opinion that he had to his. He was great enough to tell me to read the Bible for myself, to be honest with myself, and if after reading it I concluded it was not the word of God, that it was my duty to say so.

My mother died when I was but a child; and from that day—the darkest of my life—her memory has been within my heart a sacred thing, and I have felt, through all these years, her kisses on my lips.

I know that my parents—if they are conscious now —do not wish me to honor them at the expense of my manhood. I know that neither my father nor my mother would have me sacrifice upon their graves my honest thought. I know that I can only please them by being true to myself, by defending what I believe is good, by attacking what I believe is bad. Yet this minister of Christ is cruel enough, and malicious enough, to attack the reputation of the dead. What he says about my father is utterly and unqualifiedly false.

Right here, it may be well enough for me to say, that long before my father died, he threw aside, as unworthy of a place in the mind of an intelligent man, the infamous dogma of eternal fire; that he regarded with abhorrence many passages in the Old Testament; that he believed man, in another world, would have the eternal opportunity of doing right, and that the pity of God would last as long as the suffering of man. My father and my mother were good, in spite of the Old Testament. They were merciful, in spite of the one frightful doctrine in the New. They did not need the religion of Presbyterianism. Presbyterianism never made a human being better. If there is anything that will freeze the generous current of the soul, it is Calvinism. If there is any creed that will destroy charity, that will keep the tears of pity from the cheeks of men and women, it is Presbyterianism. If there is any doctrine calculated to make man bigoted, unsympathetic, and cruel, it is the doctrine of predestination. Neither my father, nor my mother, believed in the damnation of babes, nor in the inspiration of John Calvin.

Mr. Talmage professes to be a Christian. What effect has the religion of Jesus Christ had upon him? Is he the product—the natural product—of Christianity? Does the real Christian violate the sanctity of death? Does the real Christian malign the memory of the dead? Does the good Christian defame unanswering and unresisting dust?

But why should I expect kindness from a Christian? Can a minister be expected to treat with fairness a man whom his God intends to damn? If a good God is going to burn an infidel forever, in the world to come, surely a Christian should have the right to persecute him a little here.

What right has a Christian to ask anybody to love his father, or mother, or wife, or child? According to the gospels, Christ offered a reward to any one who would desert his father or his mother. He offered a premium to gentlemen for leaving their wives, and tried to bribe people to abandon their little children. He offered them happiness in this world, and a hundred fold in the next, if they would turn a deaf ear to the supplications of a father, the beseeching cry of a wife, and would leave the outstretched arms of babes. They were not even allowed to bury their fathers and their mothers. At that time they were expected to prefer Jesus to their wives and children. And now an orthodox minister says that a man ought not to express his honest thoughts, because they do not happen to be in accord with the belief of his father or mother.

Suppose Mr. Talmage should read the Bible carefully and without fear, and should come to the honest conclusion that it is not inspired, what course would he pursue for the purpose of honoring his parents? Would he say, "I cannot tell the truth, I must lie, "for the purpose of shedding a halo of glory around the memory of my mother"? Would he say: "Of course, my father and mother would a thousand times rather have their son a hypocritical Christian than an honest, manly unbeliever"? This might please Mr. Talmage, and accord perfectly with his view, but I prefer to say, that my father wished me to be an honest man. If he is in "heaven" now, I am sure that he would rather hear me attack the "inspired" word of God, honestly and bravely, than to hear me, in the solemn accents of hypocrisy, defend what I believe to be untrue.

I may be mistaken in the estimate angels put upon human beings. It may be that God likes a pretended follower better than an honest, outspoken man—one who is an infidel simply because he does not understand this God. But it seems to me, in my unregenerate condition, touched and tainted as I am by original sin, that a God of infinite power and wisdom ought to be able to make a man brave enough to have an opinion of his own. I cannot conceive of God taking any particular pride in any hypocrite he has ever made. Whatever he may say through his ministers, or whatever the angels may repeat, a manly devil stands higher in my estimation than an unmanly angel. I do not mean by this, that there are any unmanly angels, neither do I pretend that there are any manly devils. My meaning is this: If I have a Creator, I can only honor him by being true to myself, and kind and just to my fellow-men. If I wish to shed luster upon my father and mother, I can only do so by being absolutely true to myself. Never will I lay the wreath of hypocrisy upon the tombs of those I love.

Mr. Talmage takes the ground that we must defend the religious belief of our parents. He seems to forget that all parents do not believe exactly alike, and that everybody has at least two parents. Now, suppose that the father is an infidel, and the mother a Christian, what must the son do? Must he "drive the ploughshare of contempt through the grave of the father," for the purpose of honoring the mother; or must he drive the ploughshare through the grave of the mother to honor the father; or must he compromise, and talk one way and believe another? If Mr. Talmage's doctrine is correct, only persons who have no knowledge of their parents can have liberty of opinion. Foundlings would be the only free people. I do not suppose that Mr. Talmage would go so far as to say that a child would be bound by the religion of the person upon whose door-steps he was found. If he does not, then over every foundling hospital should be these words: "Home of Intellectual Liberty."

Question. Do you suppose that we will care nothing in the next world for those we loved in this? Is it worse in a man than in an angel, to care nothing for his mother?

Answer. According to Mr. Talmage, a man can be perfectly happy in heaven, with his mother in hell. He will be so entranced with the society of Christ, that he will not even inquire what has become of his wife. The Holy Ghost will keep him in such a state of happy wonder, of ecstatic joy, that the names, even, of his children will never invade his memory. It may be that I am lacking in filial affection, but I would much rather be in hell, with my parents in heaven, than be in heaven with my parents in hell. I think a thousand times more of my parents than I do of Christ. They knew me, they worked for me, they loved me, and I can imagine no heaven, no state of perfect bliss for me, in which they have no share. If God hates me, because I love them, I cannot love him.

I cannot truthfully say that I look forward with any great degree of joy, to meeting with Haggai and Habakkuk; with Jeremiah, Nehemiah, Obadiah, Zechariah or Zephaniah; with Ezekiel, Micah, or Malachi; or even with Jonah. From what little I have read of their writings, I have not formed a very high opinion of the social qualities of these gentlemen.

I want to meet the persons I have known; and if there is another life, I want to meet the really and the truly great—men who have been broad enough to be tender, and great enough to be kind.

Because I differ with my parents, because I am convinced that my father was wrong in some of his religious opinions, Mr. Talmage insists that I disgrace my parents. How did the Christian religion commence? Did not the first disciples advocate theories that their parents denied? Were they not false,—in his sense of the word,—to their fathers and mothers? How could there have been any progress in this world, if children had not gone beyond their parents? Do you consider that the inventor of a steel plow cast a slur upon his father who scratched the ground with a wooden one? I do not consider that an invention by the son is a slander upon the father; I regard each invention simply as an improvement; and every father should be exceedingly proud of an ingenious son. If Mr. Talmage has a son, it will be impossible for him to honor his father except by differing with him.

It is very strange that Mr. Talmage, a believer in Christ, should object to any man for not loving his mother and his father, when his Master, according to the gospel of Saint Luke, says: "If any man come to me, and hate not his father, and mother, and wife, and children, and brethren, and sisters, yea, and his own life also, he cannot be my disciple."

According to this, I have to make my choice between my wife, my children, and Jesus Christ. I have concluded to stand by my folks—both in this world, and in "the world to come."

Question. Mr. Talmage asks you whether, in your judgment, the Bible was a good, or an evil, to your parents?

Answer. I think it was an evil. The worst thing about my father was his religion. He would have been far happier, in my judgment, without it. I think I get more real joy out of life than he did. He was a man of a very great and tender heart. He was continually thinking—for many years of his life—of the thousands and thousands going down to eternal fire. That doctrine filled his days with gloom, and his eyes with tears. I think that my father and mother would have been far happier had they believed as I do. How any one can get any joy out of the Christian religion is past my comprehension. If that religion is true, hundreds of millions are now in hell, and thousands of millions yet unborn will be. How such a fact can form any part of the "glad tidings of great joy," is amazing to me. It is impossible for me to love a being who would create countless millions for eternal pain. It is impossible for me to worship the God of the Bible, or the God of Calvin, or the God of the Westminster Catechism.

Question. I see that Mr. Talmage challenges you to read the fourteenth chapter of Saint John. Are you willing to accept the challenge; or have you ever read that chapter?

Answer. I do not claim to be very courageous, but I have read that chapter, and am very glad that Mr. Talmage has called attention to it. According to the gospels, Christ did many miracles. He healed the sick, gave sight to the blind, made the lame walk, and raised the dead. In the fourteenth chapter of Saint John, twelfth verse, I find the following:

"Verily, verily, I say unto you: He that believeth on me, the works that I do shall he do also; and greater works than these shall he do, because I go unto my Father."

I am willing to accept that as a true test of a believer. If Mr. Talmage really believes in Jesus Christ, he ought to be able to do at least as great miracles as Christ is said to have done. Will Mr. Talmage have the kindness to read the fourteenth chapter of John, and then give me some proof, in accordance with that chapter, that he is a believer in Jesus Christ? Will he have the kindness to perform a miracle?—for instance, produce a "local flood," make a worm to smite a gourd, or "prepare a fish"?

Can he do anything of that nature? Can he even cause a "vehement east wind"? What evidence, according to the Bible, can Mr. Talmage give of his belief? How does he prove that he is a Christian? By hating infidels and maligning Christians? Let Mr. Talmage furnish the evidence, according to the fourteenth chapter of Saint John, or forever after hold his peace.

He has my thanks for calling my attention to the fourteenth chapter of Saint John.

Question. Mr. Talmage charges that you are attempting to destroy the "chief solace of the world," without offering any substitute. How do you answer this?

Answer. If he calls Christianity the "chief solace of the world," and if by Christianity he means that all who do not believe in the inspiration of the Scriptures, and have no faith in Jesus Christ, are to be eternally damned, then I admit that I am doing the best I can to take that "solace" from the human heart. I do not believe that the Bible, when properly understood, is, or ever has been, a comfort to any human being. Surely, no good man can be comforted by reading a book in which he finds that a large majority of mankind have been sentenced to eternal fire. In the doctrine of total depravity there is no "solace." In the doctrine of "election" there can be no joy until the returns are in, and a majority found for you.

Question. Mr. Talmage says that you are taking away the world's medicines, and in place of anesthetics, in place of laudanum drops, you read an essay to the man in pain, on the absurdities of morphine and nervines in general.

Answer. It is exactly the other way. I say, let us depend upon morphine, not upon prayer. Do not send for the minister—take a little laudanum. Do not read your Bible,—chloroform is better. Do not waste your time listening to meaningless sermons, but take real, genuine soporifics.

I regard the discoverer of ether as a benefactor. I look upon every great surgeon as a blessing to mankind. I regard one doctor, skilled in his profession, of more importance to the world than all the orthodox ministers.

Mr. Talmage should remember that for hundreds of years, the church fought, with all its power, the science of medicine. Priests used to cure diseases by selling little pieces of paper covered with cabalistic marks. They filled their treasuries by the sale of holy water. They healed the sick by relics—the teeth and ribs of saints, the finger-nails of departed worthies, and the hair of glorified virgins. Infidelity said: "Send for the doctor." Theology said: "Stick to the priest." Infidelity,—that is to say, science,—said: "Vaccinate him." The priest said: "Pray;—I will sell you a charm." The doctor was regarded as a man who was endeavoring to take from God his means of punishment. He was supposed to spike the artillery of Jehovah, to wet the powder of the Almighty, and to steal the flint from the musket of heavenly retribution.

Infidelity has never relied upon essays, it has never relied upon words, it has never relied upon prayers, it has never relied upon angels or gods; it has relied upon the honest efforts of men and women. It has relied upon investigation, observation, experience, and above all, upon human reason.

We, in America, know how much prayers are worth. We have lately seen millions of people upon their knees. What was the result?

In the olden times, when a plague made its appearance, the people fell upon their knees and died. When pestilence came, they rushed to their cathedrals, they implored their priests—and died. God had no pity upon his ignorant children. At last, Science came to the rescue. Science,—not in the attitude of prayer, with closed eyes, but in the attitude of investigation, with open eyes,—looked for and discovered some of the laws of health. Science found that cleanliness was far better than godliness. It said: Do not spend your time in praying;—clean your houses, clean your streets, clean yourselves. This pestilence is not a punishment. Health is not simply a favor of the gods. Health depends upon conditions, and when the conditions are violated, disease is inevitable, and no God can save you. Health depends upon your surroundings, and when these are favorable, the roses are in your cheeks.

We find in the Old Testament that God gave to Moses a thousand directions for ascertaining the presence of leprosy. Yet it never occurred to this God to tell Moses how to cure the disease. Within the lids of the Old Testament, we have no information upon a subject of such vital importance to mankind.

It may, however, be claimed by Mr. Talmage, that this statement is a little too broad, and I will therefore give one recipe that I find in the fourteenth chapter of Leviticus:

"Then shall the priest command to take for him that is to be cleansed two birds alive and clean, and cedar wood, and scarlet, and hyssop; and the priest shall command that one of the birds be killed in an earthen vessel over running water. As for the living bird, he shall take it, and the cedar wood, and the scarlet, and the hyssop, and shall dip them and the living bird in the blood of the bird that was killed over the running water. And he shall sprinkle upon him that is to be cleansed from the leprosy seven times, and shall pronounce him clean, and shall let the living bird loose into the open field."

Prophets were predicting evil—filling the country with their wails and cries, and yet it never occurred to them to tell one solitary thing of the slightest importance to mankind. Why did not these inspired men tell us how to cure some of the diseases that have decimated the world? Instead of spending forty days and forty nights with Moses, telling him how to build a large tent, and how to cut the garments of priests, why did God not give him a little useful information in respect to the laws of health?

Mr. Talmage must remember that the church has invented no anodynes, no anesthetics, no medicines, and has affected no cures. The doctors have not been inspired. All these useful things men have discovered for themselves, aided by no prophet and by no divine Savior. Just to the extent that man has depended upon the other world, he has failed to make the best of this. Just in the proportion that he has depended on his own efforts, he has advanced. The church has always said:

"Consider the lilies of the field; they toil not, neither do they spin." "Take no thought for the morrow." Whereas, the real common sense of this world has said: "No matter whether lilies toil and spin, or not, if you would succeed, you must work; you must take thought for the morrow, you must look beyond the present day, you must provide for your wife and your children."

What can I be expected to give as a substitute for perdition? It is enough to show that it does not exist. What does a man want in place of a disease? Health. And what is better calculated to increase the happiness of mankind than to know that the doctrine of eternal pain is infinitely and absurdly false?

Take theology from the world, and natural Love remains, Science is still here, Music will not be lost, the page of History will still be open, the walls of the world will still be adorned with Art, and the niches rich with Sculpture.

Take theology from the world, and we all shall have a common hope,— and the fear of hell will be removed from every human heart.

Take theology from the world, and millions of men will be compelled to earn an honest living. Impudence will not tax credulity. The vampire of hypocrisy will not suck the blood of honest toil.

Take theology from the world, and the churches can be schools, and the cathedrals universities.

Take theology from the world, and the money wasted on superstition will do away with want.

Take theology from the world, and every brain will find itself without a chain.

There is a vast difference between what is called infidelity and theology.

Infidelity is honest. When it reaches the confines of reason, it says: "I know no further."

Infidelity does not palm its guess upon an ignorant world as a demonstration.

Infidelity proves nothing by slander—establishes nothing by abuse.

Infidelity has nothing to hide. It has no "holy of holies," except the abode of truth. It has no curtain that the hand of investigation has not the right to draw aside. It lives in the cloudless light, in the very noon, of human eyes.

Infidelity has no bible to be blasphemed. It does not cringe before an angry God.

Infidelity says to every man: Investigate for yourself. There is no punishment for unbelief.

Infidelity asks no protection from legislatures. It wants no man fined because he contradicts its doctrines.

Infidelity relies simply upon evidence—not evidence of the dead, but of the living.

Infidelity has no infallible pope. It relies only upon infallible fact. It has no priest except the interpreter of Nature. The universe is its church. Its bible is everything that is true. It implores every man to verify every word for himself, and it implores him to say, if he does not believe it, that he does not.

Infidelity does not fear contradiction. It is not afraid of being laughed at. It invites the scrutiny of all doubters, of all unbelievers. It does not rely upon awe, but upon reason. It says to the whole world: It is dangerous not to think. It is dangerous not to be honest. It is dangerous not to investigate. It is dangerous not to follow where your reason leads.

Infidelity requires every man to judge for himself. Infidelity preserves the manhood of man.

Question. Mr. Talmage also says that you are trying to put out the light-houses on the coast of the next world; that you are "about to leave everybody in darkness at the narrows of death"?

Answer. There can be no necessity for these light-houses, unless the God of Mr. Talmage has planted rocks and reefs within that unknown sea. If there is no hell, there is no need of any light-house on the shores of the next world; and only those are interested in keeping up these pretended light-houses who are paid for trimming invisible wicks and supplying the lamps with allegorical oil. Mr. Talmage is one of these light-house keepers, and he knows that if it is ascertained that the coast is not dangerous, the light-house will be abandoned, and the keeper will have to find employment elsewhere. As a matter of fact, every church is a useless light-house. It warns us only against breakers that do not exist. Whenever a mariner tells one of the keepers that there is no danger, then all the keepers combine to destroy the reputation of that mariner.

No one has returned from the other world to tell us whether they have light-houses on that shore or not; or whether the light-houses on this shore—one of which Mr. Talmage is tending—have ever sent a cheering ray across the sea.

Nature has furnished every human being with a light more or less brilliant, more or less powerful. That light is Reason; and he who blows that light out, is in utter darkness. It has been the business of the church for centuries to extinguish the lamp of the mind, and to convince the people that their own reason is utterly unreliable. The church has asked all men to rely only upon the light of the church.

Every priest has been not only a light-house but a guide-board. He has threatened eternal damnation to all who travel on some other road. These guide-boards have been toll-gates, and the principal reason why the churches have wanted people to go their road is, that tolls might be collected. They have regarded unbelievers as the owners of turnpikes do people who go 'cross lots. The toll-gate man always tells you that other roads are dangerous—filled with quagmires and quicksand.

Every church is a kind of insurance society, and proposes, for a small premium, to keep you from eternal fire. Of course, the man who tells you that there is to be no fire, interferes with the business, and is denounced as a malicious meddler and blasphemer. The fires of this world sustain the same relation to insurance companies that the fires of the next do to the churches.

Mr. Talmage also insists that I am breaking up the "life-boats." Why should a ship built by infinite wisdom, by an infinite shipbuilder, carry life-boats? The reason we have life-boats now is, that we are not entirely sure of the ship. We know that man has not yet found out how to make a ship that can certainly brave all the dangers of the deep. For this reason we carry life-boats. But infinite wisdom must surely build ships that do not need life-boats. Is there to be a wreck at last? Is God's ship to go down in storm and darkness? Will it be necessary at last to forsake his ship and depend upon life-boats?

For my part, I do not wish to be rescued by a lifeboat. When the ship, bearing the whole world, goes down, I am willing to go down with it—with my wife, with my children, and with those I have loved. I will not slip ashore in an orthodox canoe with somebody else's folks,—I will stay with my own.

What a picture is presented by the church! A few in life's last storm are to be saved; and the saved, when they reach shore, are to look back with joy upon the great ship going down to the eternal depths! This is what I call the unutterable meanness of orthodox Christianity.

Mr. Talmage speaks of the "meanness of infidelity."

The meanness of orthodox Christianity permits the husband to be saved, and to be ineffably happy, while the wife of his bosom is suffering the tortures of hell.

The meanness of orthodox Christianity tells the boy that he can go to heaven and have an eternity of bliss, and that this bliss will not even be clouded by the fact that the mother who bore him writhes in eternal pain.

The meanness of orthodox Christianity allows a soul to be so captivated with the companionship of angels as to forget all the old loves and friendships of this world.

The meanness of orthodox Christianity, its unspeakable selfishness, allows a soul in heaven to exult in the fact of its own salvation, and at the same time to care nothing for the damnation of all the rest.

The orthodox Christian says that if he can only save his little soul, if he can barely squeeze into heaven, if he can only get past Saint Peter's gate, if he can by hook or crook climb up the opposite bank of Jordan, if he can get a harp in his hand, it matters not to him what becomes of brother or sister, father or mother, wife or child. He is willing that they should burn if he can sing.

Oh, the unutterable meanness of orthodox Christianity, the infinite heartlessness of the orthodox angels, who with tearless eyes will forever gaze upon the agonies of those who were once blood of their blood and flesh of their flesh!

Mr. Talmage describes a picture of the scourging of Christ, painted by Rubens, and he tells us that he was so appalled by this picture—by the sight of the naked back, swollen and bleeding—that he could not have lived had he continued to look; yet this same man, who could not bear to gaze upon a painted pain, expects to be perfectly happy in heaven, while countless billions of actual—not painted—men, women, and children writhe—not in a pictured flame, but in the real and quenchless fires of hell.

Question. Mr. Talmage also claims that we are indebted to Christianity for schools, colleges, universities, hospitals and asylums?

Answer. This shows that Mr. Talmage has not read the history of the world. Long before Christianity had a place, there were vast libraries. There were thousands of schools before a Christian existed on the earth. There were hundreds of hospitals before a line of the New Testament was written. Hundreds of years before Christ, there were hospitals in India,—not only for men, women and children, but even for beasts. There were hospitals in Egypt long before Moses was born. They knew enough then to cure insanity with music. They surrounded the insane with flowers, and treated them with kindness.

The great libraries at Alexandria were not Christian. The most intellectual nation of the Middle Ages was not Christian. While Christians were imprisoning people for saying that the earth is round, the Moors in Spain were teaching geography with globes. They had even calculated the circumference of the earth by the tides of the Red Sea.

Where did education come from? For a thousand years Christianity destroyed books and paintings and statues. For a thousand years Christianity was filled with hatred toward every effort of the human mind. We got paper from the Moors. Printing had been known thousands of years before, in China. A few manuscripts, containing a portion of the literature of Greece, a few enriched with the best thoughts of the Roman world, had been preserved from the general wreck and ruin wrought by Christian hate. These became the seeds of intellectual progress. For a thousand years Christianity controlled Europe. The Mohammedans were far in advance of the Christians with hospitals and asylums and institutions of learning.

Just in proportion that we have done away with what is known as orthodox Christianity, humanity has taken its place. Humanity has built all the asylums, all the hospitals. Humanity, not Christianity, has done these things. The people of this country are all willing to be taxed that the insane may be cared for, that the sick, the helpless, and the destitute may be provided for, not because they are Christians, but because they are humane; and they are not humane because they are Christians.

The colleges of this country have been poisoned by theology, and their usefulness almost destroyed. Just in proportion that they have gotten from ecclesiastical control, they have become a good. That college, today, which has the most religion has the least true learning; and that college which is the nearest free, does the most good. Colleges that pit Moses against modern geology, that undertake to overthrow the Copernican system by appealing to Joshua, have done, and are doing, very little good in this world.

Suppose that in the first century Pagans had said to Christians: Where are your hospitals, where are your asylums, where are your works of charity, where are your colleges and universities?

The Christians undoubtedly would have replied: We have not been in power. There are but few of us. We have been persecuted to that degree that it has been about as much as we could do to maintain ourselves.

Reasonable Pagans would have regarded such an answer as perfectly satisfactory. Yet that question could have been asked of Christianity after it had held the reins of power for a thousand years, and Christians would have been compelled to say: We have no universities, we have no colleges, we have no real asylums.

The Christian now asks of the atheist: Where is your asylum, where is your hospital, where is your university? And the atheist answers: There have been but few atheists. The world is not yet sufficiently advanced to produce them. For hundreds and hundreds of years, the minds of men have been darkened by the superstitions of Christianity. Priests have thundered against human knowledge, have denounced human reason, and have done all within their power to prevent the real progress of mankind. You must also remember that Christianity has made more lunatics than it ever provided asylums for. Christianity has driven more men and women crazy than all other religions combined. Hundreds and thousands and millions have lost their reason in contemplating the monstrous falsehoods of Christianity. Thousands of mothers, thinking of their sons in hell—thousands of fathers, believing their boys and girls in perdition, have lost their reason.

So, let it be distinctly understood, that Christianity has made ten lunatics—twenty—one hundred—where it has provided an asylum for one.

Mr. Talmage also speaks of the hospitals. When we take into consideration the wars that have been waged on account of religion, the countless thousands who have been maimed and wounded, through all the years, by wars produced by theology—then I say that Christianity has not built hospitals enough to take care of her own wounded—not enough to take care of one in a hundred. Where Christianity has bound up the wounds of one, it has pierced the bodies of a hundred others with sword and spear, with bayonet and ball. Where she has provided one bed in a hospital, she has laid away a hundred bodies in bloody graves.

Of course I do not expect the church to do anything but beg. Churches produce nothing. They are like the lilies of the field. "They toil not, neither do they spin, yet Solomon in all his glory was not arrayed like most of them."

The churches raise no corn nor wheat. They simply collect tithes. They carry the alms' dish. They pass the plate. They take toll. Of course a mendicant is not expected to produce anything. He does not support,— he is supported. The church does not help. She receives, she devours, she consumes, and she produces only discord. She exchanges mistakes for provisions, faith for food, prayers for pence. The church is a beggar. But we have this consolation: In this age of the world, this beggar is not on horseback, and even the walking is not good.

Question. Mr. Talmage says that infidels have done no good?

Answer. Well, let us see. In the first place, what is an "infidel"? He is simply a man in advance of his time. He is an intellectual pioneer. He is the dawn of a new day. He is a gentleman with an idea of his own, for which he gave no receipt to the church. He is a man who has not been branded as the property of some one else. An "infidel" is one who has made a declaration of independence. In other words, he is a man who has had a doubt. To have a doubt means that you have thought upon the subject—that you have investigated the question; and he who investigates any religion will doubt.

All the advance that has been made in the religious world has been made by "infidels," by "heretics," by "skeptics," by doubters,—that is to say, by thoughtful men. The doubt does not come from the ignorant members of your congregations. Heresy is not born of stupidity,—it is not the child of the brainless. He who is so afraid of hurting the reputation of his father and mother that he refuses to advance, is not a "heretic." The "heretic" is not true to falsehood. Orthodoxy is. He who stands faithfully by a mistake is "orthodox." He who, discovering that it is a mistake, has the courage to say so, is an "infidel."

An infidel is an intellectual discoverer—one who finds new isles, new continents, in the vast realm of thought. The dwellers on the orthodox shore denounce this brave sailor of the seas as a buccaneer.

And yet we are told that the thinkers of new thoughts have never been of value to the world. Voltaire did more for human liberty than all the orthodox ministers living and dead. He broke a thousand times more chains than Luther. Luther simply substituted his chain for that of the Catholics. Voltaire had none. The Encyclopedists of France did more for liberty than all the writers upon theology. Bruno did more for mankind than millions of "believers." Spinoza contributed more to the growth of the human intellect than all the orthodox theologians.

Men have not done good simply because they have believed this or that doctrine. They have done good in the intellectual world as they have thought and secured for others the liberty to think and to express their thoughts. They have done good in the physical world by teaching their fellows how to triumph over the obstructions of nature. Every man who has taught his fellow-man to think, has been a benefactor. Every one who has supplied his fellow-men with facts, and insisted upon their right to think, has been a blessing to his kind.

Mr. Talmage, in order to show what Christians have done, points us to Whitefield, Luther, Oberlin, Judson, Martyn, Bishop McIlvaine and Hannah More. I would not for one moment compare George Whitefield with the inventor of movable type, and there is no parallel between Frederick Oberlin and the inventor of paper; not the slightest between Martin Luther and the discoverer of the New World; not the least between Adoniram Judson and the inventor of the reaper, nor between Henry Martyn and the discoverer of photography. Of what use to the world was Bishop McIlvaine, compared with the inventor of needles? Of what use were a hundred such priests compared with the inventor of matches, or even of clothes-pins? Suppose that Hannah More had never lived? about the same number would read her writings now. It is hardly fair to compare her with the inventor of the steamship? The progress of the world—its present improved condition—can be accounted for only by the discoveries of genius, only by men who have had the courage to express their honest thoughts.

After all, the man who invented the telescope found out more about heaven than the closed eyes of prayer had ever discovered. I feel absolutely certain that the inventor of the steam engine was a greater benefactor to mankind than the writer of the Presbyterian creed. I may be mistaken, but I think that railways have done more to civilize mankind, than any system of theology. I believe that the printing press has done more for the world than the pulpit. It is my opinion that the discoveries of Kepler did a thousand times more to enlarge the minds of men than the prophecies of Daniel. I feel under far greater obligation to Humboldt than to Haggai. The inventor of the plow did more good than the maker of the first rosary—because, say what you will, plowing is better than praying; we can live by plowing without praying, but we can not live by praying without plowing. So I put my faith in the plow.

As Jehovah has ceased to make garments for his children,—as he has stopped making coats of skins, I have great respect for the inventors of the spinning-jenny and the sewing machine. As no more laws are given from Sinai, I have admiration for the real statesmen. As miracles have ceased, I rely on medicine, and on a reasonable compliance with the conditions of health.

I have infinite respect for the inventors, the thinkers, the discoverers, and above all, for the unknown millions who have, without the hope of fame, lived and labored for the ones they loved.

FIFTH INTERVIEW.

Parson. You had better join the church; it is the safer way.
Sinner. I can't live up to your doctrines, and you know it.
Parson. Well, you can come as near it in the church as out; and forgiveness will be easier if you join us.
Sinner. What do you mean by that?
Parson. I will tell you. If you join the church, and happen to back-slide now and then, Christ will say to his Father: "That man is a "friend of mine, and you may charge his account to me."

Question. What have you to say about the fifth sermon of the Rev. Mr. Talmage in reply to you?

Answer. The text from which he preached is: "Do men gather grapes of thorns, or figs of thistles?" I am compelled to answer these questions in the negative. That is one reason why I am an infidel. I do not believe that anybody can gather grapes of thorns, or figs of thistles. That is exactly my doctrine. But the doctrine of the church is, that you can. The church says, that just at the last, no matter if you have spent your whole life in raising thorns and thistles, in planting and watering and hoeing and plowing thorns and thistles—that just at the last, if you will repent, between hoeing the last thistle and taking the last breath, you can reach out the white and palsied hand of death and gather from every thorn a cluster of grapes and from every thistle an abundance of figs. The church insists that in this way you can gather enough grapes and figs to last you through all eternity.

My doctrine is, that he who raises thorns must harvest thorns. If you sow thorns, you must reap thorns; and there is no way by which an innocent being can have the thorns you raise thrust into his brow, while you gather his grapes.

But Christianity goes even further than this. It insists that a man can plant grapes and gather thorns. Mr. Talmage insists that, no matter how good you are, no matter how kind, no matter how much you love your wife and children, no matter how many self-denying acts you do, you will not be allowed to eat of the grapes you raise; that God will step between you and the natural consequences of your goodness, and not allow you to reap what you sow. Mr. Talmage insists, that if you have no faith in the Lord Jesus Christ, although you have been good here, you will reap eternal pain as your harvest; that the effect of honesty and kindness will not be peace and joy, but agony and pain. So that the church does insist not only that you can gather grapes from thorns, but thorns from grapes.

I believe exactly the other way. If a man is a good man here, dying will not change him, and he will land on the shore of another world—if there is one—the same good man that he was when he left this; and I do not believe there is any God in this universe who can afford to damn a good man. This God will say to this man: You loved your wife, your children, and your friends, and I love you. You treated others with kindness; I will treat you in the same way. But Mr. Talmage steps up to his God, nudges his elbow, and says: Although he was a very good man, he belonged to no church; he was a blasphemer; he denied the whale story, and after I explained that Jonah was only in the whale's mouth, he still denied it; and thereupon Mr. Talmage expects that his infinite God will fly in a passion, and in a perfect rage will say: What! Did he deny that story? Let him be eternally damned!

Not only this, but Mr. Talmage insists that a man may have treated his wife like a wild beast; may have trampled his child beneath the feet of his rage; may have lived a life of dishonesty, of infamy, and yet, having repented on his dying bed, having made his peace with God through the intercession of his Son, he will be welcomed in heaven with shouts of joy. I deny it. I do not believe that angels can be so quickly made from rascals. I have but little confidence in repentance without restitution, and a husband who has driven a wife to insanity and death by his cruelty—afterward repenting and finding himself in heaven, and missing his wife,—were he worthy to be an angel, would wander through all the gulfs of hell until he clasped her once again.

Now, the next question is, What must be done with those who are sometimes good and sometimes bad? That is my condition. If there is another world, I expect to have the same opportunity of behaving myself that I have here. If, when I get there, I fail to act as I should, I expect to reap what I sow. If, when I arrive at the New Jerusalem, I go into the thorn business, I expect to harvest what I plant. If I am wise enough to start a vineyard, I expect to have grapes in the early fall. But if I do there as I have done here—plant some grapes and some thorns, and harvest them together—I expect to fare very much as I have fared here. But I expect year by year to grow wiser, to plant fewer thorns every spring, and more grapes.

Question. Mr. Talmage charges that you have taken the ground that the Bible is a cruel book, and has produced cruel people?

Answer. Yes, I have taken that ground, and I maintain it. The Bible was produced by cruel people, and in its turn it has produced people like its authors. The extermination of the Canaanites was cruel. Most of the laws of Moses were bloodthirsty and cruel. Hundreds of offences were punishable by death, while now, in civilized countries, there are only two crimes for which the punishment is capital. I charge that Moses and Joshua and David and Samuel and Solomon were cruel. I believe that to read and believe the Old Testament naturally makes a man careless of human life. That book has produced hundreds of religious wars, and it has furnished the battle-cries of bigotry for fifteen hundred years.

The Old Testament is filled with cruelty, but its cruelty stops with this world, its malice ends with death; whenever its victim has reached the grave, revenge is satisfied. Not so with the New Testament. It pursues its victim forever. After death, comes hell; after the grave, the worm that never dies. So that, as a matter of fact, the New Testament is infinitely more cruel than the Old.

Nothing has so tended to harden the human heart as the doctrine of eternal punishment, and that passage: "He that believeth and is baptized shall be saved, and he that believeth not shall be damned," has shed more blood than all the other so-called "sacred books" of all this world.

I insist that the Bible is cruel. The Bible invented instruments of torture. The Bible laid the foundations of the Inquisition. The Bible furnished the fagots and the martyrs. The Bible forged chains not only for the hands, but for the brains of men. The Bible was at the bottom of the massacre of St. Bartholomew. Every man who has been persecuted for religion's sake has been persecuted by the Bible. That sacred book has been a beast of prey.

The truth is, Christians have been good in spite of the Bible. The Bible has lived upon the reputations of good men and good women,—men and women who were good notwithstanding the brutality they found upon the inspired page. Men have said: "My mother believed in the Bible; my mother was good; therefore, the Bible is good," when probably the mother never read a chapter in it.

The Bible produced the Church of Rome, and Torquemada was a product of the Bible. Philip of Spain and the Duke of Alva were produced by the Bible. For thirty years Europe was one vast battlefield, and the war was produced by the Bible. The revocation of the Edict of Nantes was produced by the sacred Scriptures. The instruments of torture—the pincers, the thumb-screws, the racks, were produced by the word of God. The Quakers of New England were whipped and burned by the Bible—their children were stolen by the Bible. The slave-ship had for its sails the leaves of the Bible. Slavery was upheld in the United States by the Bible. The Bible was the auction-block. More than this, worse than this, infinitely beyond the computation of imagination, the despotisms of the old world all rested and still rest upon the Bible. "The powers that be" were supposed to have been "ordained of God;" and he who rose against his king periled his soul.

In this connection, and in order to show the state of society when the church had entire control of civil and ecclesiastical affairs, it may be well enough to read the following, taken from the New York Sun of March 21, 1882. From this little extract, it will be easy in the imagination to reorganize the government that then existed, and to see clearly the state of society at that time. This can be done upon the same principle that one scale tells of the entire fish, or one bone of the complete animal:

"From records in the State archives of Hesse-Darmstadt, dating back to the thirteenth century, it appears that the public executioner's fee for boiling a criminal in oil was twenty-four florins; for decapitating with the sword, fifteen florins and-a-half; for quartering, the same; for breaking on the wheel, five florins, thirty kreuzers; for tearing a man to pieces, eighteen florins. Ten florins per head was his charge for hanging, and he burned delinquents alive at the rate of fourteen florins apiece. For applying the 'Spanish boot' his fee was only two florins. Five florins were paid to him every time he subjected a refractory witness to the torture of the rack. The same amount was his due for 'branding' the sign of the gallows with a red-hot iron upon 'the back, forehead, or cheek of a thief,' as well as for 'cutting off the nose and ears' of a slanderer or 'blasphemer.' Flogging with rods was a cheap punishment, its remuneration being fixed at three florins, thirty kreuzers."

The Bible has made men cruel. It is a cruel book. And yet, amidst its thorns, amidst its thistles, amidst its nettles and its swords and pikes, there are some flowers, and these I wish, in common with all good men, to save.

I do not believe that men have ever been made merciful in war by reading the Old Testament. I do not believe that men have ever been prompted to break the chain of a slave by reading the Pentateuch. The question is not whether Florence Nightingale and Miss Dix were cruel. I have said nothing about John Howard, nothing about Abbott Lawrence. I say nothing about people in this connection. The question is: Is the Bible a cruel book? not: Was Miss Nightingale a cruel woman? There have been thousands and thousands of loving, tender and charitable Mohammedans. Mohammedan mothers love their children as well as Christian mothers can. Mohammedans have died in defense of the Koran—died for the honor of an impostor. There were millions of charitable people in India—millions in Egypt—and I am not sure that the world has ever produced people who loved one another better than the Egyptians.

I think there are many things in the Old Testament calculated to make man cruel. Mr. Talmage asks:

"What has been the effect upon your children? As they have become more and more fond of the Scriptures have they become more and more fond of tearing off the wings of flies and pinning grass-hoppers and robbing birds' nests?"

I do not believe that reading the bible would make them tender toward flies or grasshoppers. According to that book, God used to punish animals for the crimes of their owners. He drowned the animals in a flood. He visited cattle with disease. He bruised them to death with hailstones—killed them by the thousand. Will the reading of these things make children kind to animals? So, the whole system of sacrifices in the Old Testament is calculated to harden the heart. The butchery of oxen and lambs, the killing of doves, the perpetual destruction of life, the continual shedding of blood—these things, if they have any tendency, tend only to harden the heart of childhood.

The Bible does not stop simply with the killing of animals. The Jews were commanded to kill their neighbors—not only the men, but the women; not only the women, but the babes. In accordance with the command of God, the Jews killed not only their neighbors, but their own brothers; and according to this book, which is the foundation, as Mr. Talmage believes, of all mercy, men were commanded to kill their wives because they differed with them on the subject of religion.

Nowhere in the world can be found laws more unjust and cruel than in the Old Testament.

Question. Mr. Talmage wants you to tell where the cruelty of the Bible crops out in the lives of Christians?

Answer. In the first place, millions of Christians have been persecutors. Did they get the idea of persecution from the Bible? Will not every honest man admit that the early Christians, by reading the Old

Testament, became convinced that it was not only their privilege, but their duty, to destroy heathen nations? Did they not, by reading the same book, come to the conclusion that it was their solemn duty to extirpate heresy and heretics? According to the New Testament, nobody could be saved unless he believed in the Lord Jesus Christ. The early Christians believed this dogma. They also believed that they had a right to defend themselves and their children from "heretics."

We all admit that a man has a right to defend his children against the assaults of a would-be murderer, and he has the right to carry this defense to the extent of killing the assailant. If we have the right to kill people who are simply trying to kill the bodies of our children, of course we have the right to kill them when they are endeavoring to assassinate, not simply their bodies, but their souls. It was in this way Christians reasoned. If the Testament is right, their reasoning was correct. Whoever believes the New Testament literally—whoever is satisfied that it is absolutely the word of God, will become a persecutor. All religious persecution has been, and is, in exact harmony with the teachings of the Old and New Testaments. Of course I mean with some of the teachings. I admit that there are passages in both the Old and New Testaments against persecution. These are passages quoted only in time of peace. Others are repeated to feed the flames of war.

I find, too, that reading the Bible and believing the Bible do not prevent even ministers from telling falsehoods about their opponents. I find that the Rev. Mr. Talmage is willing even to slander the dead,—that he is willing to stain the memory of a Christian, and that he does not hesitate to give circulation to what he knows to be untrue. Mr. Talmage has himself, I believe, been the subject of a church trial. How many of the Christian witnesses against him, in his judgment, told the truth? Yet they were all Bible readers and Bible believers. What effect, in his judgment, did the reading of the Bible have upon his enemies? Is he willing to admit that the testimony of a Bible, reader and believer is true? Is he willing to accept the testimony even of ministers?—of his brother ministers? Did reading the Bible make them bad people? Was it a belief in the Bible that colored their testimony? Or, was it a belief in the Bible that made Mr. Talmage deny the truth of their statements?

Question. Mr. Talmage charges you with having said that the Scriptures are a collection of polluted writings?

Answer. I have never said such a thing. I have said, and I still say, that there are passages in the Bible unfit to be read—passages that never should have been written—passages, whether inspired or uninspired, that can by no possibility do any human being any good. I have always admitted that there are good passages in the Bible—many good, wise and just laws—many things calculated to make men better— many things calculated to make men worse. I admit that the Bible is a mixture of good and bad, of truth and falsehood, of history and fiction, of sense and nonsense, of virtue and vice, of aspiration and revenge, of liberty and tyranny.

I have never said anything against Solomon's Song. I like it better than I do any book that precedes it, because it touches upon the human. In the desert of murder, wars of extermination, polygamy, concubinage and slavery, it is an oasis where the trees grow, where the birds sing, and where human love blossoms and fills the air with perfume. I do not regard that book as obscene. There are many things in it that are beautiful and tender, and it is calculated to do good rather than harm.

Neither have I any objection to the book of Ecclesiastes—except a few interpolations in it. That book was written by a Freethinker, by a philosopher. There is not the slightest mention of God in it, nor of another state of existence. All portions in which God is mentioned are interpolations. With some of this book I agree heartily. I believe in the doctrine of enjoying yourself, if you can, to-day. I think it foolish to spend all your years in heaping up treasures, not knowing but he who will spend them is to be an idiot. I believe it is far better to be happy with your wife and child now, than to be miserable here, with angelic expectations in some other world.

Mr. Talmage is mistaken when he supposes that all Bible believers have good homes, that all Bible readers are kind in their families. As a matter of fact, nearly all the wife-whippers of the United States are orthodox. Nine-tenths of the people in the penitentiaries are believers. Scotland is one of the most orthodox countries in the world, and one of the most intemperate. Hundreds and hundreds of women are arrested every year in Glasgow for drunkenness. Visit the Christian homes in the manufacturing districts of England. Talk with the beaters of children and whippers of wives, and you will find them believers. Go into what is known as the "Black Country," and you will have an idea of the Christian civilization of England.

Let me tell you something about the "Black Country." There women work in iron; there women do the work of men. Let me give you an instance: A commission was appointed by Parliament to examine into the condition of the women in the "Black Country," and a report was made. In that report I read the following:

"A superintendent of a brickyard where women were engaged in carrying bricks from the yard to the kiln, said to one of the women: 'Eliza, you don't appear to be very uppish this morning.' "

" 'Neither would you be very uppish, sir,' she replied, 'if you had had a child last night.' "

This gives you an idea of the Christian civilization of England.

England and Ireland produce most of the prize-fighters. The scientific burglar is a product of Great Britain. There is not the great difference that Mr. Talmage supposes, between the morality of Pekin and of New York. I doubt if there is a city in the world with more crime according to the population than New York, unless it be London, or it may be Dublin, or Brooklyn, or possibly Glasgow, where a man too pious to read a newspaper published on Sunday, stole millions from the poor.

I do not believe there is a country in the world where there is more robbery than in Christian lands—no country where more cashiers are defaulters, where more presidents of banks take the money of depositors, where there is more adulteration of food, where fewer ounces make a pound, where fewer inches make a yard, where there is more breach of trust, more respectable larceny under the name of embezzlement, or more slander circulated as gospel.

Question. Mr. Talmage insists that there are no contradictions in the Bible—that it is a perfect harmony from Genesis to Revelation—a harmony as perfect as any piece of music ever written by Beethoven or Handel?

Answer. Of course, if God wrote it, the Bible ought to be perfect. I do not see why a minister should be so perfectly astonished to find that an inspired book is consistent with itself throughout. Yet the truth is, the Bible is infinitely inconsistent.

Compare the two systems—the system of Jehovah and that of Jesus. In the Old Testament the doctrine of "an eye for an eye and a tooth for a tooth" was taught. In the New Testament, "forgive your enemies," and "pray for those who despitefully use you and persecute you." In the Old Testament it is kill, burn, massacre, destroy; in the New forgive. The two systems are inconsistent, and one is just about as far wrong as the other. To live for and thirst for revenge, to gloat over the agony of an enemy, is one extreme; to "resist not evil" is the other extreme; and both these extremes are equally distant from the golden mean of justice.

The four gospels do not even agree as to the terms of salvation. And yet, Mr. Talmage tells us that there are four cardinal doctrines taught in the Bible—the goodness of God, the fall of man, the sympathetic and forgiving nature of the Savior, and two destinies—one for believers and the other for unbelievers. That is to say:

1. That God is good, holy and forgiving.

2. That man is a lost sinner.

3. That Christ is "all sympathetic," and ready to take the whole world to his heart.

4. Heaven for believers and hell for unbelievers.

First. I admit that the Bible says that God is good and holy. But this Bible also tells what God did, and if God did what the Bible says he did, then I insist that God is not good, and that he is not holy, or forgiving. According to the Bible, this good God believed in religious persecution; this good God believed in extermination, in polygamy, in concubinage, in human slavery; this good God commanded murder and massacre, and this good God could only be mollified by the shedding of blood. This good God wanted a butcher for a priest. This good God wanted husbands to kill their wives—wanted fathers and mothers to kill their children. This good God persecuted animals on account of the crimes of their owners. This good God killed the common people because the king had displeased him. This good God killed the babe even of the maid behind the mill, in order that he might get even with a king. This good God committed every possible crime.

Second. The statement that man is a lost sinner is not true. There are thousands and thousands of magnificent Pagans—men ready to die for wife, or child, or even for friend, and the history of Pagan countries is filled with self-denying and heroic acts. If man is a failure, the infinite God, if there be one, is to blame. Is it possible that the God of Mr. Talmage could not have made man a success? According to the Bible, his God made man knowing that in about fifteen hundred years he would have to drown all his descendants.

Why would a good God create a man that he knew would be a sinner all his life, make hundreds of thousands of his fellow-men unhappy, and who at last would be doomed to an eternity of suffering? Can such a God be good? How could a devil have done worse?

Third. If God is infinitely good, is he not fully as sympathetic as Christ? Do you have to employ Christ to mollify a being of infinite mercy? Is Christ any more willing to take to his heart the whole world than his Father is? Personally, I have not the slightest objection in the world to anybody believing in an infinitely good and kind God—not the slightest objection to any human being worshiping an infinitely tender and merciful Christ—not the slightest objection to people preaching about heaven, or about the glories of the future state—not the slightest.

Fourth. I object to the doctrine of two destinies for the human race. I object to the infamous falsehood of eternal fire. And yet, Mr. Talmage is endeavoring to poison the imagination of men, women and children with the doctrine of an eternal hell. Here is what he preaches, taken from the "Constitution of the Presbyterian Church of the United States:"

"By the decrees of God, for the manifestation of his glory, some men and angels are predestinated to everlasting life, and others foreordained to everlasting death."

That is the doctrine of Mr. Talmage. He worships a God who damns people "for the manifestation of his glory,"—a God who made men, knowing that they would be damned—a God who damns babes simply to increase his reputation with the angels. This is the God of Mr. Talmage. Such a God I abhor, despise and execrate.

Question. What does Mr. Talmage think of mankind? What is his opinion of the "unconverted"? How does he regard the great and glorious of the earth, who have not been the victims of his particular superstition? What does he think of some of the best the earth has produced?

Answer. I will tell you how he looks upon all such. Read this from his "Confession of Faith:"

"Our first parents, being seduced by the subtlety of the tempter, sinned in eating the forbidden fruit. By this sin, they fell from their original righteousness and communion with God, and so became dead in sin, and wholly defiled in all the faculties and parts of soul and body; and they being the root of all mankind, the guilt of this sin was imputed, and the same death in sin and corrupted nature conveyed to all their posterity. From this original corruption—whereby we are utterly indisposed, disabled, and made opposite to all good, and wholly inclined to all evil, do proceed all actual transgressions."

This is Mr. Talmage's view of humanity.

Why did his God make a devil? Why did he allow the devil to tempt Adam and Eve? Why did he leave innocence and ignorance at the mercy of subtlety and wickedness? Why did he put "the tree of the knowledge of good and evil" in the garden? For what reason did he place temptation in the way of his children? Was it kind, was it just, was it noble, was it worthy of a good God? No wonder Christ put into his prayer: "Lead us not into temptation."

At the time God told Adam and Eve not to eat, why did he not tell them of the existence of Satan? Why were they not put upon their guard against the serpent? Why did not God make his appearance just before the sin, instead of just after. Why did he not play the role of a Savior instead of that of a detective? After he found that Adam and Eve had sinned—knowing as he did that they were then totally corrupt—knowing that all their children would be corrupt, knowing that in fifteen hundred years he would have to drown millions of them, why did he not allow Adam and Eve to perish in accordance with natural law, then kill the devil, and make a new pair?

When the flood came, why did he not drown all? Why did he save for seed that which was "perfectly and thoroughly corrupt in all its parts and faculties"? If God had drowned Noah and his sons and their families, he could have then made a new pair, and peopled the world with men not "wholly defiled in all their faculties and parts of soul and body."

Jehovah learned nothing by experience. He persisted in his original mistake. What would we think of a man who finding that a field of wheat was worthless, and that such wheat never could be raised with profit, should burn all of the field with the exception of a few sheaves, which he saved for seed? Why save such seed? Why should God have preserved Noah, knowing that he was totally corrupt, and that he would again fill the world with infamous people—people incapable of a good action? He must have known at that time, that by preserving Noah, the Canaanites would be produced, that these same Canaanites would have to be murdered, that the babes in the cradles would have to be strangled. Why did he produce them? He knew at that time, that Egypt would result from the salvation of Noah, that the Egyptians would have to be nearly destroyed, that he would have to kill their first-born, that he would have to visit even their cattle with disease and hailstones. He knew also that the Egyptians would oppress his chosen people for two hundred and fifteen years, that they would upon the back of toil inflict the lash. Why did he preserve Noah? He should have drowned all, and started with a new pair. He should have warned them against the devil, and he might have succeeded, in that way, in covering the world with gentlemen and ladies, with real men and real women.

We know that most of the people now in the world are not Christians. Most who have heard the gospel of Christ have rejected it, and the Presbyterian Church tells us what is to become of all these people. This is the "glad tidings of great joy." Let us see:

"All mankind, by their fall, lost communion with God, are under his wrath and curse, and so made liable to all the miseries of this life, to death itself, and to the pains of hell forever."

According to this good Presbyterian doctrine, all that we suffer in this world, is the result of Adam's fall. The babes of to-day suffer for the crime of the first parents. Not only so; but God is angry at us for what Adam did. We are under the wrath of an infinite God, whose brows are corrugated with eternal hatred.

Why should God hate us for being what we are and necessarily must have been? A being that God made—the devil—for whose work God is responsible, according to the Bible wrought this woe. God of his own free will must have made the devil. What did he make him for? Was it

73

necessary to have a devil in heaven? God, having infinite power, can of course destroy this devil to-day. Why does he permit him to live? Why did he allow him to thwart his plans? Why did he permit him to pollute the innocence of Eden? Why does he allow him now to wrest souls by the million from the redeeming hand of Christ?

According to the Scriptures, the devil has always been successful. He enjoys himself. He is called "the prince of the power of the air." He has no conscientious scruples. He has miraculous power. All miraculous power must come of God, otherwise it is simply in accordance with nature. If the devil can work a miracle, it is only with the consent and by the assistance of the Almighty. Is the God of Mr. Talmage in partnership with the devil? Do they divide profits?

We are also told by the Presbyterian Church—I quote from their Confession of Faith—that "there is no sin so small but it deserves damnation." Yet Mr. Talmage tells us that God is good, that he is filled with mercy and loving-kindness. A child nine or ten years of age commits a sin, and thereupon it deserves eternal damnation. That is what Mr. Talmage calls, not simply justice, but mercy; and the sympathetic heart of Christ is not touched. The same being who said: "Suffer little children to come unto me," tells us that a child, for the smallest sin, deserves to be eternally damned. The Presbyterian Church tells us that infants, as well as adults, in order to be saved, need redemption by the blood of Christ, and regeneration by the Holy Ghost.

I am charged with trying to take the consolation of this doctrine from the world. I am a criminal because I am endeavoring to convince the mother that her child does not deserve eternal punishment. I stand by the graves of those who "died in their "sins," by the tombs of the "unregenerate," over the ashes of men who have spent their lives working for their wives and children, and over the sacred dust of soldiers who died in defense of flag and country, and I say to their friends—I say to the living who loved them, I say to the men and women for whom they worked, I say to the children whom they educated, I say to the country for which they died: These fathers, these mothers, these wives, these husbands, these soldiers are not in hell.

Question. Mr. Talmage insists that the Bible is scientific, and that the real scientific man sees no contradiction between revelation and science; that, on the contrary, they are in harmony. What is your understanding of this matter?

Answer. I do not believe the Bible to be a scientific book. In fact, most of the ministers now admit that it was not written to teach any science. They admit that the first chapter of Genesis is not geologically true. They admit that Joshua knew nothing of science. They admit that four-footed birds did not exist in the days of Moses. In fact, the only way they can avoid the unscientific statements of the Bible, is to assert that the writers simply used the common language of their day, and used it, not with the intention of teaching any scientific truth, but for the purpose of teaching some moral truth. As a matter of fact, we find that moral truths have been taught in all parts of this world. They were taught in India long before Moses lived; in Egypt long before Abraham was born; in

China thousands of years before the flood. They were taught by hundreds and thousands and millions before the Garden of Eden was planted.

It would be impossible to prove the truth of a revelation simply because it contained moral truths. If it taught immorality, it would be absolutely certain that it was not a revelation from an infinitely good being. If it taught morality, it would be no reason for even suspecting that it had a divine origin. But if the Bible had given us scientific truths; if the ignorant Jews had given us the true theory of our solar system; if from Moses we had learned the nature of light and heat; if from Joshua we had learned something of electricity; if the minor prophets had given us the distances to other planets; if the orbits of the stars had been marked by the barbarians of that day, we might have admitted that they must have been inspired. If they had said anything in advance of their day; if they had plucked from the night of ignorance one star of truth, we might have admitted the claim of inspiration; but the Scriptures did not rise above their source, did not rise above their ignorant authors—above the people who believed in wars of extermination, in polygamy, in concubinage, in slavery, and who taught these things in their "sacred Scriptures."

The greatest men in the scientific world have not been, and are not, believers in the inspiration of the Scriptures. There has been no greater astronomer than Laplace. There is no greater name than Humboldt. There is no living scientist who stands higher than Charles Darwin. All the professors in all the religious colleges in this country rolled into one, would not equal Charles Darwin. All the cowardly apologists for the cosmogony of Moses do not amount to as much in the world of thought as Ernst Haeckel. There is no orthodox scientist the equal of Tyndall or Huxley. There is not one in this country the equal of John Fiske. I insist, that the foremost men today in the scientific world reject the dogma of inspiration. They reject the science of the Bible, and hold in utter contempt the astronomy of Joshua, and the geology of Moses.

Mr. Talmage tells us "that Science is a boy and Revelation is a man." Of course, like the most he says, it is substantially the other way. Revelation, so-called, was the boy. Religion was the lullaby of the cradle, the ghost-story told by the old woman, Superstition. Science is the man. Science asks for demonstration. Science impels us to investigation, and to verify everything for ourselves. Most professors of American colleges, if they were not afraid of losing their places, if they did not know that Christians were bad enough now to take the bread from their mouths, would tell their students that the Bible is not a scientific book.

I admit that I have said:

1. That the Bible is *cruel.*
2. That in many passages it is *impure.*
3. That it is *contradictory.*
4. That it is *unscientific.*

Let me now prove these propositions one by one.

First. The Bible is *cruel.*

I have opened it at random, and the very first chapter that has struck my eye is the sixth of First Samuel. In the nineteenth verse of that chapter, I find the following:

"And he smote the men of Bethshemesh, because they had looked into the ark of the Lord; even he smote of the people fifty thousand and three-score and ten men."

All this slaughter was because some people had looked into a box that was carried upon a cart. Was that cruel?

I find, also, in the twenty-fourth chapter of Second Samuel, that David was moved by God to number Israel and Judah. God put it into his heart to take a census of his people, and thereupon David said to Joab, the captain of his host:

"Go now through all the tribes of Israel, from Dan even to Beersheba, and number ye the people, that I may know the number of the people."

At the end of nine months and twenty days, Joab gave the number of the people to the king, and there were at that time, according to that census, "eight hundred thousand valiant men that drew the sword," in Israel, and in Judah, "five hundred thousand men," making a total of thirteen hundred thousand men of war. The moment this census was taken, the wrath of the Lord waxed hot against David, and thereupon he sent a seer, by the name of Gad, to David, and asked him to choose whether he would have seven years of famine, or fly three months before his enemies, or have three days of pestilence. David concluded that as God was so merciful as to give him a choice, he would be more merciful than man, and he chose the pestilence.

Now, it must be remembered that the sin of taking the census had not been committed by the people, but by David himself, inspired by God, yet the people were to be punished for David's sin. So, when David chose the pestilence, God immediately killed "seventy thousand men, from Dan even to Beersheba."

"And when the angel stretched out his hand upon Jerusalem to destroy it, the Lord repented him of the evil, and said to the angel that destroyed the people, It is enough; stay now thine hand."

Was this cruel?

Why did a God of infinite mercy destroy seventy thousand men? Why did he fill his land with widows and orphans, because King David had taken the census? If he wanted to kill anybody, why did he not kill David? I will tell you why. Because at that time, the people were considered as the property of the king. He killed the people precisely as he killed the cattle. And yet, I am told that the Bible is not a cruel book.

In the twenty-first chapter of Second Samuel, I find that there were three years of famine in the days of David, and that David inquired of the Lord the reason of the famine; and the Lord told him that it was because Saul had slain the Gibeonites. Why did not God punish Saul instead of the people? And David asked the Gibeonites how he should make atonement, and the Gibeonites replied that they wanted no silver nor gold, but they asked that seven of the sons of Saul might be delivered unto them, so that they could hang them before the Lord, in Gibeah.

And David agreed to the proposition, and thereupon he delivered to the Gibeonites the two sons of Rizpah, Saul's concubine, and the five sons of Michal, the daughter of Saul, and the Gibeonites hanged all seven of them together. And Rizpah, more tender than them all, with a woman's heart of love kept lonely vigil by the dead, "from the beginning of harvest until water dropped upon them out of heaven, and suffered neither the birds of the air to rest upon them by day, nor the beast of the field by night."

I want to know if the following, from the fifteenth chapter of First Samuel, is inspired:

"Thus saith the Lord of hosts; I remember that which Amalek did to Israel, how he laid wait for him in the way when he came up from Egypt. Now go and smite Amalek, and utterly destroy all that they have, and spare them not, but slay both man and woman, infant and suckling, ox and sheep, camel and ass."

We must remember that those he was commanded to slay had done nothing to Israel. It was something done by their forefathers, hundreds of years before; and yet they are commanded to slay the women and children and even the animals, and to spare none.

It seems that Saul only partially carried into execution this merciful command of Jehovah. He spared the life of the king. He "utterly destroyed all the people with the edge of the sword," but he kept alive the best of the sheep and oxen and of the fatlings and lambs. Then God spake unto Samuel and told him that he was very sorry he had made Saul king, because he had not killed all the animals, and because he had spared Agag; and Samuel asked Saul: "What meaneth this bleating of sheep in mine ears, and the lowing of the oxen which I hear?"

Are stories like this calculated to make soldiers merciful?

So I read in the sixth chapter of Joshua, the fate of the city of Jericho: "And they utterly destroyed all that was in the city, both man and woman, young and old, and ox, and sheep, and ass, with the edge of the sword. And they burnt the city with fire, and all that was therein." But we are told that one family was saved by Joshua, out of the general destruction: "And Joshua saved Rahab, the harlot, alive, and her father's household, and all that she had." Was this fearful destruction an act of mercy?

It seems that they saved the money of their victims: "the silver and gold and the vessels of brass and of iron they put into the treasury of the house of the Lord."

After all this pillage and carnage, it appears that there was a suspicion in Joshua's mind that somebody was keeping back a part of the treasure. Search was made, and a man by the name of Achan admitted that he had sinned against the Lord, that he had seen a Babylonish garment among the spoils, and two hundred shekels of silver and a wedge of gold of fifty shekels' weight, and that he took them and hid them in his tent. For this atrocious crime it seems that the Lord denied any victories to the Jews until they found out the wicked criminal. When they discovered poor Achan, "they took him and his sons and his daughters, and his oxen and his asses and his sheep, and all that he had, and brought them unto the valley of Achor; and all Israel stoned him with stones and burned them with fire after they had stoned them with stones."

After Achan and his sons and his daughters and his herds had been stoned and burned to death, we are told that "the Lord turned from the fierceness of "his anger."

And yet it is insisted that this God "is merciful, and that his loving-kindness is over all his works." In the eighth chapter of this same book, the infinite God, "creator of heaven and earth and all that is therein," told his general, Joshua, to lay an ambush for a city—to "lie in wait against the city, even behind the city; go not very far from the city, but be ye all ready." He told him to make an attack and then to run, as though he had been beaten, in order that the inhabitants of the city might follow, and thereupon his reserves that he had ambushed might rush into the city and set it on fire. God Almighty planned the battle. God himself laid the snare. The whole programme was carried out. Joshua made believe that he was beaten, and fled, and then the soldiers in ambush rose out of their places, entered the city, and set it on fire. Then came the slaughter. They "utterly destroyed all the inhabitants of Ai," men and maidens, women and babes, sparing only their king till evening, when they hanged him on a tree, then "took his carcass down from the tree and cast it at the entering of the gate, and raised thereon a great heap of stones which remaineth unto this day." After having done all this, "Joshua built an altar unto the Lord God of Israel, and offered burnt offerings unto the Lord." I ask again, was this cruel?

Again I ask, was the treatment of the Gibeonites cruel when they sought to make peace but were denied, and cursed instead; and although permitted to live, were yet made slaves? Read the mandate consigning them to bondage: "Now therefore ye are cursed, and there shall none of you be freed from being bondmen and hewers of wood and drawers of water for the house of my God."

Is it possible, as recorded in the tenth chapter of Joshua, that the Lord took part in these battles, and cast down great hail-stones from the battlements of heaven upon the enemies of the Israelites, so that they were more who died with hail-stones, than they whom the children of Israel slew with the sword"?

Is it possible that a being of infinite power would exercise it in that way instead of in the interest of kindness and peace?

I find, also, in this same chapter, that Joshua took Makkedah and smote it with the edge of the sword, that he utterly destroyed all the souls that were therein, that he allowed none to remain.

I find that he fought against Libnah, and smote it with the edge of the sword, and utterly destroyed all the souls that were therein, and allowed none to remain, and did unto the king as he did unto the king of Jericho.

I find that he also encamped against Lachish, and that God gave him that city, and that he "smote it with the edge of the sword, and all the souls that were therein," sparing neither old nor young, helpless women nor prattling babes.

He also vanquished Horam, King of Gezer, "and smote him and his people until he left him none remaining."

He encamped against the city of Eglon, and killed every soul that was in it, at the edge of the sword, just as he had done to Lachish and all the others.

He fought against Hebron, "and took it and smote it with the edge of the sword, and the king thereof,"—and it appears that several cities, their number not named, were included in this slaughter, for Hebron "and all the cities thereof and all the "souls that were therein," were utterly destroyed.

He then waged war against Debir and took it, and more unnumbered cities with it, and all the souls that were therein shared the same horrible fate—he did not leave a soul alive.

And this chapter of horrors concludes with this song of victory:

"So Joshua smote all the country of the hills, and of the south, and of the vale, and of the springs, and all their kings: he left none remaining, but utterly destroyed all that breathed, as the Lord God of Israel commanded. And Joshua smote them from Kadeshbarnea even unto Gaza, and all the country of Goshen, even unto Gibeon. And all these kings and their land did Joshua take at one time, because the Lord God of Israel fought for Israel." Was God, at that time, merciful?

I find, also, in the twenty-first chapter that many kings met, with their armies, for the purpose of overwhelming Israel, and the Lord said unto Joshua: "Be not afraid because of them, for to-morrow about this time I will deliver them all slain before Israel. I will hough their horses and burn their chariots with fire." Were animals so treated by the command of a merciful God?

Joshua captured Hazor, and smote all the souls that were therein with the edge of the sword, there was not one left to breathe; and he took all the cities of all the kings that took up arms against him, and utterly destroyed all the inhabitants thereof. He took the cattle and spoils as prey unto himself, and smote every man with the edge of the sword; and not only so, but left not a human being to breathe.

I find the following directions given to the Israelites who were waging a war of conquest. They are in the twentieth chapter of Deuteronomy, from the tenth to the eighteenth verses:

"When thou comest nigh unto a city to fight against it, then proclaim peace unto it. And it shall be, if it make thee an answer of peace, and open unto thee, then it shall be that all the people that is found therein shall be tributaries unto thee, and they shall serve thee. And if it will make no peace with thee, but will war against thee, then thou shalt besiege it. And when the Lord thy God hath delivered it into thine hands, thou shalt smite every male thereof with the edge of the sword; but the women, and the little ones, and the cattle, and all that is in the city, even the spoil thereof, shalt thou take unto thyself; and thou shalt eat the spoil of thine enemies, which the Lord thy God hath given thee. Thus shalt thou do unto all the cities which are very far off from thee, which are not of the cities of these nations." It will be seen from this that people could take their choice between death and slavery, provided these people lived a good ways from the Israelites. Now, let us see how they were to treat the inhabitants of the cities near to them:

"But of the cities of these people which the Lord thy God doth give thee for an inheritance, thou shalt save alive nothing that breatheth. But thou shalt utterly destroy them; namely, the Hittites, and the Amorites, the Canaanites, and the Perizzites, the Hivites and the Jebusites, as the Lord thy God hath commanded thee."

It never occurred to this merciful God to send missionaries to these people. He built them no schoolhouses, taught them no alphabet, gave them no book; they were not supplied even with a copy of the Ten Commandments. He did not say "Reform," but "Kill;" not "Educate," but "Destroy." He gave them no Bible, built them no church, sent them no preachers. He knew when he made them that he would have to have them murdered. When he created them he knew that they were not fit to live; and yet, this is the infinite God who is infinitely merciful and loves his children better than an earthly mother loves her babe.

In order to find just how merciful God is, read the twenty-eighth chapter of Deuteronomy, and see what he promises to do with people who do not keep all of his commandments and all of his statutes. He curses them in their basket and store, in the fruit of their body, in the fruit of their land, in the increase of their cattle and sheep. He curses them in the city and in the field, in their coming in and their going out. He curses them with pestilence, with consumption, with fever, with inflammation, with extreme burning, with sword, with blasting, with mildew. He tells them that the heavens shall be as brass over their heads and the earth as iron under their feet; that the rain shall be powder and dust and shall come down on them and destroy them; that they shall flee seven ways before their enemies; that their carcasses shall be meat for the fowls of the air, and the beasts of the earth; that he will smite them with the botch of Egypt, and with the scab, and with the itch, and with madness and blindness and astonishment; that he will make them grope at noonday; that they shall be oppressed and spoiled evermore; that one shall be- troth a wife and another shall have her; that they shall build a house and not dwell in it; plant a vineyard and others shall eat the grapes; that their sons and daughters shall be given to their enemies; that he will make them mad for the sight of their eyes; that he will smite them in the knees and in the legs with a sore botch that cannot be healed, and from the sole of the foot to the top of the head; that they shall be a by-word among all nations; that they shall sow much seed and gather but little; that the locusts shall consume their crops; that they shall plant vineyards and drink no wine,—that they shall gather grapes, but worms shall eat them; that they shall raise olives but have no oil; beget sons and daughters, but they shall go into captivity; that all the trees and fruit of the land shall be devoured by locusts, and that all these curses shall pursue them and overtake them, until they be destroyed; that they shall be slaves to their enemies, and be constantly in hunger and thirst and nakedness, and in want of all things. And as though this were not enough, the Lord tells them that he will bring a nation against them swift as eagles, a nation fierce and savage, that will show no mercy and no favor to old or young, and leave them neither corn, nor wine, nor oil, nor flocks, nor herds; and this nation shall besiege them in their cities until they are reduced to the necessity of eating the flesh of their own sons and daughters; so that the men would eat their wives and their children, and women eat their husbands and their own sons and daughters, and their own babes.

All these curses God pronounced upon them if they did not observe to do all the words of the law that were written in his book.

This same merciful God threatened that he would bring upon them all the diseases of Egypt—every sickness and every plague; that he would scatter them from one end of the earth to the other; that they should find no rest; that their lives should hang in perpetual doubt; that in the morning they would say: Would God it were evening! and in the evening, Would God it were morning! and that he would finally take them back to Egypt where they should be again sold for bondmen and bondwomen.

This curse, the foundation of the *Anathema maranatha;* this curse, used by the pope of Rome to prevent the spread of thought; this curse used even by the Protestant Church; this curse born of barbarism and of infinite cruelty, is now said to have issued from the lips of an infinitely merciful God. One would suppose that Jehovah had gone insane; that he had divided his kingdom like Lear, and from the darkness of insanity had launched his curses upon a world.

In order that there may be no doubt as to the mercy of Jehovah, read the thirteenth chapter of Deuteronomy:

"If thy brother, the son of thy mother, or thy son, or thy daughter, or the wife of thy bosom, or thy friend, which is as thine own soul, entice thee secretly, saying, Let us go and serve other gods, which thou hast not known, thou nor thy fathers; * * * thou shalt not consent unto him, nor hearken unto him; neither shall thine eyes pity him, neither shalt thou spare, neither shalt thou conceal him; but thou shalt surely kill him: thine hand shall be first upon him to put him to death, and afterwards the hand of all the people; and thou shalt stone him with stones that he die, because he hath sought to entice thee away from the Lord thy God."

This, according to Mr. Talmage, is a commandment of the infinite God. According to him, God ordered a man to murder his own son, his own wife, his own brother, his own daughter, if they dared even to suggest the worship of some other God than Jehovah. For my part, it is impossible not to despise such a God—a God not willing that one should worship what he must. No one can control his admiration, and if a savage at sunrise falls upon his knees and offers homage to the great light of the East, he cannot help it. If he worships the moon, he cannot help it. If he worships fire, it is because he cannot control his own spirit. A picture is beautiful to me in spite of myself. A statue compels the applause of my brain. The worship of the sun was an exceedingly natural religion, and why should a man or woman be destroyed for kneeling at the fireside of the world?

No wonder that this same God, in the very next chapter of Deuteronomy to that quoted, says to his chosen people: "Ye shall not eat of anything that dieth of itself: thou shalt give it unto the stranger that is within thy gates, that he may eat it; or thou mayest sell it unto an alien: for thou art a holy people unto the Lord thy God."

What a mingling of heartlessness and thrift—the religion of sword and trade!

In the seventh chapter of Deuteronomy, Jehovah gives his own character. He tells the Israelites that there are seven nations greater and mightier than themselves, but that he will deliver them to his chosen people, and that they shall smite them and utterly destroy them; and having some fear that a drop of pity might remain in the Jewish heart, he says:

"Thou shalt make no covenant with them, nor show mercy unto them. * * * Know therefore that the Lord thy God, he is God, the faithful God, which keepeth covenant and mercy with them that love him and keep his commandments to a thousand generations, and repayeth them that hate him to their face, to destroy them: he will not be slack to him that hateth him, he will repay him to his face." This is the description which the merciful, long-suffering Jehovah gives of himself.

So, he promises great prosperity to the Jews if they will only obey his commandments, and says: "And the Lord will take away from thee all sickness, and will put none of the evil diseases of Egypt upon thee, but will lay them upon all them that hate thee. And thou shalt consume all the people which the Lord thy God shall deliver thee; thine eye shall have no pity upon them."

Under the immediate government of Jehovah, mercy was a crime. According to the law of God, pity was weakness, tenderness was treason, kindness was blasphemy, while hatred and massacre were virtues.

In the second chapter of Deuteronomy we find another account tending to prove that Jehovah is a merciful God. We find that Sihon, king of Heshbon, would not let the Hebrews pass by him, and the reason given is, that "the Lord God hardened his "spirit and made his heart obstinate, that he might deliver him into the hand" of the Hebrews. Sihon, his heart having been hardened by God, came out against the chosen people, and God delivered him to them, and "they smote him, and his sons, and all his people, and took all his cities, and utterly destroyed the men and the women, and the little ones of every city: they left none to remain." And in this same chapter this same God promises that the dread and fear of his chosen people should be "upon all the nations that are under the whole heaven," and that "they should tremble and be in anguish because of the Hebrews."

Read the thirty-first chapter of Numbers, and see how the Midianites were slain. You will find that "the children of Israel took all the women of Midian captives, and their little ones, that they took all their cattle, and all their flocks, and all their goods," that they slew all the males, and burnt all their cities and castles with fire, that they brought the captives and the prey and the spoil unto Moses and Eleazar the priest; that Moses was wroth with the officers of his host because they had saved all the women alive, and thereupon this order was given: "Kill every male among the little ones, and kill every woman, * * * but all the women children keep alive for yourselves."

After this, God himself spake unto Moses, and said: "Take the sum of the prey that was taken, both of man and of beast, thou and Eleazar the priest * * * and divide the prey into two parts, between those who went to war, and between all the congregation, and levy a tribute unto the Lord, one soul of five hundred of the persons, and the cattle; take it of their half and give it to the priest for an offering * * * and of the children of Israel's half, take one portion of fifty of the persons and the animals and give them unto the Levites. * * * And Moses and the priest did as the Lord had commanded." It seems that they had taken six hundred and seventy-five thousand sheep, seventy-two thousand beeves, sixty-one thousand asses, and thirty-two thousand women children and maidens.

And it seems, by the fortieth verse, *that the Lord's tribute of the maidens was thirty-two,*—the rest were given to the soldiers and to the congregation of the Lord.

Was anything more infamous ever recorded in the annals of barbarism? And yet we are told that the Bible is an inspired book, that it is not a cruel book, and that Jehovah is a being of infinite mercy.

In the twenty-fifth chapter of Numbers we find that the Israelites had joined themselves unto Baal-Peor, and thereupon the anger of the Lord was kindled against them, as usual. No being ever lost his temper more frequently than this Jehovah. Upon this particular occasion, "the Lord said unto Moses, "Take all the heads of the people, and hang them up before the Lord against the sun, that the fierce anger of the Lord may be turned away from Israel."

And thereupon "Moses said unto the judges of Israel, "Slay ye every one his men that were joined unto Baal-peor."

Just as soon as these people were killed, and their heads hung up before the Lord against the sun, and a horrible double murder of a too merciful Israelite and a Midianitish woman, had been committed by Phinehas, the son of Eleazar, "the plague was stayed "from the children of Israel." Twenty-four thousand had died. Thereupon, "the Lord spake unto Moses and said"—and it is a very merciful commandment—"Vex the Midianites and smite them."

In the twenty-first chapter of Numbers is more evidence that God is merciful and compassionate.

The children of Israel had become discouraged. They had wandered so long in the desert that they finally cried out: "Wherefore have ye brought us up out of Egypt to die in the wilderness? There is no bread, there is no water, and our soul loatheth this light bread." Of course they were hungry and thirsty. Who would not complain under similar circumstances? And yet, on account of this complaint, the God of infinite tenderness and compassion sent serpents among them, and these serpents bit them—bit the cheeks of children, the breasts of maidens, and the withered faces of age. Why would a God do such an infamous thing? Why did he not, as the leader of this people, his chosen children, feed them better? Certainly an infinite God had the power to satisfy their hunger and to quench their thirst. He who overwhelmed a world with water, certainly could have made a few brooks, cool and babbling, to follow his chosen people through all their journeying. He could have supplied them with miraculous food.

How fortunate for the Jews that Jehovah was not revengeful, that he was so slow to anger, so patient, so easily pleased. What would they have done had he been exacting, easily incensed, revengeful, cruel, or blood-thirsty?

In the sixteenth chapter of Numbers, an account is given of a rebellion. It seems that Korah, Dathan and Abiram got tired of Moses and Aaron. They thought the priests were taking a little too much upon themselves. So Moses told them to have two hundred and fifty of their men bring their censers and put incense in them before the Lord, and stand in the door of the tabernacle of the congregation with Moses and Aaron. That being done, the Lord appeared, and told Moses and Aaron to separate themselves from the people, that he might consume them all in a moment. Moses and Aaron, having a little compassion, begged God not to kill everybody. The people were then divided, and Dathan and Abiram came out and stood in the door of their tents with their wives and their sons and their little children. And Moses said:

"Hereby ye shall know that the Lord hath sent me to do all these works; for I have not done them of my mine own mind. If these men die the common death of all men, or if they be visited after the common visitation of all men, then the Lord hath not sent me. But if the Lord make a new thing, and the earth open her mouth and swallow them up, with all that appertain unto them, and they go down quick into the pit, then ye shall understand that these men have provoked the Lord." The moment he ceased speaking, "the ground clave asunder that was under them; and the earth opened her mouth and swallowed them up, and their houses, and all the men that appertained unto Korah, and all their goods. They, and all that appertained to them went down alive into the pit, and the earth closed upon them, and they perished from among the congregation."

This, according to Mr. Talmage, was the act of an exceedingly merciful God, prompted by infinite kindness, and moved by eternal pity. What would he have done had he acted from motives of revenge? What would he have done had he been remorselessly cruel and wicked?

In addition to those swallowed by the earth, the two hundred and fifty men that offered the incense were consumed by "a fire that came out from the Lord." And not only this, but the same merciful Jehovah wished to consume all the people, and he would have consumed them all, only that Moses prevailed upon Aaron to take a censer and put fire therein from off the altar of incense and go quickly to the congregation and make an atonement for them. He was not quick enough. The plague had already begun; and before he could possibly get the censers and incense among the people, fourteen thousand and seven hundred had died of the plague. How many more might have died, if Jehovah had not been so slow to anger and so merciful and tender to his children, we have no means of knowing.

In the thirteenth chapter of the same book of Numbers, we find that some spies were sent over into the promised land, and that they brought back grapes and figs and pomegranates, and reported that the whole land was flowing with milk and honey, but that the people were strong, that the cities were walled, and that the nations in the promised land were mightier than the Hebrews. They reported that all the people they met were men of a great stature, that they had seen "the giants, the sons of Anak which come of giants," compared with whom the Israelites were "in their own sight as grasshoppers, and so were we in their sight." Entirely discouraged by these reports, "all the congregation lifted up their voice and cried, and the people wept that night * * * and murmured against Moses and against Aaron, and said unto them: "Would God that we had died in the land of Egypt! or would God we had died in this wilderness!" Some of them thought that it would be better to go back,— that they might as well be slaves in Egypt as to be food for giants in the promised land. They did not want their bones crunched between the teeth of the sons of Anak.

Jehovah got angry again, and said to Moses: "How long will these people provoke me? * * * I will smite them with pestilence, and disinherit them." But Moses said: "Lord, if you do this, the Egyptians will hear of it, and they will say that you were not able to bring your people into the promised land." Then he proceeded to flatter him by telling him how merciful and long-suffering he had been. Finally, Jehovah concluded to pardon the people this time, but his pardon depended upon the violation of his promise, for he said: "They shall not see the land which I sware unto their fathers, neither shall any of them that provoked me see it; but my servant Caleb, * * * him will I bring into the land." And Jehovah said to the people: "Your carcasses shall fall in this wilderness, and all that were numbered of you according to your whole number, from twenty years old and upward, which have murmured against me, ye shall not come into the land concerning which I sware to make you dwell therein, save Caleb the son of Jephunneh, and Joshua the son of Nun. But your little ones, which ye said should be a prey, them will I bring in, and they shall know the land which ye have despised. But as for you, your carcasses shall fall in this wilderness. And your children shall wander in the wilderness forty years * * * until your carcasses be wasted in the wilderness."

And all this because the people were afraid of giants, compared with whom they were but as grasshoppers.

So we find that at one time the people became exceedingly hungry. They had no flesh to eat. There were six hundred thousand men of war, and they had nothing to feed on but manna. They naturally murmured and complained, and thereupon a wind from the Lord went forth and brought quails from the sea, (quails are generally found in the sea,) and let them fall by the camp, as it were a day's journey on this side, and as it were a day's journey on the other side, round about the camp, and as it were two cubits high upon the face of the earth. And the people stood up all that day, and all that night, and all the next day, and they gathered the quails. * * * And while the flesh was yet between their teeth, ere it was chewed, the wrath of the Lord was kindled against the people, and the Lord smote the people with a very great plague."

Yet he is slow to anger, long-suffering, merciful and just.

In the thirty-second chapter of Exodus, is the account of the golden calf. It must be borne in mind that the worship of this calf by the people was before the Ten Commandments had been given to them. Christians now insist that these commandments must have been inspired, because no human being could have constructed them,—could have conceived of them.

It seems, according to this account, that Moses had been up in the mount with God, getting the Ten Commandments, and that while he was there the people had made the golden calf. When he came down and saw them, and found what they had done, having in his hands the two tables, the work of God, he cast the tables out of his hands, and broke them beneath the mount. He then took the calf which they had made, ground it to powder, strewed it in the water, and made the children of Israel drink of it. And in the twenty-seventh verse we are told what the Lord did: "Thus saith the Lord God of Israel: Put every man his sword by his side, and go in and out from gate to gate throughout the camp, and slay every man his brother, and every man his companion, and every man his neighbor. And the children of Levi did according to the word of Moses; and there fell of the people that day about three thousand men." The reason for this slaughter is thus given: "For Moses had said: Consecrate yourselves to-day to the Lord, even every man upon his son, and upon his brother, that he may bestow upon you a blessing this day."

Now, it must be remembered that there had not been as yet a promulgation of the commandment "Thou shalt have no other gods before me." This was a punishment for the infraction of a law before the law was known—before the commandment had been given. Was it cruel, or unjust?

Does the following sound as though spoken by a God of mercy: "I will make mine arrows drunk with blood, and my sword shall devour flesh"? And yet this is but a small part of the vengeance and destruction which God threatens to his enemies, as recorded in the thirty-second chapter of the book of Deuteronomy.

In the sixty-eighth Psalm is found this merciful passage: "That thy foot may be dipped in the blood of thine enemies, and the tongue of thy dogs in the same."

So we find in the eleventh chapter of Joshua the reason why the Canaanites and other nations made war upon the Jews. It is as follows: "For it was of the Lord to harden their hearts that they should come against Israel in battle, that he might destroy them utterly, and that they might have no favor, but that he might destroy them."

Read the thirtieth chapter of Exodus and you will find that God gave to Moses a recipe for making the oil of holy anointment, and in the thirty-second verse we find that no one was to make any oil like it and in the next verse it is declared that whoever compounded any like it, or whoever put any of it on a stranger, should be cut off from the Lord's people.

In the same chapter, a recipe is given for perfumery, and it is declared that whoever shall make any like it, or that smells like it, shall suffer death.

In the next chapter, it is decreed that if any one fails to keep the Sabbath "he shall be surely put to death."

There are in the Pentateuch hundreds and hundreds of passages showing the cruelty of Jehovah. What could have been more cruel than the flood? What more heartless than to overwhelm a world? What more merciless than to cover a shoreless sea with the corpses of men, women and children?

The Pentateuch is filled with anathemas, with curses, with words of vengeance, of jealousy, of hatred, and brutality. By reason of these passages, millions of people have plucked from their hearts the flowers of pity and justified the murder of women and the assassination of babes.

In the second chapter of Second Kings we find that the prophet Elisha was on his way to a place called Bethel, and as he was going, there came forth little children out of the city and mocked him and said: "Go up thou bald head; Go up thou bald head!" And he turned back and looked on them and cursed them in the name of the Lord. And there came forth two she bears out of the wood and tare forty and two children of them."

Of course he obtained his miraculous power from Jehovah; and there must have been some communication between Jehovah and the bears. Why did the bears come? How did they happen to be there? Here is a prophet of God cursing children in the name of the Lord, and thereupon these children are torn in fragments by wild beasts.

This is the mercy of Jehovah; and yet I am told that the Bible has nothing cruel in it; that it preaches only mercy, justice, charity, peace; that all hearts are softened by reading it; that the savage nature of man is melted into tenderness and pity by it, and that only the totally depraved can find evil in it.

And so I might go on, page after page, book after book, in the Old Testament, and describe the cruelties committed in accordance with the commands of Jehovah.

But all the cruelties in the Old Testament are absolute mercies compared with the hell of the New Testament. In the Old Testament God stops with the grave. He seems to have been satisfied when he saw his enemies dead, when he saw their flesh rotting in the open air, or in the beaks of birds, or in the teeth of wild beasts. But in the New Testament, vengeance does not stop with the grave. It begins there, and stops never. The enemies of Jehovah are to be pursued through all the ages of eternity. There is to be no forgiveness—no cessation, no mercy, nothing but everlasting pain.

And yet we are told that the author of hell is a being of infinite mercy.

Second; All intelligent Christians will admit that there are many passages in the Bible that, if found in the Koran, they would regard as impure and immoral.

It is not necessary for me to specify the passages, nor to call the attention of the public to such things. I am willing to trust the judgment of every honest reader, and the memory of every biblical student.

The Old Testament upholds polygamy. That is infinitely impure. It sanctions concubinage. That is impure; nothing could or can be worse. Hundreds of things are publicly told that should have remained unsaid. No one is made better by reading the history of Tamar, or the biography of Lot, or the memoirs of Noah, of Dinah, of Sarah and Abraham, or of Jacob and Leah and Rachel and others that I do not care to mention. No one is improved in his morals by reading these things.

All I mean to say is, that the Bible is like other books produced by other nations in the same stage of civilization. What one age considers pure, the next considers impure. What one age may consider just, the next may look upon as infamous. Civilization is a growth. It is continually dying, and continually being born. Old branches rot and fall, new buds appear. It is a perpetual twilight, and a perpetual dawn—the death of the old, and the birth of the new.

I do not say, throw away the Bible because there are some foolish passages in it, but I say, throw away the foolish passages. Don't throw away wisdom because it is found in company with folly; but do not say that folly is wisdom, because it is found in its company. All that is true in the Bible is true whether it is inspired or not. All that is true did not need to be

87

inspired. Only that which is not true needs the assistance of miracles and wonders. I read the Bible as I read other books. What I believe to be good, I admit is good; what I think is bad, I say is bad; what I believe to be true, I say is true, and what I believe to be false, I denounce as false.

Third. Let us see whether there are any contradictions in the Bible.

A little book has been published, called "Self Contradictions of the Bible," by J. P. Mendum, of *The Boston Investigator.* I find many of the apparent contradictions of the Bible noted in this book.

We all know that the Pentateuch is filled with the commandments of God upon the subject of sacrificing animals. We know that God declared, again and again, that the smell of burning flesh was a sweet savor to him. Chapter after chapter is filled with directions how to kill the beasts that were set apart for sacrifices; what to do with their blood, their flesh and their fat. And yet, in the seventh chapter of Jeremiah, all this is expressly denied, in the following language: "For I spake not unto your fathers, nor commanded them in the day that I brought them out of the land of Egypt, concerning burnt offerings or sacrifices."

And in the sixth chapter of Jeremiah, the same Jehovah says; "Your burnt offerings are not acceptable, nor your sacrifices sweet unto me."

In the Psalms, Jehovah derides the idea of sacrifices, and says: "Will I eat of the flesh of bulls, or drink the blood of goats? Offer unto God thanksgiving, and pay thy vows unto the Most High."

So I find in Isaiah the following: "Bring no more vain oblations; incense is an abomination unto me; the new moons and sabbaths, the calling of assemblies, I cannot away with; it is iniquity, even the solemn meeting. Your new moons and your appointed feasts my soul hateth; they are a trouble to me; I am weary to bear them." "To what purpose is the multitude of your sacrifices unto me? Saith the Lord. I am full of the burnt offerings of rams, and the fat of fed beasts; and I delight not in the blood of bullocks, or of lambs, or of he goats. When ye come to appear before me, who hath required this at your hand?"

So I find in James: "Let no man say when he is tempted: I am tempted of God; for God cannot be tempted with evil, neither tempteth he any man;" and yet in the twenty-second chapter of Genesis I find this: "And it came to pass after these things, that God did tempt Abraham."

In Second Samuel we see that he tempted David. He also tempted Job, and Jeremiah says: "O Lord, thou hast deceived me, and I was deceived." To such an extent was Jeremiah deceived, that in the fourteenth chapter and eighteenth verse we find him crying out to the Lord: "Wilt thou be altogether unto me as a liar?"

So in Second Thessalonians: "For these things God shall send them strong delusions, that they should believe a lie."

So in First Kings, twenty-second chapter: "Behold, the Lord hath put a lying spirit in the mouth of all these thy prophets, and the Lord hath spoken evil concerning thee."

So in Ezekiel: "And if the prophet be deceived when he hath spoken a thing, I, the Lord, have deceived that prophet."

So I find: "Thou shalt not bear false witness;" and in the book of Revelation: "All liars shall have their part in the lake which burneth with fire and brimstone;" yet in First Kings, twenty-second chapter, I find the following: "And the Lord said: Who shall persuade Ahab, that he may go up and fall at Ramoth-Gilead? And one said on this manner, and another said on that manner. And there came forth a spirit and stood before the Lord, and said: I will persuade him. And the Lord said unto him: Wherewith? And he said: I will go forth, and I will be a lying spirit in the mouth of all his prophets. And he said: Thou shalt persuade him, and prevail also. Go forth, and do so."

In the Old Testament we find contradictory laws about the same thing, and contradictory accounts of the same occurrences.

In the twentieth chapter of Exodus we find the first account of the giving of the Ten Commandments. In the thirty-fourth chapter another account of the same transaction is given. These two accounts could not have been written by the same person. Read them, and you will be forced to admit that both of them cannot by any possibility be true. They differ in so many particulars, and the commandments themselves are so different, that it is impossible that both can be true.

So there are two histories of the creation. If you will read the first and second chapters of Genesis, you will find two accounts inconsistent with each other, both of which cannot be true. The first account ends with the third verse of the second chapter of Genesis. By the first account, man and woman were made at the same time, and made last of all. In the second account, not to be too critical, all the beasts of the field were made before Eve was, and Adam was made before the beasts of the field; whereas in the first account, God made all the animals before he made Adam. In the first account there is nothing about the rib or the bone or the side,—that is only found in the second account. In the first account, there is nothing about the Garden of Eden, nothing about the four rivers, nothing about the mist that went up from the earth and watered the whole face of the ground; nothing said about making man from dust; nothing about God breathing into his nostrils the breath of life; yet according to the second account, the Garden of Eden was planted, and all the animals were made before Eve was formed. It is impossible to harmonize the two accounts.

So, in the first account, only the word God is used—"God said so and so,—God did so and so." In the second account he is called Lord God,— "the Lord God formed man,"—"the Lord God caused it to rain,"—"the Lord God planted a garden." It is now admitted that the book of Genesis is made up of two stories, and it is very easy to take them apart and show exactly how they were put together.

So there are two stories of the flood, differing almost entirely from each other—that is to say, so contradictory that both cannot be true.

There are two accounts of the manner in which Saul was made king, and the accounts are inconsistent with each other.

Scholars now everywhere admit that the copyists made many changes, pieced out fragments, and made additions, interpolations, and meaningless repetitions. It is now generally conceded that the speeches of Elihu, in Job, were interpolated, and most of the prophecies were made by persons whose names even are not known.

The manuscripts of the Old Testament were not alike. The Greek version differed from the Hebrew, and there was no generally received text of the Old Testament until after the beginning of the Christian era. Marks and points to denote vowels were invented probably in the seventh century after Christ; and whether these marks and points were put in the proper places, is still an open question. The Alexandrian version, or what is known as the Septuagint, translated by seventy-two learned Jews assisted by miraculous power, about two hundred years before Christ, could not, it is now said, have been translated from the Hebrew text that we now have. This can only be accounted for by supposing that we have a different Hebrew text. The early Christians adopted the Septuagint and were satisfied for a time; but so many errors were found, and so many were scanning every word in search of something to assist their peculiar views, that new versions were produced, and the new versions all differed somewhat from the Septuagint as well as from each other. These versions were mostly in Greek. The first Latin Bible was produced in Africa, and no one has ever found out which Latin manuscript was original. Many were produced, and all differed from each other. These Latin versions were compared with each other and with the Hebrew, and a new Latin version was made in the fifth century, and the old ones held their own for about four hundred years, and no one knows which version was right. Besides, there were Ethiopian, Egyptian, Armenian and several other versions, all differing from each other as well as from all others. It was not until the fourteenth century that the Bible was translated into German, and not until the fifteenth that Bibles were printed in the principal languages of Europe; and most of these Bibles differed from each other, and gave rise to endless disputes and to almost numberless crimes.

No man in the world is learned enough, nor has he time enough, even if he could live a thousand years, to find what books belonged to and constituted the Old Testament. He could not ascertain the authors of the books, nor when they were written, nor what they mean. Until a man has sufficient time to do all this, no one can tell whether he believes the Bible or not. It is sufficient, however, to say that the Old Testament is filled with contradictions as to the number of men slain in battle, as to the number of years certain kings reigned, as to the number of a woman's children, as to dates of events, and as to locations of towns and cities.

Besides all this, many of its laws are contradictory, often commanding and prohibiting the same thing.

The New Testament also is filled with contradictions. The gospels do not even agree upon the terms of salvation. They do not even agree as to the gospel of Christ, as to the mission of Christ. They do not tell the same story regarding the betrayal, the crucifixion, the resurrection or the ascension of Christ. John is the only one that ever heard of being "born again." The evangelists do not give the same account of the same miracles, and the miracles are not given in the same order. They do not agree even in the genealogy of Christ.

Fourth. Is the Bible scientific? In my judgment it is not

It is unscientific to say that this world was "created;" that the universe was produced by an infinite being, who had existed an eternity prior to such "creation." My mind is such that I cannot possibly conceive of a "creation." Neither can I conceive of an infinite being who dwelt in infinite space an infinite length of time.

I do not think it is scientific to say that the universe was made in six days, or that this world is only about six thousand years old, or that man has only been upon the earth for about six thousand years.

If the Bible is true, Adam was the first man. The age of Adam is given, the age of his children, and the time, according to the Bible, was kept and known from Adam, so that if the Bible is true, man has only been in this world about six thousand years. In my judgment, and in the judgment of every scientific man whose judgment is worth having or quoting, man inhabited this earth for thousands of ages prior to the creation of Adam. On one point the Bible is at least certain, and that is, as to the life of Adam. The genealogy is given, the pedigree is there, and it is impossible to escape the conclusion that, according to the Bible, man has only been upon this earth about six thousand years. There is no chance there to say "long periods of time," or "geological ages." There we have the years. And as to the time of the creation of man, the Bible does not tell the truth.

What is generally called "The Fall of Man" is unscientific. God could not have made a moral character for Adam. Even admitting the rest of the story to be true, Adam certainly had to make character for himself.

The idea that there never would have been any disease or death in this world had it not been for the eating of the forbidden fruit is preposterously unscientific. Admitting that Adam was made only six thousand years ago, death was in the world millions of years before that time. The old rocks are filled with remains of what were once living and breathing animals. Continents were built up with the petrified corpses of animals. We know, therefore, that death did not enter the world because of Adam's sin. We know that life and death are but successive links in an eternal chain.

So it is unscientific to say that thorns and brambles were produced by Adam's sin.

It is also unscientific to say that labor was pronounced as a curse upon man. Labor is not a curse. Labor is a blessing. Idleness is a curse.

It is unscientific to say that the sons of God, living, we suppose, in heaven, fell in love with the daughters of men, and that on account of this a flood was sent upon the earth that covered the highest mountains.

The whole story of the flood is unscientific, and no scientific man worthy of the name, believes it.

Neither is the story of the tower of Babel a scientific thing. Does any scientific man believe that God confounded the language of men for fear they would succeed in building a tower high enough to reach to heaven?

It is not scientific to say that angels were in the habit of walking about the earth, eating veal dressed with butter and milk, and making bargains about the destruction of cities.

The story of Lot's wife having been turned into a pillar of salt is extremely unscientific.

It is unscientific to say that people at one time lived to be nearly a thousand years of age. The history of the world shows that human life is lengthening instead of shortening.

It is unscientific to say that the infinite God wrestled with Jacob and got the better of him, putting his thigh out of joint.

It is unscientific to say that God, in the likeness of a flame of fire, inhabited a bush.

It is unscientific to say that a stick could be changed into a living snake. Living snakes can not be made out of sticks. There are not the necessary elements in a stick to make a snake.

It is not scientific to say that God changed water into blood. All the elements of blood are not in water.

It is unscientific to declare that dust was changed into lice.

It is not scientific to say that God caused a thick darkness over the land of Egypt, and yet allowed it to be light in the houses of the Jews.

It is not scientific to say that about seventy people could, in two hundred and fifteen years increase to three millions.

It is not scientific to say that an infinitely good God would destroy innocent people to get revenge upon a king.

It is not scientific to say that slavery was once right, that polygamy was once a virtue, and that extermination was mercy.

It is not scientific to assert that a being of infinite power and goodness went into partnership with insects,—granted letters of marque and reprisal to hornets.

It is unscientific to insist that bread was really rained from heaven.

It is not scientific to suppose that an infinite being spent forty days and nights furnishing Moses with plans and specifications for a tabernacle, an ark, a mercy seat, cherubs of gold, a table, four rings, some dishes, some spoons, one candlestick, several bowls, a few knobs, seven lamps, some snuffers, a pair of tongs, some curtains, a roof for a tent of rams' skins dyed red, a few boards, an altar with horns, ash pans, basins and flesh hooks, shovels and pots and sockets of silver and pouches of gold and pins of brass—for all of which this God brought with him patterns from heaven.

It is not scientific to say that when a man commits a sin, he can settle with God by killing a sheep.

It is not scientific to say that a priest, by laying his hands on the head of a goat, can transfer the sins of a people to the animal.

Was it scientific to endeavor to ascertain whether a woman was virtuous or not, by compelling her to drink water mixed with dirt from the floor of the sanctuary?

Is it scientific to say that a dry stick budded, blossomed, and bore almonds; or that the ashes of a red heifer mixed with water can cleanse us of sin; or that a good being gave cities into the hands of the Jews in consideration of their murdering all the inhabitants?

Is it scientific to say that an animal saw an angel, and conversed with a man?

Is it scientific to imagine that thrusting a spear through the body of a woman ever stayed a plague?

Is it scientific to say that a river cut itself in two and allowed the lower end to run off?

Is it scientific to assert that seven priests blew seven rams' horns loud enough to blow down the walls of a city?

Is it scientific to say that the sun stood still in the midst of heaven, and hasted not to go down for about a whole day, and that the moon also stayed?

Is it scientifically probable that an angel of the Lord devoured unleavened cakes and broth with fire that came out of the end of a stick, as he sat under an oak tree; or that God made known his will by letting dew fall on wool without wetting the ground around it; or that an angel of God appeared to Manoah in the absence of her husband, and that this angel afterwards went up in a flame of fire, and as the result of this visit a child was born whose strength was in his hair?

Is it scientific to say that the muscle of a man depended upon the length of his locks?

Is it unscientific to deny that water gushed from a hollow place in a dry bone?

Is it evidence of a thoroughly scientific mind to believe that one man turned over a house so large that three thousand people were on its roof?

Is it purely scientific to say that a man was once fed by the birds of the air, who brought him bread and meat every morning and evening, and that afterward an angel turned cook and prepared two suppers in one night, for the same prophet, who ate enough to last him forty days and forty nights?

Is it scientific to say that a river divided because the water had been struck with a cloak; or that a man actually went to heaven in a chariot of fire drawn by horses of fire; or that a being of infinite mercy would destroy children for laughing at a baldheaded prophet; or curse children and children's children with leprosy for a father's fault; or that he made iron float in water; or that when one corpse touched another it came to life; or that the sun went backward in heaven so that the shadow on a sundial went back ten degrees, as a sign that a miserable barbarian king would get well?

Is it scientific to say that the earth not only stopped in its rotary motion, but absolutely turned the other way,—that its motion was reversed simply as a sign to a petty king?

Is it scientific to say that Solomon made gold and silver at Jerusalem as plentiful as stones, when we know that there were kings in his day who could have thrown away the value of the whole of Palestine without missing the amount?

Is it scientific to say that Solomon exceeded all the kings of the earth in glory, when his country was barren, without roads, when his people were few, without commerce, without the arts, without the sciences, without education, without luxuries?

According to the Bible, as long as Jehovah attended to the affairs of the Jews, they had nothing but war, pestilence and famine; after Jehovah abandoned them, and the Christians ceased, in a measure, to persecute them, the Jews became the most prosperous of people. Since Jehovah in his anger cast them away, they have produced painters, sculptors, scientists, statesmen, composers, soldiers and philosophers.

It is not scientific to believe that God ever prevented rain, that he ever caused famine, that he ever sent locusts to devour the wheat and corn, that he ever relied on pestilence for the government of mankind; or that he ever killed children to get even with their parents.

It is not scientific to believe that the king of Egypt invaded Palestine with seventy thousand horsemen and twelve hundred chariots of war. There was not, at that time, a road in Palestine over which a chariot could be driven.

It is not scientific to believe that in a battle between Jeroboam and Abijah, the army of Abijah slew in one day five hundred thousand chosen men.

It is not scientific to believe that Zerah, the Ethiopian, invaded Palestine with a million of men who were overthrown and destroyed; or that Jehoshaphat had a standing army of nine hundred and sixty thousand men.

It is unscientific to believe that Jehovah advertised for a liar, as is related in Second Chronicles.

It is not scientific to believe that fire refused to burn, or that water refused to wet.

It is not scientific to believe in dreams, in visions, and in miracles.

It is not scientific to believe that children have been born without fathers, that the dead have ever been raised to life, or that people have bodily ascended to heaven taking their clothes with them.

It is not scientific to believe in the supernatural. Science dwells in the realm of fact, in the realm of demonstration. Science depends upon human experience, upon observation, upon reason.

It is unscientific to say that an innocent man can be punished in place of a criminal, and for a criminal, and that the criminal, on account of such punishment, can be justified.

It is unscientific to say that a finite sin deserves infinite punishment.

It is unscientific to believe that devils can inhabit human beings, or that they can take possession of swine, or that the devil could bodily take a man, or the Son of God, and carry him to the pinnacle of a temple.

In short, the foolish, the unreasonable, the false, the miraculous and the supernatural are unscientific.

Question. Mr. Talmage gives his reason for accepting the New Testament, and says: "You can trace it right out. Jerome and Eusebius in the first century, and Origen in the second century, gave lists of the writers of the New Testament. These lists correspond with our list of the writers of the New Testament, showing that precisely as we have it, they had it in the third and fourth centuries. Where did they get it? From Irenaeus. Where did he get it? From Polycarp. Where did Polycarp get it? From Saint John, who was a personal associate of Jesus. The line is just as clear as anything ever was clear." How do you understand this matter, and has Mr. Talmage stated the facts?

Answer. Let us examine first the witnesses produced by Mr. Talmage. We will also call attention to the great principle laid down by Mr. Talmage for the examination of evidence,—that where a witness is found false in one particular, his entire testimony must be thrown away.

Eusebius was born somewhere about two hundred and seventy years after Christ. After many vicissitudes he became, it is said, the friend of

Constantine. He made an oration in which he extolled the virtues of this murderer, and had the honor of sitting at the right hand of the man who had shed the blood of his wife and son. In the great controversy with regard to the position that Christ should occupy in the Trinity, he sided with Arius, "and lent himself to the persecution of the orthodox with Athanasius." He insisted that Jesus Christ was not the same as God, and that he was not of equal power and glory. Will Mr. Talmage admit that his witness told the truth in this? "He would not even call the Son co-eternal with God."

Eusebius must have been an exceedingly truthful man. He declared that the tracks of Pharaoh's chariots were in his day visible upon the shores of the Red Sea; that these tracks had been through all the years miraculously preserved from the action of wind and wave, as a supernatural testimony to the fact that God miraculously overwhelmed Pharaoh and his hosts.

Eusebius also relates that when Joseph and Mary arrived in Egypt they took up their abode in Hermopolis, a city of Thebaeus, in which was the superb temple of Serapis. When Joseph and Mary entered the temple, not only the great idol, but all the lesser idols fell down before him.

"It is believed by the learned Dr. Lardner, that Eusebius was the one guilty of the forgery in the passage found in Josephus concerning Christ. Unblushing falsehoods and literary forgeries of the vilest character darkened the pages of his historical writings." (Waites *History*.)

From the same authority I learn that Eusebius invented an eclipse, and some earthquakes, to agree with the account of the crucifixion. It is also believed that Eusebius quoted from works that never existed, and that he pretended a work had been written by Porphyry, entitled: "The Philosophy of Oracles," and then quoted from it for the purpose of proving the truth of the Christian religion.

The fact is, Eusebius was utterly destitute of truth. He believed, as many still believe, that he could please God by the fabrication of lies.

Irenaeus lived somewhere about the end of the second century. "Very little is known of his early history, and the accounts given in various biographies are for the most part conjectural." The writings of Irenaeus are known to us principally through Eusebius, and we know the value of his testimony.

Now, if we are to take the testimony of Irenaeus, why not take it? He says that the ministry of Christ lasted for twenty years, and that Christ was fifty years old at the time of his crucifixion. He also insisted that the "Gospel of Paul" was written by Luke, "a statement made to give sanction to the gospel of Luke."

Irenaeus insisted that there were four gospels, that there must be, and "he speaks frequently of these gospels, and argues that they should be four in number, neither more nor less, because there are four universal winds, and four quarters of the world;" and he might have added: because donkeys have four legs.

These facts can be found in "The History of the Christian Religion to A. D. 200," by Charles B. Waite,—a book that Mr. Talmage ought to read.

According to Mr. Waite, Irenaeus, in the thirty-third chapter of his fifth book, *Adversus Haereses*, cites from Papias the following sayings of

Christ: "The days will come in which vines shall grow which shall have ten thousand branches, and on each branch ten thousand twigs, and in each twig ten thousand shoots, and in each shoot ten thousand clusters, and in every one of the clusters ten thousand grapes, and every grape when pressed will give five and twenty metrets of wine." Also that "one thousand million pounds of clear, pure, fine flour will be produced from one grain of wheat." Irenaeus adds that "these things were borne witness to by Papias the hearer of John and the companion of Polycarp."

Is it possible that the eternal welfare of a human being depends upon believing the testimony of Polycarp and Irenaeus? Are people to be saved or lost on the reputation of Eusebius? Suppose a man is firmly convinced that Polycarp knew nothing about Saint John, and that Saint John knew nothing about Christ,—what then? Suppose he is convinced that Eusebius is utterly unworthy of credit,—what then? Must a man believe statements that he has every reason to think are false?

The question arises as to the witnesses named by Mr. Talmage, whether they were competent to decide as to the truth or falsehood of the gospels. We have the right to inquire into their mental traits for the purpose of giving only due weight to what they have said.

Mr. Bronson C. Keeler is the author of a book called: "A Short History of the Bible." I avail myself of a few of the facts he has there collected. I find in this book, that Irenaeus, Clement and Origen believed in the fable of the Phoenix, and insisted that God produced the bird on purpose to prove the probability of the resurrection of the body. Some of the early fathers believed that the hyena changed its sex every year. Others of them gave as a reason why good people should eat only animals with a cloven foot, the fact that righteous people lived not only in this world, but had expectations in the next. They also believed that insane people were possessed by devils; that angels ate manna; that some angels loved the daughters of men and fell; that the pains of women in childbirth, and the fact that serpents crawl on their bellies, were proofs that the account of the fall, as given in Genesis, is true; that the stag renewed its youth by eating poisonous snakes; that eclipses and comets were signs of God's anger; that volcanoes were openings into hell; that demons blighted apples; that a corpse in a cemetery moved to make room for another corpse to be placed beside it. Clement of Alexandria believed that hail storms, tempests and plagues were caused by demons. He also believed, with Mr. Talmage, that the events in the life of Abraham were typical and prophetical of arithmetic and astronomy.

Origen, another of the witnesses of Mr. Talmage, said that the sun, moon and stars were living creatures, endowed with reason and free will, and occasionally inclined to sin. That they had free will, he proved by quoting from Job; that they were rational creatures, he inferred from the fact that they moved. The sun, moon and stars, according to him, were "subject to vanity," and he believed that they prayed to God through his only begotten son.

These intelligent witnesses believed that the blighting of vines and fruit trees, and the disease and destruction that came upon animals and men, were all the work of demons; but that when they had entered into men, the sign of the cross would drive them out. They derided the idea that the earth is round, and one of them said: "About the antipodes also, one can neither hear nor speak without laughter. It is asserted as something serious that we should believe that there are men who have their feet opposite to ours. The ravings of Anaxagoras are more tolerable, who said that snow was black."

Concerning these early fathers, Professor Davidson, as quoted by Mr. Keeler, uses the following language: "Of the three fathers who contributed most to the growth of the canon, Irenaeus was credulous and blundering; Tertullian passionate and one-sided; and Clement of Alexandria, imbued with the treasures of Greek wisdom, was mainly occupied with ecclesiastical ethics. Their assertions show both ignorance and exaggeration." These early fathers relied upon by Mr. Talmage, quoted from books now regarded as apocryphal—books that have been thrown away by the church and are no longer considered as of the slightest authority. Upon this subject I again quote Mr. Keeler: "Clement quoted the 'Gospel according to 'the Hebrews,' which is now thrown away by the church; he also quoted from the Sibylline books and the Pentateuch in the same sentence. Origen frequently cited the Gospel of the Hebrews. Jerome did the same, and Clement believed in the 'Gospel 'according to the Egyptians.' The Shepherd of Hermas, a book in high repute in the early church, and one which distinctly claims to have been inspired, was quoted by Irenaeus as Scripture. "Clement of Alexandria said it was a divine revelation. Origen said it was divinely inspired, and quoted it as Holy Scripture at the same time that he cited the Psalms and Epistles of Paul. Jerome quoted the 'Wisdom of Jesus, the Son of Sirach,' as divine Scripture. Origen quotes the 'Wisdom of Solomon' as the 'Word of God' and 'the 'words of Christ himself.' Eusebius of Caesarea cites it as a 'Divine Oracle,' and St. Chrysostom used it as Scripture. So Eusebius quotes the thirteenth chapter of Daniel as Scripture, but as a matter of fact, Daniel has not a thirteenth chapter,— the church has taken it away. Clement spoke of the writer of the fourth book of Esdras as a prophet; he thought Baruch as much the word of God as any other book, and he quotes it as divine Scripture. "Clement cites Barnabas as an apostle. Origen quotes from the Epistle of Barnabas, calls it 'Holy 'Scripture,' and places it on a level with the Psalms and the Epistles of Paul; and Clement of Alexandria believed in the 'Epistle of Barnabas,' and the 'Revelation, of Peter,' and wrote comments upon these holy books."

Nothing can exceed the credulity of the early fathers, unless it may be their ignorance. They believed everything that was miraculous. They believed everything except the truth. Anything that really happened was considered of no importance by them. They looked for wonders, miracles, and monstrous things, and—generally found them. They reveled in the misshapen and the repulsive. They did not think it wrong to swear falsely in a good cause. They interpolated, forged, and changed the records to suit themselves, for the sake of Christ. They quoted from persons who never wrote. They misrepresented those who had written, and their evidence is absolutely worthless. They were ignorant, credulous, mendacious, fanatical, pious, unreasonable, bigoted, hypocritical, and for the most part, insane. Read the book of Revelation, and you will agree with me that nothing that ever emanated from a madhouse can more than equal it for incoherence. Most of the writings of the early fathers are of the same kind.

As to Saint John, the real truth is, that we know nothing certainly of him. We do not know that he ever lived.

We know nothing certainly of Jesus Christ. We know nothing of his infancy, nothing of his youth, and we are not sure that such a person ever existed.

We know nothing of Polycarp. We do not know where he was born, or where, or how he died. We know nothing for certain about Irenaeus. All the names quoted by Mr. Talmage as his witnesses are surrounded by clouds and doubts, by mist and darkness. We only know that many of their statements are false, and do not know that any of them are true.

Question. What do you think of the following statement by Mr. Talmage: "Oh, I have to tell you that no man ever died for a lie cheerfully and triumphantly"?

Answer. There was a time when men "cheerfully "and triumphantly died in defense of the doctrine of the "real presence" of God in the wafer and wine. Does Mr. Talmage believe in the doctrine of "transubstantiation"? Yet hundreds have died "cheerfully and triumphantly" for it. Men have died for the idea that baptism by immersion is the only scriptural baptism. Did they die for a lie? If not, is Mr. Talmage a Baptist?

Giordano Bruno was an atheist, yet he perished at the stake rather than retract his opinions. He did not expect to be welcomed by angels and by God. He did not look for a crown of glory. He expected simply death and eternal extinction. Does the fact that he died for that belief prove its truth?

Thousands upon thousands have died in defense of the religion of Mohammed. Was Mohammed an impostor? Thousands have welcomed death in defense of the doctrines of Buddha. Is Buddhism true?

So I might make a tour of the world, and of all ages of human history, and find that millions and millions have died "cheerfully and triumphantly" in defense of their opinions. There is not the slightest truth in Mr. Talmage's statement.

A little while ago, a man shot at the Czar of Russia. On the day of his execution he was asked if he wished religious consolation. He replied that he believed in no religion. What did that prove? It proved only the man's honesty of opinion. All the martyrs in the world cannot change, never did change, a falsehood into a truth, nor a truth into a falsehood. Martyrdom proves nothing but the sincerity of the martyr and the cruelty and meanness of his murderers. Thousands and thousands of people have imagined that they knew things, that they were certain, and have died rather than retract their honest beliefs.

Mr. Talmage now says that he knows all about the Old Testament, that the prophecies were fulfilled, and yet he does not know when the prophecies were made—whether they were made before or after the fact. He does not know whether the destruction of Babylon was told before it happened, or after. He knows nothing upon the subject. He does not know who made the pretended prophecies. He does not know that Isaiah, or Jeremiah, or Habakkuk, or Hosea ever lived in this world. He does not know who wrote a single book of the Old Testament. He knows nothing on the subject. He believes in the inspiration of the Old Testament because ancient cities finally fell into decay—were overrun and destroyed by enemies, and he accounts for the fact that the Jew does not lose his nationality by saying that the Old Testament is true.

The Jews have been persecuted by the Christians, and they are still persecuted by them; and Mr. Talmage seems to think that this persecution was a part of Gods plan, that the Jews might, by persecution, be prevented from mingling with other nationalities, and so might stand, through the instrumentality of perpetual hate and cruelty, the suffering witnesses of the divine truth of the Bible.

The Jews do not testify to the truth of the Bible, but to the barbarism and inhumanity of Christians—to the meanness and hatred of what we are pleased to call the "civilized world." They testify to the fact that nothing so hardens the human heart as religion.

There is no prophecy in the Old Testament foretelling the coming of Jesus Christ. There is not one word in the Old Testament referring to him in any way—not one word. The only way to prove this is to take your Bible, and wherever you find these words: "That it might be fulfilled," and "which was spoken," turn to the Old Testament and find what was written, and you will see that it had not the slightest possible reference to the thing recounted in the New Testament—not the slightest.

Let us take some of the prophecies of the Bible, and see how plain they are, and how beautiful they are. Let us see whether any human being can tell whether they have ever been fulfilled or not.

Here is a vision of Ezekiel: "I looked, and behold a whirlwind came out of the north, a great cloud, and a fire infolding itself, and a brightness was about it, and out of the midst thereof as the color of amber, out of the midst of the fire. Also out of the midst thereof came the likeness of four living creatures. And this was their appearance; they had the likeness of a man. And every one had four faces, and every one had four wings. And their feet were straight feet; and the sole of their feet was like the sole of a calf's foot: and they sparkled like the color of burnished brass. And they had the hands of a man under their wings on their four sides; and they four had their faces and their wings. Their wings were joined one to another; they turned not when-they went; they went every one straight forward. As for the likeness of their faces, they four had the face of a man, and the face of a lion, on the right side: and they four had the face of an ox on the left side; they four also had the face of an eagle.

"Thus were their faces: and their wings were stretched upward; two wings of every one were joined one to another, and two covered their bodies. And they went every one straight forward: whither the spirit was to go, they went; and they turned not when they went.

"As for the likeness of the living creatures, their appearance was like burning coals of fire, and like the appearance of lamps: it went up and down among the living creatures; and the fire was bright, and out of the fire went forth lightning. And the living creatures ran and returned as the appearance of a flash of lightning.

"Now as I beheld the living creatures, behold one wheel upon the earth by the living creatures, with his four faces. The appearance of the wheels and their work was like unto the color of a beryl: and they four had one likeness: and their appearance and their work was as it were a wheel in the middle of a wheel. When they went, they went upon their four sides: and they turned not when they went. As for their rings, they were so high that they were dreadful; and their rings were full of eyes round about them four. And when the living creatures went, the wheels went by them: and when the living creatures were lifted up from the earth, the wheels were lifted up. Whithersoever the spirit was to go, they went, thither was their spirit to go; and the wheels were lifted up over against them: for the spirit of the living creature was in the wheels. When those went, these went; and when those stood, these stood; and when those were lifted up from the earth, the wheels were lifted up over against them: for the spirit of the living creature was in the wheels. And the likeness of the firmament upon the heads of the living creature was as the color of the terrible crystal, stretched forth over their heads above. And under the firmament were their wings straight, the one toward the other; every one had two, which covered on this side, and every one had two, which covered on that side, their bodies."

Is such a vision a prophecy? Is it calculated o convey the slightest information? If so, what?

So, the following vision of the prophet Daniel is exceedingly important and instructive:

"Daniel spake and said: I saw in my vision by night, and behold, the four winds of the heaven strove upon the great sea. And four great beasts came up from the sea, diverse one from another. The first was like a lion, and had eagle's wings: I beheld till the wings thereof were plucked, and it was lifted up from the earth, and made stand upon the feet as a man, and a man's heart was given to it. And behold another beast, a second, like to a bear, and it raised up itself on one side, and it had three ribs in the mouth of it between the teeth of it: and they said thus unto it, Arise, devour much flesh.

"After this I beheld, and lo another, like a leopard, which had upon the back of it four wings of a fowl; the beast had also four heads, and dominion was given to it.

"After this I saw in the night visions, and behold a fourth beast, dreadful and terrible, and strong exceedingly; and it had great iron teeth; it devoured and brake in pieces, and stamped the residue with the feet of it; and it was diverse from all the beasts that were before it, and it had ten horns. I considered the horns, and, behold, there came up among them another little horn, before whom there were three of the first horns plucked up by the roots: and behold, in this horn were eyes like the eyes of man, and a mouth speaking great things."

I have no doubt that this prophecy has been literally fulfilled, but I am not at present in condition to give the time, place, or circumstances.

A few moments ago, my attention was called to the following extract from The New York Herald of the thirteenth of March, instant:

"At the Fifth Avenue Baptist Church, Dr. Armitage took as his text, 'A wheel in the middle of a wheel'—Ezekiel, i., 16. Here, said the preacher, are three distinct visions in one—the living creatures, the moving wheels and the fiery throne. We have time only to stop the wheels of this mystic chariot of Jehovah, that we may hold holy converse with Him who rides upon the wings of the wind. In this vision of the prophet we have a minute and amplified account of these magnificent symbols or hieroglyphics, this wondrous machinery which denotes immense attributes and agencies and volitions, passing their awful and mysterious course of power and intelligence in revolution after revolution of the emblematical mechanism, in steady and harmonious advancement to the object after which they are reaching. We are compelled to look upon the whole as symbolical of that tender and endearing providence of which Jesus spoke when He said, 'The very hairs of your head are numbered."

Certainly, an ordinary person, not having been illuminated by the spirit of prophecy, would never have even dreamed that there was the slightest reference in Ezekiel's vision to anything like counting hairs. As a commentator, the Rev. Dr. Armitage has no equal; and, in my judgment, no rival. He has placed himself beyond the reach of ridicule. It is impossible to say anything about his sermon as laughable as his sermon.

Question. Have you no confidence in any prophecies? Do you take the ground that there never has been a human being who could predict the future?

Answer. I admit that a man of average intelligence knows that a certain course, when pursued long enough, will bring national disaster, and it is perfectly safe to predict the downfall of any and every country in the world. In my judgment, nations, like individuals, have an average life. Every nation is mortal. An immortal nation cannot be constructed of mortal individuals. A nation has a reason for existing, and that reason sustains the same relation to the nation that the acorn does to the oak. The nation will attain its growth—other things being equal. It will reach its manhood and its prime, but it will sink into old age, and at last must die. Probably, in a few thousand years, men will be able to calculate the average life of nations, as they now calculate the average life of persons. There has been no period since the morning of history until now, that men did not know of dead and dying nations. There has always been a national cemetery. Poland is dead, Turkey is dying. In every nation are the seeds of dissolution. Not only nations die, but races of men. A nation is born, becomes powerful, luxurious, at last grows weak, is overcome, dies, and another takes its place, In this way civilization and barbarism, like day and night, alternate through all of history's years.

In every nation there are at least two classes of men: First, the enthusiastic, the patriotic, who believe that the nation will live forever,— that its flag will float while the earth has air; Second, the owls and ravens and croakers, who are always predicting disaster, defeat, and death. To the last class belong the Jeremiahs, Ezekiels, and Isaiahs of the Jews. They were always predicting the downfall of Jerusalem. They reveled in defeat and captivity. They loved to paint the horrors of famine and war. For the most part, they were envious, hateful, misanthropic and unjust.

There seems to have been a war between church and state. The prophets were endeavoring to preserve the ecclesiastical power. Every king who would listen to them, was chosen of God. He instantly became the model of virtue, and the prophets assured him that he was in the keeping of Jehovah. But if the king had a mind of his own, the prophets immediately called down upon him all the curses of heaven, and predicted the speedy destruction of his kingdom.

If our own country should be divided, if an empire should rise upon the ruins of the Republic, it would be very easy to find that hundreds and thousands of people had foretold that very thing. If you will read the political speeches of the last twenty-two years, you will find prophecies to fit any possible future state of affairs in our country. No matter what happens, you will find that somebody predicted it. If the city of London should lose her trade, if the Parliament house should become the abode of moles and bats, if "the New Zealander should sit upon the "ruins of London Bridge," all these things would be simply the fulfillment of prophecy. The fall of every nation under the sun has been predicted by hundreds and thousands of people.

The prophecies of the Old Testament can be made to fit anything that may happen, or that may not happen. They will apply to the death of a king, or to the destruction of a people,—to the loss of commerce, or the discovery of a continent. Each prophecy is a jugglery of words, of figures, of symbols, so put together, so used, so interpreted, that they can mean anything, everything, or nothing.

Question. Do you see anything "prophetic" in the fate of the Jewish people themselves? Do you think that God made the Jewish people wanderers, so that they might be perpetual witnesses to the truth of the Scriptures?

Answer. I cannot believe that an infinitely good God would make anybody a wanderer. Neither can I believe that he would keep millions of people without country and without home, and allow them to be persecuted for thousands of years, simply that they might be used as witnesses. Nothing could be more absurdly cruel than this.

The Christians justify their treatment of the Jews on the ground that they are simply fulfilling prophecy. The Jews have suffered because of the horrid story that their ancestors crucified the Son of God. Christianity, coming into power, looked with horror upon the Jews, who denied the truth of the gospel. Each Jew was regarded as a dangerous witness against Christianity. The early Christians saw how necessary it was that the people who lived in Jerusalem at the time of Christ should be convinced that he was God, and should testify to the miracles he wrought. Whenever a Jew denied it, the Christian was filled with malignity and hatred, and immediately excited the prejudice of other Christians against the man simply because he was a Jew. They forgot, in their general hatred, that Mary, the mother of Christ, was a Jewess; that Christ himself was of Jewish blood; and with an inconsistency of which, of all religions, Christianity alone could have been guilty, the Jew became an object of especial hatred and aversion.

When we remember that Christianity pretends to be a religion of love and kindness, of charity and forgiveness, must not every intelligent man be shocked by the persecution of the Jews? Even now, in learned and cultivated Germany, the Jew is treated as though he were a wild beast. The reputation of this great people has been stained by a persecution springing only from ignorance and barbarian prejudice. So in Russia, the Christians are anxious to shed every drop of Jewish blood, and thousands are to-day fleeing from their homes to seek a refuge from Christian hate. And Mr. Talmage believes that all these persecutions are kept up by the perpetual intervention of God, in order that the homeless wanderers of the seed of Abraham may testify to the truth of the Old and New Testaments. He thinks that every burning Jewish home sheds light upon the gospel,—that every gash in Jewish flesh cries out in favor of the Bible,—that every violated Jewish maiden shows the interest that God still takes in the preservation of his Holy Word.

I am endeavoring to do away with religious prejudice. I wish to substitute humanity for superstition, the love of our fellow-men, for the fear of God. In the place of ignorant worship, let us put good deeds. We should be great enough and grand enough to know that the rights of the Jew are precisely the same as our own. We cannot trample upon their rights, without endangering our own; and no man who will take liberty from another, is great enough to enjoy liberty himself.

Day by day Christians are laying the foundation of future persecution. In every Sunday school little children are taught that Jews killed the God of this universe. Their little hearts are filled with hatred against the Jewish people. They are taught as a part of the creed to despise the descendants of the only people with whom God is ever said to have had any conversation whatever.

When we take into consideration what the Jewish people have suffered, it is amazing that every one of them does not hate with all his heart and soul and strength the entire Christian world. But in spite of the persecutions they have endured, they are to-day, where they are permitted to enjoy reasonable liberty, the most prosperous people on the globe. The idea that their condition shows, or tends to show, that upon them abides the wrath of Jehovah, cannot be substantiated by the facts.

The Jews to-day control the commerce of the world. They control the money of the world. It is for them to say whether nations shall or shall not go to war. They are the people of whom nations borrow money. To their offices kings come with their hats in their hands. Emperors beg them to discount their notes. Is all this a consequence of the wrath of God?

We find upon our streets no Jewish beggars. It is a rare sight to find one of these people standing as a criminal before a court. They do not fill our alms-houses, nor our penitentiaries, nor our jails. Intellectually and morally they are the equal of any people. They have become illustrious in every department of art and science. The old cry against them is at last perceived to be ignorant. Only a few years ago, Christians would rob a Jew, strip him of his possessions, steal his money, declare him an outcast, and drive him forth. Then they would point to him as a fulfillment of prophecy.

If you wish to see the difference between some Jews and some Christians, compare the addresses of Felix Adler with the sermons of Mr. Talmage.

I cannot convince myself that an infinitely good and wise God holds a Jewish babe in the cradle of today responsible for the crimes of Caiaphas the high priest. I hardly think that an infinitely good being would pursue this little babe through all its life simply to get revenge on those who died two thousand years ago. An infinite being ought certainly to know that the child is not to blame; and an infinite being who does not know this, is not entitled to the love or adoration of any honest man.

There is a strange inconsistency in what Mr. Talmage says. For instance, he finds great fault with me because I do not agree with the religious ideas of my father; and he finds fault equally with the Jews who do. The Jews who were true to the religion of their fathers, according to Mr. Talmage, have been made a by-word and a hissing and a reproach among all nations, and only those Jews were fortunate and blest who abandoned the religion of their fathers. The real reason for this inconsistency is this: Mr. Talmage really thinks that a man can believe as he wishes. He imagines that evidence depends simply upon volition; consequently, he holds every one responsible for his belief. Being satisfied that he has the exact truth in this matter, he measures all other people by his standard, and if they fail by that measurement, he holds them personally responsible, and believes that his God does the same. If Mr. Talmage had been born in Turkey, he would in all probability have been a Mohammedan, and would now be denouncing some man who had denied the inspiration of the Koran, as the "champion blasphemer" of Constantinople. Certainly he would have been, had his parents been Mohammedans; because, according to his doctrine, he would have been utterly lacking in respect and love for his father and mother had he failed to perpetuate their errors. So, had he been born in Utah, of Mormon parents, he would now have been a defender of polygamy. He would not "run the ploughshare of contempt through the graves of his parents," by taking the ground that polygamy is wrong.

I presume that all of Mr. Talmage's forefathers were not Presbyterians. There must have been a time when one of his progenitors left the faith of his father, and joined the Presbyterian Church. According to the reasoning of Mr. Talmage, that particular progenitor was an exceedingly bad man; but had it not been for the crime of that bad man, Mr. Talmage might not now have been on the road to heaven.

I hardly think that all the inventors, the thinkers, the philosophers, the discoverers, dishonored their parents. Fathers and mothers have been made immortal by such sons. And yet these sons demonstrated the errors of their parents. A good father wishes to be excelled by his children.

104

SIXTH INTERVIEW.

It is a contradiction in terms and ideas to call anything a revelation that comes to us at secondhand, either verbally or in writing. Revelation is necessarily limited to the first communication—after this, it is only an account of something which that person says was a revelation made to him; and though he may find himself obliged to believe it, it cannot be incumbent on me to believe it in the same manner; for it was not a revelation made to me, and I have only his word for it that it was made to him.—Thomas Paine.

Question. What do you think of the arguments presented by Mr. Talmage in favor of the inspiration of the Bible?

Answer. Mr. Talmage takes the ground that there are more copies of the Bible than of any other book, and that consequently it must be inspired.

It seems to me that this kind of reasoning proves entirely too much. If the Bible is the inspired word of God, it was certainly just as true when there was only one copy, as it is to-day; and the facts contained in it were just as true before they were written, as afterwards. We all know that it is a fact in human nature, that a man can tell a falsehood so often that he finally believes it himself; but I never suspected, until now, that a mistake could be printed enough times to make it true.

There may have been a time, and probably there was, when there were more copies of the Koran than of the Bible. When most Christians were utterly ignorant, thousands of Moors were educated; and it is well known that the arts and sciences flourished in Mohammedan countries in a far greater degree than in Christian. Now, at that time, it may be that there were more copies of the Koran than of the Bible. If some enterprising Mohammedan had only seen the force of such a fact, he might have established the inspiration of the Koran beyond a doubt; or, if it had been found by actual count that the Koran was a little behind, a few years of industry spent in the multiplication of copies, might have furnished the evidence of its inspiration.

Is it not simply amazing that a doctor of divinity, a Presbyterian clergyman, in this day and age, should seriously rely upon the number of copies of the Bible to substantiate the inspiration of that book? Is it possible to conceive of anything more fig-leaflessly absurd? If there is anything at all in this argument, it is, that all books are true in proportion to the number of copies that exist. Of course, the same rule will work with newspapers; so that the newspaper having the largest circulation can consistently claim infallibility. Suppose that an exceedingly absurd statement should appear in *The New York Herald,* and some one should denounce it as utterly without any foundation in fact or probability; what would Mr. Talmage think if the editor of the *Herald,* as an evidence of the truth of the statement, should rely on the fact that his paper had the largest circulation of any in the city? One would think that the whole church had acted upon the theory that a falsehood repeated often enough was as good as the truth.

Another evidence brought forward by the reverend gentleman to prove the inspiration of the Scriptures, is the assertion that if Congress should undertake to pass a law to take the Bible from the people, thirty, millions would rise in defense of that book.

This argument also seems to me to prove too much, and as a consequence, to prove nothing. If Congress should pass a law prohibiting the reading of Shakespeare, every American would rise in defense of his right to read the works of the greatest man this world has known. Still, that would not even tend to show that Shakespeare was inspired. The fact is, the American people would not allow Congress to pass a law preventing them from reading any good book. Such action would not prove the book to be inspired; it would prove that the American people believe in liberty.

There are millions of people in Turkey who would peril their lives in defense of the Koran. A fact like this does not prove the truth of the Koran; it simply proves what Mohammedans think of that book, and what they are willing to do for its preservation.

It can not be too often repeated, that martyrdom does not prove the truth of the thing for which the martyr dies; it only proves the sincerity of the martyr and the cruelty of his murderers. No matter how many people regard the Bible as inspired,—that fact furnishes no evidence that it is inspired. Just as many people have regarded other books as inspired; just as many millions have been deluded about the inspiration of books ages and ages before Christianity was born.

The simple *belief* of one man, or of millions of men, is no *evidence* to another. Evidence must be based, not upon the belief of other people, but upon *facts*. A believer may state the facts upon which his belief is founded, and the person to whom he states them gives them the weight that according to the construction and constitution of his mind he must. But simple, bare belief is not testimony. We should build upon facts, not upon beliefs of others, nor upon the shifting sands of public opinion. So much for this argument.

The next point made by the reverend gentleman is, that an infidel cannot be elected to any office in the United States, in any county, precinct, or ward.

For the sake of the argument, let us admit that this is true. What does it prove? There was a time when no Protestant could have been elected to any office. What did that prove? There was a time when no Presbyterian could have been chosen to fill any public station. What did that prove? The same may be said of the members of each religious denomination. What does that prove?

Mr. Talmage says that Christianity must be true, because an infidel cannot be elected to office. Now, suppose that enough infidels should happen to settle in one precinct to elect one of their own number to office; would that prove that Christianity was not true in that precinct? There was a time when no man could have been elected to any office, who insisted on the rotundity of the earth; what did that prove? There was a time when no man who denied the existence of witches, wizards, spooks and devils, could hold any position of honor; what did that prove? There was a time when an abolitionist could not be elected to office in any State in this Union; what did that prove? There was a time when they were not allowed to express their honest thoughts; what does that prove? There was a time when a Quaker could not have been elected to any office; there was a time in the history of this country when but few of them were allowed to live; what does that prove? Is it necessary, in order to ascertain the truth of Christianity, to look over the election returns? Is "inspiration" a question to be settled by the ballot? I admit that it was once, in the first place, settled that way. I admit that books were voted in and voted out, and that the Bible was finally formed in accordance with a vote; but does Mr. Talmage insist that the question is not still open? Does he not know, that a fact cannot by any possibility be affected by opinion? We make laws for the whole people, by the whole people. We agree that a majority shall rule, but nobody ever pretended that a question of taste could be settled by an appeal to majorities, or that a question of logic could be affected by numbers. In the world of thought, each man is an absolute monarch, each brain is a kingdom, that cannot be invaded even by the tyranny of majorities.

No man can avoid the intellectual responsibility of deciding for himself.

Suppose that the Christian religion had been put to vote in Jerusalem? Suppose that the doctrine of the "fall" had been settled in Athens, by an appeal to the people, would Mr. Talmage have been willing to abide by their decision? If he settles the inspiration of the Bible by a popular vote, he must settle the meaning of the Bible by the same means. There are more Methodists than Presbyterians—why does the gentleman remain a Presbyterian? There are more Buddhists than Christians—why does he vote against majorities? He will remember that Christianity was once settled by a popular vote—that the divinity of Christ was submitted to the people, and the people said: "Crucify him!"

The next, and about the strongest, argument Mr. Talmage makes is, that I am an infidel because I was defeated for Governor of Illinois.

When put in plain English, his statement is this: that I was defeated because I was an infidel, and that I am an infidel because I was defeated. This, I believe, is called reasoning in a circle. The truth is, that a good many people did object to me because I was an infidel, and the probability is, that if I had denied being an infidel, I might have obtained an office. The wonderful part is, that any Christian should deride me because I preferred honor to political success. He who dishonors himself for the sake of being honored by others, will find that two mistakes have been made—one by himself, and the other, by the people.

I presume that Mr. Talmage really thinks that I was extremely foolish to avow my real opinions. After all, men are apt to judge others somewhat by themselves. According to him, I made the mistake of preserving my manhood and losing an office. Now, if I had in fact been an infidel, and had denied it, for the sake of position, then I admit that every Christian might have pointed at me the finger of contempt. But I was an infidel, and admitted it. Surely, I should not be held in contempt by Christians for having made the admission. I was not a believer in the Bible, and I said so. I was not a Christian, and I said so. I was not willing to receive the support of any man under a false impression. I thought it better to be honestly beaten, than to dishonestly succeed. According to the ethics of Mr. Talmage I made a mistake, and this mistake is brought forward as another evidence of the inspiration of the Scriptures. If I had only been elected Governor of Illinois,—that is to say, if I had been a successful hypocrite, I might now be basking in the sunshine of this gentleman's respect. I preferred to tell the truth—to be an honest man,—and I have never regretted the course I pursued.

There are many men now in office who, had they pursued a nobler course, would be private citizens. Nominally, they are Christians; actually, they are nothing; and this is the combination that generally insures political success.

Mr. Talmage is exceedingly proud of the fact that Christians will not vote for infidels. In other words, he does not believe that in our Government the church has been absolutely divorced from the state. He believes that it is still the Christian's duty to make the religious test. Probably he wishes to get his God into the Constitution. My position is this:

Religion is an individual matter—a something for each individual to settle for himself, and with which no other human being has any concern, provided the religion of each human being allows liberty to every other. When called upon to vote for men to fill the offices of this country, I do not inquire as to the religion of the candidates. It is none of my business. I ask the questions asked by Jefferson: "Is he honest; is he capable?" It makes no difference to me, if he is willing that others should be free, what creed he may profess. The moment I inquire into his religious belief, I found a little inquisition of my own; I repeat, in a small way, the errors of the past, and reproduce, in so far as I am capable, the infamy of the ignorant orthodox years.

Mr. Talmage will accept my thanks for his frankness. I now know what controls a Presbyterian when he casts his vote. He cares nothing for the capacity, nothing for the fitness, of the candidate to discharge the duties of the office to which he aspires; he simply asks: Is he a Presbyterian, is he a Protestant, does he believe our creed? and then, no matter how ignorant he may be, how utterly unfit, he receives the Presbyterian vote. According to Mr. Talmage, he would vote for a Catholic who, if he had the power, would destroy all liberty of conscience, rather than vote for an infidel who, had he the power, would destroy all the religious tyranny of the world, and allow every human being to think for himself, and to worship God, or not, as and how he pleased.

Mr. Talmage makes the serious mistake of placing the Bible above the laws and Constitution of his country. He places Jehovah above humanity. Such men are not entirely safe citizens of any republic. And yet, I am in favor of giving to such men all the liberty I ask for myself, trusting to education and the spirit of progress to overcome any injury they may do, or seek to do.

When this country was founded, when the Constitution was adopted, the churches agreed to let the State alone. They agreed that all citizens should have equal civil rights. Nothing could be more dangerous to the existence of this Republic than to introduce religion into politics. The

American theory is, that governments are founded, not by gods, but by men, and that the right to govern does not come from God, but "from the consent of the governed." Our fathers concluded that the people were sufficiently intelligent to take care of themselves—to make good laws and to execute them. Prior to that time, all authority was supposed to come from the clouds. Kings were set upon thrones by God, and it was the business of the people simply to submit. In all really civilized countries, that doctrine has been abandoned. The source of political power is here, not in heaven. We are willing that those in heaven should control affairs there; we are willing that the angels should have a government to suit themselves; but while we live here, and while our interests are upon this earth, we propose to make and execute our own laws.

If the doctrine of Mr. Talmage is the true doctrine, if no man should be voted for unless he is a Christian, then no man should vote unless he is a Christian. It will not do to say that sinners may vote, that an infidel may be the repository of political power, but must not be voted for. A decent Christian who is not willing that an infidel should be elected to an office, would not be willing to be elected to an office by infidel votes. If infidels are too bad to be voted for, they are certainly not good enough to vote, and no Christian should be willing to represent such an infamous constituency.

If the political theory of Mr. Talmage is carried out, of course the question will arise in a little while, What is a Christian? It will then be necessary to write a creed to be subscribed by every person before he is fit to vote or to be voted for. This of course must be done by the State, and must be settled, under our form of government, by a majority vote. Is Mr. Talmage willing that the question, What is Christianity? should be so settled? Will he pledge himself in advance to subscribe to such a creed? Of course he will not. He will insist that he has the right to read the Bible for himself, and that he must be bound by his own conscience. In this he would be right. If he has the right to read the Bible for himself, so have I. If he is to be bound by his conscience, so am I. If he honestly believes the Bible to be true, he must say so, in order to preserve his manhood; and if I honestly believe it to be uninspired,—filled with mistakes,—I must say so, or lose my manhood. How infamous I would be should I endeavor to deprive him of his vote, or of his right to be voted for, because he had been true to his conscience! And how infamous he is to try to deprive me of the right to vote, or to be voted for, because I am true to my conscience!

When we were engaged in civil war, did Mr. Talmage object to any man's enlisting in the ranks who was not a Christian? Was he willing, at that time, that sinners should vote to keep our flag in heaven? Was he willing that the "unconverted" should cover the fields of victory with their corpses, that this nation might not die? At the same time, Mr. Talmage knew that every "unconverted" soldier killed, went down to eternal fire. Does Mr. Talmage believe that it is the duty of a man to fight for a government in which he has no rights? Is the man who shoulders his musket in the defense of human freedom good enough to cast a ballot? There is in the heart of this priest the same hatred of real liberty that drew the sword of persecution, that built dungeons, that forged chains and made instruments of torture.

Nobody, with the exception of priests, would be willing to trust the liberties of this country in the hands of any church. In order to show the political estimation in which the clergy are held, in order to show the confidence the people at large have in the sincerity and wisdom of the clergy, it is sufficient to state, that no priest, no bishop, could by any possibility be elected President of the United States. No party could carry that load. A fear would fall upon the mind and heart of every honest man that this country was about to drift back to the Middle Ages, and that the old battles were to be refought. If the bishop running for President was of the Methodist Church, every other church would oppose him. If he was a Catholic, the Protestants would as a body combine against him. Why? The churches have no confidence in each other. Why? Because they are acquainted with each other.

As a matter of fact, the infidel has a thousand times more reason to vote against the Christian, than the Christian has to vote against the infidel. The Christian believes in a book superior to the Constitution— superior to all Constitutions and all laws. The infidel believes that the Constitution and laws are superior to any book. He is not controlled by any power beyond the seas or above the clouds. He does not receive his orders from Rome, or Sinai. He receives them from his fellow-citizens, legally and constitutionally expressed. The Christian believes in a power greater than man, to which, upon the peril of eternal pain, he must bow. His allegiance, to say the best of it, is divided. The Christian puts the fortune of his own soul over and above the temporal welfare of the entire world; the infidel puts the good of mankind here and now, beyond and over all.

There was a time in New England when only church members were allowed to vote, and it may be instructive to state the fact that during that time Quakers were hanged, women were stripped, tied to carts, and whipped from town to town, and their babes sold into slavery, or exchanged for rum. Now in that same country, thousands and thousands of infidels vote, and yet the laws are nearer just, women are not whipped and children are not sold.

If all the convicts in all the penitentiaries of the United States could be transported to some island in the sea, and there allowed to make a government for themselves, they would pass better laws than John Calvin did in Geneva. They would have clearer and better views of the rights of men, than unconvicted Christians used to have. I do not say that these convicts are better people, but I do say that, in my judgment, they would make better laws. They certainly could not make worse.

If these convicts were taken from the prisons of the United States, they would not dream of uniting church and state. They would have no religious test. They would allow every man to vote and to be voted for, no matter what his religious views might be. They would not dream of whipping Quakers, of burning Unitarians, of imprisoning or burning Universalists or infidels. They would allow all the people to guess for themselves. Some of these convicts, of course, would believe in the old ideas, and would insist upon the suppression of free thought. Those coming from Delaware would probably repeat with great gusto the opinions of Justice Comegys, and insist that the whipping-post was the handmaid of Christianity.

It would be hard to conceive of a much worse government than that founded by the Puritans. They took the Bible for the foundation of their political structure. They copied the laws given to Moses from Sinai, and the result was one of the worst governments that ever disgraced this world. They believed the Old Testament to be inspired. They believed that Jehovah made laws for all people and for all time. They had not learned the hypocrisy that believes and avoids. They did not say: This law was once just, but is now unjust; it was once good, but now it is infamous; it was given by God once, but now it can only be obeyed by the devil. They had not reached the height of biblical exegesis on which we find the modern theologian perched, and who tells us that Jehovah has reformed. The Puritans were consistent. They did what people must do who honestly believe in the inspiration of the Old Testament. If God gave laws from Sinai what right have we to repeal them?

As people have gained confidence in each other, they have lost confidence in the sacred Scriptures. We know now that the Bible can not be used as the foundation of government. It is capable of too many meanings. Nobody can find out exactly what it upholds, what it permits, what it denounces, what it denies. These things depend upon what part you read. If it is all true, it upholds everything bad and denounces everything good, and it also denounces the bad and upholds the good. Then there are passages where the good is denounced and the bad commanded; so that any one can go to the Bible and find some text, some passage, to uphold anything he may desire. If he wishes to enslave his fellow-men, he will find hundreds of passages in his favor. If he wishes to be a polygamist, he can find his authority there. If he wishes to make war, to exterminate his neighbors, there his warrant can be found. If, on the other hand, he is oppressed himself, and wishes to make war upon his king, he can find a battle-cry. And if the king wishes to put him down, he can find text for text on the other side. So, too, upon all questions of reform. The teetotaler goes there to get his verse, and the moderate drinker finds within the sacred lids his best excuse.

Most intelligent people are now convinced that the bible is not a guide; that in reading it you must exercise your reason; that you can neither safely reject nor accept all; that he who takes one passage for a staff, trips upon another; that while one text is a light, another blows it out; that it is such a mingling of rocks and quicksand, such a labyrinth of clues and snares—so few flowers among so many nettles and thorns, that it misleads rather than directs, and taken altogether, is a hindrance and not a help.

Another important point made by Mr. Talmage is, that if the Bible is thrown away, we will have nothing left to swear witnesses on, and that consequently the administration of justice will become impossible.

There was a time when the Bible did not exist, and if Mr. Talmage is correct, of course justice was impossible then, and truth must have been a stranger to human lips. How can we depend upon the testimony of those who wrote the Bible, as there was no Bible in existence while they were writing, and consequently there was no way to take their testimony, and we have no account of their having been sworn on the Bible after they got it finished. It is extremely sad to think that all the nations of antiquity were left entirely without the means of eliciting truth. No wonder that Justice was painted blindfolded.

What perfect fetishism it is, to imagine that a man will tell the truth simply because he has kissed an old piece of sheepskin stained with the saliva of all classes. A farce of this kind adds nothing to the testimony of an honest man; it simply allows a rogue to give weight to his false testimony. This is really the only result that can be accomplished by kissing the Bible. A desperate villain, for the purpose of getting revenge, or making money, will gladly go through the ceremony, and ignorant juries and superstitious judges will be imposed upon. The whole system of oaths is false, and does harm instead of good. Let every man walk into court and tell his story, and let the truth of the story be judged by its reasonableness, taking into consideration the character of the witness, the interest he has, and the position he occupies in the controversy, and then let it be the business of the jury to ascertain the real truth—to throw away the unreasonable and the impossible, and make up their verdict only upon what they believe to be reasonable and true. An honest man does not need the oath, and a rascal uses it simply to accomplish his purpose. If the history of courts proved that every man, after kissing the Bible, told the truth, and that those who failed to kiss it sometimes lied, I should be in favor of swearing all people on the Bible; but the experience of every lawyer is, that kissing the Bible is not always the preface of a true story. It is often the ceremonial embroidery of a falsehood.

If there is an infinite God who attends to the affairs of men, it seems to me almost a sacrilege to publicly appeal to him in every petty trial. If one will go into any court, and notice the manner in which oaths are administered,—the utter lack of solemnity—the matter-of-course air with which the whole thing is done, he will be convinced that it is a form of no importance. Mr. Talmage would probably agree with the judge of whom the following story is told:

A witness was being sworn. The judge noticed that he was not holding up his hand. He said to the clerk: "Let the witness hold up his right hand." "His right arm was shot off," replied the clerk. "Let him hold up his left, then." "That was shot off, too, your honor." "Well, then, let him raise one foot; no man can be sworn in this court without holding something up."

My own opinion is, that if every copy of the Bible in the world were destroyed, there would be some way to ascertain the truth in judicial proceedings; and any other book would do just as well to swear witnesses upon, or a block in the shape of a book covered with some kind of calfskin could do equally well, or just the calfskin would do. Nothing is more laughable than the performance of this ceremony, and I have never seen in court one calf kissing the skin of another, that I did not feel humiliated that such things were done in the name of Justice.

Mr. Talmage has still another argument in favor of the preservation of the Bible. He wants to know what book could take its place on the centre-table.

I admit that there is much force in this. Suppose we all admitted the Bible to be an uninspired book, it could still be kept on the centre-table. It would be just as true then as it is now. Inspiration can not add anything to a fact; neither can inspiration make the immoral moral, the unjust just, or the cruel merciful. If it is a fact that God established human slavery, that does not prove slavery to be right; it simply shows that God was wrong. If I have the right to use my reason in determining whether the Bible is inspired or not, and if in accordance with my reason I conclude that it is inspired, I have still the right to use my reason in determining whether the commandments of God are good or bad. Now, suppose we take from the Bible every word upholding slavery, every passage in favor of polygamy, every verse commanding soldiers to kill women and children, it would be just as fit for the centre-table as now. Suppose every impure word was taken from it; suppose that the history of Tamar was left out, the biography of Lot, and all other barbarous accounts of a barbarous people, it would look just as well upon the centre-table as now.

Suppose that we should become convinced that the writers of the New Testament were mistaken as to the eternity of punishment, or that all the passages now relied upon to prove the existence of perdition were shown to be interpolations, and were thereupon expunged, would not the book be dearer still to every human being with a heart? I would like to see every good passage in the Bible preserved. I would like to see, with all these passages from the Bible, the loftiest sentiments from all other books that have ever been uttered by men in all ages and of all races, bound in one volume, and to see that volume, filled with the greatest, the purest and the best, become the household book.

The average Bible, on the average centre-table, is about as much used as though it were a solid block. It is scarcely ever opened, and people who see its covers every day are unfamiliar with its every page.

I admit that some things have happened somewhat hard to explain, and tending to show that the Bible is no ordinary book. I heard a story, not long ago, bearing upon this very subject.

A man was a member of the church, but after a time, having had bad luck in business affairs, became somewhat discouraged. Not feeling able to contribute his share to the support of the church, he ceased going to meeting, and finally became an average sinner. His bad luck pursued him until he found himself and his family without even a crust to eat. At this point, his wife told him that she believed they were suffering from a visitation of God, and begged him to restore family worship, and see if God would not do something for them. Feeling that he could not possibly make matters worse, he took the Bible from its resting place on a shelf where it had quietly slumbered and collected the dust of many months, and gathered his family about him.

He opened the sacred volume, and to his utter astonishment, there, between the divine leaves, was a ten-dollar bill. He immediately dropped on his knees. His wife dropped on hers, and the children on theirs, and with streaming eyes they returned thanks to God. He rushed to the butcher's and bought some steak, to the baker's and bought some bread, to the grocer's and got some eggs and butter and tea, and joyfully hastened home. The supper was cooked, it was on the table, grace was said, and every face was radiant with joy. Just at that happy moment a knock was heard, the door was opened, and a policeman entered and arrested the father for passing counterfeit money.

Mr. Talmage is also convinced that the Bible is inspired and should be preserved because there is no other book that a mother could give her son as he leaves the old home to make his way in the world.

Thousands and thousands of mothers have presented their sons with Bibles without knowing really what the book contains. They simply followed the custom, and the sons as a rule honored the Bible, not because they knew anything of it, but because it was a gift from mother. But surely, if all the passages upholding polygamy were out, the mother would give the book to her son just as readily, and he would receive it just as joyfully. If there were not one word in it tending to degrade the mother, the gift would certainly be as appropriate. The fact that mothers have presented Bibles to their sons does not prove that the book is inspired. The most that can be proved by this fact is that the mothers believed it to be inspired. It does not even tend to show what the book is, neither does it tend to establish the truth of one miracle recorded upon its pages. We cannot believe that fire refused to burn, simply because the statement happens to be in a book presented to a son by his mother, and if all the mothers of the entire world should give Bibles to all their children, this would not prove that it was once right to murder mothers, or to enslave mothers, or to sell their babes.

The inspiration of the Bible is not a question of natural affection. It can not be decided by the love a mother bears her son. It is a question of fact, to be substantiated like other facts. If the Turkish mother should give a copy of the Koran to her son, I would still have my doubts about the inspiration of that book; and if some Turkish soldier saved his life by having in his pocket a copy of the Koran that accidentally stopped a bullet just opposite his heart, I should still deny that Mohammed was a prophet of God.

Nothing can be more childish than to ascribe mysterious powers to inanimate objects. To imagine that old rags made into pulp, manufactured into paper, covered with words, and bound with the skin of a calf or a sheep, can have any virtues when thus put together that did not belong to the articles out of which the book was constructed, is of course infinitely absurd.

In the days of slavery, negroes used to buy dried roots of other negroes, and put these roots in their pockets, so that a whipping would not give them pain. Kings have bought diamonds to give them luck. Crosses and scapularies are still worn for the purpose of affecting the inevitable march of events. People still imagine that a verse in the Bible can step in between a cause and its effect; really believe that an amulet, a charm, the bone of some saint, a piece of a cross, a little image of the Virgin, a picture of a priest, will affect the weather, will delay frost, will prevent disease, will insure safety at sea, and in some cases prevent hanging. The banditti of Italy have great confidence in these things, and whenever they start upon an expedition of theft and plunder, they take images and pictures of saints with them, such as have been blest by a priest or pope. They pray sincerely to the Virgin, to give them luck, and see not the slightest inconsistency in appealing to all the saints in the calendar to assist them in robbing honest people.

Edmund About tells a story that illustrates the belief of the modern Italian. A young man was gambling. Fortune was against him. In the room was a little picture representing the Virgin and her child. Before this picture he crossed himself, and asked the assistance of the child. Again he put down his money and again lost. Returning to the picture, he told the child that he had lost all but one piece, that he was about to hazard that, and made a very urgent request that he would favor him with divine assistance. He put down the last piece. He lost. Going to the picture and shaking his fist at the child, he cried out: "Miserable bambino, I am glad they crucified you!"

The confidence that one has in an image, in a relic, in a book, comes from the same source,—fetishism. To ascribe supernatural virtues to the skin of a snake, to a picture, or to a bound volume, is intellectually the same.

Mr. Talmage has still another argument in favor of the inspiration of the Scriptures. He takes the ground that the Bible must be inspired, because so many people believe it.

Mr. Talmage should remember that a scientific fact does not depend upon the vote of numbers;—it depends simply upon demonstration; it depends upon intelligence and investigation, not upon an ignorant multitude; it appeals to the highest, instead of to the lowest. Nothing can be settled by popular prejudice.

According to Mr. Talmage, there are about three hundred million Christians in the world. Is this true? In all countries claiming to be Christian—including all of civilized Europe, Russia in Asia, and every country on the Western hemisphere, we have nearly four hundred millions of people. Mr. Talmage claims that three hundred millions are Christians. I suppose he means by this, that if all should perish tonight, about three hundred millions would wake up in heaven—having lived and died good and consistent Christians.

There are in Russia about eighty millions of people—how many Christians? I admit that they have recently given more evidence of orthodox Christianity than formerly. They have been murdering old men; they have thrust daggers into the breasts of women; they have violated maidens—because they were Jews. Thousands and thousands are sent each year to the mines of Siberia, by the Christian government of Russia. Girls eighteen years of age, for having expressed a word in favor of human liberty, are today working like beasts of burden, with chains upon their limbs and with the marks of whips upon their backs. Russia, of course, is considered by Mr. Talmage as a Christian country—a country utterly destitute of liberty—without freedom of the press, without freedom of speech, where every mouth is locked and every tongue a prisoner—a country filled with victims, soldiers, spies, thieves and executioners. What would Russia be, in the opinion of Mr. Talmage, but for Christianity? How could it be worse, when assassins are among the best people in it? The truth is, that the people in Russia, to-day, who are in favor of human liberty, are not Christians. The men willing to sacrifice their lives for the good of others, are not believers in the Christian religion. The men who wish to break chains are infidels; the men who make chains are Christians. Every good and sincere Catholic of the Greek Church is a bad citizen, an enemy of progress, a foe of human liberty. Yet Mr. Talmage regards Russia as a Christian country.

The sixteen millions of people in Spain are claimed as Christians. Spain, that for centuries was the assassin of human rights; Spain, that endeavored to spread Christianity by flame and fagot; Spain, the soil where the Inquisition flourished, where bigotry grew, and where cruelty was worship,—where murder was prayer. I admit that Spain is a Christian nation. I admit that infidelity has gained no foothold beyond the Pyrenees. The Spaniards are orthodox. They believe in the inspiration of the Old and New Testaments. They have no doubts about miracles—no doubts about heaven, no doubts about hell. I admit that the priests, the highwaymen, the bishops and thieves, are equally true believers. The man who takes your purse on the highway, and the priest who forgives the robber, are alike orthodox.

It gives me pleasure, however, to say that even in Spain there is a dawn. Some great men, some men of genius, are protesting against the tyranny of Catholicism. Some men have lost confidence in the cathedral, and are beginning to ask the State to erect the schoolhouse. They are beginning to suspect that priests are for the most part impostors and plunderers.

According to Mr. Talmage, the twenty-eight millions in Italy are Christians. There the Christian Church was early established, and the popes are today the successors of St. Peter. For hundreds and hundreds of years, Italy was the beggar of the world, and to her, from every land, flowed streams of gold and silver. The country was covered with convents, and monasteries, and churches, and cathedrals filled with monks and nuns. Its roads were crowded with pilgrims, and its dust was on the feet of the world. What has Christianity done for Italy—Italy, its soil a blessing, its sky a smile—Italy, with memories great enough to kindle the fires of enthusiasm in any human breast?

Had it not been for a few Freethinkers, for a few infidels, for such men as Garibaldi and Mazzini, the heaven of Italy would still have been without a star.

I admit that Italy, with its popes and bandits, with its superstition and ignorance, with its sanctified beggars, is a Christian nation; but in a little while,—in a few days,—when according to the prophecy of Garibaldi priests, with spades in their hands, will dig ditches to drain the Pontine marshes; in a little while, when the pope leaves the Vatican, and seeks the protection of a nation he has denounced,—asking alms of intended victims; when the nuns shall marry, and the monasteries shall become factories, and the whirl of wheels shall take the place of drowsy prayers —then, and not until then, will Italy be,—not a Christian nation, but great, prosperous, and free.

In Italy, Giordano Bruno was burned. Someday, his monument will rise above the cross of Rome.

We have in our day one example,—and so far as I know, history records no other,—of the resurrection of a nation. Italy has been called from the grave of superstition. She is "the first fruits of them that "slept."

I admit with Mr. Talmage that Portugal is a Christian country—that she engaged for hundreds of years in the slave trade, and that she justified the infamous traffic by passages in the Old Testament. I admit, also, that she persecuted the Jews in accordance with the same divine volume. I admit that all the crime, ignorance, destitution, and superstition in that country were produced by the Catholic Church. I also admit that Portugal would be better if it were Protestant.

Every Catholic is in favor of education enough to change a barbarian into a Catholic; every Protestant is in favor of education enough to change a Catholic into a Protestant; but Protestants and Catholics alike are opposed to education that will lead to any real philosophy and science. I admit that Portugal is what it is, on account of the preaching of the gospel. I admit that Portugal can point with pride to the triumphs of what she calls civilization within her borders, and truthfully ascribe the glory to the church. But in a little while, when more railroads are built, when telegraphs connect her people with the civilized world, a spirit of doubt, of investigation, will manifest itself in Portugal.

When the people stop counting beads, and go to the study of mathematics; when they think more of plows than of prayers for agricultural purposes; when they find that one fact gives more light to the mind than a thousand tapers, and that nothing can by any possibility be more useless than a priest,—then Portugal will begin to cease to be what is called a Christian nation.

I admit that Austria, with her thirty-seven millions, is a Christian nation—including her Croats, Hungarians, Servians, and Gypsies. Austria was one of the assassins of Poland. When we remember that John Sobieski drove the Mohammedans from the gates of Vienna, and rescued from the hand of the "infidel" the beleaguered city, the propriety of calling Austria a Christian nation becomes still more apparent. If one wishes to know exactly how "Christian" Austria is, let him read the history of Hungary, let him read the speeches of Kossuth. There is one good thing about Austria: slowly but surely she is undermining the church by education. Education is the enemy of superstition. Universal education does away with the classes born of the tyranny of ecclesiasticism—classes founded upon cunning, greed, and brute strength. Education also tends to do away with intellectual cowardice. The educated man is his own priest, his own pope, his own church.

When cunning collects tolls from fear, the church prospers.

Germany is another Christian nation. Bismarck is celebrated for his Christian virtues.

Only a little while ago, Bismarck, when a bill was under consideration for ameliorating the condition of the Jews, stated publicly that Germany was a Christian nation, that her business was to extend and protect the religion of Jesus Christ, and that being a Christian nation, no laws should be passed ameliorating the condition of the Jews. Certainly a remark like this could not have been made in any other than a Christian nation. There is no freedom of the press, there is no freedom of speech, in Germany. The Chancellor has gone so far as to declare that the king is not responsible to the people. Germany must be a Christian nation. The king gets his right to govern, not from his subjects, but from God.

He relies upon the New Testament. He is satisfied that "the powers that be in Germany are ordained of God." He is satisfied that treason against the German throne is treason against Jehovah. There are millions of Freethinkers in Germany. They are not in the majority, otherwise there would be more liberty in that country. Germany is not an infidel nation, or speech would be free, and every man would be allowed to express his honest thoughts.

Wherever I see Liberty in chains, wherever the expression of opinion is a crime, I know that that country is not infidel; I know that the people are not ruled by reason. I also know that the greatest men of Germany— her Freethinkers, her scientists, her writers, her philosophers, are, for the most part, infidel. Yet Germany is called a Christian nation, and ought to be so called until her citizens are free.

France is also claimed as a Christian country. This is not entirely true. France once was thoroughly Catholic, completely Christian. At the time of the massacre of Saint Bartholomew, the French were Christians. Christian France made exiles of the Huguenots. Christian France for years and years was the property of the Jesuits. Christian France was ignorant, cruel, orthodox and infamous. When France was Christian, witnesses were cross-examined with instruments of torture.

Now France is not entirely under Catholic control, and yet she is by far the most prosperous nation in Europe. I saw, only the other day, a letter from a Protestant bishop, in which he states that there are only about a million Protestants in France, and only four or five millions of Catholics, and admits, in a very melancholy way, that thirty-four or thirty-five millions are Freethinkers. The bishop is probably mistaken in his figures, but France is the best housed, the best fed, the best clad country in Europe.

Only a little while ago, France was overrun, trampled into the very earth, by the victorious hosts of Germany, and France purchased her peace with the savings of centuries. And yet France is now rich and prosperous and free, and Germany poor, discontented and enslaved. Hundreds and thousands of Germans, unable to find liberty at home, are coming to the United States.

I admit that England is a Christian country. Any doubts upon this point can be dispelled by reading her history—her career in India, what she has done in China, her treatment of Ireland, of the American Colonies, her attitude during our Civil war; all these things show conclusively that England is a Christian nation.

Religion has filled Great Britain with war. The history of the Catholics, of the Episcopalians, of Cromwell—all the burnings, the maimings, the brandings, the imprisonments, the confiscations, the civil wars, the bigotry, the crime—show conclusively that Great Britain has enjoyed to the full the blessings of "our most holy religion."

Of course, Mr. Talmage claims the United States as a Christian country. The truth is, our country is not as Christian as it once was. When heretics were hanged in New England, when the laws of Virginia and Maryland provided that the tongue of any man who denied the doctrine of the Trinity should be bored with hot iron, and that for the second offence he should suffer death, I admit that this country was

Christian. When we engaged in the slave trade, when our flag protected piracy and murder in every sea, there is not the slightest doubt that the United States was a Christian country. When we believed in slavery, and when we deliberately stole the labor of four millions of people; when we sold women and babes, and when the people of the North enacted a law by virtue of which every Northern man was bound to turn hound and pursue a human being who was endeavoring to regain his liberty, I admit that the United States was a Christian nation. I admit that all these things were upheld by the Bible—that the slave trader was justified by the Old Testament, that the bloodhound was a kind of missionary in disguise, that the auction block was an altar, the slave pen a kind of church, and that the whipping-post was considered almost as sacred as the cross. At that time, our country was a Christian nation.

I heard Frederick Douglass say that he lectured against slavery for twenty years before the doors of a single church were opened to him. In New England, hundreds of ministers were driven from their pulpits because they preached against the crime of human slavery. At that time, this country was a Christian nation.

Only a few years ago, any man speaking in favor of the rights of man, endeavoring to break a chain from a human limb, was in danger of being mobbed by the Christians of this country. I admit that Delaware is still a Christian State. I heard a story about that State the other day.

About fifty years ago, an old Revolutionary soldier applied for a pension. He was asked his age, and he replied that he was fifty years old. He was told that if that was his age, he could not have been in the Revolutionary War, and consequently was not entitled to any pension. He insisted, however, that he was only fifty years old. Again they told him that there must be some mistake. He was so wrinkled, so bowed, had so many marks of age, that he must certainly be more than fifty years old. "Well," said the old man, "if I must explain, I will: I lived forty years in Delaware; but I never counted that time, and I hope God won't."

The fact is, we have grown less and less Christian every year from 1620 until now, and the fact is that we have grown more and more civilized, more and more charitable, nearer and nearer just.

Mr. Talmage speaks as though all the people in what he calls the civilized world were Christians. Admitting this to be true, I find that in these countries millions of men are educated, trained and drilled to kill their fellow Christians. I find Europe covered with forts to protect Christians from Christians, and the seas filled with men-of-war for the purpose of ravaging the coasts and destroying the cities of Christian nations. These countries are filled with prisons, with workhouses, with jails and with toiling, ignorant and suffering millions. I find that Christians have invented most of the instruments of death, that Christians are the greatest soldiers, fighters, destroyers. I find that every Christian country is taxed to its utmost to support these soldiers; that every Christian nation is now groaning beneath the grievous burden of monstrous debt, and that nearly all these debts were contracted in waging war. These bonds, these millions, these almost incalculable amounts, were given to pay for shot and shell, for rifle and torpedo, for men-of-war, for forts and arsenals, and all the devilish enginery of death. I find that each of these nations prays to God to assist it as against all others; and when one nation has overrun, ravaged and pillaged another, it immediately returns thanks to the Almighty, and the ravaged and pillaged kneel and thank God that it is no worse.

Mr. Talmage is welcome to all the evidence he can find in the history of what he is pleased to call the civilized nations of the world, tending to show the inspiration of the Bible.

And right here it may be well enough to say again, that the question of inspiration can not be settled by the votes of the superstitious millions. It can not be affected by numbers. It must be decided by each human being for himself. If every man in this world, with one exception, believed the Bible to be the inspired word of God, the man who was the exception could not lose his right to think, to investigate, and to judge for himself.

Question. You do not think, then, that any of the arguments brought forward by Mr. Talmage for the purpose of establishing the inspiration of the Bible, are of any weight whatever?

Answer. I do not. I do not see how it is possible to make poorer, weaker or better arguments than he has made.

Of course, there can be no "evidence" of the inspiration of the Scriptures. What is "inspiration"? Did God use the prophets simply as instruments? Did he put his thoughts in their minds, and use their hands to make a record? Probably few Christians will agree as to what they mean by "inspiration." The general idea is, that the minds of the writers of the books of the Bible were controlled by the divine will in such a way that they expressed, independently of their own opinions, the thought of God. I believe it is admitted that God did not choose the exact words, and is not responsible for the punctuation or syntax. It is hard to give any reason for claiming more for the Bible than is claimed by those who wrote it. There is no claim of "inspiration" made by the writer of First and Second Kings. Not one word about the author having been "inspired" is found in the book of Job, or in Ruth, or in Chronicles, or in the Psalms, or Ecclesiastes, or in Solomon's Song, and nothing is said about the author of the book of Esther having been "inspired." Christians now say that Matthew, Mark, Luke and John were "inspired" to write the four gospels, and yet neither Mark, nor Luke, nor John, nor Matthew claims to have been "inspired." If they were "inspired," certainly they should have stated that fact. The very first thing stated in each of the gospels should have been a declaration by the writer that he had been "inspired," and that he was about to write the book under the guidance of God, and at the conclusion of each gospel there should have been a solemn statement that the writer had put down nothing of himself, but had in all things followed the direction and guidance of the divine will. The church now endeavors to establish the inspiration of the Bible by force, by social ostracism, and by attacking the reputation of every man who denies or doubts. In all Christian countries, they begin with the child in the cradle. Each infant is told by its mother, by its father, or by some of its relatives, that "the Bible is an inspired book." This pretended fact, by repetition "in season and out of "season," is finally burned and branded into the brain to such a degree that the child of average intelligence never outgrows the conviction that the Bible is, in some peculiar sense, an "inspired" book. The question has to be settled for each generation. The evidence is not sufficient, and the foundation of Christianity is perpetually insecure. Beneath this great religious fabric there is no rock. For eighteen centuries, hundreds and thousands and millions of people have been endeavoring to establish the fact that the Scriptures are inspired, and since the dawn of science, since the first star appeared in the night of the Middle Ages, until this moment, the number of people who have doubted the fact of inspiration has steadily increased. These doubts have not been born of ignorance, they have not been suggested by the unthinking. They have forced themselves upon the thoughtful, upon the educated, and now the verdict of the intellectual world is, that the Bible is not inspired. Notwithstanding the fact that the church has taken advantage of infancy, has endeavored to control education, has filled all primers and spelling-books and readers and text books with superstition—feeding all minds with the miraculous and supernatural, the growth toward a belief in the natural and toward the rejection of the miraculous has been steady and sturdy since the sixteenth century. There has been, too, a moral growth, until many passages in the Bible have become barbarous, inhuman and infamous. The Bible has remained the same, while the world has changed. In the light of physical and moral discovery, "the inspired volume" seems in many respects absurd. If the same progress is made in the next, as in the last, century, it is very easy to predict the place that will then be occupied by the Bible. By comparing long periods of time, it is easy to measure the advance of the human race. Compare the average sermon of today with the average sermon of one hundred years ago. Compare what ministers teach today with the creeds they profess to believe, and you will see the immense distance that even the church has traveled in the last century.

The Christians tell us that scientific men have made mistakes, and that there is very little certainty in the domain of human knowledge. This I admit. The man who thought the world was flat, and who had a way of accounting for the movement of the heavenly bodies, had what he was pleased to call a philosophy. He was, in his way, a geologist and an astronomer. We admit that he was mistaken; but if we claimed that the first geologist and the first astronomer were inspired, it would not do for us to admit that any advance had been made, or that any errors of theirs had been corrected. We do not claim that the first scientists were inspired. We do not claim that the last are inspired. We admit that all scientific men are fallible. We admit that they do not know everything. We insist that they know but little, and that even in that little which they are supposed to know, there is the possibility of error. The first geologist said: "The earth is flat." Suppose that the geologists of to-day should insist that that man was inspired, and then endeavor to show that the word "flat," in the "Hebrew," did not mean quite flat, but just a little rounded; what would we think of their honesty? The first astronomer insisted that the sun and moon and stars revolved around this earth—that this little earth was the centre of the entire system. Suppose that the astronomers of today should insist that that astronomer was inspired, and should try to explain, and say that he simply used the language of the common people, and when he stated that the sun and moon and stars revolved around the earth, he merely meant that they "apparently revolved," and that the earth, in fact, turned over, would we consider them honest men? You might as well say that the first painter was inspired, or that the first sculptor had the assistance of God, as to say that the first writer, or the first bookmaker, was divinely inspired. It is more probable that the modern geologist is inspired than that the ancient one was, because the modern geologist is nearer right. It is more probable that William Lloyd Garrison was inspired upon the question of slavery than that Moses was. It is more probable that the author of the Declaration of Independence spoke by divine authority than that the author of the Pentateuch did. In other words, if there can be any evidence of "inspiration," it must lie in the fact of doing or saying the best possible thing that could have been done or said at that time or upon that subject.

To make myself clear: The only possible evidence of "inspiration" would be perfection—a perfection excelling anything that man unaided had ever attained. An "inspired" book should excel all other books; an inspired statue should be the best in this world; an inspired painting should be beyond all others. If the Bible has been improved in any particular, it was not, in that particular, "inspired." If slavery is wrong, the Bible is not inspired. If polygamy is vile and loathsome, the Bible is not inspired. If wars of extermination are cruel and heartless, the Bible is not "inspired." If there is within that book a contradiction of any natural fact; if there is one ignorant falsehood, if there is one mistake, then it is not "inspired." I do not mean mistakes that have grown out of translations; but if there was in the original manuscript one mistake, then it is not "inspired." I do not demand a miracle; I do not demand a knowledge of the future; I simply demand an absolute knowledge of the past. I demand an absolute knowledge of the then present; I demand a knowledge of the constitution of the human mind—of the facts in nature, and that is all I demand.

Question. If I understand you, you think that all political power should come from the people; do you not believe in any "special providence," and do you take the ground that God does not interest himself in the affairs of nations and individuals?

Answer. The Christian idea is that God made the world, and made certain laws for the government of matter and mind, and that he never interferes except upon special occasions, when the ordinary laws fail to work out the desired end. Their notion is, that the Lord now and then stops the horses simply to show that he is driving. It seems to me that if an infinitely wise being made the world, he must have made it the best possible; and that if he made laws for the government of matter and mind, he must have made the best possible laws. If this is true, not one of these laws can be violated without producing a positive injury. It does not seem probable that infinite wisdom would violate a law that infinite wisdom had made.

Most ministers insist that God now and then interferes in the affairs of this world; that he has not interfered as much lately as he did formerly.

When the world was comparatively new, it required altogether more tinkering and fixing than at present. Things are at last in a reasonably good condition, and consequently a great amount of interference is not necessary. In old times it was found necessary frequently to raise the dead, to change the nature of fire and water, to punish people with plagues and famine, to destroy cities by storms of fire and brimstone, to change women into salt, to cast hailstones upon heathen, to interfere with the movements of our planetary system, to stop the earth not only, but sometimes to make it turn the other way, to arrest the moon, and to make water stand up like a wall. Now and then, rivers were divided by striking them with a coat, and people were taken to heaven in chariots of fire. These miracles, in addition to curing the sick, the halt, the deaf and blind, were in former times found necessary, but since the "apostolic age," nothing of the kind has been resorted to except in Catholic countries. Since the death of the last apostle, God has appeared only to members of the Catholic Church, and all modern miracles have been performed for the benefit of Catholicism. There is no authentic account of the Virgin Mary having ever appeared to a Protestant. The bones of Protestant saints have never cured a solitary disease. Protestants now say that the testimony of the Catholics can not be relied upon, and yet, the authenticity of every book in the New Testament was established by Catholic testimony. Some few miracles were performed in Scotland, and in fact in England and the United States, but they were so small that they are hardly worth mentioning. Now and then, a man was struck dead for taking the name of the Lord in vain. Now and then, people were drowned who were found in boats on Sunday. Whenever anybody was about to commit murder, God has not interfered—the reason being that he gave man free-will, and expects to hold him accountable in another world, and there is no exception to this free-will doctrine, but in cases where men swear or violate the Sabbath. They are allowed to commit all other crimes without any interference on the part of the Lord.

My own opinion is, that the clergy found it necessary to preserve the Sabbath for their own uses, and for that reason endeavored to impress the people with the enormity of its violation, and for that purpose gave instances of people being drowned and suddenly struck dead for working or amusing themselves on that day. The clergy have objected to any other places of amusement except their own, being opened on that day. They wished to compel people either to go to church or stay at home. They have also known that profanity tended to do away with the feelings of awe they wished to cultivate, and for that reason they have insisted that swearing was one of the most terrible of crimes, exciting above all others the wrath of God.

There was a time when people fell dead for having spoken disrespectfully to a priest. The priest at that time pretended to be the visible representative of God, and as such, entitled to a degree of reverence amounting almost to worship. Several cases are given in the ecclesiastical history of Scotland where men were deprived of speech for having spoken rudely to a parson.

These stories were calculated to increase the importance of the clergy and to convince people that they were under the special care of the

Deity. The story about the bears devouring the little children was told in the first place, and has been repeated since, simply to protect ministers from the laughter of children. There ought to be carved on each side of every pulpit a bear with fragments of children in its mouth, as this animal has done so much to protect the dignity of the clergy.

Besides the protection of ministers, the drowning of breakers of the Sabbath, and striking a few people dead for using profane language, I think there is no evidence of any providential interference in the affairs of this world in what may be called modern times. Ministers have endeavored to show that great calamities have been brought upon nations and cities as a punishment for the wickedness of the people. They have insisted that some countries have been visited with earthquakes because the people had failed to discharge their religious duties; but as earthquakes happened in uninhabited countries, and often at sea, where no one is hurt, most people have concluded that they are not sent as punishments. They have insisted that cities have been burned as a punishment, and to show the indignation of the Lord, but at the same time they have admitted that if the streets had been wider, the fire departments better organized, and wooden buildings fewer, the design of the Lord would have been frustrated.

After reading the history of the world, it is somewhat difficult to find which side the Lord is really on. He has allowed Catholics to overwhelm and destroy Protestants, and then he has allowed Protestants to overwhelm and destroy Catholics. He has allowed Christianity to triumph over Paganism, and he allowed Mohammedans to drive back the hosts of the cross from the sepulcher of his son. It is curious that this God would allow the slave trade to go on, and yet punish the violators of the Sabbath. It is simply wonderful that he would allow kings to wage cruel and remorseless war, to sacrifice millions upon the altar of heartless ambition, and at the same time strike a man dead for taking his name in vain. It is wonderful that he allowed slavery to exist for centuries in the United States; that he allows polygamy now in Utah; that he cares nothing for liberty in Russia, nothing for free speech in Germany, nothing for the sorrows of the overworked, underpaid millions of the world; that he cares nothing for the innocent languishing in prisons, nothing for the patriots condemned to death, nothing for the heart-broken widows and orphans, nothing for the starving, and yet has ample time to note a sparrow's fall. If he would only strike dead the would-be murderers; if he would only palsy the hands of husbands' uplifted to strike their wives; if he would render speechless the cursers of children, he could afford to overlook the swearers and breakers of his Sabbath.

For one, I am not satisfied with the government of this world, and I am going to do what little I can to make it better. I want more thought and less fear, more manhood and less superstition, less prayer and more help, more education, more reason, more intellectual hospitality, and above all, and over all, more liberty and kindness.

Question. Do you think that God, if there be one, when he saves or damns a man, will take into consideration all the circumstances of the man's life?

Answer. Suppose that two orphan boys, James and John, are given homes. James is taken into a Christian family and John into an infidel. James becomes a Christian, and dies in the faith. John becomes an infidel, and dies without faith in Christ. According to the Christian religion, as commonly preached, James will go to heaven, and John to hell.

Now, suppose that God knew that if James had been raised by the infidel family, he would have died an infidel, and that if John had been raised by the Christian family, he would have died a Christian. What then? Recollect that the boys did not choose the families in which they were placed.

Suppose that a child, cast away upon an island in which he found plenty of food, grew to manhood; and suppose that after he had reached mature years, the island was visited by a missionary who taught a false religion; and suppose that this islander was convinced that he ought to worship a wooden idol; and suppose, further, that the worship consisted in sacrificing animals; and suppose the islander, actuated only by what he conceived to be his duty and by thankfulness, sacrificed a toad every night and every morning upon the altar of his wooden god; that when the sky looked black and threatening he sacrificed two toads; that when feeling unwell he sacrificed three; and suppose that in all this he was honest, that he really believed that the shedding of toad-blood would soften the heart of his god toward him? And suppose that after he had become fully-convinced of the truth of his religion, a missionary of the "true religion" should visit the island, and tell the history of the Jews— unfold the whole scheme of salvation? And suppose that the islander should honestly reject the true religion? Suppose he should say that he had "internal evidence" not only, but that many miracles had been performed by his god, in his behalf; that often when the sky was black with storm, he had sacrificed a toad, and in a few moments the sun was again visible, the heavens blue, and without a cloud; that on several occasions, having forgotten at evening to sacrifice his toad, he found himself unable to sleep—that his conscience smote him, he had risen, made the sacrifice, returned to his bed, and in a few moments sunk into a serene and happy slumber? And suppose, further, that the man honestly believed that the efficacy of the sacrifice depended largely on the size of the toad? Now suppose that in this belief the man had died,—what then?

It must be remembered that God knew when the missionary of the false religion went to the island; and knew that the islander would be convinced of the truth of the false religion; and he also knew that the missionary of the true religion could not, by any possibility, convince the islander of the error of his way; what then?

If God is infinite, we cannot speak of him as making efforts, as being tired. We cannot consistently say that one thing is easy to him, and another thing is hard, providing both are possible. This being so, why did not God reveal himself to every human being? Instead of having an inspired book, why did he not make inspired folks? Instead of having his commandments put on tables of stone, why did he not write them on each human brain? Why was not the mind of each man so made that every religious truth necessary to his salvation was an axiom?

Do we not know absolutely that man is greatly influenced by his surroundings? If Mr. Talmage had been born in Turkey, is it not probable that he would now be a whirling Dervish? If he had first seen the light in Central Africa, he might now have been prostrate before some enormous serpent; if in India, he might have been a Brahmin, running a prayer-machine; if in Spain, he would probably have been a priest, with his beads and holy water. Had he been born among the North American Indians, he would speak of the "Great Spirit," and solemnly smoke the pipe of peace.

Mr. Talmage teaches that it is the duty of children to perpetuate the errors of their parents; consequently, the religion of his parents determined his theology. It is with him not a question of reason, but of parents; not a question of argument, but of filial affection. He does not wish to be a philosopher, but an obedient son. Suppose his father had been a Catholic, and his mother a Protestant,—what then? Would he show contempt for his mother by following the path of his father; or would he show disrespect for his father, by accepting the religion of his mother; or would he have become a Protestant with Catholic proclivities, or a Catholic with Protestant leanings? Suppose his parents had both been infidels—what then?

Is it not better for each one to decide honestly for himself? Admitting that your parents were good and kind; admitting that they were honest in their views, why not have the courage to say, that in your opinion, father and mother were both mistaken? No one can honor his parents by being a hypocrite, or an intellectual coward. Whoever is absolutely true to himself, is true to his parents, and true to the whole world. Whoever is untrue to himself, is false to all mankind. Religion must be an individual matter. If there is a God, and if there is a day of judgment, the church that a man belongs to will not be tried, but the man will be tried.

It is a fact that the religion of most people was made for them by others; that they have accepted certain dogmas, not because they have examined them, but because they were told that they were true. Most of the people in the United States, had they been born in Turkey, would now be Mohammedans, and most of the Turks, had they been born in Spain, would now be Catholics.

It is almost, if not quite, impossible for a man to rise entirely above the ideas, views, doctrines and religions of his tribe or country. No one expects to find philosophers in Central Africa, or scientists among the Fijis. No one expects to find philosophers or scientists in any country where the church has absolute control.

If there is an infinitely good and wise God, of course he will take into consideration the surroundings of every human being. He understands the philosophy of environment, and of heredity. He knows exactly the influence of the mother, of all associates, of all associations. He will also take into consideration the amount, quality and form of each brain, and whether the brain was healthy or diseased. He will take into consideration the strength of the passions, the weakness of the judgment. He will know exactly the force of all temptation—what was resisted. He will take an account of every effort made in the right direction, and will understand all the winds and waves and quicksand and shores and shallows in, upon and around the sea of every life.

My own opinion is, that if such a being exists, and all these things are taken into consideration, we will be absolutely amazed to see how small the difference is between the "good" and the "bad." Certainly there is no such difference as would justify a being of infinite wisdom and benevolence in rewarding one with eternal joy and punishing the other with eternal pain.

Question. What are the principal reasons that have satisfied you that the Bible is not an inspired book?

Answer. The great evils that have afflicted this world are:

First. Human slavery—where men have bought and sold their fellow-men—sold babes from mothers, and have practiced) every conceivable cruelty upon the helpless.

Second. Polygamy—an institution that destroys the home, that treats woman as a simple chattel, that does away with the sanctity of marriage, and with all that is sacred in love.

Third. Wars of conquest and extermination—by which nations have been made the food of the sword.

Fourth. The idea entertained by each nation that all other nations are destitute of rights—in other words, patriotism founded upon egotism, prejudice, and love of plunder.

Fifth. Religious persecution.

Sixth. The divine right of kings—an idea that rests upon the inequality of human rights, and insists that people should be governed without their consent; that the right of one man to govern another comes from God, and not from the consent of the governed. This is caste—one of the most odious forms of slavery.

Seventh. A belief in malicious supernatural beings—devils, witches, and wizards.

Eighth. A belief in an infinite being who ordered, commanded, established and approved all these evils.

Ninth. The idea that one man can be good for another, or bad for another—that is to say, that one can be rewarded for the goodness of another, or justly punished for the sins of another.

Tenth. The dogma that a finite being can commit an infinite sin, and thereby incur the eternal displeasure of an infinitely good being, and be justly subjected to eternal torment.

My principal objection to the Bible is that it sustains all of these ten evils—that it is the advocate of human slavery, the friend of polygamy; that within its pages I find the command to wage wars of extermination; that I find also that the Jews were taught to hate foreigners—to consider all human beings as inferior to themselves; I also find persecution commanded as a religious duty; that kings were seated upon their thrones by the direct act of God, and that to rebel against a king was rebellion against God. I object to the Bible also because I find within its pages the infamous spirit of caste—I see the sons of Levi set apart as the perpetual beggars and governors of a people; because I find the air filled with demons seeking to injure and betray the sons of men; because this book is the fountain of modern superstition, the bulwark of tyranny and the fortress of caste. This book also subverts the idea of justice by threatening infinite punishment for the sins of a finite being.

At the same time, I admit—as I always have admitted—that there are good passages in the Bible—good laws, good teachings, with now and then a true line of history. But when it is asserted that every word was written by inspiration—that a being of infinite wisdom and goodness is its author,—then I raise the standard of revolt.

Question. What do you think of the declaration of Mr. Talmage that the Bible will be read in heaven throughout all the endless ages of eternity?

Answer. Of course I know but very little as to what is or will be done in heaven. My knowledge of that country is somewhat limited, and it may be possible that the angels will spend most of their time in turning over the sacred leaves of the Old Testament. I can not positively deny the statement of the Reverend Mr. Talmage as I have but very little idea as to how the angels manage to kill time.

The Reverend Mr. Spurgeon stated in a sermon that some people wondered what they would do through all eternity in heaven. He said that, as for himself, for the first hundred thousand years he would look at the wound in one of the Savior's feet, and for the next hundred thousand years he would look at the wound in his other foot, and for the next hundred thousand years he would look at the wound in one of his hands, and for the next hundred thousand years he would look at the wound in the other hand, and for the next hundred thousand years he would look at the wound in his side.

Surely, nothing could be more delightful than this. A man capable of being happy in such employment, could of course take great delight in reading even the genealogies of the Old Testament. It is very easy to see what a glow of joy would naturally overspread the face of an angel while reading the history of the Jewish wars, how the seraphim and cherubim would clasp their rosy palms in ecstasy over the fate of Korah and his company, and what laughter would wake the echoes of the New Jerusalem as some one told again the story of the children and the bears; and what happy groups, with folded pinions, would smilingly listen to the 109th Psalm.

An orthodox "state of mind"

THE TALMAGIAN CATECHISM.

As Mr. Talmage delivered the series of sermons referred to in these interviews, for the purpose of furnishing arguments to the young, so that they might not be misled by the sophistry of modern infidelity, I have thought it best to set forth, for use in Sunday schools, the pith and marrow of what he has been pleased to say, in the form of

A SHORTER CATECHISM.

Question. Who made you?
Answer. Jehovah, the original Presbyterian.

Question. What else did he make?
Answer. He made the world and all things.

Question. Did he make the world out of nothing?
Answer. No.

Question. What did he make it out of?
Answer. Out of his "omnipotence." Many infidels have pretended that if God made the universe, and if there was nothing until he did make it, he had nothing to make it out of. Of course this is perfectly absurd when we remember that he always had his omnipotence and that is, undoubtedly, the material used.

Question. Did he create his own "omnipotence"?
Answer. Certainly not, he was always omnipotent.

Question. Then if he always had "omnipotence," he did not "create" the material of which the universe is made; he simply took a portion of his "omnipotence" and changed it to "universe"?
Answer. Certainly, that is the way I understand it.

Question. Is he still omnipotent, and has he as much "omnipotence" now as he ever had?
Answer. Well, I suppose he has.

Question. How long did it take God to make the universe?
Answer. Six "good-whiles."

Question. How long is a "good-while"?
Answer. That will depend upon the future discoveries of geologists. "Good-whiles" are of such a nature that they can be pulled out, or pushed up; and it is utterly impossible for any infidel, or scientific geologist, to make any period that a "good-while" won't fit.

Question. What do you understand by "the "morning and evening" of a "good-while"?

Answer. Of course the words "morning and evening" are used figuratively, and mean simply the beginning and the ending, of each "good-while."

Question. On what day did God make vegetation?
Answer. On the third day.

Question. Was that before the sun was made?
Answer. Yes; a "good-while" before.

Question. How did vegetation grow without sunlight?
Answer. My own opinion is, that it was either "nourished by the glare of volcanoes in the moon" or "it may have gotten sufficient light from rivers of molten granite;" or, "sufficient light might have been emitted by the crystallization of rocks." It has been suggested that light might have been furnished by fire-flies and phosphorescent bugs and worms, but this I regard as going too far.

Question. Do you think that light emitted by rocks would be sufficient to produce trees?
Answer. Yes, with the assistance of the "Aurora "Borealis, or even the Aurora Australis;" but with both, most assuredly.

Question. If the light of which you speak was sufficient, why was the sun made?
Answer. To keep time with.

Question. What did God make man of?
Answer. He made man of dust and "omnipotence."

Question. Did he make a woman at the same time that he made a man?
Answer. No; he thought at one time to avoid the necessity of making a woman, and he caused all the animals to pass before Adam, to see what he would call them, and to see whether a fit companion could be found for him. Among them all, not one suited Adam, and Jehovah immediately saw that he would have to make an help-meet on purpose.

Question. What was woman made of?
Answer. She was made out of "man's side, out of his right side," and some more "omnipotence." Infidels say that she was made out of a rib, or a bone, but that is because they do not understand Hebrew.

Question. What was the object of making woman out of man's side?
Answer. So that a young man would think more of a neighbor's girl than of his own uncle or grandfather.

Question. What did God do with Adam and Eve after he got them done?
Answer. He put them into a garden to see what they would do.

Question. Do we know where the Garden of Eden was, and have we ever found any place where a "river parted and became into four heads"?

Answer. We are not certain where this garden was, and the river that parted into four heads cannot at present be found. Infidels have had a great deal to say about these four rivers, but they will wish they had even one, one of these days.

Question. What happened to Adam and Eve in the garden?

Answer. They were tempted by a snake who was an exceedingly good talker, and who probably came in walking on the end of his tail. This supposition is based upon the fact that, as a punishment, he was condemned to crawl on his belly. Before that time, of course, he walked upright.

Question. What happened then?

Answer. Our first parents gave way, ate of the forbidden fruit, and in consequence, disease and death entered the world. Had it not been for this, there would have been no death and no disease. Suicide would have been impossible, and a man could have been blown into a thousand atoms by dynamite, and the pieces would immediately have come together again. Fire would have refused to burn and water to drown; there could have been no hunger, no thirst; all things would have been equally healthy.

Question. Do you mean to say that there would have been no death in the world, either of animals, insects, or persons?

Answer. Of course.

Question. Do you also think that all briers and thorns sprang from the same source, and that had the apple not been eaten, no bush in the world would have had a thorn, and brambles and thistles would have been unknown?

Answer. Certainly.

Question. Would there have been no poisonous plants, no poisonous reptiles?

Answer. No, sir; there would have been none; there would have been no evil in the world if Adam and Eve had not partaken of the forbidden fruit.

Question. Was the snake who tempted them to eat, evil?

Answer. Certainly. '

Question. Was he in the world before the forbidden fruit was eaten?

Answer. Of course he was; he tempted them to eat it

Question. How, then, do you account for the fact that, before the forbidden fruit was eaten, an evil serpent was in the world?

Answer. Perhaps apples had been eaten in other worlds.

131

Question. Is it not wonderful that such awful consequences flowed from so small an act?

Answer. It is not for you to reason about it; you should simply remember that God is omnipotent. There is but one way to answer these things, and that is to admit their truth. Nothing so puts the Infinite out of temper as to see a human being impudent enough to rely upon his reason. The moment we rely upon our reason, we abandon God, and try to take care of ourselves. Whoever relies entirely upon God, has no need of reason, and reason has no need of him.

Question. Were our first parents under the immediate protection of an infinite God?

Answer. They were.

Question. Why did he not protect them? Why did he not warn them of this snake? Why did he not put them on their guard? Why did he not make them so sharp, intellectually, that they could not be deceived? Why did he not destroy that snake; or how did he come to make him; what did he make him for?

Answer. You must remember that, although God made Adam and Eve perfectly good, still he was very anxious to test them. He also gave them the power of choice, knowing at the same time exactly what they would choose, and knowing that he had made them so that they must choose in a certain way. A being of infinite wisdom tries experiments. Knowing exactly what will happen, he wishes to see if it will.

Question. What punishment did God inflict upon Adam and Eve for the sin of having eaten the forbidden fruit?

Answer. He pronounced a curse upon the woman, saying that in sorrow she should bring forth children, and that her husband should rule over her; that she, having tempted her husband, was made his slave; and through her, all married women have been deprived of their natural liberty. On account of the sin of Adam and Eve, God cursed the ground, saying that it should bring forth thorns and thistles, and that man should eat his bread in sorrow, and that he should eat the herb of the field.

Question. Did he turn them out of the garden because of their sin?

Answer. No. The reason God gave for turning them out of the garden was: "Behold the man is become as one of us, to know good and evil; and now, lest he put forth his hand and take of the tree of life and eat and live forever, therefore, the Lord God sent him forth from the Garden of Eden to till the ground from whence he was taken."

Question. If the man had eaten of the tree of life, would he have lived forever?

Answer. Certainly.

Question. Was he turned out to prevent his eating?

Answer. He was.

Question. Then the Old Testament tells us how we lost immortality, not that we are immortal, does it?

Answer. Yes; it tells us how we lost it.

Question. Was God afraid that Adam and Eve might get back into the garden, and eat of the fruit of the tree of life?

Answer. I suppose he was, as he placed "cherubim and a flaming sword which turned every way to guard the tree of life."

Question. Has any one ever seen any of these cherubim?

Answer. Not that I know of.

Question. Where is the flaming sword now?

Answer. Some angel has it in heaven.

Question. Do you understand that God made coats of skins, and clothed Adam and Eve when he turned them out of the garden?

Answer. Yes, sir.

Question. Do you really believe that the infinite God killed some animals, took their skins from them, cut out and sewed up clothes for Adam and Eve?

Answer. The Bible says so; we know that he had patterns for clothes, because he showed some to Moses on Mount Sinai.

Question. About how long did God continue to pay particular attention to his children in this world?

Answer. For about fifteen hundred years; and some of the people lived to be nearly a thousand years of age.

Question. Did this God establish any schools or institutions of learning? Did he establish any church? Did he ordain any ministers, or did he have any revivals?

Answer. No; he allowed the world to go on pretty much in its own way. He did not even keep his own boys at home. They came down and made love to the daughters of men, and finally the world got exceedingly bad.

Question. What did God do then?

Answer. He made up his mind that he would drown them. You see they were all totally depraved,—in every joint and sinew of their bodies, in every drop of their blood, and in every thought of their brains.

Question. Did he drown them all?

Answer. No, he saved eight, to start with again.

Question. Were these eight persons totally depraved?

Answer. Yes.

Question. Why did he not kill them, and start over again with a perfect pair? Would it not have been better to have had his flood at first, before he made anybody, and drowned the snake?

Answer. "God's way are not our ways;" and besides, you must remember that "a thousand years are as one day" with God.

Question. How did God destroy the people?
Answer. By water; it rained forty days and forty nights, and "the fountains of the great deep were broken up."

Question. How deep was the water?
Answer. About five miles.

Question. How much did it rain each day?
Answer. About eight hundred feet; though the better opinion now is, that it was a local flood. Infidels have raised objections and pressed them to that degree that most orthodox people admit that the flood was rather local.

Question. If it was a local flood, why did they put birds of the air into the ark? Certainly, birds could have avoided a local flood?
Answer. If you take this away from us, what do you propose to give us in its place? Some of the best people of the world have believed this story. Kind husbands, loving mothers, and earnest patriots have believed it, and that is sufficient.

Question. At the time God made these people, did he know that he would have to drown them all?
Answer. Of course he did.

Question. Did he know when he made them that they would all be failures?
Answer. Of course.

Question. Why, then, did he make them?
Answer. He made them for his own glory, and no man should disgrace his parents by denying it.

Question. Were the people after the flood just as bad as they were before?
Answer. About the same.

Question. Did they try to circumvent God?
Answer. They did.

Question. How?
Answer. They got together for the purpose of building a tower, the top of which should reach to heaven, so that they could laugh at any future floods, and go to heaven at any time they desired.

Question. Did God hear about this?
Answer. He did.

Question. What did he say?

Answer. He said: "Go to; let us go down," and see what the people are doing; I am satisfied they will succeed.

Question. How were the people prevented from succeeding?

Answer. God confounded their language, so that the mason on top could not cry "mort'!" to the hod-carrier below; he could not think of the word to use, to save his life, and the building stopped.

Question. If it had not been for the confusion of tongues at Babel, do you really think that all the people in the world would have spoken just the same language, and would have pronounced every word precisely the same?

Answer. Of course.

Question. If it had not been, then, for the confusion of languages, spelling books, grammars and dictionaries would have been useless?

Answer. I suppose so.

Question. Do any two people in the whole world speak the same language, now?

Answer. Of course they don't, and this is one of the great evidences that God introduced confusion into the languages. Every error in grammar, every mistake in spelling, every blunder in pronunciation, proves the truth of the Babel story.

Question. This being so, this miracle is the best attested of all?

Answer. I suppose it is.

Question. Do you not think that a confusion of tongues would bring men together instead of separating them? Would not a man unable to converse with his fellow feel weak instead of strong; and would not people whose language had been confounded cling together for mutual support?

Answer. According to nature, yes; according to theology, no; and these questions must be answered according to theology. And right here, it may be well enough to state, that in theology the unnatural is the probable, and the impossible is what has always happened. If theology were simply natural, anybody could be a theologian.

Question. Did God ever make any other special efforts to convert the people, or to reform the world?

Answer. Yes, he destroyed the cities of Sodom and Gomorrah with a storm of fire and brimstone.

Question. Do you suppose it was really brimstone?

Answer. Undoubtedly.

Question. Do you think this brimstone came from the clouds?

Answer. Let me tell you that you have no right to examine the Bible in the light of what people are pleased to call "science." The natural has nothing to do with the supernatural. Naturally there would be no brimstone in the clouds, but supernaturally there might be. God could make brimstone out of his "omnipotence." We do not know really what brimstone is, and nobody knows exactly how brimstone is made. As a matter of fact, all the brimstone in the world might have fallen at that time.

Question. Do you think that Lot's wife was changed into salt?
Answer. Of course she was. A miracle was performed. A few centuries ago, the statue of salt made by changing Lot's wife into that article, was standing. Christian travelers have seen it.

Question. Why do you think she was changed into salt?
Answer. For the purpose of keeping the event fresh in the minds of men.

Question. God having failed to keep people innocent in a garden; having failed to govern them outside of a garden; having failed to reform them by water; having failed to produce any good result by a confusion of tongues; having failed to reform them with fire and brimstone, what did he then do?
Answer. He concluded that he had no time to waste on them all, but that he would have to select one tribe, and turn his entire attention to just a few folks.

Question. Whom did he select?
Answer. A man by the name of Abram.

Question. What kind of man was Abram?
Answer. If you wish to know, read the twelfth chapter of Genesis; and if you still have any doubts as to his character, read the twentieth chapter of the same book, and you will see that he was a man who made merchandise of his wife's body. He had had such good fortune in Egypt, that he tried the experiment again on Abimelech.

Question. Did Abraham show any gratitude?
Answer. Yes; he offered to sacrifice his son, to show his confidence in Jehovah.

Question. What became of Abraham and his people?
Answer. God took such care of them, that in about two hundred and fifteen years they were all slaves in the land of Egypt.

Question. How long did they remain in slavery?
Answer. Two hundred and fifteen years.

Question. Were they the same people that God had promised to take care of?
Answer. They were.

Question. Was God at that time, in favor of slavery?

Answer. Not at that time. He was angry at the Egyptians for enslaving the Jews, but he afterwards authorized the Jews to enslave other people.

Question. What means did he take to liberate the Jews?

Answer. He sent his agents to Pharaoh, and demanded their freedom; and upon Pharaoh s refusing, he afflicted the people, who had nothing to do with it, with various plagues,—killed children, and tormented and tortured beasts.

Question. Was such conduct Godlike?

Answer. Certainly. If you have anything against your neighbor, it is perfectly proper to torture his horse, or torment his dog. Nothing can be nobler than this. You see it is much better to injure his animals than to injure him. To punish animals for the sins of their owners must be just, or God would not have done it. Pharaoh insisted on keeping the people in slavery, and therefore God covered the bodies of oxen and cows with boils. He also bruised them to death with hailstones. From this we infer, that "the loving kindness of God is over all his works."

Question. Do you consider such treatment of animals consistent with divine mercy?

Answer. Certainly. You know that under the Mosaic dispensation, when a man did a wrong, he could settle with God by killing an ox, or a sheep, or some doves. If the man failed to kill them, of course God would kill them. It was upon this principle that he destroyed the animals of the Egyptians. They had sinned, and he merely took his pay.

Question. How was it possible, under the old dispensation, to please a being of infinite kindness?

Answer. All you had to do was to take an innocent animal, bring it to the altar, cut its throat, and sprinkle the altar with its blood. Certain parts of it were to be given to the butcher as his share, and the rest was to be burnt on the altar. When God saw an animal thus butchered, and smelt the warm blood mingled with the odor of burning flesh, he was pacified, and the smile of forgiveness shed its light upon his face. Of course, infidels laugh at these things; but what can you expect of men who have not been "born "again"? "The carnal mind is enmity with God."

Question. What else did God do in order to induce Pharaoh to liberate the Jews?

Answer. He had his agents throw down a cane in the presence of Pharaoh and thereupon Jehovah changed this cane into a serpent.

Question. Did this convince Pharaoh?

Answer. No; he sent for his own magicians.

Question. What did they do?

Answer. They threw down some canes and they also were changed into serpents.

Question. Did Jehovah change the canes of the Egyptian magicians into snakes?

Answer. I suppose he did, as he is the only one capable of performing such a miracle.

Question. If the rod of Aaron was changed into a serpent in order to convince Pharaoh that God had sent Aaron and Moses, why did God change the sticks of the Egyptian magicians into serpents—why did he discredit his own agents, and render worthless their only credentials?

Answer. Well, we cannot explain the conduct of Jehovah; we are perfectly satisfied that it was for the best. Even in this age of the world God allows infidels to overwhelm his chosen people with arguments; he allows them to discover facts that his ministers can not answer, and yet we are satisfied that in the end God will give the victory to us. All these things are tests of faith. It is upon this principle that God allows geology to laugh at Genesis, that he permits astronomy apparently to contradict his holy word.

Question. What did God do with these people after Pharaoh allowed them to go?

Answer. Finding that they were not fit to settle a new country, owing to the fact that when hungry they longed for food, and sometimes when their lips were cracked with thirst insisted on having water, God in his infinite mercy had them marched round and round, back and forth, through a barren wilderness, until all, with the exception of two persons, died.

Question. Why did he do this?

Answer. Because he had promised these people that he would take them "to a land flowing with milk and honey."

Question. Was God always patient and kind and merciful toward his children while they were in the wilderness?

Answer. Yes, he always was merciful and kind and patient. Infidels have taken the ground that he visited them with plagues and disease and famine; that he had them bitten by serpents, and now and then allowed the ground to swallow a few thousands of them, and in other ways saw to it that they were kept as comfortable and happy as was consistent with good government; but all these things were for their good; and the fact is, infidels have no real sense of justice.

Question. How did God happen to treat the Israelites in this way, when he had promised Abraham that he would take care of his progeny, and when he had promised the same to the poor wretches while they were slaves in Egypt?

Answer. Because God is unchangeable in his nature, and wished to convince them that every being should be perfectly faithful to his promise.

Question. Was God driven to madness by the conduct of his chosen people?

Answer. Almost.

Question. Did he know exactly what they would do when he chose them?
Answer. Exactly.

Question. Were the Jews guilty of idolatry?
Answer. They were. They worshiped other gods—gods made of wood and stone.

Question. Is it not wonderful that they were not convinced of the power of God, by the many miracles wrought in Egypt and in the wilderness?
Answer. Yes, it is very wonderful; but the Jews, who must have seen bread rained from heaven; who saw water gush from the rocks and follow them up hill and down; who noticed that their clothes did not wear out, and did not even get shiny at the knees, while the elbows defied the ravages of time, and their shoes remained perfect for forty years; it is wonderful that when they saw the ground open and swallow their comrades; when they saw God talking face to face with Moses as a man talks with his friend; after they saw the cloud by day and the pillar of fire by night,—it is absolutely astonishing that they had more faith in a golden calf that they made themselves, than in Jehovah.

Question. How is it that the Jews had no confidence in these miracles?
Answer. Because they were there and saw them.

Question. Do you think that it is necessary for us to believe all the miracles of the Old Testament in order to be saved?
Answer. The Old Testament is the foundation of the New. If the Old Testament is not inspired, then the New is of no value. If the Old Testament is inspired, all the miracles are true, and we cannot believe that God would allow any errors, or false statements, to creep into an inspired volume, and to be perpetuated through all these years.

Question. Should we believe the miracles, whether they are reasonable or not?
Answer. Certainly; if they were reasonable, they would not be miracles. It is their unreasonableness that appeals to our credulity and our faith. It is impossible to have theological faith in anything that can be demonstrated. It is the office of faith to believe, not only without evidence, but in spite of evidence. It is impossible for the carnal mind to believe that Samson's muscle depended upon the length of his hair. "God has made the wisdom of "this world foolishness." Neither can the unconverted believe that Elijah stopped at a hotel kept by ravens. Neither can they believe that a barrel would in and of itself produce meal, or that an earthen pot could create oil. But to a Christian, in order that a widow might feed a preacher, the truth of these stories is perfectly apparent.

Question. How should we regard the wonderful stories of the Old Testament?
Answer. They should be looked upon as "types" and "symbols." They all have a spiritual significance. The reason I believe the story of Jonah is, that Jonah is a type of Christ.

Question. Do you believe the story of Jonah to be a true account of a literal fact?

Answer. Certainly. You must remember that Jonah was not swallowed by a whale. God "prepared a great fish" for that occasion. Neither is it by any means certain that Jonah was in the belly of this whale. "He probably stayed in his mouth." Even if he was in his stomach, it was very easy for him to defy the ordinary action of gastric juice by rapidly walking up and down.

Question. Do you think that Jonah was really in the whale's stomach?

Answer. My own opinion is that he stayed in his mouth. The only objection to this theory is, that it is more reasonable than the other and requires less faith. Nothing could be easier than for God to make a fish large enough to furnish ample room for one passenger in his mouth. I throw out this suggestion simply that you may be able to answer the objections of infidels who are always laughing at this story.

Question. Do you really believe that Elijah went to heaven in a chariot of fire, drawn by horses of fire?

Answer. Of course he did.

Question. What was this miracle performed for?

Answer. To convince the people of the power of God.

Question. Who saw the miracle?

Answer. Nobody but Elisha.

Question. Was he convinced before that time?

Answer. Oh yes; he was one of God's prophets.

Question. Suppose that in these days two men should leave a town together, and after a while one of them should come back having on the clothes of the other, and should account for the fact that he had his friend's clothes by saying that while they were going along the road together a chariot of fire came down from heaven drawn by fiery steeds, and thereupon his friend got into the carriage, threw him his clothes, and departed,—would you believe it?

Answer. Of course things like that don't happen in these days; God does not have to rely on wonders now.

Question. Do you mean that he performs no miracles at the present day?

Answer. We cannot say that he does not perform miracles now, but we are not in position to call attention to any particular one. Of course he supervises the affairs of nations and men and does whatever in his judgment is necessary.

Question. Do you think that Samson's strength depended on the length of his hair?

Answer. The Bible so states, and the Bible is true. A physiologist might say that a man could not use the muscle in his hair for lifting purposes, but these same physiologists could not tell you how you move a finger, nor how you lift a feather; still, actuated by the pride of intellect, they insist that the length of a man's hair could not determine his strength. God says it did; the physiologist says that it did not; we can not hesitate whom to believe. For the purpose of avoiding eternal agony I am willing to believe anything; I am willing to say that strength depends upon the length of hair, or faith upon the length of ears. I am perfectly willing to believe that a man caught three hundred foxes, and put fire brands between their tails; that he slew thousands with a bone, and that he made a bee hive out of a lion. I will believe, if necessary, that when this man's hair was short he hardly had strength enough to stand, and that when it was long, he could carry away the gates of a city, or overthrow a temple filled with people. If the infidel is right, I will lose nothing by believing, but if he is wrong, I shall gain an eternity of joy. If God did not intend that we should believe these stories, he never would have told them, and why should a man put his soul in peril by trying to disprove one of the statements of the Lord?

Question. Suppose it should turn out that some of these miracles depend upon mistranslations of the original Hebrew, should we still believe them?

Answer. The safe side is the best side. It is far better to err on the side of belief, than on the side of infidelity. God does not threaten anybody with eternal punishment for believing too much. Danger lies on the side of investigation, on the side of thought. The perfectly idiotic are absolutely safe. As they diverge from that point,—as they rise in the intellectual scale, as the brain develops, as the faculties enlarge, the danger increases. I know that some biblical students now take the ground that Samson caught no foxes,—that he only took sheaves of wheat that had been already cut and bound, set them on fire, and threw them into the grain still standing. If this is what he did, of course there is nothing miraculous about it, and the value of the story is lost. So, others contend that Elijah was not fed by the ravens, but by the Arabs. They tell us that the Hebrew word standing for "Arab" also stands for "bird," and that the word really means "migratory—going from place to place—homeless." But I prefer the old version. It certainly will do no harm to believe that ravens brought bread and flesh to a prophet of God. Where they got their bread and flesh is none of my business; how they knew where the prophet was, and recognized him; or how God talks to ravens, or how he gave them directions, I have no right to inquire. I leave these questions to the scientists, the blasphemers, and thinkers. There are many people in the church anxious to get the miracles out of the Bible, and thousands, I have no doubt, would be greatly gratified to learn that there is, in fact, nothing miraculous in Scripture; but when you take away the miraculous, you take away the supernatural; when you take away the supernatural, you destroy the ministry; and when you take away the ministry, hundreds of thousands of men will be left without employment.

Question. Is it not wonderful that the Egyptians were not converted by the miracles wrought in their country?

Answer. Yes, they all would have been, if God had not purposely hardened their hearts to prevent it. Jehovah always took great delight in furnishing the evidence, and then hardening the man's heart so that he would not believe it. After all the miracles that had been performed in Egypt,—the most wonderful that were ever done in any country, the Egyptians were as unbelieving as at first; they pursued the Israelites, knowing that they were protected by an infinite God, and failing to overwhelm them, came back and worshiped their own false gods just as firmly as before. All of which shows the unreasonableness of a Pagan, and the natural depravity of human nature.

Question. How did it happen that the Canaanites were never convinced that the Jews were assisted by Jehovah?

Answer. They must have been an exceedingly brave people to contend so many years with the chosen people of God. Notwithstanding all their cities were burned time and time again; notwithstanding all the men, women and children were put to the edge of the sword; notwithstanding the taking of all their cattle and sheep, they went right on fighting just as valiantly and desperately as ever. Each one lost his life many times, and was just as ready for the next conflict. My own opinion is, that God kept them alive by raising them from the dead after each battle, for the purpose of punishing the Jews. God used his enemies as instruments for the civilization of the Jewish people. He did not wish to convert them, because they would give him much more trouble as Jews than they did as Canaanites. He had all the Jews he could conveniently take care of. He found it much easier to kill a hundred Canaanites than to civilize one Jew.

Question. How do you account for the fact that the heathen were not surprised at the stopping of the sun and moon?

Answer. They were so ignorant that they had not the slightest conception of the real cause of the phenomenon. Had they known the size of the earth, and the relation it sustained to the other heavenly bodies; had they known the magnitude of the sun, and the motion of the moon, they would, in all probability, have been as greatly astonished as the Jews were; but being densely ignorant of astronomy, it must have produced upon them not the slightest impression. But we must remember that the sun and moon were not stopped for the purpose of converting these people, but to give Joshua more time to kill them. As soon as we see clearly the purpose of Jehovah, we instantly perceive how admirable were the means adopted.

Question. Do you not consider the treatment of the Canaanites to have been cruel and ferocious?

Answer. To a totally depraved man, it does look cruel; to a being without any good in him,—to one who has inherited the rascality of many generations, the murder of innocent women and little children does seem horrible; to one who is "contaminated in "all his parts," by original sin,—who was "conceived in sin, and brought forth in iniquity," the assassination of men, and the violation of captive maidens, do not seem consistent with infinite goodness. But when one has been "born again," when "the love of God has been shed abroad in his heart," when he loves all mankind, when he "overcomes evil with good," when he "prays for those who despitefully use him and persecute him,"—to such a man, the extermination of the Canaanites, the violation of women, the slaughter of babes, and the destruction of countless thousands, is the highest evidence of the goodness, the mercy, and the long-suffering of God. When a man has been "born again," all the passages of the Old Testament that appear so horrible and so unjust to one in his natural state, become the dearest, the most consoling, and the most beautiful of truths. The real Christian reads the accounts of these ancient battles with the greatest possible satisfaction. To one who really loves his enemies, the groans of men, the shrieks of women, and the cries of babes, make music sweeter than the zephyr's breath.

Question. In your judgment, why did God destroy the Canaanites?
Answer. To prevent their contaminating his chosen people. He knew that if the Jews were allowed to live with such neighbors, they would finally become as bad as the Canaanites themselves. He wished to civilize his chosen people, and it was therefore necessary for him to destroy the heathen.

Question. Did God succeed in civilizing the Jews after he had "removed" the Canaanites?
Answer. Well, not entirely. He had to allow the heathen he had not destroyed to overrun the whole land and make captives of the Jews. This was done for the good of his chosen people.

Question. Did he then succeed in civilizing them?
Answer. Not quite.

Question. Did he ever quite succeed in civilizing them?
Answer. Well, we must admit that the experiment never was a conspicuous success. The Jews were chosen by the Almighty 430 years before he appeared to Moses on Mount Sinai. He was their direct Governor. He attended personally to their religion and politics, and gave up a great part of his valuable time for about two thousand years, to the management of their affairs; and yet, such was the condition of the Jewish people, after they had had all these advantages, that when there arose among them a perfectly kind, just, generous and honest man, these people, with whom God had been laboring for so many centuries, deliberately put to death that good and loving man.

Question. Do you think that God really endeavored to civilize the Jews?
Answer. This is an exceedingly hard question. If he had really tried to do it, of course he could have done it. We must not think of limiting the power of the infinite. But you must remember that if he had succeeded in civilizing the Jews, if he had educated them up to the plane of intellectual liberty, and made them just and kind and merciful, like himself, they would not have crucified Christ, and you can see at once

the awful condition in which we would all be today. No atonement could have been made; and if no atonement had been made, then, according to the Christian system, the whole world would have been lost. We must admit that there was no time in the history of the Jews from Sinai to Jerusalem, that they would not have put a man like Christ to death.

Question. So you think that, after all, it was not God's intention that the Jews should become civilized?

Answer. We do not know. We can only say that "God's ways are not our ways." It may be that God took them in his special charge, for the purpose of keeping them bad enough to make the necessary sacrifice. That may have been the divine plan. In any event, it is safer to believe the explanation that is the most unreasonable.

Question. Do you think that Christ knew the Jews would crucify him?

Answer. Certainly.

Question. Do you think that when he chose Judas he knew that he would betray him?

Answer. Certainly.

Question. Did he know when Judas went to the chief priest and made the bargain for the delivery of Christ?

Answer. Certainly.

Question. Why did he allow himself to be betrayed, if he knew the plot?

Answer. Infidelity is a very good doctrine to live by, but you should read the last words of Paine and Voltaire.

Question. If Christ knew that Judas would betray him, why did he choose him?

Answer. Nothing can exceed the atrocities of the French Revolution—when they carried a woman through the streets and worshiped her as the goddess of Reason.

Question. Would not the mission of Christ have been a failure had no one betrayed him?

Answer. Thomas Paine was a drunkard, and recanted on his death-bed, and died a blaspheming infidel besides.

Question. Is it not clear that an atonement was necessary; and is it not equally clear that the atonement could not have been made unless somebody had betrayed Christ; and unless the Jews had been wicked and orthodox enough to crucify him?

Answer. Of course the atonement had to be made. It was a part of the 'divine plan' that Christ should be betrayed, and that the Jews should be wicked enough to kill him. Otherwise, the world would have been lost.

Question. Suppose Judas had understood the divine plan, what ought he to have done? Should he have betrayed Christ, or let somebody else do it; or should he have allowed the world to perish, including his own soul?

Answer. If you take the Bible away from the world, "how would it be possible to have witnesses "sworn in courts;" how would it be possible to administer justice?

Question. If Christ had not been betrayed and crucified, is it true that his own mother would be in perdition today?

Answer. Most assuredly. There was but one way by which she could be saved, and that was by the death of her son—through the blood of the atonement. She was totally depraved through the sin of Adam, and deserved eternal death. Even her love for the infant Christ was, in the sight of God,—that is to say, of her babe,—wickedness. It can not be repeated too often that there is only one way to be saved, and that is, to believe in the Lord Jesus Christ.

Question. Could Christ have prevented the Jews from crucifying him?
Answer. He could.

Question. If he could have saved his life and did not, was he not guilty of suicide?

Answer. No one can understand these questions who has not read the prophecies of Daniel, and has not a clear conception of what is meant by "the fullness of time."

Question. What became of all the Canaanites, the Egyptians, the Hindus, the Greeks and Romans and Chinese? What became of the billions who died before the promise was made to Abraham; of the billions and billions who never heard of the Bible, who never heard the name, even, of Jesus Christ—never knew of "the scheme of salvation"? What became of the millions and billions who lived in this hemisphere, and of whose existence Jehovah himself seemed perfectly ignorant?

Answer. They were undoubtedly lost. God having made them, had a right to do with them as he pleased. They are probably all in hell today, and the fact that they are damned, only adds to the joy of the redeemed. It is by contrast that we are able to perceive the infinite kindness with which God has treated us.

Question. Is it not possible that something can be done for a human soul in another world as well as in this?

Answer. No; this is the only world in which God even attempts to reform anybody. In the other world, nothing is done for the purpose of making anybody better. Here in this world, where man lives but a few days, is the only opportunity for moral improvement. A minister can do a thousand times more for a soul than its creator; and this country is much better adapted to moral growth than heaven itself. A person who lived on this earth a few years, and died without having been converted, has no hope in another world. The moment he arrives at the judgment seat, nothing remains but to damn him. Neither God, nor the Holy Ghost, nor Jesus Christ, can have the least possible influence with him there.

Question. When God created each human being, did he know exactly what would be his eternal fate?

Answer. Most assuredly he did.

Question. Did he know that hundreds and millions and billions would suffer eternal pain?

Answer. Certainly. But he gave them freedom of choice between good and evil.

Question. Did he know exactly how they would use that freedom?

Answer. Yes.

Question. Did he know that billions would use it wrong?

Answer. Yes.

Question. Was it optional with him whether he should make such people or not?

Answer. Certainly.

Question. Had these people any option as to whether they would be made or not?

Answer, No.

Question. Would it not have been far better to leave them unconscious dust?

Answer. These questions show how foolish it is to judge God according to a human standard. What to us seems just and merciful, God may regard in an exactly opposite light; and we may hereafter be developed to such a degree that we will regard the agonies of the damned as the highest possible evidence of the goodness and mercy of God.

Question. How do you account for the fact that God did not make himself known except to Abraham and his descendants? Why did he fail to reveal himself to the other nations—nations that, compared with the Jews, were learned, cultivated and powerful? Would you regard a revelation now made to the Esquimaux as intended for us; and would it be a revelation of which we would be obliged to take notice?

Answer. Of course, God could have revealed himself, not only to all the great nations, but to each individual. He could have had the Ten Commandments engraved on every heart and brain; or he could have raised up prophets in every land; but he chose, rather, to allow countless millions of his children to wander in the darkness and blackness of Nature; chose, rather, that they should redden their hands in each other's blood; chose, rather, that they should live without light, and die without hope; chose, rather, that they should suffer, not only in this world, but forever in the next. Of course we have no right to find fault with the choice of God.

Question. Now you can tell a sinner to "believe on the Lord Jesus Christ;" what could a sinner have been told in Egypt, three thousand years ago; and in what language would you have addressed a Hindu in the days of Buddha—the "divine scheme" at that time being a secret in the divine breast?

Answer. It is not for us to think upon these questions. The moment we examine the Christian system, we begin to doubt. In a little while, we shall be infidels, and shall lose the respect of those who refuse to think. It is better to go with the majority. These doctrines are too sacred to be touched. You should be satisfied with the religion of your father and your mother. "You want some book on the "centre-table," in the parlor; it is extremely handy to have a Family Record; and what book, other than the Bible, could a mother give a son as he leaves the old homestead?

Question. Is it not wonderful that all the writers of the four gospels do not give an account of the ascension of Jesus Christ?

Answer. This question has been answered long ago, time and time again.

Question. Perhaps it has, but would it not be well enough to answer it once more? Some may not have seen the answer?

Answer. Show me the hospitals that infidels have built; show me the asylums that infidels have founded.

Question. I know you have given the usual answer; but after all, is it not singular that a miracle so wonderful as the bodily ascension of a man, should not have been mentioned by all the writers of that man's life? Is it not wonderful that some of them said that he did ascend, and others that he agreed to stay with his disciples always?

Answer. People unacquainted with the Hebrew, can have no conception of these things. A story in plain English, does not sound as it does in Hebrew. Miracles seem altogether more credible, when told in a dead language.

Question. What, in your judgment, became of the dead who were raised by Christ? Is it not singular that they were never mentioned afterward?

Would not a man who had been raised from the dead naturally be an object of considerable interest, especially to his friends and acquaintances? And is it not also wonderful that Christ, after having wrought so many miracles, cured so many lame and halt and blind, fed so many thousands miraculously, and after having entered Jerusalem in triumph as a conqueror and king, had to be pointed out by one of his own disciples who was bribed for the purpose?

Answer. Of course, all these things are exceedingly wonderful, and if found in any other book, would be absolutely incredible; but we have no right to apply the same kind of reasoning to the Bible that we apply to the Koran or to the sacred books of the Hindus. For the ordinary affairs of this world, God has given us reason; but in the examination of religious questions, we should depend upon credulity and faith.

Question. If Christ came to offer himself a sacrifice, for the purpose of making atonement for the sins of such as might believe on him, why did he not make this fact known to all of his disciples?

Answer. He did. This was, and is, the gospel.

Question. How is it that Matthew says nothing about "salvation by faith," but simply says that God will be merciful to the merciful, that he will forgive the forgiving, and says not one word about the necessity of believing anything?
Answer. But you will remember that Mark says, in the last chapter of his gospel, that "whoso believeth not shall be damned."

Question. Do you admit that Matthew says nothing on the subject?
Answer. Yes, I suppose I must.

Question. Is not that passage in Mark generally admitted to be an interpolation?
Answer. Some biblical scholars say that it is.

Question. Is that portion of the last chapter of Mark found in the Syriac version of the Bible?
Answer. It is not.

Question. If it was necessary to believe in Jesus Christ, in order to be saved, how is it that Matthew failed to say so?
Answer. "There are more copies of the Bible printed today, than of any other book in the world, and it is printed in more languages than any other book."

Question. Do you consider it necessary to be "regenerated"—to be "born again"—in order to be saved?
Answer. Certainly.

Question. Did Matthew say anything on the subject of "regeneration"?
Answer. No.

Question. Did Mark?
Answer. No.

Question. Did Luke?
Answer. No.

Question. Is Saint John the only one who speaks of the necessity of being "born again"?
Answer. He is.

Question. Do you think that Matthew, Mark and Luke knew anything about the necessity of "regeneration"?
Answer. Of course they did.

Question. Why did they fail to speak of it?
Answer. There is no civilization without the Bible. The moment you throw away the sacred Scriptures, you are all at sea—you are without an anchor and without a compass.

Question. You will remember that, according to Mark, Christ said to his disciples: "Go ye into all the world, and preach the gospel to every creature." Did he refer to the gospel set forth by Mark?

Answer. Of course he did.

Question. Well, in the gospel set forth by Mark, there is not a word about "regeneration," and no word about the necessity of believing anything—except in an interpolated passage. Would it not seem from this, that "regeneration" and a "belief in the Lord Jesus Christ," are no part of the gospel?

Answer. Nothing can exceed in horror the last moments of the infidel; nothing can be more terrible than the death of the doubter. When the glories of this world fade from the vision; when ambition becomes an empty name; when wealth turns to dust in the palsied hand of death, of what use is philosophy then? Who cares then for the pride of intellect? In that dread moment, man needs something to rely on, whether it is true or not.

Question. Would it not have been more convincing if Christ, after his resurrection, had shown himself to his enemies as well as to his friends? Would it not have greatly strengthened the evidence in the case, if he had visited Pilate; had presented himself before Caiaphas, the high priest; if he had again entered the temple, and again walked the streets of Jerusalem?

Answer. If the evidence had been complete and overwhelming, there would have been no praiseworthiness in belief; even publicans and sinners would have believed, if the evidence had been sufficient. The amount of evidence required is the test of the true Christian spirit.

Question. Would it not also have been better had the ascension taken place in the presence of unbelieving thousands; it seems such a pity to have wasted such a demonstration upon those already convinced?

Answer. These questions are the natural fruit of the carnal mind, and can be accounted for only by the doctrine of total depravity. Nothing has given the church more trouble than just such questions. Unholy curiosity, a disposition to pry into the divine mysteries, a desire to know, to investigate, to explain —in short, to understand, are all evidences of a reprobate mind.

Question. How can we account for the fact that Matthew alone speaks of the wise men of the East coming with gifts to the infant Christ; that he alone speaks of the little babes being killed by Herod? Is it possible that the other writers never heard of these things?

Answer. Nobody can get any good out of the Bible by reading it in a critical spirit. The contradictions and discrepancies are only apparent, and melt away before the light of faith. That which in other books would be absolute and palpable contradiction, is, in the Bible, when spiritually discerned, a perfect and beautiful harmony. My own opinion is, that seeming contradictions are in the Bible for the purpose of testing and strengthening the faith of Christians, and for the further purpose of ensnaring infidels, "that they might believe a lie and be damned."

Question. Is it possible that a good God would take pains to deceive his children?

Answer. The Bible is filled with instances of that kind, and all orthodox ministers now know that fossil animals—that is, representations of animals in stone, were placed in the rocks on purpose to mislead men like Darwin and Humboldt, Huxley and Tyndall. It is also now known that God, for the purpose of misleading the so-called men of science, had hairy elephants preserved in ice, made stomachs for them, and allowed twigs of trees to be found in these stomachs, when, as a matter of fact, no such elephants ever lived or ever died. These men who are endeavoring to overturn the Scriptures with the lever of science will find that they have been deceived. Through all eternity they will regret their philosophy. They will wish, in the next world, that they had thrown away geology and physiology and all other "ologies" except theology. The time is coming when Jehovah will "mock at their fears and "laugh at their calamity."

Question. If Joseph was not the father of Christ, why was his genealogy given to show that Christ was of the blood of David; why would not the genealogy of any other Jew have done as well?

Answer. That objection was raised and answered hundreds of years ago.

Question. If they wanted to show that Christ was of the blood of David, why did they not give the genealogy of his mother if Joseph was not his father?

Answer. That objection was answered hundreds of years ago.

Question. How was it answered?

Answer. When Voltaire was dying, he sent for a priest.

Question. How does it happen that the two genealogies given do not agree?

Answer. Perhaps they were written by different persons.

Question. Were both these persons inspired by the same God?

Answer. Of course.

Question. Why were the miracles recorded in the New Testament performed?

Answer. The miracles were the evidence relied on to prove the supernatural origin and the divine mission of Jesus Christ.

Question. Aside from the miracles, is there any evidence to show the supernatural origin or character of Jesus Christ?

Answer. Some have considered that his moral precepts are sufficient, of themselves, to show that he was divine.

Question. Had all of his moral precepts been taught before he lived?

Answer. The same things had been said, but they did not have the same meaning.

Question. Does the fact that Buddha taught the same tend to show that he was of divine origin?

Answer. Certainly not. The rules of evidence applicable to the Bible are not applicable to other books. We examine other books in the light of reason; the Bible is the only exception. So, we should not judge of Christ as we do of any other man.

Question. Do you think that Christ wrought many of his miracles because he was good, charitable, and filled with pity?

Answer. Certainly

Question. Has he as much power now as he had when on earth?

Answer. Most assuredly.

Question. Is he as charitable and pitiful now, as he was then?

Answer. Yes.

Question. Why does he not now cure the lame and the halt and the blind?

Answer. It is well known that, when Julian the Apostate was dying, catching some of his own blood in his hand and throwing it into the air he exclaimed: "Galilean, thou hast conquered!"

Question. Do you consider it our duty to love our neighbor?

Answer. Certainly.

Question. Is virtue the same in all worlds?

Answer. Most assuredly.

Question. Are we under obligation to render good for evil, and to "pray for those who despitefully use us"?

Answer. Yes.

Question. Will Christians in heaven love their neighbors?

Answer. Yes; if their neighbors are not in hell.

Question. Do good Christians pity sinners in this world?

Answer. Yes.

Question. Why?

Answer. Because they regard them as being in great danger of the eternal wrath of God.

Question. After these sinners have died, and been sent to hell, will the Christians in heaven then pity them?

Answer. No. Angels have no pity.

Question. If we are under obligation to love our enemies, is not God under obligation to love his? If we forgive our enemies, ought not God to forgive his? If we forgive those who injure us, ought not God to forgive those who have not injured him?

Answer. God made us, and he has therefore the right to do with us as he pleases. Justice demands that he should damn all of us, and the few that he will save will be saved through mercy and without the slightest respect to anything they may have done themselves. Such is the justice of God, that those in hell will have no right to complain, and those in heaven will have no right to be there. Hell is justice, and salvation is charity.

Question. Do you consider it possible for a law to be justly satisfied by the punishment of an innocent person?
Answer. Such is the scheme of the atonement. As man is held responsible for the sin of Adam, so he will be credited with the virtues of Christ; and you can readily see that one is exactly as reasonable as the other.

Question. Suppose a man honestly reads the New Testament, and honestly concludes that it is not an inspired book; suppose he honestly makes up his mind that the miracles are not true; that the devil never really carried Christ to the pinnacle of the temple; that devils were really never cast out of a man and allowed to take refuge in swine;—I say, suppose that he is honestly convinced that these things are not true, what ought he to say?
Answer. He ought to say nothing.

Question. Suppose that the same man should read the Koran, and come to the conclusion that it is not an inspired book; what ought he to say?
Answer. He ought to say that it is not inspired; his fellow-men are entitled to his honest opinion, and it is his duty to do what he can do to destroy a pernicious superstition.

Question. Suppose then, that a reader of the Bible, having become convinced that it is not inspired—honestly convinced—says nothing—keeps his conclusion absolutely to himself, and suppose he dies in that belief, can he be saved?
Answer. Certainly not.

Question. Has the honesty of his belief anything to do with his future condition?
Answer. Nothing whatever.

Question. Suppose that he tried to believe, that he hated to disagree with his friends, and with his parents, but that in spite of himself he was forced to the conclusion that the Bible is not the inspired word of God, would he then deserve eternal punishment?
Answer. Certainly he would.

Question. Can a man control his belief?
Answer. He cannot—except as to the Bible.

Question. Do you consider it just in God to create a man who cannot believe the Bible, and then damn him because he does not?
Answer. Such is my belief.

Question. Is it your candid opinion that a man who does not believe the Bible should keep his belief a secret from his fellow-men?
Answer. It is.

Question. How do I know that you believe the Bible? You have told me that if you did not believe it, you would not tell me?
Answer. There is no way for you to ascertain, except by taking my word for it.

Question. What will be the fate of a man who does not believe it, and yet pretends to believe it?
Answer. He will be damned.

Question. Then hypocrisy will not save him?
Answer. No.

Question. And if he does not believe it, and admits that he does not believe it, then his honesty will not save him?
Answer. No. Honesty on the wrong side is no better than hypocrisy on the right side.

Question. Do we know who wrote the gospels?
Answer. Yes; we do.

Question. Are we absolutely sure who wrote them?
Answer. Of course; we have the evidence as it has come to us through the Catholic Church.

Question. Can we rely upon the Catholic Church now?
Answer. No; assuredly no! But we have the testimony of Polycarp and Irenaeus and Clement, and others of the early fathers, together with that of the Christian historian, Eusebius.

Question. What do we really know about Polycarp?
Answer. We know that he suffered martyrdom under Marcus Aurelius, and that for quite a time the fire refused to burn his body, the flames arching over him, leaving him in a kind of fiery tent; and we also know that from his body came a fragrance like frankincense, and that the Pagans were so exasperated at seeing the miracle, that one of them thrust a sword through the body of Polycarp; that the blood flowed out and extinguished the flames and that out of the wound flew the soul of the martyr in the form of a dove.

Question. Is that all we know about Polycarp?
Answer. Yes, with the exception of a few more like incidents.

Question. Do we know that Polycarp ever met St. John?
Answer. Yes; Eusebius says so.

Question. Are we absolutely certain that he ever lived?
Answer. Yes, or Eusebius could not have written about him.

Question. Do we know anything of the character of Eusebius?

Answer. Yes; we know that he was untruthful only when he wished to do good. But God can use even the dishonest. Other books have to be substantiated by truthful men, but such is the power of God, that he can establish the inspiration of the Bible by the most untruthful witnesses. If God's witnesses were honest, anybody could believe, and what becomes of faith, one of the greatest virtues?

Question. Is the New Testament now the same as it was in the days of the early fathers?

Answer. Certainly not. Many books now thrown out, and not esteemed of divine origin, were esteemed divine by Polycarp and Irenaeus and Clement and many of the early churches. These books are now called "apocryphal."

Question. Have you not the same witnesses in favor of their authenticity, that you have in favor of the gospels?

Answer. Precisely the same. Except that they were thrown out.

Question. Why were they thrown out?

Answer. Because the Catholic Church did not esteem them inspired.

Question. Did the Catholics decide for us which are the true gospels and which are the true epistles?

Answer. Yes. The Catholic Church was then the only church, and consequently must have been the true church.

Question. How did the Catholic Church select the true books?

Answer. Councils were called, and votes were taken, very much as we now pass resolutions in political meetings.

Question. Was the Catholic Church infallible then?

Answer. It was then, but it is not now.

Question. If the Catholic Church at that time had thrown out the book of Revelation, would it now be our duty to believe that book to have been inspired?

Answer. No, I suppose not.

Question. Is it not true that some of these books were adopted by exceedingly small majorities?

Answer. It is.

Question. If the Epistle to the Hebrews and to the Romans, and the book of Revelation had been thrown out, could a man now be saved who honestly believes the rest of the books?

Answer. This is doubtful.

Question. Were the men who picked out the inspired books inspired?

Answer. We cannot tell, but the probability is that they were.

Question. Do we know that they picked out the right ones?
Answer. Well, not exactly, but we believe that they did.

Question. Are we certain that some of the books that were thrown out were not inspired?
Answer. Well, the only way to tell is to read them carefully.

Question. If upon reading these apocryphal books a man concludes that they are not inspired, will he be damned for that reason?
Answer. No. Certainly not.

Question. If he concludes that some of them are inspired, and believes them, will he then be damned for that belief?
Answer. Oh, no! Nobody is ever damned for believing too much.

Question. Does the fact that the books now comprising the New Testament were picked out by the Catholic Church prevent their being examined now by an honest man, as they were examined at the time they were picked out?
Answer. No; not if the man comes to the conclusion that they are inspired.

Question. Does the fact that the Catholic Church picked them out and declared them to be inspired, render it a crime to examine them precisely as you would examine the books that the Catholic Church threw out and declared were not inspired?
Answer. I think it does.

Question. At the time the council was held in which it was determined which of the books of the New Testament are inspired, a respectable minority voted against some that were finally decided to be inspired. If they were honest in the vote they gave, and died without changing their opinions, are they now in hell?
Answer. Well, they ought to be.

Question. If those who voted to leave the book of Revelation out of the canon, and the gospel of Saint John out of the canon, believed honestly that these were not inspired books, how should they have voted?
Answer. Well, I suppose a man ought to vote as he honestly believes— except in matters of religion.

Question. If the Catholic Church was not infallible, is the question still open as to what books are, and what are not, inspired?
Answer. I suppose the question is still open—but it would be dangerous to decide it.

Question. If, then, I examine all the books again, and come to the conclusion that some that were thrown out were inspired, and some that were accepted were not inspired, ought I to say so?
Answer. Not if it is contrary to the faith of your father, or calculated to interfere with your own political prospects.

Question. Is it as great a sin to admit into the Bible books that are uninspired as to reject those that are inspired?

Answer. Well, it is a crime to reject an inspired book, no matter how unsatisfactory the evidence is for its inspiration, but it is not a crime to receive an uninspired book. God damns nobody for believing too much. An excess of credulity is simply to err in the direction of salvation.

Question. Suppose a man disbelieves in the inspiration of the New Testament—believes it to be entirely the work of uninspired men; and suppose he also believes—but not from any evidence obtained in the New Testament—that Jesus Christ was the son of God, and that he made atonement for his soul, can he then be saved without a belief in the inspiration of the Bible?

Answer. This has not yet been decided by our church, and I do not wish to venture an opinion.

Question. Suppose a man denies the inspiration of the Scriptures; suppose that he also denies the divinity of Jesus Christ; and suppose, further, that he acts precisely as Christ is said to have acted; suppose he loves his enemies, prays for those who despitefully use him, and does all the good he possibly can, is it your opinion that such a man will be saved?

Answer. No, sir. There is "none other name "given under heaven and among men," whereby a sinner can be saved but the name of Christ.

Question. Then it is your opinion that God would save a murderer who believed in Christ, and would damn another man, exactly like Christ, who failed to believe in him?

Answer. Yes; because we have the blessed promise that, out of Christ, "our God is a consuming "fire."

Question. Suppose a man read the Bible carefully and honestly, and was not quite convinced that it was true, and that while examining the subject, he died; what then?

Answer. I do not believe that God would allow him to examine the matter in another world, or to make up his mind in heaven. Of course, he would eternally perish.

Question. Could Christ now furnish evidence enough to convince every human being of the truth of the Bible?

Answer. Of course he could, because he is infinite.

Question. Are any miracles performed now?

Answer. Oh, no!

Question. Have we any testimony, except human testimony, to substantiate any miracle?

Answer. Only human testimony.

Question. Do all men give the same force to the same evidence?

Answer. By no means.

Question. Have all honest men who have examined the Bible believed it to be inspired?

Answer. Of course they have. Infidels are not honest.

Question. Could any additional evidence have been furnished?

Answer. With perfect ease.

Question. Would God allow a soul to suffer eternal agony rather than furnish evidence of the truth of his Bible?

Answer. God has furnished plenty of evidence, and altogether more than was really necessary. We should read the Bible in a believing spirit.

Question. Are all parts of the inspired books equally true?

Answer. Necessarily.

Question. According to Saint Matthew, God promises to forgive all who will forgive others; not one word is said about believing in Christ, or believing in the miracles, or in any Bible; did Matthew tell the truth?

Answer. The Bible must be taken as a whole; and if other conditions are added somewhere else, then you must comply with those other conditions. Matthew may not have stated all the conditions.

Question. I find in another part of the New Testament, that a young man came to Christ and asked him what was necessary for him to do in order that he might inherit eternal life. Christ did not tell him that he must believe the Bible, or that he must believe in him, or that he must keep the Sabbath-day; was Christ honest with that young man?

Answer. Well, I suppose he was.

Question. You will also recollect that Zaccheus said to Christ, that where he had wronged any man he had made restitution, and further, that half his goods he had given to the poor; and you will remember that Christ said to Zaccheus: "This day "hath salvation come to thy house." Why did not Christ tell Zaccheus that he "must be born again;" that he must "believe on the Lord Jesus Christ"?

Answer. Of course there are mysteries in our holy religion that only those who have been "born again" can understand. You must remember that the carnal mind is enmity with God."

Question. Is it not strange that Christ, in his Sermon on the Mount, did not speak of "regeneration," or of the "scheme of salvation"?

Answer. Well, it may be.

Question. Can a man be saved now by living exactly in accordance with the Sermon on the Mount?

Answer. He can not.

Question. Would then a man, by following the course of conduct prescribed by Christ in the Sermon on the Mount, lose his soul?

Answer. He most certainly would, because there is not one word in the Sermon on the Mount about believing on the Lord Jesus Christ; not one word about believing in the Bible; not one word about the "atonement;" not one word about "regeneration." So that, if the Presbyterian Church is right, it is absolutely certain that a man might follow the teachings of the Sermon on the Mount, and live in accordance with its every word, and yet deserve and receive the eternal condemnation of God. But we must remember that the Sermon on the Mount was preached before Christianity existed. Christ was talking to Jews.

Question. Did Christ write anything himself, in the New Testament?
Answer. Not a word.

Question. Did he tell any of his disciples to write any of his words?
Answer. There is no account of it, if he did.

Question. Do we know whether any of the disciples wrote anything?
Answer. Of course they did.

Question. How do you know?
Answer. Because the gospels bear their names.

Question. Are you satisfied that Christ was absolutely God?
Answer. Of course he was. We believe that Christ and God and the Holy Ghost are all the same, that the three form one, and that each one is three.

Question. Was Christ the God of the universe at the time of his birth?
Answer. He certainly was.

Question. Was he the infinite God, creator and controller of the entire universe, before he was born?
Answer. Of course he was. This is the mystery of "God manifest in the flesh." The infidels have pretended that he was like any other child, and was in fact supported by Nature instead of being the supporter of Nature. They have insisted that like other children, he had to be cared for by his mother. Of course he appeared to be cared for by his mother. It was a part of the plan that in all respects he should appear to be like other children.

Question. Did he know just as much before he was born as after?
Answer. If he was God of course he did.

Question. How do you account for the fact that Saint Luke tells us, in the last verse of the second chapter of his gospel, that "Jesus increased in wisdom and stature"?
Answer. That I presume is a figure of speech; because, if he was God, he certainly could not have increased in wisdom. The physical part of him could increase in stature, but the intellectual part must have been infinite all the time.

Question. Do you think that Luke was mistaken?

158

Answer. No; I believe what Luke said. If it appears untrue, or impossible, then I know that it is figurative or symbolical.

Question. Did I understand you to say that Christ was actually God?
Answer. Of course he was.

Question. Then why did Luke say in the same verse of the same chapter that "Jesus increased in "favor with God"?
Answer. I dare you to go into a room by yourself and read the fourteenth chapter of Saint John!

Question. Is it necessary to understand the Bible in order to be saved?
Answer. Certainly not; it is only necessary that you believe it.

Question. Is it necessary to believe all the miracles?
Answer. It may not be necessary, but as it is impossible to tell which ones can safely be left out, you had better believe them all.

Question. Then you regard belief as the safe way?
Answer. Of course it is better to be fooled in this world than to be damned in the next.

Question. Do you think that there are any cruelties on God's part recorded in the Bible?
Answer. At first flush, many things done by God himself, as well as by his prophets, appear to be cruel; but if we examine them closely, we will find them to be exactly the opposite.

Question. How do you explain the story of Elisha and the children,—where the two she-bears destroyed forty-two children on account of their impudence?
Answer. This miracle, in my judgment, establishes two things: 1. That children should be polite to ministers, and 2. That God is kind to animals—"giving them their meat in due season." These bears have been great educators—they are the foundation of the respect entertained by the young for theologians. No child ever sees a minister now without thinking of a bear.

Question. What do you think of the story of Daniel—you no doubt remember it? Some men told the king that Daniel was praying contrary to law, and thereupon Daniel was cast into a den of lions; but the lions could not touch him, their mouths having been shut by angels. The next morning, the king, finding that Daniel was still intact, had him taken out; and then, for the purpose of gratifying Daniels God, the king had all the men who had made the complaint against Daniel, and their wives and their little children, brought and cast into the lions' den. According to the account, the lions were so hungry that they caught these wives and children as they dropped, and broke all their bones in pieces before they had even touched the ground. Is it not wonderful that God failed to protect these innocent wives and children?

Answer. These wives and children were heathen; they were totally depraved. And besides, they were used as witnesses. The fact that they were devoured with such quickness shows that the lions were hungry. Had it not been for this, infidels would have accounted for the safety of Daniel by saying that the lions had been fed.

Question. Do you believe that Shadrach, Meshach and Abednego were cast "into a burning fiery furnace "heated one seven times hotter than it was wont to "be heated," and that they had on "their coats, their hosen and their hats," and that when they came out "not a hair of their heads was singed, nor was the smell of fire upon their garments"?
Answer. The evidence of this miracle is exceedingly satisfactory. It resulted in the conversion of Nebuchadnezzar.

Question. How do you know he was converted?
Answer. Because immediately after the miracle the king issued a decree that "every people, nation "and language that spoke anything amiss against "the God of Shadrach and Company, should be cut in pieces." This decree shows that he had become a true disciple and worshiper of Jehovah.

Question. If God in those days preserved from the fury of the fire men who were true to him and would not deny his name, why is it that he has failed to protect thousands of martyrs since that time?
Answer. This is one of the divine mysteries. God has in many instances allowed his enemies to kill his friends. I suppose this was allowed for the good of his enemies, that the heroism of the martyrs might convert them.

Question. Do you believe all the miracles?
Answer. I believe them all, because I believe the Bible to be inspired.

Question. What makes you think it is inspired?
Answer. I have never seen anybody who knew it was not; besides, my father and mother believed it.

Question. Have you any other reasons for believing it to be inspired?
Answer. Yes; there are more copies of the Bible printed than of any other book; and it is printed in more languages. And besides, it would be impossible to get along without it.

Question. Why could we not get along without it?
Answer. We would have nothing to swear wit- nesses by; no book in which to keep the family record; nothing for the centre-table, and nothing for a mother to give her son. No nation can be civilized without the Bible.

Question. Did God always know that a Bible was necessary to civilize a country?
Answer. Certainly he did.

Question. Why did he not give a Bible to the Egyptians, the Hindus, the Greeks and the Romans?

Answer. It is astonishing what perfect fools infidels are.

Question. Why do you call infidels "fools"?

Answer. Because I find in the fifth chapter of the gospel according to Matthew the following: "Whosoever shall say 'Thou fool!' shall be in danger of hell fire."

Question. Have I the right to read the Bible?

Answer. Yes. You not only have the right, but it is your duty.

Question. In reading the Bible the words make certain impressions on my mind. These impressions depend upon my brain,—upon my intelligence. Is not this true?

Answer. Of course, when you read the Bible, impressions are made upon your mind.

Question. Can I control these impressions?

Answer. I do not think you can, as long as you remain in a sinful state.

Question. How am I to get out of this sinful state?

Answer. You must believe on the Lord Jesus Christ, and you must read the Bible in a prayerful spirit and with a believing heart.

Question. Suppose that doubts force themselves upon my mind?

Answer. Then you will know that you are a sinner, and that you are depraved.

Question. If I have the right to read the Bible, have I the right to try to understand it?

Answer. Most assuredly.

Question. Do you admit that I have the right to reason about it and to investigate it?

Answer. Yes; I admit that. Of course you cannot help reasoning about what you read.

Question. Does the right to read a book include the right to give your opinion as to the truth of what the book contains?

Answer. Of course,—if the book is not inspired. Infidels hate the Bible because it is inspired, and Christians know that it is inspired because infidels say that it is not.

Question. Have I the right to decide for myself whether or not the book is inspired?

Answer. You have no right to deny the truth of God's Holy Word.

Question. Is God the author of all books?

Answer. Certainly not.

Question. Have I the right to say that God did not write the Koran?
Answer. Yes.

Question. Why?
Answer. Because the Koran was written by an impostor.

Question. How do you know?
Answer. My reason tells me so.

Question. Have you the right to be guided by your reason?
Answer. I must be.

Question. Have you the same right to follow your reason after reading the Bible?
Answer. No. The Bible is the standard of reason. The Bible is not to be judged or corrected by your reason. Your reason is to be weighed and measured by the Bible. The Bible is different from other books and must not be read in the same critical spirit, nor judged by the same standard.

Question. What did God give us reason for?
Answer. So that we might investigate other religions, and examine other so-called sacred books.

Question. If a man honestly thinks that the Bible is not inspired, what should he say?
Answer. He should admit that he is mistaken.

Question. When he thinks he is right?
Answer. Yes. The Bible is different from other books. It is the master of reason. You read the Bible, not to see if that is wrong, but to see whether your reason is right. It is the only book about which a man has no right to reason. He must believe. The Bible is addressed, not to the reason, but to the ears: "He that hath ears to hear, let him hear."

Question. Do you think we have the right to tell what the Bible means—what ideas God intended to convey, or has conveyed to us, through the medium of the Bible?
Answer. Well, I suppose you have that right. Yes, that must be your duty. You certainly ought to tell others what God has said to you.

Question. Do all men get the same ideas from the Bible?
Answer. No.

Question. How do you account for that?
Answer. Because all men are not alike; they differ in intellect, in education, and in experience.

Question. Who has the right to decide as to the real ideas that God intended to convey?

Answer. I am a Protestant, and believe in the right of private judgment. Whoever does not is a Catholic. Each man must be his own judge, but God will hold him responsible.

Question. Does God believe in the right of private judgment?
Answer. Of course he does.

Question. Is he willing that I should exercise my judgment in deciding whether the Bible is inspired or not?
Answer. No. He believes in the exercise of private judgment only in the examination and rejection of other books than the Bible.

Question. Is he a Catholic?
Answer. I cannot answer blasphemy! Let me tell you that God will "laugh at your calamity, and will mock when your fear cometh." You will be accursed.

Question. Why do you curse infidels?
Answer. Because I am a Christian.

Question. Did not Christ say that we ought to "bless those who curse us," and that we should "love our enemies"?
Answer. Yes, but he cursed the Pharisees and called them "hypocrites" and "vipers."

Question. How do you account for that?
Answer. It simply shows the difference between theory and practice.

Question. What do you consider the best way to answer infidels.
Answer. The old way is the best. You should say that their arguments are ancient, and have been answered over and over again. If this does not satisfy your hearers, then you should attack the character of the infidel—then that of his parents— then that of his children.

Question. Suppose that the infidel is a good man, how will you answer him then?
Answer. But an infidel cannot be a good man. Even if he is, it is better that he should lose his reputation, than that thousands should lose their souls. We know that all infidels are vile and infamous. We may not have the evidence, but we know that it exists.

Question. How should infidels be treated? Should Christians try to convert them?
Answer. Christians should have nothing to do with infidels. It is not safe even to converse with them. They are always talking about reason, and facts, and experience. They are filled with sophistry and should be avoided.

Question. Should Christians pray for the conversion of infidels?
Answer. Yes; but such prayers should be made in public and the name of the infidel should be given and his vile and hideous heart portrayed so that the young may be warned.

Question. Whom do you regard as infidels?

Answer. The scientists—the geologists, the astronomers, the naturalists, the philosophers. No one can overestimate the evil that has been wrought by Laplace, Humboldt, Darwin, Huxley, Haeckel, Renan, Emerson, Strauss, Bikhner, Tyndall, and their wretched followers. These men pretended to know more than Moses and the prophets. They were "dogs baying at the moon." They were "wolves" and "fools." They tried to "assassinate God," and worse than all, they actually laughed at the clergy.

Question. Do you think they did, and are doing great harm?

Answer. Certainly. Of what use are all the sciences, if you lose your own soul? People in hell will care nothing about education. The rich man said nothing about science, he wanted water. Neither will they care about books and theories in heaven. If a man is perfectly happy, it makes no difference how ignorant he is.

Question. But how can he answer these scientists?

Answer. Well, my advice is to let their arguments alone. Of course, you will deny all their facts; but the most effective way is to attack their character.

Question. But suppose they are good men,—what then?

Answer. The better they are, the worse they are. We cannot admit that the infidel is really good. He may appear to be good, and it is our duty to strip the mask of appearance from the face of unbelief. If a man is not a Christian, he is totally depraved, and why should we hesitate to make a misstatement about a man whom God is going to make miserable forever?

Question. Are we not commanded to love our enemies?

Answer. Yes, but not the enemies of God.

Question. Do you fear the final triumph of infidelity?

Answer. No. We have no fear. We believe that the Bible can be revised often enough to agree with anything that may really be necessary to the preservation of the church. We can always rely upon revision. Let me tell you that the Bible is the most peculiar of books. At the time God inspired his holy prophets to write it, he knew exactly what the discoveries and demonstrations of the future would be, and he wrote his Bible in such a way that the words could always be interpreted in accordance with the intelligence of each age, and so that the words used are capable of several meanings, so that, no matter what may hereafter be discovered, the Bible will be found to agree with it,—for the reason that the knowledge of Hebrew will grow in the exact proportion that discoveries are made in other departments of knowledge. You will therefore see, that all efforts of infidelity to destroy the Bible will simply result in giving a better translation.

Question. What do you consider is the strongest argument in favor of the inspiration of the Scriptures?

Answer. The dying words of Christians.

Question. What do you consider the strongest argument against the truth of infidelity?

Answer. The dying words of infidels. You know how terrible were the death-bed scenes of Hume, Voltaire, Paine and Hobbes, as described by hundreds of persons who were not present; while all Christians have died with the utmost serenity, and with their last words have testified to the sustaining power of faith in the goodness of God.

Question. What were the last words of Jesus Christ?

Answer. "My God, my God, why hast thou forsaken me?"

A VINDICATION
OF THOMAS PAINE.

"To argue with a man who has renounced the use and authority of reason, is like administering medicine to the dead."—Thomas Paine.

Peoria, October 8, 1877.

To the Editor of the N Y. Observer:

Sir: Last June in San Francisco, I offered a thousand dollars in gold— not as a wager, but as a gift—to any one who would substantiate the absurd story that Thomas Paine died in agony and fear, frightened by the clanking chains of devils. I also offered the same amount to any minister who would prove that Voltaire did not pass away as serenely as the coming of the dawn. Afterward I was informed that you had accepted the offer, and had called upon me to deposit the money. Acting upon this information, I sent you the following letter:

Peoria, Ill., August 31st, 1877.

To the Editor of the New York Observer:

I have been informed that you accepted, in your paper, an offer made by me to any clergyman in San Francisco. That offer was, that I would pay one thousand dollars in gold to any minister in that city who would prove that Thomas Paine died in terror because of religious opinions he had expressed, or that Voltaire did not pass away serenely as the coming of the dawn.

For many years religious journals and ministers have been circulating certain pretended accounts of the frightful agonies endured by Paine and Voltaire when dying; that these great men at the moment of death were terrified because they had given their honest opinions upon the subject of religion to their fellow-men. The imagination of the religious world has been taxed to the utmost in inventing absurd and infamous accounts of the last moments of these intellectual giants. Every Sunday school paper, thousands of idiotic tracts, and countless stupidities called sermons, have been filled with these calumnies.

Paine and Voltaire both believed in God—both hoped for immortality— both believed in special providence. But both denied the inspiration of the Scriptures—both denied the divinity of Jesus Christ. While theologians most cheerfully admit that most murderers die without fear, they deny the possibility of any man who has expressed his disbelief in the inspiration of the Bible dying except in an agony of terror. These stories are used in revivals and in Sunday schools, and have long been considered of great value.

I am anxious that these slanders shall cease. I am desirous of seeing justice done, even at this late day, to the dead.

For the purpose of ascertaining the evidence upon which these death-bed accounts really rest, I make to you the following proposition:—

First.—As to Thomas Paine: I will deposit with the First National Bank of Peoria, Illinois, one thou- sand dollars in gold, upon the following conditions: This money shall be subject to your order when you shall, in the manner hereinafter provided, substantiate that Thomas Paine admitted the Bible to be an inspired book, or that he recanted his Infidel opinions—or that he died regretting that he had disbelieved the Bible— or that he died calling upon Jesus Christ in any religious sense whatever.

In order that a tribunal may be created to try this question, you may select one man, I will select another, and the two thus chosen shall select a third, and any two of the three may decide the matter.

As there will be certain costs and expenditures on both sides, such costs and expenditures shall be paid by the defeated party.

In addition to the one thousand dollars in gold, I will deposit a bond with good and sufficient security in the sum of two thousand dollars, conditioned for the payment of all costs in case I am defeated. I shall require of you a like bond.

From the date of accepting this offer you may have ninety days to collect and present your testimony, giving me notice of time and place of taking depositions. I shall have a like time to take evidence upon my side, giving you like notice, and you shall then have thirty days to take further testimony in reply to what I may offer. The case shall then be argued before the persons chosen; and their decisions shall be final as to us.

If the arbitrator chosen by me shall die, I shall have the right to choose another. You shall have the same right. If the third one, chosen by our two, shall die, the two shall choose another; and all vacancies, from whatever cause, shall be filled upon the same principle.

The arbitrators shall sit when and where a majority shall determine, and shall have full power to pass upon all questions arising as to competency of evidence, and upon all subjects.

Second.—As to Voltaire: I make the same proposition, if you will substantiate that Voltaire died expressing remorse or showing in any way that he was in mental agony because he had attacked Catholicism—or because he had denied the inspiration of the Bible—or because he had denied the divinity of Christ.

I make these propositions because I want you to stop slandering the dead.

If the propositions do not suit you in any particular, please state your objections, and I will modify them in any way consistent with the object in view.

If Paine and Voltaire died filled with childish and silly fear, I want to know it, and I want the world to know it. On the other hand, if the believers in superstition have made and circulated these cruel slanders concerning the mighty dead, I want the world to know that.

As soon as you notify me of the acceptance of these propositions I will send you the certificate of the bank that the money has been deposited upon the foregoing conditions, together with copies of bonds for costs.

Yours truly,

R. G. Ingersoll.

In your paper of September 27, 1877, you acknowledge the receipt of the foregoing letter, and after giving an outline of its contents, say: "As not one of the affirmations, in the form stated in this letter, was contained in the offer we made, we have no occasion to substantiate them. But we are prepared to produce the evidence of the truth of our own statement, and even to go further; to show not only that Tom Paine 'died a drunken, cowardly, and beastly death,' but that for many years previous, and up to that event he lived a drunken and beastly life."

In order to refresh your memory as to what you had published, I call your attention to the following, which appeared in the *N. Y. Observer,* July 19, 1877:

"Put Down the Money.

"Col. Bob Ingersoll, in a speech full of ribaldry and blasphemy, made in San Francisco recently, said:

"I will give $1,000 in gold coin to any clergyman who can substantiate that the death of Voltaire was not as peaceful as the dawn; and of Tom Paine whom they assert died in fear and agony, frightened by the clanking chains of devils—in fact frightened to death by God. I will give $1,000 likewise to any one who can substantiate this 'absurd story'—a story without a word of truth in it."

"We have published the testimony, and the witnesses are on hand to prove that Tom Paine died a drunken, cowardly and beastly death. *Let the Colonel deposit the money with any honest man, and the absurd story, as he terms it, shall be shown to be an ower true tale. But he wont do it. His talk is Infidel 'buncombe' and nothing more.*"

On the 31st of August I sent you my letter, and on the 27th of September you say in your paper: "As not one of the affirmations in the form stated in this letter was contained in the offer we made, we have no occasion to substantiate them."

What were the affirmations contained in the offer you made? I had offered a thousand dollars in gold to any one who would substantiate *"the absurd story" that Thomas Paine died in fear and agony, frightened by the clanking chains of devils—in fact, frightened to death by God.*

In response to this offer you said: "Let the Colonel deposit the money with an honest man and the 'absurd story' as he terms it, shall be shown to be an 'ower true tale.' But he won't do it. His talk is infidel 'buncombe' and nothing more."

Did you not offer to prove that Paine died in fear and agony, frightened by the clanking chains of devils? Did you not ask me to deposit the money that you might prove the "absurd story" to be an "ower true tale" and obtain the money? Did you not in your paper of the twenty-seventh of September in effect deny that you had offered to prove this "absurd story"? As soon as I offered to deposit the gold and give bonds besides to cover costs, did you not publish a falsehood?

You have eaten your own words, and, for my part, I would rather have dined with Ezekiel than with you.

You have not met the issue. You have knowingly avoided it. The question was not as to the personal habits of Paine. The real question was and is, whether Paine was filled with fear and horror at the time of his death on account of his religious opinions. That is the question. You avoid this. In effect, you abandon that charge and make others.

To you belongs the honor of having made the most cruel and infamous charges against Thomas Paine that have ever been made. Of what you have said you cannot prove the truth of one word.

You say that Thomas Paine died a drunken, cowardly and beastly death.

I pronounce this charge to be a cowardly and beastly falsehood.

Have you any evidence that he was in a drunken condition when he died?

What did he say or do of a *cowardly* character just before, or at about the time of his death?

In what way was his death cowardly? You must answer these questions, and give your proof, or all honest men will hold you in abhorrence. You have made these charges. The man against whom you make them is dead. He cannot answer you. I can. He cannot compel you to produce your testimony, or admit by your silence that you have cruelly slandered the defenseless dead. I can and I will. You say that his death was cowardly. In what respect? Was it cowardly in him to hold the Thirty-Nine Articles in contempt? Was it cowardly *not* to call on your Lord? Was it cowardly not to be afraid? You say that his death was beastly. Again I ask, in what respect? Was it beastly to submit to the inevitable with tranquility? Was it beastly to look with composure upon the approach of death? Was it beastly to die without a complaint, without a murmur—to pass from life without a fear?

Did Thomas Paine Recant?

Mr. Paine had prophesied that fanatics would crawl and cringe around him during his last moments. He believed that they would put a lie in the mouth of Death.

When the shadow of the coming dissolution was upon him, two clergymen, Messrs. Milledollar and Cunningham, called to annoy the dying man. Mr. Cunningham had the politeness to say, "You have now a full view of death you cannot live long, and whosoever does not believe in the Lord Jesus Christ will assuredly be damned." Mr. Paine replied, "Let me have none of your popish stuff. Get away with you. Good morning."

On another occasion a Methodist minister obtruded himself when Willet Hicks was present. This minister declared to Mr. Paine "that unless he repented of his unbelief he would be damned." Paine, although at the door of death, rose in his bed and indignantly requested the clergyman to leave his room. On another occasion, two brothers by the name of Pigott, sought to convert him. He was displeased and requested their departure. Afterward Thomas Nixon and Captain Daniel Pelton visited him for the express purpose of ascertaining whether he had, in any manner, changed his religious opinions. They were assured by the dying man that he still held the principles he had expressed in his writings.

Afterward, these gentlemen hearing that William Cobbett was about to write a life of Paine, sent him the following note:

New York, April 24, 1818.

"Sir: We have been informed that you have a design to write a history of the life and writings of Thomas Paine. If you have been furnished with materials in respect to his religious opinions, or rather of his recantation of his former opinions before his death, all you have heard of his recanting is false. Being aware that such reports would be raised after his death by fanatics who infested his house at the time it was expected he would die, we, the subscribers, intimate acquaintances of Thomas Paine since the year 1776, went to his house. He was sitting up in a chair, and apparently in full vigor and use of all his mental faculties. We interrogated him upon his religious opinions, and if he had changed his mind, or repented of anything he had said or wrote on that subject. He answered, "Not at all," and appeared rather offended at our supposition that any change should take place in his mind. We took down in writing the questions put to him and his answers thereto before a number of persons then in his room, among whom were his doctor, Mrs. Bonneville, etc. paper is mislaid and cannot be found at present, but the above is the substance which can be attested by many living witnesses."

Thomas Nixon.
Daniel Pelton.

Mr. Jarvis, the artist, saw Mr. Paine one or two days before his death. To Mr. Jarvis he expressed his belief in his written opinions upon the subject of religion. B. F. Haskin, an attorney of the city of New York, also visited him and inquired as to his religious opinions. Paine was then upon the threshold of death, but he did not tremble. He was not a coward. He expressed his firm and unshaken belief in the religious ideas he had given to the world.

Dr. Manley was with him when he spoke his last words. Dr. Manley asked the dying man if he did not wish to believe that Jesus was the Son of God, and the dying philosopher answered: "I have no wish to believe on that subject." Amasa Woodsworth sat up with Thomas Paine the night before his death. In 1839 Gilbert Vale hearing that Mr. Woodsworth was living in or near Boston, visited him for the purpose of getting his statement. The statement was published in the *Beacon* of June 5, 1839, while thousands who had been acquainted with Mr. Paine were living.

The following is the article referred to.

"We have just returned from Boston. One object of our visit to that city, was to see a Mr. Amasa Woodsworth, an engineer, now retired in a handsome cottage and garden at East Cambridge, Boston. This gentleman owned the house occupied by Paine at his death—while he lived next door. As an act of kindness Mr. Woodsworth visited Mr. Paine every day for six weeks before his death. He frequently sat up with him, and did so on the last two nights of his life. He was always there with Dr. Manley, the physician, and assisted in removing Mr. Paine while his bed was prepared. He was present when Dr. Manley asked Mr. Paine "if he wished to believe that Jesus Christ was the Son of God," and he describes Mr. Paine's answer as animated. He says that lying on his back he used some action and with much emphasis, replied, "I have no wish to believe on that subject." He lived some time after this, but was not known to speak, for he died tranquilly. He accounts for the insinuating style of Dr. Manley's letter, by stating that that gentleman just after its publication joined a church. He informs us that he has openly reproved the doctor for the falsity contained in the spirit of that letter, boldly declaring be- fore Dr. Manley, who is yet living, that nothing which he saw justified the insinuations. Mr. Woodsworth assures us that he neither heard nor saw anything to justify the belief of any mental change in the opinions of Mr. Paine previous to his death; but that being very ill and in pain chiefly arising from the skin being removed in some parts by long lying, he was generally too uneasy to enjoy conversation on abstract subjects. This, then, is the best evidence that can be procured on this subject, and we publish it while the contravening parties are yet alive, and with the authority of Mr. Woodsworth.

Gilbert Vale.

A few weeks ago I received the following letter which confirms the statement of Mr. Vale:

Near Stockton, Cal., Greenwood Cottage, July 9, 1877.
Col. Ingersoll: In 1842 I talked with a gentleman in Boston. I have forgotten his name; but he was then an engineer of the Charleston navy yard. I am thus particular so that you can find his name on the books. He told me that he nursed Thomas Paine in his last illness, and closed his eyes when dead. I asked him if he recanted and called upon God to save him. He replied, "No. He died as he had taught. He had a sore upon his side and when we turned him it was very painful and he would cry out 'O God!' or something like that." "But," said the narrator, "that was nothing, for he believed in a God." I told him that I had often heard it asserted from the pulpit that Mr. Paine had recanted in his last moments. The gentleman said that it was not true, and he appeared to be an intelligent, truthful man. With respect, I remain, etc.

Philip Graves, M. D.

The next witness is Willet Hicks, a Quaker preacher. He says that during the last illness of Mr. Paine he visited him almost daily, and that Paine died firmly convinced of the truth of the religious opinions he had given to his fellow-men. It was to this same Willet Hicks that Paine applied for permission to be buried in the cemetery of the Quakers. Permission was refused. This refusal settles the question of recantation. If he had recanted, of course there could have been no objection to his body being buried by the side of the best hypocrites on the earth.

If Paine recanted why should he be denied "a little earth for charity"? Had he recanted, it would have been regarded as a vast and splendid triumph for the gospel. It would with much noise and pomp and ostentation have been heralded about the world.

I received the following letter today. The writer is well know in this city, and is a man of high character:

Peoria, Oct. 8th, 1877.

Robert G. Ingersoll, *Esteemed Friend:* My parents were Friends (Quakers). My father died when I was very young. The elderly and middle-aged Friends visited at my mother's house. We lived in the city of New York. Among the number I distinctly remember Elias Hicks, Willet Hicks, and a Mr._____ Day, who was a bookseller in Pearl street. There were many others, whose names I do not now remember. The subject of the recantation by Thomas Paine of his views about the Bible in his last illness, or at any other time, was discussed by them in my presence at different times. I learned from them that some of them had attended upon Thomas Paine in his last sickness and ministered to his wants up to the time of his death. And upon the question of whether he did recant there was but one expression. They all said that he did not recant in any manner. I often heard them say they wished he had recanted. In fact, according to them, the nearer he approached death the more positive he appeared to be in his convictions.

These conversations were from 1820 to 1822. I was at that time from ten to twelve years old, but these conversations impressed themselves upon me because many thoughtless people then blamed the Society of Friends for their kindness to that "arch Infidel," Thomas Paine.

Truly yours,
A. C. Hankinson.

A few days ago I received the following letter:

Albany, New York, Sept. 27, 1877.

Dear Sir: It is over twenty years ago that professionally I made the acquaintance of John Hogeboom, a Justice of the Peace of the county of Rensselaer, New York. He was then over seventy years of age and had the reputation of being a man of candor and integrity. He was a great admirer of Paine. He told me that he was personally acquainted with him, and used to see him frequently during the last years of his life in the city of New York, where Hogeboom then resided. I asked him if there was any truth in the charge that Paine was in the habit of getting drunk. He said that it was utterly false; that he never heard of such a thing during the life-time of Mr. Paine, and did not believe any one else did. I asked him about the recantation of his religious opinions on his death-bed, and the revolting death-bed scenes that the world had heard so much about. He said there was no truth in them, that he had received his information from persons who attended Paine in his last illness, "and that he passed peacefully away, as we may say, in the sunshine of a great soul."

Yours truly,
W. J. Hilton,

The witnesses by whom I substantiate the fact that Thomas Paine did not recant, and that he died holding the religious opinions he had published, are:

First—Thomas Nixon, Captain Daniel Pelton, B. F. Haskin. These gentlemen visited him during his last illness for the purpose of

173

ascertaining whether he had in any respect changed his views upon religion. He told them that he had not.

Second—James Cheetham. This man was the most malicious enemy Mr. Paine had, and yet he admits that "Thomas Paine died placidly, and almost without a struggle." (See *Life of Thomas Paine,* by James Cheetham).

Third—The ministers, Milledollar and Cunning- ham. These gentlemen told Mr. Paine that if he died without believing in the Lord Jesus Christ he would be damned, and Paine replied, "Let me have none of your popish stuff. Good morning." (See *Sherwin's Life of Paine,* p. 220).

Fourth—Mrs. Hedden. She told these same preachers when they attempted to obtrude them- selves upon Mr. Paine again, that the attempt to convert Mr. Paine was useless—"that if God did not change his mind no human power could."

Fifth—Andrew A. Dean. This man lived upon Paine's farm at New Rochelle, and corresponded 465 with him upon religious subjects. (See Paine's *Theological Works,* p. 308.)

Sixth—Mr. Jarvis, the artist with whom Paine lived. He gives an account of an old lady coming to Paine and telling him that God Almighty had sent her to tell him that unless he repented and believed in the blessed Savior, he would be damned. Paine replied that God would not send such a foolish old woman with such an impertinent message. (See Clio Rickman's *Life of Paine.*)

Seventh—Wm. Carver, with whom Paine boarded. Mr. Carver said again and again that Paine did not recant. He knew him well, and had every opportunity of knowing. (See *Life of Paine* by Gilbert Vale.)

Eighth—Dr. Manley, who attended him in his last sickness, and to whom Paine spoke his last words. Dr. Manley asked him if he did not wish to believe in Jesus Christ, and he replied, "I have no wish to believe on that subject."

Ninth—Willet Hicks and Elias Hicks, who were with him frequently during his last sickness, and both of whom tried to persuade him to recant. According to their testimony, Mr. Paine died as he had lived—a believer in God, and a friend of man. Willet Hicks was offered money to say something false against Thomas Paine. He was even offered money to remain silent and allow others to slander the dead. Mr. Hicks, speaking of Thomas Paine, said: "He was a good man—an honest man." (Vale's *Life of Paine.*)

Tenth—Amasa Woodsworth, who was with him every day for some six weeks immediately preceding his death, and sat up with him the last two nights of his life. This man declares that Paine did not recant and that he died tranquilly. The evidence of Mr. Woodsworth is conclusive.

Eleventh—Thomas Paine himself. *The will of Thomas Paine,* written by himself, commences as follows:

"The last will and testament of me, the subscriber, Thomas Paine, reposing confidence in my creator God, and in no other being, for I know of no other, nor believe in any other;" and closes in these words; "I have lived an honest and useful life to mankind; my time has been spent in doing good, and I die in perfect composure and resignation to the will of my creator God."

Twelfth—If Thomas Paine recanted, why do you pursue him? If he recanted, he died substantially in your belief, for what reason then do you denounce his death as cowardly? If upon his death-bed he renounced the opinions he had published, the business of defaming him should be done by Infidels, not by Christians.

I ask you if it is honest to throw away the testimony of his friends—the evidence of fair and honorable men—and take the putrid words of avowed and malignant enemies?

When Thomas Paine was dying, he was infested by fanatics—by the snaky spies of bigotry. In the shadows of death were the unclean birds of prey waiting to tear with beak and claw the corpse of him who wrote the "Rights of Man." And there lurking and crouching in the darkness were the jackals and hyenas of superstition ready to violate his grave.

These birds of prey—these unclean beasts are the witnesses produced and relied upon by you.

One by one the instruments of torture have been wrenched from the cruel clutch of the church, until within the armory of orthodoxy there remains but one weapon—Slander.

Against the witnesses that I have produced you can bring just two— Mary Roscoe and Mary Hinsdale. The first is referred to in the memoir of Stephen Grellet. She had once been a servant in his house. Grellet tells what happened between this girl and Paine. According to this account Paine asked her if she had ever read any of his writings, and on being told that she had read very *little* of them, he inquired what she thought of them, adding that from such an one as she he expected a correct answer.

Let us examine this falsehood. Why would Paine expect a correct answer about his writings from one who had read very little of them? Does not such a statement devour itself? This young lady further said that the "Age of Reason" was put in her hands and that the more she read in it the more dark and distressed she felt, and that she threw the book into the fire. Whereupon Mr. Paine remarked, "I wish all had done as you did, for if the devil ever had any agency in any work, he had it in my writing that book."

The next is Mary Hinsdale. She was a servant in the family of Willet Hicks. She, like Mary Roscoe, was sent to carry some delicacy to Mr. Paine. To this young lady Paine, according to her account, said precisely the same that he did to Mary Roscoe, and she said the same thing to Mr. Paine.

My own opinion is that Mary Roscoe and Mary Hinsdale are one and the same person, or the same story has been by mistake put in the mouth of both.

It is not possible that the same conversation should have taken place between Paine and Mary Roscoe, and between him and Mary Hinsdale.

Mary Hinsdale lived with Willet Hicks and he pronounced her story a pious fraud and fabrication. He said that Thomas Paine never said any such thing to Mary Hinsdale. (See Vale's *Life of Paine*.)

Another thing about this witness. A woman by the name of Mary Lockwood, a Hicksite Quaker, died. Mary Hinsdale met her brother about that time and told him that his sister had recanted, and wanted her to say so at her funeral. This turned out to be false.

It has been claimed that Mary Hinsdale made her statement to Charles Collins. Long after the alleged occurrence Gilbert Vale, one of the biographers of Paine, had a conversation with Collins concerning Mary Hinsdale. Vale asked him what he thought of her. He replied that some of the Friends believed that she used opiates, and that they did not give credit to her statements. He also said that he believed what the Friends said, but thought that when a young woman, she *might* have told the truth.

In 1818 William Cobbett came to New York. He began collecting materials for a life of Thomas Paine. In this he became acquainted with Mary Hinsdale and Charles Collins. Mr. Cobbett gave a full account of what happened in a letter addressed to the Norwich *Mercury* in 1819. From this account it seems that Charles Collins told Cobbett that Paine had recanted. Cobbett called for the testimony, and told Mr. Collins that he must give time, place, and the circumstances. He finally brought a statement that he stated had been made by Mary Hinsdale. Armed with this document Cobbett, in October of that year, called upon the said Mary Hinsdale, at No. 10 Anthony street, New York, and showed her the statement. Upon being questioned by Mr. Cobbett she said, "That it was so long ago that she could not speak positively to any part of the matter—that she would not say that any part of the paper was true—that she had never seen the paper—and that she had never given Charles Collins authority to say anything about the matter in her name." And so in the month of October, in the year of grace 1818, in the mist and fog of forgetful- ness disappeared forever one Mary Hinsdale—the last and only witness against the intellectual honesty of Thomas Paine.

Did Thomas Paine live the life of a drunken beast, and did he die a drunken, cowardly and beastly death?

Upon you rests the burden of substantiating these infamous charges.

You have, I suppose, produced the best evidence in your possession, and that evidence I will now proceed to examine. Your first witness is Grant Thorburn. He makes three charges against Thomas Paine, 1st. That his wife obtained a divorce from him in England for cruelty and neglect. 2d. That he was a defaulter and fled from England to America. 3d. That he was a drunkard.

These three charges stand upon the same evidence—the word of Grant Thorburn. If they are not all true Mr. Thorburn stands impeached.

The charge that Mrs. Paine obtained a divorce on account of the cruelty and neglect of her husband is utterly false. There is no such record in the world, and never was. Paine and his wife separated by mutual consent. Each respected the other. They remained friends. This charge is without any foundation in fact. I challenge the Christian world to produce the record of this decree of divorce. According to Mr. Thorburn it was granted in England. In that country public records are kept of all such decrees. Have the kindness to produce this decree showing that it was given on account of cruelty or admit that Mr. Thorburn was mistaken.

Thomas Paine was a just man. Although separated from his wife, he always spoke of her with tenderness and respect, and frequently sent her money without letting her know the source from whence it came. Was this the conduct of a drunken beast?

The second charge, that Paine was a defaulter in England and fled to America, is equally false. He did not flee from England. He came to America, not as a fugitive, but as a free man. He came with a letter of introduction signed by another Infidel, Benjamin Franklin. He came as a soldier of Freedom—an apostle of Liberty.

In this second charge there is not one word of truth.

He held a small office in England. If he was a defaulter the records of that country will show that fact.

Mr. Thorburn, unless the record can be produced to substantiate him, stands convicted of at least two mistakes.

Now, as to the third: He says that in 1802 Paine was an "old remnant of mortality, drunk, bloated and half asleep."

Can any one believe this to be a true account of the personal appearance of Mr. Paine in 1802? He had just returned from France. He had been welcomed home by Thomas Jefferson, who had said that he was entitled to the hospitality of every American.

In 1802 Mr. Paine was honored with a public dinner in the city of New York. He was called upon and treated with kindness and respect by such men as DeWitt Clinton.

In 1806 Mr. Paine wrote a letter to Andrew A. Dean upon the subject of religion. Read that letter and then say that the writer of it was an "old remnant of mortality, drunk, bloated and half asleep." Search the files of the *New York Observer* from the first issue to the last, and you will find nothing superior to this letter.

In 1803 Mr. Paine wrote a letter of considerable length, and of great force, to his friend Samuel Adams. Such letters are not written by drunken beasts, nor by remnants of old mortality, nor by drunkards. It was about the same time that he wrote his "Remarks on Robert Hall's Sermons."

These "Remarks" were not written by a drunken beast, but by a clear-headed and thoughtful man.

In 1804 he published an essay on the invasion of England, and a treatise on gunboats, full of valuable maritime information:—in 1805, a treatise on yellow fever, suggesting modes of prevention. In short, he was an industrious and thoughtful man. He sympathized with the poor and oppressed of all lands. He looked upon monarchy as a species of physical slavery. He had the goodness to attack that form of government. He regarded the religion of his day as a kind of mental slavery. He had the courage to give his reasons for his opinion. His reasons filled the churches with hatred. Instead of answering his arguments they attacked him. Men who were not fit to blacken his shoes, blackened his character.

There is too much religious cant in the statement of Mr. Thorburn. He exhibited too much anxiety to tell what Grant Thorburn said to Thomas Paine. He names Thomas Jefferson as one of the disreputable men who welcomed Paine with open arms. The testimony of a man who regarded Thomas Jefferson as a disreputable person, as to the character of anybody, is utterly without value. In my judgment, the testimony of Mr. Thorburn should be thrown aside as wholly unworthy of belief.

Your next witness is the Rev. J. D. Wickham, D. D., who tells what an elder in his church said. This elder said that Paine passed his last days on his farm at New Rochelle with a solitary female attendant. This is not true. He did not pass his last days at New Rochelle. Consequently this pious elder did not see him during his last days at that place. Upon this elder we prove an alibi. Mr. Paine passed his last days in the city of New York, in a house upon 475 Columbia street. The story of the Rev. J. D. Wickham, D.D., is simply false.

The next competent false witness is the Rev. Charles Hawley, D.D., who proceeds to state that the story of the Rev. J. D. Wickham, D.D., is corroborated by older citizens of New Rochelle. The names of these ancient residents are withheld. Ac- cording to these unknown witnesses, the account given by the deceased elder was entirely correct. But as the particulars of Mr. Paine's conduct "were too loathsome to be described in print," we are left entirely in the dark as to what he really did.

While at New Rochelle Mr. Paine lived with Mr. Purdy—with Mr. Dean—with Captain Pelton, and with Mr. Staple. It is worthy of note that all of these gentlemen give the lie direct to the statements of "older residents" and ancient citizens spoken of by the Rev. Charles Hawley, D.D., and leave him with his "loathsome particulars" existing only in his own mind.

The next gentleman you bring upon the stand is W. H. Ladd, who quotes from the memoirs of Stephen Grellet. This gentleman also has the misfortune to be dead. According to his account, Mr. Paine made his recantation to a servant girl of his by the name of Mary Roscoe. To this girl, according to the account, Mr. Paine uttered the wish that all who read his book had burned it. I believe there is a mistake in the name of this girl. Her name was probably Mary Hinsdale, as it was once claimed that Paine made the same remark to her, but this point I shall notice hereafter. These are your witnesses, and the only ones you bring forward, to support your charge that Thomas Paine lived a drunken and beastly life and died a drunken, cowardly and beastly death. All these calumnies are found in a life of Paine by a Mr. Cheetham, the convicted libeler already referred to. Mr. Cheetham was an enemy of the man whose life he pretended to write.

In order to show you the estimation in which Mr. Cheetham was held by Mr. Paine, I will give you a copy of a letter that throws light upon this point:

October 28, 1807.

"Mr. Cheetham: Unless you make a public apology for the abuse and falsehood in your paper of Tuesday, October 27th, respecting me, I will prosecute you for lying."

Thomas Paine.

In another letter, speaking of this same man, Mr. Paine says: "If an unprincipled bully cannot be reformed, he can be punished." "Cheetham has been so long in the habit of giving false information, that truth is to him like a foreign language."

Mr. Cheetham wrote the life of Paine to gratify his malice and to support religion. He was prosecuted for libel—was convicted and fined.

Yet the life of Paine written by this man is referred to by the Christian world as the highest authority.

As to the personal habits of Mr. Paine, we have the testimony of William Carver, with whom he lived; of Mr. Jarvis, the artist, with whom he lived; of Mr. Staple, with whom he lived; of Mr. Purdy, who was a tenant of Paine's; of Mr. Burger, with whom he was intimate; of Thomas Nixon and Captain Daniel Pelton, both of whom knew him well; of Amasa Woodsworth, who was with him when he died; of John Fellows, who boarded at the same house; of James Wilburn, with whom he boarded; of B. F. Haskin, a lawyer, who was well acquainted with him and called upon him during his last illness; of Walter Morton, a friend; of Clio Rickman, who had known him for many years; of Willet and Elias Hicks, Quakers, who knew him intimately and well; of Judge Herttell, H. Margary, Elihu Palmer, and many others. All these testified to the fact that Mr. Paine was a temperate man. In those days nearly everybody used spirituous liquors. Paine was not an exception; but he did not drink to excess. Mr. Lovett, who kept the City Hotel where Paine stopped, in a note to Caleb Bingham, declared that Paine drank less than any boarder he had.

Against all this evidence you produce the story of Grant Thorburn—the story of the Rev. J. D. Wickham that an elder in his church told him that Paine was a drunkard, corroborated by the Rev. Charles Hawley, and an extract from Lossing's history to the same effect. The evidence is overwhelmingly against you. Will you have the fairness to admit it? Your witnesses are merely the repeaters of the falsehoods of James Cheetham, the convicted libeler.

After all, drinking is not as bad as lying. An honest drunkard is better than a calumniator of the dead. "A remnant of old mortality, drunk, bloated and half asleep" is better than a perfectly sober defender of human slavery.

To become drunk is a virtue compared with stealing a babe from the breast of its mother.

Drunkenness is one of the beatitudes, compared with editing a religious paper devoted to the defense of slavery upon the ground that it is a divine institution.

Do you really think that Paine was a drunken beast when he wrote "Common Sense"—a pamphlet that aroused three millions of people, as people were never aroused by a pamphlet before? Was he a 479 drunken beast when he wrote the "Crisis"? Was it to a drunken beast that the following letter was addressed:

Rocky Hill, September 10, 1783.
"I have learned since I have been at this place, that you are at Bordentown.—Whether for the sake of retirement or economy I know not. Be it for either or both, or whatever it may, if you will come to this place and partake with me I shall be exceedingly happy to see you at it. Your presence may remind Congress of your past services to this country; and if it is in my power to impress them, command my best exertions with freedom, as they will be rendered cheerfully by one who entertains a lively sense of the importance of your works, and who with much pleasure subscribes himself,"
                              Your Sincere Friend,
                                 "George Washington."

179

Did any of your ancestors ever receive a letter like that?

Do you think that Paine was a drunken beast when the following letter was received by him?

"You express a wish in your letter to return to America in a national ship; Mr. Dawson, who brings over the treaty, and who will present you with this letter, is charged with orders to the captain of the *Maryland* to receive and accommodate you back, if you can be ready to depart at such a short warning. You will in general find us returned to sentiments worthy of former times; *in these it will be your glory to have steadily labored and with as much effect as any man living.* That you may live long to continue your useful labors, and reap the reward in the *thankfulness of nations,* is my sincere prayer. Accept the assurances of my high esteem and affectionate attachment."

Thomas Jefferson.

Did any of your ancestors ever receive a letter like that?

"It has been very generally propagated through the continent that I wrote the pamphlet 'Common Sense.' I could not have written anything in so manly and striking a style."—John Adams.

"A few more such *flaming* arguments as were exhibited at Falmouth and Norfolk, added to the sound doctrine and unanswerable reasoning contained in the pamphlet 'Common Sense,' will not leave numbers at a loss to decide on the propriety of a separation."—George Washington.

"It is not necessary for me to tell you how much all your countrymen— I speak of the great mass of the people—are interested in your welfare. They have not forgotten the history of their own Revolution and the difficult scenes through which they passed; nor do they review its several stages without reviving in their bosoms a due sensibility of the merits of those who served them in that great and arduous conflict. The crime of ingratitude has not yet stained, and I trust never will stain, our national character. You are considered by them as not only having rendered important services in our own Revolution, but as being on a more extensive scale the friend of human rights, and a distinguished and able defender of public liberty. To the welfare of Thomas Paine the Americans are not, nor can they be indifferent.". . James Monroe.

Did any of your ancestors ever receive a letter like that?

"No writer has exceeded Paine in ease and familiarity of style, in perspicuity of expression, happiness of elucidation, and in simple and unassuming language."'—Thomas Jefferson.

Was ever a letter like that written about an editor of the *New York Observer?*

Was it in consideration of the services of a drunken beast that the Legislature of Pennsylvania presented Thomas Paine with five hundred pounds sterling?

Did the State of New York feel indebted to a drunken beast, and confer upon Thomas Paine an estate of several hundred acres?

"I believe in the equality of man, and I believe that religious duties consist in doing justice, loving mercy, and endeavoring to make our fellow-creatures happy."

"My own mind is my own church."

"It is necessary to the happiness of man that he be mentally faithful to himself."

"Any system of religion that shocks the mind of a child cannot be a true system."

"The Word of God is the creation which we behold."

"The age of ignorance commenced with the Christian system."

"It is with a pious fraud as with a bad action—it begets a calamitous necessity of going on."

"To read the Bible without horror, we must undo everything that is tender, sympathizing and benevolent in the heart of man."

"The man does not exist who can say I have persecuted him, or that I have in any case returned evil for evil."

"Of all tyrannies that afflict mankind, tyranny in religion is the worst."

"My own opinion is, that those whose lives have been spent in doing good and endeavoring to make their fellow-mortals happy, will be happy hereafter."

"The belief in a cruel god makes a cruel man."

"The intellectual part of religion is a private affair between every man and his Maker, and in which no third party has any right to interfere. The practical part consists in our doing good to each other."

"No man ought to make a living by religion. One person cannot act religion for another—every person must perform it for himself."

"One good schoolmaster is of more use than a hundred priests."

"Let us propagate morality unfettered by superstition."

"God is the power, or first cause, Nature is the law, and matter is the subject acted upon."

"I believe in one God and no more, and I hope for happiness beyond this life."

"The key of heaven is not in the keeping of any sect nor ought the road to it to be obstructed by any."

"My religion, and the whole of it, is the fear and love of the Deity and universal philanthropy."

"I have yet, I believe, some years in store, for I have a good state of health and a happy mind. I take care of both, by nourishing the first with *temperance* and the latter with abundance."

"He lives immured within the Bastille of a word."

How perfectly that sentence describes you! The Bastille in which you are immured is the word "Calvinism."

"Man has no property in man."

What a splendid motto that would have made for the *New York Observer* in the olden time!

"The world is my country; to do good, my religion."

I ask you again whether these splendid utterances came from the lips of a drunken beast?

Did Thomas Paine die in destitution and want?

The charge has been made, over and over again, that Thomas Paine died in want and destitution—that he was an abandoned pauper—an outcast without friends and without money. This charge is just as false as the rest.

181

Upon his return to this country in 1802, he was worth $30,000, according to his own statement made at that time in the following letter addressed to Clio Rickman:

"My Dear Friend: Mr. Monroe, who is appointed minister extraordinary to France, takes charge of this, to be delivered to Mr. Este, banker in Paris, to be forwarded to you.

"I arrived at Baltimore the 30th of October, and you can have no idea of the agitation which my arrival occasioned. From New Hampshire to Georgia (an extent of 1,500 miles) every newspaper was filled with applause or abuse.

"My property in this country has been taken care of by my friends, and is now worth six thousand pounds sterling; which put in the funds will bring me £400 sterling a year.

"Remember me in affection and friendship to your wife and family, and in the circle of your friends."

Thomas Paine.

A man in those days worth thirty thousand dollars was not a pauper. That amount would bring an income of at least two thousand dollars per annum. Two thousand dollars then would be fully equal to five thousand dollars now.

On the 12th of July, 1809, the year in which he died, Mr. Paine made his will. From this instrument we learn that he was the owner of a valuable farm within twenty miles of New York. He also was the owner of thirty shares in the New York Phoenix Insurance Company, worth upwards of fifteen hundred dollars. Besides this, some personal property and ready money. By his will he gave to Walter Morton, and Thomas Addis Emmett, brother of Robert Emmett, two hundred dollars each, and one hundred to the widow of Elihu Palmer.

Is it possible that this will was made by a pauper—by a destitute outcast—by a man who suffered for the ordinary necessaries of life?

But suppose, for the sake of the argument, that he was poor and that he died a beggar, does that tend to show that the Bible is an inspired book and that Calvin did not burn Servetus? Do you really regard poverty as a crime? If Paine had died a millionaire, would you have accepted his religious opinions? If Paine had drank nothing but cold water would you have repudiated the five cardinal points of Calvin- ism? Does an argument depend for its force upon the pecuniary condition of the person making it? As a matter of fact, most reformers—most men and women of genius, have been acquainted with poverty. Beneath a covering of rags have been found some of the tenderest and bravest hearts.

Owing to the attitude of the churches for the last fifteen hundred years, truth-telling has not been a very lucrative business. As a rule, hypocrisy has worn the robes, and honesty the rags. That day is passing away. You cannot now answer the arguments of a man by pointing at holes in his coat. Thomas Paine attacked the church when it was powerful—when it had what was called honors to bestow—when it was the keeper of the public conscience—when it was strong and cruel. The church waited till he was dead then attacked his reputation and his clothes.

Once upon a time a donkey kicked a lion. The lion was dead.

CONCLUSION.

From the persistence with which the orthodox have charged for the last sixty-eight years that Thomas Paine recanted, and that when dying he was filled with remorse and fear; from the malignity of the attacks upon his personal character, I had concluded that there must be some evidence of some kind to support these charges. Even with my ideas of the average honor of believers in superstition—the disciples of fear—I did not quite believe that all these infamies rested solely upon poorly attested lies. I had charity enough to suppose that some- thing had been said or done by Thomas Paine capable of being tortured into a foundation for these calumnies. And I was foolish enough to think that even you would be willing to fairly examine the pretended evidence said to sustain these charges, and give your honest conclusion to the world. I supposed that you, being acquainted with the history of your country, felt under a certain obligation to Thomas Paine for the splendid services rendered by him in the darkest days of the Revolution. It was only reasonable to suppose that you were aware that in the midnight of Valley Forge the "Crisis," by Thomas Paine, was the first star that glittered in the wide horizon of despair. I took it for granted that you knew of the bold stand taken and the brave words spoken by Thomas Paine, in the French Convention, against the death of the king. I thought it probable that you, being an editor, had read the "Rights of Man;" that you knew that Thomas Paine was a champion of human liberty; that he was one of the founders and fathers of this Republic; that he was one of the foremost men of his age; that he had never written a word in favor of injustice; that he was a despiser of slavery; that he abhorred tyranny in all its forms; that he was in the widest and highest sense a friend of his race; that his head was as clear as his heart was good, and that he had the courage to speak his honest thought. Under these circumstances I had hoped that you would for the moment forget your religious prejudices and submit to the enlightened judgment of the world the evidence you had, or could obtain, affecting in any way the character of so great and so generous a man. This you have refused to do. In my judgment, you have mistaken the temper of even your own readers. A large majority of the religious people of this country have, to a considerable extent, outgrown the prejudices of their fathers. They are willing to know the truth and the whole truth, about the life and death of Thomas Paine. They will not thank you for having presented them the moss-covered, the maimed and distorted traditions of ignorance, prejudice, and credulity. By this course you will convince them not of the wickedness of Paine, but of your own unfairness.

What crime had Thomas Paine committed that he should have feared to die? The only answer you can give is, that he denied the inspiration of the Scriptures. If this is a crime, the civilized world is filled with criminals. The pioneers of human thought—the intellectual leaders of the world—the foremost men in every science—the kings of literature and art—those who stand in the front rank of investigation—the men who are civilizing, elevating, instructing, and refining mankind, are today unbelievers in the dogma of inspiration. Upon this question, the intellect of Christendom agrees with the conclusions reached by the genius of Thomas Paine. Centuries ago a noise was made for the purpose of frightening mankind. Orthodoxy is the echo of that noise.

The man who now regards the Old Testament as in any sense a sacred or inspired book is, in my judgment, an intellectual and moral deformity. There is in it so much that is cruel, ignorant, and ferocious that it is to me a matter of amazement that it was ever thought to be the work of a most merciful deity.

Upon the question of inspiration Thomas Paine gave his honest opinion. Can it be that to give an honest opinion causes one to die in terror and despair? Have you in your writings been actuated by the fear of such a consequence? Why should it be taken for granted that Thomas Paine, who devoted his life to the sacred cause of freedom, should have been hissed at in the hour of death by the snakes of conscience, while editors of Presbyterian papers who defended slavery as a divine institution, and cheerfully justified the stealing of babes from the breasts of mothers, are supposed to have passed smilingly from earth to the embraces of angels? Why should you think that the heroic author of the "Rights of Man" should shudderingly dread to leave this "bank and shoal of time," while Calvin, dripping with the blood of Servetus, was anxious to be judged of God? Is it possible that the persecutors—the instigators of the massacre of St. Bartholomew—the inventors and users of thumb-screws, and iron boots, and racks—the burners and tearers of human flesh—the stealers, whippers and enslavers of men—the buyers and beaters of babes and mothers—the founders of inquisitions—the makers of chains, the builders of dungeons, the slanderers of the living and the calumniators of the dead, all died in the odor of sanctity, with white, forgiven hands folded upon the breasts of peace, while the destroyers of prejudice—the apostles of humanity—the soldiers of liberty—the breakers of fetters—the creators of light—died surrounded with the fierce fiends of fear?

In your attempt to destroy the character of Thomas Paine you have failed, and have succeeded only in leaving a stain upon your own. You have written words as cruel, bitter and heartless as the creed of Calvin. Hereafter you will stand in the pillory of history as a defamer—a calumniator of the dead. You will be known as the man who said that Thomas Paine, the "Author Hero," lived a drunken, cowardly and beastly life, and died a drunken and beastly death. These infamous words will be branded upon the forehead of your reputation. They will be remembered against you when all else you may have uttered shall have passed from the memory of men.

Robert G. Ingersoll.

THE OBSERVER'S SECOND ATTACK

TOM PAINE AGAIN.

In the Observer of September 27th, in response to numerous calls from different parts of the country for information, and in fulfillment of a promise, we presented a mass of testimony, chiefly from persons with whom we had been personally acquainted, establishing the truth of our assertions in regard to the dissolute life and miserable end of Paine. It was not a pleasing subject for discussion, and an apology, or at least an explanation, is due to our readers for resuming it, and for occupying so much space, or any space, in exhibiting the truth and the proofs in regard to the character of a man who had become so debased by his intemperance, and so vile in his habits, as to be excluded, for many years before and up to the time of his death, from all decent society.

Our reasons for taking up the subject at all, and for presenting at this time so much additional testimony in regard to the facts of the case, are these: At different periods for the last fifty years, efforts have been made by Infidels to revive and honor the memory of one whose friends would honor him most by suffering his name to sink into oblivion, if that were possible. About two years since, Rev. O. B. Frothingham, of this city, came to their aid, and undertook a sort of championship of Paine, making in a public discourse this statement: "No private character has been more foully calumniated in the name of God than that of Thomas Paine." (Mr. Frothingham, it will be remembered, is the one who recently, in a public discourse, announced the downfall of Christianity, although he very kindly made the allowance that, "it may be a thousand years before its decay will be visible to all eyes." It is our private opinion that it will be at least a thousand and one.) Rev. John W. Chadwick, a minister of the same order of unbelief, who signs himself, "Minister of the Second Unitarian Society in Brooklyn," has devoted two discourses to the same end, eulogizing Paine. In one of these, which we have before us in a handsomely printed pamphlet, entitled, "Method and Value of his (Paine's) Religious Teachings," he says: "Christian usage has determined that an Infidel means one who does not believe in Christianity as a supernatural religion; in the Bible as a Supernatural book; in Jesus as a supernatural person. And in this sense Paine was an Infidel, and so, thank God, am I." It is proper to add that Unitarians generally decline all responsibility for the utterances of both of these men, and that they compose a denomination, or rather two denominations, of their own.

There is also a certain class of Infidels who are not quite prepared to meet the odium that attaches to the name; they call themselves Christians, but their sympathies are all with the enemies of Christianity, and they are not always able to conceal it. They have not the courage of their opinions, like Mr. Frothingham and Mr. Chadwick, and they work

185

only sideways toward the same end. We have been no little amused since our last article on this subject appeared, to read some of the articles that have been written on the other side, though professedly on no side, and to observe how sincerely these men deprecate the discussion of the character of Paine, as an unprofitable topic. It never appeared to them unprofitable when the discussion was on the other side.

Then, too, we have for months past been receiving letters from different parts of the country, asking authentic information on the subject and stating that the followers of Paine are making extraordinary efforts to circulate his writings against the Christian religion, and in order to give currency to these writings they are endeavoring to rescue his name from the disgrace into which it sank during the latter years of his life. Paine spent several of his last years in furnishing a commentary upon his Infidel principles. This commentary was contained in his besotted, degraded life and miserable end, but his friends do not wish the commentary to go out in connection with his writings. They prefer to have them read without the comments by their author. Hence this anxiety to free the great apostle of Infidelity from the obloquy which his life brought upon his name; to represent him as a pure, noble, virtuous man, and to make it appear that he died a peaceful, happy death, just like a philosopher.

But what makes the publication of the facts in the case still more imperative at this time is the wholesale accusation brought against the Christian public by the friends and admirers of Paine. Christian ministers as a class, and Christian journals are expressly accused of falsifying history, of defaming "the mighty dead!" (meaning Paine,) etc. In the face of all these accusations it cannot be out of place to state the facts and to fortify the statement by satisfactory evidence, as we are abundantly able to do.

The two points on which we proposed to produce the testimony are, the character of Paine's life (referring of course to his last residence in this country, for no one has intimated that he had sunk into such besotted drunkenness until about the time of his return to the United States in 1802), and the real character of his death as consistent with such a life, and as marked further by the cowardliness, which has been often exhibited by Infidels in the same circumstances.

It is nothing at all to the purpose to show, as his friends are fond of doing, that Paine rendered important service to the cause of American Independence. This is not the point under discussion and is not denied. No one ever called in question the valuable service that Benedict Arnold rendered to the country in the early part of the Revolutionary war; but this, with true Americans, does not suffice to cast a shade of loveliness or even to spread a mantle of charity over his subsequent career. Whatever share Paine had in the personal friendship of the fathers of the Revolution he forfeited by his subsequent life of beastly drunkenness and degradation, and on this account as well as on account of his blasphemy he was shunned by all decent people.

We wish to make one or two corrections of misstatements by Paine's advocates, on which a vast amount of argument has been simply wasted. We have never stated in any form, nor have we ever supposed, that Paine actually renounced his Infidelity. The accounts agree in stating that he died a blaspheming Infidel, and his horrible death we regard as one of the fruits, the fitting complement of his Infidelity. We have never seen anything that encouraged the hope that he was not abandoned of God in his last hours. But we have no doubt, on the other hand, that having become a wreck in body and mind through his intemperance, abandoned of God, deserted by his Infidel companions, and dependent upon Christian charity for the attentions he received, miserable beyond description in his condition, and seeing nothing to hope for in the future, he was afraid to die, and was ready to call upon God and upon Christ for mercy, and ready perhaps in the next minute to blaspheme. This is what we referred to in speaking of Paine's death as cowardly. It is shown in the testimony we have produced, and still more fully in that which we now present. The most wicked men are ready to call upon God in seasons of great peril, and sometimes ask for Christian ministrations when in extreme illness; but they are often ready on any alleviation of distress to turn to their wickedness again, in the expressive language of Scripture, "as the sow that was washed to her wallowing in the mire."

We have never stated or intimated, nor, so far as we are aware, has any one of our correspondents stated, that Paine died in poverty. It has been frequently and truthfully stated that Paine was dependent on Christian charity for the attentions he received in his last days, and so he was. His Infidel companions forsook him and Christian hearts and hands ministered to his wants, notwithstanding the blasphemies of his death-bed.

Nor has one of our correspondents stated, as alleged, that Paine died at New Rochelle. The Rev. Dr. Wickham, who was a resident of that place nearly fifty years ago, and who was perfectly familiar with the facts of his life, wrote that Paine spent "his latter days" on the farm presented to him by the State of New York, which was strictly true, but made no reference to it as the place of his death.

Such misrepresentations serve to show how much the advocates of Paine admire "truth."

With these explanations we produce further evidence in regard to the manner of Paine's life and the character of his death, both of which we have already characterized in appropriate terms, as the following testimony will show.

In regard to Paine's "personal habits," even before his return to this country, and particularly his aversion to soap and water, Elkana Watson, a gentleman of the highest social position, who resided in France during a part of the Revolutionary war, and who was the personal friend of Washington, Franklin, and other patriots of the period, makes some incidental statements in his "Men and Times of the Revolution." Though eulogizing Paine's efforts in behalf of American Independence, he describes him as "coarse and uncouth in his manners, loathsome in his appearance, and a disgusting egotist." On Paine's arrival at Nantes, the Mayor and other distinguished citizens called upon him to pay their respects to the American patriot. Mr. Watson says: "He was soon rid of his respectable visitors, who left the room with marks of astonishment and disgust." Mr. W., after much entreaty, and only by promising him a bundle of newspapers to read while undergoing the operation, succeeded in prevailing on Paine to "stew, for an hour, in a hot bath." Mr. W. accompanied Paine to the bath, and "instructed the keeper, in French, (which Paine did not understand,) gradually to increase the heat of the water 500 until '*le Monsieur serait bien bouille* (until the gentleman shall be well boiled;) and adds that "he became so much absorbed in his reading that he was nearly- parboiled before leaving the bath, much to his improvement and my satisfaction."

William Carver has been cited as a witness in be- half of Paine, and particularly as to his "personal habits." In a letter to Paine, dated December 2, 1776, he bears the following testimony:

"A respectable gentlemen from New Rochelle called to see me a few days back, and said that everybody was tired of you there, and no one would undertake to board and lodge you. I thought this was the case, as I found you at a tavern in a most miserable situation. You appeared as if you had not been shaved for a fortnight, and as to a shirt, it could not be said that you had one on. It was only the remains of one, and this, likewise, appeared not to have been off your back for a fortnight, and was nearly the color of tanned leather; and you had the most disagreeable smell possible; just like that of our poor beggars in England. Do you remember the pains I took to clean you? that I got a tub of warm water and soap and washed you from head to foot, and this I had to do three times before I could get you clean." (And then follow more disgusting details.)

"You say, also, that you found your own liquors during the time you boarded with me; but you should have said, 'I found only a small part of the liquor I drank during my stay with you; this part I purchased of John Fellows, which was a demijohn of brandy containing four gallons, and this did not serve me three weeks.' This can be proved, and I mean not to say anything that I cannot prove; for I hold truth as a precious jewel. It is a well-known fact, that you drank one quart of brandy per day, at my expense, during the different times that you have boarded with me, the demijohn above mentioned excepted, and the last fourteen weeks you were sick. Is not this a supply of liquor for dinner and supper?"

This chosen witness in behalf of Paine, closes his letter, which is full of loathsome descriptions of Paine's manner of life, as follows:

"Now, sir, I think I have drawn a complete portrait of your character; yet to enter upon every minutiae would be to give a history of your life, and to develop the fallacious mask of hypocrisy and deception under which you have acted in your political as well as moral capacity of life."

(Signed) "William Carver."

Carver had the same opinion of Paine to his dying day. When an old man, and an Infidel of the Paine type and habits, he was visited by the Rev. E. F. Hatfield, D.D., of this city, who writes to us of his interview with Carver, under date of Sept. 27, 1877:

"I conversed with him nearly an hour. I took special pains to learn from him all that I could about Paine, whose landlord he had been for eighteen months. He spoke of him as a base and shameless drunkard, utterly destitute of moral principle. His denunciations of the man were perfectly fearful, and fully confirmed, in my apprehension, all that had been written of Paine's immorality and repulsiveness."

Cheetham's *Life of Paine,* which was published the year that he died, and which has passed through several editions (we have three of them now before us) describes a man lost to all moral sensibility and to all sense of decency, a habitual drunkard, and it is simply incredible that a book should have appeared so soon after the death of its subject and should have been so frequently republished without being at once refuted, if the testimony were not substantially true. Many years later, when it was found necessary to bolster up the reputation of Paine, Cheetham's Memoirs were called a pack of lies. If only one-tenth part of what he publishes circumstantially in his volume, as facts in regard to Paine, were true, all that has been written against him in later years does not begin to set forth the degraded character of the man's life. And with all that has been written on the subject we see no good reason to doubt the substantial accuracy of Cheetham's portrait of the man whom he knew so well.

Dr. J. W. Francis, well-known as an eminent physician, of this city, in his Reminiscences of New York, says of Paine:

"He who, in his early days, had been associated with, and had received counsel from Franklin, was, in his old age, deserted by the humblest menial; he, whose pen has proved a very sword among nations, had shaken empires, and made kings tremble, now yielded up the mastery to the most treacherous of tyrants, King Alcohol."

The physician who attended Paine during his last illness was Dr. James R. Manley, a gentleman of the highest character. A letter of his, written in October of the year that Paine died, fully corroborates the account of his state as recorded by Stephen Grellet in his Memoirs, which we have already printed. He writes:

"New York, October 2, 1809: I was called upon by accident to visit Mr. Paine, on the 25th of February last, and found him indisposed with fever, and very apprehensive of an attack of apoplexy, as he stated that he had that disease before, and at this time felt a great degree of vertigo, and was unable to help himself as he had hitherto done, on account of an intense pain above the eyes. On inquiry of the attendants I was told that three or four days previously he had concluded to dispense with his usual quantity of accustomed stimulus and that he had on that day resumed it. To the want of his usual drink they attributed his illness, and it is highly probable that the usual quantity operating upon a state of system more excited from the above privations, was the cause of the symptoms of which he then complained. . . . And here let me be permitted to observe (lest blame might attach to those whose business it was to pay any particular attention to his cleanliness of person) that it was absolutely impossible to effect that purpose. Cleanliness appeared to make no part of his comfort; he seemed to have a singular aversion to soap and water; he would never ask to be washed, and when he was he would always make objections; and it was not unusual to wash and to dress him clean very much against his inclinations. In this deplorable state, with confirmed dropsy, attended with frequent cough, vomiting and hiccough, he continued growing from bad to worse till the morning of the 8th of June, when he died. Though I may remark that during the last three weeks of his life his situation was such that his decease was confidently expected every day, his ulcers having assumed a gangrenous appearance, being excessively fetid, and discolored blisters having taken place on the soles of his feet without any ostensible cause, which baffled the usual attempts to arrest their progress; and when we consider his former habits, his advanced age, the feebleness of his constitution, his constant habit of using ardent spirits *ad libitum* till the commencement of his last illness, so far from wondering that he died so soon, we are constrained to ask, How did he live so long? Concerning his conduct during his disease I have not much to remark, though the little I have may be somewhat interesting. Mr. Paine professed to be above the fear of death, and a great part of his conversation was principally directed to give the impression that he was perfectly willing to leave this world, and yet some parts of his conduct were with difficulty reconcilable with his belief. In the first stages of his illness he was satisfied to be left alone during the day, but he required some person to be with him at night, urging as his reason that he was afraid that he should die when unattended, and at this period his deportment and his principle seemed to be consistent; so much so that a stranger would judge from some of the remarks he would make that he was an Infidel. I recollect being with him at night, watching; he was very apprehensive of a speedy dissolution, and suffered great distress of body, and perhaps of mind (for he was waiting the event of an application to the Society of Friends for permission that his corpse might be deposited in their grave-ground, and had reason to believe that the request might be refused), when he remarked in these words, 'I think I can say what *they* made Jesus Christ to say—"My God, my God! why hast thou forsaken me?" He went on to observe on the want of that respect which he conceived he merited, when I observed to him that I thought his corpse should be matter of least concern to him; that those whom he would leave behind him would see that he was properly interred, and, further, that it would be of little consequence to *me* where I was deposited provided I was buried; upon which he answered that he had nothing else to talk about, and that he would as lief talk of his death as of anything, but that he was not so indifferent about his corpse as I appeared to be.

"During the latter part of his life, though his conversation was equivocal, his conduct was singular; he could not be left alone night or day; he not only required to have some person with him, but he must see that he or she was there, and would not allow his curtain to be closed at any time; and if, as it would sometimes unavoidably happen, he was left alone, he would scream and halloo until some person came to him. When relief from pain would admit, he seemed thoughtful and contemplative, his eyes being generally closed, and his hands folded upon his breast, although he never slept without the assistance of an anodyne. There was something remarkable in his conduct about this period (which comprises about two weeks immediately preceding his death), particularly when we reflect that Thomas Paine was the author of the 'Age of Reason.' He would call out during his paroxysms of distress, without intermission, 'O Lord help me! God help me! Jesus Christ help me! Lord help me!' etc., repeating the same expressions without the least variation, in a tone of voice that would alarm the house. It was this conduct which induced me to think that he had abandoned his former opinions, and I was more inclined to that belief when I understood from his nurse (who is a very serious and, I believe, pious woman), that he would occasionally inquire, when he saw her engaged with a book, what she was reading, and, being answered, and at the same time asked whether she should read aloud, he assented, and would appear to give particular attention.

"I took occasion during the nights of the fifth and sixth of June to test the strength of his opinions respecting revelation. I purposely made him a very late visit; it was a time which seemed to suit exactly with my errand; it was midnight, he was in great distress, constantly exclaiming in the words above mentioned, when, after a considerable preface, I addressed him in the following manner, the nurse being present: 'Mr. Paine, your opinions, by a large portion of the community, have been treated with deference, you have never been in the habit of mixing in your conversation words of coarse meaning; you have never indulged in the practice of profane swearing; you must be sensible that we are acquainted with your religious opinions as they are given to the world. What must we think of your present conduct? Why do you call upon Jesus Christ to help you? Do you believe that he can help you? Do you believe in the divinity of Jesus Christ? Come, now, answer me honestly. I want an answer from the lips of a dying man, for I verily believe that you will not live twenty-four hours.' I waited some time at the end of every question; he did not answer, but ceased to exclaim in the above manner. Again I addressed him; 'Mr. Paine, you have not answered my questions; will you answer them? Allow me to ask again, do you believe? or let me qualify the question, do you wish to believe that Jesus Christ is the Son of God?' After a pause of some minutes, he answered, 'I have no wish to believe on that subject.' I then left him, and knew not whether he afterward spoke to any person on any subject, though he lived, as I before observed, till the morning of the 8th. Such conduct, under usual circumstances, I conceive absolutely unaccountable, though, with diffidence, I would remark, not so much so in the present instance; for though the first necessary and general result of conviction be a sincere wish to atone for evil committed, yet it may be a question worthy of able consideration whether excessive pride of opinion, consummate vanity, and inordinate self-love might not prevent or retard that otherwise natural consequence. For my own part, I believe that had not Thomas Paine been such a distinguished Infidel he would have left less equivocal evidences of a change of opinion. Concerning the persons who visited Mr. Paine in his distress as his personal friends, I heard very little, though I may observe that their number was small, and of that number there were not wanting those who endeavored to support him in his deistical opinions, and to encourage him to 'die like a man,' to 'hold fast his integrity,' lest Christians, or, as they were pleased to term them, hypocrites, might take advantage of his weakness, and furnish themselves with a weapon by which they might hope to destroy their glorious system of morals. Numbers visited him from motives of benevolence and Christian charity, endeavoring to effect a change of mind in respect to his religious sentiments. The labor of such was apparently lost, and they pretty generally received such treatment from him as none but good men would risk a second time, though some of those persons called frequently."

The following testimony will be new to most of our readers. It is from a letter written by Bishop Fenwick (Roman Catholic Bishop of Boston), containing a full account of a visit which he paid to Paine in his last illness. It was printed in the *United States Catholic Magazine* for 1846; in the *Catholic Herald* of Philadelphia, October 15, 1846; in a supplement to the *Hartford Courant,* October 23, 1847; and in Littell's *Living Age* for January 22, 1848, from which we copy. Bishop Fenwick writes:

"A short time before Paine died I was sent for by him. He was prompted to this by a poor Catholic woman who went to see him in his sickness, and who told him, among other things, that in his wretched condition if anybody could do him any good it would be a Roman Catholic priest. This woman was an American convert (formerly a Shaking Quakeress) whom I had received into the church but a few weeks before. She was the bearer of this message to me from Paine. I stated this circumstance to F. Kohlmann, at breakfast, and requested him to accompany me. After some solicitation on my part he agreed to do so? at which I was greatly rejoiced, because I was at the time quite young and inexperienced in the ministry, and was glad to have his assistance, as I knew, from the great reputation of Paine, that I should have to do with one of the most impious as well as infamous of men. We shortly after set out for the house at Greenwich where Paine lodged, and on the way agreed on a mode of proceeding with him.

"We arrived at the house; a decent-looking elderly woman (probably his housekeéper,) came to the door and inquired whether we were the Catholic priests, for said she, 'Mr. Paine has been so much annoyed of late by other denominations calling upon him that he has left express orders with me to admit no one to-day but the clergymen of the Catholic Church. Upon assuring her that we were Catholic clergymen she opened the door and showed us into the parlor. She then left the room and shortly after returned to inform us that Paine was asleep, and, at the same time, expressed a wish that we would not disturb him, 'for,' said she, 'he is always in a bad humor when roused out of his sleep. It is better we wait a little till he be awake.' We accordingly sat down and resolved to await a more favorable moment. 'Gentlemen,' said the lady, after having taken her seat also, 'I really wish you may succeed with Mr. Paine, for he is laboring under great distress of mind ever since he was informed by his physicians that he cannot possibly live and must die shortly. He sent for you today because he was told that if any one could do him good you might. Possibly he may think you know of some remedy which his physicians are ignorant of. He is truly to be pitied. His cries when he is left alone are heart-rending. 'O Lord help me!' he will exclaim during his paroxysms of distress—'God help me—Jesus Christ help me!' repeating the same expressions without the least variation, in a tone of voice that would alarm the house. Sometimes he will say, 'O God, what have I done to suffer so much!' then, shortly after, 'But there is no God,' and again a little after, 'Yet if there should be, what would become of me hereafter.' Thus he will continue for some time, when on a sudden he will scream, as if in terror and agony, and call out for me by name. On one of these occasions, which are very frequent, I went to him and inquired what he wanted. 'Stay with me,' he replied, 'for God's sake, for I cannot bear to be left alone.' I then observed that I could not always be with him, as I had much to attend to in the house. 'Then,' said he, 'send even a child to stay with me, for it is a hell to be alone.' 'I never saw,' she concluded, 'a more unhappy, a more forsaken man. It seems he cannot reconcile himself to die.'

"Such was the conversation of the woman who had received us, and who probably had been employed to nurse and take care of him during his illness. She was a Protestant, yet seemed very desirous that we should afford him some relief in his state of abandonment, bordering on complete despair. Having remained thus some time in the parlor, we at length heard a noise in the adjoining passage-way, which induced us to believe that Mr. Paine, who was sick in that room, had awoke. We accordingly proposed to proceed thither, which was assented to by the woman, and she opened the door for us. On entering, we found him just getting out of his slumber. A more wretched being in appearance I never beheld. He was lying in a bed sufficiently decent of itself, but at present besmeared with filth; his look was that of a man greatly tortured in mind; his eyes haggard, his countenance forbidding, and his whole appearance that of one whose better days had been one continued scene of debauch. His only nourishment at this time, as we were informed, was nothing more than milk punch, in which he indulged to the full extent of his weak state. He had partaken, undoubtedly, but very recently of it, as the sides and corners of his mouth exhibited very unequivocal traces of it, as well as of blood, which had also followed in the track and left its mark on the pillow. His face, to a certain extent, had also been besmeared with it."

Immediately upon their making known the object of their visit, Paine interrupted the speaker by saying: "That's enough, sir; that's enough," and again interrupting him, "I see what you would be about. I wish to hear no more from you, sir. My mind is made up on that subject. I look upon the whole of the Christian scheme to be a tissue of absurdities and lies, and Jesus Christ to be nothing more than a cunning knave and impostor." He drove them out of the room, exclaiming: Away with you and your God, too; leave the room instantly; all that you have uttered are lies—filthy lies; and if I had a little more time I would prove it, as I did about your impostor, Jesus Christ."

This, we think, will suffice. We have a mass of letters containing statements confirmatory of what we have published in regard to the life and death of Paine, but nothing more can be required.

INGERSOLL'S SECOND REPLY.

Peoria, Nov. 2d, 1877.

To the Editor of the New York Observer:

You ought to have honesty enough to admit that you did, in your paper of July 19th, offer to prove that the absurd story that Thomas Paine died in terror and agony on account of the religious opinions he had expressed, was true. You ought to have fairness enough to admit that you called upon me to deposit one thousand dollars with an honest man, that you might, by proving that Thomas Paine did die in terror, obtain the money.

You ought to have honor enough to admit that you challenged me and that you commenced the controversy concerning Thomas Paine.

You ought to have goodness enough to admit that you were mistaken in the charges you made.

You ought to have manhood enough to do what you falsely asserted that Thomas Paine did:—you ought to recant. You ought to admit publicly that you slandered the dead; that you falsified history; that you defamed the defenseless; that you deliberately denied what you had published in your own paper. There is an old saying to the effect that open confession is good for the soul. To you is presented a splendid opportunity of testing the truth of this saying.

Nothing has astonished me more than your lack of common honesty exhibited in this controversy. In your last, you quote from Dr. J. W. Francis. Why did you leave out that portion in which Dr. Francis says *that Cheetham with settled malignity wrote the life of Paine?* Why did you leave out that part in which Dr. Francis says that Cheetham in the same way *slandered Alexander Hamilton and De Witt Clinton?* Is it your business to suppress the truth? Why did you not publish the entire letter of Bishop Fenwick? Was it because it proved beyond all cavil that Thomas Paine did not recant? Was it because in the light of that letter Mary Roscoe, Mary Hinsdale and Grant Thorburn appeared un- worthy of belief? Dr. J. W. Francis says in the same article from which you quoted, "*Paine clung to his Infidelity until the last moment of his life!'* Why did you not publish that? It was the first line immediately above what you did quote. You must have seen it. Why did you suppress it? A lawyer, doing a thing of this character, is denominated a shyster. I do not know the appropriate word to designate a theologian guilty of such an act.

You brought forward three witnesses, pretending to have personal knowledge about the life and death of Thomas Paine: Grant Thorburn, Mary Roscoe and Mary Hinsdale. In my reply I took the ground that Mary Roscoe and Mary Hinsdale must have been the same person. I thought it impossible that Paine should have had a conversation with Mary Roscoe, and then one *precisely* like it with Mary Hinsdale. Acting upon this conviction, I proceeded to show that the conversation never could have happened, that it was absurdly false to say that Paine asked the opinion of a girl as to his works who had never read but little of them. I then showed by the testimony of William Cobbett, that he visited Mary Hinsdale in 1819, taking with him a statement concerning the recantation of Paine, given him by Mr. Collins, and that upon being shown this statement she said that "it was so long ago that she could not speak positively to any part of the matter—that she would not say any part of the paper was true." At that time she knew nothing, and remembered nothing. I also showed that she was a kind of standing witness to prove that others recanted. Willett Hicks denounced her as unworthy of belief.

Today the following from the New York World was received, showing that I was right in my conjecture:

Tom Paine's Death-Bed.

To the Editor of the World:

Sir: I see by your paper that Bob Ingersoll discredits Mary Hinsdale's story of the scenes which occurred at the death-bed of Thomas Paine. No one who knew that good lady would for one moment doubt her veracity or question her testimony. Both she and her husband were Quaker preachers, and well known and respected inhabitants of New York City, *Ingersoll is right in his conjecture that Mary Roscoe and Mary Hinsdale was the same person.* Her maiden name was Roscoe, and she married Henry Hinsdale. My mother was a Roscoe, a niece of Mary Roscoe, and lived with her for some time. I have heard her relate the story of Tom Paine's dying remorse, as told her by her aunt, who was a witness to it. She says (in a letter I have just received from her), "he (Tom Paine) suffered fearfully from remorse, and renounced his Infidel principles, calling on God to forgive him, and wishing his pamphlets and books to be burned, saying he could not die in peace until it was done."

(Rev.) A. W. Cornell.

Harpersville, New York.

You will notice that the testimony of Mary Hinsdale has been drawing interest since 1809, and has materially increased. If Paine "suffered fearfully from remorse, renounced his Infidel opinions and called on God to forgive him," it is hardly generous for the Christian world to fasten the fangs of malice in the flesh of his reputation.

So Mary Roscoe was Mary Hinsdale, and as Mary Hinsdale has been shown by her own admission to Mr. Cobbett to have known nothing of the matter; and as Mary Hinsdale was not, according to Willet Hicks, worthy of belief—as she told a falsehood of the same kind about Mary Lockwood, and was, according to Mr. Collins, addicted to the use of opium—this disposes of her and her testimony.

There remains upon the stand Grant Thorburn. Concerning this witness, I received, yesterday, from the eminent biographer and essayist, James Parton, the following epistle:

Newburyport, Mass.

Col. R. G. Ingersoll:

Touching Grant Thorburn, I personally know him to have been a dishonest man. At the age of ninety-two he copied, with trembling hand, a piece from a newspaper and brought it to the office of the *Home Journal, as his own.* It was I who received it and detected the deliberate forgery. If you are ever going to continue this subject, I will give you the exact facts.

Fervently yours,
James Parton.

After this, you are welcome to what remains of Grant Thorburn.

There is one thing that I have noticed during this controversy regarding Thomas Paine. In no instance that I now call to mind has any Christian writer spoken respectfully of Mr. Paine. All have taken particular pains to call him "Tom" Paine. Is it not a little strange that religion should make men so coarse and ill-mannered?

I have often wondered what these same gentlemen would say if I should speak of the men eminent in the annals of Christianity in the same way. What would they say if I should write about "Tim" Dwight, old "Ad" Clark, "Tom" Scott, "Jim" McKnight, "Bill" Hamilton, "Dick" Whately, "Bill" Paley, and "Jack" Calvin?

They would say of me then, just what I *think* of them now.

Even if we have religion, do not let us try to get along without good manners. Rudeness is exceedingly unbecoming, even in a saint. Persons who forgive their enemies ought, to say the least, to treat with politeness those who have never injured them.

It is exceedingly gratifying to me that I have compelled you to say that "Paine died a blaspheming Infidel." Hereafter it is to be hoped nothing will be heard about his having recanted. As an answer to such slander his friends can confidently quote the following from the *New York Observer* of November 1st, 1877:

"WE HAVE NEVER STATED IN ANY FORM, NOR HAVE WE EVER SUPPOSED THAT PAINE ACTUALLY RENOUNCED HIS INFIDELITY. THE ACCOUNTS AGREE IN STATING THAT HE DIED A BLASPHEMING INFIDEL."

This for all coming time will refute the slanders of the churches yet to be.

Right here allow me to ask: If you never supposed that Paine renounced his Infidelity, why did you try to prove by Mary Hinsdale that which you believed to be untrue?

From the bottom of my heart I thank myself for having compelled you to admit that Thomas Paine did not recant.

For the purpose of verifying your own admission concerning the death of Mr. Paine, permit me to call your attention to the following affidavit:

Wabash, Indiana, October 27, 1877.

Col. R. G. Ingersoll:

Dear Sir: The following statement of facts is at your disposal. In the year 1833 Willet Hicks made a visit to Indiana and stayed over night at my father's house, four miles east of Richmond. In the morning at breakfast my mother asked Willet Hicks the following questions:

"Was thee with Thomas Paine during his last sickness?"

Mr. Hicks said: "I was with him every day during the latter part of his last sickness."

"Did he express any regret in regard to writing the 'Age of Reason,' as the published accounts say he did—those accounts that have the credit of emanating from his Catholic housekeeper?"

Mr. Hicks replied: "He did not in any way by word or action."

"Did he call on God or Jesus Christ, asking either of them to forgive his sins, or did he curse them or either of them?"

Mr. Hicks answered: "He did not. He died as easy as any one I ever saw die, and I have seen many die in my time."

William B Barnes.

Subscribed and sworn to before me Oct. 27, 1877.

Warren Bigler, Notary Public.

You say in your last that "Thomas Paine was abandoned of God." So far as this controversy is concerned, it seems to me that in that sentence you have most graphically described your own condition.

Wishing you success in all honest undertakings, I remain,

Yours truly,

Robert G. Ingersoll.

VOLUME SIX

Robert Ingersoll, 1876

THE CHRISTIAN RELIGION.

In the presence of eternity the mountains are as transient as the clouds.

A Profound change has taken place in the world of thought. The pews are trying to set themselves somewhat above the pulpit. The layman discusses theology with the minister, and smiles. Christians excuse themselves for belonging to the church, by denying a part of the creed. The idea is abroad that they who know the most of nature believe the least about theology. The sciences are regarded as infidels, and facts as scoffers. Thousands of most excellent people avoid churches, and, with few exceptions, only those attend prayer-meetings who wish to be alone. The pulpit is losing because the people are growing.

Of course it is still claimed that we are a Christian people, indebted to something called Christianity for all the progress we have made. There is still a vast difference of opinion as to what Christianity really is, although many warring sects have been discussing that question, with fire and sword, through centuries of creed and crime. Every new sect has been denounced at its birth as illegitimate, as a something born out of orthodox wedlock, and that should have been allowed to perish on the steps where it was found. Of the relative merits of the various denominations, it is sufficient to say that each claims to be right. Among the evangelical churches there is a substantial agreement upon what they consider the fundamental truths of the gospel. These fundamental truths, as I understand them, are:

That there is a personal God, the creator of the material universe; that he made man of the dust, and woman from part of the man; that the man and woman were tempted by the devil; that they were turned out of the Garden of Eden; that, about fifteen hundred years afterward, God's patience having been exhausted by the wickedness of mankind, he drowned his children with the exception of eight persons; that afterward he selected from their descendants Abraham, and through him the Jewish people; that he gave laws to these people, and tried to govern them in all things; that he made known his will in many ways; that he wrought a vast number of miracles; that he inspired men to write the Bible; that, in the fullness of time, it having been found impossible to reform mankind, this God came upon earth as a child born of the Virgin Mary; that he lived in Palestine; that he preached for about three years, going from place to place, occasionally raising the dead, curing the blind and the halt; that he was crucified—for the crime of blasphemy, as the Jews supposed, but that, as a matter of fact, he was offered as a sacrifice for the sins of all who might have faith in him; that he was raised from the dead and ascended into heaven, where he now is, making intercession for his followers; that he will forgive the sins of all who believe on him, and that those who do not believe will be consigned to the dungeons of eternal pain. These—it may be with the addition of the sacraments of Baptism and the Last Supper—constitute what is generally known as the Christian religion.

It is most cheerfully admitted that a vast number of people not only believe these things, but hold them in exceeding reverence, and imagine them to be of the utmost importance to mankind. They regard the Bible as the only light that God has given for the guidance of his children; that it is the one star in nature's sky—the foundation of all morality, of all law, of all order, and of all individual and national progress. They regard it as the only means we have for ascertaining the will of God, the origin of man, and the destiny of the soul.

It is needless to inquire into the causes that have led so many people to believe in the inspiration of the Scriptures. In my opinion, they were and are mistaken, and the mistake has hindered, in countless ways, the civilization of man. The Bible has been the fortress and defense of nearly every crime. No civilized country could re-enact its laws, and in many respects its moral code is abhorrent to every good and tender man. It is admitted that many of its precepts are pure, that many of its laws are wise and just, and that many of its statements are absolutely true.

Without desiring to hurt the feeling? of anybody, I propose to give a few reasons for thinking that a few passages, at least, in the Old Testament are the product of a barbarous people.

In all civilized countries it is not only admitted, but it is passionately asserted, that slavery is and always was a hideous crime; that a war of conquest is simply murder; that polygamy is the enslavement of woman, the degradation of man, and the destruction of home; that nothing is more infamous than the slaughter of decrepit men, of helpless women, and of prattling babes; that captured maidens should not be given to soldiers; that wives should not be stoned to death on account of their religious opinions, and that the death penalty ought not to be inflicted for a violation of the Sabbath. We know that there was a time, in the history of almost every nation, when slavery, polygamy, and wars of extermination were regarded as divine institutions; when women were looked upon as beasts of burden, and when, among some people, it was considered the duty of the husband to murder the wife for differing with him on the subject of religion. Nations that entertain these views to-day are regarded as savage, and, probably, with the exception of the South Sea Islanders, the Fijis, some citizens of Delaware, and a few tribes in Central Africa, no human beings can be found degraded enough to agree upon these subjects with the Jehovah of the ancient Jews. The only evidence we have, or can have, that a nation has ceased to be savage is the fact that it has abandoned these doctrines. To every one, except the theologian, it is perfectly easy to account for the mistakes, atrocities, and crimes of the past, by saying that civilization is a slow and painful growth; that the moral perceptions are cultivated through ages of tyranny, of want, of crime, and of heroism; that it requires centuries for man to put out the eyes of self and hold in lofty and in equal poise the scales of justice; that conscience is born of suffering; that mercy is the child of the imagination—of the power to put oneself in the sufferer's place, and that man advances only as he becomes acquainted with his surroundings, with the mutual obligations of life, and learns to take advantage of the forces of nature.

But the believer in the inspiration of the Bible is compelled to declare that there was a time when slavery was right—when men could buy, and women could sell, their babes. He is compelled to insist that there was a time when polygamy was the highest form of virtue; when wars of extermination were waged with the sword of mercy; when religious toleration was a crime, and when death was the just penalty for having expressed an honest thought. He must maintain that Jehovah is just as bad now as he was four thousand years ago, or that he was just as good then as he is now, but that human conditions have so changed that slavery, polygamy, religious persecutions, and wars of conquest are now perfectly devilish. Once they were right—once they were commanded by God himself; now, they are prohibited. There has been such a change in the conditions of man that, at the present time, the devil is in favor of slavery, polygamy, religious persecution, and wars of conquest. That is to say, the devil entertains the same opinion today that Jehovah held four thousand years ago, but in the meantime Jehovah has remained exactly the same—changeless and incapable of change.

We find that other nations beside the Jews had similar laws and ideas; that they believed in and practiced slavery and polygamy, murdered women and children, and exterminated their neighbors to the extent of their power. It is not claimed that they received a revelation. It is admitted that they had no knowledge of the true God. And yet, by a strange coincidence, they practiced the same crimes, of their own motion, that the Jews did by the command of Jehovah. From this it would seem that man can do wrong without a special revelation.

It will hardly be claimed, at this day, that the passages in the Bible upholding slavery, polygamy, war and religious persecution are evidences of the inspiration of that book. Suppose that there had been nothing in the Old Testament upholding these crimes, would any modern Christian suspect that it was not inspired, on account of the omission? Suppose that there had been nothing in the Old Testament but laws in favor of these crimes, would any intelligent Christian now contend that it was the work of the true God? If the devil had inspired a book, will some believer in the doctrine of inspiration tell us in what respect, on the subjects of slavery, polygamy, war, and liberty, it would have differed from some parts of the Old Testament? Suppose that we should now discover a Hindu book of equal antiquity with the Old Testament, containing a defense of slavery, polygamy, wars of extermination, and religious persecution, would we regard it as evidence that the writers were inspired by an infinitely wise and merciful God? As most other nations at that time practiced these crimes, and as the Jews would have practiced them all, even if left to themselves, one can hardly see the necessity of any inspired commands upon these subjects. Is there a believer in the Bible who does not wish that God, amid the thunders and lightnings of Sinai, had distinctly said to Moses that man should not own his fellow-man; that women should not sell their babes; that men should be allowed to think and investigate for themselves, and that the sword should never be unsheathed to shed the blood of honest men? Is there a believer in the world, who would not be delighted to find that every one of these infamous passages are interpolations, and that the skirts of God were never reddened by the blood of maiden, wife, or babe? Is there a believer who does not regret that God commanded a husband to stone his wife to death for suggesting the worship of the sun or moon? Surely, the light of experience is enough to tell us that slavery is wrong, that polygamy is infamous, and that murder is not a virtue. No one will now contend that it was worth God's while to impart the information to Moses, or to Joshua, or to anybody else, that the Jewish people might purchase slaves of the heathen, or that it was their duty to exterminate the natives of the Holy Land. The deists have contended that the Old Testament is too cruel and barbarous to be the work of a wise and loving God. To this, the theologians have replied, that nature is just as cruel; that the earthquake, the volcano, the pestilence and storm, are just as savage as the Jewish God; and to my mind this is a perfect answer.

Suppose that we knew that after "inspired" men had finished the Bible, the devil got possession of it, and wrote a few passages; what part of the sacred Scriptures would Christians now pick out as being probably his work? Which of the following passages would naturally be selected as having been written by the devil—"Love thy neighbor as thyself," or "Kill all the males among the little ones, and kill every woman; but all the women children keep alive for yourselves."?

It may be that the best way to illustrate what I have said of the Old Testament is to compare some of the supposed teachings of Jehovah with those of persons who never read an "inspired" line, and who lived and died without having received the light of revelation. Nothing can be more suggestive than a comparison of the ideas of Jehovah—the inspired words of the one claimed to be the infinite God, as recorded in the Bible—with those that have been expressed by men who, all admit, received no help from heaven.

In all ages of which any record has been preserved, there have been those who gave their ideas of justice, charity, liberty, love and law. Now, if the Bible is really the work of God, it should contain the grandest and sublimest truths. It should, in all respects, excel the works of man. Within that book should be found the best and loftiest definitions of justice; the truest conceptions of human liberty; the clearest outlines of duty; the tenderest, the highest, and the noblest thoughts,—not that the human mind has produced, but that the human mind is capable of receiving. Upon every page should be found the luminous evidence of its divine origin. Unless it contains grander and more wonderful things than man has written, we are not only justified in saying, but we are compelled to say, that it was written by no being superior to man. It may be said that it is unfair to call attention to certain bad things in the Bible, while the good are not so much as mentioned. To this it may be replied that a divine being would not put bad things in a book. Certainly a being of infinite intelligence, power, and goodness could never fall below the ideal of "depraved and barbarous" man. It will not do, after we find that the Bible upholds what we now call crimes, to say that it is not verbally inspired. If the words are not inspired, what is? It may be said that the thoughts are inspired. But this would include only the thoughts expressed without words. If ideas are inspired, they must be contained in and expressed only by inspired words; that is to say, the arrangement of the words, with relation to each other, must have been inspired. For the purpose of this perfect arrangement, the writers, according to the Christian world, were inspired. Were some sculptor inspired of God to make a statue perfect in its every part, we would not say that the marble was inspired, but the statue—the relation of part to part, the married harmony of form and function. The language, the words, take the place of the marble, and it is the arrangement of these words that Christians claim to be inspired. If there is one uninspired word,—that is, one word in the wrong place, or a word that ought not to be there,—to that extent the Bible is an uninspired book. The moment it is admitted that some words are not, in their arrangement as to other words, inspired, then, unless with absolute certainty these words can be pointed out, a doubt is cast on all the words the book contains. If it was worth God's while to make a revelation to man at all, it was certainly worth his while to see that it was correctly made. He would not have allowed the ideas and mistakes of pretended prophets and designing priests to become so mingled with the original text that it is impossible to tell where he ceased and where the priests and prophets began. Neither will it do to say that God adapted his revelation to the prejudices of mankind. Of course it was necessary for an infinite being to adapt his revelation to the intellectual capacity of man; but why should God confirm a barbarian in his prejudices? Why should he fortify a heathen in his crimes? If a revelation is of any importance whatever, it is to eradicate prejudices from the human mind. It should be a lever with which to raise the human race. Theologians Have exhausted their ingenuity in finding excuses for God. It seems to me that they would be better employed in finding excuses for men. They tell us that the Jews were so cruel and ignorant that God was compelled to justify, or nearly to justify, many of their crimes, in order to have any influence with them whatever. They tell us that if he had declared slavery and polygamy to be criminal, the Jews would have refused to receive the Ten Commandments. They insist that, under the circumstances, God did the best he could; that his real intention was to lead them along slowly, step by step, so that, in a few hundred years, they would be induced to admit that it was hardly fair to steal a babe from its mother's breast. It has always seemed reasonable that an infinite God ought to have been able to make man grand enough to know, even without a special revelation, that it is not altogether right to steal the labor, or the wife, or the child, of another. When the whole question is thoroughly examined, the world will find that Jehovah had the prejudices, the hatreds, and superstitions of his day.

If there is anything of value, it is liberty. Liberty is the air of the soul, the sunshine of life. Without it the world is a prison and the universe an infinite dungeon.

If the Bible is really inspired, Jehovah commanded the Jewish people to buy the children of the strangers that sojourned among them, and ordered that the children thus bought should be an inheritance for the children of the Jews, and that they should be bondmen and bondwomen forever. Yet Epictetus, a man to whom no revelation was made, a man whose soul followed only the light of nature, and who had never heard of the Jewish God, was great enough to say: "Will you not remember that your servants are by nature your brothers, the children of God? In saying that you have bought them, you look down on the earth, and into the pit, on the wretched law of men long since dead, but you see not the laws of the gods."

We find that Jehovah, speaking to his chosen people, assured them that their bondmen and their bondmaids must be "of the heathen that were round about them." "Of them," said Jehovah, "shall ye buy bondmen and bondmaids." And yet Cicero, a pagan, Cicero, who had never been enlightened by reading the Old Testament, had the moral grandeur to declare: "They who say that we should love our fellow-citizens, but not foreigners, destroy the universal brotherhood of mankind, with which benevolence and justice would perish forever."

If the Bible is inspired, Jehovah, God of all worlds, actually said: "And if a man smite his servant or his maid with a rod, and he die under his hand, he shall be surely punished; notwithstanding, if he continue a day or two, he shall not be punished, for he is his money." And yet Zeno, founder of the Stoics, centuries before Christ was born, insisted that no man could be the owner of another, and that the title was bad, whether the slave had become so by conquest, or by purchase. Jehovah ordered a Jewish general to make war, and gave, among others, this command: "When the Lord thy God shall drive them before thee, thou shalt smite them and utterly destroy them; thou shalt make no covenant with them, nor show mercy unto them." And yet Epictetus, whom we have already quoted, gave this marvelous rule for the guidance of human conduct: "Live with thy inferiors as thou would'st have thy superiors live with thee."

Is it possible, after all, that a being of infinite goodness and wisdom said: "I will heap mischief upon them: I will spend mine arrows upon them. They shall be burnt with hunger, and devoured with burning heat, and with bitter destruction: I will also send the teeth of beasts upon them, with the poison of serpents of the dust. The sword without, and terror within, shall destroy both the young man and the virgin, the suckling also, with the man of gray hairs"; while Seneca, an uninspired Roman, said: "The wise man will not pardon any crime that ought to be punished, but he will accomplish, in a nobler way, all that is sought in pardoning. He will spare some and watch over some, because of their youth, and others on account of their ignorance. His clemency will not fall short of justice, but will fulfill it perfectly."

Can we believe that God ever said of any one: "Let his children be fatherless and his wife a widow; let his children be continually vagabonds, and beg; let them seek their bread also out of their desolate places; let the extortioner catch all that he hath and let the stranger spoil his labor; let there be none to extend mercy unto him, neither let there be any to favor his fatherless children." If he ever said these words, surely he had never heard this line, this strain of music, from the

Hindu: "Sweet is the lute to those who have not heard the prattle of their own children."

Jehovah, "from the clouds and darkness of Sinai," said to the Jews: "Thou shalt have no other Gods before me.... Thou shalt not bow down thyself to them nor serve them; for I, the Lord thy God, am a jealous God, visiting the iniquities of the fathers upon the children, unto the third and fourth generation of them that hate me." Contrast this with the words put by the Hindu into the mouth of Brahma:

"I am the same to all mankind. They who honestly serve other gods, involuntarily worship me. I am he who partaketh of all worship, and I am the reward of all worshipers."

Compare these passages. The first, a dungeon where crawl the things begot of jealous slime; the other, great as the domed firmament inlaid with suns.

II.

Waiving the contradictory statements in the various books of the New Testament; leaving out of the question the history of the manuscripts; saying nothing about the errors in translation and the interpolations made by the fathers; and admitting, for the time being, that the books were all written at the times claimed, and by the persons whose names they bear, the questions of inspiration, probability, and absurdity still remain.

As a rule, where several persons testify to the same transaction, while agreeing in the main points, they will disagree upon many minor things, and such disagreement upon minor matters is generally considered as evidence that the witnesses have not agreed among themselves upon the story they should tell. These differences in statement we account for from the facts that all did not see alike, that all did not have the same opportunity for seeing, and that all had not equally good memories. But when we claim that the witnesses were inspired, we must admit that he who inspired them did know exactly what occurred, and consequently there should be no contradiction, even in the minutest detail. The accounts should be not only substantially, but they should be actually, the same. It is impossible to account for any differences, or any contradictions, except from the weaknesses of human nature, and these weaknesses cannot be predicated of divine wisdom. Why should there be more than one correct account of anything? Why were four gospels necessary? One inspired record of all that happened ought to be enough.

One great objection to the Old Testament is the cruelty said to have been commanded by God, but all the cruelties recounted in the Old Testament ceased with death. The vengeance of Jehovah stopped at the portal of the tomb. He never threatened to avenge himself upon the dead; and not one word, from the first mistake in Genesis to the last curse of Malachi, contains the slightest intimation that God will punish in another world. It was reserved for the New Testament to make known the frightful doctrine of eternal pain. It was the teacher of universal benevolence who rent the veil between time and eternity, and fixed the horrified gaze of man on the lurid gulfs of hell. Within the breast of non-resistance was coiled the worm that never dies.

One great objection to the New Testament is that it bases salvation upon belief. This, at least, is true of the Gospel according to John, and of many of the Epistles. I admit that Matthew never heard of the atonement, and died utterly ignorant of the scheme of salvation. I also admit that Mark never dreamed that it was necessary for a man to be born again; that he knew nothing of the mysterious doctrine of regeneration, and that he never even suspected that it was necessary to believe anything. In the sixteenth chapter of Mark, we are told that "He that believeth and is baptized shall be saved, but he that believeth not shall be damned"; but this passage has been shown to be an interpolation, and, consequently, not a solitary word is found in the Gospel according to Mark upon the subject of salvation by faith. The same is also true of the Gospel of Luke. It says not one word as to the necessity of believing on Jesus Christ, not one word as to the atonement, not one word upon the scheme of salvation, and not the slightest hint that it is necessary to believe anything here in order to be happy hereafter.

And I here take occasion to say, that with most of the teachings of the Gospels of Matthew, Mark, and Luke I most heartily agree. The miraculous parts must, of course, be thrown aside. I admit that the necessity of belief, the atonement, and the scheme of salvation are all set forth in the Gospel of John,—a gospel, in my opinion, not written until long after the others.

According to the prevailing Christian belief, the Christian religion rests upon the doctrine of the atonement. If this doctrine is without foundation, if it is repugnant to justice and mercy, the fabric falls. We are told that the first man committed a crime for which all his posterity are responsible,—in other words, that we are accountable, and can be justly punished for a sin we never in fact committed. This absurdity was the father of another, namely, that a man can be rewarded for a good action done by another. God, according to the modern theologians, made a law, with the penalty of eternal death for its infraction. All men, they say, have broken that law. In the economy of heaven, this law had to be vindicated. This could be done by damning the whole human race. Through what is known as the atonement, the salvation of a few was made possible. They insist that the law—whatever that is—demanded the extreme penalty, that justice called for its victims, and that even mercy ceased to plead. Under these circumstances, God, by allowing the innocent to suffer, satisfactorily settled with the law, and allowed a few of the guilty to escape. The law was satisfied with this arrangement. To carry out this scheme, God was born as a babe into this world. "He grew in stature and increased in knowledge." At the age of thirty-three, after having lived a life filled with kindness, charity and nobility, after having practiced every virtue, he was sacrificed as an atonement for man. It is claimed that he actually took our place, and bore our sins and our guilt; that in this way the justice of God was satisfied, and that the blood of Christ was an atonement, an expiation, for the sins of all who might believe on him.

Under the Mosaic dispensation, there was no remission of sin except through the shedding of blood. If a man committed certain sins, he must bring to the priest a lamb, a bullock, a goat, or a pair of turtle-doves. The priest would lay his hands upon the animal, and the sin of the man would be transferred. Then the animal would be killed in the place of the real sinner, and the blood thus shed and sprinkled upon the altar would be an atonement. In this way Jehovah was satisfied. The greater the crime, the greater the sacrifice—the more blood, the greater the atonement. There was always a certain ratio between the value of the animal and the enormity of the sin. The most minute directions were given about the killing of these animals, and about the sprinkling of their blood. Every priest became a butcher, and every sanctuary a slaughter-house. Nothing could be more utterly shocking to a refined and loving soul. Nothing could have been better calculated to harden the heart than this continual shedding of innocent blood. This terrible system is supposed to have culminated in the sacrifice of Christ. His blood took the place of all other. It is necessary to shed no more. The law at last is satisfied, satiated, surfeited. The idea that God wants blood is at the bottom of the atonement, and rests upon the most fearful savagery. How can sin be transferred from men to animals, and how can the shedding of the blood of animals atone for the sins of men?

The church says that the sinner is in debt to God, and that the obligation is discharged by the Savior. The best that can possibly be said of such a transaction is, that the debt is transferred, not paid. The truth is, that a sinner is in debt to the person he has injured. If a man injures his neighbor, it is not enough for him to get the forgiveness of God, but he must have the forgiveness of his neighbor. If a man puts his hand in the fire and God forgives him, his hand will smart exactly the same. You must, after all, reap what you sow. No god can give you wheat when you sow tares, and no devil can give you tares when you sow wheat.

There are in nature neither rewards nor punishments—there are consequences. The life of Christ is worth its example, its moral force, its heroism of benevolence.

To make innocence suffer is the greatest sin; how then is it possible to make the suffering of the innocent a justification for the criminal? Why should a man be willing to let the innocent suffer for him? Does not the willingness show that he is utterly unworthy of the sacrifice? Certainly, no man would be fit for heaven who would consent that an innocent person should suffer for his sin. What would we think of a man who would allow another to die for a crime that he himself had committed? What would we think of a law that allowed the innocent to take the place of the guilty? Is it possible to vindicate a just law by inflicting punishment on the innocent? Would not that be a second violation instead of a vindication?

If there was no general atonement until the crucifixion of Christ, what became of the countless millions who died before that time? And it must be remembered that the blood shed by the Jews was not for other nations. Jehovah hated foreigners. The Gentiles were left without forgiveness What has become of the millions who have died since, without having heard of the atonement? What becomes of those who have heard but have not believed? It seems to me that the doctrine of the atonement is absurd, unjust, and immoral. Can a law be satisfied by the execution of the wrong person? When a man commits a crime, the law demands his punishment, not that of a substitute; and there can be no law, human or divine, that can be satisfied by the punishment of a substitute. Can there be a law that demands that the guilty be rewarded? And yet, to reward the guilty is far nearer justice than to punish the innocent.

According to the orthodox theology, there would have been no heaven had no atonement been made. All the children of men would have been cast into hell forever. The old men bowed with grief, the smiling mothers, the sweet babes, the loving maidens, the brave, the tender, and the just, would have been given over to eternal pain. Man, it is claimed, can make no atonement for himself. If he commits one sin, and with that exception lives a life of perfect virtue, still that one sin would remain unexpiated, unatoned, and for that one sin he would be forever lost. To be saved by the goodness of another, to be a redeemed debtor forever, has in it something repugnant to manhood.

We must also remember that Jehovah took special charge of the Jewish people; and we have always been taught that he did so for the purpose of civilizing them. If he had succeeded in civilizing the Jews, he would have made the damnation of the entire human race a certainty; because, if the Jews had been a civilized people when Christ appeared,— a people whose hearts had not been hardened by the laws and teachings of Jehovah,—they would not have crucified him, and, as a consequence, the world would have been lost. If the Jews had believed in religious freedom,—in the right of thought and speech,—not a human soul could ever have been saved. If, when Christ was on his way to Calvary, some brave, heroic soul had rescued him from the holy mob, he would not only have been eternally damned for his pains, but would have rendered impossible the salvation of any human being, and, except for the crucifixion of her son, the Virgin Mary, if the church is right, would be today among the lost.

In countless ways the Christian world has endeavored, for nearly two thousand years, to explain the atonement, and every effort has ended in an admission that it cannot be understood, and a declaration that it must be believed. Is it not immoral to teach that man can sin, that he can harden his heart and pollute his soul, and that, by repenting and believing something that he does not comprehend, he can avoid the consequences of his crimes? Has the promise and hope of forgiveness ever prevented the commission of a sin? Should men be taught that sin gives happiness here; that they ought to bear the evils of a virtuous life in this world for the sake of joy in the next; that they can repent between the last sin and the last breath; that after repentance every stain of the soul is washed away by the innocent blood of another; that the serpent of regret will not hiss in the ear of memory; that the saved will not even pity the victims of their own crimes; that the goodness of another can be transferred to them; and that sins forgiven cease to affect the unhappy wretches sinned against?

Another objection is that a certain belief is necessary to save the soul. It is often asserted that to believe is the only safe way. If you wish to be safe, be honest. Nothing can be safer than that. No matter what his belief may be, no man, even in the hour of death, can regret having been honest. It never can be necessary to throw away your reason to save your soul. A soul without reason is scarcely worth saving. There is no more degrading doctrine than that of mental non-resistance. The soul has a right to defend its castle—the brain, and he who waives that right becomes a serf and slave. Neither can I admit that a man, by doing me an injury, can place me under obligation to do him a service. To render benefits for injuries is to ignore all distinctions between actions. He who treats his friends and enemies alike has neither love nor justice. The idea of non-resistance never occurred to a man with power to protect himself. This doctrine was the child of weakness, born when resistance was impossible. To allow a crime to be committed when you can prevent it, is next to committing the crime yourself. And yet, under the banner of non-resistance, the church has shed the blood of millions, and in the folds of her sacred vestments have gleamed the daggers of assassination. With her cunning hands she wove the purple for hypocrisy, and placed the crown upon the brow of crime. For a thousand years larceny held the scales of justice, while beggars scorned the princely sons of toil, and ignorant fear denounced the liberty of thought.

If Christ was in fact God, he knew all the future. Before him, like a panorama, moved the history yet to be. He knew exactly how his words would be interpreted. He knew what crimes, what horrors, what infamies, would be committed in his name. He knew that the fires of persecution would climb around the limbs of countless martyrs. He knew that brave men would languish in dungeons, in darkness, filled with pain; that the church would use instruments of torture, that his followers would appeal to whip and chain. He must have seen the horizon of the future red with the flames of the *auto da fe.* He knew all the creeds that would spring like poison fungi from every text. He saw the sects waging war against each other. He saw thousands of men, under the orders of priests, building dungeons for their fellow-men. He saw them using instruments of pain. He heard the groans, saw the faces white with agony, the tears, the blood—heard the shrieks and sobs of all the moaning, martyred multitudes. He knew that commentaries would be written on his words with swords, to be read by the light of fagots. He knew that the Inquisition would be born of teachings attributed to him. He saw all the interpolations and falsehoods that hypocrisy would write and tell. He knew that above these fields of death, these dungeons, these burnings, for a thousand years would float the dripping banner of the cross. He knew that in his name his followers would trade in human flesh, that cradles would be robbed, and women's breasts unbabed for gold, and yet he died with voiceless lips. Why did he fail to speak? Why did he not tell his disciples, and through them the world, that man should not persecute, for opinion's sake, his fellow-man? Why did he not cry, You shall not persecute in my name; you shall not burn and torment those who differ from you in creed? Why did he not plainly say, I am the Son of God? Why did he not explain the doctrine of the Trinity? Why did he not tell the manner of baptism that was pleasing to him? Why did he not say something positive, definite, and satisfactory about another world? Why did he not turn the tear-stained hope of heaven to the glad knowledge of another life? Why did he go dumbly to his death, leaving the world to misery and to doubt?

He came, they tell us, to make a revelation, and what did he reveal? "Love thy neighbor as thyself"? That was in the Old Testament. "Love God with all thy heart"? That was in the Old Testament. "Return good for evil"? That was said by Buddha seven hundred years before he was born. "Do unto others as ye would that they should do unto you"? This was the doctrine of Lao-tsze. Did he come to give a rule of action? Zoroaster had done this long before: "Whenever thou art in doubt as to whether an action is good or bad, abstain from it." Did he come to teach us of another world? The immortality of the soul had been taught by Hindus, Egyptians, Greeks, and Romans hundreds of years before he was born. Long before, the world had been told by Socrates that: "One who is injured ought not to return the injury, for on no account can it be right to do an injustice; and it is not right to return an injury, or to do evil to any man, however much we may have suffered from him." And Cicero had said:

"Let us not listen to those who think that we ought to be angry with our enemies, and who believe this to be great and manly: nothing is more praiseworthy, nothing so clearly shows a great and noble soul, as clemency and readiness to forgive."

Is there anything nearer perfect than this from Confucius: "For benefits return benefits; for injuries return justice without any admixture of revenge"?

The dogma of eternal punishment rests upon passages in the New Testament. This infamous belief subverts every idea of justice. Around the angel of immortality the church has coiled this serpent. A finite being can neither commit an infinite sin, nor a sin against the infinite. A being of infinite goodness and wisdom has no right, according to the human standard of justice, to create any being destined to suffer eternal pain. A being of infinite wisdom would not create a failure, and surely a man destined to everlasting agony is not a success.

How long, according to the universal benevolence of the New Testament, can a man be reasonably punished in the next world for failing to believe something unreasonable in this? Can it be possible that any punishment can endure forever? Suppose that every flake of snow that ever fell was a figure nine, and that the first flake was multiplied by the second, and that product by the third, and so on to the last flake. And then suppose that this total should be multiplied by every drop of rain that ever fell, calling each drop a figure nine; and that total by each blade of grass that ever helped to weave a carpet for the earth, calling each blade a figure nine; and that again by every grain of sand on every shore, so that the grand total would make a line of nines so long that it would require millions upon millions of years for light, traveling at the rate of one hundred and eighty-five thousand miles per second, to reach the end. And suppose, further, that each unit in this almost infinite total stood for billions of ages—still that vast and almost endless time, measured by all the years beyond, is as one flake, one drop, one leaf, one blade, one grain, compared with all the flakes and drops and leaves and blades and grains. Upon love's breast the church has placed the eternal asp. And yet, in the same book in which is taught this most infamous of doctrines, we are assured that "The Lord is good to all, and his tender mercies are over all his works."

III.

So far as we know, man is the author of all books. If a book had been found on the earth by the first man, he might have regarded it as the work of God; but as men were here a good while before any books were found, and as man has produced a great many books, the probability is that the Bible is no exception.

Most nations, at the time the Old Testament was written, believed in slavery, polygamy, wars of extermination, and religious persecution; and it is not wonderful that the book contained nothing contrary to such belief. The fact that it was in exact accord with the morality of its time proves that it was not the product of any being superior to man. "The inspired writers" upheld or established slavery, countenanced polygamy, commanded wars of extermination, and ordered the slaughter of women and babes. In these respects they were precisely like the uninspired savages by whom they were surrounded. They also taught and commanded religious persecution as a duty, and visited the most trivial offences with the punishment of death. In these particulars they were in exact accord with their barbarian neighbors. They were utterly ignorant of geology and astronomy, and knew no more of what had happened than of what would happen; and, so far as accuracy is concerned, their history and prophecy were about equal; in other words, they were just as ignorant as those who lived and died in nature's night.

Does any Christian believe that if God were to write a book now, he would uphold the crimes commanded in the Old Testament? Has Jehovah improved? Has infinite mercy-become more merciful? Has infinite wisdom intellectually-advanced? Will any one claim that the passages upholding slavery have liberated mankind; that we are indebted for our modern homes to the texts that made polygamy a virtue; or that religious liberty found its soil, its light, and rain in the infamous verse wherein the husband is commanded to stone to death the wife for worshiping an unknown god?

The usual answer to these objections is that no country has ever been civilized without the Bible.

The Jews were the only people to whom Jehovah made his will directly known,—the only people who had the Old Testament. Other nations were utterly neglected by their Creator. Yet, such was the effect of the Old Testament on the Jews, that they crucified a kind, loving, and perfectly innocent man. They could not have done much worse without a Bible. In the crucifixion of Christ, they followed the teachings of his Father. If, as it is now alleged by the theologians, no nation can be civilized without a Bible, certainly God must have known the fact six thousand years ago, as well as the theologians know it now. Why did he not furnish every nation with a Bible?

As to the Old Testament, I insist that all the bad passages were written by men; that those passages were not inspired. I insist that a being of infinite goodness never commanded man to enslave his fellow-man, never told a mother to sell her babe, never established polygamy, never ordered one nation to exterminate another, and never told a husband to kill his wife because she suggested the worshiping of some other God.

I also insist that the Old Testament would be a much better book with all of these passages left out; and, whatever may be said of the rest, the passages to which attention has been drawn can with vastly more propriety be attributed to a devil than to a god.

Take from the New Testament all passages upholding the idea that belief is necessary to salvation; that Christ was offered as an atonement for the sins of the world; that the punishment of the human soul will go on forever; that heaven is the reward of faith, and hell the penalty of honest investigation; take from it all miraculous stories,—and I admit that all the good passages are true. If they are true, it makes no difference whether they are inspired or not. Inspiration is only necessary to give authority to that which is repugnant to human reason. Only that which never happened needs to be substantiated by miracles. The universe is natural.

The church must cease to insist that the passages upholding the institutions of savage men were inspired of God. The dogma of the atonement must be abandoned. Good deeds must take the place of faith. The savagery of eternal punishment must be renounced. Credulity is not a virtue, and investigation is not a crime. Miracles are the children of mendacity. Nothing can be more wonderful than the majestic, unbroken, sublime, and eternal procession of causes and effects.

Reason must be the final arbiter. "Inspired" books attested by miracles cannot stand against a demonstrated fact. A religion that does not command the respect of the greatest minds will, in a little while, excite the mockery of all. Every civilized man believes in the liberty of thought. Is it possible that God is intolerant? Is an act infamous in man one of the virtues of the Deity? Could there be progress in heaven without intellectual liberty? Is the freedom of the future to exist only in perdition? Is it not, after all, barely possible that a man acting like Christ can be saved? Is a man to be eternally rewarded for believing according to evidence, without evidence, or against evidence? Are we to be saved because we are good, or because another was virtuous? Is credulity to be winged and crowned, while honest doubt is chained and damned?

Do not misunderstand me. My position is that the cruel passages in the Old Testament are not inspired; that slavery, polygamy, wars of extermination, and religious persecution always have been, are, and forever will be, abhorred and cursed by the honest, the virtuous, and the loving; that the innocent cannot justly suffer for the guilty, and that vicarious vice and vicarious virtue are equally absurd; that eternal punishment is eternal revenge; that only the natural can happen; that miracles prove the dishonesty of the few and the credulity of the many; and that, according to Matthew, Mark, and Luke, salvation does not depend upon belief, nor the atonement, nor a "second birth," but that these gospels are in exact harmony with the declaration of the great Persian: "Taking the first footstep with the good thought, the second with the good word, and the third with the good deed, I entered paradise."

The dogmas of the past no longer reach the level of the highest thought, nor satisfy the hunger of the heart. While dusty faiths, embalmed and sepulchered in ancient texts, remain the same, the sympathies of men enlarge; the brain no longer kills its young; the happy lips give liberty to honest thoughts; the mental firmament expands and lifts; the broken clouds drift by; the hideous dreams, the foul, misshapen children of the monstrous night, dissolve and fade.

Robert G. Ingersoll.

THE CHRISTIAN RELIGION,

II.

JUDGE BLACK'S REPLY
BY JEREMIAH S. BLACK.

"Gratiano speaks of an infinite deal of nothing, more than any man in all Venice: his reasons are as two grains of wheat hid in two bushels of chaff; you shall seek all day ere you find them; and when you have them they are not worth the search."—*Merchant of Venice.*

The request to answer the foregoing paper comes to me, not in the form but with the effect of a challenge, which I cannot decline without seeming to acknowledge that the religion of the civilized world is an absurd superstition, propagated by impostors, professed by hypocrites, and believed only by credulous dupes.

But why should I, an unlearned and unauthorized layman, be placed in such a predicament? The explanation is easy enough. This is no business of the priests. Their prescribed duty is to preach the word, in the full assurance that it will commend itself to all good and honest hearts by its own manifest veracity and the singular purity of its precepts. They cannot afford to turn away from their proper work, and leave willing hearers uninstructed, while they wrangle in vain with a predetermined opponent. They were warned to expect slander, indignity, and insult, and these are among the evils which they must not resist.

It will be seen that I am assuming no clerical function. I am not out on the forlorn hope of converting Mr. Ingersoll. I am no preacher exhorting a sinner to leave the seat of the scornful and come up to the bench of the penitents. My duty is more analogous to that of the policeman who would silence a rude disturber of the congregation by telling him that his clamor is false and his conduct an offence against public decency.

Nor is the Church in any danger which calls for the special vigilance of its servants. Mr. Ingersoll thinks that the rock-founded faith of Christendom is giving way before his assaults, but he is grossly mistaken. The first sentence of his essay is a preposterous blunder. It is not true that "a *profound change* has taken place in the world of *thought,*" unless a more rapid spread of the Gospel and a more faithful observance of its moral principles can be called so. Its truths are everywhere proclaimed with the power of sincere conviction, and accepted with devout reverence by uncounted multitudes of all classes. Solemn temples rise to its honor in the great cities; from every hill-top in the country you see the church-spire pointing toward heaven, and on Sunday all the paths that lead to it are crowded with worshipers. In nearly all families, parents teach their children that Christ is God, and his system of morality absolutely perfect. This belief lies so deep in the popular heart that, if every written record of it were destroyed to-day, the memory of millions could reproduce it to-morrow. Its earnestness is

214

proved by its works. Wherever it goes it manifests itself in deeds of practical benevolence. It builds, not churches alone, but almshouses, hospitals, and asylums. It shelters the poor, feeds the hungry, visits the sick, consoles the afflicted, provides for the fatherless, comforts the heart of the widow, instructs the ignorant, reforms the vicious, and saves to the uttermost them that are ready to perish. To the common observer, it does not look as if Christianity was making itself ready to be swallowed up by Infidelity. Thus far, at least, the promise has been kept that "the gates of hell shall not prevail against it."

There is, to be sure, a change in the party hostile to religion—not "a *profound* change," but a change entirely superficial—which consists, not in *thought,* but merely in modes of expression and methods of attack. The bad classes of society always hated the doctrine and discipline which reproached their wickedness and frightened them by threats of punishment in another world. Aforetime they showed their contempt of divine authority only by their actions; but now, under new leadership, their enmity against God breaks out into articulate blasphemy. They assemble themselves together, they hear with passionate admiration the bold harangue which ridicules and defies the Maker of the universe; fiercely they rage against the Highest, and loudly they laugh, alike at the justice that condemns, and the mercy that offers to pardon them. The orator who relieves them by assurances of impunity, and tells them that no supreme authority has made any law to control them, is applauded to the echo and paid a high price for his congenial labor; he pockets their money, and flatters himself that he is a great power, profoundly moving "the world of thought."

There is another totally false notion expressed in the opening paragraph, namely, that "they who know most of nature believe the least about theology." The truth is exactly the other way. The more clearly one sees "the grand procession of causes and effects," the more awful his reverence becomes for the author of the "sublime and unbroken" law which links them together. Not self-conceit and rebellious pride, but unspeakable humility, and a deep sense of the measureless distance between the Creator and the creature, fills the mind of him who looks with a rational spirit upon the works of the All-wise One. The heart of Newton repeats the solemn confession of David: "When I consider thy heavens, the work of thy fingers, the moon and the stars which thou hast ordained; what is man that thou art mindful of him or the son of man that thou visitest him?" At the same time, the lamentable fact must be admitted that "a little learning is a dangerous thing" to some persons. The sciolist with a mere smattering of physical knowledge is apt to mistake himself for a philosopher, and swelling with his own importance, he gives out, like Simon Magus, "that himself is some great one." His vanity becomes inflamed more and more, until he begins to think he knows all things. He takes every occasion to show his accomplishments by finding fault with the works of creation* and Providence; and this is an exercise in which he cannot long continue without learning to disbelieve in any Being greater than himself. It was to such a person, and not to the unpretending simpleton, that Solomon applied his often quoted aphorism: "The fool hath said in his heart, there

215

is no God." These are what Paul refers to as "vain babblings and the opposition of science, falsely so called;" but they are perfectly powerless to stop or turn aside the great current of human thought on the subject of Christian theology. That majestic stream, supplied from a thousand unfailing fountains, rolls on and will roll forever.

Labitur et labetur in omne volubilis aevum.

Mr. Ingersoll is not, as some have estimated him, the most formidable enemy that Christianity has encountered since the time of Julian the Apostate. But he stands at the head of living infidels, "by merit raised to that bad eminence." His mental organization has the peculiar defects which fit him for such a place. He is all imagination and no discretion. He rises sometimes into a region of wild poetry, where he can color everything to suit himself. His motto well expresses the character of his argumentation—"mountains are as unstable as clouds:" a fancy is as good as a fact, and a high-sounding period is rather better than a logical demonstration. His inordinate self-confidence makes him at once ferocious and fearless. He was a practical politician before he "took the stump" against Christianity, and at all times he has proved his capacity to "split the ears of the groundlings," and make the unskillful laugh. The article before us is the least objectionable of all his productions. Its style is higher, and better suited to the weight of the theme. Here the violence of his fierce invective is moderated; his scurrility gives place to an attempt at sophistry less shocking if not more true; and his coarse jokes are either excluded altogether, or else veiled in the decent obscurity of general terms. Such a paper from such a man, at a time like the present, is not wholly unworthy of a grave contradiction.

He makes certain charges which we answer by an explicit denial, and thus an issue is made, upon which, as a pleader would say, we "put ourselves upon the country." He avers that a certain "something called Christianity" is a false faith imposed on the world without evidence; that the facts it pretends to rest on are mere inventions; that its doctrines are pernicious; that its requirements are unreasonable, and that its sanctions are cruel. I deny all this, and assert, on the contrary, that its doctrines are divinely revealed; its fundamental facts incontestably proved; its morality perfectly free from all taint of error, and its influence most beneficent upon society in general, and upon all individuals who accept it and make it their rule of action.

How shall this be determined? Not by what we call divine revelation, for that would be begging the question; not by sentiment, taste, or temper, for these are as likely to be false as true; but by inductive reasoning from evidence, of which the value is to be measured according to those rules of logic which enlightened and just men everywhere have adopted to guide them in the search for truth. We can appeal only to that rational love of justice, and that detestation of falsehood, which fair-minded persons of good intelligence bring to the consideration of other important subjects when it becomes their duty to decide upon them. In short, I want a decision upon sound judicial principles.

Gibson, the great Chief-Justice of Pennsylvania, once said to certain skeptical friends of his: "Give Christianity a common-law trial; submit the evidence *pro* and *con* to an impartial jury under the direction of a competent court, and the verdict will assuredly be in its favor." This deliverance, coming from the most illustrious judge of his time, not at all given to expressions of sentimental piety, and quite incapable of speaking on any subject for mere effect, staggered the unbelief of those who heard it. I did not know him then, except by his great reputation for ability and integrity, but my thoughts were strongly influenced by his authority, and I learned to set a still higher value upon all his opinions, when, in after life, I was honored with his close and intimate friendship.

Let Christianity have a trial on Mr. Ingersoll's indictment, and give us a decision *secundum allegata et probata*. I will confine myself strictly to the record; that is to say, I will meet the accusations contained in this paper, and not those made elsewhere by him or others.

His first specification against Christianity is the belief of its disciples "that there is a personal God, the creator of the material universe." If God made the world it was a most stupendous miracle, and all miracles, according to Mr. Ingersoll's idea are "the children of mendacity." To admit the one great miracle of creation would be an admission that other miracles are at least probable, and that would ruin his whole case. But you cannot catch the leviathan of atheism with a hook. The universe, he says, is natural—it came into being of its own accord; it made its own laws at the start, and afterward improved itself considerably by spontaneous evolution. It would be a mere waste of time and space to enumerate the proofs which show that the universe was created by a pre-existent and self-conscious Being, of power and wisdom to us inconceivable. Conviction of the fact (miraculous though it be) forces itself on every one whose mental faculties are healthy and tolerably well balanced. The notion that all things owe their origin and their harmonious arrangement to the fortuitous concurrence of atoms is a kind of lunacy which very few men in these days are afflicted with. I hope I may safely assume it as certain that all, or nearly all, who read this page will have sense and reason enough to see for themselves that the plan of the universe could not have been designed without a Designer or executed without a Maker.

But Mr. Ingersoll asserts that, at all events, this material world had not a good and beneficent creator; it is a bad, savage, cruel piece of work, with its pestilences, storms, earthquakes, and volcanoes; and man, with his liability to sickness, suffering, and death, is not a success, but, on the contrary, a failure. To defend the Creator of the world against an arraignment so foul as this would be almost as unbecoming as to make the accusation. We have neither jurisdiction nor capacity to rejudge the justice of God. Why man is made to fill this particular place in the scale of creation—a little lower than the angels, yet far above the brutes; not passionless and pure, like the former, nor mere machines, like the latter; able to stand, yet free to fall; knowing the right, and accountable for going wrong; gifted with reason, and impelled by self-love to exercise the faculty—these are questions on which we may have our speculative opinions, but knowledge is out of our reach. Meantime, we do not discredit our mental independence by taking it for granted that the Supreme Being has done all things well. Our ignorance of the whole scheme makes us poor critics upon the small part that comes within our limited perceptions. Seeming defects in the structure of the world may be its most perfect ornament—all apparent harshness the tenderest of mercies.

> "All discord, harmony not understood,
> All partial evil, universal good."

But worse errors are imputed to God as moral ruler of the world than those charged against him as creator. He made man badly, but governed him worse; if the Jehovah of the Old Testament was not merely an imaginary being, then, according to Mr. Ingersoll, he was a prejudiced, barbarous, criminal tyrant. We will see what ground he lays, if any, for these outrageous assertions.

Mainly, principally, first and most important of all, is the unqualified assertion that the "moral code" which Jehovah gave to his people "is in many respects abhorrent to every good and tender man." Does Mr. Ingersoll know what he is talking about? The moral code of the Bible consists of certain immutable rules to govern the conduct of all men, at all times and all places, in their private and personal relations with one another. It is entirely separate and apart from the civil polity, the religious forms, the sanitary provisions, the police regulations, and the system of international law laid down for the special and exclusive observance of the Jewish people. This is a distinction which every intelligent man knows how to make. Has Mr. Ingersoll fallen into the egregious blunder of confounding these things? or, understanding the true sense of his words, is he rash and shameless enough to assert that the moral code of the Bible excites the abhorrence of good men? In fact, and in truth, this moral code, which he reviles, instead of being abhorred, is entitled to, and has received, the profoundest respect of all honest and sensible persons. The second table of the Decalogue is a perfect compendium of those duties which every man owes to himself, his family, and his neighbor. In a few simple words, which he can commit to memory almost in a minute, it teaches him to purify his heart from covetousness; to live decently, to injure nobody in reputation, person, or property, and to give every one his own. By the poets, the prophets, and the sages of Israel, these great elements are expanded into a volume of minuter rules, so clear, so impressive, and yet so solemn and so lofty, that no pre-existing system of philosophy can compare with it for a moment. If this vain mortal is not blind with passion, he will see, upon reflection, that he has attacked the Old Testament precisely where it is most impregnable.

Dismissing his groundless charge against the moral code, we come to his strictures on the civil government of the Jews, which he says was so bad and unjust that the Lawgiver by whom it was established must have been as savagely cruel as the Creator that made storms and pestilences; and the work of both was more worthy of a devil than a God. His language is recklessly bad, very defective in method, and altogether lacking in precision. But, apart from the ribaldry of it, which I do not feel myself bound to notice, I find four objections to the Jewish constitution—not more than four—which are definite enough to admit of an answer. These relate to the provisions of the Mosaic law on the subjects of (1) Blasphemy and Idolatry; (2) War; (3) Slavery; (4) Polygamy. In these respects he pronounces the Jewish system not only unwise but criminally unjust.

Here let me call attention to the difficulty of reasoning about justice with a man who has no acknowledged standard of right and wrong. What is justice? That which accords with law; and the supreme law is the will of God. But I am dealing with an adversary who does not admit that there is a God. Then for him there is no standard at all; one thing is as right as another, and all things are equally wrong. Without a sovereign ruler there is no law, and where there is no law there can be no transgression. It is the misfortune of the atheistic theory that it makes the moral world an anarchy; it refers all ethical questions to that confused tribunal where chaos sits as umpire and "by decision more embroils the fray." But through the whole of this cloudy paper there runs a vein of presumptuous egotism which says as plainly as words can speak it that the author holds *himself* to be the ultimate judge of all good and evil; what he approves is right, and what he dislikes is certainly wrong. Of course I concede nothing to a claim like that. I will not admit that the Jewish constitution is a thing to be condemned merely because he curses it. I appeal from his profane malediction to the conscience of men who have a rule to judge by. Such persons will readily see that his specific objections to the statesmanship which established the civil government of the Hebrew people are extremely shallow, and do not furnish the shade of an excuse for the indecency of his general abuse.

First. He regards the punishments inflicted for blasphemy and idolatry as being immoderately cruel. Considering them merely as religious offences,—as sins against God alone,—I agree that civil laws should notice them not at all. But sometimes they affect very injuriously certain social rights which it is the duty of the state to protect. Wantonly to shock the religious feelings of your neighbor is a grievous wrong. To utter blasphemy or obscenity in the presence of a Christian woman is hardly better than to strike her in the face. Still, neither policy nor justice requires them to be ranked among the highest crimes in a government constituted like ours. But things were wholly different under the Jewish theocracy, where God was the personal head of the state. There blasphemy was a breach of political allegiance; idolatry was an overt act of treason; to worship the gods of the hostile heathen was deserting to the public enemy, and giving him aid and comfort. These are crimes which every independent community has always punished with the utmost rigor. In our own very recent history, they were repressed at the cost of more lives than Judea ever contained at any one time.

Mr. Ingersoll not only ignores these considerations, but he goes the length of calling God a religious persecutor and a tyrant because he does not encourage and reward the service and devotion paid by his enemies to the false gods of the pagan world. He professes to believe that all kinds of worship are equally meritorious, and should meet the same acceptance from the true God. It is almost incredible that such drivel as this should be uttered by anybody. But Mr. Ingersoll not only expresses the thought plainly—he urges it with the most extravagant figures of his florid rhetoric. He quotes the first commandment, in which Jehovah claims for himself the exclusive worship of His people, and cites, in contrast, the promise put in the mouth of Brahma, that he will appropriate the worship of all gods to himself, and reward all worshipers alike. These passages being compared, he declares the first "a dungeon, where crawl the things begot of jealous slime;" the other, "great as the domed firmament, inlaid with suns." Why is the living God, whom Christians believe to be the Lord of liberty and Father of lights, denounced as the keeper of a loathsome dungeon? Because he refuses to encourage and reward the worship of Mammon and Moloch, of Belial and Baal; of Bacchus, with its drunken orgies, and Venus, with its wanton obscenities; the bestial religion which degraded the soul of Egypt and the "dark idolatries of alienated Judah," polluted with the moral filth of all the nations round about.

Let the reader decide whether this man, entertaining such sentiments and opinions, is fit to be a teacher, or at all likely to lead us in the way we should go.

Second. Under the constitution which God provided for the Jews, they had, like every other nation, the war-making power. They could not have lived a day without it. The right to exist implied the right to repel, with all their strength, the opposing force which threatened their destruction. It is true, also, that in the exercise of this power they did not observe those rules of courtesy and humanity which have been adopted in modern times by civilized belligerents. Why? Because their enemies, being mere savages, did not understand and would not practice, any rule whatever; and the Jews were bound *ex necessitate rei*—not merely justified by the *lex talionis*—to do as their enemies did. In your treatment of hostile barbarians, you not only may lawfully, but must necessarily, adopt their mode of warfare. If they come to conquer you, they may be conquered by you; if they give no quarter, they are entitled to none; if the death of your whole population be their purpose, you may defeat it by exterminating theirs. This sufficiently answers the silly talk of atheists and semi-atheists about the warlike wickedness of the Jews.

But Mr. Ingersoll positively, and with the emphasis of supreme and all-sufficient authority, declares that "a war of conquest is simply murder." He sustains this proposition by no argument founded in principle. He puts sentiment in place of law, and denounces aggressive fighting because it is offensive to his "tender and refined soul;" the atrocity of it is therefore proportioned to the sensibilities of his own heart. He proves war a desperately wicked thing by continually vaunting his own love for small children. Babes—sweet babes—the prattle of babes—are the subjects of his most pathetic eloquence, and his idea of music is embodied in the commonplace expression of a Hindu, that the lute is sweet only to those who have not heard the prattle of their own children. All this is very amiable in him, and the more so, perhaps, as these objects of his affection are the young ones of a race in his opinion miscreated by an evil-working chance. But his *philoprogenitiveness* proves nothing against Jew or Gentile, seeing that all have it in an equal degree, and those feel it most who make the least parade of it. Certainly it gives him no authority to malign the God who implanted it alike in the hearts of us all. But I admit that his benevolence becomes peculiar and ultra when it extends to beasts as well as babes. He is struck with horror by the sacrificial solemnities of the Jewish religion. "The killing of those animals was," he says, "a terrible system," a "shedding of innocent blood," "shocking to a refined and sensitive soul." There is such a depth of tenderness in this feeling, and such a splendor of refinement, that I give up without a struggle to the superiority of a man who merely professes it. A carnivorous American, full of beef and mutton, who mourns with indignant sorrow because bulls and goats were killed in Judea three thousand years ago, has reached the climax of sentimental goodness, and should be permitted to dictate on all questions of peace and war. Let Grotius, Vattel, and Pufendorf, as well as Moses and the prophets, hide their diminished heads.

But to show how inefficacious, for all practical purposes, a mere sentiment is when substituted for a principle, it is only necessary to recollect that Mr. Ingersoll is himself a warrior who staid not behind the mighty men of his tribe when they gathered themselves together for a war of conquest. He took the lead of a regiment as eager as himself to spoil the Philistines, "and out he went a-coloneling." How many Amalekites, and Hittites, and Amorites he put to the edge of the sword, how many wives he widowed, or how many mothers he "unbabed" cannot now be told. I do not even know how many droves of innocent oxen he condemned to the slaughter.

But it is certain that his refined and tender soul took great pleasure in the terror, conflagration, blood, and tears with which the war was attended, and in all the hard oppressions which the conquered people were made to suffer afterwards. I do not say that the war was either better or worse for his participation and approval. But if his own conduct (for which he professes neither penitence nor shame) was right, it was right on grounds which make it an inexcusable outrage to call the children of Israel savage criminals for carrying on wars of aggression to save the life of their government. These inconsistencies are the necessary consequence of having no rule of action and no guide for the conscience. When a man throws away the golden metewand of the law which God has provided, and takes the elastic cord of feeling for his measure of righteousness, you cannot tell from day to day what he will think or do.

Third. But Jehovah permitted his chosen people to hold the captives they took in war or purchased from the heathen as servants for life. This was slavery, and Mr. Ingersoll declares that "in all civilized countries it is not only admitted, but it is passionately asserted, that slavery is, and always was, a hideous crime," therefore he concludes that Jehovah was a criminal. This would be a *non sequitur,* even if the premises were true. But the premises are false; civilized countries have admitted no such thing. That slavery is a crime, under all circumstances and at all times, is a doctrine first started by the adherents of a political faction in this country, less than forty years ago. They denounced God and Christ for not agreeing with them, in terms very similar to those used here by Mr. Ingersoll. But they did not constitute the civilized world; nor were they, if the truth must be told, a very respectable portion of it. Politically, they were successful; I need not say by what means, or with what effect upon

221

the morals of the country. Doubtless Mr. Ingersoll gets a great advantage by invoking their passions and their interests to his aid, and he knows how to use it. I can only say that, whether American Abolitionism was right or wrong under the circumstances in which we were placed, my faith and my reason both assure me that the infallible God proceeded upon good grounds when he authorized slavery in Judea. Subordination of inferiors to superiors is the groundwork of human society. All improvement of our race, in this world and the next, must come from obedience to some master better and wiser than ourselves. There can be no question that, when a Jew took a neighboring savage for his bond-servant, incorporated him into his family, tamed him, taught him to work, and gave him a knowledge of the true God, he conferred upon him a most beneficent boon.

Fourth. Polygamy is another of his objections to the Mosaic constitution. Strange to say, it is not there. It is neither commanded nor prohibited; it is only discouraged. If Mr. Ingersoll were a statesman instead of a mere politician, he would see good and sufficient reasons for the forbearance to legislate directly upon the subject. It would be improper for me to set them forth here. He knows, probably, that the influence of the Christian Church alone, and without the aid of state enactments, has extirpated this bad feature of Asiatic manners wherever its doctrines were carried. As the Christian faith prevails in any community, in that proportion precisely marriage is consecrated to its true purpose, and all intercourse between the sexes refined and purified. Mr. Ingersoll got his own devotion to the principle of monogamy—his own respect for the highest type of female character—his own belief in the virtue of fidelity to one good wife—from the example and precept of his Christian parents. I speak confidently, because these are sentiments which do not grow in the heart of the natural man without being planted. Why, then, does he throw polygamy into the face of the religion which abhors it? Because he is nothing if not political. The Mormons believe in polygamy, and the Mormons are unpopular. They are guilty of having not only many wives but much property, and if a war could be hissed up against them, its fruits might be more "gaynefull pilladge than wee doe now conceyve of." It is a cunning maneuver, this, of strengthening atheism by enlisting anti-Mormon rapacity against the God of the Christians. I can only protest against the use he would make of these and other political interests. It is not argument; it is mere stump oratory.

I think I have repelled all of Mr. Ingersoll's accusations against the Old Testament that are worth noticing, and I might stop here. But I will not close upon him without letting him see, at least, some part of the case on the other side.

I do not enumerate in detail the positive proofs which support the authenticity of the Hebrew Bible, though they are at hand in great abundance, because the evidence in support of the new dispensation will establish the verity of the old—the two being so connected together that if one is true the other cannot be false.

When Jesus of Nazareth announced himself to be Christ, the Son of God, in Judea, many thousand persons who heard his words and saw his works believed in his divinity without hesitation. Since the morning of the creation, nothing has occurred so wonderful as the rapidity with which this religion spread itself abroad. Men who were in the noon of life when Jesus was put to death as a malefactor lived to see him worshiped as God by organized bodies of believers in every province of the Roman empire. In a few more years it took complete possession of the general mind, supplanted all other religions, and wrought a radical change in human society. It did this in the face of obstacles which, according to every human calculation, were insurmountable. It was antagonized by all the evil propensities, the sensual wickedness, and the vulgar crimes of the multitude, as well as the polished vices of the luxurious classes; and was most violently opposed even by those sentiments and habits of thought which were esteemed virtuous, such as patriotism and military heroism. It encountered not only the ignorance and superstition, but the learning and philosophy, the poetry, eloquence, and art of the time. Barbarism and civilization were alike its deadly enemies. The priesthood of every established religion and the authority of every government were arrayed against it. All these, combined together and roused to ferocious hostility, were overcome, not by the enticing words of man's wisdom, but by the simple presentation of a pure and peaceful doctrine, preached by obscure strangers at the daily peril of their lives. Is it Mr. Ingersoll's idea that this happened by chance, like the creation of the world? If not, there are but two other ways to account for it; either the evidence by which the Apostles were able to prove the supernatural origin of the gospel was overwhelming and irresistible, or else its propagation was provided for and carried on by the direct aid of the Divine Being himself. Between these two, infidelity may make its own choice.

Just here another dilemma presents its horns to our adversary. If Christianity was a human fabrication, its authors must have been either good men or bad. It is a moral impossibility—a mere contradiction in terms—to say that good, honest, and true men practiced a gross and willful deception upon the world. It is equally incredible that any combination of knaves, however base, would fraudulently concoct a religious system to denounce themselves, and to invoke the curse of God upon their own conduct. Men that love lies, love not such lies as that. Is there any way out of this difficulty, except by confessing that Christianity is what it purports to be—a divine revelation?

The acceptance of Christianity by a large portion of the generation contemporary with its Founder and his apostles was, under the circumstances, an adjudication as solemn and authoritative as mortal intelligence could pronounce. The record of that judgment has come down to us, accompanied by the depositions of the principal witnesses. In the course of eighteen centuries many efforts have been made to open the judgment or set it aside on the ground that the evidence was insufficient to support it. But on every rehearing the wisdom and virtue of mankind have re-affirmed it. And now comes Mr. Ingersoll, to try the experiment of another bold, bitter, and fierce reargument. I will present some of the considerations which would compel me, if I were a judge or juror in the cause, to decide it just as it was decided originally.

First. There is no good reason to doubt that the statements of the evangelists, as we have them now, are genuine. The multiplication of copies was a sufficient guarantee against any material alteration of the text. Mr. Ingersoll speaks of interpolations made by the fathers of the Church. All he knows and all he has ever heard on that subject is that some of the innumerable transcripts contained errors which were discovered and corrected. That simply proves the present integrity of the documents.

Second. I call these statements *depositions,* because they are entitled to that kind of credence which we give to declarations made under oath—but in a much higher degree, for they are more than sworn to. They were made in the immediate prospect of death. Perhaps this would not affect the conscience of an atheist,—neither would an oath,—but these people manifestly believed in a judgment after death, before a God of truth, whose displeasure they feared above all things.

Third. The witnesses could not have been mistaken. The nature of the facts precluded the possibility of any delusion about them. For every averment they had "the sensible and true avouch of their own eyes" and ears. Besides, they were plain-thinking, sober, unimaginative men, who, unlike Mr. Ingersoll, always, under all circumstances, and especially in the presence of eternity, recognized the difference between mountains and clouds. It is inconceivable how any fact could be proven by evidence more conclusive than the statement of such persons, publicly given and steadfastly persisted in through every kind of persecution, imprisonment and torture to the last agonies of a lingering death.

Fourth. Apart from these terrible tests, the more ordinary claims to credibility are not wanting. They were men of unimpeachable character. The most virulent enemies of the cause they spoke and died for have never suggested a reason for doubting their personal honesty. But there is affirmative proof that they and their fellow-disciples were held by those who knew them in the highest estimation for truthfulness. Wherever they made their report it was not only believed, but believed with a faith so implicit that thousands were ready at once to seal it with their blood.

Fifth. The tone and temper of their narrative impress us with a sentiment of profound respect. It is an artless, unimpassioned, simple story. No argument, no rhetoric, no epithets, no praises of friends, no denunciation of enemies, no attempts at concealment. How strongly these qualities commend the testimony of a witness to the confidence of judge and jury is well known to all who have any experience in such matters.

Sixth. The statements made by the evangelists are alike upon every important point, but are different in form and expression, some of them including details which the others omit. These variations make it perfectly certain that there could have been no previous concert between the witnesses, and that each spoke independently of the others, according to his own conscience and from his own knowledge. In considering the testimony of several witnesses to the same transaction, their substantial agreement upon the main facts, with circumstantial differences in the detail, is always regarded as the great characteristic of truth and honesty. There is no rule of evidence more universally adopted than this—none better sustained by general experience, or more immovably fixed in the good sense of mankind. Mr. Ingersoll, himself, admits the rule and concedes its soundness. The logical consequence of that admission is that we are bound to take this evidence as incontestably true. But mark the infatuated perversity with which he seeks to evade it. He says that when we claim that the witnesses were inspired, the rule does not apply, because the witnesses then speak what is known to him who inspired them, and all must speak exactly the same, even to the minutest detail. Mr. Ingersoll's notion of an inspired witness is that he is no witness at all, but an irresponsible medium who unconsciously and involuntarily raps out or writes down whatever he is prompted to say. But this is a false assumption, not countenanced or even suggested by anything contained in the Scriptures. The apostles and evangelists are expressly declared to be witnesses, in the proper sense of the word, called and sent to testify the truth according to their knowledge. If they had all told the same story in the same way, without variation, and accounted for its uniformity by declaring that they were inspired, and had spoken without knowing whether their words were true or false, where would have been their claim to credibility? But they testified what they knew; and here comes an infidel critic impugning their testimony because the impress of truth is stamped upon its face.

Seventh. It does not appear that the statements of the evangelists were ever denied by any person who pretended to know the facts. Many there were in that age and afterward who resisted the belief that Jesus was the Christ, the Son of God, and only Saviour of man; but his wonderful works, the miraculous purity of his life, the unapproachable loftiness of his doctrines, his trial and condemnation by a judge who pronounced him innocent, his patient suffering, his death on the cross, and resurrection from the grave,—of these not the faintest contradiction was attempted, if we except the false and feeble story which the elders and chief priests bribed the guard at the tomb to put in circulation.

Eighth. What we call the fundamental truths of Christianity consist of great public events which are sufficiently established by history without special proof. The value of mere historical evidence increases according to the importance of the facts in question, their general notoriety, and the magnitude of their visible consequences. Cornwallis surrendered to Washington at Yorktown, and changed the destiny of Europe and America. Nobody would think of calling a witness or even citing an official report to prove it. Julius Caesar was assassinated. We do not need to prove that fact like an ordinary murder. He was master of the world, and his death was followed by a war with the conspirators, the battle at Philippi, the quarrel of the victorious triumvirs, Actium, and the permanent establishment of imperial government under Augustus. The life and character, the death and resurrection, of Jesus are just as visibly connected with events which even an infidel must admit to be of equal importance. The Church rose and armed herself in righteousness for conflict with the powers of darkness; innumerable multitudes of the best and wisest rallied to her standard and died in her cause; her enemies employed the coarse and vulgar machinery of human government against her, and her professors were brutally murdered in large numbers, her triumph was complete; the gods of Greece and Rome crumbled on their altars; the world was revolutionized and human society was transformed. The course of these events, and a thousand others, which reach down to the present hour, received its first propulsion from the transcendent fact of Christ's crucifixion. Moreover, we find the memorial monuments of the original truth planted all along the way. The sacraments of baptism and the supper constantly point us back to the author and finisher of our faith. The mere historical evidence is for these reasons much stronger than what we have for other occurrences which are regarded as undeniable. When to this is added the cumulative evidence given directly and positively by eye-witnesses of irreproachable character, and wholly uncontradicted, the proof becomes so strong that the disbelief we hear of seems like a kind of insanity.

"It is the very error of the moon,
Which comes more near the earth than she was wont,
And makes men mad!"

From the facts established by this evidence, it follows irresistibly that the Gospel has come to us from God. That silences all reasoning about the wisdom and justice of its doctrines, since it is impossible, even to imagine that wrong can be done or commanded by that Sovereign Being whose will alone is the ultimate standard of all justice.

But Mr. Ingersoll is still dissatisfied. He raises objections as false, fleeting, and baseless as clouds, and insists that they are as stable as the mountains, whose everlasting foundations are laid by the hand of the Almighty. I will compress his propositions into plain words printed in *italics*, and, taking a look at his misty creations, let them roll away and vanish into air, one after another.

Christianity offers eternal salvation as the reward of belief alone. This is a misrepresentation simple and naked. No such doctrine is propounded in the Scriptures, or in the creed of any Christian church. On the contrary, it is distinctly taught that faith avails nothing without repentance, reformation, and newness of life.

The mere failure to believe it is punished in hell. I have never known any Christian man or woman to assert this. It is universally agreed that children too young to understand it do not need to believe it. And this exemption extends to adults who have never seen the evidence, or, from weakness of intellect, are incapable of weighing it. Lunatics and idiots are not in the least danger, and for aught I know, this category may, by a stretch of God's mercy, include minds constitutionally sound, but with faculties so perverted by education, habit, or passion that they are incapable of reasoning. I sincerely hope that, upon this or some other principle, Mr. Ingersoll may escape the hell he talks about so much. But there is no direct promise to save him in spite of himself. The plan of redemption contains no express covenant to pardon one who rejects it with scorn and hatred. Our hope for him rests upon the infinite compassion of that gracious Being who prayed on the cross for the insulting enemies who nailed him there.

The mystery of the second birth is incomprehensible. Christ established a new kingdom in the world, but not of it. Subjects were admitted to the privileges and protection of its government by a process equivalent to naturalization. To be born again, or regenerated is to be naturalized. The words all mean the same thing. Does Mr. Ingersoll want to disgrace his own intellect by pretending that he cannot see this simple analogy?

The doctrine of the atonement is absurd, unjust, and immoral. The plan of salvation, or any plan for the rescue of sinners from the legal operation of divine justice, could have been framed only in the councils of the Omniscient. Necessarily its heights and depths are not easily fathomed by finite intelligence. But the greatest, ablest, wisest, and most virtuous men that ever lived have given it their profoundest consideration, and found it to be not only authorized by revelation, but theoretically conformed to their best and highest conceptions of infinite goodness. Nevertheless, here is a rash and superficial man, without training or habits of reflection, who, upon a mere glance, declares that it "must be abandoned," because it *seems to him* "absurd, unjust, and immoral." I would not abridge his freedom of thought or speech, and the *argumentum ad verecundiam* would be lost upon him. Otherwise I might suggest that, when he finds all authority, human and divine, against him, he had better speak in a tone less arrogant.

He does not comprehend how justice and mercy can be blended together in the plan of redemption, and therefore it cannot be true. A thing is not necessarily false because he does not understand it: he cannot annihilate a principle or a fact by ignoring it. There are many truths in heaven and earth which no man can see through; for instance, the union of man's soul with his body, is not only an unknowable but an unimaginable mystery. Is it therefore false that a connection does exist between matter and spirit?

How, he asks, can the sufferings of an innocent person satisfy justice for the sins of the guilty? This raises a metaphysical question, which it is not necessary or possible for me to discuss here. As matter of fact, Christ died that sinners might be reconciled to God, and in that sense he died for them; that is, to furnish them with the means of averting divine justice, which their crimes had provoked.

What, he again asks, would we think of a man who allowed another to die for a crime which he himself had committed? I answer that a man who, by any contrivance, causes his own offence to be visited upon the head of an innocent person is unspeakably depraved. But are Christians guilty of this baseness because they accept the blessings of an institution which their great benefactor died to establish? Loyalty to the King who has erected a most beneficent government for us at the cost of his life—fidelity to the Master who bought us with his blood—is not the fraudulent substitution of an innocent person in place of a criminal.

The doctrine of non-resistance, forgiveness of injuries, reconciliation with enemies, as taught in the New Testament, is the child of weakness, degrading and unjust. This is the whole substance of a long, rambling diatribe, as incoherent as a sick man's dream. Christianity does not forbid the necessary defense of civil society, or the proper vindication of personal rights. But to cherish animosity, to thirst for mere revenge, to

227

hoard up wrongs, real or fancied, and lie in wait for the chance of paying them back; to be impatient, unforgiving, malicious, and cruel to all who have crossed us—these diabolical propensities are checked and curbed by the authority and spirit of the Christian religion, and the application of it has converted men from low savages into refined and civilized beings.

The punishment of sinners in eternal hell is excessive. The future of the soul is a subject on which we have very dark views. In our present state, the mind takes no idea except what is conveyed to it through the bodily senses. All our conceptions of the spiritual world are derived from some analogy to material things, and this analogy must necessarily be very remote, because the nature of the subjects compared is so diverse that a close similarity cannot be even supposed. No revelation has lifted the veil between time and eternity; but in shadowy figures we are warned that a very marked distinction will be made between the good and the bad in the next world. Speculative opinions concerning the punishment of the wicked, its nature and duration, vary with the temper and the imaginations of men. Doubtless we are many of us in error; but how can Mr. Ingersoll enlighten us? Acknowledging no standard of right and wrong in this world, he can have no theory of rewards and punishments in the next. The deeds done in the body, whether good or evil, are all morally alike in his eyes, and if there be in heaven a congregation of the just, he sees no reason why the worst rogue should not be a member of it. It is supposed, however, that man has a soul as well as a body, and that both are subject to certain laws, which cannot be violated without incurring the proper penalty—or consequence, if he likes that word better.

If Christ was God, he knew that his followers would persecute and murder men for their opinions; yet he did not forbid it. There is but one way to deal with this accusation, and that is to contradict it flatly. Nothing can be conceived more striking than the prohibition, not only of persecution, but of all the passions which lead or incite to it. No follower of Christ indulges in malice even to his enemy without violating the plainest rule of his faith. He cannot love God and hate his brother: if he says he can, St. John pronounces him a liar. The broadest benevolence, universal philanthropy, inexhaustible charity, are inculcated in every line of the New Testament. It is plain that Mr. Ingersoll never read a chapter of it; otherwise he would not have ventured upon this palpable falsification of its doctrines. Who told him that the devilish spirit of persecution was authorized, or encouraged, or not forbidden, by the Gospel? The person, whoever it was, who imposed upon his trusting ignorance should be given up to the just reprobation of his fellow-citizens.

Christians in modern times carry on wars of detraction and slander against one another. The discussions of theological subjects by men who believe in the fundamental doctrines of Christ are singularly free from harshness and abuse. Of course I cannot speak with absolute certainty, but I believe most confidently that there is not in all the religious polemics of this century as much slanderous invective as can be found in any ten lines of Mr. Ingersoll's writings. Of course I do not include political preachers among my models of charity and forbearance. They

228

are a mendacious set, but Christianity is no more responsible for their misconduct than it is for the treachery of Judas Iscariot or the wrongs done to Paul by Alexander the coppersmith.

But, says he, *Christians have been guilty of wanton and wicked Persecution.* It is true that some persons, professing Christianity, have violated the fundamental principles of their faith by inflicting violent injuries and bloody wrongs upon their fellow-men. But the perpetrators of these outrages were in fact not Christians: they were either hypocrites from the beginning or else base apostates—infidels or something worse—hireling wolves, whose gospel was their maw. Not one of them ever pretended to find a warrant for his conduct in any precept of Christ or any doctrine of his Church. All the wrongs of this nature which history records have been the work of politicians, aided often by priests and ministers who were willing to deny their Lord and desert to the enemy, for the sake of their temporal interests. Take the cases most commonly cited and see if this be not a true account of them. The *auto da fé* of Spain and Portugal, the burnings at Smithfield, and the whipping of women in Massachusetts, were the outcome of a cruel, false, and antichristian policy. Coligny and his adherents were killed by an order of Charles IX., at the instance of the Guises, who headed a hostile faction, and merely for reasons of state. Louis XIV. revoked the edict of Nantes, and banished the Waldenses under pain of confiscation and death; but this was done on the declared ground that the victims were not safe subjects. The brutal atrocities of Cromwell and the outrages of the Orange lodges against the Irish Catholics were not persecutions by religious people, but movements as purely political as those of the Know-Nothings, Plug-Uglys, and Blood-Tubs of this country. If the Gospel should be blamed for these acts in opposition to its principles, why not also charge it with the cruelties of Nero, or the present persecution of the Jesuits by the infidel republic of France?

Christianity is opposed to freedom of thought. The kingdom of Christ is based upon certain principles, to which it requires the assent of every one who would enter therein. If you are unwilling to own his authority and conform your moral conduct to his laws, you cannot expect that he will admit you to the privileges of his government. But naturalization is not forced upon you if you prefer to be an alien. The Gospel makes the strongest and tenderest appeal to the heart, reason, and conscience of man—entreats him to take thought for his own highest interest, and by all its moral influence provokes him to good works; but he is not constrained by any kind of duress to leave the service or relinquish the wages of sin. Is there anything that savors of tyranny in this? A man of ordinary judgment will say, no. But Mr. Ingersoll thinks it as oppressive as the refusal of Jehovah to reward the worship of demons.

The gospel of Christ does not satisfy the hunger of the heart. That depends upon what kind of a heart it is. If it hungers after righteousness, it will surely be filled. It is probable, also, that if it hungers for the filthy food of a godless philosophy it will get what its appetite demands. That was an expressive phrase which Carlyle used when he called modern infidelity "the gospel of dirt." Those who are greedy to swallow it will doubtless be supplied satisfactorily.

Accounts of miracles are always false. Are miracles impossible? No one will say so who opens his eyes to the miracles of creation with which we are surrounded on every hand. You cannot even show that they are *a priori* improbable. God would be likely to reveal his will to the rational creatures who were required to obey it; he would authenticate in some way the right of prophets and apostles to speak in his name; supernatural power was the broad seal which he affixed to their commission. From this it follows that the improbability of a miracle is no greater than the original improbability of a revelation, and that is not improbable at all. Therefore, if the miracles of the New Testament are proved by sufficient evidence, we believe them as we believe any other established fact. They become deniable only when it is shown that the great miracle of making the world was never performed. Accordingly Mr. Ingersoll abolishes creation first, and thus clears the way to his dogmatic conclusion that *all* miracles are "the children of mendacity."

Christianity is pernicious in its moral effect, darkens the mind, narrows the soul, arrests the progress of human society, and hinders civilization. Mr. Ingersoll, as a zealous apostle of "the gospel of dirt," must be expected to throw a good deal of mud. But this is too much: it injures himself instead of defiling the object of his assault. When I answer that all we have of virtue, justice, intellectual liberty, moral elevation, refinement, benevolence, and true wisdom came to us from that source which he reviles as the fountain of evil, I am not merely putting one assertion against the other; for I have the advantage, which he has not, of speaking what every tolerably well-informed man knows to be true. Reflect what kind of a world this was when the disciples of Christ undertook to reform it, and compare it with the condition in which their teachings have put it. In its mighty metropolis, the center of its intellectual and political power, the best men were addicted to vices so debasing that I could not even allude to them without soiling the paper I write upon. All manner of unprincipled wickedness was practiced in the private life of the whole population without concealment or shame, and the magistrates were thoroughly and universally corrupt. Benevolence in any shape was altogether unknown. The helpless and the weak got neither justice nor mercy. There was no relief for the poor, no succor for the sick, no refuge for the unfortunate. In all pagandom there was not a hospital, asylum, almshouse, or organized charity of any sort. The indifference to human life was literally frightful. The order of a successful leader to assassinate his opponents was always obeyed by his followers with the utmost alacrity and pleasure. It was a special amusement of the populace to witness the shows at which men were compelled to kill one another, to be torn in pieces by wild beasts, or otherwise "butchered, to make a Roman holiday." In every province paganism enacted the same cold-blooded cruelties; oppression and robbery ruled supreme; murder went rampaging and red over all the earth. The Church came, and her light penetrated this moral darkness like a new sun. She covered the globe with institutions of mercy, and thousands upon thousands of her disciples devoted themselves exclusively to works of charity at the sacrifice of every earthly interest. Her earliest adherents were killed without remorse—beheaded, crucified, sawn asunder, thrown to the beasts, or covered with pitch, piled up in great heaps, and slowly burnt to death. But her faith was made perfect through suffering, and the law of love rose in triumph from the ashes of her martyrs. This religion has come down to us through the ages, attended all the way by righteousness, justice, temperance, mercy, transparent truthfulness, exulting hope, and white-winged charity. Never was its influence for good more plainly perceptible than now. It has not converted, purified, and reformed all men, for its first principle is the freedom of the human will, and there are those who choose to reject it. But to the mass of mankind, directly and indirectly, it has brought uncounted benefits and blessings. Abolish it—take away the restraints which it imposes on evil passions—silence the admonitions of its preachers—let all Christians cease their labors of charity—blot out from history the records of its heroic benevolence—repeal the laws it has enacted and the institutions it has built up—let its moral principles be abandoned and all its miracles of light be extinguished—what would we come to? I need not answer this question: the experiment has been partially tried. The French nation formally renounced Christianity, denied the existence of the Supreme Being, and so satisfied the hunger of the infidel heart for a time. What followed? Universal depravity, garments rolled in blood, fantastic crimes unimagined before, which startled the earth with their sublime atrocity. The American people have and ought to have no special desire to follow that terrible example of guilt and misery.

It is impossible to discuss this subject within the limits of a review. No doubt the effort to be short has made me obscure. If Mr. Ingersoll thinks himself wronged, or his doctrines misconstrued, let him not lay my fault at the door of the Church, or cast his censure on the clergy.

"Adsum qui feci, in me convertite ferrum."

J. S. Black.

THE CHRISTIAN RELIGION.

III.

COL. INGERSOLL'S REJOINDER
BY ROBERT G. INGERSOLL.

"Apart from moral conduct, all that man thinks himself able to do, in order to become acceptable to God, is mere superstition and religious folly." Kant.

Several months ago, *The North American Review* asked me to write an article, saying that it would be published if some one would furnish a reply. I wrote the article that appeared in the August number, and by me it was entitled "Is All of the Bible Inspired?" Not until the article was written did I know who was expected to answer. I make this explanation for the purpose of dissipating the impression that Mr. Black had been challenged by me. To have struck his shield with my lance might have given birth to the impression that I was somewhat doubtful as to the correctness of my position. I naturally expected an answer from some professional theologian, and was surprised to find that a reply had been written by a "policeman," who imagined that he had answered my arguments by simply telling me that my statements were false. It is somewhat unfortunate that in a discussion like this any one should resort to the slightest personal detraction. The theme is great enough to engage the highest faculties of the human mind, and in the investigation of such a subject vituperation is singularly and vulgarly out of place. Arguments cannot be answered with insults. It is unfortunate that the intellectual arena should be entered by a "policeman," who has more confidence in concussion than discussion. Kindness is strength. Good-nature is often mistaken for virtue, and good health sometimes passes for genius. Anger blows out the lamp of the mind. In the examination of a great and important question, every one should be serene, slow-pulsed, and calm. Intelligence is not the foundation of arrogance. Insolence is not logic. Epithets are the arguments of malice. Candor is the courage of the soul. Leaving the objectionable portions of Mr. Black's reply, feeling that so grand a subject should not be blown and tainted with malicious words, I proceed to answer as best I may the arguments he has urged.

I am made to say that "the universe is natural"; that "it came into being of its own accord"; that "it made its own laws at the start, and afterward improved itself considerably by spontaneous evolution."

I did say that "the universe is natural," but I did not say that "it came into being of its own accord"; neither did I say that "it made its own laws and afterward improved itself." The universe, according to my idea, is, always was, and forever will be. It did not "come into being," it is the one eternal being,—the only thing that ever did, does, or can exist. It did not "make its own laws." We know nothing of what we call the laws of nature except as we gather the idea of law from the uniformity of phenomena springing from like conditions. To make myself clear: Water always runs down-hill. The theist says that this happens because there is behind the phenomenon an active law. As a matter of fact, law is this side of the phenomenon. Law does not cause the phenomenon, but the phenomenon causes the idea of law in our minds; and this idea is produced from the fact that under like circumstances the same phenomenon always happens. Mr. Black probably thinks that the difference in the weight of rocks and clouds was created by law; that parallel lines fail to unite only because it is illegal that diameter and circumference could have been so made that it would be a greater distance across than around a circle; that a straight line could enclose a triangle if not prevented by law, and that a little legislation could make it possible for two bodies to occupy the same space at the same time. It seems to me that law cannot be the cause of phenomena, but is an effect produced in our minds by their succession and resemblance. To put a God back of the universe, compels us to admit that there was a time when nothing existed except this God; that this God had lived from eternity in an infinite vacuum, and in absolute idleness. The mind of every thoughtful man is forced to one of these two conclusions: either that the universe is self-existent, or that it was created by a self-existent being. To my mind, there are far more difficulties in the second hypothesis than in the first.

Of course, upon a question like this, nothing can be absolutely known. We live on an atom called Earth, and what we know of the infinite is almost infinitely limited; but, little as we know, all have an equal right to give their honest thought. Life is a shadowy, strange, and winding road on which we travel for a little way—a few short steps—just from the cradle, with its lullaby of love, to the low and quiet way-side inn, where all at last must sleep, and where the only salutation is—Good-night.

I know as little as any one else about the "plan" of the universe; and as to the "design," I know just as little. It will not do to say that the universe was designed, and therefore there must be a designer. There must first be proof that it was "designed." It will not do to say that the universe has a "plan," and then assert that there must have been an infinite maker. The idea that a design must have a beginning and that a designer need not, is a simple expression of human ignorance. We find a watch, and we say: "So curious and wonderful a thing must have had a maker." We find the watch-maker, and we say: "So curious and wonderful a thing as man must have had a maker." We find God, and we then say: "He is so wonderful that he must *not* have had a maker." In other words, all things a little wonderful must have been created, but it is possible for something to be so wonderful that it always existed. One would suppose that just as the wonder increased the necessity for a creator increased, because it is the wonder of the thing that suggests the idea of creation. Is it possible that a designer exists from all eternity without design? Was there no design in having an infinite designer? For me, it is hard to see the plan or design in earthquakes and pestilences. It is somewhat difficult to discern the design or the benevolence in so making the world that billions of animals live only on the agonies of others. The justice of God is not visible to me in the history of this world. When I think of the suffering and death, of the poverty and crime, of the cruelty and malice, of the heartlessness of this "design" and "plan," where beak and claw and tooth tear and rend the quivering flesh of weakness and despair, I cannot convince myself that it is the result of infinite wisdom, benevolence, and justice.

Most Christians have seen and recognized this difficulty, and have endeavored to avoid it by giving God an opportunity in another world to rectify the seeming mistakes of this. Mr. Black, however, avoids the entire question by saying: "We have neither jurisdiction nor capacity to rejudge the justice of God." In other words, we have no right to think upon this subject, no right to examine the questions most vitally affecting human kind. We are simply to accept the ignorant statements of barbarian dead. This question cannot be settled by saying that "it would be a mere waste of time and space to enumerate the proofs which show that the Universe was created by a preexistent and self-conscious Being." The time and space should have been "wasted," and the proofs should have been enumerated. These "proofs" are what the wisest and greatest are trying to find. Logic is not satisfied with assertion. It cares nothing for the opinions of the "great,"—nothing for the prejudices of the many, and least of all for the superstitions of the dead. In the world of Science, a fact is a legal tender. Assertions and miracles are base and spurious coins. We have the right to rejudge the justice even of a god. No one should throw away his reason—the fruit of all experience. It is the intellectual capital of the soul, the only light, the only guide, and without it the brain becomes the palace of an idiot king, attended by a retinue of thieves and hypocrites.

Of course it is admitted that most of the Ten Commandments are wise and just. In passing, it may be well enough to say, that the commandment, "Thou shalt not make unto thee any graven image, or any likeness of anything that is in heaven above, or that is in the earth beneath, or that is in the water under the earth," was the absolute death of Art, and that not until after the destruction of Jerusalem was there a Hebrew painter or sculptor. Surely a commandment is not inspired that drives from the earth the living canvas and the breathing stone—leaves all walls bare and all the niches desolate. In the tenth commandment we find woman placed on an exact equality with other property, which, to say the least of it, has never tended to the amelioration of her condition.

A very curious thing about these commandments is that their supposed author violated nearly every one. From Sinai, according to the account, he said: "Thou shalt not kill," and yet he ordered the murder of millions; "Thou shalt not commit adultery," and yet he gave captured maidens to gratify the lust of captors; "Thou shalt not steal," and yet he gave to Jewish marauders the flocks and herds of others; "Thou shalt not covet thy neighbor's house, nor his wife," and yet he allowed his chosen people to destroy the homes of neighbors and to steal their wives; "Honor thy father and thy mother," and yet this same God had thousands of fathers butchered, and with the sword of war killed children yet unborn; "Thou shalt not bear false witness against thy neighbor," and yet he sent abroad "lying spirits" to deceive his own prophets, and in a hundred ways paid tribute to deceit. So far as we know, Jehovah kept only one of these commandments—he worshiped no other god.

The religious intolerance of the Old Testament is justified upon the ground that "blasphemy was a breach of political allegiance," that "idolatry was an act of overt treason," and that "to worship the gods of the hostile heathen was deserting to the public enemy, and giving him aid and comfort." According to Mr. Black, we should all have liberty of conscience except when directly governed by God. In that country where God is king, liberty cannot exist. In this position, I admit that he is upheld and fortified by the "sacred" text. Within the Old Testament there is no such thing as religious toleration. Within that volume can be found no mercy for an unbeliever. For all who think for themselves, there are threatenings, curses, and anathemas. Think of an infinite being who is so cruel, so unjust, that he will not allow one of his own children the liberty of thought! Think of an infinite God acting as the direct governor of a people, and yet not able to command their love! Think of the author of all mercy imbruing his hands in the blood of helpless men, women, and children, simply because he did not furnish them with intelligence enough to understand his law! An earthly father who cannot govern by affection is not fit to be a father; what, then, shall we say of an infinite being who resorts to violence, to pestilence, to disease, and famine, in the vain effort to obtain even the respect of a savage? Read this passage, red from the heart of cruelty:

"If thy brother, the son of thy mother, or thy son, or thy daughter, or the wife of thy bosom, or thy friend, which is as thine own soul, entice thee secretly, saying, Let us go and serve other gods which thou hast not known, thou nor thy fathers, . . . thou shalt not consent unto him, nor hearken unto him, neither shalt thine eye pity him, neither shalt thou spare, neither shalt thou conceal him, but thou shalt surely kill him; thine hand shall be first upon him to put him to death, and afterwards the hand of all the people; and thou shalt stone him with stones, that he die."

This is the religious liberty of the Bible. If you had lived in Palestine, and if the wife of your bosom, dearer to you than your own soul, had said: "I like the religion of India better than that of Palestine," it would have been your duty to kill her.

"Your eye must not pity her, your hand must be first upon her, and afterwards the hand of all the people." If she had said: "Let us worship the sun—the sun that clothes the earth in garments of green—the sun, the great fireside of the world—the sun that covers the hills and valleys with flowers—that gave me your face, and made it possible for me to look into the eyes of my babe—let us worship the sun," it was your duty to kill her. You must throw the first stone, and when against her bosom—a bosom filled with love for you—you had thrown the jagged and cruel rock, and had seen the red stream of her life oozing from the dumb lips of death, you could then look up and receive the congratulations of the God whose commandment you had obeyed. Is it possible that a being of infinite mercy ordered a husband to kill his wife for the crime of having expressed an opinion on the subject of religion? Has there been found upon the records of the savage world anything more perfectly fiendish than this commandment of Jehovah? This is justified on the ground that "blasphemy was a breach of political allegiance, and idolatry an act of overt treason." We can understand how a human king stands in need of the service of his people. We can understand how the desertion of any of his soldiers weakens his army; but were the king infinite in power, his strength would still remain the same, and under no conceivable circumstances could the enemy triumph.

I insist that, if there is an infinitely good and wise God, he beholds with pity the misfortunes of his children. I insist that such a God would know the mists, the clouds, the darkness enveloping the human mind. He would know how few stars are visible in the intellectual sky. His pity, not his wrath, would be excited by the efforts of his blind children, groping in the night to find the cause of things, and endeavoring, through their tears, to see some dawn of hope. Filled with awe by their surroundings, by fear of the unknown, he would know that when, kneeling, they poured out their gratitude to some unseen power, even to a visible idol, it was, in fact, intended for him. An infinitely good being, had he the power, would answer the reasonable prayer of an honest savage, even when addressed to wood and stone.

The atrocities of the Old Testament, the threatenings, maledictions, and curses of the "inspired book," are defended on the ground that the Jews had a right to treat their enemies as their enemies treated them; and in this connection is this remarkable statement: "In your treatment of hostile barbarians you not only may lawfully, you must necessarily, adopt their mode of warfare. If they come to conquer you, they may be conquered by you; if they give no quarter, they are entitled to none; if the death of your whole population be their purpose, you may defeat it by exterminating theirs."

For a man who is a "Christian policeman," and has taken upon himself to defend the Christian religion; for one who follows the Master who said that when smitten on one cheek you must turn the other, and who again and again enforced the idea that you must overcome evil with good, it is hardly consistent to declare that a civilized nation must of necessity adopt the warfare of savages. Is it possible that in fighting, for instance, the Indians of America, if they scalp our soldiers we should scalp theirs? If they ravish, murder, and mutilate our wives, must we treat theirs in the same manner? If they kill the babes in our cradles, must we brain theirs? If they take our captives, bind them to the trees, and if their squaws fill their quivering flesh with sharpened fagots and set them on fire, that they may die clothed with flame, must our wives, our mothers, and our daughters follow the fiendish example? Is this the conclusion of the most enlightened Christianity? Will the pulpits of the United States adopt the arguments of this "policeman"? Is this the last and most beautiful blossom of the Sermon on the Mount? Is this the echo of "Father, forgive them; they know not what they do"?

Mr. Black justifies the wars of extermination and conquest because the American people fought for the integrity of their own country; fought to do away with the infamous institution of slavery; fought to preserve the jewels of liberty and justice for themselves and for their children. Is it possible that his mind is so clouded by political and religious prejudice, by the recollections of an unfortunate administration, that he sees no difference between a war of extermination and one of self-preservation? that he sees no choice between the murder of helpless age, of weeping women and of sleeping babes, and the defense of liberty and nationality?

The soldiers of the Republic did not wage a war of extermination. They did not seek to enslave their fellow-men. They did not murder trembling age. They did not sheathe their swords in women's breasts. They gave the old men bread, and let the mothers rock their babes in peace. They fought to save the world's great hope—to free a race and put the humblest hut beneath the canopy of liberty and law.

Claiming neither praise nor dispraise for the part taken by me in the Civil war, for the purposes of this argument, it is sufficient to say that I am perfectly willing that my record, poor and barren as it is, should be compared with his.

Never for an instant did I suppose that any respectable American citizen could be found willing at this day to defend the institution of slavery; and never was I more astonished than when I found Mr. Black denying that civilized countries passionately assert that slavery is and always was a hideous crime. I was amazed when he declared that "the doctrine that slavery is a crime under all circumstances and at all times was first started by the adherents of a political faction in this country less than forty years ago." He tells us that "they denounced God and Christ for not agreeing with them," but that "they did not constitute the civilized world; nor were they, if the truth must be told, a very respectable portion of it. Politically they were successful; I need not say by what means, or with what effect upon the morals of the country."

Slavery held both branches of Congress, filled the chair of the Executive, sat upon the Supreme Bench, had in its hands all rewards, all offices; knelt in the pew, occupied the pulpit, stole human beings in the name of God, robbed the trundle-bed for love of Christ; incited mobs, led ignorance, ruled colleges, sat in the chairs of professors, dominated the public press, closed the lips of free speech, and polluted with its leprous hand every source and spring of power. The abolitionists attacked this monster. They were the bravest, grandest men of their country and their century. Denounced by thieves, hated by hypocrites, mobbed by cowards, slandered by priests, shunned by politicians, abhorred by the seekers of office,—these men "of whom the world was not worthy," in spite of all opposition, in spite of poverty and want, conquered innumerable obstacles, never faltering for one moment, never dismayed—accepting defeat with a smile born of infinite hope—knowing that they were right—insisted and persisted until every chain was broken, until slave-pens became schoolhouses, and three millions of slaves became free men, women, and children. They did not measure with "the golden metewand of God," but with "the elastic cord of human feeling." They were men the latchets of whose shoes no believer in human slavery was ever worthy to unloose. And yet we are told by this modern defender of the slavery of Jehovah that they were not even respectable; and this slander is justified because the writer is assured "that the infallible God proceeded upon good grounds when he authorized slavery in Judea."

Not satisfied with having slavery in this world, Mr. Black assures us that it will last through all eternity, and that forever and forever inferiors must be subordinated to superiors. Who is the superior man? According to Mr. Black, he is superior who lives upon the unpaid labor of the inferior. With me, the superior man is the one who uses his superiority in bettering the condition of the inferior. The superior man is strength for the weak, eyes for the blind, brains for the simple; he is the one who helps carry the burden that nature has put upon the inferior. Any man who helps another to gain and retain his liberty is superior to any infallible God who authorized slavery in Judea. For my part, I would rather be the slave than the master. It is better to be robbed than to be a robber. I had rather be stolen from than to be a thief.

According to Mr. Black, there will be slavery in heaven, and fast by the throne of God will be the auction-block, and the streets of the New Jerusalem will be adorned with the whipping post, while the music of the harp will be supplemented by the crack of the driver's whip. If some good Republican would catch Mr. Black, "incorporate him into his family, tame him, teach him to think, and give him a knowledge of the true principles of human liberty and government, he would confer upon him a most beneficent boon."

Slavery includes all other crimes. It is the joint product of the kidnapper, pirate, thief, murderer, and hypocrite. It degrades labor and corrupts leisure. To lacerate the naked back, to sell wives, to steal babes, to breed bloodhounds, to debauch your own soul—this is slavery. This is what Jehovah "authorized in Judea." This is what Mr. Black believes in still. He "measures with the golden metewand of God." I abhor slavery. With me, liberty is not merely a means—it is an end. Without that word, all other words are empty sounds.

Mr. Black is too late with his protest against the freedom of his fellow-man. Liberty is making the tour of the world. Russia has emancipated her serfs; the slave trade is prosecuted only by thieves and pirates; Spain feels upon her cheek the burning blush of shame; Brazil with proud and happy eyes is looking for the dawn of freedom's day; the people of the South rejoice that slavery is no more, and every good and honest man (excepting Mr. Black), of every land and clime, hopes that the limbs of men will never feel again the weary weight of chains.

We are informed by Mr. Black that polygamy is neither commanded nor prohibited in the Old Testament—that it is only "discouraged." It seems to me that a little legislation on that subject might have tended to its "discouragement." But where is the legislation? In the moral code, which Mr. Black assures us "consists of certain immutable rules to govern the conduct of all men at all times and at all places in their private and personal relations with others," not one word is found on the subject of polygamy. There is nothing "discouraging" in the Ten Commandments, nor in the records of any conversation Jehovah is claimed to have had with Moses upon Sinai. The life of Abraham, the story of Jacob and Laban, the duty of a brother to be the husband of the widow of his deceased brother, the life of David, taken in connection with the practice of one who is claimed to have been the wisest of men—all these things are probably relied on to show that polygamy was at least "discouraged." Certainly, Jehovah had time to instruct Moses as to the infamy of polygamy. He could have spared a few moments from a description of the patterns of tongs and basins, for a subject so important as this. A few words in favor of the one wife and the one husband—in favor of the virtuous and loving home—might have taken the place of instructions as to cutting the garments of priests and fashioning candlesticks and ouches of gold. If he had left out simply the order that rams' skins should be dyed red, and in its place had said, "A man shall have but one wife, and the wife but one husband," how much better would it have been.

All the languages of the world are not sufficient to express the filth of polygamy. It makes man a beast, and woman a slave. It destroys the fireside and makes virtue an outcast. It takes us back to the barbarism of animals, and leaves the heart a den in which crawl and hiss the slimy serpents of most loathsome lust. And yet Mr. Black insists that we owe to the Bible the present elevation of woman. Where will he find in the Old Testament the rights of wife, and mother, and daughter defined? Even in the New Testament she is told to "learn in silence, with all subjection;" that she "is not suffered to teach, nor to usurp any authority over the man, but to be in silence." She is told that "the head of every man is Christ, and the head of the woman is man, and the head of Christ is God." In other words, there is the same difference between the wife and husband that there is between the husband and Christ.

The reasons given for this infamous doctrine are that "Adam was first formed, and then Eve;" that "Adam was not deceived," but that "the woman being deceived, was in the transgression." These childish reasons are the only ones given by the inspired writers. We are also told that "a man, indeed, ought to cover his head, forasmuch as he is the image and glory of God;" but that "the woman is the glory of the man," and this is justified from the fact, and the remarkable fact, set forth in the very next verse—that "the man is not of the woman, but the woman of the man." And the same gallant apostle says: "Neither was the man created for the woman, but the woman for the man;" "Wives, submit yourselves unto your husbands as unto the Lord; for the husband is the head of the wife, even as Christ is the head of the church, and he is the savior of the body. Therefore, as the church is subject unto Christ, so let the wives be subject to their own husbands in everything." These are the passages that have liberated woman!

According to the Old Testament, woman had to ask pardon, and had to be purified, for the crime of having borne sons and daughters. If in this world there is a figure of perfect purity, it is a mother holding in her thrilled and happy arms her child. The doctrine that woman is the slave, or serf, of man—whether it comes from heaven or from hell, from God or a demon, from the golden streets of the New Jerusalem or from the very Sodom of perdition—is savagery, pure and simple.

In no country in the world had women less liberty than in the Holy Land, and no monarch held in less esteem the rights of wives and mothers than Jehovah of the Jews. The position of woman was far better in Egypt than in Palestine. Before the pyramids were built, the sacred songs of Isis were sung by women, and women with pure hands had offered sacrifices to the gods. Before Moses was born, women had sat upon the Egyptian throne. Upon ancient tombs the husband and wife are represented as seated in the same chair. In Persia women were priests, and in some of the oldest civilizations "they were reverenced on earth, and worshiped afterward as goddesses in heaven." At the advent of Christianity, in all pagan countries women officiated at the sacred altars. They guarded the eternal fire. They kept the sacred books. From their lips came the oracles of fate. Under the domination of the Christian Church, woman became the merest slave for at least a thousand years. It was claimed that through woman the race had fallen, and that her loving kiss had poisoned all the springs of life. Christian priests asserted that but for her crime the world would have been an Eden still. The ancient fathers exhausted their eloquence in the denunciation of woman, and repeated again and again the slander of St. Paul. The condition of woman has improved just in proportion that man has lost confidence in the inspiration of the Bible.

For the purpose of defending the character of his infallible God, Mr. Black is forced to defend religious intolerance, wars of extermination, human slavery, and *almost* polygamy. He admits that God established slavery; that he commanded his chosen people to buy the children of the heathen; that heathen fathers and mothers did right to sell their girls and boys; that God ordered the Jews to wage wars of extermination and conquest; that it was right to kill the old and young; that God forged manacles for the human brain; that he commanded husbands to murder their wives for suggesting the worship of the sun or moon; and that every cruel, savage passage in the Old Testament was inspired by him. Such is a "policeman's" view of God.

Will Mr. Black have the kindness to state a few of his objections to the devil?

Mr. Black should have answered my arguments, instead of calling me "blasphemous" and "scurrilous." In the discussion of these questions I have nothing to do with the reputation of my opponent. His character throws no light on the subject, and is to me a matter of perfect indifference. Neither will it do for one who enters the lists as the champion of revealed religion to say that "we have no right to rejudge the justice of God."

Such a statement is a white flag. The warrior eludes the combat when he cries out that it is a "metaphysical question." He deserts the field and throws down his arms when he admits that "no revelation has lifted the veil between time and eternity." Again I ask, why were the Jewish people as wicked, cruel, and ignorant with a revelation from God, as other nations were without? Why were the worshipers of false deities as brave, as kind, and generous as those who knew the only true and living God?

How do you explain the fact that while Jehovah was waging wars of extermination, establishing slavery, and persecuting for opinion's sake, heathen philosophers were teaching that all men are brothers, equally entitled to liberty and life? You insist that Jehovah believed in slavery and yet punished the Egyptians for enslaving the Jews. Was your God once an abolitionist? Did he at that time "denounce Christ for not agreeing with him"? If slavery was a crime in Egypt, was it a virtue in Palestine? Did God treat the Canaanites better than Pharaoh did the Jews? Was it right for Jehovah to kill the children of the people because of Pharaoh's sin? Should the peasant be punished for the king's crime? Do you not know that the worst thing that can be said of Nero, Caligula, and Commodus is that they resembled the Jehovah of the Jews? Will you tell me why God failed to give his Bible to the whole world? Why did he not give the Scriptures to the Hindu, the Greek, and Roman? Why did he fail to enlighten the worshipers of "Mammon" and Moloch, of Belial and Baal, of Bacchus and Venus? After all, was not Bacchus as good as Jehovah? Is it not better to drink wine than to shed blood? Was there anything in the worship of Venus worse than giving captured maidens to satisfy the victor's lust? Did "Mammon" or Moloch do anything more infamous than to establish slavery? Did they order their soldiers to kill men, women, and children, and to save alive nothing that had breath? Do not answer these questions by saying that "no veil has been lifted between time and eternity," and that "we have no right to rejudge the justice of God."

If Jehovah was in fact God, he knew the end from the beginning. He knew that his Bible would be a breastwork behind which tyranny and hypocrisy would crouch; that it would be quoted by tyrants; that it would be the defense of robbers, called kings, and of hypocrites called priests. He knew that he had taught the Jewish people but little of importance. He knew that he found them free and left them captives. He knew that he had never fulfilled the promises made to them. He knew that while other nations had advanced in art and science, his chosen people were savage still. He promised them the world, and gave them a desert. He promised them liberty, and he made them slaves. He promised them victory, and he gave them defeat. He said they should be kings, and he made them serfs. He promised them universal empire, and gave them exile. When one finishes the Old Testament, he is compelled to say: Nothing can add to the misery of a nation whose king is Jehovah!

And here I take occasion to thank Mr. Black for having admitted that Jehovah gave no commandment against the practice of polygamy, that he established slavery, waged wars of extermination, and persecuted for opinion's sake even unto death. Most theologians endeavor to putty, patch, and paint the wretched record of inspired crime, but Mr. Black has been bold enough and honest enough to admit the truth. In this age of fact and demonstration it is refreshing to find a man who believes so thoroughly in the monstrous and miraculous, the impossible and immoral—who still clings lovingly to the legends of the bib and rattle—who through the bitter experiences of a wicked world has kept the credulity of the cradle, and finds comfort and joy in thinking about the Garden of Eden, the subtle serpent, the flood, and Babel's tower, stopped by the jargon of a thousand tongues—who reads with happy eyes the story of the burning brimstone storm that fell upon the cities of the plain, and smilingly explains the transformation of the retrospective

Mrs. Lot—who laughs at Egypt's plagues and Pharaoh's whelmed and drowning hosts—eats manna with the wandering Jews, warms himself at the burning bush, sees Korah's company by the hungry earth devoured, claps his wrinkled hands with glee above the heathens' butchered babes, and longingly looks back to the patriarchal days of concubines and slaves. How touching when the learned and wise crawl back in cribs and ask to hear the rhymes and fables once again! How charming in these hard and scientific times to see old age in Superstition's lap, with eager lips upon her withered breast!

Mr. Black comes to the conclusion that the Hebrew Bible is in exact harmony with the New Testament, and that the two are "connected together;" and "that if one is true the other cannot be false."

If this is so, then he must admit that if one is false the other cannot be true; and it hardly seems possible to me that there is a right-minded, sane man, except Mr. Black, who now believes that a God of infinite kindness and justice ever commanded one nation to exterminate another; ever ordered his soldiers to destroy men, women, and babes; ever established the institution of human slavery; ever regarded the auction-block as an altar, or a bloodhound as an apostle.

Mr. Black contends (after having answered my indictment against the Old Testament by admitting the allegations to be true) that the rapidity with which Christianity spread "proves the supernatural origin of the Gospel, or that it was propagated by the direct aid of the Divine Being himself."

Let us see. In his efforts to show that the "infallible God established slavery in Judea," he takes occasion to say that "the doctrine that slavery is a crime under all circumstances was first started by the adherents of a political faction in this, country less than forty years ago;" that "they denounced God and Christ for not agreeing with them;" but that "they did not constitute the civilized world; nor were they, if the truth must be told, a very respectable portion of it." Let it be remembered that this was only forty years ago; and yet, according to Mr. Black, a few disreputable men changed the ideas of nearly fifty millions of people, changed the Constitution of the United States, liberated a race from slavery, clothed three millions of people with political rights, took possession of the Government, managed its affairs for more than twenty years, and have compelled the admiration of the civilized world. Is it Mr. Black's idea that this happened by chance? If not, then according to him, there are but two ways to account for it; either the rapidity with which Republicanism spread proves its supernatural origin, "or else its propagation was provided for and carried on by the direct aid of the Divine Being himself." Between these two, Mr. Black may make his choice. He will at once see that the rapid rise and spread of any doctrine does not even tend to show that it was divinely revealed.

This argument is applicable to all religions. Mohammedans can use it as well as Christians. Mohammed was a poor man, a driver of camels. He was without education, without influence, and without wealth, and yet in a few years he consolidated thousands of tribes, and made millions of men confess that there is "one God, and Mohammed is his prophet." His success was a thousand times greater during his life than that of Christ. He was not crucified; he was a conqueror. "Of all men, he exercised the greatest influence upon the human race." Never in the world's history did a religion spread with the rapidity of his. It burst like a storm over the fairest portions of the globe. If Mr. Black is right in his position that rapidity is secured only by the direct aid of the Divine Being, then Mohammed was most certainly the prophet of God. As to wars of extermination and slavery, Mohammed agreed with Mr. Black, and upon polygamy, with Jehovah. As to religious toleration, he was great enough to say that "men holding to any form of faith might be saved, provided they were virtuous." In this, he was far in advance both of Jehovah and Mr. Black.

It will not do to take the ground that the rapid rise and spread of a religion demonstrates its divine character. Years before Gautama died, his religion was established, and his disciples were numbered by millions. His doctrines were not enforced by the sword, but by an appeal to the hopes, the fears, and the reason of mankind; and more than one-third of the human race are to-day the followers of Gautama. His religion has outlived all that existed in his time; and according to Dr. Draper, "there is no other country in the world except India that has the religion to-day it had at the birth of Jesus Christ." Gautama believed in the equality of all men; abhorred the spirit of caste, and proclaimed justice, mercy, and education for all.

Imagine a Mohammedan answering an infidel; would he not use the argument of Mr. Black, simply substituting Mohammed for Christ, just as effectually as it has been used against me? There was a time when India was the foremost nation of the world. Would not your argument, Mr. Black, have been just as good in the mouth of a Brahmin then, as it is in yours now? Egypt, the mysterious mother of mankind, with her pyramids built thirty-four hundred years before Christ, was once the first in all the earth, and gave to us our Trinity, and our symbol of the cross. Could not a priest of Isis and Osiris have used your arguments to prove that his religion was divine, and could he not have closed by saying: "From the facts established by this evidence it follows irresistibly that our religion came to us from God"? Do you not see that your argument proves too much, and that it is equally applicable to all the religions of the world?

Again, it is urged that "the acceptance of Christianity by a large portion of the generation contemporary with its founder and his apostles was, under the circumstances, an adjudication as solemn and authoritative as mortal intelligence could pronounce." If this is true, then "the acceptance of Buddhism by a large portion of the generation contemporary with its founder was an adjudication as solemn and authoritative as mortal intelligence could pronounce." The same could be said of Mohammedanism, and, in fact, of every religion that has ever benefited or cursed this world. This argument, when reduced to its simplest form, is this: All that succeeds is inspired.

The old argument that if Christianity is a human fabrication its authors must have been either good men or bad men, takes it for granted that there are but two classes of persons—the good and the bad. There is at least one other class—*the mistaken,* and both of the other classes may belong to this. Thousands of most excellent people have been deceived, and the history of the world is filled with instances where men have honestly supposed that they had received communications from angels and gods.

In thousands of instances these pretended communications contained the purest and highest thoughts, together with the most important truths; yet it will not do to say that these accounts are true; neither can they be proved by saying that the men who claimed to be inspired were good. What we must say is, that being good men, they were mistaken; and it is the charitable mantle of a mistake that I throw over Mr. Black, when I find him defending the institution of slavery. He seems to think it utterly incredible that any "combination of knaves, however base, would fraudulently concoct a religious system to denounce themselves, and to invoke the curse of God upon their own conduct." How did religions other than Christianity and Judaism arise? Were they all "concocted by a combination of knaves"? The religion of Gautama is filled with most beautiful and tender thoughts, with most excellent laws, and hundreds of sentences urging mankind to deeds of love and self-denial. Was Gautama inspired?

Does not Mr. Black know that thousands of people charged with witchcraft actually confessed in open court their guilt? Does he not know that they admitted that they had spoken face to face with Satan, and had sold their souls for gold and power? Does he not know that these admissions were made in the presence and expectation of death? Does he not know that hundreds of judges, some of them as great as the late lamented Gibson, believed in the existence of an impossible crime?

We are told that "there is no good reason to doubt that the statements of the Evangelists, as we have them now, are genuine." The fact is, no one knows who made the "statements of the Evangelists."

There are three important manuscripts upon which the Christian world relies. "The first appeared in the catalogue of the Vatican, in 1475. This contains the Old Testament. Of the New, it contains the four gospels,—the Acts, the seven Catholic Epistles, nine of the Pauline Epistles, and the Epistle to the Hebrews, as far as the fourteenth verse of the ninth chapter,"—and nothing more. This is known as the Codex Vatican. "The second, the Alexandrine, was presented to King Charles the First, in 1628. It contains the Old and New Testaments, with some exceptions; passages are wanting in Matthew, in John, and in II. Corinthians. It also contains the Epistle of Clemens Romanus, a letter of Athanasius, and the treatise of Eusebius on the Psalms." The last is the Sinaitic Codex, discovered about 1850, at the Convent of St. Catherine's, on Mount Sinai. "It contains the Old and New Testaments, and in addition the entire Epistle of Barnabas, and a portion of the Shepherd of Hermas—two books which, up to the beginning of the fourth century, were looked upon by many as Scripture." In this manuscript, or codex, the gospel of St. Mark concludes with the eighth verse of the sixteenth chapter, leaving out the frightful passage: "Go ye into all the world, and preach the gospel to every creature. He that believeth and is baptized shall be saved; but he that believeth not shall be damned."

In matters of the utmost importance these manuscripts disagree, but even if they all agreed it would not furnish the slightest evidence of their truth. It will not do to call the statements made in the gospels "depositions," until it is absolutely established who made them, and the circumstances under which they were made. Neither can we say that "they were made in the immediate prospect of death," until we know who made them. It is absurd to say that "the witnesses could not have been mistaken, because the nature of the facts precluded the possibility of any delusion about them." Can it be pretended that the witnesses could not have been mistaken about the relation the Holy Ghost is alleged to have sustained to Jesus Christ? Is there no possibility of delusion about a circumstance of that kind? Did the writers of the four gospels have "'the sensible and true avouch of their own eyes' and ears" in that behalf? How was it possible for any one of the four Evangelists to know that Christ was the Son of God, or that he was God? His mother wrote nothing on the subject. Matthew says that an angel of the Lord told Joseph in a dream, but Joseph never wrote an account of this wonderful vision. Luke tells us that the angel had a conversation with Mary, and that Mary told Elizabeth, but Elizabeth never wrote a word. There is no account of Mary or Joseph or Elizabeth or the angel, having had any conversation with Matthew, Mark, Luke, or John in which one word was said about the miraculous origin of Jesus Christ. The persons who knew did not write, so that the account is nothing but hearsay. Does Mr. Black pretend that such statements would be admitted as evidence in any court? But how do we know that the disciples of Christ wrote a word of the gospels? How did it happen that Christ wrote nothing? How do we know that the writers of the gospels "were men of unimpeachable character"?

All this is answered by saying "that nothing was said by the most virulent enemies against the personal honesty of the Evangelists." How is this known? If Christ performed the miracles recorded in the New Testament, why would the Jews put to death a man able to raise their dead? Why should they attempt to kill the Master of Death? How did it happen that a man who had done so many miracles was so obscure, so unknown, that one of his disciples had to be bribed to point him out? Is it not strange that the ones he had cured were not his disciples? Can we believe, upon the testimony of those about whose character we know nothing, that Lazarus was raised from the dead? What became of Lazarus? We never hear of him again. It seems to me that he would have been an object of great interest. People would have said: "He is the man who was once dead." Thousands would have inquired of him about the other world; would have asked him where he was when he received the information that he was wanted on the earth. His experience would have been vastly more interesting than everything else in the New Testament. A returned traveler from the shores of Eternity—one who had walked twice through the valley of the shadow—would have been the most interesting of human beings. When he came to die again, people would have said: "He is not afraid; he has had experience; he knows what death is." But, strangely enough, this Lazarus fades into obscurity with "the wise men of the East," and with the dead who came out of their graves on the night of the crucifixion. How is it known that it was claimed, during the life of Christ, that he had wrought a miracle? And if the claim was made, how is it known that it was not denied? Did the Jews believe that Christ was clothed with miraculous power? Would they have dared to crucify a man who had the power to clothe the dead with life? Is it not wonderful that no one at the trial of Christ said one word about the miracles he had wrought? Nothing about the sick he had healed, nor the dead he had raised?

Is it not wonderful that Josephus, the best historian the Hebrews produced, says nothing about the life or death of Christ; nothing about the massacre of the infants by Herod; not one word about the wonderful star that visited the sky at the birth of Christ; nothing about the darkness that fell upon the world for several hours in the midst of day; and failed entirely to mention that hundreds of graves were opened, and that multitudes of Jews arose from the dead, and visited the Holy City? Is it not wonderful that no historian ever mentioned any of these prodigies? and is it not more amazing than all the rest, that Christ himself concealed from Matthew, Mark, and Luke the dogma of the atonement, the necessity of belief, and the mystery of the second birth?

Of course I know that two letters were said to have been written by Pilate to Tiberius, concerning the execution of Christ, but they have been shown to be forgeries. I also know that "various letters were circulated attributed to Jesus Christ," and that one letter is said to have been written by him to Abgarus, king of Edessa; but as there was no king of Edessa at that time, this letter is admitted to have been a forgery. I also admit that a correspondence between Seneca and St. Paul was forged.

Here in our own country, only a few years ago, men claimed to have found golden plates upon which was written a revelation from God. They founded a new religion, and, according to their statement, did many miracles. They were treated as outcasts, and their leader was murdered. These men made their "depositions" "in the immediate prospect of death." They were mobbed, persecuted, derided, and yet they insisted that their prophet had miraculous power, and that he, too, could swing back the hingeless door of death. The followers of these men have increased, in these few years, so that now the murdered prophet has at least two hundred thousand disciples. It will be hard to find a contradiction of these pretended miracles, although this is an age filled with papers, magazines, and books. As a matter of fact, the claims of Joseph Smith were so preposterous that sensible people did not take the pains to write and print denials. When we remember that eighteen hundred years ago there were but few people who could write, and that a manuscript did not become public in any modern sense, it was possible for the gospels to have been written with all the foolish claims in reference to miracles without exciting comment or denial. There is not, in all the contemporaneous literature of the world, a single word about Christ or his apostles. The paragraph in Josephus is admitted to be an interpolation, and the letters, the account of the trial, and several other documents forged by the zeal of the early fathers, are now admitted to be false.

Neither will it do to say that "the statements made by the Evangelists are alike upon every important point." If there is anything of importance in the New Testament, from the theological standpoint, it is the ascension of Jesus Christ. If that happened, it was a miracle great enough to surfeit wonder. Are the statements of the inspired witnesses alike on this important point? Let us see.

Matthew says nothing upon the subject. Either Matthew was not there, had never heard of the ascension,—or, having heard of it, did not believe it, or, having seen it, thought it too unimportant to record. To this wonder of wonders Mark devotes one verse: "So then, after the Lord had spoken unto them, he was received up into heaven, and sat on the right-hand of God." Can we believe that this verse was written by one who witnessed the ascension of Jesus Christ; by one who watched his Master slowly rising through the air till distance left him from his tearful sight? Luke, another of the witnesses, says: "And it came to pass, while he blessed them, he was parted from them, and carried up into heaven." John corroborates Matthew by saying nothing on the subject. Now, we find that the last chapter of Mark, after the eighth verse, is an interpolation; so that Mark really says nothing about the occurrence. Either the ascension of Christ must be given up, or it must be admitted that the witnesses do not agree, and that three of them never heard of that most stupendous event.

Again, if anything could have left its "form and pressure" on the brain, it must have been the last words of Jesus Christ. The last words, according to Matthew, are: "Go ye, therefore, and teach all nations, baptizing them in the name of the Father, and of the Son, and of the Holy Ghost; teaching them to observe all things whatsoever I have commanded you: and lo, I am with you always, even unto the end of the world." The last words, according to the inspired witness known as Mark, are: "And these signs shall follow them that believe: in my name shall they cast out devils; they shall speak with new tongues; they shall take up serpents; and if they drink any deadly thing, it shall not hurt them; they shall lay hands on the sick, and they shall recover." Luke tells us that the last words uttered by Christ, with the exception of a blessing, were: "And behold, I send forth the promise of my Father upon you; but tarry ye in the city of Jerusalem, until ye be endued with power from on high." The last words, according to John, were: "Peter, seeing Him, saith to Jesus: Lord, and what shall this man do? Jesus saith unto him, If I will that he tarry till I come, what is that to thee? follow thou me."

An account of the ascension is also given in the Acts of the Apostles; and the last words of Christ, according to that inspired witness, are: "But ye shall receive power, after that the Holy Ghost is come upon you; and ye shall be witnesses unto me, both in Jerusalem and in all Judea, and in Samaria, and unto the uttermost part of the earth." In this account of the ascension we find that two men stood by the disciples in white apparel, and asked them: "Ye men of Galilee, why stand ye gazing up into heaven? This same Jesus, which is taken up from you into heaven, shall so come in like manner as ye have seen him go into heaven." Matthew says nothing of the two men. Mark never saw them. Luke may have forgotten them when writing his gospel, and John may have regarded them as optical illusions.

Luke testifies that Christ ascended on the very day of his resurrection. John deposes that eight days after the resurrection Christ appeared to the disciples and convinced Thomas. In the Acts we are told that Christ remained on earth for forty days after his resurrection. These "depositions" do not agree. Neither do Matthew and Luke agree in their histories of the infancy of Christ. It is impossible for both to be true. One of these "witnesses" must have been mistaken.

The most wonderful miracle recorded in the New Testament, as having been wrought by Christ, is the resurrection of Lazarus. While all the writers of the gospels, in many instances, record the same wonders and the same conversations, is it not remarkable that the greatest miracle is mentioned alone by John?

Two of the witnesses, Matthew and Luke, give the genealogy of Christ. Matthew says that there were forty-two generations from Abraham to Christ. Luke insists that there were forty-two from Christ to David, while Matthew gives the number as twenty-eight. It may be said that this is an old objection. An objection-remains young until it has been answered. Is it not wonderful that Luke and Matthew do not agree on a single name of Christ's ancestors for thirty-seven generations?

There is a difference of opinion among the "witnesses" as to what the gospel of Christ is. If we take the "depositions" of Matthew, Mark, and Luke, then the gospel of Christ amounts simply to this: That God will forgive the forgiving, and that he will be merciful to the merciful. According to three witnesses, Christ knew nothing of the doctrine of the atonement; never heard of the second birth; and did not base salvation, in whole nor in part, on belief. In the "deposition" of John, we find that we must be born again; that we must believe on the Lord Jesus Christ; and that an atonement was made for us. If Christ ever said these things to, or in the hearing of, Matthew, Mark, and Luke, they forgot to mention them.

To my mind, the failure of the evangelists to agree as to what is necessary for man to do in order to insure the salvation of his soul, is a demonstration that they were not inspired.

Neither do the witnesses agree as to the last words of Christ when he was crucified. Matthew says that he cried: "My God, my God, why hast thou forsaken me?" Mark agrees with Matthew. Luke testifies that his last words were: "Father, into thy hands I commend my spirit." John states that he cried: "It is finished."

Luke says that Christ said of his murderers: "Father, forgive them; for they know not what they do." Matthew, Mark, and John do not record these touching words. John says that Christ, on the day of his resurrection, said to his disciples: "Whosoever sins ye remit, they are remitted unto them; and whosoever sins ye retain, they are retained."

The other disciples do not record this monstrous passage. They did not hear the abdication of God. They were not present when Christ placed in their hands the keys of heaven and hell, and put a world beneath the feet of priests.

It is easy to account for the differences and contradictions in these "depositions" (and there are hundreds of them) by saying that each one told the story as he remembered it, or as he had heard it, or that the accounts have been changed, but it will not do to say that the witnesses were inspired of God. We can account for these contradictions by the infirmities of human nature; but, as I said before, the infirmities of human nature cannot be predicated of a divine being.

Again, I ask, why should there be more than one inspired gospel? Of what use were the other three? There can be only one true account of anything. All other true accounts must simply be copies of that. And I ask again, why should there have been more than one inspired gospel? That which is the test of truth as to ordinary witnesses is a demonstration against their inspiration. It will not do at this late day to say that the miracles worked by Christ demonstrated his divine origin or mission. The wonderful works he did, did not convince the people with whom he lived. In spite of the miracles, he was crucified. He was charged with blasphemy. "Policemen" denounced the "scurrility" of his words, and the absurdity of his doctrines. He was no doubt told that it was "almost a crime to utter blasphemy in the presence of a Jewish woman;" and it may be that he was taunted for throwing away "the golden metewand" of the "infallible God who authorized slavery in Judea," and taking the "elastic cord of human feeling."

Christians tell us that the citizens of Mecca refused to believe on Mohammed because he was an impostor, and that the citizens of Jerusalem refused to believe on Jesus Christ because he was *not* an impostor.

If Christ had wrought the miracles attributed to him—if he had cured the maimed, the leprous, and the halt—if he had changed the night of blindness into blessed day—if he had wrested from the fleshless hand of avaricious death the stolen jewel of a life, and clothed again with throbbing flesh the pulseless dust, he would have won the love and adoration of mankind. If ever there shall stand upon this earth the king of death, all human knees will touch the ground.

We are further informed that "what we call the fundamental truths of Christianity consist of great public events which are sufficiently established by history without special proof."

Of course, we admit that the Roman Empire existed; that Julius Caesar was assassinated; and we may admit that Rome was founded by Romulus and Remus; but will some one be kind enough to tell us how the assassination of Caesar even tends to prove that Romulus and Remus were suckled by a wolf? We will all admit that, in the sixth century after Christ, Mohammed was born at Mecca; that his victorious hosts vanquished half the Christian world; that the crescent triumphed over the cross upon a thousand fields; that all the Christians of the earth were not able to rescue from the hands of an impostor the empty grave of Christ. We will all admit that the Mohammedans cultivated the arts and sciences; that they gave us our numerals; taught us the higher mathematics; gave us our first ideas of astronomy, and that "science was thrust into the brain of Europe on the point of a Moorish lance;" and yet we will not admit that Mohammed was divinely inspired, nor that he had frequent conversations with the angel Gabriel, nor that after his death his coffin was suspended in mid-air.

A little while ago, in the city of Chicago, a gentleman addressed a number of Sunday-school children. In his address, he stated that some people were wicked enough to deny the story of the deluge; that he was a traveler; that he had been to the top of Mount Ararat, and had brought with him a stone from that sacred locality. The children were then invited to form in procession and walk by the pulpit, for the purpose of seeing this wonderful stone. After they had looked at it, the lecturer said: "Now, children, if you ever hear anybody deny the story of the deluge, or say that the ark did not rest on Mount Ararat, you can tell them that you know better, because you have seen with your own eyes a stone from that very mountain."

The fact that Christ lived in Palestine does not tend to show that he was in any way related to the Holy Ghost; nor does the existence of the Christian religion substantiate the ascension of Jesus Christ. We all admit that Socrates lived in Athens, but we do not admit that he had a familiar spirit. I am satisfied that John Wesley was an Englishman, but I hardly believe that God postponed a rain because Mr. Wesley wanted to preach. All the natural things in the world are not sufficient to establish the supernatural. Mr. Black reasons in this way: There was a hydra-headed monster. We know this, because Hercules killed him. There must have been such a woman as Proserpine, otherwise Pluto could not have carried her away. Christ must have been divine, because the Holy Ghost was his father. And there must have been such a being as the Holy Ghost, because without a father Christ could not have existed. Those who are disposed to deny everything because a part is false, reason exactly the other way. They insist that because there was no hydra-headed monster, Hercules did not exist. The true position, in my judgment, is that the natural is not to be discarded because found in the company of the miraculous, neither should the miraculous be believed because associated with the probable. There was in all probability such a man as Jesus Christ. He may have lived in Jerusalem. He may have been crucified, but that he was the Son of God, or that he was raised from the dead, and ascended bodily to heaven, has never been, and, in the nature of things, can never be, substantiated.

Apparently tired with his efforts to answer what I really said, Mr. Black resorted to the expedient of "compressing" my propositions and putting them in italics. By his system of "compression" he was enabled to squeeze out what I really said, and substitute a few sentences of his own. I did not say that "Christianity offers eternal salvation as the reward of belief alone," but I did say that no salvation is offered without belief. There must be a difference of opinion in the minds of Mr. Black's witnesses on this subject. In one place we are told that a man is "justified by faith without the deeds of the law;" and in another, "to him that worketh not, but believeth on him that justifieth the ungodly, his faith is counted to him for righteousness;" and the following passages seem to show the necessity of belief:

"He that believeth on Him is not condemned; but he that believeth not is condemned already, because he hath not believed in the name of the only begotten Son of God." "He that believeth on the Son hath everlasting life: and he that believeth not the Son, shall not see life; but the wrath of God abideth on him." "Jesus said unto her, I am the resurrection and the life;

he that believeth in Me, though he were dead, yet shall he live." "And whosoever liveth and believeth in Me, shall never die." "For the gifts and calling of God are without repentance." "For by grace are ye saved through faith; and that not of yourselves; it is the gift of God." "Not of works, lest any man should boast." "Whosoever shall confess that Jesus is the Son of God, God dwelleth in him, and he in God." "Whosoever believeth not shall be damned."

I do not understand that the Christians of to-day insist that simple belief will secure the salvation of the soul. I believe it is stated in the Bible that "the very devils believe;" and it would seem from this that belief is not such a meritorious thing, after all. But Christians do insist that without belief no man can be saved; that faith is necessary to salvation, and that there is "none other name under heaven given among men whereby we can be saved," except that of Christ. My doctrine is that there is only one way to be saved, and that is to act in harmony with your surroundings—to live in accordance with the facts of your being. A Being of infinite wisdom has no right to create a person destined to everlasting pain. For the honest infidel, according to the American Evangelical pulpit, there is no heaven. For the upright atheist, there is nothing in another world but punishment. Mr. Black admits that lunatics and idiots are in no danger of hell. This being so, his God should have created only lunatics and idiots. Why should the fatal gift of brain be given to any human being, if such gift renders him liable to eternal hell? Better be a lunatic here and an angel there. Better be an idiot in this world, if you can be a seraph in the next.

As to the doctrine of the atonement, Mr. Black has nothing to offer except the barren statement that it is believed by the wisest and the best. A Mohammedan, speaking in Constantinople, will say the same of the Koran. A Brahmin, in a Hindu temple, will make the same remark, and so will the American Indian, when he endeavors to enforce something upon the young of his tribe. He will say: "The best, the greatest of our tribe have believed in this." This is the argument of the cemetery, the philosophy of epitaphs, the logic of the coffin. Who are the greatest and wisest and most virtuous of mankind? This statement, that it has been believed by the best, is made in connection with an admission that it cannot be fathomed by the wisest. It is not claimed that a thing is necessarily false because it is not understood, but I do claim that it is not necessarily true because it cannot be comprehended. I still insist that "the plan of redemption," as usually preached, is absurd, unjust, and immoral.

For nearly two thousand years Judas Iscariot has been execrated by mankind; and yet, if the doctrine of the atonement is true, upon his treachery hung the plan of salvation. Suppose Judas had known of this plan—known that he was selected by Christ for that very purpose, that Christ was depending on him. And suppose that he also knew that only by betraying Christ could he save either himself or others; what ought Judas to have done? Are you willing to rely upon an argument that justifies the treachery of that wretch?

I insisted upon knowing how the sufferings of an innocent man could satisfy justice for the sins of the guilty. To this, Mr. Black replies as follows: "This raises a metaphysical question, which it is not necessary or possible for me to discuss here." Is this considered an answer? Is it in this way that "my misty creations are made to roll away and vanish into air one after another?" Is this the best that can be done by one of the disciples of the infallible God who butchered babes in Judea? Is it possible for a "policeman" to "silence a rude disturber" in this way? To answer an argument, is it only necessary to say that it "raises a metaphysical question"? Again I say: The life of Christ is worth its example, its moral force, its heroism of benevolence. And again I say: The effort to vindicate a law by inflicting punishment on the innocent is a second violation instead of a vindication.

Mr. Black, under the pretence of "compressing," puts in my mouth the following: "The doctrine of non-resistance, forgiveness of injuries, reconciliation with enemies, as taught in the New Testament, is the child of weakness, degrading and unjust."

This is entirely untrue. What I did say is this: "The idea of non-resistance never occurred to a man who had the power to protect himself. This doctrine was the child of weakness, born when resistance was impossible." I said not one word against the forgiveness of injuries, not one word against the reconciliation of enemies—not one word. I believe in the reconciliation of enemies. I believe in a reasonable forgiveness of injuries. But I do not believe in the doctrine of non-resistance. Mr. Black proceeds to say that Christianity forbids us "to cherish animosity, to thirst for mere revenge, to hoard up wrongs real or fancied, and lie in wait for the chance of paying them back; to be impatient, unforgiving, malicious, and cruel to all who have crossed us." And yet the man who thus describes Christianity tells us that it is not only our right, but our duty, to fight savages as savages fight us; insists that where a nation tries to exterminate us, we have a right to exterminate them. This same man, who tells us that "the diabolical propensities of the human heart are checked and curbed by the spirit of the Christian religion," and that this religion "has converted men from low savages into refined and civilized beings," still insists that the author of the Christian religion established slavery, waged wars of extermination, abhorred the liberty of thought, and practiced the divine virtues of retaliation and revenge. If it is our duty to forgive our enemies, ought not God to forgive his? Is it possible that God will hate his enemies when he tells us that we must love ours? The enemies of God cannot injure him, but ours can injure us. If it is the duty of the injured to forgive, why should the uninjured insist upon having revenge? Why should a being who destroys nations with pestilence and famine expect that his children will be loving and forgiving?

Mr. Black insists that without a belief in God there can be no perception of right and wrong, and that it is impossible for an atheist to have a conscience. Mr. Black, the Christian, the believer in God, upholds wars of extermination. I denounce such wars as murder. He upholds the institution of slavery. I denounce that institution as the basest of crimes. Yet I am told that I have no knowledge of right and wrong; that I measure with "the elastic cord of human feeling," while the believer in slavery and wars of extermination measures with "the golden metewand of God."

What is right and what is wrong? Everything is right that tends to the happiness of mankind, and everything is wrong that increases the sum of human misery. What can increase the happiness of this world more than to do away with every form of slavery, and with all war? What can increase the misery of mankind more than to increase wars and put chains upon more human limbs? What is conscience? If man were incapable of suffering, if man could not feel pain, the word "conscience" never would have passed his lips. The man who puts himself in the place of another, whose imagination has been cultivated to the point of feeling the agonies suffered by another, is the man of conscience. But a man who justifies slavery, who justifies a God when he commands the soldier to rip open the mother and to pierce with the sword of war the child unborn, is controlled and dominated, not by conscience, but by a cruel and remorseless superstition.

Consequences determine the quality of an action. If consequences are good, so is the action. If actions had no consequences, they would be neither good nor bad. Man did not get his knowledge of the consequences of actions from God, but from experience and reason. If man can, by actual experiment, discover the right and wrong of actions, is it not utterly illogical to declare that they who do not believe in God can have no standard of right and wrong? Consequences are the standard by which actions are judged. They are the children that testify as to the real character of their parents. God or no God, larceny is the enemy of industry—industry is the mother of prosperity—prosperity is a good, and therefore larceny is an evil. God or no God, murder is a crime. There has always been a law against larceny, because the laborer wishes to enjoy the fruit of his toil. As long as men object to being killed, murder will be illegal.

According to Mr. Black, the man who does not believe in a supreme being acknowledges no standard of right and wrong in this world, and therefore can have no theory of rewards and punishments in the next. Is it possible that only those who believe in the God who persecuted for opinion's sake have any standard of right and wrong? Were the greatest men of all antiquity without this standard? In the eyes of intelligent men of Greece and Rome, were all deeds, whether good or evil, morally alike? Is it necessary to believe in the existence of an infinite intelligence before you can have any standard of right and wrong? Is it possible that a being cannot be just or virtuous unless he believes in some being infinitely superior to himself? If this doctrine be true, how can God be just or virtuous? Does he believe in some being superior to himself?

It may be said that the Pagans believed in a god, and consequently had a standard of right and wrong. But the Pagans did not believe in the "true" God. They knew nothing of Jehovah. Of course it will not do to believe in the wrong God. In order to know the difference between right and wrong, you must believe in the right God—in the one who established slavery. Can this be avoided by saying that a false god is better than none?

The idea of justice is not the child of superstition—it was not born of ignorance; neither was it nurtured by the passages in the Old Testament upholding slavery, wars of extermination, and religious persecution.

Every human being necessarily has a standard of right and wrong; and where that standard has not been polluted by superstition, man abhors slavery, regards a war of extermination as murder, and looks upon religious persecution as a hideous crime. If there is a God, infinite in power and wisdom, above him, poised in eternal calm, is the figure of Justice. At the shrine of Justice the infinite God must bow, and in her impartial scales the actions even of Infinity must be weighed. There is no world, no star, no heaven, no hell, in which gratitude is not a virtue and where slavery is not a crime.

According to the logic of this "reply," all good and evil become mixed and mingled—equally good and equally bad, unless we believe in the existence of the infallible God who ordered husbands to kill their wives. We do not know right from wrong now, unless we are convinced that a being of infinite mercy waged wars of extermination four thousand years ago. We are incapable even of charity, unless we worship the being who ordered the husband to kill his wife for differing with him on the subject of religion.

We know that acts are good or bad only as they effect the actors, and others. We know that from every good act good consequences flow, and that from every bad act there are only evil results. Every virtuous deed is a star in the moral firmament. There is in the moral world, as in the physical, the absolute and perfect relation of cause and effect. For this reason, the atonement becomes an impossibility. Others may suffer by your crime, but their suffering cannot discharge you; it simply increases your guilt and adds to your burden. For this reason happiness is not a reward—it is a consequence. Suffering is not a punishment—it is a result.

It is insisted that Christianity is not opposed to freedom of thought, but that "it is based on certain principles to which it requires the assent of all." Is this a candid statement? Are we only required to give our assent to certain principles in order to be saved? Are the inspiration of the Bible, the divinity of Christ, the atonement, and the Trinity, principles? Will it be admitted by the orthodox world that good deeds are sufficient unto salvation—that a man can get into heaven by living in accordance with certain principles? This is a most excellent doctrine, but it is not Christianity. And right here, it may be well enough to state what I mean by Christianity. The morality of the world is not distinctively Christian. Zoroaster, Gautama, Mohammed, Confucius, Christ, and, in fact, all founders of religions, have said to their disciples: You must not steal; You must not murder; You must not bear false witness; You must discharge your obligations. Christianity is the ordinary moral code, *plus* the miraculous origin of Jesus Christ, his crucifixion, his resurrection, his ascension, the inspiration of the Bible, the doctrine of the atonement, and the necessity of belief. Buddhism is the ordinary moral code, *plus* the miraculous illumination of Buddha, the performance of certain ceremonies, a belief in the transmigration of the soul, and in the final absorption of the human by the infinite. The religion of Mohammed is the ordinary moral code, *plus* the belief that Mohammed was the prophet of God, total abstinence from the use of intoxicating drinks, a harem for the faithful here and hereafter, ablutions, prayers, alms, pilgrimages, and fasts.

The morality in Christianity has never opposed the freedom of thought. It has never put, nor tended to put, a chain on a human mind, nor a manacle on a human limb; but the doctrines distinctively Christian—the necessity of believing a certain thing; the idea that eternal punishment awaited him who failed to believe; the idea that the innocent can suffer for the guilty—these things have opposed, and for a thousand years substantially destroyed, the freedom of the human mind. All religions have, with ceremony, magic, and mystery, deformed, darkened, and corrupted the soul. Around the sturdy oaks of morality have grown and clung the parasitic, poisonous vines of the miraculous and monstrous.

I have insisted, and I still insist, that it is impossible for a finite man to commit a crime deserving infinite punishment; and upon this subject Mr. Black admits that "no revelation has lifted the veil between time and eternity;" and, consequently, neither the priest nor the "policeman" knows anything with certainty regarding another world. He simply insists that "in shadowy figures we are warned that a very marked distinction will be made between the good and bad in the next world." There is "a very marked distinction" in this; but there is this rainbow on the darkest human cloud: The worst have hope of reform. All I insist is, if there is another life, the basest soul that finds its way to that dark or radiant shore will have the everlasting chance of doing right. Nothing but the most cruel ignorance, the most heartless superstition, the most ignorant theology, ever imagined that the few days of human life spent here, surrounded by mists and clouds of darkness, blown over life's sea by storms and tempests of passion, fixed for all eternity the condition of the human race. If this doctrine be true, this life is but a net, in which Jehovah catches souls for hell.

The idea that a certain belief is necessary to salvation unsheathed the swords and lighted the fagots of persecution. As long as heaven is the reward of creed instead of deed, just so long will every orthodox church be a Bastille, every member a prisoner, and every priest a turnkey.

In the estimation of good orthodox Christians, I am a criminal, because I am trying to take from loving mothers, fathers, brothers, sisters, husbands, wives, and lovers the consolations naturally arising from a belief in an eternity of grief and pain. I want to tear, break, and scatter to the winds the God that priests erected in the fields of innocent pleasure—a God made of sticks, called creeds, and of old clothes, called myths. I have tried to take from the coffin its horror, from the cradle its curse, and put out the fires of revenge kindled by the savages of the past. Is it necessary that heaven should borrow its light from the glare of hell? Infinite punishment is infinite cruelty, endless injustice, immortal meanness. To worship an eternal gaoler hardens, debases, and pollutes the soul. While there is one sad and breaking heart in the universe, no perfectly good being can be perfectly happy. Against the heartlessness of this doctrine every grand and generous soul should enter its solemn protest. I want no part in any heaven where the saved, the ransomed, and redeemed drown with merry shouts the cries and sobs of hell—in which happiness forgets misery—where the tears of the lost increase laughter and deepen the dimples of joy. The idea of hell was born of ignorance, brutality, fear, cowardice, and revenge. This idea tends to show that our remote ancestors were the lowest beasts. Only from dens, lairs, and caves—only from mouths filled with cruel fangs—only from hearts of fear and hatred—only from the conscience of hunger and lust—only from the lowest and most debased, could come this most cruel, heartless, and absurd of all dogmas.

Our ancestors knew but little of nature. They were too astonished to investigate. They could not divest themselves of the idea that everything happened with reference to them; that they caused storms and earthquakes; that they brought the tempest and the whirlwind; that on account of something they had done, or omitted to do, the lightning of vengeance leaped from the darkened sky. They made up their minds that at least two vast and powerful beings presided over this world; that one was good and the other bad; that both of these beings wished to get control of the souls of men; that they were relentless enemies, eternal foes; that both welcomed recruits and hated deserters; that one offered rewards in this world, and the other in the next. Man saw cruelty and mercy in nature, because he imagined that phenomena were produced to punish or to reward him. It was supposed that God demanded worship; that he loved to be flattered; that he delighted in sacrifice; that nothing made him happier than to see ignorant faith upon its knees; that above all things he hated and despised doubters and heretics, and regarded investigation as rebellion. Each community felt it a duty to see that the enemies of God were converted or killed. To allow a heretic to live in peace was to invite the wrath of God. Every public evil—every misfortune—was accounted for by something the community had permitted or done. When epidemics appeared, brought by ignorance and welcomed by filth, the heretic was brought out and sacrificed to appease the anger of God. By putting intention behind what man called good, God was produced. By putting intention behind what man called bad, the Devil was created. Leave this "intention" out, and gods and devils fade away. If not a human being existed, the sun would continue to shine, and tempest now and then would devastate the earth; the rain would fall in pleasant showers; violets would spread their velvet bosoms to the sun, the earthquake would devour, birds would sing and daisies bloom and roses blush, and volcanoes fill the heavens with their lurid glare; the procession of the seasons would not be broken, and the stars would shine as serenely as though the world were filled with loving hearts and happy homes. Do not imagine that the doctrine of eternal revenge belongs to Christianity alone. Nearly all religions have had this dogma for a corner-stone. Upon this burning foundation nearly all have built. Over the abyss of pain rose the glittering dome of pleasure. This world was regarded as one of trial. Here, a God of infinite wisdom experimented with man. Between the outstretched paws of the Infinite, the mouse—man—was allowed to play. Here, man had the opportunity of hearing priests and kneeling in temples. Here, he could read, and hear read, the sacred books. Here, he could have the example of the pious and the counsels of the holy. Here, he could build churches and cathedrals. Here, he could burn incense, fast, wear hair-cloth, deny himself all the pleasures of life, confess to priests, construct instruments of torture, bow before pictures and images, and persecute all who had the courage to despise superstition, and the goodness to tell their honest thoughts. After death, if he died out of the church, nothing could be done to make him better. When he should come into the presence of God, nothing was left except to damn him. Priests might convert him here, but God could do nothing there. All of which shows how much more a priest can do for a soul than its creator. Only here, on the earth, where the devil is constantly active, only where his agents attack every soul, is there the slightest hope of moral improvement. Strange! that a world cursed by God, filled with temptations, and thick with fiends, should be the only place where man can repent, the only place where reform is possible!

Masters frightened slaves with the threat of hell, and slaves got a kind of shadowy revenge by whispering back the threat. The imprisoned imagined a hell for their gaolers; the weak built this place for the strong; the arrogant for their rivals; the vanquished for their victors; the priest for the thinker; religion for reason; superstition for science. All the meanness, all the revenge, all the selfishness, all the cruelty, all the hatred, all the infamy of which the heart of man is capable, grew, blossomed, and bore fruit in this one word—Hell. For the nourishment of this dogma, cruelty was soil, ignorance was rain, and fear was light.

Why did Mr. Black fail to answer what I said in relation to the doctrine of inspiration? Did he consider that a "metaphysical question"? Let us see what inspiration really is. A man looks at the sea, and the sea says something to him. It makes an impression on his mind. It awakens memory, and this impression depends upon his experience—upon his intellectual capacity. Another looks upon the same sea. He has a different brain; he has a different experience. The sea may speak to him of joy, to the other of grief and tears. The sea cannot tell the same thing to any two human beings, because no two human beings have had the same experience. One may think of wreck and ruin, and another, while listening to the "multitudinous laughter of the sea," may say: Every drop has visited all the shores of earth; every one has been frozen in the vast and icy North, has fallen in snow, has whirled in storms around the mountain peaks, been kissed to vapor by the sun, worn the seven-hued robe of light, fallen in pleasant rain, gurgled from springs, and laughed in brooks while lovers wooed upon the banks. Everything in nature tells a different story to all eyes that see and to all ears that hear. So, when we look upon a flower, a painting, a statue, a star, or a violet, the more we know, the more we have experienced, the more we have thought, the more we remember, the more the statue, the star, the painting, the violet has to tell. Nature says to me all that I am capable of understanding— gives all that I can receive. As with star, or flower, or sea, so with a book. A thoughtful man reads Shakespeare. What does he get? All that he has the mind to understand. Let another read him, who knows nothing of the drama, nothing of the impersonations of passion, and what does he get? Almost nothing. Shakespeare has a different story for each reader. He is a world in which each recognizes his acquaintances. The impression that nature makes upon the mind, the stories told by sea and star and flower, must be the natural food of thought. Leaving out for the moment the impressions gained from ancestors, the hereditary fears and drifts and trends—the natural food of thought must be the impressions made upon the brain by coming in contact through the medium of the senses with what we call the outward world. The brain is natural; its food is natural; the result, thought, must be natural. Of the supernatural we have no conception. Thought may be deformed, and the thought of one may be strange to, and denominated unnatural by, another; but it cannot be supernatural. It may be weak, it may be insane, but it is not supernatural. Above the natural, man cannot rise. There can be deformed ideas, as there are deformed persons. There may be religions monstrous and misshapen, but they were naturally produced. The world is to each man according to each man. It takes the world as it really is and that man to make that man's world.

You may ask, And what of all this? I reply, As with everything in nature, so with the Bible. It has a different story for each reader. Is, then, the Bible a different book to every human being who reads it? It is. Can God, through the Bible, make precisely the same revelation to two persons? He cannot. Why? Because the man who reads is not inspired. God should inspire readers as well as writers.

You may reply: God knew that his book would be understood differently by each one, and intended that it should be understood as it is understood by each. If this is so, then my understanding of the Bible is the real revelation to me. If this is so, I have no right to take the understanding of another. I must take the revelation made to me through my understanding, and by that revelation I must stand. Suppose then, that I read this Bible honestly, fairly, and when I get through am compelled to say, "The book is not true." If this is the honest result, then you are compelled to say, either that God has made no revelation to me, or that the revelation that it is not true is the revelation made to me, and by which I am bound. If the book and my brain are both the work of the same infinite God, whose fault is it that the book and brain do not agree? Either God should have written a book to fit my brain, or should have made my brain to fit his book. The inspiration of the Bible depends on the credulity of him who reads. There was a time when its geology, its astronomy, its natural history, were thought to be inspired; that time has passed. There was a time when its morality satisfied the men who ruled the world of thought; that time has passed.

Mr. Black, continuing his process of compressing my propositions, attributes to me the following statement: "The gospel of Christ does not satisfy the hunger of the heart." I did not say this. What I did say is: "The dogmas of the past no longer reach the level of the highest thought, nor satisfy the hunger of the heart." In so far as Christ taught any doctrine in opposition to slavery, in favor of intellectual liberty, upholding kindness, enforcing the practice of justice and mercy, I most cheerfully admit that his teachings should be followed. Such teachings do not need the assistance of miracles. They are not in the region of the supernatural. They find their evidence in the glad response of every honest heart that superstition has not touched and stained. The great question under discussion is, whether the immoral, absurd, and infamous can be established by the miraculous. It cannot be too often repeated, that truth scorns the assistance of miracle. That which actually happens sets in motion innumerable effects, which, in turn, become causes producing other effects. These are all "witnesses" whose "depositions" continue. What I insist on is, that a miracle cannot be established by human testimony. We have known people to be mistaken. We know that all people will not tell the truth. We have never seen the dead raised. When people assert that they have, we are forced to weigh the probabilities, and the probabilities are on the other side. It will not do to assert that the universe was created, and then say that such creation was miraculous, and, therefore, all miracles are possible. We must be sure of our premises. Who knows that the universe was created? If it was not; if it has existed from eternity; if the present is the necessary child of all the past, then the miraculous is the impossible. Throw away all the miracles of the New Testament, and the good teachings of Christ remain—all that is worth preserving will be there still. Take from what is now known as Christianity the doctrine of the atonement, the fearful dogma of eternal punishment, the absurd idea that a certain belief is necessary to salvation, and with most of the remainder the good and intelligent will most heartily agree.

Mr. Black attributes to me the following expression: "Christianity is pernicious in its moral effect, darkens the mind, narrows the soul, arrests the progress of human society, and hinders civilization." I said no such thing. Strange, that he is only able to answer what I did not say. I endeavored to show that the passages in the Old Testament upholding slavery, polygamy, wars of extermination, and religious intolerance had filled the world with blood and crime. I admitted that there are many wise and good things in the Old Testament. I also insisted that the doctrine of the atonement—that is to say, of moral bankruptcy—the idea that a certain belief is necessary to salvation, and the frightful dogma of eternal pain, had narrowed the soul, had darkened the mind, and had arrested the progress of human society. Like other religions, Christianity is a mixture of good and evil. The church has made more orphans than it has fed. It has never built asylums enough to hold the insane of its own making. It has shed more blood than light.

Mr. Black seems to think that miracles are the most natural things imaginable, and wonders that anybody should be insane enough to deny the probability of the impossible. He regards all who doubt the miraculous origin, the resurrection and ascension of Jesus Christ, as afflicted with some "error of the moon," and declares that their "disbelief seems like a kind of insanity."

To ask for evidence is not generally regarded as a symptom of a brain diseased. Delusions, illusions, phantoms, hallucinations, apparitions, chimeras, and visions are the common property of the religious and the insane. Persons blessed with sound minds and healthy bodies rely on facts, not fancies—on demonstrations instead of dreams. It seems to me that the most orthodox Christians must admit that many of the miracles recorded in the New Testament are extremely childish. They must see that the miraculous draught of fishes, changing water into wine, fasting for forty days, inducing devils to leave an insane man by allowing them to take possession of swine, walking on the water, and using a fish for a pocket-book, are all unworthy of an infinite being, and are calculated to provoke laughter—to feed suspicion and engender doubt.

Mr. Black takes the ground that if a man believes in the creation of the universe—that being the most stupendous miracle of which the mind can conceive—he has no right to deny anything. He asserts that God created the universe; that creation was a miracle; that "God would be likely to reveal his will to the rational creatures who were required to obey it," and that he would authenticate his revelation by giving his prophets and apostles supernatural power.

After making these assertion, he triumphantly exclaims: "It therefore follows that the improbability of a miracle is no greater than the original improbability of a revelation, and that is not improbable at all."

How does he know that God made the universe? How does he know what God would be likely to do? How does he know that any revelation was made? And how did he ascertain that any of the apostles and prophets were entrusted with supernatural power? It will not do to prove your premises by assertions, and then claim that your conclusions are correct, because they agree with your premises.

If "God would be likely to reveal his will to the rational creatures who were required to obey it," why did he reveal it only to the Jews? According to Mr. Black, God is the only natural thing in the universe.

We should remember that ignorance is the mother of credulity; that the early Christians believed everything but the truth, and that they accepted Paganism, admitted the reality of all the Pagan miracles—taking the ground that they were all forerunners of their own. Pagan miracles were never denied by the Christian world until late in the seventeenth century. Voltaire was the third man of note in Europe who denied the truth of Greek and Roman mythology. "The early Christians cited Pagan oracles predicting in detail the sufferings of Christ. They forged prophecies, and attributed them to the heathen sibyls, and they were accepted as genuine by the entire church."

St. Irenaeus assures us that all Christians possessed the power of working miracles; that they prophesied, cast out devils, healed the sick, and even raised the dead. St. Epiphanius asserts that some rivers and fountains were annually transmuted into wine, in attestation of the miracle of Cana, adding that he himself had drunk of these fountains. St. Augustine declares that one was told in a dream where the bones of St. Stephen were buried, that the bones were thus discovered, and brought to Hippo, and that they raised five dead persons to life, and that in two years seventy miracles were performed with these relics. Justin Martyr states that God once sent some angels to guard the human race, that these angels fell in love with the daughters of men, and became the fathers of innumerable devils.

For hundreds of years, miracles were about the only things that happened. They were wrought by thousands of Christians, and testified to by millions. The saints and martyrs, the best and greatest, were the witnesses and workers of wonders. Even heretics, with the assistance of the devil, could suspend the "laws of nature." Must we believe these wonderful accounts because they were written by "good men," by Christians, "who made their statements in the presence and expectation of death"? The truth is that these "good men" were mistaken. They expected the miraculous. They breathed the air of the marvelous. They fed their minds on prodigies, and their imaginations feasted on effects without causes. They were incapable of investigating. Doubts were regarded as "rude disturbers of the congregation." Credulity and sanctity walked hand in hand. Reason was danger. Belief was safety. As the philosophy of the ancients was rendered almost worthless by the credulity of the common people, so the proverbs of Christ, his religion of forgiveness, his creed of kindness, were lost in the mist of miracle and the darkness of superstition.

If Mr. Black is right, there were no virtue, justice, intellectual liberty, moral elevation, refinement, benevolence, or true wisdom, until Christianity was established. He asserts that when Christ came, "benevolence, in any shape, was altogether unknown."

He insists that "the infallible God who authorized slavery in Judea" established a government; that he was the head and king of the Jewish people; that for this reason heresy was treason. Is it possible that God established a government in which benevolence was unknown? How did it happen that he established no asylums for the insane? How do you account for the fact that your God permitted some of his children to become insane? Why did Jehovah fail to establish hospitals and schools? Is it reasonable to believe that a good God would assist his chosen people to exterminate or enslave his other children? Why would your God people a world, knowing that it would be destitute of benevolence for four thousand years? Jehovah should have sent missionaries to the heathen. He ought to have reformed the inhabitants of Canaan. He should have sent teachers, not soldiers—missionaries, not murderers. A God should not exterminate his children; he should reform them.

Mr. Black gives us a terrible picture of the condition of the world at the coming of Christ; but did the God of Judea treat his own children, the Gentiles, better than the Pagans treated theirs? When Rome enslaved mankind—when with her victorious armies she sought to conquer or to exterminate tribes and nations, she but followed the example of Jehovah. Is it true that benevolence came with Christ, and that his coming heralded the birth of pity in the human heart? Does not Mr. Black know that, thousands of years before Christ was born, there were hospitals and asylums for orphans in China? Does he not know that in Egypt, before Moses lived, the insane were treated with kindness and wooed back to natural thought by music's golden voice? Does he not know that in all times, and in all countries, there have been great and loving souls who wrought, and toiled, and suffered, and died that others might enjoy? Is it possible that he knows nothing of the religion of Buddha—a religion based upon equality, charity and forgiveness? Does he not know that, centuries before the birth of the great Peasant of Palestine, another, upon the plains of India, had taught the doctrine of forgiveness; and that, contrary to the tyranny of Jehovah, had given birth to the sublime declaration that all men are by nature free and equal? Does he not know that a religion of absolute trust in God had been taught thousands of years before Jerusalem was built—a religion based upon absolute special providence, carrying its confidence to the extremist edge of human thought, declaring that every evil is a blessing in disguise, and that every step taken by mortal man, whether in the rags of poverty or the royal robes of kings, is the step necessary to be taken by that soul in order to reach perfection and eternal joy? But how is it possible for a man who believes in slavery to have the slightest conception of benevolence, justice or charity? If Mr. Black is right, even Christ believed and taught that man could buy and sell his fellow-man. Will the Christians of America admit this? Do they believe that Christ from heaven's throne mocked when colored mothers, reft of babes, knelt by empty cradles and besought his aid?

For the man Christ—for the reformer who loved his fellow-men—for the man who believed in an Infinite Father, who would shield the innocent and protect the just—for the martyr who expected to be rescued from the cruel cross, and who at last, finding that his hope was dust, cried out in the gathering gloom of death: "My God! My God! Why hast thou forsaken me?"—for that great and suffering man, mistaken though he was, I have the highest admiration and respect. That man did not, as I believe, claim a miraculous origin; he did not pretend to heal the sick nor raise the dead. He claimed simply to be a man, and taught his fellow-men that love is stronger far than hate. His life was written by reverent ignorance. Loving credulity belittled his career with feats of jugglery and magic art, and priests, wishing to persecute and slay, put in his mouth the words of hatred and revenge. The theological Christ is the impossible union of the human and divine—man with the attributes of God, and God with the limitations and weaknesses of man.

After giving a terrible description of the Pagan world, Mr. Black says: "The church came, and her light penetrated the moral darkness like a new sun; she covered the globe with institutions of mercy."

Is this true? Do we not know that when the Roman empire fell, darkness settled on the world? Do we not know that this darkness lasted for a thousand years, and that during all that time the church of Christ held, with bloody hands, the sword of power? These years were the starless midnight of our race. Art died, law was forgotten, toleration ceased to exist, charity fled from the human breast, and justice was unknown. Kings were tyrants, priests were pitiless, and the poor multitude were slaves. In the name of Christ, men made instruments of torture, and the auto da fê took the place of the gladiatorial show. Liberty was in chains, honesty in dungeons, while Christian superstition ruled mankind. Christianity compromised with Paganism. The statues of Jupiter were used to represent Jehovah. Isis and her babe were changed to Mary and the infant Christ. The Trinity of Egypt became the Father, Son, and Holy Ghost. The simplicity of the early Christians was lost in heathen rites and Pagan pomp. The believers in the blessedness of poverty became rich, avaricious, and grasping, and those who had said, "Sell all, and give to the poor," became the ruthless gatherers of tithes and taxes. In a few years the teachings of Jesus were forgotten. The gospels were interpolated by the designing and ambitious. The church was infinitely corrupt. Crime was crowned, and virtue scourged. The minds of men were saturated with superstition. Miracles, apparitions, angels, and devils had possession of the world. "The nights were filled with incubi and succubi; devils', clad in wondrous forms, and imps in hideous shapes, sought to tempt or fright the soldiers of the cross. The maddened spirits of the air sent hail and storm. Sorcerers wrought sudden death, and witches worked with spell and charm against the common weal." In every town the stake arose. Faith carried fagots to the feet of philosophy. Priests—not "politicians"—fed and fanned the eager flames. The dungeon was the foundation of the cathedral.

Priests sold charms and relics to their flocks to keep away the wolves of hell. Thousands of Christians, failing to find protection in the church, sold their poor souls to Satan for some magic wand. Suspicion sat in every house, families were divided, wives denounced husbands, husbands denounced wives, and children their parents. Every calamity then, as now, increased the power of the church. Pestilence supported the' pulpit, and famine was the right hand of faith. Christendom was insane.

Will Mr. Black be kind enough to state at what time "the church covered the globe with institutions of mercy"? In his reply, he conveys the impression that these institutions were organized in the first century, or at least in the morning of Christianity. How many hospitals for the sick were established by the church during a thousand years? Do we not know that for hundreds of years the Mohammedans erected more hospitals and asylums than the Christians? Christendom was filled with racks and thumbscrews, with stakes and fagots, with chains and dungeons, for centuries before a hospital was built. Priests despised doctors. Prayer was medicine. Physicians interfered with the sale of charms and relics. The church did not cure—it killed. It practiced surgery with the sword. The early Christians did not build asylums for the insane. They charged them with witchcraft, and burnt them. They built asylums, not for the mentally diseased, but for the mentally developed. These asylums were graves.

All the languages of the world have not words of horror enough to paint the agonies of man when the church had power. Tiberius, Caligula, Claudius, Nero, Domitian, and Commodus were not as cruel, false, and base as many of the Christians Popes. Opposite the names of these imperial criminals write John the XII., Leo the VIII., Boniface the VII., Benedict the IX., Innocent the III., and Alexander the VI.

Was it under these pontiffs that the "church penetrated the moral darkness like a new sun," and covered the globe with institutions of mercy? Rome was far better when Pagan than when Catholic. It was better to allow gladiators and criminals to fight than to burn honest men. The greatest of the Romans denounced the cruelties of the arena. Seneca condemned the combats even of wild beasts. He was tender enough to say that "we should have a bond of sympathy for all sentient beings, knowing that only the depraved and base take pleasure in the sight of blood and suffering." Aurelius compelled the gladiators to fight with blunted swords. Roman lawyers declared that all men are by nature free and equal. Woman, under Pagan rule in Rome, became as free as man. Zeno, long before the birth of Christ, taught that virtue alone establishes a difference between men. We know that the Civil Law is the foundation of our codes. We know that fragments of Greek and Roman art—a few manuscripts saved from Christian destruction, some inventions and discoveries of the Moors—were the seeds of modern civilization. Christianity, for a thousand years, taught memory to forget and reason to believe. Not one step was taken in advance. Over the manuscripts of philosophers and poets, priests with their ignorant tongues thrust out, devoutly scrawled the forgeries of faith. For a thousand years the torch of progress was extinguished in the blood of Christ, and his disciples, moved by ignorant zeal, by insane, cruel creeds, destroyed with flame and sword a hundred millions of their fellow-men. They made this world a hell. But if cathedrals had been universities—if dungeons of the Inquisition had been laboratories—if Christians had believed in character instead of creed—if they had taken from the Bible all the good and thrown away the wicked and absurd—if domes of temples had been observatories—if priests had been philosophers—if missionaries had taught the useful arts—if astrology had been astronomy—if the black art had been chemistry—if superstition had been science—if religion had been humanity—it' would have been a heaven filled with love, with liberty, and joy.

We did not get our freedom from the church. The great truth, that all men are by nature free, was never told on Sinai's barren crags, nor by the lonely shores of Galilee.

The Old Testament filled this world with tyranny and crime, and the New gives us a future filled with pain for nearly all the sons of men. The Old describes the hell of the past, and the New the hell of the future. The Old tells us the frightful things that God has done—the New the cruel things that he will do. These two books give us the sufferings of the past and future—the injustice, the agony, the tears of both worlds. If the Bible is true—if Jehovah is God—if the lot of countless millions is to be eternal pain—better a thousand times that all the constellations of the shoreless vast were eyeless darkness and eternal space. Better that all that is should cease to be. Better that all the seeds and springs of things should fail and wither from great Nature's realm. Better that causes and effects should lose relation and become unmeaning phrases and forgotten sounds. Better that every life should change to breathless death, to voiceless blank, and every world to blind oblivion and to moveless naught.

Mr. Black justifies all the crimes and horrors, excuses all the tortures of all the Christian years, by denouncing the cruelties of the French Revolution. Thinking people will not hasten to admit that an infinitely good being authorized slavery in Judea, because of the atrocities of the French Revolution. They will remember the sufferings of the Huguenots. They will remember the massacre of St. Bartholomew. They will not forget the countless cruelties of priest and king. They will not forget the dungeons of the Bastille. They will know that the Revolution was an effect, and that liberty was not the cause—that atheism was not the cause. Behind the Revolution they will see altar and throne—sword and fagot—palace and cathedral—king and priest—master and slave—tyrant and hypocrite. They will see that the excesses, the cruelties, and crimes were but the natural fruit of seeds the church had sown. But the

Revolution was not entirely evil. Upon that cloud of war, black with the myriad miseries of a thousand years, dabbled with blood of king and queen, of patriot and priest, there was this bow: "Beneath the flag of France all men are free." In spite of all the blood and crime, in spite of deeds that seem insanely base, the People placed upon a Nation's brow these stars:—Liberty, Fraternity, Equality—grander words than ever issued from Jehovah's lips.

Robert G. Ingersoll.

FAITH OR AGNOSTICISM.

[Ingersoll-Field.]

THE FIELD-INGERSOLL DISCUSSION.
An Open Letter to Robert G. Ingersoll.

Dear Sir: I am glad that I know you, even though some of my brethren look upon you as a monster because of your unbelief. I shall never forget the long evening I spent at your house in Washington; and in what I have to say, however it may fail to convince you, I trust you will feel that I have not shown myself unworthy of your courtesy or confidence.

Your conversation, then and at other times, interested me greatly. I recognized at once the elements of your power over large audiences, in your wit and dramatic talent—personating characters and imitating tones of voice and expressions of countenance—and your remarkable use of language, which even in familiar talk often rose to a high degree of eloquence. All this was a keen intellectual stimulus. I was, for the most part, a listener; but as we talked freely of religious matters, I protested against your unbelief as utterly without reason. Yet there was no offence given or taken, and we parted, I trust, with a feeling of mutual respect.

Still further, we found many points of sympathy. I do not hesitate to say that there are many things in which I agree with you, in which I love what you love and hate what you hate. A man's hatreds are not the least important part of him; they are among the best indications of his character. You love truth, and hate lying and hypocrisy—all the petty arts and deceits of the world by which men represent themselves to be other than they are—as well as the pride and arrogance, in which they assume superiority over their fellow-beings. Above all, you hate every form of injustice and oppression. Nothing moves your indignation so much as "man's inhumanity to man," and you mutter "curses, not loud but deep," on the whole race of tyrants and oppressors, whom you would sweep from the face of the earth. And yet, you do not hate oppression more than I; nor love liberty more. Nor will I admit that you have any stronger desire for that intellectual freedom, to the attainment of which you look forward as the last and greatest emancipation of mankind.

Nor have you a greater horror of superstition. Indeed, I might say that you cannot have so great, for the best of all reasons, that you have not seen so much of it; you have not stood on the banks of the Ganges, and seen the Hindus by tens of thousands rushing madly to throw themselves into the sacred river, even carrying the ashes of their dead to cast them upon the waters. It seems but yesterday that I was sitting on the back of an elephant, looking down on this horrible scene of human degradation. Such superstition overthrows the very foundations of morality. In place of the natural sense of right and wrong, which is written in men's consciences and hearts, it introduces an artificial standard, by which the order of things is totally reversed: right is made wrong, and wrong is made right. It makes that a virtue which is not a virtue, and that a crime which is not a crime. Religion consists in a round of observances that have no relation whatever to natural goodness, but which rather exclude it by being a substitute for it. Penances and pilgrimages take the place of justice and mercy, benevolence and charity. Such a religion, so far from being a purifier, is the greatest corrupter of morals; so that it is no extravagance to say of the Hindus, who are a gentle race, that they might be virtuous and good if they were not so religious. But this colossal superstition weighs upon their very existence, crushing out even natural virtue. Such a religion is an immeasurable curse.

I hope this language is strong enough to satisfy even your own intense hatred of superstition. You cannot loathe it more than I do. So far we agree perfectly. But unfortunately you do not limit your crusade to the religions of Asia, but turn the same style of argument against the religion of Europe and America, and, indeed, against the religious belief and worship of every country and clime. In this matter you make no distinctions: you would sweep them all away; church and cathedral must go with the temple and the pagoda, as alike manifestations of human credulity, and proofs of the intellectual feebleness and folly of mankind. While under the impression of that memorable evening at your house, I took up some of your public addresses, and experienced a strange revulsion of feeling. I could hardly believe my eyes as I read, so inexpressibly was I shocked. Things which I held sacred you not only rejected with unbelief, but sneered at with contempt. Your words were full of a bitterness so unlike anything I had heard from your lips, that I could not reconcile the two, till I reflected that in Robert Ingersoll (as in the most of us) there were two men, who were not only distinct, but contrary the one to the other—the one gentle and sweet-tempered; the other delighting in war as his native element. Between the two, I have a decided preference for the former. I have no dispute with the quiet and peaceable gentleman, whose kindly spirit makes sunshine in his home; but it is *that other man* over yonder, who comes forth into the arena like a gladiator, defiant and belligerent, that rouses my antagonism. And yet I do not intend to *stand up* even against him; but if he will only *sit down* and listen patiently, and answer in those soft tones of voice which he knows so well how to use, we can have a quiet talk, which will certainly do him no harm, while it relieves my troubled mind.

What then is the basis of this religion which you despise? At the foundation of every form of religious faith and worship, is the idea of God. Here you take your stand; you do not believe in God. Of course you do not deny absolutely the existence of a Creative Power: for that would be to assume a knowledge which no human being can possess. How small is the distance that we can see before us! The candle of our intelligence throws its beams but a little way, beyond which the circle of light is compassed by universal darkness. Upon this no one insists more than yourself. I have heard you discourse upon the insignificance of man in a way to put many preachers to shame. I remember your illustration from the myriads of creatures that live on plants, from which you picked out, to represent human insignificance, an insect too small to be seen by the naked eye, whose world was a leaf, and whose life lasted but a single day! Surely a creature that can only be seen with a microscope, cannot know that a Creator does not exist!

This, I must do you the justice to say, you do not affirm. All that you can say is, that if there be no knowledge on one side, neither is there on the other; that it is only a matter of probability; and that, judging from such evidence as appeals to your senses and your understanding, you do not *believe* that there is a God. Whether this be a reasonable conclusion or not, it is at least an intelligible state of mind.

Now I am not going to argue against what the Catholics call "invincible ignorance"—an incapacity on account of temperament—for I hold that the belief in God, like the belief in all spiritual things, comes to some minds by a kind of intuition. There are natures so finely strung that they are sensitive to influences which do not touch others. You may say that it is mere poetical rhapsody when Shelley writes:

> "The awful shadow of some unseen power,
> Floats, though unseen, among us."

But there are natures which are not at all poetical or dreamy, only most simple and pure, which, in moments of spiritual exaltation, are almost *conscious* of a Presence that is not of this world. But this, which is a matter of experience, will have no weight with those who do not have that experience. For the present, therefore, I would not be swayed one particle by mere sentiment, but look at the question in the cold light of reason alone.

The idea of God is, indeed, the grandest and most awful that can be entertained by the human mind. Its very greatness overpowers us, so that it seems impossible that such a Being should exist. But if it is hard to conceive of Infinity, it is still harder to get any intelligible explanation of the present order of things without admitting the existence of an intelligent Creator and Upholder of all. Galileo, when he swept the sky with his telescope, traced the finger of God in every movement of the heavenly bodies. Napoleon, when the French savants on the voyage to Egypt argued that there was no God, disdained any other answer than to point upward to the stars and ask, "Who made all these?" This is the first question, and it is the last. The farther we go, the more we are forced to one conclusion. No man ever studied nature with a more simple desire to know the truth than Agassiz, and yet the more he explored, the more he was startled as he found himself constantly face to face with the evidences of mind.

Do you say this is "a great mystery," meaning that it is something that we do not know anything about? Of course, it is "a mystery." But do you think to escape mystery by denying the Divine existence? You only exchange one mystery for another. The first of all mysteries is, not that God exists, but that *we* exist. Here we are. How did we come here? We go back to our ancestors; but that does not take away the difficulty; it only removes it farther off. Once begin to climb the stairway of past generations, and you will find that it is a Jacob's ladder, on which you mount higher and higher until you step into the very presence of the Almighty.

But even if we know that there is a God, what can we know of His character? You say, "God is whatever we conceive Him to be." We frame an image of Deity out of our consciousness—it is simply a reflection of our own personality, cast upon the sky like the image seen in the Alps in certain states of the atmosphere—and then fall down and worship that which we have created, not indeed with our hands, but out of our minds. This may be true to some extent of the gods of mythology, but not of the God of Nature, who is as inflexible as Nature itself. You might as well say that the laws of nature are whatever we imagine them to be. But we do not go far before we find that, instead of being pliant to our will, they are rigid and inexorable, and we dash ourselves against them to our own destruction. So God does not bend to human thought any more than to human will. The more we study Him the more we find that He is *not* what we imagined him to be; that He is far greater than any image of Him that we could frame.

But, after all, you rejoin that the conception of a Supreme Being is merely an abstract idea, of no practical importance, with no bearing upon human life. I answer, it is of immeasurable importance. Let go the idea of God, and you have let go the highest moral restraint. There is no Ruler above man; he is a law unto himself—a law which is as impotent to produce order, and to hold society together, as man is with his little hands to hold the stars in their courses.

I know how you reason against the Divine existence from the moral disorder of the world. The argument is one that takes strong hold of the imagination, and may be used with tremendous effect. You set forth in colors none too strong the injustice that prevails in the relations of men to one another—the inequalities of society; the haughtiness of the rich and the misery of the poor; you draw lurid pictures of the vice and crime which run riot in the great capitals which are the centers of civilization; and when you have wound up your audience to the highest pitch, you ask, "How can it be that there is a just God in heaven, who looks down upon the earth and sees all this horrible confusion, and yet does not lift His hand to avenge the innocent or punish the guilty?" To this I will make but one answer: Does it convince yourself? I do not mean to imply that you are conscious of insincerity. But an orator is sometimes carried away by his own eloquence, and states things more strongly than he would in his cooler moments. So I venture to ask: With all your tendency to skepticism, do you really believe that there is no moral government of the world—no Power behind nature "making for righteousness?" Are there no retributions in history? When Lincoln stood on the field of Gettysburg, so lately drenched with blood, and, reviewing the carnage of that terrible day, accepted it as the punishment of our national sins, was it a mere theatrical flourish in him to lift his hand to heaven, and exclaim, "Just and true are Thy ways, Lord God Almighty!"

Having settled it to your own satisfaction that there is no God, you proceed in the same easy way to dispose of that other belief which lies at the foundation of all religion—the immortality of the soul. With an air of modesty and diffidence that would carry an audience by storm, you confess your ignorance of what, perhaps, others are better acquainted with, when you say, "This world is all that *I* know anything about, *so far as I recollect."* This is very wittily put, and some may suppose it contains an argument; but do you really mean to say that you do not know anything except what you "recollect," or what you have seen with your eyes? Perhaps you never saw your grandparents; but have you any more doubt of their existence than of that of your father and mother whom you did see?

Here, as when you speak of the existence of God, you carefully avoid any positive affirmation: you neither affirm nor deny. You are ready for whatever may "turn up." In your jaunty style, if you find yourself hereafter in some new and unexpected situation, you will accept it and make the best of it, and be "as ready as the next man to enter on any remunerative occupation!"

But while airing this pleasant fancy, you plainly regard the hope of another life as a beggar's dream—the momentary illusion of one who, stumbling along life's highway, sets him down by the roadside, footsore and weary, cold and hungry, and falls asleep, and dreams of a time when he shall have riches and plenty. Poor creature! let him dream; it helps him to forget his misery, and may give him a little courage for his rude awaking to the hard reality of life. But it is all a dream, which dissolves in thin air, and floats away and disappears. This illustration I do not take from you, but simply choose to set forth what (as I infer from the sentences above quoted and many like expressions) may describe, not unfairly, your state of mind. Your treatment of the subject is one of trifling. You do not speak of it in a serious way, but lightly and flippantly, as if it were all a matter of fancy and conjecture, and not worthy of sober consideration.

Now, does it never occur to you that there is something very cruel in this treatment of the belief of your fellow-creatures, on whose hope of another life hangs all that relieves the darkness of their present existence? To many of them life is a burden to carry, and they need all the helps to carry it that can be found in reason, in philosophy, or in religion. But what support does your hollow creed supply? You are a man of warm heart, of the tenderest sympathies. Those who know you best, and love you most, tell me that you cannot bear the sight of suffering even in animals; that your natural sensibility is such that you find no pleasure in sports, in hunting or fishing; to shoot a robin would make you feel like a murderer. If you see a poor man in trouble your first impulse is to help him. You cannot see a child in tears but you want to take up the little fellow in your arms, and make him smile again. And yet, with all your sensibility, you hold the most remorseless and pitiless creed in the world—a creed in which there is not a gleam of mercy or of hope. A mother has lost her only son. She goes to his grave and throws herself upon it, the very picture of woe. One thought only keeps her from despair: it is that beyond this life there is a world where she may once more clasp her boy in her arms. What will you say to that mother? You are silent, and your silence is a sentence of death to her hopes. By that grave you cannot speak; for if you were to open your lips and tell that mother what you really believe, it would be that her son is blotted out of existence, and that she can never look upon his face again. Thus with your iron heel do you trample down and crush the last hope of a broken heart.

When such sorrow comes to you, you feel it as keenly as any man. With your strong domestic attachments one cannot pass out of your little circle without leaving a great void in your heart, and your grief is as eloquent as it is hopeless. No sadder words ever fell from human lips than these, spoken over the coffin of one to whom you were tenderly attached: "Life is but a narrow vale, between the cold and barren peaks of two eternities!" This is a doom of annihilation, which strikes a chill to the stoutest heart. Even you must envy the faith which, as it looks upward, sees those "peaks of two eternities," not "cold and barren," but warm with the glow of the setting sun, which gives promise of a happier to-morrow!

I think I hear you say, "So might it be! Would that I could believe it!" for no one recognizes more the emptiness of life as it is. I do not forget the tone in which you said: "Life is very sad to me; it is very pitiful; there isn't much to it." True indeed! With your belief, or want of belief, there is very little to it; and if this were all, it would be a fair question whether life were worth living. In the name of humanity, let us cling to all that is left us that can bring a ray of hope into its darkness, and thus lighten its otherwise impenetrable gloom.

I observe that you not infrequently entertain yourself and your audiences by caricaturing certain doctrines of the Christian religion. The "Atonement," as you look upon it, is simply "punishing the wrong man"—letting the guilty escape and putting the innocent to death. This is vindicating justice by permitting injustice. But is there not another side to this? Does not the idea of sacrifice run through human life, and ennoble human character? You see a mother denying herself for her children, foregoing every comfort, enduring every hardship, till at last, worn out by her labor and her privation, she folds her hands upon her breast. May it not be said truly that she *gives her life* for the life of her children? History is full of sacrifice, and it is the best part of history. I will not speak of "the noble army of martyrs," but of heroes who have died for their country or for liberty—what is it but this element of devotion for the good of others that gives such glory to their immortal names? How then should it be thought a thing without reason that a Deliverer of the race should give His life for the life of the world?

So, too, you find a subject for caricature in the doctrine of "Regeneration." But what is regeneration but a change of character shown in a change of life? Is that so very absurd? Have you never seen a drunkard reformed? Have you never seen a man of impure life, who, after running his evil course, had, like the prodigal, "come to himself"— that is, awakened to his shame, and turning from it, come back to the path of purity, and finally regained a true and noble manhood? Probably you would admit this, but say that the change was the result of reflection, and of the man's own strength of will. The doctrine of regeneration only adds to the will of man the power of God. We believe that man is weak, but that God is mighty; and that when man tries to raise himself, an arm is stretched out to lift him up to a height which he could not attain alone. Sometimes one who has led the worst life, after being plunged into such remorse and despair that he feels as if he were enduring the agonies of hell, turns back and takes another course: he becomes "a new creature," whom his friends can hardly recognize as he "sits clothed and in his right mind." The change is from darkness to light, from death to life; and he who has known but one such case will never say that the language is too strong which describes that man as "born again."

If you think that I pass lightly over these doctrines, not bringing out all the meaning which they bear, I admit it. I am not writing an essay in theology, but would only show, in passing, by your favorite method of illustration, that the principles involved are the same with which you are familiar in everyday life.

But the doctrine which excites your bitterest animosity is that of Future Retribution. The prospect of another life, reaching on into an unknown futurity, you would contemplate with composure were it not for the dark shadow hanging over it. But to live only to suffer; to live when asking to die; to "long for death, and not be able to find it"—is a prospect which arouses the anger of one who would look with calmness upon death as an eternal sleep. The doctrine loses none of its terrors in passing through your hands; for it is one of the means by which you work upon the feelings of your hearers. You pronounce it "the most horrible belief that ever entered the human mind: that the Creator should bring beings into existence to destroy them! This would make Him the most fearful tyrant in the universe—a Moloch devouring his own children!" I shudder when I recall the fierce energy with which you spoke as you said, "Such a God I hate with all the intensity of my being!"

But gently, gently, Sir! We will let this burst of fury pass before we resume the conversation. When you are a little more tranquil, I would modestly suggest that perhaps you are fighting a figment of your imagination. I never heard of any Christian teacher who said that "the Creator brought beings into the world to destroy them!" Is it not better to moderate yourself to exact statements, especially when, with all modifications, the subject is one to awaken a feeling the most solemn and profound?

Now I am not going to enter into a discussion of this doctrine. I will not quote a single text. I only ask you whether it is not a scientific truth that *the effect of everything which is of the nature of a cause is eternal.* Science has opened our eyes to some very strange facts in nature. The theory of vibrations is carried by the physicists to an alarming extent. They tell us that it is literally and mathematically true that you cannot throw a ball in the air but it shakes the solar system. Thus all things act upon all. What is true in space may be true in time, and the law of physics may hold in the spiritual realm. When the soul of man departs out of the body, being released from the grossness of the flesh, it may enter on a life a thousand times more intense than this: in which it will not need the dull senses as avenues of knowledge, because the spirit itself will be all eye, all ear, all intelligence; while memory, like an electric flash, will in an instant bring the whole of the past into view; and the moral sense will be quickened as never before. Here then we have all the conditions of retribution—a world which, however shadowy it may be seem, is yet as real as the homes and habitations and activities of our present state; with memory trailing the deeds of a lifetime behind it, and conscience, more inexorable than any judge, giving its solemn and final verdict.

With such conditions assumed, let us take a case which would awaken your just indignation—that of a selfish, hardhearted, and cruel man; who sacrifices the interests of everybody to his own; who grinds the faces of the poor, robbing the widow and the orphan of their little all; and who, so far from making restitution, dies with his ill-gotten gains held fast in his clenched hand. How long must the night be to sleep away the memory of such a hideous life? If he wakes, will not the recollection cling to him still? Are there any waters of oblivion that can cleanse his miserable soul? If not—if he cannot *forget*—surely he cannot *forgive* himself for the baseness which now he has no opportunity to repair. Here, then, is a retribution which is inseparable from his being, which is a part of his very existence. The undying memory brings the undying pain.

Take another case—alas! too sadly frequent. A man of pleasure betrays a young, innocent, trusting woman by the promise of his love, and then casts her off, leaving her to sink down, down, through every degree of misery and shame, till she is lost in depths, which plummet never sounded, and disappears. Is he not to suffer for this poor creature's ruin? Can he rid himself of it by fleeing beyond "that bourne from whence no traveler returns"? Not unless he can flee from himself: for in the lowest depths of the under-world—a world in which the sun never shines—that image will still pursue him. As he wanders in its gloomy shades a pale form glides by him like an affrighted ghost. The face is the same, beautiful even in its sorrow, but with a look upon it as of one who has already suffered an eternity of woe. In an instant all the past comes back again. He sees the young, unblessed mother wandering in some lonely place, that only the heavens may witness her agony and her despair. There he sees her holding up in her arms the babe that had no right to be born, and calling upon God to judge her betrayer. How far in the future must he travel to forget that look? Is there any escape except by plunging into the gulf of annihilation?

Thus far in this paper I have taken a tone of defense. But I do not admit that the Christian religion needs any apology,—it needs only to be rightly understood to furnish its own complete vindication. Instead of considering its "evidences," which is but going round the outer walls, let us enter the gates of the temple and see what is within. Here we find something better than "towers and bulwarks" in the character of Him who is the Founder of our Religion, and not its Founder only but its very core and being. Christ *is* Christianity. Not only is He the Great Teacher, but the central subject of what He taught, so that the whole stands or falls with Him.

In our first conversation, I observed that, with all your sharp comments on things sacred, you professed great respect for the ethics of Christianity, and for its author. "Make the Sermon on the Mount your religion," you said, "and there I am with you." Very well! So far, so good.

And now, if you will go a little further, you may find still more food for reflection.

All who have made a study of the character and teachings of Christ, even those who utterly deny the supernatural, stand in awe and wonder before the gigantic figure which is here revealed. Renan closes his "Life of Jesus" with this as the result of his long study: "Jesus will never be surpassed. His worship will be renewed without ceasing; his story [légende] will draw tears from beautiful eyes without end; his sufferings will touch the finest natures; ALL THE AGES WILL PROCLAIM THAT AMONG THE SONS OF MEN THERE HAS NOT RISEN A GREATER THAN JESUS;" while Rousseau closes his immortal eulogy by saying, "SOCRATES DIED LIKE A PHILOSOPHER, BUT JESUS CHRIST LIKE A GOD!"

Here is an argument for Christianity to which I pray you to address yourself. As you do not believe in miracles, and are ready to explain everything by natural causes, I beg you to tell us how came it to pass that a Hebrew peasant, born among the hills of Judea, had a wisdom above that of Socrates or Plato, of Confucius or Buddha? This is the greatest of miracles, that such a Being has lived and died on the earth.

Since this is the chief argument for Religion, does it not become one who undertakes to destroy it to set himself first to this central position, instead of wasting his time on mere outposts? When you next address one of the great audiences that hang upon your words, is it unfair to ask that you lay aside such familiar topics as Miracles or Ghosts, or a reply to Talmage, and tell us what you think of Jesus Christ; whether you look upon Him as an impostor, or merely as a dreamer—a mild and harmless enthusiast; or are you ready to acknowledge that He is entitled to rank among the great teachers of mankind?

But if you are compelled to admit the greatness of Christ, you take your revenge on the Apostles, whom you do not hesitate to say that you "don't think much of." In fact, you set them down in a most peremptory way as "a poor lot." It did seem rather an unpromising "lot," that of a boat-load of fishermen, from which to choose the apostles of a religion—almost as unpromising as it was to take a rail-splitter to be the head of a nation in the greatest crisis of its history! But perhaps in both cases there was a wisdom higher than ours, that chose better than we. It might puzzle even you to give a better definition of religion than this of the Apostle James: "Pure religion and undefiled before God and the Father is this: to visit the fatherless and widows in their affliction, and to keep himself unspotted from the world," or to find among those sages of antiquity, with whose writings you are familiar, a more complete and perfect delineation of that which is the essence of all goodness and virtue, than Paul's description of the charity which "suffereth long and is kind;" or to find in the sayings of Confucius or of Buddha anything more sublime than this aphorism of John: "God is love, and he that dwelleth in love dwelleth in God, and God in him."

And here you must allow me to make a remark, which is not intended as a personal retort, but simply in the interest of that truth which we both profess to seek, and to count worth more than victory. Your language is too sweeping to indicate the careful thinker, who measures his words and weighs them in a balance. Your lectures remind me of the pictures of Gustave Doré, who preferred to paint on a large canvas, with figures as gigantesque as those of Michael Angelo in his Last Judgment. The effect is very powerful, but if he had softened his colors a little,—if there were a few delicate touches, a mingling of light and shade, as when twilight is stealing over the earth,—the landscape would be more true to nature. So, believe me, your words would be more weighty if they were not so strong. But whenever you touch upon religion you seem to lose control of yourself, and a vindictive feeling takes possession of you, which causes you to see things so distorted from their natural appearance that you cannot help running into the broadest caricature. You swing your sentences as the woodman swings his axe. Of course, this "slashing" style is very effective before a popular audience, which does not care for nice distinctions, or for evidence that has to be sifted and weighed; but wants opinions off hand, and likes to have its prejudices and hatreds echoed back in a ringing voice. This carries the crowd, but does not convince the philosophic mind. The truth-seeker cannot cut a road through the forest with sturdy blows; he has a hidden path to trace, and must pick his way with slow and cautious step to find that which is more precious than gold.

But if it were possible for you to sweep away the "evidences of Christianity," you have not swept away Christianity itself; it still lives, not only in tradition, but in the hearts of the people, entwined with all that is sweetest in their domestic life, from which it must be torn out with unsparing hand before it can be exterminated. To begin with, you turn your back upon history. All that men have done and suffered for the sake of religion was folly. The Pilgrims, who crossed the sea to find freedom to worship God in the forests of the New World, were miserable fanatics. There is no more place in the world for heroes and martyrs. He who sacrifices his life for a faith, or an idea, is a fool. The only practical wisdom is to have a sharp eye to the main chance. If you keep on in this work of demolition, you will soon destroy all our ideals. Family life withers under the cold sneer—half pity and half scorn—with which you look down on household worship. Take from our American firesides such scenes as that pictured in the *Cotter's Saturday Night,* and you have taken from them their most sacred hours and their tenderest memories.

The same destructive spirit which intrudes into our domestic as well as our religious life, would take away the beauty of our villages as well as the sweetness of our homes. In the weary round of a week of toil, there comes an interval of rest; the laborer lays down his burden, and for a few hours breathes a serener air. The Sabbath morning has come:

> "Sweet day I so cool, so calm, so bright,
> The bridal of the earth and sky."

At the appointed hour the bell rings across the valley, and sends its echoes among the hills; and from all the roads the people come trooping to the village church. Here they gather, old and young, rich and poor; and as they join in the same act of worship, feel that God is the maker of them all? Is there in our national life any influence more elevating than this—one which tends more to bring a community together; to promote neighborly feeling; to refine the manners of the people; to breed true courtesy, and all that makes a Christian village different from a cluster of Indian wigwams—a civilized community different from a tribe of savages?

All this you would destroy: you would abolish the Sabbath, or have it turned into a holiday; you would tear down the old church, so full of tender associations of the living and the dead, or at least have it "razeed," cutting off the tall spire that points upward to heaven; and the interior you would turn into an Assembly room—a place of entertainment, where the young people could have their merry-makings, except perchance in the warm' Summer-time, when they could dance on the village green! So far you would have gained your object. But would that be a more orderly community, more refined or more truly happy?

You may think this a mere sentiment—that we care more for the picturesque than for the true. But there is one result which is fearfully real: the destructive creed, or no creed, which despoils our churches and our homes, attacks society in its first principles by taking away the support of morality. I do not believe that general morality can be upheld without the sanctions of religion. There may be individuals of great natural force of character, who can stand alone—men of superior intellect and strong will. But in general human nature is weak, and virtue is not the spontaneous growth of childish innocence. Men do not become pure and good by instinct. Character, like mind, has to be developed by education; and it needs all the elements of strength which can be given it, from without as well as from within, from the government of man and the government of God. To let go of these restraints is a peril to public morality.

You feel strong in the strength of a robust manhood, well poised in body and mind, and in the centre of a happy home, where loving hearts cling to you like vines round the oak. But many to whom you speak are quite otherwise. You address thousands of young men who have come out of country homes, where they have been brought up in the fear of God, and have heard the morning and evening prayer. They come into a city full of temptations, but are restrained from evil by the thought of father and mother, and reverence for Him who is the Father of us all—a feeling which, though it may not have taken the form of any profession, is yet at the bottom of their hearts, and keeps them from many a wrong and wayward step. A young man, who is thus "guarded and defended" as by unseen angels, some evening when he feels very lonely, is invited to "go and hear Ingersoll," and for a couple of hours listens to your caricatures of religion, with descriptions of the prayers and the psalm-singing, illustrated by devout grimaces and nasal tones, which set the house in roars of laughter, and are received with tumultuous applause. When it is all over, and the young man finds himself again under the flaring lamps of the city streets, he is conscious of a change; the faith of his childhood has been rudely torn from him, and with it "a glory has passed away from the earth;" the Bible which his mother gave him, the morning that he came away, is "a mass of fables;" the sentence which she wished him to hang on the wall, "Thou, God, seest me," has lost its power, for there is no God that sees him, no moral government, no law and no retribution. So he reasons as he walks slowly homeward, meeting the temptations which haunt these streets at night—temptations from which he has hitherto turned with a shudder, but which he now meets with a diminished power of resistance. Have you done that young man any good in taking from him what he held sacred before? Have you not left him morally weakened? From sneering at religion, it is but a step to sneering at morality, and then but one step more to a vicious and profligate career. How are you going to stop this downward tendency? When you have stripped him of former restraints, do you leave him anything in their stead, except indeed a sense of honor, self-respect, and self-interest?—worthy motives, no doubt, but all too feeble to withstand the fearful temptations that assail him. Is the chance of his resistance as good as it was before? Watch him as he goes along that street at midnight! He passes by the places of evil resort, of drinking and gambling—those open mouths of hell; he hears the sound of music and dancing, and for the first time pauses to listen. How long will it be before he will venture in?

With such dangers in his path, it is a grave responsibility to loosen the restraints which hold such a young man to virtue. These gibes and sneers which you utter so lightly, may have a sad echo in a lost character and a wretched life. Many a young man has been thus taunted until he has pushed off from the shore, under the idea of gaining his "liberty," and ventured into the rapids, only to be carried down the stream, and left a wreck in the whirlpool below.

You tell me that your object is to drive fear out of the world. That is a noble ambition; if you succeed, you will be indeed a deliverer. Of course you mean only irrational fears. You would not have men throw off the fear of violating the laws of nature; for that would lead to incalculable misery. You aim only at the terrors born of ignorance and superstition. But how are you going to get rid of these? You trust to the progress of science, which has dispelled so many fears arising from physical phenomena, by showing that calamities ascribed to spiritual agencies are explained by natural causes. But science can only go a certain way, beyond which we come into the sphere of the unknown, where all is dark as before. How can you relieve the fears of others—indeed how can you rid yourself of fear, believing as you do that there is no Power above which can help you in any extremity; that you are the sport of accident, and may be dashed in pieces by the blind agency of nature? If I believed this, I should feel that I was in the grasp of some terrible machinery which was crushing me to atoms, with no possibility of escape.

Not so does Religion leave man here on the earth, helpless and hopeless—in abject terror, as he is in utter darkness as to his fate—but opening the heaven above him, it discovers a Great Intelligence, compassing all things, seeing the end from the beginning, and ordering our little lives so that even the trials that we bear, as they call out the finer elements of character, conduce to our future happiness. God is our Father. We look up into His face with childlike confidence, and find that "His service is perfect freedom." "Love casts out fear." That, I beg to assure you, is the way, and the only way, by which man can be delivered from those fears by which he is all his lifetime subject to bondage.

In your attacks upon Religion you do violence to your own manliness. Knowing you as I do, I feel sure that you do not realize where your blows fall, or whom they wound, or you would not use your weapons so freely. The faiths of men are as sacred as the most delicate manly or womanly sentiments of love and honor. They are dear as the beloved faces that have passed from our sight. I should think myself wanting in respect to the memory of my father and mother if I could speak lightly of the faith in which they lived and died. Surely this must be mere thoughtlessness, for I cannot believe that you find pleasure in giving pain. I have not forgotten the gentle hand that was laid upon your shoulder, and the gentle voice which said, "Uncle Robert wouldn't hurt a fly." And yet you bruise the tenderest sensibilities, and trample down what is most cherished by millions of sisters and daughters and mothers, little heeding that you are sporting with 'human creatures' lives."

You are waging a hopeless war—a war in which you are certain only of defeat. The Christian Religion began to be nearly two thousand years before you and I were born, and it will live two thousand years after we are dead. Why is it that it lives on and on, while nations and kingdoms perish? Is not this "the survival of the fittest?" Contend against it with all your wit and eloquence, you will fail, as all have failed before you. You cannot fight against the instincts of humanity. It is as natural for men to look up to a Higher Power as it is to look up to the stars. Tell them that there is no God! You might as well tell them that there is no Sun in heaven, even while on that central light and heat all life on earth depends.

I do not presume to, think that I have convinced you, or changed your opinion; but it is always right to appeal to a man's "sober second thought"—to that better judgment that comes with increasing knowledge and advancing years; and I will not give up hope that you will yet see things more clearly, and recognize the mistake you have made in not distinguishing Religion from Superstition—two things as far apart as "the hither from the utmost pole." Superstition is the greatest enemy of Religion. It is the nightmare of the mind, filling it with all imaginable terrors—a black cloud which broods over half the world. Against this you may well invoke the light of science to scatter its darkness. Whoever helps to sweep it away, is a benefactor of his race. But when this is done, and the moral atmosphere is made pure and sweet, then you as well as we may be conscious of a new Presence coming into the hushed and vacant air, as Religion, daughter of the skies, descends to earth to bring peace and good will to men.

Henry M. Field.

A REPLY TO THE REV. HENRY M. FIELD, D.D.

"Doubt is called the beacon of the wise."

My Dear Mr. Field:

I answer your letter because it is manly, candid and generous. It is not often that a minister of the gospel of universal benevolence speaks of an unbeliever except in terms of reproach, contempt and hatred. The meek are often malicious. The statement in your letter, that some of your brethren look upon me as a monster on account of my unbelief, tends to show that those who love God are not always the friends of their fellowmen.

Is it not strange that people who admit that they ought to be eternally damned, that they are by nature totally depraved, and that there is no soundness or health in them, can be so arrogantly egotistic as to look upon others as "monsters"? And yet "some of your brethren," who regard unbelievers as infamous, rely for salvation entirely on the goodness of another, and expect to receive as alms an eternity of joy.

The first question that arises between us, is as to the innocence of honest error—as to the right to express an honest thought.

You must know that perfectly honest men differ on many important subjects. Some believe in free trade, others are the advocates of protection. There are honest Democrats and sincere Republicans. How do you account for these differences? Educated men, presidents of colleges, cannot agree upon questions capable of solution—questions that the mind can grasp, concerning which the evidence is open to all and where the facts can be with accuracy ascertained. How do you explain this? If such differences can exist consistently with the good faith of those who differ, can you not conceive of honest people entertaining different views on subjects about which nothing can be positively known?

You do not regard me as a monster. "Some of your brethren" do. How do you account for this difference? Of course, your brethren—their hearts having been softened by the Presbyterian God—are governed by charity and love. They do not regard me as a monster because I have committed an infamous crime, but simply for the reason that I have expressed my honest thoughts.

What should I have done? I have read the Bible with great care, and the conclusion has forced itself upon my mind not only that it is not inspired, but that it is not true. Was it my duty to speak or act contrary to this conclusion? Was it my duty to remain silent? If I had been untrue to myself, if I had joined the majority,—if I had declared the book to be the inspired word of God,—would your brethren still have regarded me as a monster? Has religion had control of the world so long that an honest man seems monstrous?

According to your creed—according to your Bible—the same Being who made the mind of man, who fashioned every brain, and sowed within those wondrous fields the seeds of every thought and deed, inspired the Bible's every word, and gave it as a guide to all the world. Surely the book should satisfy the brain. And yet, there are millions who do not believe in the inspiration of the Scriptures. Some of the greatest and best have held the claim of inspiration in contempt. No Presbyterian ever stood higher in the realm of thought than Humboldt. He was familiar with Nature from sands to stars, and gave his thoughts, his discoveries and conclusions, "more precious than the tested gold," to all mankind. Yet he not only rejected the religion of your brethren, but denied the existence of their God. Certainly, Charles Darwin was one of the greatest and purest of men,—as free from prejudice as the mariner's compass,—desiring only to find amid the mists and clouds of ignorance the star of truth. No man ever exerted a greater influence on the intellectual world. His discoveries, carried to their legitimate conclusion, destroy the creeds and sacred Scriptures of mankind. In the light of "Natural Selection," "The Survival of the Fittest," and "The Origin of Species," even the Christian religion becomes a gross and cruel superstition. Yet Darwin was an honest, thoughtful, brave and generous man.

Compare, I beg of you, these men, Humboldt and Darwin, with the founders of the Presbyterian Church. Read the life of Spinoza, the loving pantheist, and then that of John Calvin, and tell me, candidly, which, in your opinion, was a "monster." Even your brethren do not claim that men are to be eternally punished for having been mistaken as to the truths of geology, astronomy, or mathematics. A man may deny the rotundity and rotation of the earth, laugh at the attraction of gravitation, scout the nebular hypothesis, and hold the multiplication table in abhorrence, and yet join at last the angelic choir. I insist upon the same freedom of thought in all departments of human knowledge. Reason is the supreme and final test.

If God has made a revelation to man, it must have been addressed to his reason. There is no other faculty that could even decipher the address. I admit that reason is a small and feeble flame, a flickering torch by stumblers carried in the starless night,—blown and flared by passion's storm,—and yet it is the only light. Extinguish that, and nought remains.

You draw a distinction between what you are pleased to call "superstition" and religion. You are shocked at the Hindu mother when she gives her child to death at the supposed command of her God. What do you think of Abraham, of Jephthah? What is your opinion of Jehovah himself? Is not the sacrifice of a child to a phantom as horrible in Palestine as in India? Why should a God demand a sacrifice from man? Why should the infinite ask anything from the finite? Should the sun beg of the glow-worm, and should the momentary spark excite the envy of the source of light?

You must remember that the Hindu mother believes that her child will be forever blest—that it will become the especial care of the God to whom it has been given. This is a sacrifice through a false belief on the part of the mother. She breaks her heart for the love of her babe. But what do you think of the Christian mother who expects to be happy in heaven, with her child a convict in the eternal prison—a prison in which none die, and from which none escape? What do you say of those Christians who believe that they, in heaven, will be so filled with ecstasy that all the loved of earth will be forgotten—that all the sacred relations of life, and all the passions of the heart, will fade and die, so that they will look with stony, un-replying, happy eyes upon the miseries of the lost?

You have laid down a rule by which superstition can be distinguished from religion. It is this: "It makes that a crime which is not a crime, and that a virtue which is not a virtue." Let us test your religion by this rule.

Is it a crime to investigate, to think, to reason, to observe? Is it a crime to be governed by that which to you is evidence, and is it infamous to express your honest thought? There is also another question: Is credulity a virtue? Is the open mouth of ignorant wonder the only entrance to Paradise?

According to your creed, those who believe are to be saved, and those who do not believe are to be eternally lost. When you condemn men to everlasting pain for unbelief—that is to say, for acting in accordance with that which is evidence to them—do you not make that a crime which is not a crime? And when you reward men with an eternity of joy for simply believing that which happens to be in accord with their minds, do you not make that a virtue which is not a virtue? In other words, do you not bring your own religion exactly within your own definition of superstition?

The truth is, that no one can justly be held responsible for his thoughts. The brain thinks without asking our consent. We believe, or we disbelieve, without an effort of the will. Belief is a result. It is the effect of evidence upon the mind. The scales turn in spite of him who watches. There is no opportunity of being honest or dishonest in the formation of an opinion. The conclusion is entirely independent of desire. We must believe, or we must doubt, in spite of what we wish.

That which must be, has the right to be.

We think in spite of ourselves. The brain thinks as the heart beats, as the eyes see, as the blood pursues its course in the old accustomed ways.

The question then is, not have we the right to think,—that being a necessity,—but have we the right to express our honest thoughts? You certainly have the right to express yours, and you have exercised that right. Some of your brethren, who regard me as a monster, have expressed theirs. The question now is, have I the right to express mine? In other words, have I the right to answer your letter? To make that a crime in me which is a virtue in you, certainly comes within your definition of superstition. To exercise a right yourself which you deny to me is simply the act of a tyrant. Where did you get your right to express your honest thoughts? When, and where, and how did I lose mine?

You would not burn, you would not even imprison me, because I differ with you on a subject about which neither of us knows anything. To you the savagery of the Inquisition is only a proof of the depravity of man. You are far better than your creed. You believe that even the Christian world is outgrowing the frightful feeling that fagot, and dungeon, and thumb-screw are legitimate arguments, calculated to convince those upon whom they are used, that the religion of those who use them was founded by a God of infinite compassion. You will admit that he who now persecutes for opinion's sake is infamous. And yet, the God you worship will, according to your creed, torture through all the endless years the man who entertains an honest doubt. A belief in such a God is the foundation and cause of all religious persecution. You may reply that only the belief in a false God causes believers to be inhuman. But you must admit that the Jews believed in the true God, and you are forced to say that they were so malicious, so cruel, so savage, that they crucified the only Sinless Being who ever lived. This crime was Committed, not in spite of their religion, but in accordance with it. They simply obeyed the command of Jehovah. And the followers of this Sinless Being, who, for all these centuries, have denounced the cruelty of the Jews for crucifying a man on account of his opinion, have destroyed millions and millions of their fellow-men for differing with them. And this same Sinless Being threatens to torture in eternal fire countless myriads for the same offence. Beyond this, inconsistency cannot go. At this point absurdity becomes infinite.

Your creed transfers the Inquisition to another world, making it eternal. Your God becomes, or rather is, an infinite Torquemada, who denies to his countless victims even the mercy of death. And this you call "a consolation."

You insist that at the foundation of every religion is the idea of God. According to your creed, all ideas of God, except those entertained by those of your faith, are absolutely false. You are not called upon to defend the Gods of the nations dead; nor the Gods of heretics. It is your business to defend the God of the Bible—the God of the Presbyterian Church. When in the ranks doing battle for your creed, you must wear the uniform of your church. You dare not say that it is sufficient to insure the salvation of a soul to believe in *a* god, or in *some* god. According to your creed, man must believe in *your* God. All the nations dead believed in gods, and all the worshipers of Zeus, and Jupiter, and Isis, and Osiris, and Brahma prayed and sacrificed in vain. Their petitions were not answered, and their souls were not saved. Surely you do not claim that it is sufficient to believe in any one of the heathen gods.

What right have you to occupy the position of the deists, and to put forth arguments that even Christians have answered? The deist denounced the God of the Bible because of his cruelty, and at the same time lauded the God of Nature. The Christian replied that the God of Nature was as cruel as the God of the Bible. This answer was complete.

I feel that you are entitled to the admission that none have been, that none are, too ignorant, too degraded, to believe in the supernatural; and I freely give you the advantage of this admission. Only a few—and they among the wisest, noblest, and purest of the human race—have regarded all gods as monstrous myths. Yet a belief in "the true God" does not seem to make men charitable or just. For most people, theism is the easiest solution of the universe. They are satisfied with saying that there must be a Being who created and who governs the world. But the universality of a belief does not tend to establish its truth. The belief in the existence of a malignant Devil has been as universal as the belief in a beneficent God, yet few intelligent men will say that the universality of this belief in an infinite demon even tends to prove his existence. In the world of thought, majorities count for nothing. Truth has always dwelt with the few.

Man has filled the world with impossible monsters, and he has been the sport and prey of these phantoms born of ignorance and hope and fear. To appease the wrath of these monsters man has sacrificed his fellow-man. He has shed the blood of wife and child; he has fasted and prayed; he has suffered beyond the power of language to express, and yet he has received nothing from these gods—they have heard no supplication, they have answered no prayer.

You may reply that your God "sends his rain on the just and on the unjust," and that this fact proves that he is merciful to all alike. I answer, that your God sends his pestilence on the just and on the unjust—that his earthquakes devour and his cyclones rend and wreck the loving and the vicious, the honest and the criminal. Do not these facts prove that your God is cruel to all alike? In other words, do they not demonstrate the absolute impartiality of divine negligence?

Do you not believe that any honest man of average intelligence, having absolute control of the rain, could do vastly better than is being done? Certainly there would be no droughts or floods; the crops would not be permitted to wither and die, while rain was being wasted in the sea. Is it conceivable that a good man with power to control the winds would not prevent cyclones? Would you not rather trust a wise and honest man with the lightning?

Why should an infinitely wise and powerful God destroy the good and preserve the vile? Why should he treat all alike here, and in another world make an infinite difference? Why should your God allow his worshipers, his adorers, to be destroyed by his enemies? Why should he allow the honest, the loving, the noble, to perish at the stake? Can you answer these questions? Does it not seem to you that your God must have felt a touch of shame when the poor slave mother—one that had been robbed of her babe—knelt and with clasped hands, in a voice broken with sobs, commenced her prayer with the words "Our Father"?

It gave me pleasure to find that, notwithstanding your creed, you are philosophical enough to say that some men are incapacitated, by reason of temperament, for believing in the existence of God. Now, if a belief in God is necessary to the salvation of the soul, why should God create a soul without this capacity? Why should he create souls that he knew would be lost? You seem to think that it is necessary to be poetical, or dreamy, in order to be religious, and by inference, at least, you deny certain qualities to me that you deem necessary. Do you account for the atheism of Shelley by saying that he was not poetic, and do you quote his lines to prove the existence of the very God whose being he so passionately denied? Is it possible that Napoleon—one of the most infamous of men—had a nature so finely strung that he was sensitive to the divine influences? Are you driven to the necessity of proving the existence of one tyrant by the words of another? Personally, I have but little confidence in a religion that satisfied the heart of a man who, to gratify his ambition, filled half the world with widows and orphans. In regard to Agassiz, it is just to say that he furnished a vast amount of testimony in favor of the truth of the theories of Charles Darwin, and then denied the correctness of these theories—preferring the good opinions of Harvard for a few days to the lasting applause of the intellectual world.

I agree with you that the world is a mystery, not only, but that everything in nature is equally mysterious, and that there is no way of escape from the mystery of life and death. To me, the crystallization of the snow is as mysterious as the constellations. But when you endeavor to explain the mystery of the universe by the mystery of God, you do not even exchange mysteries—you simply make one more.

Nothing can be mysterious enough to become an explanation.

The mystery of man cannot be explained by the mystery of God. That mystery still asks for explanation. The mind is so that it cannot grasp the idea of an infinite personality. That is beyond the circumference. This being so, it is impossible that man can be convinced by any evidence of the existence of that which he cannot in any measure comprehend. Such evidence would be equally incomprehensible with the incomprehensible fact sought to be established by it, and the intellect of man can grasp neither the one nor the other.

You admit that the God of Nature—that is to say, your God—is as inflexible as nature itself. Why should man worship the inflexible? Why should he kneel to the unchangeable? You say that your God "does not bend to human thought any more than to human will," and that "the more we study him, the more we find that he is not what we imagined him to be." So that, after all, the only thing you are really certain of in relation to your God is, that he is not what you think he is. Is it not almost absurd to insist that such a state of mind is necessary to salvation, or that it is a moral restraint, or that it is the foundation of social order?

The most religious nations have been the most immoral, the cruelest and the most unjust. Italy was far worse under the Popes than under the Caesars. Was there ever a barbarian nation more savage than the Spain of the sixteenth century? Certainly you must know that what you call religion has produced a thousand civil wars, and has severed with the sword all the natural ties that produce "the unity and married calm of States." Theology is the fruitful mother of discord; order is the child of reason. If you will candidly consider this question—if you will for a few moments forget your preconceived opinions—you will instantly see that the instinct of self-preservation holds society together. Religion itself was born of this instinct. People, being ignorant, believed that the Gods were jealous and revengeful. They peopled space with phantoms that demanded worship and delighted in sacrifice and ceremony, phantoms that could be flattered by praise and changed by prayer. These ignorant people wished to preserve themselves. They supposed that they could in this way avoid pestilence and famine, and postpone perhaps the day of death. Do you not see that self-preservation lies at the foundation of worship? Nations, like individuals, defend and protect themselves.

Nations, like individuals, have fears, have ideals, and live for the accomplishment of certain ends. Men defend their property because it is of value. Industry is the enemy of theft. Men, as a rule, desire to live, and for that reason murder is a crime. Fraud is hateful to the victim. The majority of mankind work and produce the necessities, the comforts, and the luxuries of life. They wish to retain the fruits of their labor. Government is one of the instrumentalities for the preservation of what man deems of value. This is the foundation of social order, and this holds society together.

Religion has been the enemy of social order, because it directs the attention of man to another world. Religion teaches its votaries to sacrifice this world for the sake of that other. The effect is to weaken the ties that hold families and States together. Of what consequence is anything in this world compared with eternal joy?

You insist that man is not capable of self-government, and that God made the mistake of filling a world with failures—in other words, that man must be governed not by himself, but by your God, and that your God produces order, and establishes and preserves all the nations of the earth. This being so, your God is responsible for the government of this world. Does he preserve order in Russia? Is he accountable for Siberia? Did he establish the institution of slavery? Was he the founder of the Inquisition?

You answer all these questions by calling my attention to "the retributions of history." What are the retributions of history? The honest were burned at the stake; the patriotic, the generous, and the noble were allowed to die in dungeons; whole races were enslaved; millions of mothers were robbed of their babes. What were the retributions of history? They who committed these crimes wore crowns, and they who justified these infamies were adorned with the tiara.

You are mistaken when you say that Lincoln at Gettysburg said: "Just and true are thy judgments, Lord God Almighty." Something like this occurs in his last inaugural, in which he says,—speaking of his hope that the war might soon be ended,—"If it shall continue until every drop of blood drawn by the lash shall be paid by another drawn with the sword, still it must be said, 'The judgments of the Lord are true and righteous altogether.'" But admitting that you are correct in the assertion, let me ask you one question: Could one standing over the body of Lincoln, the blood slowly oozing from the madman's wound, have truthfully said: "Just and true are thy judgments, Lord God Almighty"?

Do you really believe that this world is governed by an infinitely wise and good God? Have you convinced even yourself of this? Why should God permit the triumph of injustice? Why should the loving be tortured? Why should the noblest be destroyed? Why should the world be filled with misery, with ignorance, and with want? What reason have you for believing that your God will do better in another world than he has done and is doing in this? Will he be wiser? Will he have more power? Will he be more merciful?

When I say "your God," of course I mean the God described in the Bible and the Presbyterian Confession of Faith. But again I say, that in the nature of things, there can be no evidence of the existence of an infinite being.

An infinite being must be conditionless, and for that reason there is nothing that a finite being can do that can by any possibility affect the well-being of the conditionless. This being so, man can neither owe nor discharge any debt or duty to an infinite being. The infinite cannot want, and man can do nothing for a being who wants nothing. A conditioned being can be made happy, or miserable, by changing conditions, but the conditionless is absolutely independent of cause and effect.

I do not say that a God does not exist, neither do I say that a God does exist; but I say that I do not know—that there can be no evidence to my mind of the existence of such a being, and that my mind is so that it is incapable of even thinking of an infinite personality. I know that in your creed you describe God as "without body, parts, or passions." This, to my mind, is simply a description of an infinite vacuum. I have had no experience with gods. This world is the only one with which I am acquainted, and I was surprised to find in your letter the expression that "perhaps others are better acquainted with that of which I am so ignorant." Did you, by this, intend to say that you know anything of any other state of existence—that you have inhabited some other planet—that you lived before you were born, and that you recollect something of that other world, or of that other state?

Upon the question of immortality you have done me, unintentionally, a great injustice. With regard to that hope, I have never uttered "a flippant or a trivial" word. I have said a thousand times, and I say again, that the idea of immortality, that, like a sea, has ebbed and flowed in the human heart, with its countless waves of hope and fear beating against the shores and rocks of time and fate, was not born of any book, nor of any creed, nor of any religion. It was born of human affection, and it will continue to ebb and flow beneath the mists and clouds of doubt and darkness as long as love kisses the lips of death.

I have said a thousand times, and I say again, that we do not know, we cannot say, whether death is a wall or a door—the beginning, or end, of a day—the spreading of pinions to soar, or the folding forever of wings—the rise or the set of a sun, or an endless life, that brings rapture and love to every one.

The belief in immortality is far older than Christianity. Thousands of years before Christ was born billions of people had lived and died in that hope. Upon countless graves had been laid in love and tears the emblems of another life. The heaven of the New Testament was to be in this world. The dead, after they were raised, were to live here. Not one satisfactory word was said to have been uttered by Christ—nothing philosophic, nothing clear, nothing that adorns, like a bow of promise, the cloud of doubt.

According to the account in the New Testament, Christ was dead for a period of nearly three days. After his resurrection, why did not some one of his disciples ask him where he had been? Why did he not tell them what world he had visited? There was the opportunity to "bring life and immortality to light." And yet he was as silent as the grave that he had left—speechless as the stone that angels had rolled away.

How do you account for this? Was it not infinitely cruel to leave the world in darkness and in doubt, when one word could have filled all time with hope and light?

The hope of immortality is the great oak round which have climbed the poisonous vines of superstition. The vines have not supported the oak— the oak has supported the vines. As long as men live and love and die, this hope will blossom in the human heart.

All I have said upon this subject has been to express my hope and confess my lack of knowledge. Neither by word nor look have I expressed any other feeling than sympathy with those who hope to live again—for those who bend above their dead and dream of life to come. But I have denounced the selfishness and heartlessness of those who expect for themselves an eternity of joy, and for the rest of mankind predict, without a tear, a world of endless pain. Nothing can be more contemptible than such a hope—a hope that can give satisfaction only to the hyenas of the human race.

When I say that I do not know—when I deny the existence of perdition, you reply that "there is something very cruel in this treatment of the belief of my fellow-creatures."

You have had the goodness to invite me to a grave over which a mother bends and weeps for her only son. I accept your invitation. We will go together. Do not, I pray you, deal in splendid generalities. Be explicit. Remember that the son for whom the loving mother weeps was not a Christian, not a believer in the inspiration of the Bible nor in the divinity of Jesus Christ. The mother turns to you for consolation, for some star of hope in the midnight of her grief. What must you say? Do not desert the Presbyterian creed. Do not forget the threatenings of Jesus Christ. What must you say? Will you read a portion of the Presbyterian Confession of Faith? Will you read this?

"Although the light of Nature, and the works of creation and Providence, do so far manifest the goodness, wisdom, and power of God as to leave man inexcusable, yet they are not sufficient to give that knowledge of God and of his will which is necessary to salvation."

Or, will you read this?

"By the decree of God, for the manifestation of his glory, some men and angels are predestined unto everlasting life and others foreordained to everlasting death. These angels and men, thus predestined and foreordained, are particularly and unchangeably designed, and their number is so certain and definite that it cannot be either increased or diminished."

Suppose the mother, lifting her tear-stained face, should say: "My son was good, generous, loving and kind. He gave his life for me. Is there no hope for him?" Would you then put this serpent in her breast?

"Men not professing the Christian religion cannot be saved in any other way whatsoever, be they never so diligent to conform their lives according to the light of Nature. We cannot by our best works merit pardon of sin. There is no sin so small but that it deserves damnation. Works done by unregenerate men, although, for the matter of that, they may be things which God commands, and of good use both to themselves and others, are sinful and cannot please God or make a man meet to receive Christ or God."

And suppose the mother should then sobbingly ask: "What has become of my son? Where is he now?" Would you still read from your Confession of Faith, or from your Catechism—this?

"The souls of the wicked are cast into hell, where they remain in torment and utter darkness, reserved to the judgment of the great day. At the last day the righteous shall come into everlasting life, but the wicked shall be cast into eternal torment and punished with everlasting destruction. The wicked shall be cast into hell, to be punished with unspeakable torment, both of body and soul, with the devil and his angels forever."

If the poor mother still wept, still refused to be comforted, would you thrust this dagger in her heart?

"At the Day of Judgment you, being caught up to Christ in the clouds, shall be seated at his right hand and there openly acknowledged and acquitted, and you shall join with him in the damnation of your son."

If this failed to still the beatings of her aching heart, would you repeat these words which you say came from the loving soul of Christ?

"They who believe and are baptized shall be saved, and they who believe not shall be damned; and these shall go away into everlasting fire prepared for the devil and his angels."

Would you not be compelled, according to your belief, to tell this mother that "there is but one name given under heaven and among men whereby" the souls of men can enter the gates of Paradise? Would you not be compelled to say: "Your son lived in a Christian land. The means of grace were within his reach. He died not having experienced a change of heart, and your son is forever lost. You can meet your son again only by dying in your sins; but if you will give your heart to God you can never clasp him to your breast again."
What could I say? Let me tell you:

"My dear madam, this reverend gentleman knows nothing of another world. He cannot see beyond the tomb. He has simply stated to you the superstitions of ignorance, of cruelty and fear. If there be in this universe a God, he certainly is as good as you are. Why should he have loved your son in life—loved him, according to this reverend gentleman, to that degree that he gave his life for him; and why should that love be changed to hatred the moment your son was dead?

"My dear woman, there are no punishments, there are no rewards—there are consequences; and of one thing you may rest assured, and that is, that every soul, no matter what sphere it may inhabit, will have the everlasting opportunity of doing right.

"If death ends all, and if this handful of dust over which you weep is all there is, you have this consolation: Your son is not within the power of this reverend gentleman's God—that is something. Your son does not suffer. Next to a life of joy is the dreamless sleep of death."

Does it not seem to you infinitely absurd to call orthodox Christianity "a consolation"? Here in this world, where every human being is enshrouded in cloud and mist,—where all lives are filled with mistakes,—where no one claims to be perfect, is it "a consolation" to say that "the smallest sin deserves eternal pain"? Is it possible for the ingenuity of man to extract from the doctrine of hell one drop, one ray, of "consolation"? If that doctrine be true, is not your God an infinite criminal? Why should he have created uncounted billions destined to suffer forever? Why did he not leave them unconscious dust? Compared with this crime, any crime that man can by any possibility commit is a virtue.

Think for a moment of your God,—the keeper of an infinite penitentiary filled with immortal convicts,—your God an eternal turnkey, without the pardoning power. In the presence of this infinite horror, you complacently speak of the atonement,—a scheme that has not yet gathered within its horizon a billionth part of the human race,—an atonement with one-half the world remaining undiscovered for fifteen hundred years after it was made.

If there could be no suffering, there could be no sin. To unjustly cause suffering is the only possible crime. How can a God accept the suffering of the innocent in lieu of the punishment of the guilty?

According to your theory, this infinite being, by his mere will, makes right and wrong. This I do not admit. Right and wrong exist in the nature of things—in the relation they bear to man, and to sentient beings. You have already admitted that "Nature is inflexible, and that a violated law calls for its consequences." I insist that no God can step between an act and its natural effects. If God exists, he has nothing to do with punishment, nothing to do with reward. From certain acts flow certain consequences; these consequences increase or decrease the happiness of man; and the consequences must be borne.

A man who has forfeited his life to the commonwealth may be pardoned, but a man who has violated a condition of his own well-being cannot be pardoned—there is no pardoning power. The laws of the State are made, and, being made, can be changed; but the facts of the universe cannot be changed. The relation of act to consequence cannot be altered. This is above all power, and, consequently, there is no analogy between the laws of the State and the facts in Nature. An infinite God could not change the relation between the diameter and circumference of the circle.

A man having committed a crime may be pardoned, but I deny the right of the State to punish an innocent man in the place of the pardoned—no matter how willing the innocent man may be to suffer the punishment. There is no law in Nature, no fact in Nature, by which the innocent can be justly punished to the end that the guilty may go free. Let it be understood once for all: Nature cannot pardon.

You have recognized this truth. You have asked me what is to become of one who seduces and betrays, of the criminal with the blood of his victim upon his hands? Without the slightest hesitation I answer, whoever commits a crime against another must, to the utmost of his power in this world and in another, if there be one, make full and ample restitution, and in addition must bear the natural consequences of his offence. No man can be perfectly happy, either in this world or in any other, who has by his perfidy broken a loving and confiding heart. No power can step between acts and consequences—no forgiveness, no atonement.

But, my dear friend, you have taught for many years, if you are a Presbyterian, or an evangelical Christian, that a man may seduce and betray, and that the poor victim, driven to insanity, leaping from some wharf at night where ships strain at their anchors in storm and darkness—you have taught that this poor girl may be tormented forever by a God of infinite compassion. This is not all that you have taught. You have said to the seducer, to the betrayer, to the one who would not listen to her wailing cry,—who would not even stretch forth his hand to catch her fluttering garments,—you have said to him: "Believe in the Lord Jesus Christ, and you shall be happy forever; you shall live in the realm of infinite delight, from which you can, without a shadow falling upon your face, observe the poor girl, your victim, writhing in the agonies of hell." You have taught this. For my part, I do not see how an angel in heaven meeting another angel whom he had robbed on the earth, could feel entirely blissful. I go further. Any decent angel, no matter if sitting at the right hand of God, should he see in hell one of his victims, would leave heaven itself for the purpose of wiping one tear from the cheek of the damned.

You seem to have forgotten your statement in the commencement of your letter, that your God is as inflexible as Nature—that he bends not to human thought nor to human will. You seem to have forgotten the line which you emphasized with italics: "*The effect of everything which is of the nature of a cause, is eternal.*" In the light of this sentence, where do you find a place for forgiveness—for your atonement? Where is a way to escape from the effect of a cause that is eternal? Do you not see that this sentence is a cord with which I easily tie your hands? The scientific part of your letter destroys the theological. You have put "new wine into old bottles," and the predicted result has followed. Will the angels in heaven, the redeemed of earth, lose their memory? Will not all the redeemed rascals remember their rascality? Will not all the redeemed assassins remember the faces of the dead? Will not all the seducers and betrayers remember her sighs, her tears, and the tones of her voice, and will not the conscience of the redeemed be as inexorable as the conscience of the damned?

If memory is to be forever "the warder of the brain," and if the redeemed can never forget the sins they committed, the pain and anguish they caused, then they can never be perfectly happy; and if the lost can never forget the good they did, the kind actions, the loving words, the heroic deeds; and if the memory of good deeds gives the slightest pleasure, then the lost can never be perfectly miserable. Ought not the memory of a good action to live as long as the memory of a bad one? So that the undying memory of the good, in heaven, brings undying pain, and the undying memory of those in hell brings undying pleasure. Do you not see that if men have done good and bad, the future can have neither a perfect heaven nor a perfect hell?

I believe in the manly doctrine that every human being must bear the consequences of his acts, and that no man can be justly saved or damned on account of the goodness or the wickedness of another.

If by atonement you mean the natural effect of self-sacrifice, the effects following a noble and disinterested action; if you mean that the life and death of Christ are worth their effect upon the human race,—which your letter seems to show,—then there is no question between us. If you have thrown away the old and barbarous idea that a law had been broken, that God demanded a sacrifice, and that Christ, the innocent, was offered up for us, and that he bore the wrath of God and suffered in our place, then I congratulate you with all my heart.

It seems to me impossible that life should be exceedingly joyous to any one who is acquainted with its miseries, its burdens, and its tears. I know that as darkness follows light around the globe, so misery and misfortune follow the sons of men. According to your creed, the future state will be worse than this. Here, the vicious may reform; here, the wicked may repent; here, a few gleams of sunshine may fall upon the darkest life. But in your future state, for countless billions of the human race, there will be no reform, no opportunity of doing right, and no possible gleam of sunshine can ever touch their souls. Do you not see that your future state is infinitely worse than this? You seem to mistake the glare of hell for the light of morning.

Let us throw away the dogma of eternal retribution. Let us "cling to all that can bring a ray of hope into the darkness of this life."

You have been kind enough to say that I find a subject for caricature in the doctrine of regeneration. If, by regeneration, you mean reformation,— if you mean that there comes a time in the life of a young man when he feels the touch of responsibility, and that he leaves his foolish or vicious ways, and concludes to act like an honest man,—if this is what you mean by regeneration, I am a believer. But that is not the definition of regeneration in your creed—that is not Christian regeneration. There is some mysterious, miraculous, supernatural, invisible agency, called, I believe, the Holy Ghost, that enters and changes the heart of man, and this mysterious agency is like the wind, under the control, apparently, of no one, coming and going when and whither it listeth. It is this illogical and absurd view of regeneration that I have attacked.

You ask me how it came to' pass that a Hebrew peasant, born among the hills of Galilee, had a wisdom above that of Socrates or Plato, of Confucius or Buddha, and you conclude by saying, "This is the greatest of miracles—that such a being should live and die on the earth."

I can hardly admit your conclusion, because I remember that Christ said nothing in favor of the family relation. As a matter of fact, his life tended to cast discredit upon marriage. He said nothing against the institution of slavery; nothing against the tyranny of government; nothing of our treatment of animals; nothing about education, about intellectual progress; nothing of art, declared no scientific truth, and said nothing as to the rights and duties of nations.

You may reply that all this is included in "Do unto others as you would be done by;" and "Resist not evil." More than this is necessary to educate the human race. It is not enough to say to your child or to your pupil, "Do right." The great question still remains: What is right? Neither is there any wisdom in the idea of non-resistance. Force without mercy is tyranny. Mercy without force is but a waste of tears. Take from virtue the right of self-defense and vice becomes the master of the world.

Let me ask you how it came to pass that an ignorant driver of camels, a man without family, without wealth, became master of hundreds of millions of human beings? How is it that he conquered and overran more than half of the Christian world? How is it that on a thousand fields the banner of the cross went down in blood, while that of the crescent floated in triumph? How do you account for the fact that the flag of this impostor floats to-day above the sepulcher of Christ? Was this a miracle? Was Mohammed inspired? How do you account for Confucius, whose name is known wherever the sky bends? Was he inspired—this man who for many centuries has stood first, and who has been acknowledged the superior of all men by hundreds and thousands of millions of his fellow-men? How do you account for Buddha,—in many respects the greatest religious teacher this world has ever known,—the broadest, the most intellectual of them all; he who was great enough, hundreds of years before Christ was born, to declare the universal brotherhood of man, great enough to say that intelligence is the only lever capable of raising mankind? How do you account for him, who has had more followers than any other? Are you willing to say that all success is divine? How do you account for Shakespeare, born of parents who could neither read nor write, held in the lap of ignorance and love, nursed at the breast of poverty—how do you account for him, by far the greatest of the human race, the wings of whose imagination still fill the horizon of human thought; Shakespeare, who was perfectly acquainted with the human heart, knew all depths of sorrow, all heights of joy, and in whose mind were the fruit of all thought, of all experience, and a prophecy of all to be; Shakespeare, the wisdom and beauty and depth of whose words increase with the intelligence and civilization of mankind? How do you account for this miracle? Do you believe that any founder of any religion could have written "Lear" or "Hamlet"? Did Greece produce a man who could by any possibility have been the author of "Troilus and Cressida"? Was there among all the countless millions of almighty Rome an intellect that could have written the tragedy of "Julius Caesar"? Is not the play of "Antony and Cleopatra" as Egyptian as the Nile? How do you account for this man, within whose veins there seemed to be the blood of every race, and in whose brain there were the poetry and philosophy of a world?

You ask me to tell my opinion of Christ. Let me say here, once for all, that for the man Christ—for the man who, in the darkness, cried out,

"My God, why hast thou forsaken me!" —for that man I have the greatest possible respect. And let me say, once for all, that the place where man has died for man is holy ground. To that great and serene peasant of Palestine I gladly pay the tribute of my admiration and my tears. He was a reformer in his day—an infidel in his time. Back of the theological mask, and in spite of the interpolations of the New Testament, I see a great and genuine man.

It is hard to see how you can consistently defend the course pursued by Christ himself. He attacked with great bitterness "the religion of others." It did not occur to him that "there was something very cruel in this treatment of the belief of his fellow-creatures." He denounced the chosen people of God as a "generation of vipers." He compared them to "whited sepulchers." How can you sustain the conduct of missionaries? They go to other lands and attack the sacred beliefs of others. They tell the people of India and of all heathen lands, not only that their religion is a lie, not only that their gods are myths, but that the ancestors of these people—their fathers and mothers who never heard of God, of the Bible, or of Christ—are all in perdition. Is not this a cruel treatment of the belief of a fellow-creature?

A religion that is not manly and robust enough to bear attack with smiling fortitude is unworthy of a place in the heart or brain. A religion that takes refuge in sentimentality, that cries out: "Do not, I pray you, tell me any truth calculated to hurt my feelings," is fit only for asylums.

You believe that Christ was God, that he was infinite in power. While in Jerusalem he cured the sick, raised a few from the dead, and opened the eyes of the blind. Did he do these things because he loved mankind, or did he do these miracles simply to establish the fact that he was the very Christ? If he was actuated by love, is he not as powerful now as he was then? Why does he not open the eyes of the blind now? Why does he not with a touch make the leper clean? If you had the power to give sight to the blind, to cleanse the leper, and would not exercise it, what would be thought of you? What is the difference between one who can and will not cure, and one who causes disease?

Only the other day I saw a beautiful girl—a paralytic, and yet her brave and cheerful spirit shone over the wreck and ruin of her body like morning on the desert. What would I think of myself, had I the power by a word to send the blood through all her withered limbs freighted again with life, should I refuse?

Most theologians seem to imagine that the virtues have been produced by and are really the children of religion.

Religion has to do with the supernatural. It defines our duties and obligations to God. It prescribes a certain course of conduct by means of which happiness can be attained in another world. The result here is only an incident. The virtues are secular. They have nothing whatever to do with the supernatural, and are of no kindred to any religion. A man may be honest, courageous, charitable, industrious, hospitable, loving and pure, without being religious—that is to say, without any belief in the supernatural; and a man may be the exact opposite and at the same time a sincere believer in the creed of any church—that is to say, in the existence of a personal God, the inspiration of the Scriptures and in the divinity of Jesus Christ. A man who believes in the Bible may or may not be kind to his family, and a man who is kind and loving in his family may or may not believe in the Bible.

In order that you may see the effect of belief in the formation of character, it is only necessary to call your attention to the fact that your Bible shows that the devil himself is a believer in the existence of your God, in the inspiration of the Scriptures, and in the divinity of Jesus Christ. He not only believes these things, but he knows them, and yet, in spite of it all, he remains a devil still.

Few religions have been bad enough to destroy all the natural goodness in the human heart. In the deepest midnight of superstition some natural virtues, like stars, have been visible in the heavens. Man has committed every crime in the name of Christianity—or at least crimes that involved the commission of all others. Those who paid for labor with the lash, and who made blows a legal tender, were Christians. Those who engaged in the slave trade were believers in a personal God. One slave ship was called "The Jehovah." Those who pursued with hounds the fugitive led by the Northern star prayed fervently to Christ to crown their efforts with success, and the stealers of babes, just before falling asleep, commended their souls to the keeping of the Most High.

As you have mentioned the apostles, let me call your attention to an incident.

You remember the story of Ananias and Sapphira. The apostles, having nothing themselves, conceived the idea of having all things in common. Their followers who had something were to sell what little they had, and turn the proceeds over to these theological financiers. It seems that Ananias and Sapphira had a piece of land. They sold it, and after talking the matter over, not being entirely satisfied with the collaterals, concluded to keep a little—just enough to keep them from starvation if the good and pious bankers should abscond.

When Ananias brought the money, he was asked whether he had kept back a part of the price. He said that he had not. Whereupon God, the compassionate, struck him dead. As soon as the corpse was removed, the apostles sent for his wife. They did not tell her that her husband had been killed. They deliberately set a trap for her life. Not one of them was good enough or noble enough to put her on her guard; they allowed her to believe that her husband had told his story, and that she was free to corroborate what he had said. She probably felt that they were giving more than they could afford, and, with the instinct of woman, wanted to keep a little. She denied that any part of the price had been kept back. That moment the arrow of divine vengeance entered her heart.

Will you be kind enough to tell me your opinion of the apostles in the light of this story? Certainly murder is a greater crime than mendacity.

You have been good enough, in a kind of fatherly way, to give me some advice. You say that I ought to soften my colors, and that my words would be more weighty if not so strong. Do you really desire that I should add weight to my words? Do you really wish me to succeed? If the commander of one army should send word to the general of the other that his men were firing too high, do you think the general would be misled? Can you conceive of his changing his orders by reason of the message?

I deny that "the Pilgrims crossed the sea to find freedom to worship God in the forests of the new world." They came not in the interest of freedom. It never entered their minds that other men had the same right to worship God according to the dictates of their consciences that the Pilgrims themselves had. The moment they had power they were ready to whip and brand, to imprison and burn. They did not believe in religious freedom. They had no more idea of liberty of conscience than Jehovah.

I do not say that there is no place in the world for heroes and martyrs. On the contrary, I declare that the liberty we now have was won for us by heroes and by martyrs, and millions of these martyrs were burned, or flayed alive, or torn in pieces, or assassinated by the church of God. The heroism was shown in fighting the hordes of religious superstition.

Giordano Bruno was a martyr. He was a hero. He believed in no God, in no heaven, and in no hell, yet he perished by fire. He was offered liberty on condition that he would recant. There was no God to please, no heaven to expect, no hell to fear, and yet he died by fire, simply to preserve the unstained whiteness of his soul.

For hundreds of years every man who attacked the church was a hero. The sword of Christianity has been wet for many centuries with the blood of the noblest. Christianity has been ready with whip and chain and fire to banish freedom from the earth.

Neither is it true that "family life withers under the cold sneer—half pity and half scorn—with which I look down on household worship."

Those who believe in the existence of God, and believe that they are indebted to this divine being for the few gleams of sunshine in this life, and who thank God for the little they have enjoyed, have my entire respect. Never have I said one word against the spirit of thankfulness. I understand the feeling of the man who gathers his family about him after the storm, or after the scourge, or after long sickness, and pours out his heart in thankfulness to the supposed God who has protected his fireside. I understand the spirit of the savage who thanks his idol of stone, or his fetish of wood. It is not the wisdom of the one or of the other that I respect, it is the goodness and thankfulness that prompt the prayer.

I believe in the family. I believe in family life; and one of my objections to Christianity is that it divides the family. Upon this subject I have said hundreds of times, and I say again, that the roof-tree is sacred, from the smallest fiber that feels the soft, cool clasp of earth, to the topmost flower that spreads its bosom to the sun, and like a spendthrift gives its perfume to the air. The home where virtue dwells with love is like a lily with a heart of fire, the fairest flower in all this world.

What did Christianity in the early centuries do for the home? What have nunneries and monasteries, and what has the glorification of celibacy done for the family? Do you not know that Christ himself offered rewards in this world and eternal happiness in another to those who would desert their wives and children and follow him? What effect has that promise had upon family life?

As a matter of fact, the family is regarded as nothing. Christianity teaches that there is but one family, the family of Christ, and that all other relations are as nothing compared with that. Christianity teaches the husband to desert the wife, the wife to desert the husband, children to desert their parents, for the miserable and selfish purpose of saving their own little, shriveled souls.

It is far better for a man to love his fellow-men than to love God. It is better to love wife and children than to love Christ. It is better to serve your neighbor than to serve your God—even if God exists. The reason is palpable. You can do nothing for God. You can do something for wife and children. You can add to the sunshine of a life. You can plant flowers in the pathway of another.

It is true that I am an enemy of the orthodox Sabbath. It is true that I do not believe in giving one-seventh of our time to the service of superstition. The whole scheme of your religion can be understood by any intelligent man in one day. Why should he waste a seventh of his whole life in hearing the same thoughts repeated again and again?

Nothing is more gloomy than an orthodox Sabbath. The mechanic who has worked during the week in heat and dust, the laboring man who has barely succeeded in keeping his soul in his body, the poor woman who has been sewing for the rich, may go to the village church which you have described. They answer the chimes of the bell, and what do they hear in this village church? Is it that God is the Father of the human race; is that all? If that were all, you never would have heard an objection from my lips. That is not all. If all ministers said: Bear the evils of this life; your Father in heaven counts your tears; the time will come when pain and death and grief will be forgotten words; I should have listened with the rest. What else does the minister say to the poor people who have answered the chimes of your bell? He says: "The smallest sin deserves eternal pain." "A vast majority of men are doomed to suffer the wrath of God forever." He fills the present with fear and the future with fire. He has heaven for the few, hell for the many. He describes a little grass-grown path that leads to heaven, where travelers are "few and far between," and a great highway worn with countless feet that leads to everlasting death.

Such Sabbaths are immoral. Such ministers are the real savages. Gladly would I abolish such a Sabbath. Gladly would I turn it into a holiday, a day of rest and peace, a day to get acquainted with your wife and children, a day to exchange civilities with your neighbors; and gladly would I see the church in which such sermons are preached changed to a place of entertainment. Gladly would I have the echoes of orthodox sermons—the owls and bats among the rafters, the snakes in crevices and corners—driven out by the glorious music of Wagner and Beethoven. Gladly would I see the Sunday school where the doctrine of eternal fire is taught, changed to a happy dance upon the village green.

Music refines. The doctrine of eternal punishment degrades. Science civilizes. Superstition looks longingly back to savagery.

You do not believe that general morality can be upheld without the sanctions of religion.

Christianity has sold, and continues to sell, crime on a credit. It has taught, and it still teaches, that there is forgiveness for all. Of course it teaches morality. It says: "Do not steal, do not murder;" but it adds, "but if you do both, there is a way of escape: believe on the Lord Jesus Christ and thou shalt be saved." I insist that such a religion is no restraint. It is far better to teach that there is no forgiveness, and that every human being must bear the consequences of his acts.

The first great step toward national reformation is the universal acceptance of the idea that there is no escape from the consequences of our acts. The young men who come from their country homes into a city filled with temptations, may be restrained by the thought of father and mother. This is a natural restraint. They may be restrained by their knowledge of the fact that a thing is evil on account of its consequences, and that to do wrong is always a mistake. I cannot conceive of such a man being more liable to temptation because he has heard one of my lectures in which I have told him that the only good is happiness—that the only way to attain that good is by doing what he believes to be right. I cannot imagine that his moral character will be weakened by the statement that there is no escape from the consequences of his acts. You seem to think that he will be instantly led astray—that he will go off under the flaring lamps to the riot of passion. Do you think the Bible calculated to restrain him? To prevent this would you recommend him to read the lives of Abraham, of Isaac, and of Jacob, and the other holy polygamists of the Old Testament? Should he read the life of David, and of Solomon? Do you think this would enable him to withstand temptation? Would it not be far better to fill the young man's mind with facts so that he may know exactly the physical consequences of such acts? Do you regard ignorance as the foundation of virtue? Is fear the arch that supports the moral nature of man?

You seem to think that there is danger in knowledge, and that the best chemists are most likely to poison themselves.

You say that to sneer at religion is only a step from sneering at morality, and then only another step to that which is vicious and profligate.

The Jews entertained the same opinion of the teachings of Christ. He sneered at their religion. The Christians have entertained the same opinion of every philosopher. Let me say to you again—and let me say it once for all—that morality has nothing to do with religion. Morality does not depend upon the supernatural. Morality does not walk with the crutches of miracles. Morality appeals to the experience of mankind. It cares nothing about faith, nothing about sacred books. Morality depends upon facts, something that can be seen, something known, the product of which can be estimated. It needs no priest, no ceremony, no mummery. It believes in the freedom of the human mind. It asks for investigation. It is founded upon truth. It is the enemy of all religion, because it has to do with this world, and with this world alone.

My object is to drive fear out of the world. Fear is the jailer of the mind. Christianity, superstition—that is to say, the supernatural— makes every brain a prison and every soul a convict. Under the government of a personal deity, consequences partake of the nature of punishments and rewards.

Under the government of Nature, what you call punishments and rewards are simply consequences. Nature does not punish. Nature does not reward. Nature has no purpose. When the storm comes, I do not think: "This is being done by a tyrant." When the sun shines, I do not say: "This is being done by a friend." Liberty means freedom from personal dictation. It does not mean escape from the relations we sustain to other facts in Nature. I believe in the restraining influences of liberty. Temperance walks hand in hand with freedom. To remove a chain from the body puts an additional responsibility upon the soul. Liberty says to the man: You injure or benefit yourself; you increase or decrease your own well-being. It is a question of intelligence. You need not bow to a supposed tyrant, or to infinite goodness. You are responsible to yourself and to those you injure, and to none other.

I rid myself of fear, believing as I do that there is no power above which can help me in any extremity, and believing as I do that there is no power above or below that can injure me in any extremity. I do not believe that I am the sport of accident, or that I may be dashed in pieces by the blind agency of Nature. There is no accident, and there is no agency. That which happens must happen. The present is the necessary child of all the past, the mother of all the future.

Does it relieve mankind from fear to believe that there is some God who will help them in extremity? What evidence have they on which to found this belief? When has any God listened to the prayer of any man? The water drowns, the cold freezes, the flood destroys, the fire burns, the bolt of heaven falls—when and where has the prayer of man been answered?

Is the religious world to-day willing to test the efficacy of prayer? Only a few years ago it was tested in the United States. The Christians of Christendom, with one accord, fell upon their knees and asked God to spare the life of one man. You know the result. You know just as well as I that the forces of Nature produce the good and bad alike. You know that the forces of Nature destroy the good and bad alike. You know that the lightning feels the same keen delight in striking to death the honest man that it does or would in striking the assassin with his knife lifted above the bosom of innocence.

Did God hear the prayers of the slaves? Did he hear the prayers of imprisoned philosophers and patriots? Did he hear the prayers of martyrs, or did he allow fiends, calling themselves his followers, to pile the fagots round the forms of glorious men? Did he allow the flames to devour the flesh of those whose hearts were his? Why should any man depend on the goodness of a God who created countless millions, knowing that they would suffer eternal grief?

The faith that you call sacred—"sacred as the most delicate manly or womanly sentiment of love and honor"—is the faith that nearly all of your fellow-men are to be lost. Ought an honest man to be restrained from denouncing that faith because those who entertain it say that their feelings are hurt? You say to me: "There is a hell. A man advocating the opinions you advocate will go there when he dies." I answer: "There is no hell. The Bible that teaches it is not true." And you say: "How can you hurt my feelings?"

You seem to think that one who attacks the religion of his parents is wanting in respect to his father and his mother.

Were the early Christians lacking in respect for their fathers and mothers? Were the Pagans who embraced Christianity heartless sons and daughters? What have you to say of the apostles? Did they not heap contempt upon the religion of their fathers and mothers? Did they not join with him who denounced their people as a "generation of vipers"? Did they not follow one who offered a reward to those who would desert fathers and mothers? Of course you have only to go back a few generations in your family to find a Field who was not a Presbyterian. After that you find a Presbyterian. Was he base enough and infamous enough to heap contempt upon the religion of his father and mother? All the Protestants in the time of Luther lacked in respect for the religion of their fathers and mothers. According to your idea, Progress is a Prodigal Son. If one is bound by the religion of his father and mother, and his father happens to be a Presbyterian and his mother a Catholic, what is he to do? Do you not see that your doctrine gives intellectual freedom only to foundlings?

If by Christianity you mean the goodness, the spirit of forgiveness, the benevolence claimed by Christians to be a part, and the principal part, of that peculiar religion, then I do not agree with you when you say that "Christ is Christianity and that it stands or falls with him." You have narrowed unnecessarily the foundation of your religion. If it should be established beyond doubt that Christ never existed, all that is of value in Christianity would remain, and remain unimpaired. Suppose that we should find that Euclid was a myth, the science known as mathematics would not suffer. It makes no difference who painted or chiseled the greatest pictures and statues, so long as we have the pictures and statues. When he who has given the world a truth passes from the earth, the truth is left. A truth dies only when forgotten by the human race. Justice, love, mercy, forgiveness, honor, all the virtues that ever blossomed in the human heart, were known and practiced for uncounted ages before the birth of Christ.

You insist that religion does not leave man in "abject terror"—does not leave him "in utter darkness as to his fate."

Is it possible to know who will be saved? Can you read the names mentioned in the decrees of the Infinite? Is it possible to tell who is to be eternally lost? Can the imagination conceive a worse fate than your religion predicts for a majority of the race? Why should not every human being be in "abject terror" who believes your doctrine? How many loving and sincere women are in the asylums to-day fearing that they have committed "the unpardonable sin"—a sin to which your God has attached the penalty of eternal torment, and yet has failed to describe the offence? Can tyranny go beyond this—fixing the penalty of eternal pain for the violation of a law not written, not known, but kept in the secrecy of infinite darkness? How much happier it is to know nothing about it, and to believe nothing about it! How much better to have no God!

You discover a "Great Intelligence ordering our little lives, so that even the trials that we bear, as they call out the finer elements of character, conduce to our future happiness." This is an old explanation—probably as good as any. The idea is, that this world is a school in which man

300

becomes educated through tribulation—the muscles of character being developed by wrestling with misfortune. If it is necessary to live this life in order to develop character, in order to become worthy of a better world, how do you account for the fact that billions of the human race die in infancy, and are thus deprived of this necessary education and development? What would you think of a schoolmaster who should kill a large proportion of his scholars during the first day, before they had even had the opportunity to look at "A"?

You insist that "there is a power behind Nature making for righteousness."

If Nature is infinite, how can there be a power outside of Nature? If you mean by "a power making for righteousness" that man, as he becomes civilized, as he becomes intelligent, not only takes advantage of the forces of Nature for his own benefit, but perceives more and more clearly that if he is to be happy he must live in harmony with the conditions of his being, in harmony with the facts by which he is surrounded, in harmony with the relations he sustains to others and to things; if this is what you mean, then there is "a power making for righteousness." But if you mean that there is something supernatural back of Nature directing events, then I insist that there can by no possibility be any evidence of the existence of such a power.

The history of the human race shows that nations rise and fall. There is a limit to the life of a race; so that it can be said of every dead nation, that there was a period when it laid the foundations of prosperity, when the combined intelligence and virtue of the people constituted a power working for righteousness, and that there came a time when this nation became a spendthrift, when it ceased to accumulate, when it lived on the labors of its youth, and passed from strength and glory to the weakness of old age, and finally fell palsied to its tomb.

The intelligence of man guided by a sense of duty is the only power that makes for righteousness.

You tell me that I am waging "a hopeless war," and you give as a reason that the Christian religion began to be nearly two thousand years before I was born, and that it will live two thousand years after I am dead.

Is this an argument? Does it tend to convince even yourself? Could not Caiaphas, the high priest, have said substantially this to Christ? Could he not have said: "The religion of Jehovah began to be four thousand years before you were born, and it will live two thousand years after you are dead"? Could not a follower of Buddha make the same illogical remark to a missionary from Andover with the glad tidings? Could he not say: "You are waging a hopeless war. The religion of Buddha began to be twenty-five hundred years before you were born, and hundreds of millions of people still worship at Great Buddha's shrine"?

Do you insist that nothing except the right can live for two thousand years? Why is it that the Catholic Church "lives on and on, while nations and kingdoms perish"? Do you consider that the "survival of the fittest"?

Is it the same Christian religion now living that lived during the Middle Ages? Is it the same Christian religion that founded the Inquisition and invented the thumbscrew? Do you see no difference between the religion of Calvin and Jonathan Edwards and the Christianity of to-day? Do you really think that it is the same Christianity that has been living all these years? Have you noticed any change in the last generation? Do you remember when scientists endeavored to prove a theory by a passage from the Bible, and do you now know that believers in the Bible are exceedingly anxious to prove its truth by some fact that science has demonstrated? Do you know that the standard has changed? Other things are not measured by the Bible, but the Bible has to submit to another test. It no longer owns the scales. It has to be weighed,—it is being weighed,—it is growing lighter and lighter every day. Do you know that only a few years ago "the glad tidings of great joy" consisted mostly in a description of hell? Do you know that nearly every intelligent minister is now ashamed to preach about it, or to read about it, or to talk about it? Is there any change? Do you know that but few ministers now believe in the "plenary inspiration" of the Bible, that from thousands of pulpits people are now told that the creation according to Genesis is a mistake, that it, never was as wet as the flood, and that the miracles of the Old Testament are considered simply as myths or mistakes?

How long will what you call Christianity endure, if it changes as rapidly during the next century as it has during the last? What will there be left of the supernatural?

It does not seem possible that thoughtful people can, for many years, believe that a being of infinite wisdom is the author of the Old Testament, that a being of infinite purity and kindness upheld polygamy and slavery, that he ordered his chosen people to massacre their neighbors, and that he commanded husbands and fathers to persecute wives and daughters unto death for opinion's sake.

It does not seem within the prospect of belief that Jehovah, the cruel, the jealous, the ignorant, and the revengeful, is the creator and preserver of the universe.

Does it seem possible that infinite goodness would create a world in which life feeds on life, in which everything devours and is devoured? Can there be a sadder fact than this: Innocence is not a certain shield?

It is impossible for me to believe in the eternity of punishment. If that doctrine be true, Jehovah is insane.

Day after day there are mournful processions of men and women, patriots and mothers, girls whose only crime is that the word Liberty burst into flower between their pure and loving lips, driven like beasts across the melancholy wastes of Siberian snow. These men, these women, these daughters, go to exile and to slavery, to a land where hope is satisfied with death. Does it seem possible to you that an "Infinite Father" sees all this and sits as silent as a god of stone?

And yet, according to your Presbyterian creed, according to your inspired book, according to your Christ, there is another procession, in which are the noblest and the best, in which you will find the wondrous spirits of this world, the lovers of the human race, the teachers of their fellow-men, the greatest soldiers that ever battled for the right; and this procession of countless millions, in which you will find the most generous and the most loving of the sons and daughters of men, is moving on to the Siberia of God, the land of eternal exile, where agony becomes immortal.

How can you, how can any man with brain or heart, believe this infinite lie?

Is there not room for a better, for a higher philosophy? After all, is it not possible that we may find that everything has been necessarily produced, that all religions and superstitions, all mistakes and all crimes, were simply necessities? Is it not possible that out of this perception may come not only love and pity for others, but absolute justification for the individual? May we not find that every soul has, like Mazeppa, been lashed to the wild horse of passion, or like Prometheus to the rocks of fate?

You ask me to take the "sober second thought." I beg of you to take the first, and if you do, you will throw away the Presbyterian creed; you will instantly perceive that he who commits the "smallest sin" no more deserves eternal pain than he who does the smallest virtuous deed deserves eternal bliss; you will become convinced that an infinite God who creates billions of men knowing that they will suffer through all the countless years is an infinite demon; you will be satisfied that the Bible, with its philosophy and its folly, with its goodness and its cruelty, is but the work of man, and that the supernatural does not and cannot exist.

For you personally, I have the highest regard and the sincerest respect, and I beg of you not to pollute the soul of childhood, not to furrow the cheeks of mothers, by preaching a creed that should be shrieked in a mad-house. Do not make the cradle as terrible as the coffin. Preach, I pray you, the gospel of Intellectual Hospitality—the liberty of thought and speech. Take from loving hearts the awful fear. Have mercy on your fellow-men. Do not drive to madness the mothers whose tears are falling on the pallid faces of those who died in unbelief. Pity the erring, wayward, suffering, weeping world. Do not proclaim as "tidings of great joy" that an Infinite Spider is weaving webs to catch the souls of men.

Robert G. Ingersoll.

A LAST WORD TO ROBERT G. INGERSOLL

My Dear Colonel Ingersoll:

I have read your Reply to my Open Letter half a dozen times, and each time with new appreciation of your skill as an advocate. It is written with great ingenuity, and furnishes probably as complete an argument as you are able to give for the faith (or want of faith) that is in you. Doubtless you think it unanswerable, and so it will seem to those who are predisposed to your way of thinking. To quote a homely saying of Mr. Lincoln, in which there is as much of wisdom as of wit, "For those who like that sort of thing, no doubt that is the sort of thing they do like." You may answer that we, who cling to the faith of our fathers, are equally prejudiced, and that it is for that reason that we are not more impressed by the force of your pleading. I do not deny a strong leaning that way, and yet our real interest is the same—to get at the truth; and, therefore, I have tried to give due weight to whatever of argument there is in the midst of so much eloquence; but must confess that, in spite of all, I remain in the same obdurate frame of mind as before. With all the candor that I can bring to bear upon the question, I find on reviewing my Open Letter scarcely a sentence to change and nothing to withdraw; and am quite willing to leave it as my Declaration of Faith, to stand side by side with your Reply, for intelligent and candid men to judge between us. I need only to add a few words in taking leave of the subject.

You seem a little disturbed that "some of my brethren" should look upon you as "a monster" because of your unbelief. I certainly do not approve of such language, although they would tell me that it is the only word which is a fit response to your ferocious attacks upon what they hold most sacred. You are a born gladiator, and when you descend into the arena, you strike heavy blows, which provoke blows in return. In this very Reply you manifest a particular animosity against Presbyterians. Is it because you were brought up in that Church, of which your father, whom you regard with filial respect and affection, was an honored minister? You even speak of "the Presbyterian God!" as if we assumed to appropriate the Supreme Being, claiming to be the special objects of His favor. Is there any ground for this imputation of narrowness? On the contrary, when we bow our knees before our Maker, it is as the God and Father of all mankind; and the expression you permit yourself to use, can only be regarded as grossly offensive. Was it necessary to offer this rudeness to the religious denomination in which you were born?

And this may explain, what you do not seem fully to understand, why it is that you are sometimes treated to sharp epithets by the religious press and public. You think yourself persecuted for your opinions. But others hold the same opinions without offence. Nor is it because you express your opinions. Nobody would deny you the same freedom which is accorded to Huxley or Herbert Spencer. It is not because you exercise your liberty of judgment or of speech, but because of the way in which you attack others, holding up their faith to all manner of ridicule, and speaking of those who profess it as if they must be either knaves or fools. It is not in human nature not to resent such imputations on that which, however incredible to you, is very precious to them. Hence it is that they think you a rough antagonist; and when you shock them by such expressions as I have quoted, you must expect some pretty strong language in return. I do not join them in this, because I know you, and appreciate that other side of you which is manly and kindly and chivalrous. But while I recognize these better qualities, I must add in all frankness that I am compelled to look upon you as a man so embittered against religion that you cannot think of it except as associated with cant, bigotry, and hypocrisy. In such a state of mind it is hardly possible for you to judge fairly of the arguments for its truth.

I believe with you, that reason was given us to be exercised, and that when man seeks after truth, his mind should be, as you say Darwin's was, "as free from prejudice as the mariner's compass." But if he is warped by passion so that he cannot see things truly, then is he responsible. It is the moral element which alone makes the responsibility. Nor do I believe that any man will be judged in this world or the next for what does not involve a moral wrong. Hence your appalling statement, "The God you worship will, according to your creed, torture (!) through all the endless years the man who entertains an honest doubt," does not produce the effect intended, simply because I do not affirm nor believe any such thing. I believe that, in the future world, every man will be judged according to the deeds done in the body, and that the judgment, whatever it may be, will be transparently just. God is more merciful than man. He desireth not the death of the wicked. Christ forgave, where men would condemn, and whatever be the fate of any human soul, it can never be said that the Supreme Ruler was wanting either in justice or mercy. This I emphasize because you dwell so much upon the subject of future retribution, giving it an attention so constant as to be almost exclusive. Whatever else you touch upon, you soon come back to this as the black thunder-cloud that darkens all the horizon, casting its mighty shadows over the life that now is and that which is to come. Your denunciations of this "inhuman" belief are so reiterated that one would be left to infer that there is nothing else in Religion; that it is all wrath and terror. But this is putting a part for the whole. Religion is a vast system, of which this is but a single feature: it is but one doctrine of many; and indeed some whom no one will deny to be devout Christians, do not hold it at all, or only in a modified form, while with all their hearts they accept and profess the Religion that Christ came to bring into the world.

Archdeacon Farrar, of Westminster Abbey, the most eloquent preacher in the Church of England, has written a book entitled "Eternal Hope," in which he argues from reason and the Bible, that this life is not "the be-all and end-all" of human probation; but that in the world to come there will be another opportunity, when countless millions, made wiser by unhappy experience, will turn again to the paths of life; and that so in the end the whole human race, with the exception of perhaps a few who remain irreclaimable, will be recovered and made happy forever. Others look upon "eternal death" as merely the extinction of being, while immortality is the reward of pre-eminent virtue, interpreting in that sense the words, "The wages of sin is death but the gift of God is eternal life through Jesus Christ our Lord." The latter view might recommend itself to you as the application of "the survival of the fittest" to another world, the worthless, the incurably bad, of the human race being allowed to drop out of existence (an end which can have no terrors for you, since you look upon it as the common lot of all men,) while the good are continued in being forever. The acceptance of either of these theories would relieve your mind of that "horror of great darkness" which seems to come over it whenever you look forward to retribution beyond the grave.

But while conceding all liberty to others I cannot so easily relieve myself of this stern and rugged truth. To me moral evil in the universe is a tremendous reality, and I do not see how to limit it within the bounds of time. Retribution is to me a necessary part of the Divine law. A law without a penalty for its violations is no law. But I rest the argument for it, not on the Bible, but on *principles which you yourself acknowledge.* You say, "There are no punishments, no rewards: there are consequences." Very well, take the "consequences," and see where they lead you. When a man by his vices has reduced his body to a wreck and his mind to idiocy, you say this is the "consequence" of his vicious life. Is it a great stretch of language to say that it is his "punishment," and nonetheless punishment because self-inflicted? To the poor sufferer raving in a madhouse, it matters little what it is called, so long as he is experiencing the agonies of hell. And here your theory of "consequences," if followed up, will lead you very far. For if man lives after death, and keeps his personal identity, do not the "consequences" of his past life follow him into the future? And if his existence is immortal, are not the consequences immortal also? And what is this but endless retribution?

But you tell me that the moral effect of retribution is destroyed by the easy way in which a man escapes the penalty. He has but to repent, and he is restored to the same condition before the law as if he had not sinned. Not so do I understand it. "I believe in the forgiveness of sins," but forgiveness does not reverse the course of nature; it does not prevent the operation of natural law. A drunkard may repent as he is nearing his end, but that does not undo the wrong that he has done, nor avert the consequences. In spite of his tears, he dies in an agony of shame and remorse. The inexorable law must be fulfilled.

And so in the future world. Even though a man be forgiven, he does not wholly escape the evil of his past life. A retribution follows him even within the heavenly gates; for if he does not *suffer*, still that bad life has so shriveled up his moral nature as to diminish his power of enjoyment. There are degrees of happiness, as one star differeth from another star in glory; and he who begins wrong, will find that it is not as well to sin and repent of it as not to sin at all. He enters the other world in a state of spiritual infancy, and will have to begin at the bottom and climb slowly upward.

We might go a step farther, and say that perhaps heaven itself has not only its lights but its shadows, in the reflections that must come even there. We read of "the book of God's remembrance," but is there not another book of remembrance in the mind itself—a book which any man may well fear to open and to look thereon? When that book is opened, and we read its awful pages, shall we not all think "what might have been?" And will those thoughts be wholly free from sadness? The drunken brute who breaks the heart that loved him may weep bitterly, and his poor wife may forgive him with her dying lips; but *he cannot forgive himself*, and *never* can he recall without grief that bowed head and that broken heart. This preserves the element of retribution, while it does not shut the door to forgiveness and mercy.

But we need not travel over again the round of Christian doctrines. My faith is very simple; it revolves around two words; God and Christ. These are the two centers, or, as an astronomer might say, the double-star, or double-sun, of the great orbit of religious truth.

As to the first of these, you say "There can be no evidence to my mind of the existence of such a being, and my mind is so that it is incapable of even thinking of an infinite personality;" and you gravely put to me this question: "Do you really believe that this world is governed by an infinitely wise and good God? Have you convinced even yourself of this?" Here are two questions—one as to the existence of God, and the other as to His benevolence. I will answer both in language as plain as it is possible for me to use.

First, Do I believe in the existence of God? I answer that it is impossible for me *not* to believe it. I could not disbelieve it if I would. You insist that belief or unbelief is not a matter of choice or of the will, but of evidence. You say "the brain thinks as the heart beats, as the eyes see." Then let us stand aside with all our prepossessions, and open our eyes to what we can see.

When Robinson Crusoe in his desert island came down one day to the seashore, and saw in the sand the print of a human foot, could he help the instantaneous conviction that a man had been there? You might have tried to persuade him that it was all chance,—that the sand had been washed up by the waves or blown by the winds, and taken this form, or that some marine insect had traced a figure like a human foot,—you would not have moved him a particle. The imprint was there, and the conclusion was irresistible: he did not believe—he knew that some human being, whether friend or foe, civilized or savage, had set his foot upon that desolate shore. So when I discover in the world (as I think I do) mysterious footprints that are certainly not human, it is not a question whether I shall believe or not: I cannot help believing that some Power greater than man has set foot upon the earth.

It is a fashion among atheistic philosophers to make light of the argument from design; but "my mind is so that it is incapable" of resisting the conclusion to which it leads me. And (since personal questions are in order) I beg to ask if it is possible for *you* to take in your hands a watch, and believe that there was no "design" in its construction; that it was not made to keep time, but only "happened" so; that it is the product of some freak of nature, which brought together its parts and set it going. Do you not *know* with as much positiveness as can belong to any conviction of your mind, that it was *not* the work of accident, but of design; and that if there was a design, there was a designer? And if the watch was made to keep time, was not the eye made to see and the ear to hear? Skeptics may fight against this argument as much as they please, and try to evade the inevitable conclusion, and yet it remains forever entwined in the living frame of man as well as imbedded in the solid foundations of the globe. Wherefore I repeat, it is not a question with me whether I *will* believe or not—I cannot help believing; and I am not only surprised, but amazed, that you or any thoughtful man can come to any other conclusion.' In wonder and astonishment I ask, "Do you really believe" that in all the wide universe there is no Higher Intelligence than that of the poor human creatures that creep on this earthly ball? For myself, it is with the pro-foundest conviction as well as the deepest reverence that I repeat the first sentence of my faith: "I believe in God the Father Almighty."

And not the Almighty only, but the Wise and the Good. Again I ask, How can I help believing what I see every day of my life? Every morning, as the sun rises in the East, sending light and life over the world, I behold a glorious image of the beneficent Creator. The exquisite beauty of the dawn, the dewy freshness of the air, the fleecy clouds floating in the sky—all speak of Him. And when the sun goes down, sending shafts of light through the dense masses that would hide his setting, and casting a glory over the earth and sky, this wondrous illumination is to me but the reflection of Him who "spreadeth out the heavens like a curtain; who maketh the clouds His chariot; who walketh upon the wings of the wind."

How much more do we find the evidences of goodness in man himself: in the power of thought; of acquiring knowledge; of penetrating the mysteries of nature and climbing among the stars. Can a being endowed with such transcendent gifts doubt the goodness of his Creator?

Yes, I believe with all my heart and soul in One who is not only Infinitely Great, but Infinitely Good; who loves all the creatures He has made; bending over them as the bow in the cloud spans the arch of heaven, stretching from horizon to horizon; looking down upon them with a tenderness compared to which all human love is faint and cold. "Like as a father pitieth his children, so the Lord pitieth them that fear Him; for He knoweth our frame, He remembereth that we are dust."

On the question of immortality you are equally "at sea." You know nothing and believe nothing; or, rather, you know only that you do *not* know, and believe that you do not believe. You confess indeed to a faint hope, and admit a bare possibility, that there may be another life, though you are in an uncertainty about it that is altogether bewildering and desperate. But your mind is so poetical that you give a certain attractiveness even to the prospect of annihilation. You strew the sepulcher with such flowers as these:

"I have said a thousand times, and I say again, that the idea of immortality, that like a sea has ebbed and flowed in the human heart, with its countless waves of hope and fear beating against the shores and rocks of time and fate, was not born of any book, nor of any creed, nor of any religion. It was born of human affection, and it will continue to ebb and flow beneath the mists and clouds of doubt and darkness as long as love kisses the lips of death.

"I have said a thousand times, and I say again, that we do not know, we cannot say, whether death is a wall or a door; the beginning or end of a day; the spreading of pinions to soar, or the folding forever of wings; the rise or the set of a sun, or an endless life that brings rapture and love to every one."

Beautiful words! But inexpressibly sad! It is a silver lining to the cloud, and yet the cloud is there, dark and impenetrable. But perhaps we ought not to expect anything clearer and brighter from one who recognizes no light but that of Nature.

That light is very dim. If it were all we had, we should be just where Cicero was, and say with him, and with you, that a future life was "to be hoped for rather than believed." But does not that very uncertainty show the need of a something above Nature, which is furnished in Him who "was crucified, dead and buried, and the third day rose again from the dead?" It is the Conqueror of Death who calls to the fainthearted: "I am the Resurrection and the Life." Since He has gone before us, lighting up the dark passage of the grave, we need not fear to follow, resting on the word of our Leader: "Because I live, ye shall live also."

This faith in another life is a precious inheritance, which cannot be torn from the agonized bosom without a wrench that tears every heartstring; and it was to this I referred as the last refuge of a poor, suffering, despairing soul, when I asked: "Does it never occur to you that there is something very cruel in this treatment of the belief of your fellow-creatures, on whose hope of another life hangs all that relieves the darkness of their present existence?" The imputation of cruelty you repel with some warmth, saying (with a slight variation of my language): "When I deny the existence of perdition, you reply that there is something very cruel in this treatment of the belief of my fellow-creatures." Of course, this change of words, putting perdition in the place of immortal life and hope, was a mere inadvertence. But it was enough to change the whole character of what I wrote. As I described "the treatment of the belief of my fellow-creatures," I did think it "very cruel," and I think so still.

While correcting this slight misquotation, I must remove from your mind a misapprehension, which is so very absurd as to be absolutely comical. In my Letter referring to your disbelief of immortality, I had said: "With an air of modesty and diffidence that would carry an audience by storm, you confess your ignorance of what perhaps others are better acquainted with, when you say, 'This world is all that I know anything about, so far as I recollect'." Of course "what perhaps others are better acquainted with" was a part of what you said, or at least implied by your manner (for you do not convey your meaning merely by words, but by a tone of voice, by arched eyebrows, or a curled lip); and yet, instead of taking the sentence in its plain and obvious sense, you affect to understand it as an assumption on my part to have some private and mysterious knowledge of another world (!), and gravely ask me, "Did you by this intend to say that you know anything of any other state of existence; that you have inhabited some other planet; that you lived before you were born; and that you recollect something of that other world or of that other state?" No, my dear Colonel! I have been a good deal of a traveler, and have seen all parts of this world, but I have never visited any other. In reading your sober question, if I did not know you to be one of the brightest wits of the day, I should be tempted to quote what Sidney Smith says of a Scotchman, that "you cannot get a joke into his head except by a surgical operation!"

But to return to what is serious: you make light of our faith and our hopes, because you know not the infinite solace they bring to the troubled human heart. You sneer at the idea that religion can be a "consolation." Indeed! Is it not a consolation to have an Almighty Friend? Was it a light matter for the poor slave mother, who sat alone in her cabin, having been robbed of her children, to sing in her wild, wailing accents:

"Nobody knows the sorrows I've seen:
Nobody knows but Jesus?"

Would you rob her of that Unseen Friend—the only Friend she had on earth or in heaven?

But I will do you the justice to say that your want of religious faith comes in part from your very sensibility and tenderness of heart. You cannot recognize an overruling Providence, because your mind is so harassed by scenes that you witness. Why, you ask, do men suffer so? You draw frightful pictures of the misery which exists in the world, as a proof of the incapacity of its Ruler and Governor, and do not hesitate to say that "any honest man of average intelligence could do vastly better." If you could have your way, you would make everybody happy; there should be no more poverty, and no more sickness or pain. This is a pleasant picture to look at, and yet you must excuse me for saying that it is rather a child's picture than that of a stalwart man. The world is not a playground in which men are to be petted and indulged like children: spoiled children they would soon become. It is an arena of conflict, in which we are to develop the manhood that is in us. We all have to take the "rough-and-tumble" of life, and are the better for it—physically, intellectually, and morally. If there be any true manliness within us, we come out of the struggle stronger and better; with larger minds and kinder hearts; a broader wisdom and a gentler charity. Perhaps we should not differ on this point if we could agree as to the true end of life. But here I fear the difference is irreconcilable. You think that end is happiness: I think it is character. I do not believe that the highest end of life upon earth is to "have a good time to get from it the utmost amount of enjoyment;" but to be truly and greatly GOOD; and that to that end no discipline can be too severe which leads us "to suffer and be strong." That discipline answers its end when it raises the spirit to the highest pitch of courage and endurance. The splendor of virtue never appears so bright as when set against a dark background. It was in prisons and dungeons that the martyrs showed the greatest degree of moral heroism, the power of

"Man's unconquerable mind."

But I know well that these illustrations do not cover the whole case. There is another picture to be added to those of heroic struggle and martyrdom—that of silent suffering, which makes of life one long agony, and which often comes upon the good, so that it seems as if the best suffered the most. And yet when you sit by a sick bed, and look into a face whiter than the pillow on which it rests, do you not sometimes mark how that very suffering refines the nature that bears it so meekly? This is the Christian theory: that suffering, patiently borne, is a means of the greatest elevation of character, and, in the end, of the highest enjoyment. Looking at it in this light, we can understand how it should be that "the sufferings of this present time are not worthy to be compared [or even to be named] with the glory which shall be revealed." When the heavenly morning breaks, brighter than any dawn that blushes "o'er the world," there will be "a restitution of all things:" the poor will be made rich, and the most suffering the most serenely happy; as in the vision of the Apocalypse, when it is asked "What are these which are arrayed in white robes, and whence came they?" the answer is, "These are they which came our of great tribulation."

In this conclusion, which is not adopted lightly, but after innumerable struggles with doubt, after the experience and the reflection of years, I feel "a great peace." It is the glow of sunset that gilds the approach of evening. For (we must confess it) it is towards that you and I are advancing. The sun has passed the meridian, and hastens to his going down. Whatever of good this life has for us (and I am far from being one of those who look upon it as a vale of tears) will soon be behind us. I see the shadows creeping on; yet I welcome the twilight that will soon darken into night, for I know that it will be a night all glorious with stars. As I look upward, the feeling of awe is blended with a strange, overpowering sense of the Infinite Goodness, which surrounding me like an atmosphere:

"And so beside the Silent Sea,
I wait the muffled oar;
No harm from Him can come to me
On ocean or on shore.

I know not where His Islands lift
Their fronded palms in air;
I only know I cannot drift
Beyond His love and care."

Would that you could share with me this confidence and this hope! But you seem to be receding farther from any kind of faith. In one of your closing paragraphs, you give what is to you "the conclusion of the whole matter." After repudiating religion with scorn, you ask, "Is there not room for a better, for a higher philosophy?" and thus indicate the true answer to be given, to which no words can do justice but your own:

"After all, is it not possible that we may find that everything has been necessarily produced; that all religions and superstitions, all mistakes and all crimes, were simply necessities? Is it not possible that out of this perception may come not only love and pity for others, but absolute justification for the individual? May we not find that every soul has, like Mazeppa, been lashed to the wild horse of passion, or like Prometheus to the rocks of fate?"

If this be the end of all philosophy, it is equally the end of "all things." Not only does it make an end of us and of our hopes of futurity, but of all that makes the present life worth living—of all freedom, and hence of all virtue. There are no more any moral distinctions in the world—no good and no evil, no right and no wrong; nothing but grim necessity. With such a creed, I wonder how you can ever stand at the bar, and argue for the conviction of a criminal. Why should he be convicted and punished for what he could not help? Indeed he is not a criminal, since there is no such thing as crime. He is not to blame. Was he not "lashed to the wild horse of passion," carried away by a power beyond his control?

What cruelty to thrust him behind iron bars! Poor fellow! he deserves our pity. Let us hasten to relieve him from a position which must be so painful, and make our humble apology for having presumed to punish him for an act in which he only obeyed an impulse which he could not resist. This will be "absolute justification for the individual." But what will become of society, you do not tell us.

Are you aware that in this last attainment of "a better, a higher philosophy" (which is simply absolute fatalism), you have swung round to the side of John Calvin, and gone far beyond him? That you, who have exhausted all the resources of the English language in denouncing his creed as the most horrible of human beliefs—brainless, soulless, heartless; who have held it up to scorn and derision; now hold to the blackest Calvinism that was ever taught by man? You cannot find words sufficient to express your horror of the doctrine of Divine decrees; and yet here you have decrees with a vengeance—predestination and damnation, both in one. Under such a creed, man is a thousand times worse off than under ours: for he has absolutely no hope. You may say that at any rate he cannot suffer forever. You do not know even that; but at any rate *he suffers as long as he exists*. There is no God above to show him pity, and grant him release; but as long as the ages roll, he is "lashed to the rocks of fate," with the insatiate vulture tearing at his heart!

In reading your glittering phrases, I seem to be losing hold of everything, and to be sinking, sinking, till I touch the lowest depths of an abyss; while from the blackness above me a sound like a death-knell tolls the midnight of the soul. If I believed this I should cry, God help us all! Or no—for there would be no God, and even this last consolation would be denied us: for why should we offer a prayer which can neither be heard nor answered? As well might we ask mercy from "the rocks of fate" to which we are chained forever!

Recoiling from this Gospel of Despair, I turn to One in whose face there is something at once human and divine—an indescribable majesty, united with more than human tenderness and pity; One who was born among the poor, and had not where to lay His head, and yet went about doing good; poor, yet making many rich; who trod the world in deepest loneliness, and yet whose presence lighted up every dwelling into which He came; who took up little children in His arms, and blessed them; a giver of joy to others, and yet a sufferer himself; who tasted every human sorrow, and yet was always ready to minister to others' grief; weeping with them that wept; coming to Bethany to comfort Mary and Martha concerning their brother; rebuking the proud, but gentle and pitiful to the most abject of human creatures; stopping amid the throng at the cry of a blind beggar by the wayside; willing to be known as "the friend of sinners," if He might recall them into the way of peace; who did not scorn even the fallen woman who sank at His feet, but by His gentle word, "Neither do I condemn thee; go and sin no more," lifted her up, and set her in the path of a virtuous womanhood; and who, when dying on the cross, prayed: "Father, forgive them, for they know not what they do." In this Friend of the friendless, Comforter of the comfortless, Forgiver of the penitent, and Guide of the erring, I find a greatness that I had not found in any of the philosophers or teachers of the world. No voice in all the ages thrills me like that which whispers close to my heart, "Come unto me and I will give you rest," to which I answer: This is my Master, and I will follow Him.

Henry M. Field.

A LETTER TO DR. FIELD.

My Dear Mr. Field:

With great pleasure I have read your second letter, in which you seem to admit that men may differ even about religion without being responsible for that difference; that every man has the right to read the Bible for himself, state freely the conclusion at which he arrives, and that it is not only his privilege, but his duty to speak the truth; that Christians can hardly be happy in heaven, while those they loved on earth are suffering with the lost; that it is not a crime to investigate, to think, to reason, to observe, and to be governed by evidence; that credulity is not a virtue, and that the open mouth of ignorant wonder is not the only entrance to Paradise; that belief is not necessary to salvation, and that no man can justly be made to suffer eternal pain for having expressed an intellectual conviction.

You seem to admit that no man can justly be held responsible for his thoughts; that the brain thinks without asking our consent, and that we believe or disbelieve without an effort of the will.

I congratulate you upon the advance that you have made. You not only admit that we have the right to think, but that we have the right to express our honest thoughts. You admit that the Christian world no longer believes in the fagot, the dungeon, and the thumbscrew. Has the Christian world outgrown its God? Has man become more merciful than his maker? If man will not torture his fellow-man on account of a difference of opinion, will a God of infinite love torture one of his children for what is called the sin of unbelief? Has man outgrown the Inquisition, and will God forever be the warden of a penitentiary? The walls of the old dungeons have fallen, and light now visits the cell where brave men perished in darkness. Is Jehovah to keep the cells of perdition in repair forever, and are his children to be the eternal prisoners?

It seems hard for you to appreciate the mental condition of one who regards all gods as substantially the same; that is to say, who thinks of them all as myths and phantoms born of the imagination,—characters in the religious fictions of the race. To you it probably seems strange that a man should think far more of Jupiter than of Jehovah. Regarding them both as creations of the mind, I choose between them, and I prefer the God of the Greeks, on the same principle that I prefer Portia to Iago; and yet I regard them, one and all, as children of the imagination, as phantoms born of human fears and human hopes.

Surely nothing was further from my mind than to hurt the feelings of any one by speaking of the Presbyterian God. I simply intended to speak of the God of the Presbyterians. Certainly the God of the Presbyterian is not the God of the Catholic, nor is he the God of the Mohammedan or Hindu. He is a special creation suited only to certain minds. These minds have naturally come together, and they form what we call the Presbyterian Church. As a matter of fact, no two churches can by any possibility have precisely the same God; neither can any two human beings conceive of precisely the same Deity. In every man's God there is, to say the least, a part of that man. The lower the man, the lower his conception of God. The higher the man, the grander his Deity must be. The savage who adorns his body with a belt from which hang the scalps of enemies slain in battle, has no conception of a loving, of a forgiving God; his God, of necessity, must be as revengeful, as heartless, as infamous as the God of John Calvin.

You do not exactly appreciate my feeling. I do not hate Presbyterians; I hate Presbyterianism. I hate with all my heart the creed of that church, and I most heartily despise the God described in the Confession of Faith. But some of the best friends I have in the world are afflicted with the mental malady known as Presbyterianism. They are the victims of the consolation growing out of the belief that a vast majority of their fellow-men are doomed to suffer eternal torment, to the end that their Creator may be eternally glorified. I have said many times, and I say again, that I do not despise a man because he has the rheumatism; I despise the rheumatism because it has a man.

But I do insist that the Presbyterians have assumed to appropriate to themselves their Supreme Being, and that they have claimed, and that they do claim, to be the "special objects of his favor." They do claim to be the very elect, and they do insist that God looks upon them as the objects of his special care. They do claim that the light of Nature, without the torch of the Presbyterian creed, is insufficient to guide any soul to the gate of heaven. They do insist that even those who never heard of Christ, or never heard of the God of the Presbyterians, will be eternally lost; and they not only claim this, but that their fate will illustrate not only the justice but the mercy of God. Not only so, but they insist that the morality of an unbeliever is displeasing to God, and that the love of an unconverted mother for her helpless child is nothing less than sin.

When I meet a man who really believes the Presbyterian creed, I think of the Laocoon. I feel as though looking upon a human being helpless in the coils of an immense and poisonous serpent. But I congratulate you with all my heart that you have repudiated this infamous, this savage creed; that you now admit that reason was given us to be exercised; that God will not torture any man for entertaining an honest doubt, and that in the world to come "every man will be judged according to the deeds done in the body."

Let me quote your exact language: "I believe that in the future world every man will be judged according to the deeds done in the body." Do you not see that you have bidden farewell to the Presbyterian Church? In that sentence you have thrown away the atonement, you have denied the efficacy of the blood of Jesus Christ, and you have denied the necessity of belief. If we are to be judged by the deeds done in the body, that is the end of the Presbyterian scheme of salvation. I sincerely congratulate you for having repudiated the savagery of Calvinism.

It also gave me great pleasure to find that you have thrown away, with a kind of glad shudder, that infamy of infamies, the dogma of eternal pain. I have denounced that inhuman belief; I have denounced every creed that had coiled within it that viper; I have denounced every man who preached it, the book that contains it, and with all my heart the God who threatens it; and at last I have the happiness of seeing the editor of the New York *Evangelist* admit that devout Christians do not believe that lie, and quote with approbation the words of a minister of the Church of England to the effect that all men will be finally recovered and made happy.

Do you find this doctrine of hope in the Presbyterian creed? Is this star, that sheds light on every grave, found in your Bible? Did Christ have in his mind the shining truth that all the children of men will at last be filled with joy, when he uttered these comforting words: "Depart from me, ye cursed, into everlasting fire prepared for the devil and his angels"?

Do you find in this flame the bud of hope, or the flower of promise?

You suggest that it is possible that "the incurably bad will be annihilated," and you say that such a fate can have no terrors for me, as I look upon annihilation as the common lot of all. Let us examine this position. Why should a God of infinite wisdom create men and women whom he knew would be "incurably bad"? What would you say of a mechanic who was forced to destroy his own productions on the ground that they were "incurably bad"? Would you say that he was an infinitely wise mechanic? Does infinite justice annihilate the work of infinite wisdom? Does God, like an ignorant doctor, bury his mistakes?

Besides, what right have you to say that I "look upon annihilation as the common lot of all"? Was there any such thought in my Reply? Do you find it in any published words of mine? Do you find anything in what I have written tending to show that I believe in annihilation? Is it not true that I say now, and that I have always said, that I do not know? Does a lack of knowledge as to the fate of the human soul imply a belief in annihilation? Does it not equally imply a belief in immortality?

You have been—at least until recently—a believer in the inspiration of the Bible and in the truth of its every word. What do you say to the following: "For that which befalleth the sons of men befalleth beasts; even one thing befalleth them: as the one dieth, so dieth the other; yea, they have all one breath; so that a man hath no pre-eminence above a beast." You will see that the inspired writer is not satisfied with admitting that he does not know. "As the cloud is consumed and vanisheth away; so he that goeth down to the grave shall come up no more." Was it not cruel for an inspired man to attack a sacred belief?

You seem surprised that I should speak of the doctrine of eternal pain as "the black thunder-cloud that darkens all the horizon, casting its mighty shadows over the life that now is and that which is to come." If that doctrine be true, what else is there worthy of engaging the attention of the human mind? It is the blackness that extinguishes every star. It is the abyss in which every hope must perish. It leaves a universe without justice and without mercy—a future without one ray of light, and a present with nothing but fear. It makes heaven an impossibility, God an infinite monster, and man an eternal victim. Nothing can redeem a religion in which this dogma is found. Clustered about it are all the snakes of the Furies.

But you have abandoned this infamy, and you have admitted that we are to be judged according to the deeds done in the body. Nothing can be nearer self-evident than the fact that a finite being cannot commit an infinite sin; neither can a finite being do an infinitely good deed. That is to say, no one can deserve for any act eternal pain, and no one for any deed can deserve eternal joy. If we are to be judged by the deeds done in the body, the old orthodox hell and heaven both become impossible.

So, too, you have recognized the great and splendid truth that sin cannot be predicated of an intellectual conviction. This is the first great step toward the liberty of soul. You admit that there is no morality and no immorality in belief—that is to say, in the simple operation of the mind in weighing evidence, in observing facts, and in drawing conclusions. You admit that these things are without sin and without guilt. Had all men so believed there never could have been religious persecution—the Inquisition could not have been built, and the idea of eternal pain never could have polluted the human heart.

You have been driven to the passions for the purpose of finding what you are pleased to call "sin" and "responsibility" and you say, speaking of a human being, "but if he is warped by passion so that he cannot see things truly, then is he responsible." One would suppose that the use of the word "cannot" is inconsistent with the idea of responsibility. What is passion? There are certain desires, swift, thrilling, that quicken the action of the heart—desires that fill the brain with blood, with fire and flame—desires that bear the same relation to judgment that storms and waves bear to the compass on a ship. Is passion necessarily produced? Is there an adequate cause for every effect? Can you by any possibility think of an effect without a cause, and can you by any possibility think of an effect that is not a cause, or can you think of a cause that is not an effect? Is not the history of real civilization the slow and gradual emancipation of the intellect, of the judgment, from the mastery of passion? Is not that man civilized whose reason sits the crowned monarch of his brain—whose passions are his servants?

Who knows the strength of the temptation to another? Who knows how little has been resisted by those who stand, how much has been resisted by those who fall? Who knows whether the victor or the victim made the braver and the more gallant fight? In judging of our fellow-men we must take into consideration the circumstances of ancestry, of race, of nationality, of employment, of opportunity, of education, and of the thousand influences that tend to mold or mar the character of man. Such a view is the mother of charity, and makes the God of the Presbyterians impossible.

At last you have seen the impossibility of forgiveness. That is to say, you perceive that after forgiveness the crime remains, and its children, called consequences, still live. You recognize the lack of philosophy in that doctrine. You still believe in what you call "the forgiveness of sins," but you admit that forgiveness cannot reverse the course of nature, and cannot prevent the operation of natural law. You also admit that if a man lives after death, he preserves his personal identity, his memory, and that the consequences of his actions will follow him through all the eternal years. You admit that consequences are immortal. After making this admission, of what use is the old idea of the forgiveness of sins? How can the criminal be washed clean and pure in the blood of another? In spite of this forgiveness, in spite of this blood, you have taken the ground that consequences, like the dogs of Actaeon, follow even a Presbyterian, even one of the elect, within the heavenly gates. If you wish to be logical, you must also admit that the consequences of good deeds, like winged angels, follow even the atheist within the gates of hell.

You have had the courage of your convictions, and you have said that we are to be judged according to the deeds done in the body. By that judgment I am willing to abide. But, whether willing or not, I must abide, because there is no power, no God that can step between me and the consequences of my acts. I wish no heaven that I have not earned, no happiness to which I am not entitled. I do not wish to become an immortal pauper; neither am I willing to extend unworthy hands for alms.

My dear Mr. Field, you have outgrown your creed—as every Presbyterian must who grows at all. You are far better than the spirit of the Old Testament; far better, in my judgment, even than the spirit of the New. The creed that you have left behind, that you have repudiated, teaches that a man may be guilty of every crime—that he may have driven his wife to insanity, that his example may have led his children to the penitentiary, or to the gallows, and that yet, at the eleventh hour, he may, by what is called "repentance," be washed absolutely pure by the blood of another and receive and wear upon his brow the laurels of eternal peace. Not only so, but that creed has taught that this wretch in heaven could look back on the poor earth and see the wife, whom he swore to love and cherish, in the mad-house, surrounded by imaginary serpents, struggling in the darkness of night, made insane by his heartlessness—that creed has taught and teaches that he could look back and see his children in prison cells, or on the scaffold with the noose about their necks, and that these visions would not bring a shade of sadness to his redeemed and happy face. It is this doctrine, it is this dogma—so bestial, so savage as to beggar all the languages of men—that I have denounced. All the words of hatred, loathing and contempt, found in all the dialects and tongues of men, are not sufficient to express my hatred, my contempt, and my loathing of this creed.

You say that it is impossible for you not to believe in the existence of God. With this statement, I find no fault. Your mind is so that a belief in the existence of a Supreme Being gives satisfaction and content. Of course, you are entitled to no credit for this belief, as you ought not to be rewarded for believing that which you cannot help believing; neither should I be punished for failing to believe that which I cannot believe.

You believe because you see in the world around you such an adaptation of means to ends that you are satisfied there is design. I admit that when Robinson Crusoe saw in the sand the print of a human foot, like and yet unlike his own, he was justified in drawing the conclusion that a human being had been there. The inference was drawn from his own experience, and was within the scope of his own mind. But I do not agree with you that he "knew" a human being had been there; he had only sufficient evidence upon which to found a belief. He did not know the footsteps of all animals; he could not have known that no animal except man could have made that footprint: In order to have known that it was the foot of man, he must have known that no other animal was capable of making it, and he must have known that no other being had produced in the sand the likeness of this human foot.

You see what you call evidences of intelligence in the universe, and you draw the conclusion that there must be an infinite intelligence. Your conclusion is far wider than your premise. Let us suppose, as Mr. Hume supposed, that there is a pair of scales, one end of which is in darkness, and you find that a pound weight, or a ten-pound weight, placed upon that end of the scale in the light is raised; have you the right to say that there is an infinite weight on the end in darkness, or are you compelled to say only that there is weight enough on the end in darkness to raise the weight on the end in light?

It is illogical to say, because of the existence of this earth and of what you can see in and about it, that there must be an infinite intelligence. You do not know that even the creation of this world, and of all planets discovered, required an infinite power, or infinite wisdom. I admit that it is impossible for me to look at a watch and draw the inference that there was no design in its construction, or that it only happened. I could not regard it as a product of some freak of nature, neither could I imagine that its various parts were brought together and set in motion by chance. I am not a believer in chance. But there is a vast difference between what man has made and the materials of which he has constructed the things he has made. You find a watch, and you say that it exhibits, or shows design. You insist that it is so wonderful it must have had a designer—in other words, that it is too wonderful not to have been constructed. You then find the watchmaker, and you say with regard to him that he too must have had a designer, for he is more wonderful than the watch. In imagination you go from the watchmaker to the being you call God, and you say he designed the watchmaker, but he himself was not designed because he is too wonderful to have been designed. And yet in the case of the watch and of the watchmaker, it was the wonder that suggested design, while in the case of the maker of the watchmaker the wonder denied a designer. Do you not see that this argument devours itself?

If wonder suggests a designer, can it go on increasing until it denies that which it suggested?

You must remember, too, that the argument of design is applicable to all. You are not at liberty to stop at sunrise and sunset and growing corn and all that adds to the happiness of man; you must go further. You must admit that an infinitely wise and merciful God designed the fangs of serpents, the machinery by which the poison is distilled, the ducts by which it is carried to the fang, and that the same intelligence impressed this serpent with a desire to deposit this deadly virus in the flesh of man. You must believe that an infinitely wise God so constructed this world, that in the process of cooling, earthquakes would be caused—earthquakes that devour and overwhelm cities and states. Do you see any design in the volcano that sends its rivers of lava over the fields and the homes of men? Do you really think that a perfectly good being designed the invisible parasites that infest the air, that inhabit the water, and that finally attack and destroy the health and life of man? Do you see the same design in cancers that you do in wheat and corn? Did God invent tumors for the brain? Was it his ingenuity that so designed the human race that millions of people should be born deaf and dumb, that millions should be idiotic? Did he knowingly plant in the blood or brain the seeds of insanity? Did he cultivate those seeds? Do you see any design in this?

Man calls that good which increases his happiness, and that evil which gives him pain. In the olden time, back of the good he placed a God; back of the evil a devil; but now the orthodox world is driven to admit that the God is the author of all.

For my part, I see no goodness in the pestilence—no mercy in the bolt that leaps from the cloud and leaves the mark of death on the breast of a loving mother. I see no generosity in famine, no goodness in disease, no mercy in want and agony.

And yet you say that the being who created parasites that live only by inflicting pain—the being responsible for all the sufferings of mankind—you say that he has "a tenderness compared to which all human love is faint and cold." Yet according to the doctrine of the orthodox world, this being of infinite love and tenderness so created nature that its light misleads, and left a vast majority of the human race to blindly grope their way to endless pain.

You insist that a knowledge of God—a belief in God—is the foundation of social order; and yet this God of infinite tenderness has left for thousands and thousands of years nearly all of his children without a revelation. Why should infinite goodness leave the existence of God in doubt? Why should he see millions in savagery destroying the lives of each other, eating the flesh of each other, and keep his existence a secret from man? Why did he allow the savages to depend on sunrise and sunset and clouds? Why did he leave this great truth to a few half-crazed prophets, or to a cruel, heartless, and ignorant church? The sentence "There is a God", could have been imprinted on every blade of grass, on every leaf, on every star. An infinite God has no excuse for leaving his children in doubt and darkness.

There is still another point. You know that for thousands of ages men worshiped wild beasts as God. You know that for countless generations they knelt by coiled serpents, believing those serpents to be gods. Why did the real God secrete himself and allow his poor, ignorant, savage children to imagine that he was a beast, a serpent? Why did this God allow mothers to sacrifice their babes? Why did he not emerge from the darkness? Why did he not say to the poor mother, "Do not sacrifice your babe; keep it in your arms; press it to your bosom; let it be the solace of your declining years. I take no delight in the death of children; I am not what you suppose me to be; I am not a beast; I am not a serpent; I am full of love and kindness and mercy, and I want my children to be happy in this world"? Did the God who allowed a mother to sacrifice her babe through the mistaken idea that he, the God, demanded the sacrifice, feel a tenderness toward that mother "compared to which all human love is faint and cold"? Would a good father allow some of his children to kill others of his children to please him?

There is still another question. Why should God, a being of infinite tenderness, leave the question of immortality in doubt? How is it that there is nothing in the Old Testament on this subject? Why is it that he who made all the constellations did not put in his heaven the star of hope? How do you account for the fact that you do not find in the Old Testament, from the first mistake in Genesis, to the last curse in Malachi, a funeral service? Is it not strange that some one in the Old Testament did not stand by an open grave of father or mother and say: "We shall meet again"? Was it because the divinely inspired men did not know?

You taunt me by saying that I know no more of the immortality of the soul than Cicero knew. I admit it. I know no more than the lowest savage, no more than a doctor of divinity—that is to say, nothing.

Is it not, however, a curious fact that there is less belief in the immortality of the soul in Christian countries than in heathen lands—that the belief in immortality, in an orthodox church, is faint and cold and speculative, compared with that belief in India, in China, or in the Pacific Isles? Compare the belief in immortality in America, of Christians, with that of the followers of Mohammed. Do not Christians weep above their dead? Does a belief in immortality keep back their tears? After all, the promises are so far away, and the dead are so near— the echoes of words said to have been spoken more than eighteen centuries ago are lost in the sounds of the clods that fall on the coffin, And yet, compared with the orthodox hell, compared with the prison-house of God, how ecstatic is the grave—the grave without a sigh, without a tear, without a dream, without a fear. Compared with the immortality promised by the Presbyterian creed, how beautiful annihilation seems. To be nothing—how much better than to be a convict forever. To be unconscious dust—how much better than to be a heartless angel.

There is not, there never has been, there never will be, any consolation in orthodox Christianity. It offers no consolation to any good and loving man. I prefer the consolation of Nature, the consolation of hope, the consolation springing from human affection. I prefer the simple desire to live and love forever.

Of course, it would be a consolation to know that we have an "Almighty Friend" in heaven; but an "Almighty Friend" who cares nothing for us, who allows us to be stricken by his lightning, frozen by his winter, starved by his famine, and at last imprisoned in his hell, is a friend I do not care to have.

I remember "the poor slave mother who sat alone in her cabin, having been robbed of her children;" and, my dear Mr. Field, I also remember that the people who robbed her justified the robbery by reading passages from the sacred Scriptures. I remember that while the mother wept, the robbers, some of whom were Christians, read this: "Buy of the heathen round about, and they shall be your bondmen and bondwomen forever." I remember, too, that the robbers read: "Servants be obedient unto your masters;" and they said, this passage is the only message from the heart of God to the scarred back of the slave. I remember this, and I remember, also, that the poor slave mother upon her knees in wild and wailing accents called on the "Almighty Friend," and I remember that her prayer was never heard, and that her sobs died in the negligent air.

You ask me whether I would "rob this poor woman of such a friend?" My answer is this: I would give her liberty; I would break her chains. But let me ask you, did an "Almighty Friend" see the woman he loved "with a tenderness compared to which all human love is faint and cold," and the woman who loved him, robbed of her children? What was the "Almighty Friend" worth to her? She preferred her babe.

How could the "Almighty Friend" see his poor children pursued by hounds—his children whose only crime was the love of liberty—how could he see that, and take sides with the hounds? Do you believe that the "Almighty Friend" then governed the world? Do you really think that he

"Bade the slave-ship speed from coast to coast,
Fanned by the wings of the Holy Ghost"?

Do you believe that the "Almighty Friend" saw all of the tragedies that were enacted in the jungles of Africa—that he watched the wretched slave-ships, saw the miseries of the middle passage, heard the blows of all the whips, saw all the streams of blood, all the agonized faces of women, all the tears that were shed? Do you believe that he saw and knew all these things, and that he, the "Almighty Friend," looked coldly down and stretched no hand to save?

You persist, however, in endeavoring to account for the miseries of the world by taking the ground that happiness is not the end of life. You say that "the real end of life is character, and that no discipline can be too severe which leads us to suffer and be strong." Upon this subject you use the following language: "If you could have your way you would make everybody happy; there would be no more poverty, and no more sickness or pain." And this you say, is a "child's picture, hardly worthy of a stalwart man." Let me read you another "child's picture," which you will find in the twenty-first chapter of Revelation, supposed to have been written by St. John, the Divine: "And I heard a great voice out of heaven saying, behold the tabernacle of God is with men, and he will dwell with them, and they shall be his people, and God himself shall be with them, and be their God; and God shall wipe away all tears from their eyes, and there shall be no more death, neither sorrow, nor crying, neither shall there be any more pain.".

If you visited some woman living in a tenement, supporting by her poor labor a little family—a poor woman on the edge of famine, sewing, it may be, her eyes blinded by tears—would you tell her that "the world is not a playground in which men are to be petted and indulged like children."? Would you tell her that to think of a world without poverty, without tears, without pain, is "a child's picture"? If she asked you for a little assistance, would you refuse it on the ground that by being helped she might lose character? Would you tell her: "God does not wish to have you happy; happiness is a very foolish end; character is what you want, and God has put you here with these helpless, starving babes, and he has put this burden on your young life simply that you may suffer and be strong. I would help you gladly, but I do not wish to defeat the plans of your Almighty Friend"? You can reason one way, but you would act the other.

I agree with you that work is good, that struggle is essential; that men are made manly by contending with each other and with the forces of nature; but there is a point beyond which struggle does not make character; there is a point at which struggle becomes failure.

Can you conceive of an "Almighty Friend" deforming his children because he loves them? Did he allow the innocent to languish in dungeons because he was their friend? Did he allow the noble to perish upon the scaffold, the great and the self-denying to be burned at the stake, because he had the power to save? Was he restrained by love? Did this "Almighty Friend" allow millions of his children to be enslaved to the end that the "splendor of virtue might have a dark background"? You insist that "suffering patiently borne, is a means of the greatest elevation of character, and in the end of the highest enjoyment." Do you not then see that your "Almighty Friend" has been unjust to the happy— that he is cruel to those whom we call the fortunate—that he is indifferent to the men who do not suffer—that he leaves all the happy and prosperous and joyous without character, and that in the end, according to your doctrine, they are the losers?

But, after all, there is no need of arguing this question further. There is one fact that destroys forever your theory—and that is the fact that millions upon millions die in infancy. Where do they get "elevation of character"? What opportunity is given to them to "suffer and be strong"? Let us admit that we do not know. Let us say that the mysteries of life, of good and evil, of joy and pain, have never been explained. Is character of no importance in heaven? How is it possible for angels, living in "a child's picture," to "suffer and be strong"? Do you not see that, according to your philosophy, only the damned can grow great—only the lost can become sublime?

You do not seem to understand what I say with regard to what I call the higher philosophy. When that philosophy is accepted, of course there will be good in the world, there will be evil, there will still be right and wrong. What is good? That which tends to the happiness of sentient beings. What is evil? That which tends to the misery, or tends to lessen the happiness of sentient beings. What is right? The best thing to be done under the circumstances—that is to say, the thing that will increase or preserve the happiness of man. What is wrong? That which tends to the misery of man.

What you call liberty, choice, morality, responsibility, have nothing whatever to do with this. There is no difference between necessity and liberty. He who is free, acts from choice. What is the foundation of his choice? What we really mean by liberty is freedom from personal dictation—we do not wish to be controlled by the will of others. To us the nature of things does not seem to be a master—Nature has no will.

Society has the right to protect itself by imprisoning those who prey upon its interests; but it has no right to punish. It may have the right to destroy the life of one dangerous to the community; but what has freedom to do with this? Do you kill the poisonous serpent because he knew better than to bite? Do you chain a wild beast because he is morally responsible? Do you not think that the criminal deserves the pity of the virtuous?

I was looking forward to the time when the individual might feel justified—when the convict who had worn the garment of disgrace might know and feel that he had acted as he must.

There is an old Hindu prayer to which I call your attention:

"Have mercy, God, upon the vicious; Thou hast already had mercy upon the just by making them just."

Is it not possible that we may find that everything has been necessarily produced? This, of course, would end in the justification of men. Is not that a desirable thing? Is it not possible that intelligence may at last raise the human race to that sublime and philosophic height?

You insist, however, that this is Calvinism. I take it for granted that you understand Calvinism—but let me tell you what it is. Calvinism asserts that man does as he must, and that, notwithstanding this fact, he is responsible for what he does—that is to say, for what he is compelled to do—that is to say, for what God does with him; and that, for doing that which he must, an infinite God, who compelled him to do it, is justified in punishing the man in eternal fire; this, not because the man ought to be damned, but simply for the glory of God.

Starting from the same declaration, that man does as he must, I reach the conclusion that we shall finally perceive in this fact justification for every individual. And yet you see no difference between my doctrine and Calvinism. You insist that damnation and justification are substantially the same; and yet the difference is as great as human language can express. You call the justification of all the world "the Gospel of Despair," and the damnation of nearly all the human race the "Consolation of Religion."

After all, my dear friend, do you not see that when you come to speak of that which is really good, you are compelled to describe your ideal human being? It is the human in Christ, and only the human, that you by any possibility can understand. You speak of one who was born among the poor, who went about doing good, who sympathized with those who suffered. You have described, not only one, but many millions of the human race, Millions of others have carried light to those sitting in darkness; millions and millions have taken children in their arms; millions have wept that those they love might smile. No language can express the goodness, the heroism, the patience and self-denial of the many millions, dead and living, who have preserved in the family of man the jewels of the heart. You have clad one being in all the virtues of the race, in all the attributes of gentleness, patience, goodness, and love, and yet that being, according to the New Testament, had to his character another side. True, he said, "Come unto me and I will give you rest;" but what did he say to those who failed to come? You pour out your whole heart in thankfulness to this one man who suffered for the right, while I thank not only this one, but all the rest. My heart goes out to all the great, the self-denying and the good,—to the founders of nations, singers of songs, builders of homes; to the inventors, to the artists who have filled the world with beauty, to the composers of music, to the soldiers of the right, to the makers of mirth, to honest men, and to all the loving mothers of the race.

Compare, for one moment, all that the Savior did, all the pain and suffering that he relieved,—compare all this with the discovery of anesthetics. Compare your prophets with the inventors, your Apostles with the Keplers, the Humboldts and the Darwins.

I belong to the great church that holds the world within its starlit aisles; that claims the great and good of every race and clime; that finds with joy the grain of gold in every creed, and floods with light and love the germs of good in every soul.

Most men are provincial, narrow, one sided, only partially developed. In a new country we often see a little patch of land, a clearing in which the pioneer has built his cabin. This little clearing is just large enough to support a family, and the remainder of the farm is still forest, in which snakes crawl and wild beasts occasionally crouch. It is thus with the brain of the average man. There is a little clearing, a little patch, just large enough to practice medicine with, or sell goods, or practice law; or preach with, or do some kind of business, sufficient to obtain bread and food and shelter for a family, while all the rest of the brain is covered with primeval forest, in which lie coiled the serpents of superstition and from which spring the wild beasts of orthodox religion.

Neither in the interest of truth, nor for the benefit of man, is it necessary to assert what we do not know. No cause is great enough to demand a sacrifice of candor. The mysteries of life and death, of good and evil, have never yet been solved.

I combat those only who, knowing nothing of the future, prophesy an eternity of pain—those only who sow the seeds of fear in the hearts of men—those only who poison all the springs of life, and seat a skeleton at every feast.

Let us banish the shriveled hags of superstition; let us welcome the beautiful daughters of truth and joy.

Robert G. Ingersoll.

CONTROVERSY ON CHRISTIANTY

[Ingersoll-Gladstone.]

COLONEL INGERSOLL ON CHRISTIANITY;
SOME REMARKS ON HIS REPLY TO DR. FIELD.

By Hon. Wm. E. Gladstone.

As a listener from across the broad Atlantic to the clash of arms in the combat between Colonel Ingersoll and Dr. Field on the most momentous of all subjects, I have not the personal knowledge which assisted these doughty champions in making reciprocal acknowledgments, as broad as could be desired, with reference to personal character and motive. Such acknowledgments are of high value in keeping the issue clear, if not always of all adventitious, yet of all venomous matter. Destitute of the experience on which to found them as original testimonies, still, in attempting partially to criticize the remarkable Reply of Colonel Ingersoll, I can both accept in good faith what has been said by Dr. Field, and add that it seems to me consonant with the strain of the pages I have set before me. Having said this, I shall allow myself the utmost freedom in remarks, which will be addressed exclusively to the matter, not the man.

Let me begin by making several acknowledgments of another kind, but which I feel to be serious. The Christian Church has lived long enough in external triumph and prosperity to expose those of whom it is composed to all such perils of error and misfeasance, as triumph and prosperity bring with them. Belief in divine guidance is not of necessity belief that such guidance can never be frustrated by the laxity, the infirmity, the perversity of man, alike in the domain of action and in the domain of thought. Believers in the perpetuity of the life of the Church are not tied to believing in the perpetual health of the Church. Even the great Latin Communion, and that communion even since the Council of the Vatican in 1870, theoretically admits, or does not exclude, the possibility of a wide range of local and partial error in opinion as well as conduct. Elsewhere the admission would be more unequivocal. Of such errors in tenet, or in temper and feeling more or less hardened into tenet, there has been a crop alike abundant and multifarious. Each Christian party is sufficiently apt to recognize this fact with regard to every other Christian party; and the more impartial and reflective minds are aware that no party is exempt from mischiefs, which lie at the root of the human constitution in its warped, impaired, and dislocated condition. Naturally enough, these deformities help to indispose men towards belief; and when this indisposition has been developed into a system of negative warfare, all the faults of all the Christian bodies, and sub-divisions of bodies, are, as it was natural to expect they would be, carefully raked together, and become part and parcel of the indictment against the divine scheme of redemption. I notice these things in the mass, without particularity, which might be invidious, for two important purposes. First, that we all, who hold by the Gospel and the Christian Church, may learn humility and modesty, as well as charity and indulgence, in the treatment of opponents, from our consciousness that we all, alike by our exaggerations and our shortcomings in belief, no less than by faults of conduct, have contributed to bring about this condition of fashionable hostility to religious faith: and, secondly, that we may resolutely decline to be held bound to tenets, or to consequences of tenets, which represent not the great Christendom of the past and present, but only some hole and corner of its vast organization; and not the heavenly treasure, but the rust or the canker to which that treasure has been exposed through the incidents of its custody in earthen vessels.

I do not remember ever to have read a composition, in which the merely local coloring of particular, and even very limited sections of Christianity, was more systematically used as if it had been available and legitimate argument against the whole, than in the Reply before us. Colonel Ingersoll writes with a rare and enviable brilliancy, but also with an impetus which he seems unable to control. Denunciation, sarcasm, and invective, may in consequence be said to constitute the staple of his work; and, if argument or some favorable admission here and there peeps out for a moment, the writer soon leaves the dry and barren heights for his favorite and more luxurious galloping grounds beneath. Thus, when the Reply has consecrated a line (N. A. R., No. 372, p. 473) to the pleasing contemplation of his opponent as "manly, candid, and generous," it immediately devotes more than twelve to a declamatory denunciation of a practice (as if it were his) altogether contrary to generosity and to candor, and reproaches those who expect (*ibid.*) "to receive as alms an eternity of joy." I take this as a specimen of the mode of statement which permeates the whole Reply. It is not the statement of an untruth. The Christian receives as alms all whatsoever he receives at all. *Qui salvandos salvas gratis* is his song of thankful praise. But it is the statement of one-half of a truth, which lives only in its entirety, and of which the Reply gives us only a mangled and bleeding *frustum.* For the gospel teaches that the faith which saves is a living and energizing faith, and that the most precious part of the alms which we receive lies in an ethical and spiritual process, which partly qualifies for, but also and emphatically composes, this conferred eternity of joy. Restore this ethical element to the doctrine from which the Reply has rudely displaced it, and the whole force of the assault is gone, for there is now a total absence of point in the accusation; it conies only to this, that "mercy and judgment are met together," and that "righteousness and peace have kissed each other" (Psalms lxxxv. 10).

Perhaps, as we proceed, there will be supplied ampler means of judging whether I am warranted in saying that the instance I have here given is a normal instance of a practice so largely followed as to divest the entire Reply of that calmness and sobriety of movement which are essential to the just exercise of the reasoning power in subject matter not only grave, but solemn. Pascal has supplied us, in the "Provincial Letters," with an unique example of easy, brilliant, and fascinating treatment of a theme both profound and complex. But where shall we find another Pascal? And, if we had found him, he would be entitled to point out to us that the famous work was not less close and logical than it was witty. In this case, all attempt at continuous argument appears to be deliberately abjured, not only as to pages, but, as may almost be said, even as to lines. The paper, noteworthy as it is, leaves on my mind the impression of a battle-field where every man strikes at every man, and all is noise, hurry, and confusion. Better surely had it been, and worthier of the great weight and elevation of the subject, if the controversy had been waged after the pattern of those engagements where a chosen champion on either side, in a space carefully limited and reserved, does battle on behalf of each silent and expectant host. The promiscuous crowds represent all the lower elements which enter into human conflicts: the chosen champions, and the order of their proceeding, signify the dominion of reason over force, and its just place as the sovereign arbiter of the great questions that involve the main destiny of man.

I will give another instance of the tumultuous method in which the Reply conducts, not, indeed, its argument, but its case. Dr. Field had exhibited an example of what he thought superstition, and had drawn a distinction between superstition and religion. But to the author of the Reply all religion is superstition, and, accordingly, he writes as follows (p. 475): "You are shocked at the Hindu mother, when she gives her child to death at the supposed command of her God. What do you think of Abraham? of Jephthah? What is your opinion of Jehovah himself?"

Taking these three appeals in the reverse order to that in which they are written, I will briefly ask, as to the closing challenge, "What do you think of Jehovah himself?" whether this is the tone in which controversy ought to be carried on? Not only is the name of Jehovah encircled in the heart of every believer with the profoundest reverence and love, but the Christian religion teaches, through the Incarnation, a doctrine of personal union with God so lofty that it can only be approached in a deep, reverential calm. I do not deny that a person who deems a given religion to be wicked may be led onward by logical consistency to impugn in strong terms the character of the Author and Object of that religion. But he is surely bound by the laws of social morality and decency to consider well the terms and the manner of his indictment. If he founds it upon allegations of fact, these allegations should be carefully stated, so as to give his antagonists reasonable evidence that it is truth and not temper which wrings from him a sentence of condemnation, delivered in sobriety and sadness, and not without a due commiseration for those, whom he is attempting to undeceive, who think he is himself both deceived and a deceiver, but who surely are entitled, while this question is in process of decision, to require that He whom they adore should at least be treated with those decent reserves which are deemed essential when a human being, say a parent, wife, or sister, is in question. But here a contemptuous reference to Jehovah follows, not upon a careful investigation of the cases of Abraham and of Jephthah, but upon a mere summary citation of them to surrender themselves, so to speak, as culprits; that is to say, a summons to accept at once, on the authority of the Reply, the view which the writer is pleased to take of those cases. It is true that he assures us in another part of his paper that he has read the scriptures with care; and I feel bound to accept this assurance, but at the same time to add that if it had not been given I should, for one, not have made the discovery, but might have supposed that the author had galloped, not through, but about, the sacred volume, as a man glances over the pages of an ordinary newspaper or novel.

Although there is no argument as to Abraham or Jephthah expressed upon the surface, we must assume that one is intended, and it seems to be of the following kind: "You are not entitled to reprove the Hindu mother who cast her child under the wheels of the car of Juggernaut, for you approve of the conduct of Jephthah, who (probably) sacrificed his daughter in fulfillment of a vow (Judges xi. 31) that he would make a burnt offering of whatsoever, on his safe return, he should meet coming forth from the doors of his dwelling." Now the whole force of this rejoinder depends upon our supposed obligation as believers to approve the conduct of Jephthah. It is, therefore, a very serious question whether we are or are not so obliged. But this question the Reply does not condescend either to argue, or even to state. It jumps to an extreme conclusion without the decency of an intermediate step. Are not such methods of proceeding more suited to placards at an election, than to disquisitions on these most solemn subjects?

I am aware of no reason why any believer in Christianity should not be free to canvass, regret, condemn the act of Jephthah. So far as the narration which details it is concerned, there is not a word of sanction given to it more than to the falsehood of Abraham in Egypt, or of Jacob and Rebecca in the matter of the hunting (Gen. xx. 1-18, and Gen. xxiii.); or to the dissembling of St. Peter in the case of the Judaizing converts (Gai. ii. 11). I am aware of no color of approval given to it elsewhere. But possibly the author of the Reply may have thought he found such an approval in the famous eleventh chapter of the Epistle to the Hebrews, where the apostle, handling his subject with a discernment and care very different from those of the Reply, writes thus (Heb. xi. 32): "And what shall I say more? For the time would fail me to tell of Gideon, and of Barak, and of Samson, and of Jephthah: of David also, and Samuel, and of the prophets."

Jephthah, then, is distinctly held up to us by a canonical writer as an object of praise. But of praise on what account? Why should the Reply assume that it is on account of the sacrifice of his child? The writer of the Reply has given us no reason, and no rag of a reason, in support of such a proposition. But this was the very thing he was bound by every consideration to prove, upon making his indictment against the Almighty. In my opinion, he could have one reason only for not giving a reason, and that was that no reason could be found.

The matter, however, is so full of interest, as illustrating both the method of the Reply and that of the Apostolic writer, that I shall enter farther into it, and draw attention to the very remarkable structure of this noble chapter, which is to Faith what the thirteenth of Cor. I. is to Charity. From the first to the thirty-first verse, it commemorates the achievements of faith in ten persons: Abel, Enoch, Noah, Abraham,

Sarah, Isaac, Jacob, Joseph, Moses (in greater detail than any one else), and finally Rahab, in whom, I observe in passing, it will hardly be pretended that she appears in this list on account of the profession she had pursued. Then comes the rapid recital (v. 31), without any specification of particulars whatever, of these four names: Gideon, Barak, Samson, Jephthah. Next follows a kind of recommencement, indicated by the word *also;* and the glorious acts and sufferings of the prophets are set forth largely with a singular power and warmth, headed by the names of David and Samuel, the rest of the sacred band being mentioned only in the mass.

Now, it is surely very remarkable that, in the whole of this recital, the Apostle, whose "feet were shod with the preparation of the gospel of peace," seems with a tender instinct to avoid anything like stress on the exploits of warriors. Of the twelve persons having a share in the detailed expositions, David is the only warrior, and his character as a man of war is eclipsed by his greater attributes as a prophet, or declarer of the Divine counsels. It is yet more noteworthy that Joshua, who had so fair a fame, but who was only a warrior, is never named in the chapter, and we are simply told that "by faith the walls of Jericho fell down, after they had been compassed about seven times" (Hebrews xi. 30). But the series of four names, which are given without any specification of their title to appear in the list, are all names of distinguished warriors. They had all done great acts of faith and patriotism against the enemies of Israel,— Gideon against the Midianites, Barak against the hosts of Syria, Samson against the Philistines, and Jephthah against the children of Ammon. Their title to appear in the list at all is in their acts of war, and the mode of their treatment as men of war is in striking accordance with the analogies of the chapter. All of them had committed errors. Gideon had again and again demanded a sign, and had made a golden ephod, "which thing became a snare unto Gideon and to his house" (Judges viii. 27). Barak had refused to go up against Jabin unless Deborah would join the venture (Judges v. 8). Samson had been in dalliance with Delilah. Last came Jephthah, who had, as we assume, sacrificed his daughter in fulfillment of a rash vow. No one supposes that any of the others are honored by mention in the chapter on account of his sin or error: why should that supposition be made in the case of Jephthah, at the cost of all the rules of orderly interpretation?

Having now answered the challenge as to Jephthah, I proceed to the case of Abraham. It would not be fair to shrink from touching it in its tenderest point. That point is nowhere expressly touched by the commendations bestowed upon Abraham in Scripture. I speak now of the special form, of the words that are employed. He is not commended because, being a father, he made all the preparations antecedent to plunging the knife into his son. He is commended (as I read the text) because, having received a glorious promise, a promise that his wife should be a mother of nations, and that kings should be born of her (Gen. xvii. 6), and that by his seed the blessings of redemption should be conveyed to man, and the fulfillment of this promise depending solely upon the life of Isaac, he was, nevertheless, willing that the chain of these promises should be broken by the extinction of that life, because his faith assured him that the Almighty would find the way to give effect to His own designs (Heb. xi. 17-19). The offering of Isaac is mentioned as a completed offering, and the intended blood-shedding, of which I shall speak presently, is not here brought into view.

The facts, however, which we have before us, and which are treated in Scripture with caution, are grave and startling. A father is commanded to sacrifice his son. Before consummation, the sacrifice is interrupted. Yet the intention of obedience had been formed, and certified by a series of acts. It may have been qualified by a reserve of hope that God would interpose before the final act, but of this we have no distinct statement, and it can only stand as an allowable conjecture. It may be conceded that the narrative does not supply us with a complete statement of particulars. That being so, it behooves us to tread cautiously in approaching it. Thus much, however, I think, may further be said: the command was addressed to Abraham under conditions essentially different from those which now determine for us the limits of moral obligation.

For the conditions, both socially and otherwise, were indeed very different. The estimate of human life at the time was different. The position of the father in the family was different: its members were regarded as in some sense his property. There is every reason to suppose that, around Abraham in "the land of Moriah," the practice of human sacrifice as an act of religion was in vigor. But we may look more deeply into the matter. According to the Book of Genesis, Adam and Eve were placed under a law, not of consciously perceived right and wrong, but of simple obedience. The tree, of which alone they were forbidden to eat, was the tree of the knowledge of good and evil. Duty lay for them in following the command of the Most High, before and until they, or their descendants, should become capable of appreciating it by an ethical standard. Their condition was greatly analogous to that of the infant, who has just reached the stage at which he can comprehend that he is ordered to do this or that, but not the nature of the thing so ordered. To the external standard of right and wrong, and to the obligation it entails *per se,* the child is introduced by a process gradually unfolded with the development of his nature, and the opening out of what we term a moral sense. If we pass at once from the epoch of Paradise to the period of the prophets, we perceive the important progress that has been made in the education of the race. The Almighty, in His mediate intercourse with Israel, deigns to appeal to an independently conceived criterion, as to an arbiter between His people and Himself. "Come, now, and let us reason together, saith the Lord" (Isaiah i. 18). "Yet ye say the way of the Lord is not equal. Hear now, O house of Israel, is not my way equal, are not your ways unequal?" (Ezekiel xvii. 25). Between these two epochs how wide a space of moral teaching has been traversed! But Abraham, so far as we may judge from the pages of Scripture, belongs essentially to the Adamic period, far more than to the prophetic. The notion of righteousness and sin was not indeed hidden from him: transgression itself had opened that chapter, and it was never to be closed: but as yet they lay wrapped up, so to speak, in Divine command and prohibition. And what God commanded, it was for Abraham to believe that He himself would adjust to the harmony of His own character.

The faith of Abraham, with respect to this supreme trial, appears to have been centered in this, that he would trust God to all extremities, and in despite of all appearances. The command received was obviously inconsistent with the promises which had preceded it. It was also inconsistent with the morality acknowledged in later times, and perhaps too definitely reflected in our minds, by an anachronism easy to conceive, on the day of Abraham. There can be little doubt, as between these two points of view, that the strain upon his faith was felt mainly, to say the least, in connection with the first mentioned. This faith is not wholly unlike the faith of Job; for Job believed, in despite of what was to the eye of flesh an unrighteous government of the world. If we may still trust the Authorized Version, his cry was, "though he slay me, yet will I trust in him" (Job xiii. 15). This cry was, however, the expression of one who did not expect to be slain; and it may be that Abraham, when he said, "My son, God will provide Himself a lamb for a burnt offering," not only believed explicitly that God would do what was right, but, moreover, believed implicitly that a way of rescue would be found for his son. I do not say that this case is like the case of Jephthah, where the introduction of difficulty is only gratuitous. I confine myself to these propositions. Though the law of moral action is the same everywhere and always, it is variously applicable to the human being, as we know from experience, in the various stages of his development; and its first form is that of simple obedience to a superior whom there is every ground to trust. And further, if the few straggling rays of our knowledge in a case of this kind rather exhibit a darkness lying around us than dispel it, we do not even know all that was in the mind of Abraham, and are not in a condition to pronounce upon it, and cannot, without departure from sound reason, abandon that anchorage by which he probably held, that the law of Nature was safe in the hands of the Author of Nature, though the means of the reconciliation between the law and the appearances have not been fully placed within our reach.

But the Reply is not entitled to so wide an answer as that which I have given. In the parallel with the case of the Hindu widow, it sins against first principles. An established and habitual practice of child-slaughter, in a country of an old and learned civilization, presents to us a case totally different from the issue of a command which was not designed to be obeyed and which belongs to a period when the years of manhood were associated in great part with the character that appertains to childhood.

It will already have been seen that the method of this Reply is not to argue seriously from point to point, but to set out in masses, without the labor of proof, crowds of imputations, which may overwhelm an opponent like balls from a *mitrailleuse*. As the charges lightly run over in a line or two require pages for exhibition and confutation, an exhaustive answer to the Reply within the just limits of an article is on this account out of the question; and the only proper course left open seems to be to make a selection of what appears to be the favorite, or the most formidable and telling assertions, and to deal with these in the serious way which the grave interests of the theme, not the manner of their presentation, may deserve.

It was an observation of Aristotle that weight attaches to the undemonstrated propositions of those who are able to speak on any given subject matter from experience. The Reply abounds in undemonstrated propositions. They appear, however, to be delivered without any sense of a necessity that either experience or reasoning are required in order to give them a title to acceptance. Thus, for example, the system of Mr. Darwin is hurled against Christianity as a dart which cannot but be fatal (p. 475):

"His discoveries, carried to their legitimate conclusion, destroy the creeds and sacred Scriptures of mankind."

This wide-sweeping proposition is imposed upon us with no exposition of the how or the why; and the whole controversy of belief one might suppose is to be determined, as if from St. Petersburgh, by a series of *ukases.* It is only advanced, indeed, to decorate the introduction of Darwin's name in support of the proposition, which I certainly should support and not contest, that error and honesty are compatible.

On what ground, then, and for what reason, is the system of Darwin fatal to Scriptures and to creeds? I do not enter into the question whether it has passed from the stage of working hypothesis into that of demonstration, but I assume, for the purposes of the argument, all that, in this respect, the Reply can desire.

It is not possible to discover, from the random language of the Reply, whether the scheme of Darwin is to sweep away all theism, or is to be content with extinguishing revealed religion. If the latter is meant, I should reply that the moral history of man, in its principal stream, has been distinctly an evolution from the first until now; and that the succinct though grand account of the Creation in Genesis is singularly accordant with the same idea, but is wider than Darwinism, since it includes in the grand progression the inanimate world as well as the history of organisms. But, as this could not be shown without much detail, the Reply reduces me to the necessity of following its own unsatisfactory example in the bald form of an assertion, that there is no colorable ground for assuming evolution and revelation to be at variance with one another.

If, however, the meaning be that theism is swept away by Darwinism, I observe that, as before, we have only an unreasoned dogma or dictum to deal with, and, dealing perforce with the unknown, we are in danger of striking at a will of the wisp. Still, I venture on remarking that the doctrine of Evolution has acquired both praise and dispraise which it does not deserve. It is lauded in the skeptical camp because it is supposed to get rid of the shocking idea of what are termed sudden acts of creation; and it is as unjustly dispraised, on the opposing side, because it is thought to bridge over the gap between man and the inferior animals, and to give emphasis to the relationship between them. But long before the day either of Mr. Darwin or his grandfather, Dr. Erasmus Darwin, this relationship had been stated, perhaps even more emphatically by one whom, were it not that I have small title to deal in undemonstrated assertion, I should venture to call the most cautious, the most robust, and the most comprehensive of our philosophers. Suppose, says Bishop Butler (*Analogy,* Part 2, Chap. 2), that it were

334

implied in the natural immortality of brutes, that they must arrive at great attainments, and become (like us) rational and moral agents; even this would be no difficulty, since we know not what latent powers and capacities they may be endowed with. And if pride causes us to deem it an indignity that our race should have proceeded by propagation from an ascending scale of inferior organisms, why should it be a more repulsive idea to have sprung immediately from something less than man in brain and body, than to have been fashioned according to the expression in Genesis (Chap. II., v. 7), "out of the dust of the ground?" There are halls and galleries of introduction in a palace, but none in a cottage; and this arrival of the creative work at its climax through an ever aspiring preparatory series, rather than by transition at a step from the inanimate mould of earth, may tend rather to magnify than to lower the creation of man on its physical side. But if belief has (as commonly) been premature in its alarms, has non-belief been more reflective in its exulting anticipations, and its paeans on the assumed disappearance of what are strangely enough termed sudden acts of creation from the sphere of our study and contemplation?

One striking effect of the Darwinian theory of descent is, so far as I understand, to reduce the breadth of all intermediate distinctions in the scale of animated life. It does not bring all creatures into a single lineage, but all diversities are to be traced back, at some point in the scale and by stages indefinitely minute, to a common ancestry. All is done by steps, nothing by strides, leaps, or bounds; all from protoplasm up to Shakespeare, and, again, all from primal night and chaos up to protoplasm. I do not ask, and am incompetent to judge, whether this is among the things proven, but I take it so for the sake of the argument; and I ask, first, why and whereby does this doctrine eliminate the idea of creation? Does the new philosophy teach that if the passage from pure reptile to pure bird is achieved by a spring (so to speak) over a chasm, this implies and requires creation; but that if reptile passes into bird, and rudimental into finished bird, by a thousand slight and but just discernible modifications, each one of these is so small that they are not entitled to a name so lofty, may be set down to any cause or no cause, as we please? I should have supposed it miserably unphilosophical to treat the distinction between creative and non-creative function as a simply quantitative distinction. As respects the subjective effect on the human mind, creation in small, when closely regarded, awakens reason to admiring wonder, not less than creation in great: and as regards that function itself, to me it appears no less than ridiculous to hold that the broadly outlined and large advances of so-called Mosaism are creation, but the refined and stealthy onward steps of Darwinism are only manufacture, and relegate the question of a cause into obscurity, insignificance, or oblivion.

But does not reason really require us to go farther, to turn the tables on the adversary, and to contend that evolution, by how much it binds more closely together the myriad ranks of the living, aye, and of all other orders, by so much the more consolidates, enlarges, and enhances the true argument of design, and the entire theistic position? If orders are not mutually related, it is easier to conceive of them as sent at haphazard into the world. We may, indeed, sufficiently, draw an argument of design from each separate structure, but we have no further title to build upon the position which each of them holds as towards any other. But when the connection between these objects has been established, and so established that the points of transition are almost as indiscernible as the passage from day to night, then, indeed, each preceding stage is a prophecy of the following, each succeeding one is a memorial of the past, and, throughout the immeasurable series, every single member of it is a witness to all the rest. The Reply ought surely to dispose of these, and probably many more arguments in the case, before assuming so absolutely the rights of dictatorship, and laying it down that Darwinism, carried to its legitimate conclusion (and I have nowhere endeavored to cut short its career), destroys the creeds and Scriptures of mankind. That I maybe the more definite in my challenge, I would, with all respect, ask the author of the Reply to set about confuting the succinct and clear argument of his countryman, Mr. Fiske, who, in the earlier part of the small work entitled *Man's Destiny* (Macmillan, London, 1887) has given what seems to me an admissible and also striking interpretation of the leading Darwinian idea in its bearings on the theistic argument. To this very partial treatment of a great subject I must at present confine myself; and I proceed to another of the notions, as confident as they seem to be crude, which the Reply has drawn into its wide-casting net (p. 475):

"Why should God demand a sacrifice from; man? Why should the Infinite ask anything from the finite? Should the sun beg of the glow-worm, and should the momentary spark excite the envy of the source of light?"

This is one of the cases in which happy or showy illustration is, in the Reply before me, set to carry with a rush the position which argument would have to approach more laboriously and more slowly. The case of the glow-worm with the sun cannot but move a reader's pity, it seems so very hard. But let us suppose for a moment that the glow-worm was so constituted, and so related to the sun that an interaction between them was a fundamental condition of its health and life; that the glowworm must, by the law of its nature, like the moon, reflect upon the sun, according to its strength and measure, the light which it receives, and that only by a process involving that reflection its own store of vitality could be upheld? It will be said that this is a very large *petitio* to import into the glowworm's case. Yes, but it is the very *petitio* which is absolutely requisite in order to make it parallel to the case of the Christian. The argument which the Reply has to destroy is and must be the Christian argument, and not some figure of straw, fabricated at will. It is needless, perhaps, but it is refreshing, to quote the noble Psalm (Ps. 1. 10, 12, 14, 15), in which this assumption of the Reply is rebuked. "All the beasts of the forest are mine; and so are the cattle upon a thousand hills. . . . If I be hungry I will not tell thee; for the whole world is mine, and all that is therein.... Offer unto God thanksgiving; and pay thy vows unto the Most Highest, and call upon Me in the time of trouble; so will I hear thee, and thou shalt praise Me." Let me try my hand at a counter-illustration. If the Infinite is to make no demand upon the finite, by parity of reasoning the great and strong should scarcely make them on the weak and small. Why then should the father make demands of love, obedience, and sacrifice, from his young child? Is there not some flavor of the sun and glow-worm here? But every man does so make them, if he is a man of sense and feeling; and he makes them for the sake and in the interest of the son himself, whose nature, expanding in the warmth of affection and pious care, requires, by an inward law, to return as well as to receive. And so God asks of us, in order that what we give to Him may be far more our own than it ever was before the giving, or than it could have been unless first rendered up to Him, to become a part of what the gospel calls our treasure in heaven.

Although the Reply is not careful to supply us with whys, it does not hesitate to ask for them (p. 479):

"Why should an infinitely wise and powerful God destroy the good and preserve the vile? Why should He treat all alike here, and in another world make an infinite difference? Why should your God allow His worshipers, His adorers, to be destroyed by His enemies? Why should He allow the honest, the loving, the noble, to perish at the stake?"

The upholders of belief or of revelation, from Claudian down to Cardinal Newman (see the very remarkable passage of the *Apologia pro vitâ suâ,* pp. 376-78), cannot and do not, seek to deny that the methods of divine government, as they are exhibited by experience, present to us many and varied moral problems, insoluble by our understanding. Their existence may not, and should not, be dissembled. But neither should they be exaggerated. Now exaggeration by mere suggestion is the fault, the glaring fault, of these queries. One who had no knowledge of mundane affairs beyond the conception they insinuate would assume that, as a rule, evil has the upper hand in the management of the world. Is this the grave philosophical conclusion of a careful observer, or is it a crude, hasty, and careless overstatement?

It is not difficult to conceive how, in times of sadness and of storm, when the suffering soul can discern no light at any point of the horizon, place is found for such an idea of life. It is, of course, opposed to the Apostolic declaration that godliness hath the promise of the life that now is (1 Tim. iv. 8), but I am not to expect such a declaration to be accepted as current coin, even of the meanest value, by the author of the Reply. Yet I will offer two observations founded on experience in support of it, one taken from a limited, another from a larger and more open sphere. John Wesley, in the full prime of his mission, warned the converts whom he was making among English laborers of a spiritual danger that lay far ahead. It was that, becoming godly, they would become careful, and, becoming careful, they would become wealthy. It was a just and sober forecast, and it represented with truth the general rule of life, although it be a rule perplexed with exceptions. But, if this be too narrow a sphere of observation, let us take a wider one, the widest of all. It is comprised in the brief statement that Christendom rules the world, and rules it, perhaps it should be added, by the possession of a vast surplus of material as well as moral force. Therefore the assertions carried by implication in the queries of the Reply, which are general, are because general untrue, although they might have been true within those prudent limitations which the method of this Reply appears especially to eschew.

Taking, then, these challenges as they ought to have been given, I admit that great believers, who have been also great masters of wisdom and knowledge, are not able to explain the inequalities of adjustment between human beings and the conditions in which they have been set down to work out their destiny. The climax of these inequalities is perhaps to be found in the fact that, whereas rational belief, viewed at large, founds the Providential government of the world upon the hypothesis of free agency, there are so many cases in which the overbearing mastery of circumstance appears to reduce it to extinction or paralysis. Now, in one sense, without doubt, these difficulties are matter for our legitimate and necessary cognizance. It is a duty incumbent upon us respectively, according to our means and opportunities, to decide for ourselves, by the use of the faculty of reason given us, the great questions of natural and revealed religion. They are to be decided according to the evidence; and, if we cannot trim the evidence into a consistent whole, then according to the balance of the evidence. We are not entitled, either for or against belief, to set up in this province any rule of investigation, except such as common-sense teaches us to use in the ordinary conduct of life. As in ordinary conduct, so in considering the basis of belief, we are bound to look at the evidence as a whole. We have no right to demand demonstrative proofs, or the removal of all conflicting elements, either in the one sphere or in the other. What guides us sufficiently in matters of common practice has the very same authority to guide us in matters of speculation; more properly, perhaps, to be called the practice of the soul. If the evidence in the aggregate shows the being of a moral Governor of the world, with the same force as would suffice to establish an obligation to act in a matter of common conduct, we are bound in duty to accept it, and have no right to demand as a condition previous that all occasions of doubt or question be removed out of the way. Our demands for evidence must be limited by the general reason of the case. Does that general reason of the case make it probable that a finite being, with a finite place in a comprehensive scheme, devised and administered by a Being who is infinite, would be able either to embrace within his view, or rightly to appreciate, all the motives and the aims that may have been in the mind of the Divine Disposer? On the contrary, a demand so unreasonable deserves to be met with the scornful challenge of Dante (Paradise xix. 79):

> Or tu chi sei, che vuoi sedere a scranna
> Per giudicar da lungi mille miglia
> Colla veduta corta d'una spanna?

Undoubtedly a great deal here depends upon the question whether, and in what degree, our knowledge is limited. And here the Reply seems to be by no means in accord with Newton and with Butler. By its contempt for authority, the Reply seems to cut off from us all knowledge that is not at first hand; but then also it seems to assume an original and first hand knowledge of all possible kinds of things. I will take an instance, all the easier to deal with because it is outside the immediate sphere of controversy. In one of those pieces of fine writing with which the Reply abounds, it is determined *obiter* by a backhanded stroke (*N.A.R.*, p. 491) that Shakespeare is "by far the greatest of the human race." I do not feel entitled to assert that he is not; but how vast and complex a question is here determined for us in this airy manner! Has the writer of the Reply really weighed the force, and measured the sweep of his own words? Whether Shakespeare has or has not the primacy of genius over a very few other names which might be placed in competition with his, is a question which has not yet been determined by the general or deliberate judgment of lettered mankind. But behind it lies another question, inexpressibly difficult, except for the Reply, to solve. That question is, what is the relation of human genius to human greatness. Is genius the sole constitutive element of greatness, or with what other elements, and in what relations to them, is it combined? Is every man great in proportion to his genius? Was Goldsmith, or was Sheridan, or was Burns, or was Byron, or was Goethe, or was Napoleon, or was Alcibiades, no smaller, and was Johnson, or was Howard, or was Washington, or was Phocion, or Leonidas, no greater, than in proportion to his genius properly so-called? How are we to find a common measure, again, for different kinds of greatness; how weigh, for example, Dante against Julius Caesar? And I am speaking of greatness properly so called, not of goodness properly so called. We might seem to be dealing with a writer whose contempt for authority in general is fully balanced, perhaps outweighed, by his respect for one authority in particular.

The religions of the world, again, have in many cases given to many men material for life-long study. The study of the Christian Scriptures, to say nothing of Christian life and institutions, has been to many and justly famous men a study "never ending, still beginning"; not, like the world of Alexander, too limited for the powerful faculty that ranged over it; but, on the contrary, opening height on height, and with deep answering to deep, and with increase of fruit ever prescribing increase of effort. But the Reply has sounded all these depths, has found them very shallow, and is quite able to point out (p. 490) the way in which the Saviour of the world might have been a much greater teacher than He actually was; had He said anything, for instance, of the family relation, had He spoken against slavery and tyranny, had He issued a sort of *code Napoleon* embracing education, progress, scientific truth, and international law. This observation on the family relation seems to me beyond even the usual measure of extravagance when we bear in mind that, according to the Christian scheme, the Lord of heaven and earth "was subject" (St. Luke ii. 51) to a human mother and a reputed human father, and that He taught (according to the widest and, I believe, the best opinion) the absolute indissolubility of marriage. I might cite many other instances in reply. But the broader and the true answer to the objection is, that the Gospel was promulgated to teach principles and not a code; that it included the foundation of a society in which those principles were to be conserved, developed, and applied; and that down to this day there is not a moral question of all those which the Reply does or does not enumerate, nor is there a question of duty arising in the course of life for any of us, that is not determinable in all its essentials by applying to it as a touchstone the principles declared in the Gospel. Is not, then, the *hiatus,* which the Reply has discovered in the teaching of our Lord, an imaginary *hiatus?* Nay, are the suggested improvements of that teaching really gross deteriorations? Where would have been the wisdom of delivering to an uninstructed population of a particular age a codified religion, which was to serve for all nations, all ages, all states of civilization? Why was not room to be left for the career of human thought in finding out, and in working out, the adaptation of Christianity to the ever varying movement of the world? And how is it that they who will not admit that a revelation is in place when it has in view the great and necessary work of conflict against sin, are so free in recommending enlargements of that Revelation for purposes, as to which no such necessity can be pleaded?

I have known a person who, after studying the old classical or Olympian religion for the third part of a century, at length began to hope that he had some partial comprehension of it, some inkling of what it meant. Woe is him that he was not conversant either with the faculties or with the methods of the Reply, which apparently can dispose in half an hour of any problem, dogmatic, historical, or moral: and which accordingly takes occasion to assure us that Buddha was "in many respects the greatest religious teacher this world has ever known, the broadest, the most intellectual of them all" (p. 491). On this I shall only say that an attempt to bring Buddha and Buddhism into line together is far beyond my reach, but that every Christian, knowing in some degree what Christ is, and what He has done for the world, can only be the more thankful if Buddha, or Confucius, or any other teacher has in any point, and in any measure, come near to the outskirts of His ineffable greatness and glory.

It is my fault or my misfortune to remark, in this Reply, an inaccuracy of reference, which would of itself suffice to render it remarkable. Christ, we are told (pp. 492, 500), denounced the chosen people of God as "a generation of vipers." This phrase is applied by the Baptist to the crowd who came to seek baptism from him; but it is only applied by our Lord to Scribes or Pharisees (Luke iii. 7, Matthew xxiii. 33, and xii.34), who are so commonly placed by Him in contrast with the people. The error is repeated in the mention of whited sepulchers. Take again the version of the story of Ananias and Sapphira. We are told (p. 494) that the Apostles conceived the idea "of having all things in common." In the narrative there is no statement, no suggestion of the kind; it is a pure interpolation (Acts iv. 32-7). Motives of a reasonable prudence are stated as a matter of fact to have influenced the offending couple—another pure interpolation. After the catastrophe of Ananias "the Apostles sent for his wife"—a third interpolation. I refer only to these points as exhibitions of an habitual and dangerous inaccuracy, and without any attempt at present to discuss the case, in which the judgments of God are exhibited on their severer side, and in which I cannot, like the Reply, undertake summarily to determine for what causes the Almighty should or should not take life, or delegate the power to take it.

Again, we have (p. 486) these words given as a quotation from the Bible:

"They who believe and are baptized shall be saved, and they who believe not shall be damned; and these shall go away into everlasting fire, prepared for the devil and his angels."

The second clause thus reads as if applicable to the persons mentioned in the first; that is to say, to those who reject the tidings of the Gospel. But instead of its being a continuous passage, the latter section is brought out of another gospel (St. Matthew's) and another connection; and it is really written, not of those who do not believe, but those who refuse to perform offices of charity to their neighbor in his need. It would be wrong to call this intentional misrepresentation; but can it be called less than somewhat reckless negligence?

It is a more special misfortune to find a writer arguing on the same side with his critic, and yet for the critic not to be able to agree with him. But so it is with reference to the great subject of immortality, as treated in the Reply.

"The idea of immortality, that, like a sea, has ebbed and flowed in the human heart, with its countless waves of hope and fear beating against the shores and rocks of time and fate, was not born of any book, nor of any creed, nor of any religion. It was born of human affection; and it will continue to ebb and flow beneath the mist and clouds of doubt and darkness, as long as love kisses the lips of death" (p. 483).

Here we have a very interesting chapter of the history of human opinion disposed of in the usual summary way, by a statement which, as it appears to me, is developed out of the writer's inner consciousness. If the belief in immortality is not connected with any revelation or religion, but is simply the expression of a subjective want, then plainly we may expect the expression of it to be strong and clear in proportion to the various degrees in which faculty is developed among the various races of mankind. But how does the matter stand historically? The Egyptians were not a people of high intellectual development, and yet their religious system was strictly associated with, I might rather say founded on, the belief in immortality. The ancient Greeks, on the other hand, were a race of astonishing, perhaps unrivalled, intellectual capacity. But not only did they, in prehistoric ages, derive their scheme of a future world from Egypt; we find also that, with the lapse of time and the advance of the Hellenic civilization, the constructive ideas of the system lost all life and definite outline, and the most powerful mind of the Greek philosophy, that of Aristotle, had no clear perception whatever of a personal existence in a future state.

The favorite doctrine of the Reply is the immunity of all error in belief from moral responsibility. In the first page (p. 473) this is stated with reserve as the "innocence of *honest* error." But why such a limitation? The Reply warms with its subject; it shows us that no error can be otherwise than honest, inasmuch as nothing which involves honesty, or its reverse, can, from the constitution of our nature, enter into the formation of opinion. Here is the full blown exposition (p. 476):

"The brain thinks without asking our consent. We believe, or we disbelieve, without an effort of the will. Belief is a result. It is the effect of evidence upon the mind. The scales turn in spite of him who watches. *There is no opportunity of being honesty or dishonest, in the formation of an opinion.* The conclusion is entirely independent of desire."

The reasoning faculty is, therefore, wholly extrinsic to our moral nature, and no influence is or can be received or imparted between them. I know not whether the meaning is that all the faculties of our nature are like so many separate departments in one of the modern shops that supply all human wants; that will, memory, imagination, affection, passion, each has its own separate domain, and that they meet only for a comparison of results, just to tell one another what they have severally been doing. It is difficult to conceive, if this be so, wherein consists the personality, or individuality or organic unity of man. It is not difficult to see that while the Reply aims at uplifting human nature, it in reality plunges us (p. 475) into the abyss of degradation by the destruction of moral freedom, responsibility, and unity. For we are justly told that "reason is the supreme and final test." Action may be merely instinctive and habitual, or it may be consciously founded on formulated thought; but, in the cases where it is instinctive and habitual, it passes over, so soon as it is challenged, into the other category, and finds a basis for itself in some form of opinion. But, says the Reply, we have no responsibility for our opinions: we cannot help forming them according to the evidence as it presents itself to us. Observe, the doctrine embraces every kind of opinion, and embraces all alike, opinion on subjects where we like or dislike, as well as upon subjects where we merely affirm or deny in some medium absolutely colorless. For, if a distinction be taken between the colorless and the colored medium, between conclusions to which passion or propensity or imagination inclines us, and conclusions to which these have nothing to say, then the whole ground will be cut away from under the feet of the Reply, and it will have to build again *ab initio*. Let us try this by a test case. A father who has believed his son to have been through life upright, suddenly finds that charges are made from various quarters against his integrity. Or a friend, greatly dependent for the work of his life on the co-operation of another friend, is told that that comrade is counterworking and betraying him. I make no assumption now as to the evidence or the result; but I ask which of them could approach the investigation without feeling a desire to be able to acquit? And what shall we say of the desire to condemn? Would Elizabeth have had no leaning towards finding Mary Stuart implicated in a conspiracy? Did English judges and juries approach with an unbiased mind the trials for the Popish plot? Were the opinions formed by the English Parliament on the Treaty of Limerick formed without the intervention of the will? Did Napoleon judge according to the evidence when he acquitted himself in the matter of the Duc d' Enghien? Does the intellect sit in a solitary chamber, like Galileo in the palace of the Vatican, and pursue celestial observation all untouched, while the turmoil of earthly business is raging everywhere around? According to the Reply, it must be a mistake to suppose that there is anywhere in the world such a thing as bias, or prejudice, or prepossession: they are words without meaning in regard to our judgments, for even if they could raise a clamor from without, the intellect sits within, in an atmosphere of serenity, and, like Justice, is deaf and blind, as well as calm.

In addition to all other faults, I hold that this philosophy, or phantasm of philosophy, is eminently retrogressive. Human nature, in its compound of flesh and spirit, becomes more complex with the progress of civilization; with the steady multiplication of wants, and of means for their supply. With complication, introspection has largely extended, and I believe that, as observation extends its field, so far from isolating the intelligence and making it autocratic, it tends more and more to enhance and multiply the infinitely subtle, as well as the broader and more palpable modes, in which the interaction of the human faculties is carried on. Who among us has not had occasion to observe, in the course of his experience, how largely the intellectual power of a man is affected by the demands of life on his moral powers, and how they open and grow, or dry up and dwindle, according to the manner in which those demands are met.

Genius itself, however purely a conception of the intellect, is not exempt from the strong influences of joy and suffering, love and hatred, hope and fear, in the development of its powers. It may be that Homer, Shakespeare, Goethe, basking upon the whole in the sunshine of life, drew little supplementary force from its trials and agitations. But the history of one not less wonderful than any of these, the career of Dante, tells a different tale; and one of the latest and most searching investigators of his history (Scartazzini, Dante Alighieri, *seine zeit, sein leben, und seine werkes,* B. II. Ch. 5, p. 119; also pp. 438, 9. Biel, 1869) tells and shows us, how the experience of his life co-operated with his extraordinary natural gifts and capabilities to make him what he was. Under the three great heads of love, belief, and patriotism, his life was a continued course of ecstatic or agonizing trials. The strain of these trials was discipline; discipline was experience; and experience was elevation. No reader of his greatest work will, I believe, hold with the Reply that his thoughts, conclusions, judgments, were simple results of an automatic process, in which the will and affections had no share, that reasoning operations are like the whir of a clock running down, and we can no more arrest the process or alter the conclusion than the wheels can stop the movement or the noise.[1]

---

[1] I possess the confession of an illiterate criminal, made, I think, in 1834, under the following circumstances: The new poor law had just been passed in England, and it required persons needing relief to go into the workhouse as a condition of receiving it. In some parts of the country, this provision produced a profound popular panic. The man in question was destitute at the time. He was (I think) an old widower with four very young sons. He rose in the night and strangled them all, one after another, with a blue handkerchief, not from want of fatherly affection, but to keep them out of the workhouse. The confession of this peasant, simple in phrase, but intensely impassioned, strongly reminds me of the Ugolino of Dante, and appears to make some approach to its sublimity. Such, in given circumstances, is the effect of moral agony on mental power.

The doctrine taught in the Reply, that belief is, as a general, nay, universal law, independent of the will, surely proves, when examined, to be a plausibility of the shallowest kind. Even in arithmetic, if a boy, through dislike of his employment, and consequent lack of attention, brings out a wrong result for his sum, it can hardly be said that his conclusion is absolutely and in all respects independent of his will. Moving onward, point by point, toward the centre of the argument, I will next take an illustration from mathematics. It has (I apprehend) been demonstrated that the relation of the diameter to the circumference of a circle is not susceptible of full numerical expression. Yet, from time to time, treatises are published which boldly announce that they set forth the quadrature of the circle. I do not deny that this may be purely intellectual error; but would it not, on the other hand, be hazardous to assert that no grain of egotism or ambition has ever entered into the composition of any one of such treatises? I have selected these instances as, perhaps, the most favorable that can be found to the doctrine of the Reply. But the truth is that, if we set aside matters of trivial import, the enormous majority of human judgments are those into which the biasing power off likes and dislikes more or less largely enters. I admit, indeed, that the illative faculty works under rules upon which choice and inclination ought to exercise no influence whatever. But even if it were granted that in fact the faculty of discourse is exempted from all such influence within its own province, yet we come no nearer to the mark, because that faculty has to work upon materials supplied to it by other faculties; it draws conclusions according to premises, and the question has to be determined whether our conceptions set forth in those premises are or are not influenced by moral causes. For, if they be so influenced, then in vain will be the proof that the understanding has dealt loyally and exactly with the materials it had to work upon; inasmuch as, although the intellectual process be normal in itself, the operation may have been tainted *ab initio* by coloring and distorting influences which have falsified the primary conceptions.

Let me now take an illustration from the extreme opposite quarter to that which I first drew upon. The system called Thuggism, represented in the practice of the Thugs, taught that the act, which we describe as murder, was innocent. Was this an honest error? Was it due, in its authors as well as in those who blindly followed them, to an automatic process of thought, in which the will was not consulted, and which accordingly could entail no responsibility? If it was, then it is plain that the whole foundations, not of belief, but of social morality, are broken up. If it was not, then the sweeping doctrine of the present writer on the necessary blamelessness of erroneous conclusions tumbles to the ground like a house of cards at the breath of the child who built it.

In truth, the pages of the Reply, and the Letter which has more recently followed it,[2] themselves demonstrate that what the writer has asserted wholesale he overthrows and denies in detail.

---

[2] North American Review for January, 1888, "Another Letter to Dr. Field."

"You will admit," says the Reply (p. 477), "that he who now persecutes for opinion's sake is infamous." But why? Suppose he thinks that by persecution he can bring a man from soul-destroying falsehood to soul-saving truth, this opinion may reflect on his intellectual debility: but that is his misfortune, not his fault. His brain has thought without asking his consent; he has believed or disbelieved without an effort of the will (p. 476). Yet the very writer, who has thus established his title to think, is the first to hurl at him an anathema for thinking. And again, in the Letter to Dr. Field (N. A. R., vol. 146, p. 33), "the dogma of eternal pain" is described as "that infamy of infamies." I am not about to discuss the subject of future retribution. If I were, it would be my first duty to show that this writer has not adequately considered either the scope of his own arguments (which in no way solve the difficulties he presents) or the meaning of his words; and my second would be to recommend his perusal of what Bishop Butler has suggested on this head. But I am at present on ground altogether different. I am trying another issue. This author says we believe or disbelieve without the action of the will, and, consequently, belief or disbelief is not the proper subject of praise or blame. And yet, according to the very same authority, the dogma of eternal pain is what?—not "an error of errors," but an "infamy of infamies;" and though to hold a negative may not be a subject of moral reproach, yet to hold the affirmative may. Truly it may be asked, is not this a fountain which sends forth at once sweet waters and bitter?

Once more. I will pass away from tender ground, and will endeavor to lodge a broader appeal to the enlightened judgment of the author. Says Odysseus in the Iliad (B. II.) οὐκ ἀγαθὸν πολυκοιρανίη: and a large part of the world, stretching this sentiment beyond its original meaning, have held that the root of civil power is not in the community, but in its head. In opposition to this doctrine, the American written Constitution, and the entire American tradition, teach the right of a nation to self-government. And these propositions, which have divided and still divide the world, open out respectively into vast systems of irreconcilable ideas and laws, practices and habits of mind. Will any rational man, above all will any American, contend that these conflicting systems have been adopted, upheld, and enforced on one side and the other, in the daylight of pure reasoning only, and that moral, or immoral, causes have had nothing to do with their adoption? That the intellect has worked impartially, like a steam-engine, and that selfishness, love of fame, love of money, love of power, envy, wrath, and malice, or again bias, in its least noxious form, have never had anything to do with generating the opposing movements, or the frightful collisions in which they have resulted? If we say that they have not, we contradict the universal judgment of mankind. If we say they have, then mental processes are not automatic, but may be influenced by the will and by the passions, affections, habits, fancies that sway the will; and this writer will not have advanced a step toward proving the universal innocence of error, until he has shown that propositions of religion are essentially unlike almost all other propositions, and that no man ever has been, or from the nature of the case can be, affected in their acceptance or rejection by moral causes.[3]

To sum up. There are many passages in these noteworthy papers, which, taken by themselves, are calculated to command warm sympathy. Towards the close of his final, or latest letter, the writer expresses himself as follows (N. A. R., vol. 146, p. 46.):

"Neither in the interest of truth, nor for the benefit of man, is it necessary to assert what we do not know. No cause is great enough to demand a sacrifice of candor. The mysteries of life and death, of good and evil, have never yet been solved." How good, how wise are these words! But coming at the close of the controversy, have they not some of the ineffectual features of a death-bed repentance? They can hardly be said to represent in all points the rules under which the pages preceding them have been composed; or he, who so justly says that we ought not to assert what we do not know, could hardly have laid down the law as we find it a few pages earlier (ibid, p. 40) when it is pronounced that "an infinite God has no excuse for leaving his children in doubt and darkness." Candor and upright intention are indeed every where manifest amidst the flashing coruscations which really compose the staple of the articles. Candor and upright intention also impose upon a commentator the duty of formulating his animadversions. I sum them up under two heads. Whereas we are placed in an atmosphere of mystery, relieved only by a little sphere of light round each of us, like a clearing in an American forest (which this writer has so well described), and rarely can see farther than is necessary for the direction of our own conduct from day to day, we find here, assumed by a particular person, the character of an universal judge without appeal. And whereas the highest self-restraint is necessary in these dark but, therefore, all the more exciting inquiries, in order to maintain the ever quivering balance of our faculties, this rider chooses to ride an unbroken horse, and to throw the reins upon his neck. I have endeavored to give a sample of the results.

W. E. Gladstone.

---

[3] The chief part of these observations were written before I had received the January number of the *Review,* with Col. Ingersoll's additional letter to Dr. Field. Much, of this letter is specially pointed at Dr. Field, who can defend himself, and at Calvin, whose ideas I certainly cannot undertake to defend all along the line. I do not see that the Letter adds to those, the most salient, points of the earlier article which I have endeavored to select for animadversion.

COL. INGERSOLL
TO MR. GLADSTONE.

To The Right Honorable W. E. Gladstone, M. P.:

My Dear Sir:

At the threshold of this Reply, it gives me pleasure to say that for your intellect and character I have the greatest respect; and let me say further, that I shall consider your arguments, assertions, and inferences entirely apart from your personality—apart from the exalted position that you occupy in the estimation of the civilized world. I gladly acknowledge the inestimable services that you have rendered, not only to England, but to mankind. Most men are chilled and narrowed by the snows of age; their thoughts are darkened by the approach of night. But you, for many years, have hastened toward the light, and your mind has been "an autumn that grew the more by reaping."

Under no circumstances could I feel justified in taking advantage of the admissions that you have made as to the "errors" the "misfeasance" the "infirmities and the perversity" of the Christian Church.

It is perfectly apparent that churches, being only aggregations of people, contain the prejudice, the ignorance, the vices and the virtues of ordinary human beings. The perfect cannot be made out of the imperfect.

A man is not necessarily a great mathematician because he admits the correctness of the multiplication table. The best creed may be believed by the worst of the human race. Neither the crimes nor the virtues of the church tend to prove or disprove the supernatural origin of religion. The massacre of St. Bartholomew tends no more to establish the inspiration of the Scriptures, than the bombardment of Alexandria.

But there is one thing that cannot be admitted, and that is your statement that the constitution of man is in a "warped, impaired, and dislocated condition," and that "these deformities indispose men to belief." Let us examine this.

We say that a thing is "warped" that was once nearer level, flat, or straight; that it is "impaired" when it was once nearer perfect, and that it is "dislocated" when once it was united. Consequently, you have said that at some time the human constitution was unwarped, unimpaired, and with each part working in harmony with all. You seem to believe in the degeneracy of man, and that our unfortunate race, starting at perfection, has traveled downward through all the wasted years.

It is hardly possible that our ancestors were perfect. If history proves anything, it establishes the fact that civilization was not first, and savagery afterwards. Certainly the tendency of man is not now toward barbarism. There must have been a time when language was unknown, when lips had never formed a word. That which man knows, man must have learned. The victories of our race have been slowly and painfully won. It is a long distance from the gibberish of the savage to the sonnets of Shakespeare—a long and weary road from the pipe of Pan to the great orchestra voiced with every tone from the glad warble of a mated bird to the hoarse thunder of the sea. The road is long that lies between the discordant cries uttered by the barbarian over the gashed body of his foe and the marvelous music of Wagner and Beethoven. It is hardly possible to conceive of the years that lie between the caves in which crouched our naked ancestors crunching the bones of wild beasts, and the home of a civilized man with its comforts, its articles of luxury and use,—with its works of art, with its enriched and illuminated walls. Think of the billowed years that must have rolled between these shores. Think of the vast distance that man has slowly groped from the dark dens and lairs of ignorance and fear to the intellectual conquests of our day.

Is it true that these deformities, these warped, impaired, and dislocated constitutions indispose men to belief? Can we in this way account for the doubts entertained by the intellectual leaders of mankind?

It will not do, in this age and time, to account for unbelief in this deformed and dislocated way. The exact opposite must be true. Ignorance and credulity sustain the relation of cause and effect. Ignorance is satisfied with assertion, with appearance. As man rises in the scale of intelligence he demands evidence. He begins to look back of appearance. He asks the priest for reasons. The most ignorant part of Christendom is the most orthodox.

You have simply repeated a favorite assertion of the clergy, to the effect that man rejects the gospel because he is naturally depraved and hard of heart—because, owing to the sin of Adam and Eve, he has fallen from the perfection and purity of Paradise to that "impaired" condition in which he is satisfied with the filthy rags of reason, observation and experience.

The truth is, that what you call unbelief is only a higher and holier faith. Millions of men reject Christianity because of its cruelty. The Bible was never rejected by the cruel. It has been upheld by countless tyrants—by the dealers in human flesh—by the destroyers of nations—by the enemies of intelligence—by the stealers of babes and the whippers of women.

It is also true that it has been held as sacred by the good, the self-denying, the virtuous and the loving, who clung to the sacred volume on account of the good it contains and in spite of all its cruelties and crimes.

You are mistaken when you say that all "the faults of all the Christian bodies and subdivisions of bodies have been carefully raked together," in my Reply to Dr. Field, "and made part and parcel of the indictment against the divine scheme of salvation."

No thoughtful man pretends that any fault of any Christian body can be used as an argument against what you call the "divine scheme of redemption."

I find in your Remarks the frequent charge that I am guilty of making assertions and leaving them to stand without the assistance of argument or fact, and it may be proper, at this particular point, to inquire how you know that there is "a divine scheme of redemption."

My objections to this "divine scheme of redemption" are: *first,* that there is not the slightest evidence that it is divine; *second,* that it is not in any sense a "scheme," human or divine; and *third,* that it cannot, by any possibility, result in the redemption of a human being.

It cannot be divine, because it has no foundation in the nature of things, and is not in accordance with reason. It is based on the idea that right and wrong are the expression of an arbitrary will, and not words applied to and descriptive of acts in the light of consequences. It rests upon the absurdity called "pardon," upon the assumption that when a crime has been committed justice will be satisfied with the punishment of the innocent. One person may suffer, or reap a benefit, in consequence of the act of another, but no man can be justly punished for the crime, or justly rewarded for the virtues, of another. A "scheme" that punishes an innocent man for the vices of another can hardly be called divine. Can a murderer find justification in the agonies of his victim? There is no vicarious vice; there is no vicarious virtue. For me it is hard to understand how a just and loving being can charge one of his children with the vices, or credit him with the virtues, of another.

And why should we call anything a "divine scheme" that has been a failure from the "fall of man" until the present moment? What race, what nation, has been redeemed through the instrumentality of this "divine scheme"? Have not the subjects of redemption been for the most part the enemies of civilization? Has not almost every valuable book since the invention of printing been denounced by the believers in the "divine scheme"? Intelligence, the development of the mind, the discoveries of science, the inventions of genius, the cultivation of the imagination through art and music, and the practice of virtue will redeem the human race. These are the saviors of mankind.

You admit that the "Christian churches have by their exaggerations and shortcomings, and by their faults of conduct, contributed to bring about a condition of hostility to religious faith."

If one wishes to know the worst that man has done, all that power guided by cruelty can do, all the excuses that can be framed for the commission of every crime, the infinite difference that can exist between that which is professed and that which is practiced, the marvelous malignity of meekness, the arrogance of humility and the savagery of what is known as "universal love," let him read the history of the Christian Church.

Yet, I not only admit that millions of Christians have been honest in the expression of their opinions, but that they have been among the best and noblest of our race.

And it is further admitted that a creed should be examined apart from the conduct of those who have assented to its truth. The church should be judged as a whole, and its faults should be accounted for either by the weakness of human nature, or by reason of some defect or vice in the religion taught,—or by both.

Is there anything in the Christian religion—anything in what you are pleased to call the "Sacred Scriptures" tending to cause the crimes and atrocities that have been committed by the church?

It seems to be natural for man to defend himself and the ones he loves. The father slays the man who would kill his child—he defends the body. The Christian father burns the heretic—he defends the soul.

If "orthodox Christianity" be true, an infidel has not the right to live. Every book in which the Bible is attacked should be burned with its author. Why hesitate to burn a man whose constitution is "warped, impaired and dislocated," for a few moments, when hundreds of others will be saved from eternal flames?

In Christianity you will find the cause of persecution. The idea that belief is essential to salvation—this ignorant and merciless dogma—accounts for the atrocities of the church. This absurd declaration built the dungeons, used the instruments of torture, erected the scaffolds and lighted the fagots of a thousand years.

What, I pray you, is the "heavenly treasure" in the keeping of your church? Is it a belief in an infinite God? That was believed thousands of years before the serpent tempted Eve. Is it the belief in the immortality of the soul? That is far older. Is it that man should treat his neighbor as himself? That is more ancient. What is the treasure in the keeping of the church? Let me tell you. It is this: That there is but one true religion—Christianity,—and that all others are false; that the prophets, and Christs, and priests of all others have been and are impostors, or the victims of insanity; that the Bible is the one inspired book—the one authentic record of the words of God; that all men are naturally depraved and deserve to be punished with unspeakable torments forever; that there is only one path that leads to heaven, while countless highways lead to hell; that there is only one name under heaven by which a human being can be saved; that we must believe in the Lord Jesus Christ; that this life, with its few and fleeting years, fixes the fate of man; that the few will be saved and the many forever lost. This is "the heavenly treasure" within the keeping of your church.

And this "treasure" has been guarded by the cherubim of persecution, whose flaming swords were wet for many centuries with the best and bravest blood. It has been guarded by cunning, by hypocrisy, by mendacity, by honesty, by calumniating the generous, by maligning the good, by thumbscrews and racks, by charity and love, by robbery and assassination, by poison and fire, by the virtues of the ignorant and the vices of the learned, by the violence of mobs and the whirlwinds of war, by every hope and every fear, by every cruelty and every crime, and by all there is of the wild beast in the heart of man.

With great propriety it may be asked: In the keeping of which church is this "heavenly treasure"? Did the Catholics have it, and was it taken by Luther? Did Henry the VIII. seize it, and is it now in the keeping of the Church of England? Which of the warring sects in America has this treasure; or have we, in this country, only the "rust and cankers"? Is it in an Episcopal Church, that refuses to associate with a colored man for whom Christ died, and who is good enough for the society of the angelic host?

But wherever this "heavenly treasure" has been, about it have always hovered the Stymphalian birds of superstition, thrusting their brazen beaks and claws deep into the flesh of honest men.

You were pleased to point out as the particular line justifying your assertion "that denunciation, sarcasm, and invective constitute the staple of my work," that line in which I speak of those who expect to receive as alms an eternity of joy, and add: "I take this as a specimen of the mode of statement which permeates the whole."

Dr. Field commenced his Open Letter by saying: "I am glad that I know you, *even though some of my brethren look upon you as a monster, because of your unbelief.*"

In reply I simply said: "The statement in your Letter that some of your brethren look upon me as a monster on account of my unbelief tends to show that those who love God are not always the friends of their fellow-men. Is it not strange that people who admit that they ought to be eternally damned—that they are by nature depraved—that there is no soundness or health in them, can be so arrogantly egotistic as to look upon others as monsters? And yet some of your brethren, who regard unbelievers as infamous, rely for salvation entirely on the goodness of another, and expect to receive as alms an eternity of joy." Is there any denunciation, sarcasm or invective in this?

Why should one who admits that he himself is totally depraved call any other man, by way of reproach, a monster? Possibly, he might be justified in addressing him as a fellow-monster.

I am not satisfied with your statement that "the Christian receives as alms all whatsoever he receives at all." Is it true that man deserves only punishment? Does the man who makes the world better, who works and battles for the right, and dies for the good of his fellow-men, deserve nothing but pain and anguish? Is happiness a gift or a consequence? Is heaven only a well-conducted poorhouse? Are the angels in their highest estate nothing but happy paupers? Must all the redeemed feel that they are in heaven simply because there was a miscarriage of justice? Will the lost be the only ones who will know that the right thing has been done, and will they alone appreciate the "ethical elements of religion"? Will they repeat the words that you have quoted: "Mercy and judgment are met together; righteousness and peace have kissed each other"? or will those words be spoken by the redeemed as they joyously contemplate the writhings of the lost?

No one will dispute "that in the discussion of important questions calmness and sobriety are essential." But solemnity need not be carried to the verge of mental paralysis. In the search for truth,—that everything in nature seems to hide,—man needs the assistance of all his faculties. All the senses should be awake. Humor should carry a torch, Wit should give its sudden light, Candor should hold the scales, Reason, the final arbiter, should put his royal stamp on every fact, and Memory, with a miser's care, should keep and guard the mental gold.

The church has always despised the man of humor, hated laughter, and encouraged the lethargy of solemnity. It is not willing that the mind should subject its creed to every test of truth. It wishes to overawe. It does not say, "He that hath a mind to think, let him think;" but, "He that hath ears to hear, let him hear." The church has always abhorred wit,—that is to say, it does not enjoy being struck by the lightning of the soul.

The foundation of wit is logic, and it has always been the enemy of the supernatural, the solemn and absurd.

You express great regret that no one at the present day is able to write like Pascal. You admire his wit and tenderness, and the unique, brilliant, and fascinating manner in which he treated the profoundest and most complex themes. Sharing in your admiration and regret, I call your attention to what might be called one of his religious generalizations: "Disease is the natural state of a Christian." Certainly it cannot be said that I have ever mingled the profound and complex in a more fascinating manner.

Another instance is given of the "tumultuous method in which I conduct, not, indeed, my argument, but my case."

Dr. Field had drawn a distinction between superstition and religion, to which I replied: "You are shocked at the Hindu mother when she gives her child to death at the supposed command of her God. What do you think of Abraham, of Jephthah? What is your opinion of Jehovah himself?"

These simple questions seem to have excited you to an unusual degree, and you ask in words of some severity:

"Whether this is the tone in which controversies ought be carried on?" And you say that—"not only is the name of Jehovah encircled in the heart of every believer with the profoundest reverence and love, but that the Christian religion teaches, through the incarnation, a personal relation with God so lofty that it can only be approached in a deep, reverential calm." You admit that "a person who deems a given religion to be wicked, may be led onward by logical consistency to impugn in strong terms the character of the author and object of that religion," but you insist that such person is "bound by the laws of social morality and decency to consider well the terms and meaning of his indictment."

Was there any lack of "reverential calm" in my question? I gave no opinion, drew no indictment, but simply asked for the opinion of another. Was that a violation of the "laws of social morality and decency"?

It is not necessary for me to discuss this question with you. It has been settled by Jehovah himself. You probably remember the account given in the eighteenth chapter of I. Kings, of a contest between the prophets of Baal and the prophets of Jehovah. There were four hundred and fifty prophets of the false God who endeavored to induce their deity to consume with fire from heaven the sacrifice upon his altar. According to the account, they were greatly in earnest. They certainly appeared to have some hope of success, but the fire did not descend.

"And it came to pass at noon, that Elijah mocked them and said 'Cry aloud, for he is a god; either he is talking, or he is pursuing, or he is in a journey, or peradventure, he sleepeth and must be awaked.'"

Do you consider that the proper way to attack the God of another? Did not Elijah know that the name of Baal "was encircled in the heart of every believer with the profoundest reverence and love"? Did he "violate the laws of social morality and decency"?

But Jehovah and Elijah did not stop at this point. They were not satisfied with mocking the prophets of Baal, but they brought them down to the brook Kishon—four hundred and fifty of them—and there they murdered every one.

Does it appear to you that on that occasion, on the banks of the brook Kishon—"Mercy and judgment met together, and that righteousness and peace kissed each other"?

The question arises: Has every one who reads the Old Testament the right to express his thought as to the character of Jehovah? You will admit that as he reads his mind will receive some impression, and that when he finishes the "inspired volume" he will have some opinion as to the character of Jehovah. Has he the right to express that opinion? Is the Bible a revelation from God to man? Is it a revelation to the man who reads it, or to the man who does not read it? If to the man who reads it, has he the right to give to others the revelation that God has given to him? If he comes to the conclusion at which you have arrived,—that Jehovah is God,—has he the right to express that opinion?

If he concludes, as I have done, that Jehovah is a myth, must he refrain from giving his honest thought? Christians do not hesitate to give their opinion of heretics, philosophers, and infidels. They are not restrained by the "laws of social morality and decency." They have persecuted to the extent of their power, and their Jehovah pronounced upon unbelievers every curse capable of being expressed in the Hebrew dialect. At this moment, thousands of missionaries are attacking the gods of the heathen world, and heaping contempt on the religion of others.

But as you have seen proper to defend Jehovah, let us for a moment examine this deity of the ancient Jews.

There are several tests of character. It may be that all the virtues can be expressed in the word "kindness," and that nearly all the vices are gathered together in the word "cruelty."

Laughter is a test of character. When we know what a man laughs at, we know what he really is. Does he laugh at misfortune, at poverty, at honesty in rags, at industry without food, at the agonies of his fellow-men? Does he laugh when he sees the convict clothed in the garments of shame—at the criminal on the scaffold? Does he rub his hands with glee over the embers of an enemy's home? Think of a man capable of laughing while looking at Marguerite in the prison cell with her dead babe by her side. What must be the real character of a God who laughs at the calamities of his children, mocks at their fears, their desolation, their distress and anguish? Would an infinitely loving God hold his ignorant children in derision? Would he pity, or mock? Save, or destroy? Educate, or exterminate? Would he lead them with gentle hands toward the light, or lie in wait for them like a wild beast? Think of the echoes of Jehovah's laughter in the rayless caverns of the eternal prison. Can a good man mock at the children of deformity? Will he deride the misshapen? Your Jehovah deformed some of his own children, and then held them up to scorn and hatred. These divine mistakes—these blunders of the infinite—were not allowed to enter the temple erected in honor of him who had dishonored them. Does a kind father mock his

353

deformed child? What would you think of a mother who would deride and taunt her misshapen babe?

There is another test. How does a man use power? Is he gentle or cruel? Does he defend the weak, succor the oppressed, or trample on the fallen?

If you will read again the twenty-eighth chapter of Deuteronomy, you will find how Jehovah, the compassionate, whose name is enshrined in so many hearts, threatened to use his power.

"The Lord shall smite thee with a consumption, and with a fever, and with an inflammation, and with an extreme burning, and with the sword, and with blasting and mildew. And thy heaven that is over thy head shall be brass, and the earth that is under thee shall be iron. The Lord shall make the rain of thy land powder and dust.". . . . "And thy carcass shall be meat unto all fowls of the air and unto the beasts of the earth.". . . . "The Lord shall smite thee with madness and blindness. And thou shalt eat of the fruit of thine own body, the flesh of thy sons and thy daughters. The tender and delicate woman among you,... her eye shall be evil. . . toward her young one and toward her children which she shall bear; for she shall eat them."

Should it be found that these curses were in fact uttered by the God of hell, and that the translators had made a mistake in attributing them to Jehovah, could you say that the sentiments expressed are inconsistent with the supposed character of the Infinite Fiend?

A nation is judged by its laws—by the punishment it inflicts. The nation that punishes ordinary offences with death is regarded as barbarous, and the nation that tortures before it kills is denounced as savage.

What can you say of the government of Jehovah, in which death was the penalty for hundreds of offences?—death for the expression of an honest thought—death for touching with a good intention a sacred ark—death for making hair oil—for eating shew bread—for imitating incense and perfumery?

In the history of the world a more cruel code cannot be found. Crimes seem to have been invented to gratify a fiendish desire to shed the blood of men.

There is another test: How does a man treat the animals in his power—his faithful horse—his patient ox—his loving dog?

How did Jehovah treat the animals in Egypt? Would a loving God, with fierce hail from heaven, bruise and kill the innocent cattle for the crimes of their owners? Would he torment, torture and destroy them for the sins of men?

Jehovah was a God of blood. His altar was adorned with the horns of a beast. He established a religion in which every temple was a slaughter-house, and every priest a butcher—a religion that demanded the death of the first-born, and delighted in the destruction of life.

There is still another test: The civilized man gives to others the rights that he claims for himself. He believes in the liberty of thought and expression, and abhors persecution for conscience sake.

Did Jehovah believe in the innocence of thought and the liberty of expression? Kindness is found with true greatness. Tyranny lodges only in the breast of the small, the narrow, the shriveled and the selfish. Did Jehovah teach and practice generosity? Was he a believer in religious liberty? If he was and is, in fact, God, he must have known, even four thousand years ago, that worship must be free, and that he who is forced upon his knees cannot, by any possibility, have the spirit of prayer.

Let me call your attention to a few passages in the thirteenth chapter of Deuteronomy:

"If thy brother, the son of thy mother, or thy son, or thy daughter, or the wife of thy bosom, or thy friend, which is as thine own soul, entice thee secretly, saying, Let us go and serve other gods, . . . thou shalt not consent unto him, nor hearken unto him; neither shall thine eye pity him, neither shalt thou spare, neither shalt thou conceal him; but thou shalt surely kill him; thine hand shall be first upon him to put him to death, and afterwards the hand of all the people. And thou shalt stone him with stones, that he die."

Is it possible for you to find in the literature of this world more awful passages than these? Did ever savagery, with strange and uncouth marks, with awkward forms of beast and bird, pollute the dripping walls of caves with such commands? Are these the words of infinite mercy? When they were uttered, did "righteousness and peace kiss each other"? How can any loving man or woman "encircle the name of Jehovah"— author of these words—"with profoundest reverence and love"? Do I rebel because my "constitution is warped, impaired and dislocated"? Is it because of "total depravity" that I denounce the brutality of Jehovah? If my heart were only good—if I loved my neighbor as myself—would I then see infinite mercy in these hideous words? Do I lack "reverential calm"?

These frightful passages, like coiled adders, were in the hearts of Jehovah's chosen people when they crucified "the Sinless Man."

Jehovah did not tell the husband to reason with his wife. She was to be answered only with death. She was to be bruised and mangled to a bleeding, shapeless mass of quivering flesh, for having breathed an honest thought.

If there is anything of importance in this world, it is the family, the home, the marriage of true souls, the equality of husband and wife—the true republicanism of the heart—the real democracy of the fireside.

Let us read the sixteenth verse of the third chapter of Genesis:

"Unto the woman he said, I will greatly multiply thy sorrow and thy conception; in sorrow thou shalt bring forth children; and thy desire shall be to thy husband, and he shall rule over thee."

Never will I worship any being who added to the sorrows and agonies of maternity. Never will I bow to any God who introduced slavery into every home—who made the wife a slave and the husband a tyrant.

The Old Testament shows that Jehovah, like his creators, held women in contempt. They were regarded as property: "Thou shalt not covet thy neighbor's wife,—nor his ox."

Why should a pure woman worship a God who upheld polygamy? Let us finish this subject: The institution of slavery involves all crimes. Jehovah was a believer in slavery. This is enough. Why should any civilized man worship him? Why should his name "be encircled with love and tenderness in any human heart"?

He believed that man could become the property of man—that it was right for his chosen people to deal in human flesh—to buy and sell mothers and babes. He taught that the captives were the property of the captors and directed his chosen people to kill, to enslave, or to pollute.

In the presence of these commandments, what becomes of the fine saying, "Love thy neighbor as thyself"? What shall we say of a God who established slavery, and then had the effrontery to say, "Thou shalt not steal"?

It may be insisted that Jehovah is the Father of all—and that he has "made of one blood all the nations of the earth." How then can we account for the wars of extermination? Does not the commandment "Love thy neighbor as thyself," apply to nations precisely the same as to individuals? Nations, like individuals, become great by the practice of virtue. How did Jehovah command his people to treat their neighbors?

He commanded his generals to destroy all, men, women and babes: "Thou shalt save nothing alive that breatheth."

"I will make mine arrows drunk with blood, and my sword shall devour flesh."

"That thy foot may be dipped in the blood of thine enemies, and the tongue of thy dogs in the same."

". . . I will also send the teeth of beasts upon them, with the poison of serpents of the dust. . . ."

"The sword without and terror within shall destroy both the young man and the virgin, the suckling also, with the man of gray hairs."

Is it possible that these words fell from the lips of the Most Merciful?

You may reply that the inhabitants of Canaan were unfit to live—that they were ignorant and cruel. Why did not Jehovah, the "Father of all," give them the Ten Commandments? Why did he leave them without a bible, without prophets and priests? Why did he shower all the blessings of revelation on one poor and wretched tribe, and leave the great world in ignorance and crime—and why did he order his favorite children to murder those whom he had neglected?

By the question I asked of Dr. Field, the intention was to show that Jephthah, when he sacrificed his daughter to Jehovah, was as much the slave of superstition as is the Hindu mother when she throws her babe into the yellow waves of the Ganges.

It seems that this savage Jephthah was in direct communication with Jehovah at Mizpeh, and that he made a vow unto the Lord and said:

"If thou shalt without fail deliver the children of Ammon into mine hands, then it shall be that whatsoever cometh forth of the doors of my house to meet me, when I return in peace from the children of Ammon, shall surely be the Lord's, and I will offer it up as a burnt offering."

In the first place, it is perfectly clear that the sacrifice intended was a human sacrifice, from the words: "that whatsoever cometh forth of the doors of my house to meet me." Some human being—wife, daughter, friend, was expected to come. According to the account, his daughter—his only daughter—his only child—came first.

If Jephthah was in communication with God, why did God allow this man to make this vow; and why did he allow the daughter that he loved to be first, and why did he keep silent and allow the vow to be kept, while flames devoured the daughter's flesh?

St. Paul is not authority. He praises Samuel, the man who hewed Agag in pieces; David, who compelled hundreds to pass under the saws and harrows of death, and many others who shed the blood of the innocent and helpless. Paul is an unsafe guide. He who commends the brutalities of the past, sows the seeds of future crimes.

If "believers are not obliged to approve of the conduct of Jephthah" are they free to condemn the conduct of Jehovah? If you will read the account you will see that the "spirit of the Lord was upon Jephthah" when he made the cruel vow. If Paul did not commend Jephthah for keeping this vow, what was the act that excited his admiration? Was it because Jephthah slew on the banks of the Jordan "forty and two thousand" of the sons of Ephraim?

In regard to Abraham, the argument is precisely the same, except that Jehovah is said to have interfered, and allowed an animal to be slain instead.

One of the answers given by you is that "it may be allowed that the narrative is not within our comprehension"; and for that reason you say that "it behooves us to tread cautiously in approaching it." Why cautiously?

These stories of Abraham and Jephthah have cost many an innocent life. Only a few years ago, here in my country, a man by the name of Freeman, believing that God demanded at least the show of obedience—believing what he had read in the Old Testament that "without the shedding of blood there is no remission," and so believing, touched with insanity, sacrificed his little girl—plunged into her innocent breast the dagger, believing it to be God's will, and thinking that if it were not God's will his hand would be stayed.

I know of nothing more pathetic than the story of this crime told by this man.

Nothing can be more monstrous than the conception of a God who demands sacrifice—of a God who would ask of a father that he murder his son—of a father that he would burn his daughter. It is far beyond my comprehension how any man ever could have believed such an infinite, such a cruel absurdity.

At the command of the real God—if there be one—I would not sacrifice my child, I would not murder my wife. But as long as there are people in the world whose minds are so that they can believe the stories of Abraham and Jephthah, just so long there will be men who will take the lives of the ones they love best.

You have taken the position that the conditions are different; and you say that: "According to the book of Genesis, Adam and Eve were placed under a law, not of consciously perceived right and wrong, but of simple obedience. The tree of which alone they were forbidden to eat was the tree of the knowledge of good and evil; duty lay for them in following the command of the Most High, before and until they became capable of appreciating it by an ethical standard. Their knowledge was but that of an infant who has just reached the stage at which he can comprehend that he is ordered to do this or that, but not the nature of the things so ordered.".

If Adam and Eve could not "consciously perceive right and wrong," how is it possible for you to say that "duty lay for them in following the command of the Most High"? How can a person "incapable of perceiving right and wrong" have an idea of duty? You are driven to say that Adam and Eve had no moral sense. How under such circumstances could they have the sense of guilt, or of obligation? And why should such persons be punished? And why should the whole human race become tainted by the offence of those who had no moral sense?

Do you intend to be understood as saying that Jehovah allowed his children to enslave each other because "duty lay for them in following the command of the Most High"? Was it for this reason that he caused them to exterminate each other? Do you account for the severity of his punishments by the fact that the poor creatures punished were not aware of the enormity of the offences they had committed? What shall we say of a God who has one of his children stoned to death for picking up sticks on Sunday, and allows another to enslave his fellow-man? Have you discovered any theory that will account for both of these facts?

Another word as to Abraham:—You defend his willingness to kill his son because "the estimate of human life at the time was different"—because "the position of the father in the family was different; its members were regarded as in some sense his property;" and because "there is every reason to suppose that around Abraham in the 'land of Moriah' the practice of human sacrifice as an act of religion was in full vigor."

Let us examine these three excuses: Was Jehovah justified in putting a low estimate on human life? Was he in earnest when he said "that whoso sheddeth man's blood, by man shall his blood be shed"? Did he pander to the barbarian view of the worthlessness of life? If the estimate of human life was low, what was the sacrifice worth?

Was the son the property of the father? Did Jehovah uphold this savage view? Had the father the right to sell or kill his child?

Do you defend Jehovah and Abraham because the ignorant wretches in the "land of Moriah," knowing nothing of the true God, cut the throats of their babes "as an act of religion"?

Was Jehovah led away by the example of the Gods of Moriah? Do you not see that your excuses are simply the suggestions of other crimes?

You see clearly that the Hindu mother, when she throws her babe into the Ganges at the command of her God, "sins against first principles";

but you excuse Abraham because he lived in the childhood of the race. Can Jehovah be excused because of his youth? Not satisfied with your explanation, your defenses and excuses, you take the ground that when Abraham said: "My son, God will provide a lamb for a burnt offering," he may have "believed implicitly that a way of rescue would be found for his son." In other words, that Abraham did not believe that he would be required to shed the blood of Isaac. So that, after all, the faith of Abraham consisted in "believing implicitly" that Jehovah was not in earnest.

You have discovered a way by which, as you think, the neck of orthodoxy can escape the noose of Darwin, and in that connection you use this remarkable language:

"I should reply that the moral history of man, in its principal stream, has been distinctly an evolution from the first until now." It is hard to see how this statement agrees with the one in the beginning of your Remarks, in which you speak of the human constitution in its "warped, impaired and dislocated" condition. When you wrote that line you were certainly a theologian—a believer in the Episcopal creed—and your mind, by mere force of habit, was at that moment contemplating man as he is supposed to have been created—perfect in every part. At that time you were endeavoring to account for the unbelief now in the world, and you did this by stating that the human constitution is "warped, impaired and dislocated"; but the moment you are brought face to face with the great truths uttered by Darwin, you admit "that the moral history of man has been distinctly an evolution from the first until now." Is not this a fountain that brings forth sweet and bitter waters?

I insist, that the discoveries of Darwin do away absolutely with the inspiration of the Scriptures—with the account of creation in Genesis, and demonstrate not simply the falsity, not simply the wickedness, but the foolishness of the "sacred volume." There is nothing in Darwin to show that all has been evolved from "primal night and from chaos." There is no evidence of "primal night." There is no proof of universal chaos. Did your Jehovah spend an eternity in "primal night," with no companion but chaos.

It makes no difference how long a lower form may require to reach a higher. It makes no difference whether forms can be simply modified or absolutely changed. These facts have not the slightest tendency to throw the slightest light on the beginning or on the destiny of things.

I most cheerfully admit that gods have the right to create swiftly or slowly. The reptile may become a bird in one day, or in a thousand billion years—this fact has nothing to do with the existence or non-existence of a first cause, but it has something to do with the truth of the Bible, and with the existence of a personal God of infinite power and wisdom.

Does not a gradual improvement in the thing created show a corresponding improvement in the creator? The church demonstrated the falsity and folly of Darwin's theories by showing that they contradicted the Mosaic account of creation, and now the theories of Darwin having been fairly established, the church says that the Mosaic account is true, because it is in harmony with Darwin. Now, if it should turn out that Darwin was mistaken, what then?

To me it is somewhat difficult to understand the mental processes of one who really feels that "the gap between man and the inferior animals or their relationship was stated, perhaps, even more emphatically by Bishop Butler than by Darwin."

Butler answered deists, who objected to the cruelties of the Bible, and yet lauded the God of Nature by showing that the God of Nature is as cruel as the God of the Bible. That is to say, he succeeded in showing that both Gods are bad. He had no possible conception of the splendid generalizations of Darwin—the great truths that have revolutionized the thought of the world.

But there was one question asked by Bishop Butler that throws a flame of light upon the probable origin of most, if not all, religions: "Why might not whole communities and public bodies be seized with fits of insanity as well as individuals?"

If you are convinced that Moses and Darwin are in exact accord, will you be good enough to tell who, in your judgment, were the parents of Adam and Eve? Do you find in Darwin any theory that satisfactorily accounts for the "inspired fact" that a Rib, commencing with Monogonic Propagation—falling into halves by a contraction in the middle—reaching, after many ages of Evolution, the Amphigonie stage, and then, by the Survival of the Fittest, assisted by Natural Selection, molded and modified by Environment, became at last, the mother of the human race?

Here is a world in which there are countless varieties of life—these varieties in all probability related to each other—all living upon each other—everything devouring something, and in its turn devoured by something else—everywhere claw and beak, hoof and tooth,—everything seeking the life of something else—every drop of water a battle-field, every atom being for some wild beast a jungle—every place a Golgotha—and such a world is declared to be the work of the infinitely wise and compassionate.

According to your idea, Jehovah prepared a home for his children—first a garden in which they should be tempted and from which they should be driven; then a world filled with briers and thorns and wild and poisonous beasts—a world in which the air should be filled with the enemies of human life—a world in which disease should be contagious, and in which it was impossible to tell, except by actual experiment, the poisonous from the nutritious. And these children were allowed to live in dens and holes and fight their way against monstrous serpents and crouching beasts—were allowed to live in ignorance and fear—to have false ideas of this good and loving God—ideas so false, that they made of him a fiend—ideas so false, that they sacrificed their wives and babes to appease the imaginary wrath of this monster. And this God gave to different nations different ideas of himself, knowing that in consequence of that these nations would meet upon countless fields of death and drain each other's veins.

Would it not have been better had the world been so that parents would transmit only their virtues—only their perfections, physical and mental,—allowing their diseases and their vices to perish with them?

In my reply to Dr. Field I had asked: Why should God demand a sacrifice from man? Why should the infinite ask anything from the finite? Should the sun beg from the glowworm, and should the momentary spark excite the envy of the source of light?

Upon which you remark, "that if the infinite is to make no demands upon the finite, by parity of reasoning, the great and strong should scarcely make them on the weak and small." Can this be called reasoning? Why should the infinite demand a sacrifice from man? In the first place, the infinite is conditionless—the infinite cannot want—the infinite has. A conditioned being may want; but the gratification of a want involves a change of condition. If God be conditionless, he can have no wants—consequently, no human being can gratify the infinite.

But you insist that "if the infinite is to make no demands upon the finite, by parity of reasoning, the great and strong should scarcely make them on the weak and small."

The great have wants. The strong are often in need, in peril, and the great and strong often need the services of the small and weak. It was the mouse that freed the lion. England is a great and powerful nation—yet she may need the assistance of the weakest of her citizens. The world is filled with illustrations.

The lack of logic is in this: The infinite cannot want anything; the strong and the great may, and as a fact always do. The great and the strong cannot help the infinite—they can help the small and the weak, and the small and the weak can often help the great and strong.

You ask: "Why then should the father make demands of love, obedience, and sacrifice from his young child?"

No sensible father ever demanded love from his child. Every civilized father knows that love rises like the perfume from a flower. You cannot command it by simple authority.

It cannot obey. A father demands obedience from a child for the good of the child and for the good of himself. But suppose the father to be infinite—why should the child sacrifice anything for him?

But it may be that you answer all these questions, all these difficulties, by admitting, as you have in your Remarks, "that these problems are insoluble by our understanding."

Why, then, do you accept them? Why do you defend that which you cannot understand? Why does your reason volunteer as a soldier under the flag of the incomprehensible?

I asked of Dr. Field, and I ask again, this question: Why should an infinitely wise and powerful God destroy the good and preserve the vile?

What do I mean by this question? Simply this: The earthquake, the lightning, the pestilence, are no respecters of persons. The vile are not always destroyed, the good are not always saved. I asked: Why should God treat all alike in this world, and in another make an infinite difference? This, I suppose, is "insoluble to our understanding."

Why should Jehovah allow his worshipers, his adorers, to be destroyed by his enemies? Can you by any possibility answer this question?

You may account for all these inconsistencies, these cruel contradictions, as John Wesley accounted for earthquakes when he insisted that they were produced by the wickedness of men, and that the only way to prevent them was for everybody to believe on the Lord Jesus Christ. And you may have some way of showing that Mr. Wesley's idea is entirely consistent with the theories of Mr. Darwin.

You seem to think that as long as there is more goodness than evil in the world—as long as there is more joy than sadness—we are compelled to infer that the author of the world is infinitely good, powerful, and wise, and that as long as a majority are out of gutters and prisons, the "divine scheme" is a success.

According to this system of logic, if there were a few more unfortunates—if there was just a little more evil than good—then we would be driven to acknowledge that the world was created by an infinitely malevolent being.

As a matter of fact, the history of the world has been such that not only your theologians but your apostles, and not only your apostles but your prophets, and not only your prophets but your Jehovah, have all been forced to account for the evil, the injustice and the suffering, by the wickedness of man, the natural depravity of the human heart and the wiles and machinations of a malevolent being second only in power to Jehovah himself.

Again and again you have called me to account for "mere suggestions and assertions without proof"; and yet your remarks are filled with assertions and mere suggestions without proof.

You admit that "great believers are not able to explain the inequalities of adjustment between human beings and the conditions in which they have been set down to work out their destiny."

How do you know "that they have been set down to work out their destiny"? If that was, and is, the purpose, then the being who settled the "destiny," and the means by which it was to be "worked out," is responsible for all that happens.

And is this the end of your argument, "That you are not able to explain the inequalities of adjustment between human beings"? Is the solution of this problem beyond your power? Does the Bible shed no light? Is the Christian in the presence of this question as dumb as the agnostic? When the injustice of this world is so flagrant that you cannot harmonize that awful fact with the wisdom and goodness of an infinite God, do you not see that you have surrendered, or at least that you have raised a flag of truce beneath which your adversary accepts as final your statement that you do not know and that your imagination is not sufficient to frame an excuse for God?

It gave me great pleasure to find that at last even you have been driven to say that: "it is a duty incumbent upon us respectively according to our means and opportunities, to decide by the use of the faculty of reason given us, the great questions of natural and revealed religion."

You admit "that I am to decide for myself, by the use of my reason," whether the Bible is the word of God or not—whether there is any revealed religion—and whether there be or be not an infinite being who created and who governs this world.

You also admit that we are to decide these questions according to the balance of the evidence.

Is this in accordance with the doctrine of Jehovah? Did Jehovah say to the husband that if his wife became convinced, according to her means and her opportunities, and decided according to her reason, that it was better to worship some other God than Jehovah, then that he was to say to her: "You are entitled to decide according to the balance of the evidence as it seems to you"?

Have you abandoned Jehovah? Is man more just than he? Have you appealed from him to the standard of reason? Is it possible that the leader of the English Liberals is nearer civilized than Jehovah?

Do you know that in this sentence you demonstrate the existence of a dawn in your mind? This sentence makes it certain that in the East of the midnight of Episcopal superstition there is the herald of the coming day. And if this sentence shows a dawn, what shall I say of the next:

"We are not entitled, either for or against belief, to set up in this province any rule of investigation except such as common sense teaches us to use in the ordinary conduct of life"?

This certainly is a morning star. Let me take this statement, let me hold it as a torch, and by its light I beg of you to read the Bible once again.

Is it in accordance with reason that an infinitely good and loving God would drown a world that he had taken no means to civilize—to whom he had given no bible, no gospel,—taught no scientific fact and in which the seeds of art had not been sown; that he would create a world that ought to be drowned? That a being of infinite wisdom would create a rival, knowing that the rival would fill perdition with countless souls destined to suffer eternal pain? Is it according to common sense that an infinitely good God would order some of his children to kill others? That he would command soldiers to rip open with the sword of war the bodies of women—wreaking vengeance on babes unborn? Is it according to reason that a good, loving, compassionate, and just God would establish slavery among men, and that a pure God would uphold polygamy? Is it according to common sense that he who wished to make men merciful and loving would demand the sacrifice of animals, so that his altars would be wet with the blood of oxen, sheep, and doves? Is it according to reason that a good God would inflict tortures upon his ignorant children—that he would torture animals to death—and is it in accordance with common sense and reason that this God would create countless billions of people knowing that they would be eternally damned?

What is common sense? Is it the result of observation, reason and experience, or is it the child of credulity?

There is this curious fact: The far past and the far future seem to belong to the miraculous and the monstrous. The present, as a rule, is the realm of common sense. If you say to a man: "Eighteen hundred years ago the dead were raised," he will reply: "Yes, I know that." And if you say: "A hundred thousand years from now all the dead will be raised," he will probably reply: "I presume so." But if you tell him: "I saw a dead man raised today," he will ask, "From what madhouse have you escaped?"

The moment we decide "according to reason," "according to the balance of evidence," we are charged with "having violated the laws of social morality and decency," and the defender of the miraculous and the incomprehensible takes another position.

The theologian has a city of refuge to which he flies—an old breastwork behind which he kneels—a rifle-pit into which he crawls. You have described this city, this breastwork, this rifle-pit and also the leaf under which the ostrich of theology thrusts its head. Let me quote:

"Our demands for evidence must be limited by the general reason of the case. Does that general reason of the case make it probable that a finite being, with a finite place in a comprehensive scheme devised and administered by a being who is infinite, would be able even to embrace within his view, or rightly to appreciate all the motives or aims that there may have been in the mind of the divine disposer?"

And this is what you call "deciding by the use of the faculty of reason," "according to the evidence," or at least "according to the balance of evidence." This is a conclusion reached by a "rule of investigation such as common sense teaches us to use in the ordinary conduct of life." Will you have the kindness to explain what it is to act contrary to evidence, or contrary to common sense? Can you imagine a superstition so gross that it cannot be defended by that argument?

Nothing, it seems to me, could have been easier than for Jehovah to have reasonably explained his scheme. You may answer that the human intellect is not sufficient to understand the explanation. Why then do not theologians stop explaining? Why do they feel it incumbent upon them to explain that which they admit God would have explained had the human mind been capable of understanding it?

How much better would it have been if Jehovah had said a few things on these subjects. It always seemed wonderful to me that he spent several days and nights on Mount Sinai explaining to Moses how he could detect the presence of leprosy, without once thinking to give him a prescription for its cure.

There were thousands and thousands of opportunities for this God to withdraw from these questions the shadow and the cloud. When Jehovah out of the whirlwind asked questions of Job, how much better it would have been if Job had asked and Jehovah had answered.

You say that we should be governed by evidence and by common sense. Then you tell us that the questions are beyond the reach of reason, and with which common sense has nothing to do. If we then ask for an explanation, you reply in the scornful challenge of Dante.

You seem to imagine that every man who gives an opinion, takes his solemn oath that the opinion is the absolute end of all investigation on that subject.

In my opinion, Shakespeare was, intellectually, the greatest of the human race, and my intention was simply to express that view. It never occurred to me that any one would suppose that I thought Shakespeare a greater actor than Garrick, a more wonderful composer than Wagner, a better violinist than Remenyi, or a heavier man than Daniel Lambert. It is to be regretted that you were misled by my words and really supposed that I intended to say that Shakespeare was a greater general than Caesar. But, after all, your criticism has no possible bearing on the point at issue. Is it an effort to avoid that which cannot be met? The real question is this: If we cannot account for Christ without a miracle, how can we account for Shakespeare? Dr. Field took the ground that Christ himself was a miracle; that it was impossible to account for such a being in any natural way; and, guided by common sense, guided by the rule of investigation such as common sense teaches, I called attention to Buddha, Mohammed, Confucius, and Shakespeare.

In another place in your Remarks, when my statement about Shakespeare was not in your mind, you say: "All is done by steps—nothing by strides, leaps or bounds—all from protoplasm up to Shakespeare." Why did you end the series with Shakespeare? Did you intend to say Dante, or Bishop Butler?

It is curious to see how much ingenuity a great man exercises when guided by what he calls "the rule of investigation as suggested by common sense." I pointed out some things that Christ did not teach—among others, that he said nothing with regard to the family relation, nothing against slavery, nothing about education, nothing as to the rights and duties of nations, nothing as to any scientific truth. And this is answered by saying that "I am quite able to point out the way in which the Savior of the world might have been much greater as a teacher than he actually was."

Is this an answer, or is it simply taking refuge behind a name? Would it not have been better if Christ had told his disciples that they must not persecute; that they had no right to destroy their fellow-men; that they must not put heretics in dungeons, or destroy them with flames; that they must not invent and use instruments of torture; that they must not appeal to brutality, nor endeavor to sow with bloody hands the seeds of peace? Would it not have been far better had he said: "I come not to bring a sword, but peace"? Would not this have saved countless cruelties and countless lives?

You seem to think that you have fully answered my objection when you say that Christ taught the absolute indissolubility of marriage.

Why should a husband and wife be compelled to live with each other after love is dead? Why should the wife still be bound in indissoluble chains to a husband who is cruel, infamous, and false? Why should her life be destroyed because of his? Why should she be chained to a criminal and an outcast? Nothing can be more unphilosophic than this. Why fill the world with the children of indifference and hatred?

The marriage contract is the most important, the most sacred, that human beings can make. It will be sacredly kept by good men and by good women. But if a loving woman—tender, noble, and true—makes this contract with a man whom she believed to be worthy of all respect and love, and who is found to be a cruel, worthless wretch, why should her life be lost?

Do you not know that the indissolubility of the marriage contract leads to its violation, forms an excuse for immorality, eats out the very heart of truth, and gives to vice that which alone belongs to love?

But in order that you may know why the objection was raised, I call your attention to the fact that Christ offered a reward, not only in this world but in another, to any husband who would desert his wife. And do you know that this hideous offer caused millions to desert their wives and children?

Theologians have the habit of using names instead of arguments—of appealing to some man, great in some direction, to establish their creed; but we all know that no man is great enough to be an authority, except in that particular domain in which he won his eminence; and we all know that great men are not great in all directions. Bacon died a believer in the Ptolemaic system of astronomy. Tycho Brahe kept an imbecile in his service, putting down with great care the words that fell from the hanging lip of idiocy, and then endeavored to put them together in a way to form prophecies. Sir Matthew Hale believed in witchcraft not only, but in its lowest and most vulgar forms; and some of the greatest men of antiquity examined the entrails of birds to find the secrets of the future.

It has always seemed to me that reasons are better than names.

After taking the ground that Christ could not have been a greater teacher than he actually was, you ask: "Where would have been the wisdom of delivering to an uninstructed population of a particular age a codified religion which was to serve for all nations, all ages, all states of civilization?"

Does not this question admit that the teachings of Christ will not serve for all nations, all ages and all states of civilization?

But let me ask: If it was necessary for Christ "to deliver to an uninstructed population of a particular age a certain religion suited only for that particular age," why should a civilized and scientific age eighteen hundred years afterwards be absolutely bound by that religion? Do you not see that your position cannot be defended, and that you have provided no way for retreat? If the religion of Christ was for that age, is it for this? Are you willing to admit that the Ten Commandments are not for all time? If, then, four thousand years before Christ, commandments were given not simply for "an uninstructed population of a particular age, but for all time," can you give a reason why the religion of Christ should not have been of the same character?

In the first place you say that God has revealed himself to the world—that he has revealed a religion; and in the next place, that "he has not revealed a perfect religion, for the reason that no room would be left for the career of human thought."

Why did not God reveal this imperfect religion to all people instead of to a small and insignificant tribe, a tribe without commerce and without influence among the nations of the world? Why did he hide this imperfect light under a bushel? If the light was necessary for one, was it not necessary for all? And why did he drown a world to whom he had not even given that light? According to your reasoning, would there not have been left greater room for the career of human thought, had no revelation been made?

You say that "you have known a person who after studying the old classical or Olympian religion for a third part of a century, at length began to hope that he had some partial comprehension of it—some inkling of what is meant." You say this for the purpose of showing how impossible it is to understand the Bible. If it is so difficult, why do you call it a revelation? And yet, according to your creed, the man who does not understand the revelation and believe it, or who does not believe it, whether he understands it or not, is to reap the harvest of everlasting pain. Ought not the revelation to be revealed?

In order to escape from the fact that Christ denounced the chosen people of God as "a generation of vipers" and as "whited sepulchers," you take the ground that the scribes and pharisees were not the chosen people. Of what blood were they? It will not do to say that they were not the people. Can you deny that Christ addressed the chosen people when he said: "Jerusalem, which killest the prophets and stonest them that are sent unto thee"?

You have called me to an account for what I said in regard to Ananias and Sapphira. First, I am charged with having said that the apostles conceived the idea of having all things in common, and you denounce this as an interpolation; second, "that motives of prudence are stated as a matter of fact to have influenced the offending couple"—and this is charged as an interpolation; and, third, that I stated that the apostles sent for the wife of Ananias—and this is characterized as a pure invention.

To me it seems reasonable to suppose that the idea of having all things in common was conceived by those who had nothing, or had the least, and not by those who had plenty. In the last verses of the fourth chapter of the Acts, you will find this:

"Neither was there any among them that lacked, for as many as were possessed of lands or houses sold them, and brought the prices of the things that were sold, and laid them down at the apostles' feet: and distribution was made unto every man according as he had need. And Joses, who by the apostles was surnamed Barnabas (which is, being interpreted, the son of consolation), a Levite and of the country of Cyprus, having land, sold it, and brought the money, and laid it at the apostles' feet."

Now it occurred to me that the idea was in all probability suggested by the men at whose feet the property was laid. It never entered my mind that the idea originated with those who had land for sale. There may be a different standard by which human nature is measured in your country, than in mine; but if the thing had happened in the United States, I feel absolutely positive that it would have been at the suggestion of the apostles.

"Ananias, with Sapphira, his wife, sold a possession and kept back part of the price, his wife also being privy to it, and brought a certain part and laid it at the apostles' feet."

In my Letter to Dr. Field I stated—not at the time pretending to quote from the New Testament—that Ananias and Sapphira, after talking the matter over, not being entirely satisfied with the collaterals, probably concluded to keep a little—just enough to keep them from starvation if the good and pious bankers should abscond. It never occurred to me that any man would imagine that this was a quotation, and I feel like asking your pardon for having led you into this error. We are informed in the Bible that "they kept back a part of the price." It occurred to me, "judging by the rule of investigation according to common sense," that there was a reason for this, and I could think of no reason except that they did not care to trust the apostles with all, and that they kept back just a little, thinking it might be useful if the rest should be lost.

According to the account, after Peter had made a few remarks to Ananias,

"Ananias fell down and gave up the ghost;.... and the young men arose, wound him up, and carried him out, and buried him. And it was about the space of three hours after, when his wife, not knowing what was done, came in."

Whereupon Peter said:

" 'Tell me whether ye sold the land for so much?' And she said, 'Yea, for so much.' Then Peter said unto her, 'How is it that ye have agreed together to tempt the spirit of the Lord? Behold, the feet of them which have buried thy husband are at the door, and shall carry thee out.' Then fell she down straightway at his feet, and yielded up the ghost; and the young men came in, and found her dead, and, carrying her forth, buried her by her husband."

The only objection found to this is, that I inferred that the apostles had sent for her. Sending for her was not the offence. The failure to tell her what had happened to her husband was the offence—keeping his fate a secret from her in order that she might be caught in the same net that had been set for her husband by Jehovah. This was the offence. This was the mean and cruel thing to which I objected. Have you answered that?

Of course, I feel sure that the thing never occurred—the probability being that Ananias and Sapphira never lived and never died. It is probably a story invented by the early church to make the collection of subscriptions somewhat easier.

And yet, we find a man in the nineteenth century, foremost of his fellow-citizens in the affairs of a great nation, upholding this barbaric view of God.

Let me beg of you to use your reason "according to the rule suggested by common sense." Let us do what little we can to rescue the reputation, even of a Jewish myth, from the calumnies of Ignorance and Fear.

So, again, I am charged with having given certain words as a quotation from the Bible in which two passages are combined—"They who believe and are baptized shall be saved, and they who believe not shall be damned. And these shall go away into everlasting fire prepared for the devil and his angels."

They were given as two passages. No one for a moment supposed that they would be read together as one, and no one imagined that any one in answering the argument would be led to believe that they were intended as one. Neither was there in this the slightest negligence, as I was answering a man who is perfectly familiar with the Bible. The objection was too small to make. It is hardly large enough to answer—and had it not been made by you it would not have been answered.

You are not satisfied with what I have said upon the subject of immortality. What I said was this: The idea of immortality, that like a sea has ebbed and flowed in the human heart, with its countless waves of hope and fear beating against the shores and rocks of time and fate, was not born of any book, nor of any creed, nor of any religion. It was born of human affection, and it will continue to ebb and flow beneath the mists and clouds of doubt and darkness as long as love kisses the lips of death.

You answer this by saying that "the Egyptians were believers in immortality, but were not a people of high intellectual development."

How such a statement tends to answer what I have said, is beyond my powers of discernment. Is there the slightest connection between my statement and your objection?

You make still another answer, and say that "the ancient Greeks were a race of perhaps unparalleled intellectual capacity, and that notwithstanding that, the most powerful mind of the Greek philosophy, that of Aristotle, had no clear conception of a personal existence in a future state." May I be allowed to ask this simple question: Who has?

Are you urging an objection to the dogma of immortality, when you say that a race of unparalleled intellectual capacity had no confidence in it? Is that a doctrine believed only by people who lack intellectual capacity? I stated that the idea of immortality was born of love, You reply, "the Egyptians believed it, but they were not intellectual." Is not this a *non sequitur?* The question is: Were they a loving people?

Does history show that there is a moral governor of the world? What witnesses shall we call? The billions of slaves who were paid with blows?—the countless mothers whose babes were sold? Have we time to examine the Waldenses, the Covenanters of Scotland, the Catholics of Ireland, the victims of St. Bartholomew, of the Spanish Inquisition, all those who have died in flames? Shall we hear the story of Bruno? Shall we ask Servetus? Shall we ask the millions slaughtered by Christian swords in America—all the victims of ambition, of perjury, of ignorance, of superstition and revenge, of storm and earthquake, of famine, flood and fire?

Can all the agonies and crimes, can all the inequalities of the world be answered by reading the "noble Psalm" in which are found the words: "Call upon me in the day of trouble, so I will hear thee, and thou shalt praise me"? Do you prove the truth of these fine words, this honey of Trebizond, by the victims of religious persecution? Shall we hear the sighs and sobs of Siberia?

Another thing. Why should you, from the page of Greek history, with the sponge of your judgment, wipe out all names but one, and tell us that the most powerful mind of the Greek philosophy was that of Aristotle? How did you ascertain this fact? Is it not fair to suppose that you merely intended to say that, according to your view, Aristotle had the most powerful mind among all the philosophers of Greece? I should not call attention to this, except for your criticism on a like remark of mine as to the intellectual superiority of Shakespeare. But if you knew the trouble I have had in finding out your meaning, from your words, you would pardon me for calling attention to a single line from Aristotle: "Clearness is the virtue of style."

To me Epicurus seems far greater than Aristotle, He had clearer vision. His cheek was closer to the breast of nature, and he planted his philosophy nearer to the bed-rock of fact. He was practical enough to know that virtue is the means and happiness the end; that the highest philosophy is the art of living. He was wise enough to say that nothing is of the slightest value to man that does not increase or preserve his wellbeing, and he was great enough to know and courageous enough to declare that all the gods and ghosts were monstrous phantoms born of ignorance and fear.

I still insist that human affection is the foundation of the idea of immortality; that love was the first to speak that word, no matter whether they who spoke it were savage or civilized, Egyptian or Greek. But if we are immortal—if there be another world—why was it not clearly set forth in the Old Testament? Certainly, the authors of that book had an opportunity to learn it from the Egyptians. Why was it not revealed by Jehovah? Why did he waste his time in giving orders for the consecration of priests—in saying that they must have sheep's blood put on their right ears and on their right thumbs and on their right big toes? Could a God with any sense of humor give such directions, or watch without huge laughter the performance of such a ceremony? In order to see the beauty, the depth and tenderness of such a consecration, is it essential to be in a state of "reverential calm"?

Is it not strange that Christ did not tell of another world distinctly, clearly, without parable, and without the mist of metaphor?

The fact is that the Hindus, the Egyptians, the Greeks, and the Romans taught the immortality of the soul, not as a glittering guess—a possible perhaps—but as a clear and demonstrated truth for many centuries before the birth of Christ.

If the Old Testament proves anything, it is that death ends all. And the New Testament, by basing immortality on the resurrection of the body, but "keeps the word of promise to our ear and breaks it to our hope."

In my Reply to Dr. Field, I said: "The truth is, that no one can justly be held responsible for his thoughts. The brain thinks without asking our consent; we believe, or disbelieve, without an effort of the will. Belief is a result. It is the effect of evidence upon the mind. The scales turn in spite of him who watches. There is no opportunity of being honest or dishonest in the formation of an opinion. The conclusion is entirely independent of desire. We must believe, or we must doubt, in spite of what we wish."

Does the brain think without our consent? Can we control our thought? Can we tell what we are going to think tomorrow?

Can we stop thinking?

Is belief the result of that which to us is evidence, or is it a product of the will? Can the scales in which reason weighs evidence be turned by the will? Why then should evidence be weighed? If it all depends on the will, what is evidence? Is there any opportunity of being dishonest in the formation of an opinion? Must not the man who forms the opinion know what it is? He cannot knowingly cheat himself. He cannot be deceived with dice that he loads. He cannot play unfairly at solitaire without knowing that he has lost the game. He cannot knowingly weigh with false scales and believe in the correctness of the result.

You have not even attempted to answer my arguments upon these points, but you have unconsciously avoided them. You did not attack the citadel. In military parlance, you proceeded to "shell the woods." The noise is precisely the same as though every shot had been directed against the enemy's position, but the result is not. You do not seem willing to implicitly trust the correctness of your aim. You prefer to place the target after the shot.

The question is whether the will knowingly can change evidence, and whether there is any opportunity of being dishonest in the formation of an opinion. You have changed the issue. You have erased the word formation and interpolated the word expression.

Let us suppose that a man has given an opinion, knowing that it is not based on any fact. Can you say that he has given his opinion? The moment a prejudice is known to be a prejudice, it disappears. Ignorance is the soil in which prejudice must grow. Touched by a ray of light, it dies. The judgment of man may be warped by prejudice and passion, but it cannot be consciously warped. It is impossible for any man to be influenced by a known prejudice, because a known prejudice cannot exist.

I am not contending that all opinions have been honestly expressed. What I contend is that when a dishonest opinion has been expressed it is not the opinion that was formed.

The cases suggested by you are not in point. Fathers are honestly swayed, if really swayed, by love; and queens and judges have pretended to be swayed by the highest motives, by the clearest evidence, in order that they might kill rivals, reap rewards, and gratify revenge. But what has all this to do with the fact that he who watches the scales in which evidence is weighed knows the actual result?

Let us examine your case: If a father is *consciously* swayed by his love for his son, and for that reason says that his son is innocent, then he has not expressed his opinion. If he is unconsciously swayed and says that his son is innocent, then he has expressed his opinion. In both instances his opinion was independent of his will; but in the first instance he did not express his opinion. You will certainly see this distinction between the formation and the expression of an opinion.

The same argument applies to the man who consciously has a desire to condemn. Such a *conscious* desire cannot affect the testimony— cannot affect the opinion. Queen Elizabeth undoubtedly desired the death of Mary Stuart, but this conscious desire could not have been the foundation on which rested Elizabeth's opinion as to the guilt or innocence of her rival. It is barely possible that Elizabeth did not express her real opinion. Do you believe that the English judges in the matter of the Popish Plot gave judgment in accordance with their opinions? Are you satisfied that Napoleon expressed his real opinion when he justified himself for the assassination of the Duc d'Enghien?

If you answer these questions in the affirmative, you admit that I am right. If you answer in the negative, you admit that you are wrong. The moment you admit that the opinion formed cannot be changed by expressing a pretended opinion, your argument is turned against yourself.

It is admitted that prejudice strengthens, weakens and colors evidence; but prejudice is honest. And when one acts knowingly against the evidence, that is not by reason of prejudice.

According to my views of propriety, it would be unbecoming for me to say that your argument on these questions is "a piece of plausible shallowness." Such language might be regarded as lacking "reverential calm," and I therefore refrain from even characterizing it as plausible.

Is it not perfectly apparent that you have changed the issue, and that instead of showing that opinions are creatures of the will, you have discussed the quality of actions? What have corrupt and cruel judgments pronounced by corrupt and cruel judges to do with their real opinions? When a judge forms one opinion and renders another he is called corrupt. The corruption does not consist in forming his opinion, but in rendering one that he did not form. Does a dishonest creditor, who incorrectly adds a number of items making the aggregate too large, necessarily change his opinion as to the relations of numbers? When an error is known, it is not a mistake; but a conclusion reached by a mistake, or by a prejudice, or by both, is a necessary conclusion. He who pretends to come to a conclusion by a mistake which he knows is not a mistake, knows that he has not expressed his real opinion.

Can any thing be more illogical than the assertion that because a boy reaches, through negligence in adding figures, a wrong result, that he is accountable for his opinion of the result? If he knew he was negligent, what must his opinion of the result have been?

So with the man who boldly announces that he has discovered the numerical expression of the relation sustained by the diameter to the circumference of a circle. If he is honest in the announcement, then the announcement was caused not by his will but by his ignorance. His will cannot make the announcement true, and he could not by any possibility have supposed that his will could affect the correctness of his announcement. The will of one who thinks that he has invented or discovered what is called perpetual motion, is not at fault. The man, if honest, has been misled; if not honest, he endeavors to mislead others. There is prejudice, and prejudice does raise a clamor, and the intellect is affected and the judgment is darkened and the opinion is deformed; but the prejudice is real and the clamor is sincere and the judgment is upright and the opinion is honest.

The intellect is not always supreme. It is surrounded by clouds. It sometimes sits in darkness. It is often misled—sometimes, in superstitious fear, it abdicates. It is not always a white light. The passions and prejudices are prismatic—they color thoughts. Desires betray the judgment and cunningly mislead the will.

You seem to think that the fact of responsibility is in danger unless it rests upon the will, and this will you regard as something without a cause, springing into being in some mysterious way, without father or mother, without seed or soil, or rain or light. You must admit that man is a conditioned being—that he has wants, objects, ends, and aims, and that these are gratified and attained only by the use of means. Do not these wants and these objects have something to do with the will, and does not the intellect have something to do with the means? Is not the will a product? Independently of conditions, can it exist? Is it not necessarily produced? Behind every wish and thought, every dream and fancy, every fear and hope, are there not countless causes? Man feels shame. What does this prove? He pities himself. What does this demonstrate?

The dark continent of motive and desire has never been explored. In the brain, that wondrous world with one inhabitant, there are recesses dim and dark, treacherous sands and dangerous shores, where seeming sirens tempt and fade; streams that rise in unknown lands from hidden springs, strange seas with ebb and flow of tides, resistless billows urged by storms of flame, profound and awful depths hidden by mist of dreams, obscure and phantom realms where vague and fearful things are half revealed, jungles where passion's tigers crouch, and skies of cloud and blue where fancies fly with painted wings that dazzle and mislead; and the poor sovereign of this pictured world is led by old desires and ancient hates, and stained by crimes of many vanished years, and pushed by hands that long ago were dust, until he feels like some bewildered slave that Mockery has throned and crowned.

No one pretends that the mind of man is perfect—that it is not affected by desires, colored by hopes, weakened by fears, deformed by ignorance and distorted by superstition. But all this has nothing to do with the innocence of opinion.

It may be that the Thugs were taught that murder is innocent; but did the teachers believe what they taught? Did the pupils believe the teachers? Did not Jehovah teach that the act that we describe as murder was a duty? Were not his teachings practiced by Moses and Joshua and Jephthah and Samuel and David? Were they honest? But what has all this to do with the point at issue?

Society has the right to protect itself, even from honest murderers and conscientious thieves. The belief of the criminal does not disarm society; it protects itself from him as from a poisonous serpent, or from a beast that lives on human flesh. We are under no obligation to stand still and allow ourselves to be murdered by one who honestly thinks that it is his duty to take our lives. And yet according to your argument, we have no right to defend ourselves from honest Thugs. Was Saul of Tarsus a Thug when he persecuted Christians "even unto strange cities"? Is the Thug of India more ferocious than Torquemada, the Thug of Spain?

If belief depends upon the will, can all men have correct opinions who will to have them? Acts are good or bad, according to their consequences, and not according to the intentions of the actors. Honest opinions may be wrong, and opinions dishonestly expressed may be right.

Do you mean to say that because passion and prejudice, the reckless "pilots 'twixt the dangerous shores of will and judgment," sway the mind, that the opinions which you have expressed in your Remarks to me are not your opinions? Certainly you will admit that in all probability you have prejudices and passions, and if so, can the opinions that you have expressed, according to your argument, be honest? My lack of confidence in your argument gives me perfect confidence in your candor. You may remember the philosopher who retained his reputation for veracity, in spite of the fact that he kept saying: "There is no truth in man."

Are only those opinions honest that are formed without any interference of passion, affection, habit or fancy? What would the opinion of a man without passions, affections, or fancies be worth? The alchemist gave up his search for an universal solvent upon being asked in what kind of vessel he expected to keep it when found.

It may be admitted that Biel "shows us how the life of Dante co-operated with his extraordinary natural gifts and capabilities to make him what he was," but does this tend to show that Dante changed his opinions by an act of his will, or that he reached honest opinions by knowingly using false weights and measures?

You must admit that the opinions, habits and religions of men depend, at least in some degree, on race, occupation, training and capacity. Is not every thoughtful man compelled to agree with Edgar Fawcett, in whose brain are united the beauty of the poet and the subtlety of the logician,

> "Who sees how vice her venom wreaks
> On the frail babe before it speaks,
> And how heredity enslaves
> With ghostly hands that reach from graves"?

Why do you hold the intellect criminally responsible for opinions, when you admit that it is controlled by the will? And why do you hold the will responsible, when you insist that it is swayed by the passions and affections? But all this has nothing to do with the fact that every opinion has been honestly formed, whether honestly expressed or not.

No one pretends that all governments have been honestly formed and honestly administered. All vices, and some virtues are represented in most nations. In my opinion a republic is far better than a monarchy. The legally expressed will of the people is the only rightful sovereign. This sovereignty, however, does not embrace the realm of thought or opinion. In that world, each human being is a sovereign,—throned and crowned: One is a majority. The good citizens of that realm give to others all rights that they claim for themselves, and those who appeal to force are the only traitors.

The existence of theological despotisms, of God-anointed kings, does not tend to prove that a known prejudice can determine the weight of evidence. When men were so ignorant as to suppose that God would destroy them unless they burned heretics, they lighted the fagots in self defense.

Feeling as I do that man is not responsible for his opinions, I characterized persecution for opinion's sake as infamous. So, it is perfectly clear to me, that it would be the infamy of infamies for an infinite being to create vast numbers of men knowing that they would suffer eternal pain. If an infinite God creates a man on purpose to damn him, or creates him knowing that he will be damned, is not the crime the same? We make mistakes and failures because we are finite; but can you conceive of any excuse for an infinite being who creates failures? If you had the power to change, by a wish, a statue into a human being, and you knew that this being would die without a "change of heart" and suffer endless pain, what would you do?

Can you think of any excuse for an earthly father, who, having wealth, learning and leisure, leaves his own children in ignorance and darkness? Do you believe that a God of infinite wisdom, justice and love, called countless generations of men into being, knowing that they would be used as fuel for the eternal fire?

Many will regret that you did not give your views upon the main questions—the principal issues—involved, instead of calling attention, for the most part, to the unimportant. If men were discussing the causes and results of the Franco-Prussian war, it would hardly be worth while for a third person to interrupt the argument for the purpose of calling attention to a misspelled word in the terms of surrender.

If we admit that man is responsible for his opinions and his thoughts, and that his will is perfectly free, still these admissions do not even tend to prove the inspiration of the Bible, or the "divine scheme of redemption."

In my judgment, the days of the supernatural are numbered. The dogma of inspiration must be abandoned. As man advances,—as his intellect enlarges,—as his knowledge increases,—as his ideals become nobler, the bibles and creeds will lose their authority—the miraculous will be classed with the impossible, and the idea of special providence will be discarded. Thousands of religions have perished, innumerable gods have died, and why should the religion of our time be exempt from the common fate?

Creeds cannot remain permanent in a world in which knowledge increases. Science and superstition cannot peaceably occupy the same brain. This is an age of investigation, of discovery and thought. Science destroys the dogmas that mislead the mind and waste the energies of man. It points out the ends that can be accomplished; takes into consideration the limits of our faculties; fixes our attention on the affairs of this world, and erects beacons of warning on the dangerous shores. It seeks to ascertain the conditions of health, to the end that life may be enriched and lengthened, and it reads with a smile this passage:

"And God-wrought special miracles by the hands of Paul, so that from his body were brought unto the sick handkerchiefs or aprons, and the diseases departed from them, and the evil spirits went out of them."

Science is the enemy of fear and credulity. It invites investigation, challenges the reason, stimulates inquiry, and welcomes the unbeliever. It seeks to give food and shelter, and raiment, education and liberty to the human race. It welcomes every fact and every truth. It has furnished a foundation for morals, a philosophy for the guidance of man. From all books it selects the good, and from all theories, the true. It seeks to civilize the human race by the cultivation of the intellect and' heart. It refines through art, music and the drama—giving voice and expression to every noble thought. The mysterious does not excite the feeling of worship, but the ambition to understand. It does not pray—it works. It does not answer inquiry with the malicious cry of "blasphemy." Its feelings are not hurt by contradiction, neither does it ask to be protected by law from the laughter of heretics. It has taught man that he cannot walk beyond the horizon—that the questions of origin and destiny cannot be answered—that an infinite personality cannot be comprehended by a finite being, and that the truth of any system of religion based on the supernatural cannot by any possibility be established—such a religion not being within the domain of evidence. And, above all, it teaches that all our duties are here—that all our obligations are to sentient beings; that intelligence, guided by kindness, is the highest possible wisdom; and that "man believes not what he would, but what he can."

And after all, it may be that "to ride an unbroken horse with the reins thrown upon his neck"—as you charge me with doing—gives a greater variety of sensations, a keener delight, and a better prospect of winning the race than to sit solemnly astride of a dead one, in "a deep reverential calm," with the bridle firmly in your hand.

Again assuring you of my profound respect, I remain, Sincerely yours,
Robert G. Ingersoll.

ROME OR REASON.

The Gladstone-Ingersoll Controversy.

THE CHURCH ITS OWN WITNESS,
By Cardinal Manning.

The Vatican Council, in its Decree on Faith has these words: "The Church itself, by its marvelous propagation, its eminent sanctity, its inexhaustible fruitfulness in all good things, its catholic unity and invincible stability, is a vast and perpetual motive of credibility, and an irrefragable witness of its own Divine legation."[4] Its Divine Founder said: "I am the light of the world;" and, to His Apostles, He said also, "Ye are the light of the world," and of His Church He added, "A city seated on a hill cannot be hid." The Vatican Council says, "The Church is its own witness." My purpose is to draw out this assertion more fully.

These words affirm that the Church is self-evident, as light is to the eye, and through sense, to the intellect. Next to the sun at noonday, there is nothing in the world more manifest than the one visible Universal Church. Both the faith and the infidelity of the world bear witness to it. It is loved and hated, trusted and feared, served and assaulted, honored and blasphemed: it is Christ or Antichrist, the Kingdom of God or the imposture of Satan. It pervades the civilized world. No man and no nation can ignore it, none can be indifferent to it. Why is all this? How is its existence to be accounted for?

Let me suppose that I am an unbeliever in Christianity, and that some *friend* should make me promise to examine the evidence to show that Christianity is a Divine revelation; I should then sift and test the evidence as strictly as if it were in a court of law, and in a cause of life and death; my will would be in suspense: it would in no way control the process of my intellect. If it had any inclination from the equilibrium, it would be towards mercy and hope; but this would not add a feather's weight to the evidence, nor sway the intellect a hair's breadth.

After the examination has been completed, and my intellect convinced, the evidence being sufficient to prove that Christianity is a divine revelation, nevertheless I am not yet a Christian. All this sifting brings me to the conclusion of a chain of reasoning; but I am not yet a believer. The last act of reason has brought me to the brink of the first act of faith. They are generically distinct and separable. The acts of reason are intellectual, and jealous of the interference of the will. The act of faith is an imperative act of the will, founded on and justified by the process and conviction of the intellect. Hitherto I have been a critic: henceforward, if I will, I become a disciple.

It may here be objected that no man can so far suspend the inclination of the will when the question is, has God indeed spoken to man or no? is

---

[4] "Const. Dogm. de Fide Catholica, c. iii.

the revealed law of purity, generosity, perfection, divine, or only the poetry of imagination? Can a man be indifferent between two such sides of the problem? Will he not desire the higher and better side to be true? and if he desire, will he not incline to the side that he desires to find true? Can a moral being be absolutely indifferent between two such issues? and can two such issues be equally attractive to a moral agent? Can it be indifferent and all the same to us whether God has made Himself and His will known to us or not? Is there no attraction in light, no repulsion in darkness? Does not the intrinsic and eternal distinction of good and evil make itself felt in spite of the will? Are we not responsible to "receive the truth in the love of it?" Nevertheless, evidence has its own limits and quantities, and cannot be made more or less by any act of the will. And yet, what is good or bad, high or mean, lovely or hateful, ennobling or degrading, must attract or repel men as they are better or worse in their moral sense; for an equilibrium between good and evil, to God or to man, is impossible.

The last act of my reason, then, is distinct from my first act of faith precisely in this: so long as I was uncertain I suspended the inclination of my will, as an act of fidelity to conscience and of loyalty to truth; but the process once complete, and the conviction once attained, my will imperatively constrains me to believe, and I become a disciple of a Divine revelation.

My friend next tells me that there are Christian Scriptures, and I go through precisely the same process of critical examination and final conviction, the last act of reasoning preceding, as before, the first act of faith.

He then tells me that there is a Church claiming to be divinely founded, divinely guarded, and divinely guided in its custody of Christianity and of the Christian Scriptures.

Once more I have the same twofold process of reasoning and of believing to go through.

There is, however, this difference in the subject-matter: Christianity is an order of supernatural truth appealing intellectually to my reason; the Christian Scriptures are voiceless, and need a witness. They cannot prove their own mission, much less their own authenticity or inspiration. But the Church is visible to the eye, audible to the ear, self-manifesting and self-asserting: I cannot escape from it. If I go to the east, it is there; if I go to the west, it is there also. If I stay at home, it is before me, seated on the hill; if I turn away from it, I am surrounded by its light. It pursues me and calls to me. I cannot deny its existence; I cannot be indifferent to it; I must either listen to it or willfully stop my ears; I must heed it or defy it, love it or hate it. But my first attitude towards it is to try it with forensic strictness, neither pronouncing it to be Christ nor Antichrist till I have tested its origin, claim, and character. Let us take down the case in short-hand.

1. It says that it interpenetrates all the nations of the civilized world. In some it holds the whole nation in its unity, in others it holds fewer; but in all it is present, visible, audible, naturalized, and known as the one Catholic Church, a name that none can appropriate. Though often claimed and controversially assumed, none can retain it; it falls off. The

world knows only one Catholic Church, and always restores the name to the right owner.

2. It is not a national body, but extra-national, accused of its foreign relations and foreign dependence. It is international, and independent in a supernational unity.

3. In faith, divine worship, sacred ceremonial, discipline, government, from the highest to the lowest, it is the same in every place.

4. It speaks all languages in the civilized world.

5. It is obedient to one Head, outside of all nations, except one only; and in that nation, his headship is not national but world-wide.

6. The world-wide sympathy of the Church in all lands with its Head has been manifested in our days, and before our eyes, by a series of public assemblages in Rome, of which nothing like or second to it can be found. In 1854, 350 Bishops of all nations surrounded their Head when he defined the Immaculate Conception. In 1862, 400 Bishops assembled at the canonization of the Martyrs of Japan. In 1867, 500 Bishops came to keep the eighteenth centenary of St. Peter's martyrdom. In 1870, 700 Bishops assembled in the Vatican Council. On the Feast of the Epiphany, 1870, the Bishops of thirty nations during two whole hours made profession of faith in their own languages, kneeling before their head. Add to this, that in 1869, in the sacerdotal jubilee of Pius IX., Rome was filled for months by pilgrims from all lands in Europe and beyond the sea, from the Old World and from the New, bearing all manner of gifts and oblations to the Head of the Universal Church. To this, again, must be added the world-wide outcry and protest of all the Catholic unity against the seizure and sacrilege of September, 1870, when Rome was taken by the Italian Revolution.

7. All this came to pass not only by reason of the great love of the Catholic world for Pius IX., but because they revered him as the successor of St. Peter and the Vicar of Jesus Christ. For that undying reason the same events have been reproduced in the time of Leo XIII. In the early months of this year Rome was once more filled with pilgrims of all nations, coming in thousands as representatives of millions in all nations, to celebrate the sacerdotal jubilee of the Sovereign Pontiff. The courts of the Vatican could not find room for the multitude of gifts and offerings of every kind which were sent from all quarters of the world.

8. These things are here said, not because of any other importance, but because they set forth in the most visible and self-evident way the living unity and the luminous universality of the One Catholic and Roman Church.

9. What has thus far been said is before our eyes at this hour. It is no appeal to history, but to a visible and palpable fact. Men may explain it as they will; deny it, they cannot. They see the Head of the Church year by year speaking to the nations of the world; treating with Empires, Republics and Governments. There is no other man on earth that can so bear himself. Neither from Canterbury nor from Constantinople can such a voice go forth to which rulers and people listen.

This is the century of revolutions. Rome has in our time been besieged three times; three Popes have been driven out of it, two have been shut up in the Vatican. The city is now full of the Revolution. The whole

Church has been tormented by Falck laws, Mancini laws, and Crispi laws. An unbeliever in Germany said some years ago, "The net is now drawn so tight about the Church, that if it escapes this time I will believe in it." Whether he believes, or is even alive now to believe, I cannot say.

Nothing thus far has been said as proof. The visible, palpable facts, which are at this moment before the eyes of all men, speak for themselves. There is one, and only one, worldwide unity of which these things can be said. It is a fact and a phenomenon for which an intelligible account must be rendered. If it be only a human system built up by the intellect, will and energy of men, let the adversaries prove it. The burden is upon them; and they will have more to do as we go on.

Thus far we have rested upon the evidence of sense and fact. We must now go on to history and reason.

Every religion and every religious body known to history has varied from itself and broken up. Brahminism has given birth to Buddhism; Mahometanism is parted into the Arabian and European Khalifates; the Greek schism into the Russian, Constantinopolitan, and Bulgarian autocephalous fragment; Protestantism into its multitudinous diversities. All have departed from their original type, and all are continually developing new and irreconcilable, intellectual and ritualistic, diversities and repulsions. How is it that, with all diversities of language, civilization, race, interest, and conditions, social and political, including persecution and warfare, the Catholic nations are at this day, even when in warfare, in unchanged unity of faith, communion, worship and spiritual sympathy with each other and with their Head? This needs a rational explanation.

It may be said in answer, endless divisions have come out of the Church, from Arius to Photius, and from Photius to Luther.

Yes, but they all came out. There is the difference. They did not remain in the Church, corrupting the faith. They came out, and ceased to belong to the Catholic unity, as a branch broken from a tree ceases to belong to the tree. But the identity of the tree remains the same. A branch is not a tree, nor a tree a branch. A tree may lose branches, but it rests upon its root, and renews its loss. Not so the religions, so to call them, that have broken away from unity. Not one has retained its members or its doctrines. Once separated from the sustaining unity of the Church, all separations lose their spiritual cohesion, and then their intellectual identity. *Ramus procisus arescit.*

For the present it is enough to say that no human legislation, authority or constraint can ever create internal unity of intellect and will; and that the diversities and contradictions generated by all human systems prove the absence of Divine authority. Variations or contradictions are proof of the absence of a Divine mission to mankind. All natural causes run to disintegration. Therefore, they can render no account of the world-wide unity of the One Universal Church.

Such, then, are the facts before our eyes at this day. We will seek out the origin of the body or system called the Catholic Church, and pass at once to its outset eighteen hundred years ago.

I affirm, then, three things: (1) First, that no adequate account can be given of this undeniable fact from natural causes; (2) that the history of the Catholic Church demands causes above nature; and (3) that it has always claimed for itself a Divine origin and Divine authority.

I. And, first, before we examine what it was and what it has done, we will recall to mind what was the world in the midst of which it arose.

The most comprehensive and complete description of the old world, before Christianity came in upon it, is given in the first chapter of the Epistle to the Romans. Mankind had once the knowledge of God: that knowledge was obscured by the passions of sense; in the darkness of the human intellect, with the light of nature still before them, the nations worshiped the creature—that is, by pantheism, polytheism, idolatry; and, having lost the knowledge of God and of His perfections, they lost the knowledge of their own nature and of its laws, even of the natural and rational laws, which thenceforward ceased to guide, restrain, or govern them. They became perverted and inverted with every possible abuse, defeating the end and destroying the powers of creation. The lights of nature were put out, and the world rushed headlong into confusions, of which the beasts that perish were innocent. This is analytically the history of all nations but one. A line of light still shone from Adam to Enoch, from Enoch to Abraham, to whom the command was given, "Walk before Me and be perfect." And it ran on from Abraham to Caiaphas, who crucified the founder of Christianity. Through all anthropomorphisms of thought and language this line of light still passed inviolate and inviolable. But in the world, on either side of that radiant stream, the whole earth was dark. The intellectual and moral state of the Greek world may be measured in its highest excellence in Athens; and of the Roman world in Rome. The 'state of Athens—its private, domestic, and public morality—may be seen in Aristophanes.

The state of Rome is visible in Juvenal, and in the fourth book of St. Augustine's "City of God." There was only one evil wanting-. The world was not Atheist. Its polytheism was the example and the warrant of all forms of moral abominations. *Imitary quod colis* plunged the nations in crime. Their theology was their degradation; their text-book of an elaborate corruption of intellect and will.

Christianity came in "the fullness of time." What that fullness may mean, is one of the mysteries of times and seasons which it is not for us to know. But one motive for the long delay of four thousand years is not far to seek. It gave time, full and ample, for the utmost development and consolidation of all the falsehood and evil of which the intellect and will of man are capable. The four great empires were each of them the concentration of a supreme effort of human power. The second inherited from the first, the third from both, the fourth from all three. It was, as it was foretold or described, as a beast, "exceeding terrible; his teeth and claws were of iron; he devoured and broke in pieces; and the rest he stamped upon with his feet."[5] The empire of man over man was never so widespread, so absolute, so hardened into one organized mass, as in Imperial Rome. The world had never seen a military power so disciplined, irresistible, invincible; a legislation so just, so equitable, so

---

[5] Daniel, vii. 19.

strong in its execution; a government so universal, so local, so minute. It seemed to be imperishable. Rome was called the eternal. The religions of all nations were enshrined in Dea Roma; adopted, practiced openly, and taught. They were all *religiones licitae,* known to the law; not tolerated only, but recognized. The theologies of Egypt, Greece, and of the Latin world, met in an empyreum, consecrated and guarded by the Imperial law, and administered by the Pontifex Maximus. No fanaticism ever surpassed the religious cruelties of Rome. Add to all this the colluvies of false philosophies of every land, and of every date. They both blinded and hardened the intellect of public opinion and of private men against the invasion of anything except contempt, and hatred of both the philosophy of sophists and of the religion of the people. Add to all this the sensuality of the most refined and of the grossest luxury the world had ever seen, and a moral confusion and corruption which violated every law of nature.

The god of this world had built his city. From foundation to parapet, everything that the skill and power of man could do had been done without stint of means or limit of will. The Divine hand was stayed, or rather, as St. Augustine says, an unsurpassed natural greatness was the reward of certain natural virtues, degraded as they were in unnatural abominations. Rome was the climax of the power of man without God, the apotheosis of the human will, the direct and supreme antagonist of God in His own world. In this the fullness of time was come. Man built all this for himself. Certainly, man could not also build the City of God. They are not the work of one and the same architect, who capriciously chose to build first the city of confusion, suspending for a time his skill and power to build some day the City of God. Such a hypothesis is folly. Of two things, one. Disputers must choose one or the other. Both cannot be asserted, and the assertion needs no answer—it refutes itself. So much for the first point.

II. In the reign of Augustus, and in a remote and powerless Oriental race, a Child was born in a stable of a poor Mother. For thirty years He lived a hidden life; for three years He preached the Kingdom of God, and gave laws hitherto unknown to men. He died in ignominy upon the Cross; on the third day He rose again; and after forty days He was seen no more. This unknown Man created the world-wide unity of intellect and will which is visible to the eye, and audible, in all languages, to the ear. It is in harmony with the reason and moral nature of all nations, in all ages, to this day. What proportion is there between the cause and the effect? What power was there in this isolated Man? What unseen virtues went out of Him to change the world? For change the world He did; and that not in the line or on the level of nature as men had corrupted it, but in direct contradiction to all that was then supreme in the world. He taught the dependence of the intellect against its self-trust, the submission of the will against its license, the subjugation of the passions by temperate control or by absolute subjection against their willful indulgence. This was to reverse what men believed to be the laws of nature: to make water climb upward and fire to point downward. He taught mortification of the lusts of the flesh, contempt of the lusts of the eyes, and hatred of the pride of life. What hope was there that such a teacher should convert imperial Rome? that such a doctrine should exorcise the fullness of human pride and lust? Yet so it has come to pass; and how? Twelve men more obscure than Himself, absolutely without authority or influence of this world, preached throughout the empire and beyond it. They asserted two facts: the one, that God had been made man; the other, that He died and rose again. What could be more incredible? To the Jews the unity and spirituality of God were axioms of reason and faith; to the Gentiles, however cultured, the resurrection of the flesh was impossible. The Divine Person Who had died and risen could not be called in evidence as the chief witness. He could not be produced in court. Could anything be more suspicious if credible, or less credible even if He were there to say so? All that they could do was to say, "We knew Him for three years, both before His death and after He rose from the dead. If you will believe us, you will believe what we say. If you will not believe us, we can say no more. He is not here, but in heaven. We cannot call him down." It is true, as we read, that Peter cured a lame man at the gate of the Temple. The Pharisees could not deny it, but they would not believe what Peter said; they only told him to hold his tongue. And yet thousands in one day in Jerusalem believed in the Incarnation and the Resurrection; and when the Apostles were scattered by persecution, wherever they went men believed their word. The most intense persecution was from the Jews, the people of faith and of Divine traditions. In the name of God and of religion they stoned Stephen, and sent Saul to persecute at Damascus. More than this, they stirred up the Romans in every place. As they had forced Pilate to crucify Jesus of Nazareth, so they swore to slay Paul. And yet, in spite of all, the faith spread.

It is true, indeed, that the Empire of Alexander, the spread of the Hellenistic Greek, the prevalence of Greek in Rome itself, the Roman roads which made the Empire traversable, the Roman peace which sheltered the preachers of the faith in the outset of their work, gave them facilities to travel and to be understood. But these were only external facilities, which in no way rendered more credible or more acceptable the voice of penance and mortification, or the mysteries of the faith, which was immutably "to the Jews a stumbling-block and to the Greeks foolishness." It was in changeless opposition to nature as man had marred it; but it was in absolute harmony with nature as God had made it to His own likeness. Its power was its persuasiveness; and its persuasiveness was in its conformity to the highest and noblest aspirations and aims of the soul in man. The master-key so long lost was found at last; and its conformity to the wards of the lock was its irrefragable witness to its own mission and message.

But if it is beyond belief that Christianity in its outset made good its foothold by merely human causes and powers, how much more does this become incredible in every age as we come down from the first century to the nineteenth, and from the Apostolic mission to the world-wide Church, Catholic and Roman, at this day.

Not only did the world in the fullness of its power give to the Christian faith no help to root or to spread itself, but it wreaked all the fullness of its power upon it to uproot and to destroy it, Of the first thirty Pontiffs in Rome, twenty-nine were martyred. Ten successive persecutions, or rather one universal and continuous persecution of two hundred years, with ten more bitter excesses of enmity in every province of the Empire, did all that man can do to extinguish the Christian name. The Christian name may be blotted out here and there in blood, but the Christian faith can nowhere be slain. It is inscrutable, and beyond the reach of man. In nothing is the blood of the martyrs more surely the seed of the faith. Every martyrdom was a witness to the faith, and the ten persecutions were the sealing of the work of the twelve Apostles. The destroyer defeated himself. Christ crucified was visibly set forth before all the nations, the world was a Calvary, and the blood of the martyrs preached in every tongue the Passion of Jesus Christ. The world did its worst, and ceased only for weariness and conscious defeat.

Then came the peace, and with peace the peril of the Church. The world outside had failed; the world inside began to work. It no longer destroyed life; it perverted the intellect, and, through intellectual perversion, assailed the faith at its centre, The Angel of light preached heresy. The Baptismal Creed was assailed all along the line; Gnosticism assailed the Father-and Creator of all things; Arianism, the God-head of the Son; Nestorianism, the unity of His person; Monophysites, the two natures; Monothelites, the divine and human wills; Macedonians, the person of the Holy Ghost So throughout the centuries, from Nicaea to the Vatican, every article has been in succession perverted by heresy and defined by the Church. But of this we shall speak hereafter. If the human intellect could fasten its perversions on the Christian faith, it would have done so long ago; and if the Christian faith had been guarded by no more than human intellect, it would long ago have been disintegrated, as we see in every religion outside the unity of the one Catholic Church. There is no example in which fragmentary Christianities have not departed from their original type. No human system is immutable; no thing human is changeless. The human intellect, therefore, can give no sufficient account of the identity of the Catholic faith in all places and in all ages by any of its own natural processes or powers. The force of this argument is immensely increased when we trace the tradition of the faith through the nineteen Ecumenical Councils which, with one continuous intelligence, have guarded and unfolded the deposit of faith, defining every truth as it has been successively assailed, in absolute harmony and unity of progression.

What the Senate is to your great Republic, or the Parliament to our English monarchy, such are the nineteen Councils of the Church, with this only difference: the secular Legislatures must meet year by year with short recesses; Councils have met on the average once in a century. The reason of this is that the mutabilities of national life, which are as the water-floods, need constant remedies; the stability of the Church seldom needs new legislation. The faith needs no definition except in rare intervals of periodical intellectual disorder. The discipline of the Church reigns by an universal common law which seldom needs a change, and by local laws which are provided on the spot. Nevertheless, the legislation of the Church, the Corpus Juris, or Canon Law, is a creation of wisdom and justice, to which no Statutes at large or Imperial pandects can bear comparison. Human intellect has reached its climax in jurisprudence, but the world-wide and secular legislation of the Church has a higher character. How the Christian law corrected, elevated, and completed the Imperial law, may be seen in a learned and able work by an American author, far from the Catholic faith, but in the main just and accurate in his facts and arguments—the *Gesta Christi* of Charles Loring Brace. Water cannot rise above its source, and if the Church by mere human wisdom corrected and perfected the Imperial law, its source must be higher than the sources of the world. This makes a heavy demand on our credulity.

Starting from St. Peter to Leo XIII., there have been some 258 Pontiffs claiming to be, and recognized by the whole Catholic unity as, successors of St. Peter and Vicars of Jesus Christ. To them has been rendered in every age not only the external obedience of outward submission, but the internal obedience of faith. They have borne the onset of the nations who destroyed Imperial Rome, and the tyranny of heretical Emperors of Byzantium; and, worse than this, the alternate despotism and patronage of the Emperors of the West, and the substraction of obedience in the great Western schisms, when the unity of the Church and the authority of its Head were, as men thought, gone for ever. It was the last assault—the forlorn hope of the gates of hell. Every art of destruction had been tried: martyrdom, heresy, secularity, schism; at last, two, and three, and four claimants, or, as the world says, rival Popes, were set up, that men might believe that St. Peter had no longer a successor, and our Lord no Vicar, upon earth; for, though all might be illegitimate, only one could be the lawful and true Head of the Church. Was it only by the human power of man that the unity, external and internal, which for fourteen hundred years had been supreme, was once more restored in the Council of Constance, never to be broken again? The succession of the English monarchy has been, indeed, often broken, and always restored, in these thousand years. But here is a monarchy of eighteen hundred years, powerless in worldly force or support, claiming and receiving not only outward allegiance, but inward unity of intellect and will. If any man tell us that these two phenomena are on the same level of merely human causes, it is too severe a tax upon our natural reason to believe it.

But the inadequacy of human causes to account for the universality, unity, and immutability of the Catholic Church, will stand out more visibly if we look at the intellectual and moral revolution which Christianity has wrought in the world and upon mankind.

The first effect of Christianity was to fill the world with the true knowledge of the One True God, and to destroy utterly all idols, not by fire but by light. Before the Light of the world no false god and no polytheism could stand. The unity and spirituality of God swept away all theogonies and theologies of the first four thousand years. The stream of light which descended from the beginning expanded into a radiance, and the radiance into a flood, which illuminated all nations, as it had been foretold, "The earth is filled with the knowledge of the Lord, as the covering waters of the sea;" "And idols shall be utterly destroyed."[6] In

---

[6] Isaias, xi. 9-11, 18.

this true knowledge of the Divine Nature was revealed to men their own relation to a Creator as of sons to a father. The Greeks called the chief of the gods *Zeus Pater,* and the Latins *Jupiter;* but neither realized the dependence and love of sonship as revealed by the Founder of Christianity.

The monotheism of the world comes down from a primeval and Divine source. Polytheism is the corruption of men and of nations. Yet in the multiplicity of all polytheisms, one supreme Deity was always recognized. The Divine unity was imperishable. Polytheism is of human imagination: it is of men's manufacture. The deification of nature and passions and heroes had filled the world with an elaborate and tenacious superstition, surrounded by reverence, fear, religion, and awe. Every perversion of what is good in man surrounded it with authority; everything that is evil in man guarded it with jealous care. Against this world-wide and imperious demonology the science of one God, all holy and supreme, advanced with resistless force. Beelzebub is not divided against himself; and if polytheism is not Divine, monotheism must be. The overthrow of idolatry and demonology was the mastery of forces that are above nature. This conclusion is enough for our present purpose.

A second visible effect of Christianity of which nature cannot offer any adequate cause is to be found in the domestic life of the Christian world. In some nations the existence of marriage was not so much as recognized. In others, if recognized, it was dishonored by profuse concubinage. Even in Israel, the most advanced nation, the law of divorce was permitted for the hardness of their hearts. Christianity republished the primitive law by which marriage unites only one man and one woman indissolubly in a perpetual contract. It raised their mutual and perpetual contract to a sacrament. This at one blow condemned all other relations between man and woman, all the legal gradations of the Imperial law, and all forms and pleas of divorce. Beyond this the spiritual legislation of the Church framed most elaborate tables of consanguinity and affinity, prohibiting all marriages between persons in certain degrees of kinship or relation. This law has created the purity and peace of domestic life. Neither the Greek nor the Roman world had any true conception of a home. The *Eoria* or Vesta was a sacred tradition guarded by vestals like a temple worship. It was not a law and a power in the homes of the people. Christianity, by enlarging the circles of prohibition within which men and women were as brothers and sisters, has created the home with all its purities and safeguards.

Such a law of unity and indissolubility, encompassed by a multitude of prohibitions, no mere human legislation could impose on the passions and will of mankind. And yet the Imperial laws gradually yielded to its resistless pressure, and incorporated it in its world-wide legislation. The passions and practices of four thousand years were against the change; yet it was accomplished, and it reigns inviolate to this day, though the relaxations of schism in the East and the laxities of the West have revived the abuse of divorces, and have partially abolished the wise and salutary prohibitions which guard the homes of the faithful. These relaxations prove that all natural forces have been, and are, hostile to the indissoluble law of Christian marriage. Certainly, then, it was not by natural forces that the Sacrament of Matrimony and the legislation springing from it were enacted. If these are restraints of human liberty and license, either they do not spring from nature, or they have had a supernatural cause whereby they exist. It was this that redeemed woman from the traditional degradation in which the world had held her. The condition of women in Athens and in Rome—which may be taken as the highest points of civilization—is too well known to need recital. Women had no rights, no property, no independence. Plato looked upon them as State property; Aristotle as chattels; the Greeks wrote of them as κύνεξ, γυναῖκεξ, καί τά ἀλλά κτή ματα.

They were the prey, the sport, the slaves of man. Even in Israel, though they were raised incomparably higher than in the Gentile world, they were far below the dignity and authority of Christian women. Libanius, the friend of Julian, the Apostate, said, "O ye gods of Greece, how great are the women of the Christians!" Whence came the elevation of womanhood? Not from the ancient civilization, for it degraded them; not from Israel, for among the Jews the highest state of womanhood was the marriage state. The daughter of Jepthe went into the mountains to mourn not her death but her virginity. The marriage state in the Christian world, though holy and good, is not the highest state. The state of virginity unto death is the highest condition of man and woman. But this is above the law of nature. It belongs to a higher order. And this life of virginity, in repression of natural passion and lawful instinct, is both above and against the tendencies of human nature. It begins in a mortification, and ends in a mastery, over the movements and ordinary laws of human nature. Who will ascribe this to natural causes? and, if so, why did it not appear in the first four thousand years? And when has it ever appeared except in a handful of vestal virgins, or in Oriental recluses, with what reality history shows? An exception proves a rule. No one will imagine that a life of chastity is impossible to nature; but the restriction is a repression of nature which individuals may acquire, but the multitude have never attained. A religion which imposes chastity on the unmarried, and upon its priesthood, and upon the multitudes of women in every age who devote themselves to the service of One Whom they have never seen, is a mortification of nature in so high a degree as to stand out as a fact and a phenomenon, of which mere natural causes afford no adequate solution. Its existence, not in a handful out of the millions of the world, but its prevalence and continuity in multitudes scattered throughout the Christian world, proves the presence of a cause higher than the laws of nature. So true is this, that jurists teach that the three vows of chastity, poverty, and obedience are contrary to "the policy of the law," that is, to the interests of the commonwealth, which desires the multiplication, enrichment, and liberty of its members.

To what has been said may be added the change wrought by Christianity upon the social, political, and international relations of the world. The root of this ethical change, private and public, is the Christian home. The authority of parents, the obedience of children, the love of brotherhood, are the three active powers which have raised the society of man above the level of the old world. Israel was head and shoulders above the world around it; but Christendom is high above

Israel. The new Commandment of brotherly love, and the Sermon on the Mount, have wrought a revolution, both in private and public life. From this come the laws of justice and sympathy which bind together the nations of the Christian world. In the old world, even the most refined races, worshiped by our modern philosophers, held and taught that man could hold property in man. In its chief cities there were more slaves than free men. Who has taught the equality of men before the law, and extinguished the impious thought that man can hold property in man? It was no philosopher: even Aristotle taught that a slave was ὄργανον ζῷον. It was no lawgiver, for all taught the lawfulness of slavery till Christianity denied it. The Christian law has taught that man can lawfully sell his labor, but that he cannot lawfully be sold, or sell himself.

The necessity of being brief, the impossibility of drawing out the picture of the old world, its profound immoralities, its unimaginable cruelties, compels me to argue with my right hand tied behind me. I can do no more than point again to Mr. Brace's "Gesta Christi," or to Dr. Dollinger's "Gentile and Jew," as witnesses to the facts which I have stated or implied. No one who has not read such books, or mastered their contents by original study, can judge of the force of the assertion that Christianity has reformed the world by direct antagonism to the human will, and by a searching and firm repression of human passion. It has ascended the stream of human license, *contra ictum fluminis,* by a power mightier than nature, and by laws of a higher order than the relaxations of this world.

Before Christianity came on earth, the civilization of man by merely natural force had culminated. It could not rise above its source; all that it could do was done; and the civilization in every race and empire had ended in decline and corruption. The old civilization was not regenerated. It passed away to give place to a new. But the new had a higher source, nobler laws and supernatural powers. The highest excellence of men and of nations is the civilization of Christianity. The human race has ascended into what we call Christendom, that is, into the new creation of charity and justice among men. Christendom was created by the worldwide Church as we see it before our eyes at this day. Philosophers and statesmen believe it to be the work of their own hands: they did not make it; but they have for three hundred years been unmaking it by reformations and revolutions. These are destructive forces. They build up nothing. It has been well said by Donoso Cortez that "the history of civilization is the history of Christianity, the history of Christianity is the history of the Church, the history of the Church is the history of the Pontiffs, the greatest statesmen and rulers that the world has ever seen."

Some years ago, a Professor of great literary reputation in England, who was supposed even then to be, as his subsequent writings have proved, a skeptic or non-Christian, published a well-known and very candid book, under the title of "Ecce Homo." The writer placed himself, as it were, outside of Christianity. He took, not the Church in the world as in this article, but the Christian Scriptures as a historical record, to be judged with forensic severity and absolute impartiality of mind. To the credit of the author, he fulfilled this pledge; and his conclusion shall here be given. After an examination of the life and character of the Author of Christianity, he proceeded to estimate His teaching and its effects under the following heads:

1. The Christian Legislation.
2. The Christian Republic.
3. Its Universality.
4. The Enthusiasm of Humanity.
5. The Lord's Supper.
6. Positive Morality.
7. Philanthropy.
8. Edification.
9. Mercy.
10. Resentment.
11. Forgiveness.

He then draws his conclusion as follows:

"The achievement of Christ in founding by his single will and power a structure so durable and so universal is like no other achievement which history records. The masterpieces of the men of action are coarse and commonplace in comparison with it, and the masterpieces of speculation flimsy and unsubstantial. When we speak of it the commonplaces of admiration fail us altogether. Shall we speak of the originality of the design, of the skill displayed in the execution? All such terms are inadequate. Originality and contriving skill operate indeed, but, as it were, implicitly. The creative effort which produced that against which it is said the gates of hell shall not prevail cannot be analyzed. No architect's designs were furnished for the New Jerusalem; no committee drew up rules for the universal commonwealth. If in the works of nature we can trace the indications of calculation, of a struggle with difficulties, of precaution, of ingenuity, then in Christ's work it may be that the same indications occur. But these inferior and secondary powers were not consciously exercised; they were implicitly present in the manifold yet single creative act. The inconceivable work was done in calmness; before the eyes of mea it was noiselessly accomplished, attracting little attention. Who can describe that which unites men? Who has entered into the formation of speech, which is the symbol of their union? Who can describe exhaustively the origin of civil society? He who can do these things can explain the origin of the Christian Church. For others it must be enough to say, 'The Holy Ghost fell on those that believed'. No man saw the building of the New Jerusalem, the workmen crowded together, the unfinished walls and unpaved streets; no man heard the clink of trowel and pickaxe: 'it descended out of heaven from God.' "[7]

And yet the writer is, as he was then, still outside of Christianity.

---

[7] "Ece Homo," Conclusion, p. 329, Fifth Edition. Macmillan, 1886.

III. We come now to our third point, that Christianity has always claimed a Divine origin and a Divine presence as the source of its authority and powers.

To prove this by texts from the New Testament would be to transcribe the volume; and if the evidence of the whole New Testament were put in, not only might some men deny its weight as evidence, but we should place our whole argument upon a false foundation. Christianity was anterior to the New Testament and is independent of it. The Christian Scriptures presuppose both the faith and the Church as already existing, known, and believed. *Prior liber quam stylus:* as Tertullian argued. The Gospel was preached before it was written. The four books were written to those who already believed, to confirm their faith. They were written at intervals: St. Matthew in Hebrew in the year 39, in Greek in 45. St. Mark in 43, St. Luke in 57, St. John about 90, in different places and for different motives. Four Gospels did not exist for sixty years, or two generations of men. St. Peter and St. Paul knew of only three of our four. In those sixty years the faith had spread from east to west. Saints and Martyrs had gone up to their crown who never saw a sacred book. The Apostolic Epistles prove the antecedent existence of the Churches to which they were addressed. Rome and Corinth, and Galatia and Ephesus, Philippi and Colossae, were Churches with pastors and people before St. Paul wrote to them. The Church had already attested and executed its Divine legation before the New Testament existed; and when all its books were written they were not as yet collected into a volume. The earliest collection was about the beginning of the second century, and in the custody of the Church in Rome. We must, therefore, seek to know what was and is Christianity before and outside of the written books; and we have the same evidence for the oral tradition of the faith as we have for the New Testament itself. Both alike were in the custody of the Church; both are delivered to us by the same witness and on the same evidence. To reject either, is logically to reject both. Happily men are not saved by logic, but by faith. The millions of men in all ages have believed by inheritance of truth divinely guarded and delivered to them. They have no need of logical analysis. They have believed from their childhood. Neither children nor those who *infantibus aequiparantur* are logicians. It is the penance of the doubter and the unbeliever to regain by toil his lost inheritance. It is a hard penance, like the suffering of those who eternally debate on "predestination, freewill, fate."

Between the death of St. John and the mature lifetime of St. Irenaeus fifty years elapsed. St. Polycarp was disciple of St. John. St. Irenaeus was disciple of St. Polycarp. The mind of St. John and the mind of St. Irenaeus had only one intermediate intelligence, in contact with each. It would be an affectation of minute criticism to treat the doctrine of St. Irenaeus as a departure from the doctrine of St. Polycarp, or the doctrine of St. Polycarp as a departure from the doctrine of St. John. Moreover, St. John ruled the Church at Ephesus, and St. Irenaeus was born in Asia Minor about the year A. D. 120—that is, twenty years after St. John's death, when the Church in Asia Minor was still full of the light of his teaching and of the accents of his voice. Let us see how St. Irenaeus describes the faith and the Church. In his work against

Heresies, in Book iii. chap. i., he says, "We have known the way of our salvation by those through whom the Gospel came to us; which, indeed, they then preached, but afterwards, by the will of God, delivered to us in Scriptures, the future foundation and pillar of our faith. It is not lawful to say that they preached before they had perfect knowledge, as some dare to affirm, boasting themselves to be correctors of the Apostles. For after our Lord rose from the dead, and when they had been clothed with the power of the Holy Ghost, Who came upon them from on high, they were filled with all truths, and had knowledge which was perfect." In chapter ii. he adds that, "When they are refuted out of Scripture, they turn and accuse the Scriptures as erroneous, unauthoritative, and of various readings, so that the truth cannot be found by those who do not know tradition"—that is, their own. "But when we challenge them to come to the tradition of the Apostles, which is in custody of the succession of Presbyters in the Church, they turn against tradition, saying that they are not only wiser than the Presbyters, but even the Apostles, and have found the truth." "It therefore comes to pass that they will not agree either with the Scriptures or with tradition." (Ibid. c. iii.) "Therefore, all who desire to know the truth ought to look to the tradition of the Apostles, which is manifest in all the world and in all the Church. We are able to count up the Bishops who were instituted in the Church by the Apostles, and their successors to our day. They never taught nor knew such things as these men madly assert." "But as it would be too long in such a book as this to enumerate the successions of all the Churches, we point to the tradition of the greatest, most ancient Church, known to all, founded and constituted in Rome by the two glorious Apostles Peter and Paul, and to the faith announced to all men, coming down to us by the succession of Bishops, thereby confounding all those who, in any way, by self-pleasing, or vainglory, or blindness, or an evil mind, teach as they ought not. For with this Church, by reason of its greater principality, it is necessary that all churches should agree; that is, the faithful, wheresoever they be, for in that Church the tradition of the Apostles has been preserved." No comment need be made on the words the "greater principality," which have been perverted by every anti-Catholic writer from the time they were written to this day. But if any one will compare them with the words of St. Paul to the Colossians (chap. i. 18), describing the primacy of the Head of the Church in heaven, it will appear almost certain that the original Greek of St. Irenaeus, which is unfortunately lost, contained either τά πρωτεία, or some inflection of πρωτεύ ω which signifies primacy. However this may be, St. Irenaeus goes on: "The blessed Apostles, having founded and instructed the Church, gave in charge the Episcopate, for the administration of the same, to Linus. Of this Linus, Paul, in his Epistle to Timothy, makes mention. To him succeeded Anacletus, and after him, in the third place from the Apostles, Clement received the Episcopate, he who saw the Apostles themselves and conferred with them, while as yet he had the preaching of the Apostles in his ears and the tradition before his eyes; and not he only, but many who had been taught by the Apostles still survived. In the time of this Clement, when no little dissension had arisen among the brethren in

Corinth, the Church in Rome wrote very powerful letters *potentissimas litteras* to the Corinthians, recalling them to peace, restoring their faith, and declaring the tradition which it had so short a time ago received from the Apostles." These letters of St. Clement are well known, but have lately become more valuable and complete by the discovery of fragments published in a new edition by Light-foot. In these fragments there is a tone of authority fully explaining the words of St. Irenaeus. He then traces the succession of the Bishops of Rome to his own day, and adds: "This demonstration is complete to show that it is one and the same life-giving faith which has been preserved in the Church from the Apostles until now, and is handed on in truth." "Polycarp was not only taught by the Apostles, and conversed with many of those who had seen our Lord, but he also was constituted by the Apostles in Asia to be Bishop in the Church of Smyrna. We also saw him in our early youth, for he lived long, and when very old departed from this life most gloriously and nobly by martyrdom. He ever taught that what he had learned from the Apostles, and what the Church had delivered, those things only are true." In the fourth chapter, St. Irenaeus goes on to say: "Since, then, there are such proofs (of the faith), the truth is no longer to be sought for among others, which it is easy to receive from the Church, forasmuch as the Apostles laid up all truth in fullness in a rich depository, that all who will may receive from it the water of life." "But what if the Apostles had not left us the Scriptures: ought we not to follow the order of tradition, which they gave in charge to them to whom they entrusted the Churches? To which order (of tradition) many barbarous nations yield assent, who believe in Christ without paper and ink, having salvation written by the Spirit in their hearts, and diligently holding the ancient tradition." In the twenty-sixth chapter of the same book he says: "Therefore, it is our duty to obey the Presbyters who are in the Church, who have succession from the Apostles, as we have already shown; who also with the succession of the Episcopate have the *charisma veritatis certum,"* the spiritual and certain gift of truth.

I have quoted these passages at length, not so much as proofs of the Catholic Faith as to show the identity of the Church at its outset with the Church before our eyes at this hour, proving that the acorn has grown up into its oak, or, if you will, the identity of the Church at this hour with the Church of the Apostolic mission. These passages show the Episcopate, its central principality, its succession, its custody of the faith, its subsequent reception and guardianship of the Scriptures, Its Divine tradition, and the *charisma* or Divine assistance by which its perpetuity is secured in the succession of the Apostles. This is almost verbally, after eighteen hundred years, the decree of the Vatican Council: *Veritatis et fidei nunquam deficientis charisma.*[8]

But St. Irenaeus draws out in full the Church of this day. He shows the parallel of the first creation and of the second; of the first Adam and the Second; and of the analogy between the Incarnation or natural body, and the Church or mystical body of Christ. He says:

---

[8] "Const. Dogmatica Prima de Ecclesia Christi," cap. iv.

Our faith "we received from the Church, and guard. . . . as an excellent gift in a noble vessel, always full of youth, and making youthful the vessel itself in which it is. For this gift of God is entrusted to the Church, as the breath of life (was imparted) to the first man, so this end, that all the members partaking of it might be quickened with life. And thus the communication of Christ is imparted; that is, the Holy Ghost, the earnest of incorruption, the confirmation of the faith, the way of ascent to God. For in the Church (St. Paul says) God placed Apostles, Prophets, Doctors, and all other operations of the Spirit, of which none are partakers who do not come to the Church, thereby depriving themselves of life by a perverse mind and worse deeds. For where the Church is, there is also the Spirit of God; and where the Spirit of God is, there is the Church, and all grace. But the Spirit is truth. Wherefore, they who do not partake of Him (the Spirit), and are not nurtured unto life at the breast of the mother (the Church), do not receive of that most pure fountain which proceeds from the Body of Christ, but dig out for themselves broken pools from the trenches of the earth, and drink water soiled with mire, because they turn aside from the faith of the Church lest they should be convicted, and reject the Spirit lest they should be taught."[9] Again he says: "The Church, scattered throughout the world, even unto the ends of the earth, received from the Apostles and their disciples the faith in one God the Father Almighty, that made the heaven and the earth, and the seas, and all things that are in them." etc.[10]

He then recites the doctrines of the Holy Trinity, the Incarnation, the Passion, Resurrection, and Ascension of our Lord Jesus Christ, and His coming again to raise all men, to judge men and angels, and to give sentence of condemnation or of life everlasting. How much soever the language may vary from other forms, such is the substance of the Baptismal Creed. He then adds:

"The Church having received this preaching and this faith, as we have said before, although it be scattered abroad through the whole world, carefully preserves it, dwelling as in one habitation, and believes alike in these (doctrines) as though she had one soul and the same heart: and in strict accord, as though she had one mouth, proclaims, and teaches, and delivers onward these things. And although there may be many diverse languages in the world, yet the power of the tradition is one and the same. And neither do the Churches planted in Germany believe otherwise, or otherwise deliver (the faith), nor those in Iberia, nor among the Celtae, nor in the East, nor in Egypt, nor in Libya, nor they that are planted in the mainland. But as the sun, which is God's creature, in all the world is one and the same, so also the preaching of the truth shineth everywhere, and lightened all men that are willing to come to the knowledge of the truth. And neither will any ruler of the Church, though he be mighty in the utterance of truth, teach otherwise than thus (for no man is above the master), nor will he that is weak in the same diminish from the tradition; for the faith being one and the same, he that is able

---

[9] St. Irenaeus, Cont. Haeret lib. iii. cap. xxiv.
[10] Lib. i. cap. x.

to say most of it hath nothing over, and he that is able to say least hath no lack."[11]

To St. Irenaeus, then, the Church was "the irrefragable witness of its own legation." When did it cease so to be? It would be easy to multiply quotations from Tertullian in A. D. 200, from St. Cyprian a. d. 250, from St. Augustine and St. Optatus in A. d. 350, from St. Leo in a. d. 450, all of which are on the same traditional lines of faith in a divine mission to the world and of a divine assistance in its discharge. But I refrain from doing so because I should have to write not an article but a folio. Any Catholic theology will give the passages which are now before me; or one such book as the *Loci Theologici* of Melchior Canus will suffice to show the continuity and identity of the tradition of St. Irenaeus and the tradition of the Vatican Council, in which the universal church last declared the immutable faith and its own legation to mankind.

The world-wide testimony of the Catholic Church is a sufficient witness to prove the coming of the Incarnate Son to redeem mankind, and to return to His Father; it is also sufficient to prove the advent of the Holy Ghost to abide with us for ever. The work of the Son in this world was accomplished by the Divine acts and facts of His three-and-thirty years of life, death, Resurrection, and Ascension. The office of the Holy Ghost is perpetual, not only as the Illuminator and Sanctifier of all who believe, but also as the Life and Guide of the Church. I may quote now the words of the Founder of the Church: "It is expedient to you that I go: for if I go not, the Paraclete will not come to you; but if I go, I will send Him to you."[12] "I will ask the Father, and He shall give you another Paraclete, that He may abide with you for ever."[13] "The Spirit of Truth, Whom the world cannot receive, because it seeth Him not nor knoweth Him; but you shall know Him, because He shall abide with you and shall be in you."[14]

St. Paul in the Epistles to the Ephesians describes the Church as a body of which the Head is in heaven, and the Author of its indefectible life abiding in it as His temple. Therefore the words, "He that heareth you heareth Me." This could not be if the witness of the Apostles had been only human. A Divine guidance was attached to the office they bore. They were, therefore, also judges of right and wrong, and teachers by Divine guidance of the truth. But the presence and guidance of the Spirit of Truth is as full at this day as when St. Irenaeus wrote. As the Churches then were witnesses, judges, and teachers, so is the Church at this hour a world-wide witness, an unerring judge and teacher, divinely guided and guarded in the truth. It is therefore not only a human and historical, but a Divine witness. This is the chief Divine truth which the last three hundred years have obscured. Modern Christianity believes in the one advent of the Redeemer, but rejects the full and personal advent of the Holy Ghost. And yet the same evidence

---

[11] St. Irenaeus, lib. i. c. x.

[12] St. John, xvi. 7.

[13] Ibid, xiv. 16.

[14] St. John, xiv. 16, 17.

proves both. The Christianity of reformers, always returns to Judaism, because they reject the full, or do not believe the personal, advent of the Holy Ghost. They deny that there is an infallible teacher, among men; and therefore they return to the types and shadows of the Law before the Incarnation, when the Head was not yet incarnate, and the Body of Christ did not as yet exist.

But perhaps some one will say, "I admit your description of the Church as it is now and as it was in the days of St. Irenaeus; but the eighteen hundred years of which you have said nothing were ages of declension, disorder, superstition, demoralization." I will answer by a question: was not this foretold? Was not the Church to be a field of wheat and tares growing together till the harvest at the end of the world? There were Cathari of old, and Puritans since, impatient at the patience of God in bearing with the perversities and corruptions of the human intellect and will. The Church, like its Head in heaven, is both human and divine. "He was crucified in weakness," but no power of man could wound His divine nature. So with the Church, which is His Body. Its human element may corrupt and die; its divine life, sanctity, authority, and structure cannot die; nor can the errors of human intellect fasten upon its faith, nor the immoralities of the human will fasten upon its sanctity. Its organization of Head and Body is of divine creation, divinely guarded by the Holy Ghost, who quickens it by His indwelling, and guides it by His light. It is in itself incorrupt and incorruptible in the midst of corruption, as the light of heaven falls upon all the decay and corruption in the world, unsullied and unalterably pure. We are never concerned to deny or to cloak the sins of Christians or of Catholics. They may destroy themselves, but they cannot infect the Church from which they fall. The fall of Lucifer left no stain behind him.

When men accuse the Church of corruption, they reveal the fact that to them the Church is a human institution, of voluntary aggregation or of legislative enactment. They reveal the fact that to them the Church is not an object of Divine faith, as the Real Presence in the Sacrament of the Altar. They do not perceive or will not believe that the articles of the Baptismal Creed are objects of faith, divinely revealed or divinely created. "I believe in the Holy Ghost, the Holy Catholic Church, the Communion of Saints, the forgiveness of sins," are all objects of faith in a Divine order. They are present in human history, but the human element which envelops them has no power to infect or to fasten upon them. Until this is perceived there can be no true or full belief in the advent and office of the Holy Ghost, or in the nature and sacramental action of the Church. It is the visible means and pledge of light and of sanctification to all who do not bar their intellect and their will against its inward and spiritual grace. The Church is not on probation. It is the instrument of probation to the world. As the light of the world, it is changeless as the firmament As the source of sanctification, it is inexhaustible as the River of Life. The human and external history of men calling themselves Christian and Catholic has been at times as degrading and abominable as any adversary is pleased to say. But the sanctity of the Church is no more affected by human sins than was Baptism by the hypocrisy of Simon Magus. The Divine foundation, and office, and mission of the Church is a part of Christianity. They who deny it deny an article of faith; they who believe it imperfectly are the followers of a fragmentary Christianity of modern date. Who can be a disciple of Jesus Christ who does not believe the words? "On this rock I will build My Church, and the gates of hell shall not prevail against it;" "As the Father hath sent Me, I also send you;"[15] "I dispose to you, as My Father hath disposed to Me, a kingdom;"[16] "All power in heaven and earth is given unto Me. Go, therefore, and teach all nations;"[17] "He that heareth you heareth Me;"[18] "I will be with you always, even unto the end of the world;"[19] "When the days of Pentecost were accomplished they were all together in one place: and suddenly there came a sound from heaven as of a mighty wind coming, and there appeared to them parted tongues, as it were, of fire;" "And they were all filled with the Holy Ghost;"[20] "It seemed good to the Holy Ghost and to us to lay upon you no other burdens."(vii)[21] But who denies that the Apostles claimed a Divine mission? and who can deny that the Catholic and Roman Church from St. Irenaeus to Leo XIII. has ever and openly claimed the same, invoking in all its supreme acts as witness, teacher, and legislator the presence, light, and guidance of the Holy Ghost? As the preservation of all created things is by the same creative power produced in perpetual and universal action, so the indefectibility of the Church and of the faith is by the perpetuity of the presence and office of the Third Person of the Holy Trinity. Therefore, St. Augustine calls the day of Pentecost, *Natalis Spiritus Sancti.*

It is more than time that I should make an end; and to do so it will be well to sum up the heads of our argument. The Vatican Council declares that the world-wide Church is the irrefragable witness of its own legation or mission to mankind.

In proof of this I have affirmed:

1. That the imperishable existence of Christianity, and the vast and undeniable revolution that it has wrought in men and in nations, in the moral elevation of manhood and of womanhood, and in the domestic, social and political life of the Christian world, cannot be accounted for by any natural causes, or by any forces that are, as philosophers say, *intra possibilitatem naturae,* within the limits of what is possible to man.

2. That this world-wide and permanent elevation of the Christian world, in comparison with both the old world and the modern world outside of Christianity, demands a cause higher than the possibility of nature.

3. That the Church has always claimed a Divine origin and a Divine office and authority in virtue of a perpetual Divine assistance. To this

---

[15] St. John, xx. 21.
[16] St. Luke, xxii. 29.
[17] St. Matthew, xxviii. 18, 19.
[18] St. Luke, x. 10.
[19] St. Matthew, xxviii. 20.
[20] Acts, ii. 1-5.
[21] Acts, xv. 28.

even the Christian world, in all its fragments external to the Catholic unity, bears witness. It is turned to our reproach. They rebuke us for holding the teaching of the Church to be infallible. We take the rebuke as a testimony of our changeless faith. It is not enough for men to say that they refuse to believe this account of the visible and palpable fact of the imperishable Christianity of the Catholic and Roman Church. They must find a more reasonable, credible, and adequate account for it. This no man has yet done. The denials are many and the solutions are many; but they do not agree together. Their multiplicity is proof of their human origin. The claim of the Catholic Church to a Divine authority and to a Divine assistance is one and the same in every age, and is identical in every place. Error is not the principle of unity, nor truth of variations.

The Church has guarded the doctrine of the Apostles, by Divine assistance, with unerring fidelity. The articles of the faith are to-day the same in number as in the beginning. The explicit definition of their implicit meaning has expanded from age to age, as the ever-changing denials and perversions of the world have demanded new definitions of the ancient truth. The world is against all dogma, because it is impatient of definiteness and certainty in faith. It loves open questions and the liberty of error. The Church is dogmatic for fear of error. Every truth defined adds to its treasure. It narrows the field of error and enlarges the inheritance of truth. The world and the Church are ever moving in opposite directions. As the world becomes more vague and uncertain, the Church becomes more definite. It moves against wind and tide, against the stress and storm of the world. There was never a more luminous evidence of this supernatural fact than in the Vatican Council. For eight months all that the world could say and do, like the four winds of heaven, was directed upon it. Governments, statesmen, diplomatists, philosophers, intriguers, mockers, and traitors did their utmost and their worst against it. They were in dread lest the Church should declare that by Divine assistance its Head in faith and morals cannot err; for if this be true, man did not found it, man cannot reform it, man cannot teach it to interpret its history or its acts. It knows its own history, and is the supreme witness of its own legation.

I am well aware that I have been writing truisms, and repeating trite and trivial arguments. They are trite because the feet of the faithful for nearly nineteen hundred years have worn them in their daily life; they are trivial because they point to the one path in which the wayfarer, though a fool, shall not err.

Henry Edward, (Cardinal Manning),
Card. Archbishop of Westminster.

ROME OR REASON:
A REPLY TO CARDINAL MANNING.

Superstition "has ears more deaf than adders to the voice of any true decision."

PART I.

Cardinal Manning has stated the claims of the Roman Catholic Church with great clearness, and apparently without reserve. The age, position and learning of this man give a certain weight to his words, apart from their worth. He represents the oldest of the Christian churches. The questions involved are among the most important that can engage the human mind. No one having the slightest regard for that superb thing known as intellectual honesty, will avoid the issues tendered, or seek in any way to gain a victory over truth.

Without candor, discussion, in the highest sense, is impossible. All have the same interest, whether they know it or not, in the establishment of facts. All have the same to gain, the same to lose. He loads the dice against himself who scores a point against the right.

Absolute honesty is to the intellectual perception what light is to the eyes. Prejudice and passion cloud the mind. In each disputant should be blended the advocate and judge.

In this spirit, having in view only the ascertainment of the truth, let us examine the arguments, or rather the statements and conclusions, of Cardinal Manning.

The proposition is that "The church itself, by its marvelous propagation, its eminent sanctity, its inexhaustible fruitfulness in all good things, its catholic unity and invincible stability, is a vast and perpetual motive of credibility, and an irrefragable witness of its own divine legation."

The reasons given as supporting this proposition are:

That the Catholic Church interpenetrates all the nations of the civilized world; that it is extranational and independent in a supernatural unity; that it is the same in every place; that it speaks all languages in the civilized world; that it is obedient to one head; that as many as seven hundred bishops have knelt before the pope; that pilgrims from all nations have brought gifts to Rome, and that all these things set forth in the most self-evident way the unity and universality of the Roman Church.

It is also asserted that "men see the Head of the Church year by year speaking to the nations of the world, treating with Empires, Republics and Governments;" that "there is no other man on earth that can so bear himself," and that "neither from Canterbury nor from Constantinople can such a voice go forth to which rulers and people listen."

It is also claimed that the Catholic Church has enlightened and purified the world; that it has given us the peace and purity of domestic life; that it has destroyed idolatry and demonology; that it gave us a body of law from a higher source than man; that it has produced the civilization of Christendom; that the popes were the greatest of statesmen and rulers; that celibacy is better than marriage, and that the revolutions and reformations of the last three hundred years have been destructive and calamitous.

We will examine these assertions as well as some others.

No one will dispute that the Catholic Church is the best witness of its own existence. The same is true of every thing that exists—of every church, great and small, of every man, and of every insect.

But it is contended that the marvelous growth or propagation of the church is evidence of its divine origin. Can it be said that success is supernatural? All success in this world is relative. Majorities are not necessarily right. If anything is known—if anything can be known—we are sure that very large bodies of men have frequently been wrong. We believe in what is called the progress of mankind. Progress, for the most part, consists in finding new truths and getting rid of old errors—that is to say, getting nearer and nearer in harmony with the facts of nature, seeing with greater clearness the conditions of well-being.

There is no nation in which a majority leads the way. In the progress of mankind, the few have been the nearest right. There have been centuries in which the light seemed to emanate only from a handful of men, while the rest of the world was enveloped in darkness. Some great man leads the way—he becomes the morning star, the prophet of a coming day. Afterward, many millions accept his views. But there are still heights above and beyond; there are other pioneers, and the old day, in comparison with the new, becomes a night. So, we cannot say that success demonstrates either divine origin or supernatural aid.

We know, if we know anything, that wisdom has often been trampled beneath the feet of the multitude. We know that the torch of science has been blown out by the breath of the hydra-headed. We know that the whole intellectual heaven has been darkened again and again. The truth or falsity of a proposition cannot be determined by ascertaining the number of those who assert, or of those who deny.

If the marvelous propagation of the Catholic Church proves its divine origin, what shall we say of the marvelous propagation of Mohammedanism?

Nothing can be clearer than that Christianity arose out of the ruins of the Roman Empire—that is to say, the ruins of Paganism. And it is equally clear that Mohammedanism arose out of the wreck and ruin of Catholicism.

After Mohammed came upon the stage, "Christianity was forever expelled from its most glorious seats—from Palestine, the scene of its most sacred recollections; from Asia Minor, that of its first churches; from Egypt, whence issued the great doctrine of Trinitarian Orthodoxy, and from Carthage, who imposed her belief on Europe." Before that time "the ecclesiastical chiefs of Rome, of Constantinople, and of Alexandria were engaged in a desperate struggle for supremacy, carrying out their purposes by weapons and in ways revolting to the conscience of man. Bishops were concerned in assassinations, poisonings, adulteries, blindings, riots, treasons, civil war. Patriarchs and primates were excommunicating and anathematizing one another in their rivalries for earthly power—bribing eunuchs with gold and courtesans and royal females with concessions of Episcopal love. Among legions of monks who carried terror into the imperial armies and riot into the great cities arose hideous clamors for theological dogmas, but never a voice for intellectual liberty or the outraged rights of man.

"Under these circumstances, amid these atrocities and crimes, Mohammed arose, and raised his own nation from Fetishism, the adoration of the meteoric stone, and from the basest idol worship, and irrevocably wrenched from Christianity more than half—and that by far the best half—of her possessions, since it included the Holy Land, the birth-place of the Christian faith, and Africa, which had imparted to it its Latin form; and now, after a lapse of more than a thousand years that continent, and a very large part of Asia, remain permanently attached to the Arabian doctrine."

It may be interesting in this connection to say that the Mohammedan now proves the divine mission of his apostle by appealing to the marvelous propagation of the faith. If the argument is good in the mouth of a Catholic, is it not good in the mouth of a Moslem? Let us see if it is not better.

According to Cardinal Manning, the Catholic Church triumphed only over the institutions of men—triumphed only over religions that had been established by men,—by wicked and ignorant men. But Mohammed triumphed not only over the religions of men, but over the religion of God. This ignorant driver of camels, this poor, unknown, unlettered boy, unassisted by God, unenlightened by supernatural means, drove the armies of the true cross before him as the winter's storm drives withered leaves. At his name, priests, bishops, and cardinals fled with white faces—popes trembled, and the armies of God, fighting for the true faith, were conquered on a thousand fields.

If the success of a church proves its divinity, and after that another church arises and defeats the first, what does that prove?

Let us put this question in a milder form: Suppose the second church lives and flourishes in spite of the first, what does that prove?

As a matter of fact, however, no church rises with everything against it. Something is favorable to it, or it could not exist. If it succeeds and grows, it is absolutely certain that the conditions are favorable. If it spreads rapidly, it simply shows that the conditions are exceedingly favorable, and that the forces in opposition are weak and easily overcome.

Here, in my own country, within a few years, has arisen a new religion. Its foundations were laid in an intelligent community, having had the advantages of what is known as modern civilization. Yet this new faith—founded on the grossest absurdities, as gross as we find in the Scriptures—in spite of all opposition began to grow, and kept growing. It was subjected to persecution, and the persecution increased its strength. It was driven from State to State by the believers in universal love, until it left what was called civilization, crossed the wide plains, and took up its abode on the shores of the Great Salt Lake. It continued to grow. Its founder, as he declared, had frequent conversations with God, and received directions from that source. Hundreds of miracles were performed—multitudes upon the desert were miraculously fed—the sick were cured—the dead were raised, and the Mormon Church continued to grow, until now, less than half a century after the death of its founder, there are several hundred thousand believers in the new faith.

Do you think that men enough could join this church to prove the truth of its creed?

Joseph Smith said that he found certain golden plates that had been buried for many generations, and upon these plates, in some unknown language, had been engraved this new revelation, and I think he insisted that by the use of miraculous mirrors this language was translated. If there should be Mormon bishops in all the countries of the world, eighteen hundred years from now, do you think a cardinal of that faith could prove the truth of the golden plates simply by the fact that the faith had spread and that seven hundred bishops had knelt before the head of that church?

It seems to me that a "supernatural" religion—that is to say, a religion that is claimed to have been divinely founded and to be authenticated by miracles, is much easier to establish among an ignorant people than any other—and the more ignorant the people, the easier such a religion could be established. The reason for this is plain. All ignorant tribes, all savage men, believe in the miraculous, in the supernatural. The conception of uniformity, of what may be called the eternal consistency of nature, is an idea far above their comprehension. They are forced to think in accordance with their minds, and as a consequence they account for all phenomena by the acts of superior beings—that is to say, by the supernatural. In other words, that religion having most in common with the savage, having most that was satisfactory to his mind, or to his lack of mind, would stand the best chance of success.

It is probably safe to say that at one time, or during one phase of the development of man, everything was miraculous. After a time, the mind slowly developing, certain phenomena, always happening under like conditions, were called "natural," and none suspected any special interference. The domain of the miraculous grew less and less—the domain of the natural larger; that is to say, the common became the natural, but the uncommon was still regarded as the miraculous. The rising and setting of the sun ceased to excite the wonder of mankind— there was no miracle about that; but an eclipse of the sun was miraculous. Men did not then know that eclipses are periodical, that they happen with the same certainty that the sun rises. It took many observations through many generations to arrive at this conclusion. Ordinary rains became "natural," floods remained "miraculous."

But it can all be summed up in this: The average man regards the common as natural, the uncommon as supernatural. The educated man—and by that I mean the developed man—is satisfied that all phenomena are natural, and that the supernatural does not and can not exist.

As a rule, an individual is egotistic in the proportion that he lacks intelligence. The same is true of nations and races. The barbarian is egotistic enough to suppose that an Infinite Being is constantly doing something, or failing to do something, on his account. But as man rises in the scale of civilization, as he becomes really great, he comes to the conclusion that nothing in Nature happens on his account—that he is hardly great enough to disturb the motions of the planets.

Let us make an application of this: To me, the success of Mormonism is no evidence of its truth, because it has succeeded only with the superstitious. It has been recruited from communities brutalized by other forms of superstition. To me, the success of Mohammed does not tend to show that he was right—for the reason that he triumphed only over the ignorant, over the superstitious. The same is true of the Catholic Church. Its seeds were planted in darkness. It was accepted by the credulous, by men incapable of reasoning upon such questions. It did not, it has not, it can not triumph over the intellectual world. To count its many millions does not tend to prove the truth of its creed. On the contrary, a creed that delights the credulous gives evidence against itself.

Questions of fact or philosophy cannot be settled simply by numbers. There was a time when the Copernican system of astronomy had but few supporters—the multitude being on the other side. There was a time when the rotation of the earth was not believed by the majority.

Let us press this idea further. There was a time when Christianity was not in the majority, anywhere. Let us suppose that the first Christian missionary had met a prelate of the Pagan faith, and suppose this prelate had used against the Christian missionary the Cardinal's argument—how could the missionary have answered if the Cardinal's argument is good?

But, after all, is the success of the Catholic Church a marvel? If this church is of divine origin, if it has been under the especial care, protection and guidance of an Infinite Being, is not its failure far more wonderful than its success? For eighteen centuries it has persecuted and preached, and the salvation of the world is still remote. This is the result, and it may be asked whether it is worth while to try to convert the world to Catholicism.

Are Catholics better than Protestants? Are they nearer honest, nearer just, more charitable? Are Catholic nations better than Protestant? Do the Catholic nations move in the van of progress? Within their jurisdiction are life, liberty and property safer than anywhere else? Is Spain the first nation of the world?

Let me ask another question: Are Catholics or Protestants better than Freethinkers? Has the Catholic Church produced a greater man than Humboldt? Has the Protestant produced a greater than Darwin? Was not Emerson, so far as purity of life is concerned, the equal of any true believer? Was Pius IX., or any other vicar of Christ, superior to Abraham Lincoln?

But it is claimed that the Catholic Church is universal, and that its universality demonstrates its divine origin.

According to the Bible, the apostles were ordered to go into all the world and preach the gospel—yet not one of them, nor one of their converts at any time, nor one of the vicars of God, for fifteen hundred years afterward, knew of the existence of the Western Hemisphere. During all that time, can it be said that the Catholic Church was universal? At the close of the fifteenth century, there was one-half of the world in which the Catholic faith had never been preached, and in the other half not one person in ten had ever heard of it, and of those who had heard of it, not one in ten believed it. Certainly the Catholic Church was not then universal.

Is it universal now? What impression has Catholicism made upon the many millions of China, of Japan, of India, of Africa? Can it truthfully be said that the Catholic Church is now universal? When any church becomes universal, it will be the only church. There cannot be two universal churches, neither can there be one universal church and any other.

The Cardinal next tries to prove that the Catholic Church is divine, "by its eminent sanctity and its inexhaustible fruitfulness in all good things."

And here let me admit that there are many millions of good Catholics— that is, of good men and women who are Catholics. It is unnecessary to charge universal dishonesty or hypocrisy, for the reason that this would be only a kind of personality. Many thousands of heroes have died in defense of the faith, and millions of Catholics have killed and been killed for the sake of their religion.

And here it may be well enough to say that martyrdom does not even tend to prove the truth of a religion. The man who dies in flames, standing by what he believes to be true, establishes, not the truth of what he believes, but his sincerity.

Without calling in question the intentions of the Catholic Church, we can ascertain whether it has been "inexhaustibly fruitful in all good things," and whether it has been "eminent for its sanctity."

In the first place, nothing can be better than goodness. Nothing is more sacred, or can be more sacred, than the wellbeing of man. All things that tend to increase or preserve the happiness of the human race are good—that is to say, they are sacred. All things that tend to the destruction of man's well-being, that tend to his unhappiness, are bad, no matter by whom they are taught or done.

It is perfectly certain that the Catholic Church has taught, and still teaches, that intellectual liberty is dangerous—that it should not be allowed. It was driven to take this position because it had taken another. It taught, and still teaches, that a certain belief is necessary to salvation. It has always known that investigation and inquiry led, or might lead, to doubt; that doubt leads, or may lead, to heresy, and that heresy leads to hell. In other words, the Catholic Church has something more important than this world, more important than the well-being of man here. It regards this life as an opportunity for joining that church, for accepting that creed, and for the saving of your soul.

If the Catholic Church is right in its premises, it is right in its conclusion. If it is necessary to believe the Catholic creed in order to obtain eternal joy, then, of course, nothing else in this world is, comparatively speaking, of the slightest importance. Consequently, the Catholic Church has been, and still is, the enemy of intellectual freedom, of investigation, of inquiry—in other words, the enemy of progress in secular things.

The result of this was an effort to compel all men to accept the belief necessary to salvation. This effort naturally divided itself into persuasion and persecution.

It will be admitted that the good man is kind, merciful, charitable, forgiving and just. A church must be judged by the same standard. Has the church been merciful? Has it been "fruitful in the good things" of justice, charity and forgiveness? Can a good man, believing a good doctrine, persecute for opinion's sake? If the church imprisons a man for the expression of an honest opinion, is it not certain, either that the doctrine of the church is wrong, or that the church is bad? Both cannot be good. "Sanctity" without goodness is impossible. Thousands of "saints" have been the most malicious of the human race. If the history of the world proves anything, it proves that the Catholic Church was for many centuries the most merciless institution that ever existed among men. I cannot believe that the instruments of persecution were made and used by the eminently good; neither can I believe that honest people were imprisoned, tortured, and burned at the stake by a church that was "inexhaustibly fruitful in all good things."

And let me say here that I have no Protestant prejudices against Catholicism, and have no Catholic prejudices against Protestantism. I regard all religions either without prejudice or with the same prejudice. They were all, according to my belief, devised by men, and all have for a foundation ignorance of this world and fear of the next. All the Gods have been made by men. They are all equally powerful and equally useless. I like some of them better than I do others, for the same reason that I admire some characters in fiction more than I do others. I prefer Miranda to Caliban, but have not the slightest idea that either of them existed. So I prefer Jupiter to Jehovah, although perfectly satisfied that both are myths. I believe myself to be in a frame of mind to justly and fairly consider the claims of different religions, believing as I do that all are wrong, and admitting as I do that there is some good in all.

When one speaks of the "inexhaustible fruitfulness in all good things" of the Catholic Church, we remember the horrors and atrocities of the Inquisition—the rewards offered by the Roman Church for the capture and murder of honest men. We remember the Dominican Order, the members of which, upheld by the vicar of Christ, pursued the heretics like sleuth hounds, through many centuries.

The church, "inexhaustible in fruitfulness in all good things," not only imprisoned and branded and burned the living, but violated the dead. It robbed graves, to the end that it might convict corpses of heresy—to the end that it might take from widows their portions and from orphans their patrimony.

We remember the millions in the darkness of dungeons—the millions who perished by the sword—the vast multitudes destroyed in flames—those who were flayed alive—those who were blinded—those whose tongues were cut out—those into whose ears were poured molten lead—those whose eyes were deprived of their lids—those who were tortured and tormented in every way by which pain could be inflicted and human nature overcome.

And we remember, too, the exultant cry of the church over the bodies of her victims: "Their bodies were burned here, but their souls are now tortured in hell."

We remember that the church, by treachery, bribery, perjury, and the commission of every possible crime, got possession and control of Christendom, and we know the use that was made of this power—that it was used to brutalize, degrade, stupefy, and "sanctify" the children of men. We know also that the vicars of Christ were persecutors for opinion's sake—that they sought to destroy the liberty of thought through fear—that they endeavored to make every brain a Bastille in which the mind should be a convict—that they endeavored to make every tongue a prisoner, watched by a familiar of the Inquisition—and that they threatened punishment here, imprisonment here, burnings here, and, in the name of their God, eternal imprisonment and eternal burnings hereafter.

We know, too, that the Catholic Church was, during all the years of its power, the enemy of every science. It preferred magic to medicine, relics to remedies, priests to physicians. It thought more of astrologers than of astronomers. It hated geologists—it persecuted the chemist, and imprisoned the naturalist, and opposed every discovery calculated to improve the condition of mankind.

It is impossible to forget the persecutions of the Cathari, the Albigenses, the Waldenses, the Hussites, the Huguenots, and of every sect that had the courage to think just a little for itself. Think of a woman—the mother of a family—taken from her children and burned, on account of her view as to the three natures of Jesus Christ. Think of the Catholic Church,—an institution with a Divine Founder, presided over by the agent of God—punishing a woman for giving a cup of cold water to a fellow-being who had been anathematized. Think of this church, "fruitful in all good things," launching its curse at an honest man—not only cursing him from the crown of his head to the soles of his feet with a fiendish particularity, but having at the same time the impudence to call on God, and the Holy Ghost, and Jesus Christ, and the Virgin Mary, to join in the curse; and to curse him not only here, but forever hereafter—calling upon all the saints and upon all the redeemed to join in a hallelujah of curses, so that earth and heaven should reverberate with countless curses launched at a human being simply for having expressed an honest thought.

This church, so "fruitful in all good things," invented crimes that it might punish. This church tried men for a "suspicion of heresy"—imprisoned them for the vice of being suspected—stripped them of all they had on earth and allowed them to rot in dungeons, because they were guilty of the crime of having been suspected. This was a part of the Canon Law.

It is too late to talk about the "invincible stability" of the Catholic Church.

It was not invincible in the seventh, in the eighth, or in the ninth centuries. It was not invincible in Germany in Luther's day. It was not invincible in the Low Countries. It was not invincible in Scotland, or in England. It was not invincible in France. It is not invincible in Italy, It is not supreme in any intellectual centre of the world. It does not triumph in Paris, or Berlin; it is not dominant in London, in England; neither is it triumphant in the United States. It has not within its fold the philosophers, the statesmen, and the thinkers, who are the leaders of the human race.

It is claimed that Catholicism "interpenetrates all the nations of the civilized world," and that "in some it holds the whole nation in its unity."

I suppose the Catholic Church is more powerful in Spain than in any other nation. The history of this nation demonstrates the result of Catholic supremacy, the result of an acknowledgment by a people that a certain religion is too sacred to be examined.

Without attempting in an article of this character to point out the many causes that contributed to the adoption of Catholicism by the Spanish people, it is enough to say that Spain, of all nations, has been and is the most thoroughly Catholic, and the most thoroughly interpenetrated and dominated by the spirit of the Church of Rome.

Spain used the sword of the church. In the name of religion it endeavored to conquer the Infidel world. It drove from its territory the Moors, not because they were bad, not because they were idle and dishonest, but because they were Infidels. It expelled the Jews, not because they were ignorant or vicious, but because they were unbelievers. It drove out the Moriscoes, and deliberately made outcasts of the intelligent, the industrious, the honest and the useful, because they were not Catholics. It leaped like a wild beast upon the Low Countries, for the destruction of Protestantism. It covered the seas with its fleets, to destroy the intellectual liberty of man. And not only so—it established the Inquisition within its borders. It imprisoned the honest, it burned the noble, and succeeded after many years of devotion to the true faith, in destroying the industry, the intelligence, the usefulness, the genius, the nobility and the wealth of a nation. It became a wreck, a jest of the conquered, and excited the pity of its former victims.

In this period of degradation, the Catholic Church held "the whole nation in its unity."

At last Spain began to deviate from the path of the church It made a treaty with an Infidel power. In 1782 it became humble enough, and wise enough, to be friends with Turkey. It made treaties with Tripoli and Algiers and the Barbary States. It had become too poor to ransom the prisoners taken by these powers. It began to appreciate the fact that it could neither conquer nor convert the world by the sword.

Spain has progressed in the arts and sciences, in all that tends to enrich and ennoble a nation, in the precise proportion that she has lost faith in the Catholic Church. This may be said of every other nation in Christendom. Torquemada is dead; Castelar is alive. The dungeons of the Inquisition are empty, and a little light has penetrated the clouds and mists—not much, but a little. Spain is not yet clothed and in her right mind. A few years ago the cholera visited Madrid and other cities. Physicians were mobbed. Processions of saints carried the host through the streets for the purpose of staying the plague. The streets were not cleaned; the sewers were filled. Filth and faith, old partners, reigned supreme. The church, "eminent for its sanctity," stood in the light and cast its shadow on the ignorant and the prostrate. The church, in its "inexhaustible fruitfulness in all good things," allowed its children to perish through ignorance, and used the diseases it had produced as an instrumentality to further enslave its votaries and its victims.

No one will deny that many of its priests exhibited heroism of the highest order in visiting the sick and administering what are called the consolations of religion to the dying, and in burying the dead. It is necessary neither to deny or disparage the self-denial and goodness of these men. But their religion did more than all other causes to produce the very evils that called for the exhibition of self-denial and heroism. One scientist in control of Madrid could have prevented the plague. In such cases, cleanliness is far better than "godliness;" science is superior to superstition; drainage much better than divinity; therapeutics more excellent than theology. Goodness is not enough—intelligence is necessary. Faith is not sufficient, creeds are helpless, and prayers fruitless.

It is admitted that the Catholic Church exists in many nations; that it is dominated, at least in a great degree, by the Bishop of Rome—that it is international in that sense, and that in that sense it has what may be called a "supernational unity." The same, however, is true of the Masonic fraternity. It exists in many nations, but it is not a national body. It is in the same sense extranational, in the same sense international, and has in the same sense a supernational unity. So the same may be said of other societies. This, however, does not tend to prove that anything supernational is supernatural.

It is also admitted that in faith, worship, ceremonial, discipline and government, the Catholic Church is substantially the same wherever it exists. This establishes the unity, but not the divinity, of the institution. The church that does not allow investigation, that teaches that all doubts are wicked, attains unity through tyranny, that is, monotony by repression. Wherever man has had something like freedom, differences have appeared, heresies have taken root, and the divisions have become permanent—new sects have been born and the Catholic Church has been weakened. The boast of unity is the confession of tyranny.

It is insisted that the unity of the church substantiates its claim to divine origin. This is asserted over and over again, in many ways; and yet in the Cardinal's article is found this strange mingling of boast and confession: "Was it only by the human power of man that the unity, external and internal, which for fourteen hundred years had been supreme, was once more restored in the Council of Constance, never to be broken again?"

By this it is admitted that the internal and external unity of the Catholic Church had been broken, and that it required more than human power to restore it. Then the boast is made that it will never be broken again. Yet it is asserted that the internal and external unity of the Catholic Church is the great fact that demonstrates its divine origin.

Now, if this internal and external unity was broken, and remained broken for years, there was an interval during which the church had no internal or external unity, and during which the evidence of divine origin failed. The unity was broken in spite of the Divine Founder. This is admitted by the use of the word "again." The unbroken unity of the church is asserted, and upon this assertion is based the claim of divine origin; it is then admitted that the unity was broken. The argument is then shifted, and the claim is made that it required more than human power to restore the internal and external unity of the church, and that the restoration, not the unity, is proof of the divine origin. Is there any contradiction beyond this?

Let us state the case in another way. Let us suppose that a man has a sword which he claims was made by God, stating that the reason he knows that God made the sword is that it never had been and never could be broken. Now, if it was afterwards ascertained that it had been broken, and the owner admitted that it had been, what would be thought of him if he then took the ground that it had been welded, and that the welding was the evidence that it was of divine origin?

A prophecy is then indulged in, to the effect that the internal and external unity of the church can never be broken again. It is admitted that it was broken—it is asserted that it was divinely restored—and then it is declared that it is never to be broken again. No reason is given for this prophecy; it must be born of the facts already stated. Put in a form to be easily understood, it is this:

We know that the unity of the church can never be broken, because the church is of divine origin.

We know that it was broken; but this does not weaken the argument, because it was restored by God, and it has not been broken since.

Therefore, it never can be broken again.

It is stated that the Catholic Church is immutable, and that its immutability establishes its claim to divine origin. Was it immutable when its unity, internal and external, was broken? Was it precisely the same after its unity was broken that it was before? Was it precisely the same after its unity was divinely restored that it was while broken? Was it universal while it was without unity? Which of the fragments was universal—which was immutable?

The fact that the Catholic Church is obedient to the pope, establishes, not the supernatural origin of the church, but the mental slavery of its members. It establishes the fact that it is a successful organization; that it is cunningly devised; that it destroys the mental independence, and that whoever absolutely submits to its authority loses the jewel of his soul.

The fact that Catholics are to a great extent obedient to the pope, establishes nothing except the thoroughness of the organization.

How was the Roman empire formed? By what means did that Great Power hold in bondage the then known world? How is it that a despotism is established? How is it that the few enslave the many? How is it that the nobility live on the labor of peasants? The answer is in one word, Organization. The organized few triumph over the unorganized many. The few hold the sword and the purse. The unorganized are overcome in detail—terrorized, brutalized, robbed, conquered.

We must remember that when Christianity was established the world was ignorant, credulous and cruel. The gospel with its idea of forgiveness—with its heaven and hell—was suited to the barbarians among whom it was preached. Let it be understood, once for all, that

408

Christ had but little to do with Christianity. The people became convinced—being ignorant, stupid and credulous—that the church held the keys of heaven and hell. The foundation for the most terrible mental tyranny that has existed among men was in this way laid. The Catholic Church enslaved to the extent of its power. It resorted to every possible form of fraud; it perverted every good instinct of the human heart; it rewarded every vice; it resorted to every artifice that ingenuity could devise, to reach the highest round of power. It tortured the accused to make them confess; it tortured witnesses to compel the commission of perjury; it tortured children for the purpose of making them convict their parents; it compelled men to establish their own innocence; it imprisoned without limit; it had the malicious patience to wait; it left the accused without trial, and left them in dungeons until released by death. There is no crime that the Catholic Church did not commit,—no cruelty that it did not practice,—no form of treachery that it did not reward, and no virtue that it did not persecute. It was the greatest and most powerful enemy of human rights. It did all that organization, cunning, piety, self-denial, heroism, treachery, zeal and brute force could do to enslave the children of men. It was the enemy of intelligence, the assassin of liberty, and the destroyer of progress. It loaded the noble with chains and the infamous with honors. In one hand it carried the alms dish, in the other a dagger. It argued with the sword, persuaded with poison, and convinced with the fagot.

It is impossible to see how the divine origin of a church can be established by showing that hundreds of bishops have visited the pope.

Does the fact that millions of the faithful visit Mecca establish the truth of the Koran? Is it a scene for congratulation when the bishops of thirty nations kneel before a man? Is it not humiliating to know that man is willing to kneel at the feet of man? Could a noble man demand, or joyfully receive, the humiliation of his fellows?

As a rule, arrogance and humility go together. He who in power compels his fellow-man to kneel, will himself kneel when weak. The tyrant is a cringer in power; a cringer is a tyrant out of power. Great men stand face to face. They meet on equal terms. The cardinal who kneels in the presence of the pope, wants the bishop to kneel in his presence; and the bishop who kneels demands that the priest shall kneel to him; and the priest who kneels demands that they in lower orders shall kneel; and all, from pope to the lowest—that is to say, from pope to exorcist, from pope to the one in charge of the bones of saints— all demand that the people, the laymen, those upon whom they live, shall kneel to them.

The man of free and noble spirit will not kneel. Courage has no knees.

Fear kneels, or falls upon its ashen face.

The Cardinal insists that the pope is the vicar of Christ, and that all popes have been. What is a vicar of Christ? He is a substitute in office. He stands in the place, or occupies the position in relation to the church, in relation to the world, that Jesus Christ would occupy were he the pope at Rome. In other words, he takes Christ's place; so that, according to the doctrine of the Catholic Church, Jesus Christ himself is present in the person of the pope.

We all know that a good man may employ a bad agent. A good king might leave his realm and put in his place a tyrant and a wretch. The good man and the good king cannot certainly know what manner of man the agent is—what kind of person the vicar is—consequently the bad may be chosen. But if the king appointed a bad vicar, knowing him to be bad, knowing that he would oppress the people, knowing that he would imprison and burn the noble and generous, what excuse can be imagined for such a king?

Now, if the church is of divine origin, and if each pope is the vicar of Jesus Christ, he must have been chosen by Jesus Christ; and when he was chosen, Christ must have known exactly what his vicar would do. Can we believe that an infinitely wise and good Being would choose immoral, dishonest, ignorant, malicious, heartless, fiendish, and inhuman vicars?

The Cardinal admits that "the history of Christianity is the history of the church, and that the history of the church is the history of the Pontiffs," and he then declares that "the greatest statesmen and rulers that the world has ever seen are the Popes of Rome."

Let me call attention to a few passages in Draper's "History of the Intellectual Development of Europe."

"Constantine was one of the vicars of Christ. Afterwards, Stephen IV. was chosen. The eyes of Constantine were then put out by Stephen, acting in Christ's place. The tongue of the Bishop Theodorus was amputated by the man who had been substituted for God. This bishop was left in a dungeon to perish of thirst. Pope Leo III. was seized in the street and forced into a church, where the nephews of Pope Adrian attempted to put out his eyes and cut off his tongue. His successor, Stephen V., was driven ignominiously from Rome. His successor, Paschal I., was accused of blinding and murdering two ecclesiastics in the Lateran Palace. John VIII., unable to resist the Mohammedans, was compelled to pay them tribute.

"At this time, the Bishop of Naples was in secret alliance with the Mohammedans, and they divided with this Catholic bishop the plunder they collected from other Catholics. This bishop was excommunicated by the pope; afterwards he gave him absolution because he betrayed the chief Mohammedans, and assassinated others. There was an ecclesiastical conspiracy to murder the pope, and some of the treasures of the church were seized, and the gate of St. Pancrazia was opened with false keys to admit the Saracens. Formosus, who had been engaged in these transactions, who had been excommunicated as a conspirator for the murder of Pope John, was himself elected pope in 891. Boniface VI. was his successor. He had been deposed from the diaconate and from the priesthood for his immoral and lewd life. Stephen VII. was the next pope, and he had the dead body of Formosus taken from the grave, clothed in papal habiliments, propped up in a chair and tried before a Council. The corpse was found guilty, three fingers were cut off and the body cast into the Tiber. Afterwards Stephen VII., this Vicar of Christ, was thrown into prison and strangled.

"From 896 to 900, five popes were consecrated. Leo V., in less than two months after he became pope, was cast into prison by Christopher, one of his chaplains. This Christopher usurped his place, and in a little while was expelled from Rome by Sergius III., who became pope in 905. This pope lived in criminal intercourse with the celebrated Theodora, who with her daughters Marozia and Theodora, both prostitutes, exercised an extraordinary control over him. The love of Theodora was also shared by John X. She gave him the Archbishopric of Revenna, and made him pope in 915. The daughter of Theodora overthrew this pope. She surprised him in the Lateran Palace. His brother, Peter, was killed; the pope was thrown into prison, where he was afterward murdered. Afterward, this Marozia, daughter of Theodora, made her own son pope, John XI. Many affirmed that Pope Sergius was his father, but his mother inclined to attribute him to her husband Alberic, whose brother Guido she afterward married. Another of her sons, Alberic, jealous of his brother John, the pope, cast him and their mother into prison. Alberic's son was then elected pope as John XII.

"John was nineteen years old when he became the vicar of Christ. His reign was characterized by the most shocking immoralities, so that the Emperor Otho I. was compelled by the German clergy to interfere. He was tried. It appeared that John had received bribes for the consecration of bishops; that he had ordained one who was only ten years old; that he was charged with incest, and with so many adulteries that the Lateran Palace had become a brothel. He put out the eyes of one ecclesiastic; he maimed another—both dying in consequence of their injuries. He was given to drunkenness and to gambling. He was deposed at last, and Leo VII. elected in his stead. Subsequently he got the upper hand. He seized his antagonists; he cut off the hand of one, the nose, the finger, and the tongue of others. His life was eventually brought to an end by the vengeance of a man whose wife he had seduced."

And yet, I admit that the most infamous popes, the most heartless and fiendish bishops, friars, and priests were models of mercy, charity, and justice when compared with the orthodox God—with the God they worshiped. These popes, these bishops, these priests could persecute only for a few years—they could burn only for a few moments—but their God threatened to imprison and burn forever; and their God is as much worse than they were, as hell is worse than the Inquisition.

"John XIII. was strangled in prison. Boniface VII. imprisoned Benedict VII., and starved him to death. John XIV. was secretly put to death in the dungeons of the castle of St. Angelo. The corpse of Boniface was dragged by the populace through the streets."

It must be remembered that the popes were assassinated by Catholics—murdered by the faithful—that one vicar of Christ strangled another vicar of Christ, and that these men were "the greatest rulers and the greatest statesmen of the earth."

"Pope John XVI. was seized, his eyes put out, his nose cut off, his tongue torn from his mouth, and he was sent through the streets mounted on an ass, with his face to the tail. Benedict IX., a boy of less than twelve years of age, was raised to the apostolic throne. One of his successors, Victor III., declared that the life of Benedict was so shameful, so foul, so execrable, that he shuddered to describe it. He ruled like a captain of banditti. The people, unable to bear longer his adulteries, his homicides and his abominations, rose against him, and in despair of maintaining his position, he put up the papacy to auction, and it was bought by a presbyter named John, who became Gregory VI., in the year of grace 1045. Well may we ask, Were these the vicegerents of God upon earth—these, who had truly reached that goal beyond which the last effort of human wickedness cannot pass?"

It may be sufficient to say that there is no crime that man can commit that has not been committed by the vicars of Christ. They have inflicted every possible torture, violated every natural right. Greater monsters the human race has not produced.

Among the "some two hundred and fifty-eight" Vicars of Christ there were probably some good men. This would have happened even if the intention had been to get all bad men, for the reason that man reaches perfection neither in good nor in evil; but if they were selected by Christ himself, if they were selected by a church with a divine origin and under divine guidance, then there is no way to account for the selection of a bad one. If one hypocrite was duly elected pope—one murderer, one strangler, one starver—this demonstrates that all the popes were selected by men, and by men only, and that the claim of divine guidance is born of zeal and uttered without knowledge.

But who were the vicars of Christ? How many have there been? Cardinal Manning himself does not know. He is not sure. He says: "Starting from St. Peter to Leo XIII., there have been *some* two hundred and fifty-eight Pontiffs claiming to be recognized by the whole Catholic unity as successors of St. Peter and Vicars of Jesus Christ." Why did he use the word "some"? Why "claiming"? Does he not positively know? Is it possible that the present Vicar of Christ is not certain as to the number of his predecessors? Is he infallible in faith and fallible in fact?

Robert G. Ingersoll.

A REPLY TO CARDINAL MANNING

"If we live thus tamely,—
To be thus jaded by a piece of scarlet,—
Farewell nobility."

PART II.

No one will deny that "the pope speaks to many people in many nations; that he treats with empires and governments," and that "neither from Canterbury nor from Constantinople such a voice goes forth."

How does the pope speak? What does he say?

He speaks against the liberty of man—against the progress of the human race. He speaks to calumniate thinkers, and to warn the faithful against the discoveries of science. He speaks for the destruction of civilization.

Who listens? Do astronomers, geologists and scientists put the hand to the ear fearing that an accent may be lost? Does France listen? Does Italy hear? Is not the church weakest at its centre? Do those who have raised Italy from the dead, and placed her again among the great nations, pay attention? Does Great Britain care for this voice—this moan, this groan—of the Middle Ages? Do the words of Leo XIII. impress the intelligence of the Great Republic? Can anything be more absurd than for the vicar of Christ to attack a demonstration of science with a passage of Scripture, or a quotation from one of the "Fathers"?

Compare the popes with the kings and queens of England. Infinite wisdom had but little to do with the selection of these monarchs, and yet they were far better than any equal number of consecutive popes. This is faint praise, even for kings and queens, but it shows that chance succeeded in getting better rulers for England than "Infinite Wisdom" did for the Church of Rome. Compare the popes with the presidents of the Republic elected by the people. If Adams had murdered Washington, and Jefferson had imprisoned Adams, and if Madison had cut out Jefferson's tongue, and Monroe had assassinated Madison, and John Quincy Adams had poisoned Monroe, and General Jackson had hung Adams and his Cabinet, we might say that presidents had been as virtuous as popes. But if this had happened, the verdict of the world would be that the people are not capable of selecting their presidents.

But this voice from Rome is growing feebler day by day; so feeble that the Cardinal admits that the vicar of God, and the supernatural church, "are being tormented by Falck laws, by Mancini laws and by Crispi laws." In other words, this representative of God, this substitute of Christ, this church of divine origin, this supernatural institution—pervaded by the Holy Ghost—are being "tormented" by three politicians. Is it possible that this patriotic trinity is more powerful than the other?

It is claimed that if the Catholic Church "be only a human system, built up by the intellect, will and energy of men, the adversaries must prove it—that the burden is upon them."

As a general thing, institutions are natural. If this church is supernatural, it is the one exception. The affirmative is with those who claim that it is of divine origin. So far as we know, all governments and all creeds are the work of man. No one believes that Rome was a supernatural production, and yet its beginnings were as small as those of the Catholic Church. Commencing in weakness, Rome grew, and fought, and conquered, until it was believed that the sky bent above a subjugated world. And yet all was natural. For every effect there was an efficient cause.

The Catholic asserts that all other religions have been produced by man—that Brahminism and Buddhism, the religion of Isis and Osiris, the marvelous mythologies of Greece and Rome, were the work of the human mind. From these religions Catholicism has borrowed. Long before Catholicism was born, it was believed that women had borne children whose fathers were gods. The Trinity was promulgated in Egypt centuries before the birth of Moses. Celibacy was taught by the ancient Nazarenes and Essenes, by the priests of Egypt and India, by mendicant monks, and by the piously insane of many countries long before the apostles lived. The Chinese tell us that "when there were but one man and one woman upon the earth, the woman refused to sacrifice her virginity even to people the globe; and the gods, honoring her purity, granted that she should conceive beneath the gaze of her lover's eyes, and a virgin mother became the parent of humanity."

The founders of many religions have insisted that it was the duty of man to renounce the pleasures of sense, and millions before our era took the vows of chastity, poverty and obedience, and most cheerfully lived upon the labor of others.

The sacraments of baptism and confirmation are far older than the Church of Rome. The Eucharist is pagan. Long before popes began to murder each other, pagans ate cakes—the flesh of Ceres, and drank wine—the blood of Bacchus. Holy water flowed in the Ganges and Nile, priests interceded for the people, and anointed the dying.

It will not do to say that every successful religion that has taught unnatural doctrines, unnatural practices, must of necessity have been of divine origin. In most religions there has been a strange mingling of the good and bad, of the merciful and cruel, of the loving and malicious. Buddhism taught the universal brotherhood of man, insisted on the development of the mind, and this religion was propagated not by the sword, but by preaching, by persuasion, and by kindness—yet in many things it was contrary to the human will, contrary to the human passions, and contrary to good sense. Buddhism succeeded. Can we, for this reason, say that it is a supernatural religion? Is the unnatural the supernatural?

It is insisted that, while other churches have changed, the Catholic Church alone has remained the same, and that this fact demonstrates its divine origin.

Has the creed of Buddhism changed in three thousand years? Is intellectual stagnation a demonstration of divine origin? When anything refuses to grow, are we certain that the seed was planted by God? If the Catholic Church is the same to-day that it has been for many centuries, this proves that there has been no intellectual development. If men do not differ upon religious subjects, it is because they do not think.

Differentiation is the law of growth, of progress. Every church must gain or lose: it cannot remain the same; it must decay or grow. The fact that the Catholic Church has not grown—that it has been petrified from the first—does not establish divine origin; it simply establishes the fact that it retards the progress of man. Everything in nature changes—every atom is in motion—every star moves. Nations, institutions and individuals have youth, manhood, old age, death. This is and will be true of the Catholic Church. It was once weak—it grew stronger—it reached its climax of power—it began to decay—it never can rise again. It is confronted by the dawn of Science. In the presence of the nineteenth century it cowers.

It is not true that "All natural causes run to disintegration."

Natural causes run to integration as well as to disintegration. All growth is integration, and all growth is natural. All decay is disintegration, and all decay is natural. Nature builds and nature destroys. When the acorn grows—when the sunlight and rain fall upon it and the oak rises—so far as the oak is concerned "all natural causes" do not "run to disintegration." But there comes a time when the oak has reached its limit, and then the forces of nature run towards disintegration, and finally the old oak falls. But if the Cardinal is right— if "all natural causes run to disintegration," then every success must have been of divine origin, and nothing is natural but destruction. This is Catholic science: "All natural causes run to disintegration." What do these causes find to disintegrate? Nothing that is natural. The fact that the thing is not disintegrated shows that it was and is of supernatural origin. According to the Cardinal, the only business of nature is to disintegrate the supernatural. To prevent this, the supernatural needs the protection of the Infinite. According to this doctrine, if anything lives and grows, it does so in spite of nature. Growth, then, is not in accordance with, but in opposition to nature. Every plant is supernatural—it defeats the disintegrating influences of rain and light. The generalization of the Cardinal is half the truth. It would be equally true to say: All natural causes run to integration. But the whole truth is that growth and decay are equal.

The Cardinal asserts that "Christendom was created by the world-wide church as we see it before our eyes at this day."

Philosophers and statesmen believe it to be the work of their own hands; they did not make it, but they have for three hundred years been unmaking it by reformations and revolutions.

The meaning of this is that Christendom was far better three hundred years ago than now; that during these three centuries Christendom has been going toward barbarism. It means that the supernatural church of God has been a failure for three hundred years; that it has been unable to withstand the attacks of philosophers and statesmen, and that it has been helpless in the midst of "reformations and revolutions."

What was the condition of the world three hundred years ago, the period, according to the Cardinal, in which the church reached the height of its influence, and since which it has been unable to withstand the rising tide of reformation and the whirlwind of revolution?

In that blessed time, Philip II. was king of Spain—he with the cramped head and the monstrous jaw. Heretics were hunted like wild and poisonous beasts; the Inquisition was firmly established, and priests were busy with rack and fire. With a zeal born of the hatred of man and the love of God, the church, with every instrument of torture, touched every nerve in the human body.

In those happy days, the Duke of Alva was devastating the homes of Holland; heretics were buried alive—their tongues were torn from their mouths, their lids from their eyes; the Armada was on the sea for the destruction of the heretics of England, and the Moriscoes—a million and a half of industrious people—were being driven by sword and flame from their homes. The Jews had been expelled from Spain. This Catholic country had succeeded in driving intelligence and industry from its territory; and this had been done with a cruelty, with a ferocity, unequaled, in the annals of crime.

Nothing was left but ignorance, bigotry, intolerance, credulity, the Inquisition, the seven sacraments and the seven deadly sins. And yet a Cardinal of the nineteenth century, living in the land of Shakespeare, regrets the change that has been wrought by the intellectual efforts, by the discoveries, by the inventions and heroism of three hundred years.

Three hundred years ago, Charles IX., in France, son of Catherine de Medici, in the year of grace 1572—after nearly sixteen centuries of Catholic Christianity—after hundreds of vicars of Christ had sat in St. Peter's chair—after the natural passions of man had been "softened" by the creed of Rome—came the Massacre of St. Bartholomew, the result of a conspiracy between the Vicar of Christ, Philip II., Charles IX., and his fiendish mother. Let the Cardinal read the account of this massacre once more, and, after reading it, imagine that he sees the gashed and mutilated bodies of thousands of men and women, and then let him say that he regrets the revolutions and reformations of three hundred years.

About three hundred years ago Clement VIII., Vicar of Christ, acting in God's place, substitute of the Infinite, persecuted Giordano Bruno even unto death. This great, this sublime man, was tried for heresy. He had ventured to assert the rotary motion of the earth; he had hazarded the conjecture that there were in the fields of infinite space worlds larger and more glorious than ours. For these low and groveling thoughts, for this contradiction of the word and vicar of God, this man was imprisoned for many years. But his noble spirit was not broken, and finally, in the year 1600, by the orders of the infamous vicar, he was chained to the stake. Priests believing in the doctrine of universal forgiveness—priests who when smitten upon one cheek turned the other—carried with a kind of ferocious joy fagots to the feet of this incomparable man. These disciples of "Our Lord" were made joyous as the flames, like serpents, climbed around the body of Bruno. In a few moments the brave thinker was dead, and the priests who had burned him fell upon their knees and asked the infinite God to continue the blessed work forever in hell.

There are two things that cannot exist in the same universe—an infinite God and a martyr.

Does the Cardinal regret that kings and emperors are not now engaged in the extermination of Protestants? Does he regret that dungeons of the Inquisition are no longer crowded with the best and bravest? Does he long for the fires of the auto da fé.?

In coming to a conclusion as to the origin of the Catholic Church—in determining the truth of the claim of infallibility—we are not restricted to the physical achievements of that church, or to the history of its propagation, or to the rapidity of its growth.

This church has a creed; and if this church is of divine origin—if its head is the vicar of Christ, and, as such, infallible in matters of faith and morals, this creed must be true. Let us start with the supposition that God exists, and that he is infinitely wise, powerful and good—and this is only a supposition. Now, if the creed is foolish, absurd and cruel, it cannot be of divine origin. We find in this creed the following:

"Whosoever will be saved, before all things it is necessary that he hold the Catholic faith."

It is not necessary, before all things, that he be good, honest, merciful, charitable and just. Creed is more important than conduct. The most important of all things is, that he hold the Catholic faith. There were thousands of years during which it was not necessary to hold that faith, because that faith did not exist; and yet during that time the virtues were just as important as now, just as important as they ever can be.

Millions of the noblest of the human race never heard of this creed. Millions of the bravest and best have heard of it, examined, and rejected it. Millions of the most infamous have believed it, and because of their belief, or notwithstanding their belief, have murdered millions of their fellows. We know that men can be, have been, and are just as wicked with it as without it. We know that it is not necessary to believe it to be good, loving, tender, noble and self-denying. We admit that millions who have believed it have also been self-denying and heroic, and that millions, by such belief, were not prevented from torturing and destroying the helpless.

Now, if all who believed it were good, and all who rejected it were bad, then there might be some propriety in saying that "whoever will be saved, before all things it is necessary that he hold the Catholic faith." But as the experience of mankind is otherwise, the declaration becomes absurd, ignorant and cruel.

There is still another clause:

"Which faith, except every one do keep entire and inviolate, without doubt, he shall everlastingly perish."

We now have both sides of this wonderful truth: The believer will be saved, the unbeliever will be lost. We know that faith is not the child or servant of the will. We know that belief is a conclusion based upon what the mind supposes to be true. We know that it is not an act of the will. Nothing can be more absurd than to save a man because he is not intelligent enough to accept the truth, and nothing can be more infamous than to damn a man because he is intelligent enough to reject the false. It resolves itself into a question of intelligence. If the creed is true, then a man rejects it because he lacks intelligence. Is this a crime for which a man should everlastingly perish? If the creed is false, then a man accepts it because he lacks intelligence. In both cases the crime is exactly the same.

If a man is to be damned for rejecting the truth, certainly he should not be saved for accepting the false. This one clause demonstrates that a being of infinite wisdom and goodness did not write it. It also demonstrates that it was the work of men who had neither wisdom nor a sense of justice.

What is this Catholic faith that must be held? It is this:

"That we worship one God in Trinity and Trinity in Unity, neither confounding the persons nor dividing the substance." Why should an Infinite Being demand worship? Why should one God wish to be worshiped as three? Why should three Gods wished to be worshiped as one? Why should we pray to one God and think of three, or pray to three Gods and think of one? Can this increase the happiness of the one or of the three? Is it possible to think of one as three, or of three as one? If you think of three as one, can you think of one as none, or of none as one? When you think of three as one, what do you do with the other two? You must not "confound the persons"—they must be kept separate. When you think of one as three, how do you get the other two? You must not "divide the substance." Is it possible to write greater contradictions than these?

This creed demonstrates the human origin of the Catholic Church. Nothing could be more unjust than to punish man for unbelief—for the expression of honest thought—for having been guided by his reason—for having acted in accordance with his best judgment.

Another claim is made, to the effect "that the Catholic Church has filled the world with the true knowledge of the one true God, and that it has destroyed all idols by light instead of by fire."

The Catholic Church described the true God as a being who would inflict eternal pain on his weak and erring children; described him as a fickle, quick-tempered, unreasonable deity, whom honesty enraged, and whom flattery governed; one who loved to see fear upon its knees, ignorance with closed eyes and open mouth; one who delighted in useless self-denial, who loved to hear the sighs and sobs of suffering nuns, as they lay prostrate on dungeon floors; one who was delighted when the husband deserted his family and lived alone in some cave in the far wilderness, tormented by dreams and driven to insanity by prayer and penance, by fasting and faith.

According to the Catholic Church, the true God enjoyed the agonies of heretics. He loved the smell of their burning flesh; he applauded with wide palms when philosophers were flayed alive, and to him the *auto da fé* was a divine comedy. The shrieks of wives, the cries of babes when fathers were being burned, gave contrast, heightened the effect and filled his cup with joy. This true God did not know the shape of the earth he had made, and had forgotten the orbits of the stars. "The stream of light which descended from the beginning" was propagated by fagot to fagot, until Christendom was filled with the devouring fires of faith.

It may also be said that the Catholic Church filled the world with the true knowledge of the one true Devil. It filled the air with malicious phantoms, crowded innocent sleep with leering fiends, and gave the world to the domination of witches and wizards, spirits and spooks, goblins and ghosts, and butchered and burned thousands for the commission of impossible crimes.

It is contended that: "In this true knowledge of the Divine Nature was revealed to man their own relation to a Creator as sons to a Father."

This tender relation was revealed by the Catholics to the Pagans, the Arians, the Cathari, the Waldenses, the Albigenses, the heretics, the Jews, the Moriscoes, the Protestants—to the natives of the West Indies, of Mexico, of Peru—to philosophers, patriots and thinkers. All these victims were taught to regard the true God as a loving father, and this lesson was taught with every instrument of torture—with brandings and burnings, with flayings and flames. The world was filled with cruelty and credulity, ignorance and intolerance, and the soil in which all these horrors grew was the true knowledge of the one true God, and the true knowledge of the one true Devil. And yet, we are compelled to say, that the one true Devil described by the Catholic Church was not as malevolent as the one true God.

Is it true that the Catholic Church overthrew idolatry? What is idolatry? What shall we say of the worship of popes—of the doctrine of the Real Presence, of divine honors paid to saints, of sacred vestments, of holy water, of consecrated cups and plates, of images and relics, of amulets and charms?

The Catholic Church filled the world with the spirit of idolatry. It abandoned the idea of continuity in nature, it denied the integrity of cause and effect. The government of the world was the composite result of the caprice of God, the malice of Satan, the prayers of the faithful— softened, it may be, by the charity of Chance. Yet the Cardinal asserts, without the preface of a smile, that "Demonology was overthrown by the church, with the assistance of forces that were above nature;" and in the same breath gives birth to this enlightened statement: "Beelzebub is not divided against himself." Is a belief in Beelzebub a belief in demonology? Has the Cardinal forgotten the Council of Nice, held in the year of grace 787, that declared the worship of images to be lawful? Did that infallible Council, under the guidance of the Holy Ghost, destroy idolatry?

The Cardinal takes the ground that marriage is a sacrament, and therefore indissoluble, and he also insists that celibacy is far better than marriage,—holier than a sacrament,—that marriage is not the highest state, but that "the state of virginity unto death is the highest condition of man and woman."

The highest ideal of a family is where all are equal—where love has superseded authority—where each seeks the good of all, and where none obey—where no religion can sunder hearts, and with which no church can interfere.

The real marriage is based on mutual affection—the ceremony is but the outward evidence of the inward flame. To this contract there are but two parties. The church is an impudent intruder. Marriage is made public to the end that the real contract may be known, so that the world can see that the parties have been actuated by the highest and holiest motives that find expression in the acts of human beings. The man and woman are not joined together by God, or by the church, or by the state.

The church and state may prescribe certain ceremonies, certain formalities—but all these are only evidence of the existence of a sacred fact in the hearts of the wedded. The indissolubility of marriage is a dogma that has filled the lives of millions with agony and tears. It has given a perpetual excuse for vice and immorality. Fear has borne children begotten by brutality. Countless women have endured the insults, indignities and cruelties of fiendish husbands, because they thought that it was the will of God. The contract of marriage is the most important that human beings can make; but no contract can be so important as to release one of the parties from the obligation of performance; and no contract, whether made between man and woman, or between them and God, after a failure of consideration caused by the willful act of the man or woman, can hold and bind the innocent and honest.

Do the believers in indissoluble marriage treat their wives better than others? A little while ago, a woman said to a man who had raised his hand to strike her: "Do not touch me; you have no right to beat me; I am not your wife."

About a year ago a husband, whom God in his infinite wisdom had joined to a loving and patient woman in the indissoluble sacrament of marriage, becoming enraged, seized the helpless wife and tore out one of her eyes. She forgave him. A few weeks ago he deliberately repeated this frightful crime, leaving his victim totally blind. Would it not have been better if man, before the poor woman was blinded, had put asunder whom God had joined together? Thousands of husbands, who insist that marriage is indissoluble, are the beaters of wives.

The law of the church has created neither the purity nor the peace of domestic life. Back of all churches is human affection. Back of all theologies is the love of the human heart. Back of all your priests and creeds is the adoration of the one woman by the one man, and of the one man by the one woman. Back of your faith is the fireside; back of your folly is the family; and back of all your holy mistakes and your sacred absurdities is the love of husband and wife, of parent and child.

It is not true that neither the Greek nor the Roman world had any true conception of a home. The splendid story of Ulysses and Penelope, the parting of Hector and Andromache, demonstrate that a true conception of home existed among the Greeks. Before the establishment of Christianity, the Roman matron commanded the admiration of the then known world. She was free and noble. The church degraded woman— made her the property of the husband, and trampled her beneath its brutal feet. The "fathers" denounced woman as a perpetual temptation, as the cause of all evil. The church worshiped a God who had upheld polygamy, and had pronounced his curse on woman, and had declared that she should be the serf of the husband. This church followed the teachings of St. Paul. It taught the uncleanness of marriage, and insisted that all children were conceived in sin. This church pretended to have been founded by one who offered a reward in this world, and eternal joy in the next, to husbands who would forsake their wives and children and follow him. Did this tend to the elevation of woman? Did this detestable doctrine "create the purity and peace of domestic life"? Is it true that a monk is purer than a good and noble father?—that a nun is holier than a loving mother?

Is there anything deeper and stronger than a mother's love? Is there anything purer, holier than a mother holding her dimpled babe against her billowed breast?

The good man is useful, the best man is the most useful. Those who fill the nights with barren prayers and holy hunger, torture themselves for their own good and not for the benefit of others. They are earning eternal glory for themselves—they do not fast for their fellow-men—their selfishness is only equaled by their foolishness. Compare the monk in his selfish cell, counting beads and saying prayers for the purpose of saving his barren soul, with a husband and father sitting by his fireside with wife and children. Compare the nun with the mother and her babe.

Celibacy is the essence of vulgarity. It tries to put a stain upon motherhood, upon marriage, upon love—that is to say, upon all that is holiest in the human heart. Take love from the world, and there is nothing left worth living for. The church has treated this great, this sublime, this unspeakably holy passion, as though it polluted the heart. They have placed the love of God above the love of woman, above the love of man. Human love is generous and noble. The love of God is selfish, because man does not love God for God's sake, but for his own.

Yet the Cardinal asserts "that the change wrought by Christianity in the social, political and international relations of the world"—"that the root of this ethical change, private and public, is the Christian home." A moment afterward, this prelate insists that celibacy is far better than marriage. If the world could be induced to live in accordance with the "highest state," this generation would be the last. Why were men and women created? Why did not the Catholic God commence' with the sinless and sexless? The Cardinal ought to take the ground that to talk well is good, but that to be dumb is the highest condition; that hearing is a pleasure, but that deafness is ecstasy; and that to think, to reason, is very well, but that to be a Catholic is far better.

Why should we desire the destruction of human passions? Take passions from human beings and what is left? The great object should be not to destroy passions, but to make them obedient to the intellect. To indulge passion to the utmost is one form of intemperance—to destroy passion is another. The reasonable gratification of passion under the domination of the intellect is true wisdom and perfect virtue.

The goodness, the sympathy, the self-denial of the nun, of the monk, all come from the mother-instinct, the father-instinct—all were produced by human affection, by the love of man for woman, of woman for man. Love is a transfiguration. It ennobles, purifies and glorifies. In true marriage two hearts burst into flower. Two lives unite. They melt in music. Every moment is a melody. Love is a revelation, a creation. From love the world borrows its beauty and the heavens their glory. Justice, self-denial, charity and pity are the children of love. Lover, wife, mother, husband, father, child, home—these words shed light—they are the gems of human speech. Without love all glory fades, the noble falls from life, art dies, music loses meaning and becomes mere motions of the air, and virtue ceases to exist.

It is asserted that this life of celibacy is above and against the tendencies of human nature; and the Cardinal then asks: "Who will ascribe this to natural causes, and, if so, why did it not appear in the first four thousand years?"

If there is in a system of religion a doctrine, a dogma, or a practice against the tendencies of human nature—if this religion succeeds, then it is claimed by the Cardinal that such religion must be of divine origin. Is it "against the tendencies of human nature" for a mother to throw her child into the Ganges to please a supposed God? Yet a religion that insisted on that sacrifice succeeded, and has, to-day, more believers than the Catholic Church can boast.

Religions, like nations and individuals, have always gone along the line of least resistance. Nothing has "ascended the stream of human license by a power mightier than nature." There is no such power. There never was, there never can be, a miracle. We know that man is a conditioned being. We know that he is affected by a change of conditions. If he is ignorant he is superstitious; this is natural. If his brain is developed—if he perceives clearly that all things are naturally produced, he ceases to be superstitious, and becomes scientific. He is not a saint, but a savant—not a priest, but a philosopher. He does not worship, he works; he investigates; he thinks; he takes advantage, through intelligence, of the forces of nature. He is no longer the victim of appearances, the dupe of his own ignorance, and the persecutor of his fellow-men.

He then knows that it is far better to love his wife and children than to love God. He then knows that the love of man for woman, of woman for man, of parent for child, of child for parent, is far better, far holier than the love of man for any phantom born of ignorance and fear.

It is illogical to take the ground that the world was cruel and ignorant and idolatrous when the Catholic Church was established, and that because the world is better now than then, the church is of divine origin.

What was the world when science came? What was it in the days of Galileo, Copernicus and Kepler? What-was it when printing was invented? What was it when the Western World was found? Would it not be much easier to prove that science is of divine origin?

Science does not persecute. It does not shed blood—it fills the world with light. It cares nothing for heresy; it develops the mind, and enables man to answer his own prayers.

Cardinal Manning takes the ground that Jehovah practically abandoned the children of men for four thousand years, and gave them over to every abomination. He claims that Christianity came "in the fullness of time," and it is then admitted that "what the fullness of time may mean is one of the mysteries of times and seasons, that it is not for us to know." Having declared that it is a mystery, and one that we are not to know, the Cardinal explains it: "One motive for the long delay of four thousand years is not far to seek—it gave time, full and ample, for the utmost development and consolidation of all the falsehood and evil of which the intellect and will of man are capable."

Is it possible to imagine why an infinitely good and wise being "gave time full and ample for the utmost development and consolidation of falsehood and evil"? Why should an infinitely wise God desire this development and consolidation? What would be thought of a father who should refuse to teach his son and deliberately allow him to go into every possible excess, to the end that he might "develop all the falsehood and evil of which his intellect and will were capable"? If a supernatural religion is a necessity, and if without it all men simply develop and consolidate falsehood and evil, why was not a supernatural religion given to the first man? The Catholic Church, if this be true, should have been founded in the Garden of Eden.

Was it not cruel to drown a world just for the want of a supernatural religion—a religion that man, by no possibility, could furnish? Was there "husbandry in heaven"?

But the Cardinal contradicts himself by not only admitting, but declaring, that the world had never seen a legislation so just, so equitable, as that of Rome.

Is it possible that a nation in which falsehood and evil had reached their highest development was, after all, so wise, so just and so equitable?

Was not the civil law far better than the Mosaic—more philosophical, nearer just?

The civil law was produced without the assistance of God.

According to the Cardinal, it was produced by men in whom all the falsehood and evil of which they were capable had been developed and consolidated, while the cruel and ignorant Mosaic code came from the lips of infinite wisdom and compassion.

It is declared that the history of Rome shows what man can do without God, and I assert that the history of the Inquisition shows what man can do when assisted by a church of divine origin, presided over, by the infallible vicars of God.

The fact that the early Christians not only believed incredible things, but persuaded others of their truth, is regarded by the Cardinal as a miracle. This is only another phase of the old argument that success is the test of divine origin. All supernatural religions have been founded in precisely the same way. The credulity of eighteen hundred years ago believed everything except the truth.

A religion is a growth, and is of necessity adapted in some degree to the people among whom it grows. It is shaped and molded by the general ignorance, the superstition and credulity of the age in which it lives. The key is fashioned by the lock.

Every religion that has succeeded has in some way supplied the wants of its votaries, and has to a certain extent harmonized with their hopes, their fears, their vices, and their virtues.

If, as the Cardinal says, the religion of Christ is in absolute harmony with nature, how can it be supernatural? The Cardinal also declares that "the religion of Christ is in harmony with the reason and moral nature in all nations and all ages to this day."

What becomes of the argument that Catholicism must be of divine origin because "it has ascended the stream of human license, *contra ictum fluminis,* by a power mightier than nature"?

If "it is in harmony with the reason and moral nature of all nations and all ages to this day," it has gone with the stream, and not against it.

If "the religion of Christ is in harmony with the reason and moral nature of all nations," then the men who have rejected it are unnatural, and these men have gone against the stream. How then can it be said that Christianity has been in changeless opposition to nature as man has marred it? To what extent has man marred it?

In spite of the marring by man, we are told that the reason and moral nature of all nations in all ages to this day is in harmony with the religion of Jesus Christ.

Are we justified in saying that the Catholic Church is of divine origin because the Pagans failed to destroy it by persecution?

We will put the Cardinal's statement in form:

Paganism failed to destroy Catholicism by persecution, therefore Catholicism is of divine origin.

Let us make an application of this logic:

Paganism failed to destroy Catholicism by persecution; therefore, Catholicism is of divine origin.

Catholicism failed to destroy Protestantism by persecution; therefore, Protestantism is of divine origin.

Catholicism and Protestantism combined failed to destroy Infidelity; therefore, Infidelity is of divine origin.

Let us make another application:

Paganism did not succeed in destroying Catholicism; therefore, Paganism was a false religion.

Catholicism did not succeed in destroying Protestantism; therefore, Catholicism is a false religion.

Catholicism and Protestantism combined failed to destroy Infidelity; therefore, both Catholicism and Protestantism are false religions.

The Cardinal has another reason for believing the Catholic Church of divine origin. He declares that the "Canon Law is a creation of wisdom and justice to which no statutes at large or imperial pandects can bear comparison;" "that the world-wide and secular legislation of the church was of a higher character, and that as water cannot rise above its source, the church could not, by mere human wisdom, have corrected and perfected the imperial law, and therefore its source must have been higher than the sources of the world."

When Europe was the most ignorant, the Canon Law was supreme.

As a matter of fact, the good in the Canon Law was borrowed—the bad was, for the most part, original. In my judgment, the legislation of the Republic of the United States is in many respects superior to that of Rome, and yet we are greatly indebted to the Civil Law. Our legislation is superior in many particulars to that of England, and yet we are greatly indebted to the Common Law; but it never occurred to me that our Statutes at Large are divinely inspired.

If the Canon Law is, in fact, the legislation of infinite wisdom, then it should be a perfect code. Yet, the Canon Law made it a crime next to robbery and theft to take interest for money. Without the right to take interest the business of the whole world, would to a large extent, cease and the prosperity of mankind end. There are railways enough in the United States to make six tracks around the globe, and every mile was built with borrowed money on which interest was paid or promised. In no other way could the savings of many thousands have been brought together and a capital great enough formed to construct works of such vast and continental importance.

It was provided in this same wonderful Canon Law that a heretic could not be a witness against a Catholic. The Catholic was at liberty to rob and wrong his fellow-man, provided the fellow-man was not a fellow Catholic, and in a court established by the vicar of Christ, the man who had been robbed was not allowed to open his mouth. A Catholic could enter the house of an unbeliever, of a Jew, of a heretic, of a Moor, and before the eyes of the husband and father murder his wife and children, and the father could not pronounce in the hearing of a judge the name of the murderer.

The world is wiser now, and the Canon Law, given to us by infinite wisdom, has been repealed by the common sense of man.

In this divine code it was provided that to convict a cardinal bishop, seventy-two witnesses were required; a cardinal presbyter, forty-four; a cardinal deacon, twenty-four; a sub deacon, acolyte, exorcist, reader, ostiarius, seven; and in the purgation of a bishop, twelve witnesses were invariably required; of a presbyter, seven; of a deacon, three. These laws, in my judgment, were made, not by God, but by the clergy.

So too in this cruel code it was provided that those who gave aid, favor, or counsel, to excommunicated persons, should be anathema, and that those who talked with, consulted, or sat at the same table with or gave anything in charity to the excommunicated should be anathema.

Is it possible that a being of infinite wisdom made hospitality a crime? Did he say: "Whoso giveth a cup of cold water to the excommunicated shall wear forever a garment of fire"? Were not the laws of the Romans much better? Besides all this, under the Canon Law the dead could be tried for heresy, and their estates confiscated—that is to say, their widows and orphans robbed.

The most brutal part of the common law of England is that in relation to the rights of women—all of which was taken from the *Corpus Juris Canonici,* "the law that came from a higher source than man."

The only cause of absolute divorce as laid down by the pious canonists was *propter infidelitatem,* which was when one of the parties became Catholic, and would not live with the other who continued still an unbeliever. Under this divine statute, a pagan wishing to be rid of his wife had only to join the Catholic Church, provided she remained faithful to the religion of her fathers. Under this divine law, a man marrying a widow was declared to be a bigamist.

It would require volumes to point out the cruelties, absurdities and inconsistencies of the Canon Law. It has been thrown away by the world. Every civilized nation has a code of its own, and the Canon Law is of interest only to the historian, the antiquarian, and the enemy of theological government.

Under the Canon Law, people were convicted of being witches and wizards, of holding intercourse with devils. Thousands perished at the stake, having been convicted of these impossible crimes. Under the Canon Law, there was such a crime as the suspicion of heresy. A man or woman could be arrested, charged with being suspected, and under this

Canon Law, flowing from the intellect of infinite wisdom, the presumption was in favor of guilt. The suspected had to prove themselves innocent. In all civilized courts, the presumption of innocence is the shield of the indicted, but the Canon Law took away this shield, and put in the hand of the priest the sword of presumptive guilt.

If the real pope is the vicar of Christ, the true shepherd of the sheep, this fact should be known not only to the vicar, but to the sheep. A divinely founded and guarded church ought to know its own shepherd, and yet the Catholic sheep have not always been certain who the shepherd was.

The Council of Pisa, held in 1409, deposed two popes—rivals—Gregory and Benedict—that is to say, deposed the actual vicar of Christ and the pretended. This action was taken because a council, enlightened by the Holy Ghost, could not tell the genuine from the counterfeit. The council then elected another vicar, whose authority was afterwards denied. Alexander V. died, and John XXIII. took his place; Gregory XII. insisted that he was the lawful pope; John resigned, then he was deposed, and afterward imprisoned; then Gregory XII. resigned, and Martin V. was elected. The whole thing reads like the annals of a South American revolution.

The Council of Constance restored, as the Cardinal declares, the unity of the church, and brought back the consolation of the Holy Ghost. Before this great council John Huss appeared and maintained his own tenets. The council declared that the church was not bound to keep its promise with a heretic. Huss was condemned and executed on the 6th of July, 1415. His disciple, Jerome of Prague, recanted, but having relapsed, was put to death, May 30, 1416. This cursed council shed the blood of Huss and Jerome.

The Cardinal appeals to the author of "Ecce Homo" for the purpose of showing that Christianity is above nature, and the following passages, among others, are quoted:

"Who can describe that which unites men? Who has entered into the formation of speech, which is the symbol of their union? Who can describe exhaustively the origin of civil society? He who can do these things can explain the origin of the Christian Church."

These passages should not have been quoted by the Cardinal. The author of these passages simply says that the origin of the Christian Church is no harder to find and describe than that which unites men—than that which has entered into the formation of speech, the symbol of their union—no harder to describe than the origin of civil society—because he says that one who can describe these can describe the other.

Certainly none of these things are above nature. We do not need the assistance of the Holy Ghost in these matters. We know that men are united by common interests, common purposes, common dangers—by race, climate and education. It is no more wonderful that people live in families, tribes, communities and nations, than that birds, ants and bees live in flocks and swarms.

If we know anything, we know that language is natural—that it is a physical science. But if we take the ground occupied by the Cardinal, then we insist that everything that cannot be accounted for by man, is supernatural. Let me ask, by what man? What man must we take as the standard?

Cosmas or Humboldt, St. Irenaeus or Darwin? If everything that we cannot account for is above nature, then ignorance is the test of the supernatural. The man who is mentally honest, stops where his knowledge stops. At that point he says that he does not know. Such a man is a philosopher. Then the theologian steps forward, denounces the modesty of the philosopher as blasphemy, and proceeds to tell what is beyond the horizon of the human intellect.

Could a savage account for the telegraph, or the telephone, by natural causes? How would he account for these wonders? He would account for them precisely as the Cardinal accounts for the Catholic Church.

Belonging to no rival church, I have not the slightest interest in the primacy of Leo XIII., and yet it is to be regretted that this primacy rests upon such a narrow and insecure foundation.

The Cardinal says that "it will appear almost certain that the original Greek of St. Irenaeus, *which is unfortunately lost,* contained either τά πρωτεία, or some inflection of πρωτεύω, which signifies primacy."

From this it appears that the primacy of the Bishop of Rome rests on some "inflection" of a Greek word—and that this supposed inflection was in a letter supposed to have been written by St. Irenaeus, which has certainly been lost. Is it possible that the vast fabric of papal power has this, and only this, for its foundation? To this "inflection" has it come at last?

The Cardinal's case depends upon the intelligence and veracity of his witnesses. The Fathers of the church were utterly incapable of examining a question of fact. They were all believers in the miraculous. The same is true of the apostles. If St. John was the author of the Apocalypse, he was undoubtedly insane. If Polycarp said the things attributed to him by Catholic writers, he was certainly in the condition of his master. What is the testimony of St. John worth in the light of the following? "Cerinthus, the heretic, was in a bathhouse. St. John and another Christian were about to enter. St. John cried out: 'Let us run away, lest the house fall upon us while the enemy of truth is in it.'" Is it possible that St. John thought that God would kill two eminent Christians for the purpose of getting even with one heretic?

Let us see who Polycarp was. He seems to have been a prototype of the Catholic Church, as will be seen from the following statement concerning this Father: "When any heretical doctrine was spoken in his presence he would stop his ears." After this, there can be no question of his orthodoxy. It is claimed that Polycarp was a martyr—that a spear was run through his body, and that from the wound his soul, in the shape of a bird, flew away. The history of his death is just as true as the history of his life.

Irenaeus, another witness, took the ground that there was to be a millennium—a thousand years of enjoyment in which celibacy would not be the highest form of virtue. If he is called as a witness for the purpose of establishing the divine origin of the church, and if one of his "inflections" is the basis of papal supremacy, is the Cardinal also willing to take his testimony as to the nature of the millennium?

All the Fathers were infinitely credulous. Every one of them believed, not only in the miracles said to have been wrought by Christ, by the apostles, and by other Christians, but every one of them believed in the Pagan miracles. All of these Fathers were familiar with wonders and impossibilities. Nothing was so common with them as to work miracles, and on many occasions they not only cured diseases, not only reversed the order of nature, but succeeded in raising the dead.

It is very hard, indeed, to prove what the apostles said, or what the Fathers of the church wrote. There were many centuries filled with forgeries—many generations in which the cunning hands of ecclesiastics erased, obliterated or interpolated the records of the past—during which they invented books, invented authors, and quoted from works that never existed.

The testimony of the "Fathers" is without the slightest value. They believed everything—they examined nothing. They received as a waste-basket receives. Whoever accepts their testimony will exclaim with the Cardinal: "Happily, men are not saved by logic."

Robert G. Ingersoll.

IS DIVORCE WRONG?

By Cardinal Gibbons, Bishop Henry C. Potter,
and Colonel Robert G. Ingersoll.

The attention of the public has been particularly directed of late to the abuses of divorce, and to the facilities afforded by the complexities of American law, and by the looseness of its administration, for the disruption of family ties. Therefore the *North American Review* has opened its pages for the thorough discussion of the subject in its moral, social, and religious aspects, and some of the most eminent leaders of modern thought have contributed their opinions. The Rev. S. W. Dike, LL.D., who is a specialist on the subject of divorce, has prepared some statistics touching the matter, and, with the assistance of Bishop Potter, the four following questions have been formulated as a basis for the discussion:

1. Do you believe in the principle of divorce under any circumstances?
2. Ought divorced people to be allowed to marry under any circumstances?
3. What is the effect of divorce on the integrity of the family?
4. Does the absolute prohibition of divorce where it exists contribute to the moral purity of society?

Editor *North American Review,*

Introduction

by the Rev. S. W. Dike, LL.D.

I am to introduce this discussion with some facts and make a few suggestions upon them. In the dozen years of my work at this problem I have steadily insisted upon a broad basis of fact as the only foundation of sound opinion. We now have a great statistical advance in the report of the Department of labor. A few of these statistics will serve the present purpose.

There were in the United States 9,937 divorces reported for the year 1867 and 25,535 for 1886, or a total 328,716 in the twenty years. This increase is more than twice as great as the population, and has been remarkably uniform throughout the period. With the exception of New York, perhaps Delaware, and the three or four States where special legislative reforms have been secured, the increase covers the country and has been more than twice the gain in population. The South apparently felt the movement later than the North and West, but its greater rapidity there will apparently soon obliterate most existing differences. The movement is well-nigh as universal in Europe as here. Thirteen European countries, including Canada, had 6,540 divorces in 1876 and 10,909 in 1886—an increase of 67 per cent. In the same period the increase with us was 72.5 per cent. But the ratios of divorce to population are here generally three or four times greater than in Europe. The ratios to marriage in the United States are sometimes as high as 1 to 10, 1 to 9, or even a little more for single years. In heathen Japan for three years they were more than 1 to 3. But divorce there is almost wholly left to the regulation of the family, and practically optional with the parties. It is a re-transference of the wife by a simple writing to her own family.

1. The increase of divorce is one of several evils affecting the family. Among these are hasty or ill-considered marriages, the decline of marriage and the decrease of children,—too generally among classes pecuniarily best able to maintain domestic life,—the probable increase in some directions of marital infidelity and sexual vice, and last, but not least, a tendency to reduce the family to a minimum of force in the life of society. All these evils should be studied and treated in their relations to each other. Carefully-conducted investigations alone can establish these latter statements beyond dispute, although there can be little doubt of their general correctness as here carefully made. And the conclusion is forced upon us that the toleration of the increase of divorce, touching as it does the vital bond of the family, is so far forth a confession of our western civilization that it despairs of all remedies for ills of the family, and is becoming willing, in great degree, to look away from all true remedies to a dissolution of the family by the courts in all serious cases. If this were our settled purpose, it would look like giving up the idea of producing and protecting a family increasingly capable of enduring to the end of its natural existence. If the drift of things on this subject during the present century may be taken as prophetic, our civilization moves in an opposite direction in its treatment of the family from its course with the individual.

2. Divorce, including these other evils related to the family, is preeminently a social problem. It should therefore be reached by all the forces of our great social institutions—religious, educational, industrial, and political. Each of these should be brought to bear on it proportionately and in cooperation with the others. But I can here take up only one or two lines for further suggestion.

3. The causes of divorces, like those of most social evils, are often many and intricate. The statistics for this country, when the forty-three various statutory causes are reduced to a few classes, show that 20 per cent, of the divorces were based on adultery, 16 on cruelty, 38 were granted for desertion, 4 for drunkenness, less than 3 for neglect to provide, and so on. But these tell very little, except that it is easier or more congenial to use one or another of the statutory causes, just as the old "omnibus clause," which gave general discretion to the courts in Connecticut, and still more in some other States, was made to cover many cases. A special study of forty-five counties in twelve States, however, shows that drunkenness was a direct or indirect cause in 20.1 per cent, of 29,665 cases. That is, it could be found either alone or in conjunction with others, directly or indirectly, in one-fifth of the cases.

4. Laws and their administration affect divorce. New York grants absolute divorce for only one cause, and New Jersey for two. Yet New York has many more divorces in proportion to population, due largely to a looser system of administration. In seventy counties of twelve States

68 per cent, of the applications are granted. The enactment of a more stringent law is immediately followed by a decrease of divorces, from which there is a tendency to recover. Personally, I think stricter methods of administration, restrictions upon remarriage, proper delays in hearing suits, and some penal inflictions for cruelty, desertion, neglect of support, as well as for adultery, would greatly reduce divorces, even without removing a single statutory cause. There would be fewer unhappy families, not more. For people would then look to real remedies instead of confessing the hopelessness of remedy by appeals to the courts. A multitude of petty ills and many utterly wicked frauds and other abuses would disappear. "Your present methods," said a Nova Scotian to a man from Maine a few years ago, "are simply ways of multiplying and magnifying domestic ills." There is much force in this. But let us put reform of marriage laws along with these measures.

5. The evils of conflicting and diverse marriage and divorce laws are doing immense harm. The mischief through which innocent parties are defrauded, children rendered illegitimate, inheritance made uncertain, and actual imprisonments for bigamy grow out of divorce and remarriage, are well known to most. Uniformity through a national law or by conventions of the States has been strongly urged for many years. Uniformity is needed. But for one, I have long discouraged too early action, because the problem is too difficult, the consequences too serious, and the elements of it still too far out of our reach for any really wise action at present. The government report grew immediately out of this conviction. It will, I think, abundantly justify the caution. For it shows that uniformity could affect at the utmost only a small percentage of the total divorces in the United States. *Only 19.9 percent of all the divorced who were married in this country obtained their divorces in a different State from the one in which their marriage had taken place, in all these twenty years, 80.1 per cent, having been divorced in the State where married.* Now, marriage on the average lasts 9.17 years before divorce occurs, which probably is nearly two-fifths the length of a married life before its dissolution by death. From this 19.9 per cent, there must, therefore, be subtracted the large migration of married couples for legitimate purposes, in order to get any fair figure to express the migration for divorce. But the movement of the native population away from the State of birth is 22 or 23 per cent. This, however, includes all ages. For all who believe that divorce itself is generally a great evil, the conclusion is apparently inevitable that the question of uniformity, serious as it is, is a very small part of the great legal problem demanding solution at our hands. This general problem, aside from its graver features in the more immediate sphere of sociology and religion, must evidently tax our publicists and statesmen severely. The old temptation to meet special evils by general legislation besets us on this subject. I think comparative and historical study of the law of the family, (the *Familienrecht* of the Germans), especially if the movement of European law be seen, points toward the need of a pretty comprehensive and thorough examination of our specific legal problem of divorce and marriage law in this fuller light, before much legislation is undertaken.

Samuel W. Dike.

However much men may differ in their views of the nature and attributes of the matrimonial contract, and in their concept of the rights and obligations of the marriage state, no one will deny that these are grave questions; since upon marriage rests the family, and upon the family rest society, civilization, and the highest interests of religion and the state. Yet, strange to say, divorce, the deadly enemy of marriage, stalks abroad today bold and unblushing, a monster licensed by the laws of Christian states to break hearts, wreck homes and ruin souls. And passing strange is it, too, that so many, wise and far-seeing in less weighty concerns, do not appear to see in the ever-growing power of divorce a menace not only to the sacredness of the marriage institution, but even to the fair social fabric reared upon matrimony as its corner-stone.

God instituted in Paradise the marriage state and sanctified it. He established its law of unity and declared its indissolubility. By divine authority Adam spoke when of his wife he said: "This now is bone of my bones, and flesh of my flesh; she shall be called woman, because she was taken out of man. Wherefore a man shall leave father and mother, and shall cleave to his wife: and they shall be two in one flesh."[22]

But like other things on earth, marriage suffered in the fall; and little by little polygamy and divorce began to assert themselves against the law of matrimonial unity and indissolubility. Yet the ideal of the marriage institution never faded away. It survived, not only among the chosen people, but even among the nations of heathendom, disfigured much, 'tis true, but with its ancient beauty never wholly destroyed.

When, in the fullness of time, Christ came to restore the things that were perishing, he reasserted in clear and unequivocal terms the sanctity, unity, and indissolubility of marriage. Nay, more. He gave to this state added holiness and a dignity higher far than it had "from the beginning." He made marriage a sacrament, made it the type of his own never-ending union with his one spotless spouse, the church. St. Paul, writing to the Ephesians, says: "Husbands, love your wives, as Christ also loved the church, and delivered himself up for it, that he might sanctify it, cleansing it by the laver of water in the word of life, that he might present it to himself a glorious church, not having spot or wrinkle, or any such thing, but that it should be holy and without blemish. So also ought men to love their wives as their own bodies. . . . For this cause shall a man leave his father and mother, and shall cleave to his wife, and they shall be two in one flesh."[23]

In defense of Christian marriage, the church was compelled from the earliest days of her existence to do frequent and stern battle. But cultured pagan, and rough barbarian, and haughty Christian lord were met and conquered. Men were taught to master passion, and Christian marriage, with all its rights secured and reverenced, became a ruling power in the world.

The Council of Trent, called, in the throes of the mighty moral upheaval of the sixteenth century, to deal with the new state of things,

---

[22] Gen., ii., 23-24.
[23] Ephes., v., 25-31.

again proclaimed to a believing and an unbelieving world the Catholic doctrine of the holiness, unity, and indissolubility of marriage, and the unlawfulness of divorce. The council declared no new dogmas: it simply reaffirmed the common teaching of the church for centuries. But some of the most hallowed attributes of marriage seemed to be objects of peculiar detestation to the new teachers, and their abolition was soon demanded. "The leaders in the changes of matrimonial law," writes Professor Woolsey, "were the Protestant reformers themselves, and that almost from the beginning of the movement. . . . The reformers, when they discarded the sacramental view of marriage and the celibacy of the clergy, had to make out a new doctrine of marriage and of divorce."[24] The "new doctrine of marriage and of divorce," pleasing as it was to the sensual man, was speedily learned and as speedily put in practice. The sacredness with which Christian marriage had been hedged around began to be more and more openly trespassed upon, and restive shoulders wearied more and more quickly of the marriage yoke when divorce promised freedom for newer joys.

To our own time the logical consequences of the "new doctrine" have come. To-day "abyss calls upon abyss," change calls for change, laxity calls for license. Divorce is now a recognized presence in high life and low; and polygamy, the first-born of divorce, sits shameless in palace and in hovel. Yet the teacher that feared not to speak the words of truth in bygone ages is not silent now. In no uncertain tones, the church proclaims to the world to-day the unchangeable law of the strict unity and absolute indissolubility of valid and consummated Christian marriage.

To the question then, "Can divorce from the bond of marriage ever be allowed?" the Catholic can only answer no.

And for this no, his first and last and best reason can be but this: *"Thus saith the Lord."*

As time goes on the wisdom of the church in absolutely forbidding divorce from the marriage bond grows more and more plain even to the many who deny to this prohibition a divine and authoritative sanction. And nowhere is this more true than in our own country. Yet our experience of the evils of divorce is but the experience of every people that has cherished this monster.

Let us take but a hasty view of the consequences of divorce in ancient times. Turn only to pagan Greece and Rome, two peoples that practiced divorce most extensively. In both we find divorce weakening their primitive virtue and making their latter corruption more corrupt. Among the Greeks morality declined as material civilization advanced. Divorce grew easy and common, and purity and peace were banished from the family circle. Among the Romans divorce was not common until the latter days of the Republic. Then the flood-gates of immorality were opened, and, with divorce made easy, came rushing in corruption of morals among both sexes and in every walk of life. "Passion, interest, or

---

[24] "Divorce and Divorce Legislation," by Theodore D. Woolsey, 2d Ed., p. 126.

caprice," Gibbon, the historian, tells us, "suggested daily motives for the dissolution of marriage; a word, a sign, a message, a letter, the mandate of a freedman, declared the separation; the most tender of human connections was degraded to a transient society of profit or pleasure."[25] Each succeeding generation witnessed moral corruption more general, moral degradation more profound; men and women were no longer ashamed of licentiousness; until at length the nation that became mighty because built on a pure family fell when its corner-stone crumbled away in rottenness.

Heedless of the lessons taught by history, modern nations, too, have made trial of divorce. In Europe, wherever the new gospel of marriage and divorce has had! notable influence, divorce has been legalized; and in due proportion to the extent of that influence causes for divorce have been multiplied, the bond of marriage more and more recklessly broken, and the obligations of that sacred state more and more shamelessly disregarded. In our own country the divorce evil has grown more rapidly than our growth and strengthened more rapidly than our strength. Mr. Carroll D. Wright, in a special report on the statistics of marriage and divorce made to Congress in February, 1889, places the number of divorces in the United States in 1867 at 9,937, and the number in 1886 at 25,535. These figures show an increase of the divorce evil much out of proportion to our increase in population. The knowledge that divorces can easily be procured encourages hasty marriages and equally hasty preparations. Legislators and judges in some States are encouraging inventive genius in the art of finding new causes for divorce. Frequently the most trivial and even ridiculous pretexts are recognized as sufficient for the rupture of the marriage bond; and in some States divorce can be obtained "without publicity," and even without the knowledge of the defendant—in such cases generally an innocent wife. Crime has sometimes been committed for the very purpose of bringing about a divorce, and cases are not rare in which plots have been laid to blacken the reputation of a virtuous spouse in order to obtain legal freedom for new nuptials. Sometimes, too, there is a collusion between the married parties to obtain divorce. One of them trumps up charges; the other does not oppose the suit; and judgment is entered for the plaintiff. Every daily newspaper tells us of divorces applied for or granted, and the public sense of decency is constantly being shocked by the disgusting recital of divorce-court scandals.

We are filled with righteous indignation at Mormonism; we brand it as a national disgrace, and justly demand its suppression. Why? Because, forsooth, the Mormons are polygamists. Do we forget that there are two species of polygamy—simultaneous and successive? Mormons practice without legal recognition the first species; while among us the second species is indulged in, and with the sanction of law, by thousands in whose nostrils Mormonism is a stench and an abomination. The Christian press and pulpit of the land denounce the Mormons as "an

---

[25] "Decline and Fall of the Roman Empire," Milman's Ed., Vol. III., p. 236.

adulterous generation," but too often deal very tenderly with Christian polygamists. Why? Is Christian polygamy less odious in the eyes of God than Mormon polygamy? Among us, 'tis true, the one is looked upon as more respectable than the other. Yet we know that the Mormons as a class, care for their wives and children; while Christian polygamists but too often leave wretched wives to starve, slave, or sin, and leave miserable children a public charge. "O divorced and much-married Christian," says the polygamous dweller by Salt Lake, "pluck first the beam from thy own eye, and then shalt thou see to pluck the mote from the eye of thy much-married, but undivorced, Mormon brother." It follows logically from the Catholic doctrine of the unity and indissolubility of marriage, and the consequent prohibition of divorce from the marital bond, that no one, even though divorced a vinculo by the civil power, can be allowed by the church to take another consort during the lifetime of the true wife or husband, and such connection the church can but hold as sinful. It is written: "Whosoever shall put away his wife and marry another committeth adultery against her. And if the wife shall put away her husband, and be married to another, she committeth adultery."[26]

Of course, I am well aware that upon the words of our Saviour as found in St. Matthew, Chap. xix., 9, many base the right of divorce from the marriage bond for adultery, with permission to remarry. But, as is well known, the Catholic Church, upon the concurrent testimony of the Evangelists Mark[27] and Luke,[28] and upon the teaching of St. Paul,[29] interprets our Lord's words quoted by St. Matthew as simply permitting, on account of adultery, divorce from bed and board, with no right to either party to marry another.

But even if divorce *a vinculo* were not forbidden by divine law, how inadequate a remedy would it be for the evils for which so many deem it a panacea. "Divorce *a vinculo,*" as Dr. Brownson truly says, "logically involves divorce *ad libitum.*"[30] Now, what reason is there to suppose that parties divorced and remated will be happier in the new connection than in the old? As a matter of fact, many persons have been divorced a number of times. Sometimes, too, it happens that, after a period of separation, divorced parties repent of their folly, reunite, and are again divorced. Indeed, experience clearly proves that unhappiness among married people frequently does not arise so much from "mutual incompatibility" as from causes inherent in one or both of the parties— causes that would be likely to make a new union as wretched as the old one. There is wisdom in the pithy saying of a recent writer: "Much ill comes, not because men and women are married, but because they are fools."[31]

---

26 Mark, x., ii, 12.
27 Mark, x., n, 12.
28 Luke, xvi., 18. J I.
29 Cor.,vii., 10, 11.
30 Essay on "The Family—Christian and Pagan."
31 Prof. David Swing in Chicago Journal.

There are some who think that the absolute prohibition of divorce does not contribute to the purity of society, and are therefore of opinion that divorce with liberty to remarry does good in this regard. He who believes the matrimonial bond indissoluble, divorce a vinculo *evil,* and the connection resulting from it criminal, can only say: "Evil should not be done that good may come." But, after all, would even passing good come from this greater freedom? In a few exceptional cases—*Yes:* in the vast majority of cases—*No.* The trying of divorce as a safeguard of purity is an old experiment, and an unsuccessful one. In Rome adulteries increased as divorces were multiplied. After speaking of the facility and frequency of divorce among the Romans, Gibbon adds:

"A specious theory is confuted by this free and perfect experiment, which demonstrates that the liberty of divorce does not contribute to happiness and virtue. The facility of separation would destroy all mutual confidence, and inflame every trifling dispute. The minute difference between a husband and a stranger, which might so easily be removed, might still more easily be forgotten."[32]

How apropos in this connection are the words of Professor Woolsey:

"Nothing is more startling than to pass from the first part of the eighteenth to this latter part of the nineteenth century, and to observe how law has changed and opinion has altered in regard to marriage, the great foundation of society, and to divorce; and how, almost *pari passu,* various offences against chastity, such as concubinage, prostitution, illegitimate births, abortion, disinclination to family life, have increased also—not, indeed, at the same pace everywhere, or all of them equally in all countries, yet have decidedly increased on the whole."[33]

Surely in few parts of the wide world is the truth of these strong words more evident than in those parts of our own country where loose divorce laws have long prevailed.

It should be noted that, while never allowing the dissolution of the marriage bond, the Catholic Church has always permitted, for grave causes and under certain conditions, a temporary or permanent "separation from bed and board." The causes which, *positis ponendis,* justify such separation may be briefly given thus: mutual consent, adultery, and grave peril of soul or body.

It may be said that there are persons so unhappily mated and so constituted that for them no relief can come save from divorce *a vinculo,* with permission to remarry. I shall not linger here to point out to such the need of seeking from a higher than earthly power the grace to suffer and be strong. But for those whose reasoning on this subject is of the earth, earthy, I shall add some words of practical worldly wisdom from eminent jurists. In a note to his edition of Blackstone's "Commentaries," Mr. John Taylor Coleridge says:

---

[32] "Decline and Fall of the Roman Empire," Milman's Ed., Vol. III., p. 236.
[33] "Divorce and Divorce Legislation," 2d Ed., p. 274.

"It is no less truly than beautifully said by Sir W. Scott, in the case of Evans *v.* Evans, that 'though in particular cases the repugnance of the law to dissolve the obligation of matrimonial cohabitation may operate with great severity upon individuals, yet it must be carefully remembered that the general happiness of the married life is secured by its indissolubility.' When people understand that they *must* live together, except for a few reasons known to the law, they learn to soften by mutual accommodation that yoke which they know they cannot shake off: they become good husbands and good wives from the necessity of remaining husbands and wives: for necessity is a powerful master in teaching the duties which it imposes. If it were once understood that upon mutual disgust married persons might be legally separated, many couples who now pass through the world with mutual comfort, with attention to their common offspring, and to the moral order of civil society, might have been at this moment living in a state of mutual unkindness, in a state of estrangement from their common offspring, and in a state of the most licentious and unrestrained immorality. In this case, as in many other cases, the happiness of some individuals must be sacrificed to the greater and more general good."

The facility and frequency of divorce, and its lamentable consequences, are nowadays calling much attention to measures of "divorce reform." "How can divorce reform be best secured?" it may be asked. Believing, as I do, that divorce is evil, I also believe that its "reformation" and its death must be simultaneous. It should cease to be. Divorce as we know it began when marriage was removed from the domain of the church: divorce shall cease when the old order shall be restored. Will this ever come to pass? Perhaps so—after many days. Meanwhile, something might be done, something should be done, to lessen the evils of divorce. Our present divorce legislation must be presumed to be such as the majority of the people wish it. A first step, therefore, in the way of "divorce reform" should be the creation of a more healthy public sentiment on this question. Then will follow measures that will do good in proportion to their stringency. A few practical suggestions as to the salient features of remedial divorce legislation may not be out of place. Persons seeking at the hands of the civil law relief in matrimonial troubles should have the right to ask for divorce *a vinculo,* or simple separation *a mensâ et thoro,* as they may elect. The number of legally-recognized grounds for divorce should be lessened, and "noiseless" divorces forbidden. "Rapid-transit" facilities for passing through divorce courts should be cut off, and divorce "agencies" should be suppressed. The plaintiff in a divorce case should be a *bona fide* resident of the judicial district in which his petition is filed, and in every divorce case the legal representatives of the State should appear for the defendant, and, by all means, the right of remarriage after divorce should be restricted. If divorce cannot be legislated out of existence, let, at least, its power for evil be diminished.

James Cardinal Gibbons.

I am asked certain questions with regard to the attitude of the Episcopal Church towards the matter of divorce. In undertaking to answer them, it is to be remembered that there is a considerable variety of opinion which is held in more or less precise conformity with doctrinal or canonical declarations of the church. With these variations this paper, except in so far as it may briefly indicate them, is not concerned. Nor is it an expression of individual opinion. That is not what has been asked for or attempted.

The doctrine and law of the Protestant Episcopal Church on the subject of divorce is contained in canon 13, title II., of the "Digest of the Canons," 1887. That, canon has been to a certain extent interpreted by Episcopal judgments under section IV. The "public opinion" of the clergy or laity can only be ascertained in the usual way; especially by examining their published treatises, letters, etc., and perhaps most satisfactorily by the reports of discussion in the diocesan and general conventions on the subject of divorce. Among members of the Protestant Episcopal Church divorce is excessively rare, cases of uncertainty in the application of the canon, are much more rare, and the practice of the clergy is almost perfectly uniform. There is, however, by no means the same uniformity in their opinions either as to divorce or marriage.

As divorce is necessarily a mere accident of marriage, and as divorce is impossible without a precedent marriage, much practical difficulty might arise, and much difference of opinion does arise, from the fact that the Protestant Episcopal Church has nowhere defined marriage. Negatively, it is explicitly affirmed (Article XXV.) that "matrimony is not to be counted for a sacrament of the Gospel." This might seem to reduce matrimony to a civil contract. And accordingly the first rubric in the *Form of Solemnization of Matrimony* directs, on the ground of differences of laws in the various States, that "the minister is left to the direction of those laws in everything that regards the civil contract between the parties." Laws determining what persons shall be capable of contracting would seem to be included in "everything that regards the civil contract;" and unquestionably the laws of most of the States render all persons legally divorced capable of at once contracting a new marriage. Both the first section of canon 13 and the *Form of Solemnization,* affirm that, "if any persons be joined together otherwise than as God's word doth allow, their marriage is not lawful." But it is nowhere excepting as to divorce, declared *what the impediments are.* The Protestant Episcopal Church has never, by canon or express legislation, published, for instance, a table of prohibited degrees.

On the matter of divorce, however, canon 13, title II., supersedes, for the members of the Protestant Episcopal Church, both a part of the civil law relating to the persons capable of contracting marriage, and also all private judgment as to the teaching of "the Word of God" on that subject. No minister is allowed, as a rule, to solemnize the marriage of any man or woman who has a divorced husband or wife still living. But if the person seeking to be married is the innocent party in the divorce for adultery, that person, whether man or woman, may be married by a minister of the church. With the above exception, the clergy are forbidden to administer the sacraments to any divorced and remarried person without the express permission of the bishop, unless that person be "penitent" and "in imminent danger of death." Any doubts "as to the facts of any case under section II. of this canon" must be referred to the bishop. Of course, where there is no reasonable doubt the minister may proceed. It may be added that the sacraments are to be refused also to persons who may be reasonably supposed to have contracted marriage "otherwise," in any respect, "than as the Word of God and the discipline of this Church doth allow." These impediments are nowhere defined; and accordingly it has happened that a man who had married a deceased wife's sister and the woman he had married were, by the private judgment of a priest, refused the holy communion. The civil courts do not seem inclined to protect the clergy from consequences of interference with the civil law. In Southbridge, Mass., a few weeks ago, a man who had been denounced from the altar for marrying again after a divorce obtained a judgment for $1,720 damages. The law of the church would seem to be that, even though a legal divorce may have been obtained, remarriage is absolutely forbidden, excepting to the innocent party, whether man or woman, in a divorce for adultery. The penalty for breach of this law might involve, for the officiating clergyman, deposition from the ministry; for the offending man or woman, exclusion from the sacraments, which, in the judgment of a very large number of the clergy, involves everlasting damnation.

It is obvious, then, that the Protestant Episcopal Church allows the complete validity of a divorce *a vinculo* in the case of adultery, and the right of remarriage to the innocent party. But that church has not determined in what manner either the grounds of the divorce or the "innocence" of either party is to be ascertained. The canon does not require a clergyman to demand, nor can the church enable him to secure, the production of a copy of the record or decree of the court of law by which a divorce is granted, nor would such decree indicate the "innocence" of one party, though it might prove the guilt of the other.

The effect of divorce upon the integrity of the family is too obvious to require stating. As the father and mother are the heads of the family, their separation must inevitably destroy the common family life. On the other hand, it is often contended that the destruction has been already completed, and that a divorce is only the legal recognition of what has already taken place; "the integrity of the family" can scarcely remain when either a father or mother, or both, are living in violation of the law on which that integrity rests. The question may be asked whether the absolute prohibition of divorce would contribute to the moral purity of society. It is difficult to answer such a question, because anything on the subject must be comparatively worthless until verified by experience. It is quite certain that the prohibition of divorce never prevents illicit sexual connections, as was abundantly proved when divorce in England was put within the reach of persons who were not able to afford the expense of a special act of Parliament. It is, indeed, so palpable a fact that any amount of evidence or argument is wholly superfluous.

The *law* of the Protestant Episcopal Church is by no means identical with the opinion of either the clergy or the laity. In the judgment of many, the existing law is far too lax, or, at least, the whole doctrine of marriage is far too inadequately dealt with in the authoritative teaching of the church. The opinion of this school finds, perhaps, its most adequate expression in the report of a committee of the last General Convention forming Appendix XIII. of the "Journal" of that convention. It is, substantially, that the Mosaic law of marriage is still binding upon the church, unless directly abrogated by Christ himself; that it was abrogated by him only so far that all divorce was forbidden by him, excepting for the cause of fornication; that a woman might not claim divorce for any reason whatever; that the marriage of a divorced person until the death of the other party is wholly forbidden; that marriage is not merely a civil contract, but a spiritual and supernatural union, requiring for its mutual obligation a supernatural, divine grace; that such grace is only imparted in the sacrament of matrimony, which is a true sacrament and does actually confer grace; that marriage is wholly within the jurisdiction of the church, though the State may determine such rules and guarantees as may secure publicity and sufficient evidence of a marriage, etc.; that severe penalties should be inflicted by the State, on the demand of the church, for the suppression of all offences against the seventh commandment and sundry other parts of the Mosaic legislation, especially in relation to "prohibited degrees."

There is another school, equally earnest and sincere in its zeal for the integrity of the family and sexual purity, which would nevertheless repudiate much the greater part of the above assumption. This school, if one may so venture to combine scattered opinions, argues substantially as follows: The type of all Mosaic legislation was circumcision; that rite was of universal obligation and divine authority. St. Paul so regarded it. The abrogation of the law requiring circumcision was, therefore, the abrogation of the whole of the Mosaic legislation. The "burden of proof," therefore, rests upon those who affirm the present obligation of what formed a part of the Mosaic law; and they must show that it has been reenacted by Christ and his Apostles or forms some part of some other and independent system of law or morals still in force. Christ's words about divorce are not to be construed as a positive law, but as expressing the ideal of marriage, and corresponding to his words about eunuchs, which not everybody "can receive." So far as Christ's words seem to indicate an inequality as to divorce between man and woman, they are explained by the authoritative and inspired assertion of St. Paul: "In Christ Jesus there is neither male nor female." A divine law is equally authoritative by whomsoever declared—whether by the Son Incarnate or by the Holy Ghost speaking through inspired Apostles. If, then, a divine law was ever capable of suspension or modification, it may still be capable of such suspension or modification in corresponding circumstances. The circumstances which justified a modification of the original divine law of marriage do still exist in many conditions of society and even of individual life. The Protestant Episcopal Church cannot, alone, speak with such authority on disputed passages of Scripture as to justify her ministers in direct disobedience to the civil authority, which is also "ordained of God." The exegesis of the early church was closely connected with theories about matter, and about the inferiority of women and of married life, which are no longer believed.

Of course this is a very brief statement. As a matter of fact the actual effect of the doctrine and discipline of the Protestant Episcopal Church on marriage and divorce is that divorce among her members is excessively rare; that it is regarded with extreme aversion; and that the public opinion of the church maintains the law as it now is, but could not be trusted to execute laws more stringent. A member of the committee of the General Convention whose report has been already referred to closes that report with the following protest:

"The undersigned finds himself unable to concur in so much of the [proposed] canon as forbids the holy communion to a truly pious and godly woman who has been compelled by long years of suffering from a drunken and brutal husband to obtain a divorce, and has regularly married some suitable person according to the established laws of the land. And also from so much of the [proposed] canon as may seem to forbid marriage with a deceased wife's sister."

The final action on these points, which has already been stated, indicates that the proposed report thus referred to was, in one particular at least, in advance of the sentiment of the church as expressed in her General Convention.

Henry C. Potter.

Question (1.) *Do you believe in the principle of divorce under any circumstances?*

The world for the most part is ruled by the tomb, and the living are tyrannized over by the dead. Old ideas, long after the conditions under which they were produced have passed away, often persist in surviving. Many are disposed to worship the ancient—to follow the old paths, without inquiring where they lead, and without knowing exactly where they wish to go themselves.

Opinions on the subject of divorce have been, for the most part, inherited from the early Christians. They have come to us through theological and priestly channels. The early Christians believed that the world was about to be destroyed, or that it was to be purified by fire; that all the wicked were to perish, and that the good were to be caught up in the air to meet their Lord—to remain there, in all probability, until the earth was prepared as a habitation for the blessed. With this thought or belief in their minds, the things of this world were of comparatively no importance. The man who built larger barns in which to store his grain was regarded as a foolish farmer, who had forgotten, in his greed for gain, the value of his own soul. They regarded prosperous people as the children of Mammon, and the unfortunate, the wretched and diseased, as the favorites of God. They discouraged all worldly pursuits, except the soliciting of alms. There was no time to marry or to be given in marriage; no time to build homes and have families. All their thoughts were centered upon the heaven they expected to inherit. Business, love, all secular things, fell into disrepute.

Nothing is said in the Testament about the families of the apostles; nothing of family life, of the sacredness of home; nothing about the necessity of education, the improvement and development of the mind. These things were forgotten, for the reason that nothing, in the presence of the expected event, was considered of any importance, except to be ready when the Son of Man should come. Such was the feeling, that rewards were offered by Christ himself to those who would desert their wives and children. Human love was spoken of with contempt. "Let the dead bury their dead. What is that to thee? Follow thou me." They not only believed these things, but acted in accordance with them; and, as a consequence, all the relations of life were denied or avoided, and their obligations disregarded. Marriage was discouraged. It was regarded as only one degree above open and unbridled vice, and was allowed only in consideration of human weakness. It was thought far better not to marry—that it was something grander for a man to love God than to love woman. The exceedingly godly, the really spiritual, believed in celibacy, and held the opposite sex in a kind of pious abhorrence. And yet, with that inconsistency so characteristic of theologians, marriage was held to be a sacrament. The priest said to the man who married: "Remember that you are caught for life. This door opens but once. Before this den of matrimony the tracks are all one way." This was in the nature of a punishment for having married. The theologian felt that the contract of marriage, if not contrary to God's command, was at least contrary to his advice, and that the married ought to suffer in some way, as a matter of justice. The fact that there could be no divorce, that a mistake could not be corrected, was held up as a warning. At every wedding feast this skeleton stretched its fleshless finger towards bride and groom.

Nearly all intelligent people have given up the idea that the world is about to come to an end. They do not now believe that prosperity is a certain sign of wickedness, or that poverty and wretchedness are sure certificates of virtue. They are hardly convinced that Dives should have been sent to hell simply for being rich, or that Lazarus was entitled to eternal joy on account of his poverty. We now know that prosperous people may be good, and that unfortunate people may be bad. We have reached the conclusion that the practice of virtue tends in the direction of prosperity, and that a violation of the conditions of well-being brings, with absolute certainty, wretchedness and misfortune.

There was a time when it was believed that the sin of an individual was visited upon the tribe, the community, or the nation to which he belonged. It was then thought that if a man or woman had made a vow to God, and had failed to keep the vow, God might punish the entire community; therefore it was the business of the community to see to it that the vow was kept. That idea has been abandoned. As we progress, the rights of the individual are perceived, and we are now beginning dimly to discern that there are no rights higher than the rights of the individual. There was a time when nearly all believed in the reforming power of punishment—in the beneficence of brute force. But the world is changing. It was at one time thought that the Inquisition was the savior of society; that the persecution of the philosopher was requisite to the preservation of the state, and that, no matter what happened, the state should be preserved. We have now more light. And standing upon this luminous point that we call the present, let me answer your questions.

Marriage is the most important, the most sacred, contract that human beings can make. No matter whether we call it a contract, or a sacrament, or both, it remains precisely the same. And no matter whether this contract is entered into in the presence of magistrate or priest, it is exactly the same. A true marriage is a natural concord and agreement of souls, a harmony in which discord is not even imagined; it is a mingling so perfect that only one seems to exist; all other considerations are lost; the present seems to be eternal. In this supreme moment there is no shadow—or the shadow is as luminous as light. And when two beings thus love, thus unite, this is the true marriage of soul and soul. That which is said before the altar, or minister, or magistrate, or in the presence of witnesses, is only the outward evidence of that which has already happened within; it simply testifies to a union that has already taken place—to the uniting of two mornings of hope to reach the night together. Each has found the ideal; the man has found the one woman of all the world—the impersonation of affection, purity, passion, love, beauty, and grace; and the woman has found the one man of all the world, her ideal, and all that she knows of romance, of art, courage, heroism, honesty, is realized in him. The idea of contract is lost. Duty and obligation are instantly changed into desire and joy, and two lives, like uniting streams, flow on as one. Nothing can add to the sacredness of this marriage, to the obligation and duty of each to each. There is nothing in the ceremony except the desire on the part of the man and woman that the whole world should know that they are really married and that their souls have been united.

Every marriage, for a thousand reasons, should be public, should be recorded, should be known; but, above all, to the end that the purity of the union should appear. These ceremonies are not only for the good and for the protection of the married, but also for the protection of their children, and of society as well. But, after all, the marriage remains a contract of the highest possible character—a contract in which each gives and receives a heart.

The question then arises, Should this marriage, under any circumstances, be dissolved? It is easy to understand the position taken by the various churches; but back of theological opinions is the question of contract.

In this contract of marriage, the man agrees to protect and cherish his wife. Suppose that he refuses to protect; that he abuses, assaults, and tramples upon the woman he wed. What is her redress? Is she under any obligation to him? He has violated the contract. He has failed to protect, and, in addition, he has assaulted her like a wild beast. Is she under any obligation to him? Is she bound by the contract he has broken? If so, what is the consideration for this obligation? Must she live with him for his sake? or, if she leaves him to preserve her life, must she remain his wife for his sake? No intelligent man will answer these questions in the affirmative.

If, then, she is not bound to remain his wife for the husband's sake, is she bound to remain his wife because the marriage was a sacrament? Is there any obligation on the part of the wife to remain with the brutal husband for the sake of God? Can her conduct affect in any way the happiness of an infinite being? Is it possible for a human being to increase or diminish the well-being of the Infinite?

The next question is as to the right of society in this matter. It must be admitted that the peace of society will be promoted by the separation of such people. Certainly society cannot insist upon a wife remaining with a husband who bruises and mangles her flesh. Even married women have a right to personal security. They do not lose, either by contract or sacrament, the right of self-preservation; this they share in common, to say the least of it, with the lowest living creatures.

This will probably be admitted by most of the enemies of divorce; but they will insist that while the wife has the right to flee from her husband's roof and seek protection of kindred or friends, the marriage—the sacrament—must remain unbroken. Is it to the interest of society that those who despise each other should live together? Ought the world to be peopled by the children of hatred or disgust, the children of lust and loathing, or by the welcome babes of mutual love? Is it possible that an infinitely wise and compassionate God insists that a helpless woman shall remain the wife of a cruel wretch? Can this add to the joy of Paradise, or tend to keep one harp in tune? Can anything be more infamous than for a government to compel a woman to remain the wife of a man she hates—of one whom she justly holds in abhorrence? Does any decent man wish the assistance of a constable, a sheriff, a judge, or a church, to keep his wife in his house? Is it possible to conceive of a more contemptible human being than a man who would appeal to force in such a case? It may be said that the woman is free to go, and that the courts will protect her from the brutality of the man who promised to be her protector; but where shall the woman go? She may have no friends; or they may be poor; her kindred may be dead. Has she no right to build another home? Must this woman, full of kindness, affection, health, be tied and chained to this living corpse? Is there no future for her? Must she be an outcast forever—deceived and betrayed for her whole life? Can she never sit by her own hearth, with the arms of her children about her neck, and with a husband who loves and protects her? Is she to become a social pariah, and is this for the benefit of society?—or is it for the sake of the wretch who destroyed her life?

The ground has been taken that woman would lose her dignity if marriage could be annulled. Is it necessary to lose your liberty in order to retain your moral character—in order to be pure and womanly? Must a woman, in order to retain her virtue, become a slave, a serf, with a beast for a master, or with society for a master, or with a phantom for a master?

If an infinite being is one of the parties to the contract, is it not the duty of this being to see to it that the contract is carried out? What consideration does the infinite being give? What consideration does he receive? If a wife owes no duty to her husband because the husband has violated the contract, and has even assaulted her life, is it possible for her to feel toward him any real thrill of affection? If she does not, what is there left of marriage? What part of this contract or sacrament remains in living force? She can not sustain the relation of wife, because she abhors him; she cannot remain under the same roof, for fear that she may be killed. They sustain, then, only the relations of hunter and hunted—of tyrant and victim. Is it desirable that this relation should last through life, and that it should be rendered sacred by the ceremony of a church?

Again I ask, Is it desirable to have families raised under such circumstances? Are we in need of children born of such parents? Can the virtue of others be preserved only by this destruction of happiness, by this perpetual imprisonment?

A marriage without love is bad enough, and a marriage for wealth or position is low enough; but what shall we say of a marriage where the parties actually abhor each other? Is there any morality in this? any virtue in this? Is there virtue in retaining the name of wife, or husband, without the real and true relation? Will any good man say, will any good woman declare, that a true, loving woman should be compelled to be the mother of children whose father she detests? Is there a good woman in the world who would not shrink from this herself; and is there a woman so heartless and so immoral that she would force another to bear that from which she would shudderingly and shriekingly shrink?

Marriages are made by men and women; not by society; not by the state; not by the church; not by supernatural beings. By this time we should know that nothing is moral that does not tend to the well-being of sentient beings; that nothing is virtuous the result of which is not good. We know now, if we know anything, that all the reasons for doing right, and all the reasons against doing wrong, are here in this world. We should have imagination enough to put ourselves in the place of another. Let a man suppose himself a helpless woman beaten by a brutal husband—would he advocate divorces then?

Few people have an adequate idea of the sufferings of women and children, of the number of wives who tremble when they hear the footsteps of a returning husband, of the number of children who hide when they hear the voice of a father. Few`people know the number of blows that fall on the flesh of the helpless every day, and few know the nights of terror passed by mothers who hold babes to their breasts. Compared with these, all the hardships of poverty borne by those who love each other are as nothing. Men and women truly married bear the sufferings and misfortunes of poverty together. They console each other. In the darkest night they see the radiance of a star, and their affection gives to the heart of each perpetual sunshine.

The good home is the unit of the good government. The hearthstone is the corner-stone of civilization. Society is not interested in the preservation of hateful homes, of homes where husbands and wives are selfish, cold, and cruel. It is not to the interest of society that good women should be enslaved, that they should live in fear, or that they should become mothers by husbands whom they hate. Homes should be filled with kind and generous fathers, with true and loving mothers; and when they are so filled, the world will be civilized. Intelligence will rock the cradle; justice will sit in the courts; wisdom in the legislative halls; and above all and over all, like the dome of heaven, will be the spirit of liberty.

Although marriage is the most important and the most sacred contract that human beings can make, still when that contract has been violated, courts should have the power to declare it null and void upon such conditions as may be just.

As a rule, the woman dowers the husband with her youth, her beauty, her love—with all she has; and from this contract certainly the husband should never be released, unless the wife has broken the conditions of that contract. Divorces should be granted publicly, precisely as the marriage should be solemnized. Every marriage should be known, and there should be witnesses, to the end that the character of the contract entered into should be understood; the record should be open and public. And the same is true of divorces. The conditions should be determined, the property should be divided by a court of equity, and the custody of the children given under regulations prescribed.

Men and women are not virtuous by law. Law does not of itself create virtue, nor is it the foundation or fountain of love. Law should protect virtue, and law should protect the wife, if she has kept her contract, and the husband, if he has fulfilled his. But the death of love is the end of marriage. Love is natural. Back of all ceremony burns and will forever burn the sacred flame. There has been no time in the world's history when that torch was extinguished. In all ages, in all climes, among all people, there has been true, pure, and unselfish love. Long before a ceremony was thought of, long before a priest existed, there were true and perfect marriages. Back of public opinion is natural modesty, the affections of the heart; and in spite of all law, there is and forever will be the realm of choice. Wherever love is, it is pure; and everywhere, and at all times, the ceremony of marriage testifies to that which has happened within the temple of the human heart.

Question (2). Ought divorced people to be allowed to marry under any circumstances?

This depends upon whether marriage is a crime. If it is not a crime, why should any penalty be attached? Can any one conceive of any reason why a woman obtaining a divorce, without fault on her part, should be compelled as a punishment to remain forever single? Why should she be punished for the dishonesty or brutality of another? Why should a man who faithfully kept his contract of marriage, and who was deserted by an unfaithful wife, be punished for the benefit of society? Why should he be doomed to live without a home?

There is still another view. We must remember that human passions are the same after as before divorce. To prevent remarriage is to give excuse for vice.

Question (3). What is the effect of divorce upon the integrity of the family?

The real marriage is back of the ceremony, and the real divorce is back of the decree. When love is dead, when husband and wife abhor each other, they are divorced. The decree records in a judicial way what has really taken place, just as the ceremony of marriage attests a contract already made.

The true family is the result of the true marriage, and the institution of the family should above all things be preserved. What becomes of the sacredness of the home, if the law compels those who abhor each other to sit at the same hearth? This lowers the standard, and changes the happy haven of home into the prison-cell. If we wish to preserve the integrity of the family, we must preserve the democracy of the fireside, the republicanism of the home, the absolute and perfect equality of husband and wife. There must be no exhibition of force, no specter of fear. The mother must not remain through an order of court, or the command of a priest, or by virtue of the tyranny of society; she must sit in absolute freedom, the queen of herself, the sovereign of her own soul and of her own body. Real homes can never be preserved through force, through slavery, or superstition. Nothing can be more sacred than a home, no altar purer than the hearth.

Question (4). *Does the absolute prohibition of divorce where it exists contribute to the moral purity of society?*

We must define our terms. What is moral purity? The intelligent of this world seek the well-being of themselves and others. They know that happiness is the only good; and this they strive to attain. To live in accordance with the conditions of well-being is moral in the highest sense. To use the best instrumentalities to attain the highest ends is our highest conception of the moral. In other words, morality is the melody of the perfection of conduct. A man is not moral because he is obedient through fear or ignorance. Morality lives in the realm of perceived obligation, and where a being acts in accordance with perceived obligation, that being is moral. Morality is not the child of slavery. Ignorance is not the corner-stone of virtue.

The first duty of a human being is to himself. He must see to it that he does not become a burden upon others. To be self-respecting, he must endeavor to be self-sustaining. If by his industry and intelligence he accumulates a margin, then he is under obligation to do with that margin all the good he can. He who lives to the ideal does the best he can. In true marriage men and women give not only their bodies, but their souls. This is the ideal marriage; this is moral. They who give their bodies, but not their souls, are not married, whatever the ceremony may be; this is immoral.

If this be true, upon what principle can a woman continue to sustain the relation of wife after love is dead? Is there some other consideration that can take the place of genuine affection? Can she be bribed with money, or a home, or position, or by public opinion, and still remain a virtuous woman? Is it for the good of society that virtue should be thus crucified between church and state? Can it be said that this contributes to the moral purity of the human race?

Is there a higher standard of virtue in countries where divorce is prohibited than in those where it is granted? Where husbands and wives who have ceased to love cannot be divorced, there are mistresses and lovers.

The sacramental view of marriage is the shield of vice. The world looks at the wife who has been abused, who has been driven from the home of her husband, and the world pities; and when this wife is loved by some other man, the world excuses. So, too, the husband who cannot live in peace, who leaves his home, is pitied and excused.

Is it possible to conceive of anything more immoral than for a husband to insist on living with a wife who has no love for him? Is not this a perpetual crime? Is the wife to lose her personality? Has she no right of choice? Is her modesty the property of another? Is the man she hates the lord of her desire? Has she no right to guard the jewels of her soul? Is there a depth below this? And is this the foundation of morality? this the corner-stone of society? this the arch that supports the dome of civilization? Is this pathetic sacrifice on the one hand, this sacrilege on the other, pleasing in the sight of heaven?

To me, the tenderest word in our language, the most pathetic fact within our knowledge, is maternity. Around this sacred word cluster the joys and sorrows, the agonies and ecstasies, of the human race. The mother walks in the shadow of death that she may give another life. Upon the altar of love she puts her own life in pawn. When the world is civilized, no wife will become a mother against her will. Man will then know that to enslave another is to imprison himself.

Robert G. Ingersoll.

DIVORCE.

A little while ago the North American Review propounded the following questions:

1. Do you believe in the principle of divorce under any circumstances?

2. Ought divorced people to be allowed to marry, under any circumstances?

3. What is the effect of divorce on the integrity of the family?

4. Does the absolute prohibition of divorce, where it exists, contribute to the moral purity of society?

These questions were answered in the November number of the *Review*, 1889, by Cardinal Gibbons, Bishop Henry C. Potter and myself. In the December number, the same questions were again answered by W. E. Gladstone, Justice Bradley and Senator Dolph. In the following month Mary A. Livermore, Amelia E. Barr, Rose Terry Cooke, Elizabeth Stuart Phelps and Jennie June gave their opinions upon the subject of divorce; and in the February number of this year, Margaret Lee and the Rev. Phillip S. Moxom contributed articles upon this subject.

I propose to review these articles, and, first, let me say a few words in answer to Cardinal Gibbons.

REPLY TO CARDINAL GIBBONS.

The indissolubility of marriage was a reaction from polygamy. Man naturally rushes from one extreme to the other. The Cardinal informs us that "God instituted in Paradise the marriage state, and sanctified it;" that "he established its law of unity and declared its indissolubility." The Cardinal, however, accounts for polygamy and divorce by saying that, "marriage suffered in the fall."

If it be true that God instituted marriage in the Garden of Eden, and declared its unity and indissolubility, how do you account for the fact that this same God afterwards upheld polygamy? How is it that he forgot to say anything on the subject when he gave the Ten Commandments to Moses? How does it happen that in these commandments he puts women on an equality with other property—"Thou shalt not covet thy neighbor's wife, or thy neighbor's ox, or anything that is thy neighbor's"? How did it happen that Jacob, who was in direct communication with God, married, not his deceased wife's sister, but both sisters, while both were living? Is there any way of accounting for the fact that God upheld concubinage?

Neither is it true that "Christ reasserted in clear and unequivocal terms, the sanctity, unity, and indissolubility of marriage." Neither is it true that "Christ gave to this state an added holiness and a dignity higher far than it had 'from the beginning.'" If God declared the unity and indissolubility of marriage in the Garden of Eden, how was it possible for Christ to have "added a holiness and dignity to marriage higher far than it had from the beginning"? How did Christ make marriage a sacrament? There is nothing on that subject in the new

Testament; besides, Christ did apparently allow divorce, for one cause at least. He is reported to have said: "Whosoever putteth away his wife, save for fornication, causeth her to commit adultery."

The Cardinal answers the question, "Can divorce from the bonds of marriage ever be allowed?" with an emphatic theological "NO," and as a reason for this "no," says, "Thus saith the Lord."

It is true that we regard Mormonism as a national disgrace, and that we so regard it because the Mormons are polygamists. At the same time, intelligent people admit that polygamy is no worse in Utah, than it was in Palestine—no worse under Joseph Smith, than under Jehovah—that it has been and must be forever the same, in all countries and in all times. The Cardinal takes the ground that "there are two species of polygamy—simultaneous and successive," and yet he seems to regard both species with equal horror. If a wife dies and the husband marries another woman, is not that successive polygamy?

The Cardinal takes the ground that while no dissolution of the marriage bond should be allowed, yet for grave causes a temporary or permanent separation from bed and board may be obtained, and these causes he enumerates as "mutual consent, adultery, and grave peril of soul or body." To those, however, not satisfied with this doctrine, and who are "so unhappily mated and so constituted that for them no relief can come save from absolute divorce," the Cardinal says, in a very sympathetic way, that he "Will not linger here to point out to such the need of seeking from a higher than earthly power, the grace to suffer and be strong."

At the foundation and upon the very threshold of this inquiry, one thing ought to be settled, and that is this: Are we to answer these questions in the light of human experience; are we to answer them from the standpoint of what is better here, in this world, for men and women—what is better for society here and now—or are we to ask: What is the will of God? And in order to find out what is this will of God, are we to ask the church, or are we to read what are called "the sacred writings" for ourselves? In other words, are these questions to be settled by theological and ecclesiastical authority, or by the common sense of mankind? No one, in my judgment, should marry for the sake of God, and no one should be divorced for the sake of God, and no man and woman should live together as husband and wife, for the sake of God. God being an infinite being, cannot be rendered unhappy by any action of man, neither can his well-being be increased; consequently, the will of God has nothing whatever to do with this matter. The real question then must be: What is best for man?

Only the other day, a husband sought out his wife and with his own hand covered her face with sulfuric acid, and in a moment afterward she was blind. A Cardinal of the Catholic Church tells this woman, sitting in darkness, that it is her duty to "suffer and be strong"; that she must still remain the wife of this wretch; that to break the bond that binds them together, would be an act of sacrilege. So, too, two years ago, a husband deserted his wife in Germany. He came to this country. She was poor. She had two children—one a babe. Holding one in her arm, and leading the other by the hand, she walked hundreds of miles to the shore of the sea. Overcome by fatigue, she was taken sick, and for months remained in a hospital. Having recovered, she went to work, and finally got enough money to pay her passage to New York. She came to this city, bringing her children with her. Upon her arrival, she commenced a search for her husband. One day overcome by exertion, she fainted in the street. Persons took pity upon her and carried her upstairs into a room. By a strange coincidence, a few moments afterward her husband entered. She recognized him. He fell upon her like a wild beast, and threw her down the stairs. She was taken up from the pavement bleeding, and carried to a hospital.

The Cardinal says to this woman: Remain the wife of this man; it will be very pleasing to God; "suffer and be strong." But I say to this woman: Apply to some Court; get a decree of absolute divorce; cling to your children, and if at any time hereafter some good and honest man offers you his hand and heart, and you can love him, accept him and build another home, to the end that you may sit by your own fireside, in your old age, with your children about you.

It is not true that the indissolubility of marriage preserves the virtue of mankind. The fact is exactly the opposite. If the Cardinal wishes to know why there are more divorces now than there were fifty or a hundred years ago, let me tell him: Women are far more intelligent—some of them are no longer the slaves either of husbands, or priests. They are beginning to think for themselves. They can see no good reason why they should sacrifice their lives to please Popes or Gods. They are no longer deceived by theological prophecies. They are not willing to suffer here, with the hope of being happy beyond the clouds—they want their happiness now.

REPLY TO BISHOP POTTER.

Bishop Potter does not agree with the Cardinal, yet they both study substantially the same bible—both have been set apart for the purpose of revealing the revelation. They are the persons whose duty it is to enlighten the common people. Cardinal Gibbons knows that he represents the only true church, and Bishop Potter is just as sure that he occupies that position. What is the ordinary man to do?

The Cardinal states, without the slightest hesitation, that "Christ made marriage a sacrament—made it the type of his own never-ending union with his one sinless spouse, the church." The Bishop does not agree with the Cardinal. He says: "Christ's words about divorce are not to be construed as a positive law, but as expressing the ideal of marriage, and corresponding to his words about eunuchs, which not everybody can receive." Ought not the augurs to agree among themselves? What is a man who has only been born once, to do?

The Cardinal says explicitly that marriage is a sacrament, and the Bishop cites Article xxv., that "matrimony is not to be accounted for a sacrament of the gospel," and then admits that "this might seem to reduce matrimony to a civil contract." For the purpose of bolstering up that view, he says, "The first rubric in the Form of Solemnization of Matrimony declares that the minister is left to the direction of those laws in every thing that regards a civil contract between the parties.'" He admits that "no minister is allowed, *as a rule,* to solemnize the marriage of any man or woman who has a divorced husband or wife still living." As a matter of fact, we know that hundreds of Episcopalians do marry where a wife or a husband is still living, and they are not turned out of the Episcopal Church for this offence. The Bishop admits that the church can do very little on the subject, but seems to gather a little consolation from the fact, that "the penalty for breach of this law might involve, for the officiating clergyman, deposition from the ministry—for the offending man or woman exclusion from the sacraments, which, in the judgment of a very large number of the clergy, involves everlasting damnation."

The Cardinal is perfectly satisfied that the prohibition of divorce is the foundation of morality, and the Bishop is equally certain that "the prohibition of divorce never prevents illicit sexual connections."

The Bishop also gives us the report of a committee of the last General Convention, forming Appendix xiii of the Journal. This report, according to the Bishop, is to the effect "that the Mosaic law of marriage is still binding upon the church unless directly abrogated by Christ himself, that it-was abrogated by him only so far that all divorce was forbidden by him excepting for the cause of fornication; that a woman might not claim divorce for any reason whatever; that the marriage of a divorced person until the death of the other party, is wholly forbidden; that marriage is not merely a civil contract but a spiritual and supernatural union, requiring for its mutual obligations a supernatural divine grace, and that such grace is only imparted in the sacrament of matrimony."

The most beautiful thing about this report is, that a woman might not claim divorce for any reason whatever. I must admit that the report is in exact accordance with the words of Jesus Christ. On the other hand, the Bishop, not to leave us entirely without hope, says that "there is in his church another school, equally earnest and sincere in its zeal for the integrity of the family, which would nevertheless repudiate the greater part of the above report."

There is one thing, however, that I was exceedingly glad to see, and that is, that according to the Bishop the ideas of the early church are closely connected with theories about matter, and about the inferiority of woman, and about married life, which are no longer believed. The Bishop has, with great clearness, stated several sides of this question; but I must say, that after reading the Cardinal and the Bishop, the earnest theological seeker after truth would find himself, to say the least of it, in some doubt.

As a matter of fact, who cares what the Old Testament says upon this subject? Are we to be bound forever by the ancient barbarians?

Mr. Gladstone takes the ground, first, "that marriage is essentially a contract for life, and only expires when life itself expires"; second, "that Christian marriage involves a vow before God"; third, "that no authority has been given to the Christian Church to cancel such a vow"; fourth, "that it lies beyond the province of tie civil legislature, which, from the necessity of things, has a veto within the limits of reason, upon the making of it, but has no competency to annul it when once made"; fifth, "that according to the laws of just interpretation, remarriage is forbidden by the text of Holy Scripture"; and sixth, "that while divorce of any kind impairs the integrity of the family, divorce with remarriage destroys it root and branch; that the parental and the conjugal relations are joined together by the hand of the Almighty no less than the persons united by the marriage tie, to one another." First. Undoubtedly, a real marriage was never entered into unless the parties expected to live together as long as they lived. It does not enter into the imagination of the real lover that the time is coming when he is to desert the being he adores, neither does it enter into the imagination of his wife, or of the girl about to become a wife. But how and in what way, does a Christian marriage involve a vow before God? Is God a party to the contract? If yes, he ought to see to it that the contract is carried out. If there are three parties—the man, the woman, and God—each one should be bound to do something, and what is God bound to do? Is he to hold the man to his contract, when the woman has violated hers? Is it his business to hold the woman to the contract, when the man has violated his? And what right has he to have anything to say on the subject, unless he has agreed to do something by reason of this vow? Otherwise, it would be simply a *nudum pactum*—a vow without consideration.

Mr. Gladstone informs us that no authority has been given to the Christian Church to cancel such a vow. If he means by that, that God has not given any such authority to the Christian Church, I most cheerfully admit it.[34]

JUSTICE BRADLEY.

Cardinal Gibbons, Bishop Potter, and Mr. Gladstone represent the theological side—that is to say, the impracticable, the supernatural, the unnatural. After reading their opinions, it is refreshing to read those of Justice Bradley. It is like coming out of the tomb into the fresh air.

Speaking of the law, whether regarded as divine or human or both, Justice Bradley says: "I know no other law on the subject but the moral law, which does not consist of arbitrary enactments and decrees, but is adapted to our condition as human beings. This is so, whether it is conceived of as the will of an all-wise creator, or as the voice of humanity speaking from its experience, its necessities and its higher instincts. And that law surely does not demand that the injured party to

---

[34] Note.—This abrupt termination, together with the unfinished replies to Justice Bradley and Senator Dolph, which follow, shows that the author must have been interrupted in his work, and on next taking it up concluded that the colloquial and concrete form would better serve his turn than the more formal and didactic style above employed. He thereupon dictated his reply to the Gibbon and Gladstone arguments in the following form which will be regarded as a most interesting instance of the author's wonderful versatility of style.

This unfinished matter was found among Col. Ingersoll's manuscripts, and is given as transcribed from the stenographic notes of Mr. I. N. Baker, his secretary, without revision by the author.

the marriage bond should be forever tied to one who disregards and violates every obligation that it imposes—to one with whom it is impossible to cohabit—to one whose touch is contamination. Nor does it demand that such injured party, if legally free, should be forever debarred from forming other ties through which the lost hopes of happiness for life may be restored. It is not reason, and it can not be law—divine, or moral—that unfaithfulness, or willful and obstinate desertion, or persistent cruelty of the stronger party, should afford no ground for relief. . . . If no redress be legalized, the law itself will be set at defiance, and greater injury to soul and body will result from clandestine methods of relief."

Surely, this is good, wholesome, practical common sense.

SENATOR DOLPH.

Senator Dolph strikes a strong blow, and takes the foundation from under the idiotic idea of legal separation without divorce. He says: "As there should be no partial divorce, which leaves the parties in the condition aptly described by an eminent jurist as 'a wife without a husband and a husband without a wife,' so, as a matter of public expediency, and in the interest of public morals, whenever and however the marriage is dissolved, both parties should be left free to remarry." Again: "Prohibition of remarriage is likely to injure society more than the remarriage of the guilty party;" and the Senator says, with great force: "Divorce for proper causes, free from fraud and collusion, conserves the moral integrity of the family."

In answering the question as to whether absolute prohibition of divorce tends to morality or immorality, the Senator cites the case of South Carolina. In that State, divorces were prohibited, and in consequence of this prohibition, the proportion of his property which a married man might give to his concubine was regulated by law.

THE ARGUMENT CONTINUED,
IN COLLOQUIAL FORM.

Those who have written on the subject of divorce seem to be divided into two classes—the supernaturalists and the naturalists. The first class rely on tradition, inspired books, the opinions of theologians as expressed in creeds, and the decisions of ecclesiastical tribunals. The second class take into account the nature of human beings, their own experience, and the facts of life, as they know them. The first class live for another world; the second, for this—the one in which we live.

The theological theorists regard men and women as depraved, in consequence of what they are pleased to call "the fall of man," while the men and women of common sense know that the race has slowly and painfully progressed through countless years of suffering and toil. The priests insist that marriage is a sacrament; the philosopher, that it is a contract.

The question as to the propriety of granting divorces cannot now be settled by quoting passages of Scripture, or by appealing to creeds, or by citing the acts of legislatures or the decisions of courts. With intelligent millions, the Scriptures are no longer considered as of the slightest authority. They pay no more regard to the Bible than to the Koran, the Zend-Avestas, or the Popol Vuh—neither do they care for the various creeds that were formulated by barbarian ancestors, nor for the laws and decisions based upon the savagery of the past.

In the olden times when religions were manufactured—when priest-craft and lunacy governed the world—the women were not consulted. They were regarded and treated as serfs and menials—looked upon as a species of property to be bought and sold like the other domestic animals. This view or estimation of woman was undoubtedly in the mind of the author of the Ten Commandments when he said: "Thou shalt not covet thy neighbor's wife,—nor his ox."

Such, however, has been the advance of woman in all departments of knowledge—such advance having been made in spite of the efforts of the church to keep her the slave of faith—that the obligations, rights and remedies growing out of the contract of marriage and its violation, cannot be finally determined without her consent and approbation. Legislators and priests must consult with wives and mothers. They must become acquainted with their wants and desires—with their profound aversions, their pure hatreds, their loving self-denials, and, above all, with the religion of the body that moulds and dominates their lives.

We have learned to suspect the truth of the old, because it is old, and for that reason was born in the days of slavery and darkness—because the probability is that the parents of the old were ignorance and superstition. We are beginning to be wise enough to take into consideration the circumstances of our own time—the theories and aspirations of the present—the changed conditions of the world—the discoveries and inventions that have modified or completely changed the standards of the greatest of the human race. We are on the eve of discovering that nothing should be done for the sake of gods, but all for the good of man—nothing for another world—everything for this.

All the theories must be tested by experience, by facts. The moment a supernatural theory comes in contact with a natural fact, it falls to chaos. Let us test all these theories about marriage and divorce—all this sacramental, indissoluble imbecility, with a real case—with a fact in life.

A few years ago a man and woman fell in love and were married in a German village. The woman had a little money and this was squandered by the husband. When the money was gone, the husband deserted his wife and two little children, leaving them to live as best they might. She had honestly given her hand and heart, and believed that if she could only see him once more—if he could again look into her eyes—he would come back to her. The husband had fled to America. The wife lived four hundred miles from the sea. Taking her two little children with her, she traveled on foot the entire distance. For eight weeks she journeyed, and when she reached the sea—tired, hungry, worn out, she fell unconscious in the street. She was taken to the hospital, and for many weeks fought for life upon the shore of death. At last she recovered, and sailed for New York. She was enabled to get just enough money to buy a steerage ticket.

A few days ago, while wandering in the streets of New York in search of her husband, she sank unconscious to the sidewalk. She was taken into the home of another. In a little while her husband entered. He caught sight of his wife. She ran toward him, threw her arms about his neck, and cried: "At last I have found you!" "With an oath, he threw her to the floor; he bruised her flesh with his feet and fists; he dragged her into the hall, and threw her into the street."

Let us suppose that this poor wife sought out Cardinal Gibbons and the Right Honorable William E. Gladstone, for the purpose of asking their advice. Let us imagine the conversation:

The Wife. My dear Cardinal, I was married four years ago. I loved my husband and I was sure that he loved me. Two babes were born. He deserted me without cause. He left me in poverty and want. Feeling that he had been overcome by some delusion—tempted by something more than he could bear, and dreaming that if I could look upon his face again he would return, I followed-him on foot. I walked, with my children in my arms, four hundred miles. I crossed the sea. I found him at last—and instead of giving me again his love, he fell upon me like a wild beast. He bruised and blackened my flesh. He threw me from him, and for my proffered love I received curses and blows. Another man, touched by the evidence of my devotion, made my acquaintance—came to my relief—supplied my wants—gave me and my children comfort, and then offered me his hand and heart, in marriage. My dear Cardinal, I told him that I was a married woman, and he told me that I should obtain a divorce, and so I have come to ask your counsel.

The Cardinal. My dear woman, God instituted in Paradise the marriage state and sanctified it, and he established its law of unity and declared its indissolubility.

The Wife. But, Mr. Cardinal, if it be true that "God instituted marriage in the Garden of Eden, and declared its unity and indissolubility," how do you account for the fact that this same God afterward upheld polygamy? How is it that he forgot to say anything on the subject when he gave the Ten Commandments to Moses?

The Cardinal. You must remember that the institution of marriage suffered in the fall of man.

The Wife. How does that throw any light upon my case? That was long ago. Surely, I was not represented at that time, and is it right that I should be punished for what was done by others in the very beginning of the world?

The Cardinal. Christ reasserted in clear and unequivocal terms, the sanctity, unity and indissolubility of marriage, and Christ gave to this state an added holiness, and a dignity higher far than it had from the beginning.

The Wife. How did it happen that Jacob, while in direct communication with God, married, not his deceased wife's sister, but both sisters while both were living? And how, my dear Cardinal, do you account for the fact that God upheld concubinage?

The Cardinal. Marriage is a sacrament. You seem to ask me whether divorce from the bond of marriage can ever be allowed? I answer with an emphatic theological No; and as a reason for this No, I say, Thus saith the Lord. To allow a divorce and to permit the divorced parties, or either of them, to remarry, is one species of polygamy. There are two kinds—the simultaneous and the successive.

The Wife. But why did God allow simultaneous polygamy in Palestine? Was it any better in Palestine then than it is in Utah now? If a wife dies, and the husband marries another wife, is not that successive polygamy?

The Cardinal. Curiosity leads to the commission of deadly sins. We should be satisfied with a Thus saith the Lord, and you should be satisfied with a Thus saith the Cardinal. If you have the right to inquire—to ask questions—then you take upon yourself the right of deciding after the questions have been answered. This is the end of authority. This undermines the cathedral. You must remember the words of our Lord: "What God hath joined together, let not man put asunder."

The Wife. Do you really think that God joined us together? Did he at the time know what kind of man he was joining to me? Did he then know that he was a wretch, an ingrate, a kind of wild beast? Did he then know that this husband would desert me—leave me with two babes in my arms, without raiment and without food? Did God put his seal upon this bond of marriage, upon this sacrament, and it was well-pleasing in his sight that my life should be sacrificed, and does he leave me now to crawl toward death, in poverty and tears?

The Cardinal. My dear woman, I will not linger here to point out to you the need of seeking from a higher than an earthly power the grace to suffer and be strong.

The Wife. Mr. Cardinal, am I under any obligation to God? Will it increase the happiness of the infinite for me to remain homeless and husbandless? Another offers to make me his wife and to give me a home,—to take care of my children and to fill my heart with joy. If I accept, will the act lessen the felicity or ecstasy of heaven? Will it add to the grief of God? Will it in any way affect his well-being?

The Cardinal. Nothing that we can do can effect the well-being of God. He is infinitely above his children.

The Wife. Then why should he insist upon the sacrifice of my life? Mr. Cardinal, you do not seem to sympathize with me. You do not understand the pangs I feel. You are too far away from my heart, and your words of consolation do not heal the bruise; they leave me as I now leave you—without hope. I will ask the advice of the Right Honorable William E. Gladstone.

The Wife. Mr. Gladstone, you know my story, and so I ask that you will give me the benefit of your knowledge, of your advice.

Mr. Gladstone. My dear woman, marriage is essentially a contract for life, and only expires when life itself expires. I say this because Christian marriage involves a vow before God, and no authority has been given to the Christian Church to cancel such a vow.

The Wife. Do you consider that God was one of the contracting parties in my marriage? Must all vows made to God be kept? Suppose the vow was made in ignorance, in excitement—must it be absolutely fulfilled? Will it make any difference to God whether it is kept or not? Does not an infinite God know the circumstances under which every vow is made?

Will he not take into consideration the imperfections, the ignorance, the temptations and the passions of his children? Will God hold a poor girl to the bitter dregs of a mistaken bargain? Have I not suffered enough? Is it necessary that my heart should break? Did not God know at the time the vow was made that it ought not to have been made? If he feels toward me as a father should, why did he give no warning? Why did he accept the vow? Why did he allow a contract to be made giving only to death the annulling power? Is death more merciful than God?

Mr. Gladstone. All vows that are made to God must be kept. Do you not remember that Jephthah agreed to sacrifice the first one who came out of his house to meet him, and that he fulfilled the vow, although in doing so, he murdered his own daughter. God makes no allowance for ignorance, for temptation, for passion—nothing. Besides, my dear woman, to cancel the contract of marriage lies beyond the province of the civil legislature; it has no competency to annul the contract of marriage when once made.

The Wife. The man who has rescued me from the tyranny of my husband—the man who wishes to build me a home and to make my life worth living, wishes to make with me a contract of marriage. This will give my babes a home.

Mr. Gladstone. My dear madam, while divorce of any kind impairs the integrity of the family, divorce with remarriage destroys it root and branch.

The Wife. The integrity of my family is already destroyed. My husband deserted his home—left us in the very depths of want. I have in my arms two helpless babes. I love my children, and I love the man who has offered to give them and myself another fireside. Can you say that this is only destruction? The destruction has already occurred. A remarriage gives a home to me and mine.

Mr. Gladstone. But, my dear mistaken woman, the parental and the conjugal relations are joined together by the hand of the Almighty.

The Wife. Do you believe that the Almighty was cruel enough, in my case, to join the parental and the conjugal relations, to the end that they should endure as long as I can bear the sorrow? If there were three parties to my marriage, my husband, myself, and God, should each be bound by the contract to do something? What did God bind himself to do? If nothing, why should he interfere? If nothing, my vow to him was without consideration. You are as cruel and unsympathetic, Mr. Gladstone, as the Cardinal. You have not the imagination to put yourself in my place.

Mr. Gladstone. My dear madam, we must be governed by the law of Christ, and there must be no remarriage. The husband and wife must remain husband and wife until a separation is caused by death.

The Wife. If Christ was such a believer in the sacredness of the marriage relation, why did he offer rewards not only in this world, but in the next, to husbands who would desert their wives and follow him?

Mr. Gladstone. It is not for us to inquire. God's ways are not our ways.

The Wife. Nature is better than you. A mother's love is higher and deeper than your philosophy. I will follow the instincts of my heart. I will provide a home for my babes, and for myself. I will be freed from the infamous man who betrayed me. I will become the wife of another—of one who loves me—and after having filled his life with joy, I hope to die in his arms, surrounded by my children.

A few months ago, a priest made a confession—he could carry his secret no longer. He admitted that he was married—that he was the father of two children—that he had violated his priestly vows. He was unfrocked and cast out. After a time he came back and asked to be restored into the bosom of the church, giving as his reason that he had abandoned his wife and babes. This throws a flood of light on the theological view of marriage.

I know of nothing equal to this, except the story of the Sandwich Island chief who was converted by the missionaries, and wished to join the church. On cross-examination, it turned out that he had twelve wives, and he was informed that a polygamist could not be a Christian. The next year he presented himself again for the purpose of joining the church, and stated that he was not a polygamist—that he had only one wife. When the missionaries asked him what he had done with the other eleven he replied: "I ate them."

The indissoluble marriage was a reaction from polygamy. The church has always pretended that it was governed by the will of God, and that for all its dogmas it had a "thus saith the Lord." Reason and experience were branded as false guides. The priests insisted that they were in direct communication with the Infinite—that they spoke by the authority of God, and that the duty of the people was to obey without question and to submit with at least the appearance of gladness.

We now know that no such communication exists—that priests spoke without authority, and that the duty of the people was and is to examine for themselves. We now know that no one knows what the will of God is, or whether or not such a being exists. We now know that nature has furnished all the light there is, and that the inspired books are like all books, and that their value depends on the truth, the beauty, and the wisdom they contain. We also know that it is now impossible to substantiate the supernatural. Judging from experience—reasoning from known facts—we can safely say that society has no right to demand the sacrifice of an innocent individual.

Society has no right, under the plea of self-preservation, to compel women to remain the wives of men who have violated the contract of marriage, and who have become objects of contempt and loathing to their wives. It is not to the best interest of society to maintain such firesides—such homes.

The time has not arrived, in my judgment, for the Congress of the United States, under an amendment to the Constitution, to pass a general law applicable to all the States, fixing the terms and conditions of divorce. The States of the Union are not equally enlightened. Some are far more conservative than others. Let us wait until a majority of the States have abandoned the theological theories upon this subject.

Upon this question light comes from the West, where men have recently laid the foundations of States, and where the people are not manacled and burdened with old constitutions and statutes and decisions, and where with a large majority the tendency is to correct the mistakes of their ancestors.

Let the States in their own way solve this question, and the time will come when the people will be ready to enact sensible and reasonable laws touching this important subject, and then the Constitution can be amended and the whole subject controlled by Federal law.

The law, as it now exists in many of the States, is to the last degree absurd and cruel. In some States the husband can obtain a divorce on the ground that the wife has been guilty of adultery, but the wife cannot secure a divorce from the husband simply for the reason that he has been guilty of the same offence. So, in most of the States where divorce is granted on account of desertion for a certain number of years, the husband can return on the last day of the time fixed, and the poor wife who has been left in want is obliged to receive the wretch with open arms. In some States nothing is considered cruelty that does not endanger life or limb or health. The whole question is in great confusion, but after all there are some States where the law is reasonable, and the consequence is, that hundreds and thousands of suffering wives are released from a bondage worse than death.

The idea that marriage is something more than a contract is at the bottom of all the legal and judicial absurdities that surround this subject. The moment that it is regarded from a purely secular standpoint the infamous laws will disappear. We shall then take into consideration the real rights and obligations of the parties to the contract of marriage. We shall have some respect for the sacred feelings of mothers—for the purity of woman—the freedom of the fireside—the real democracy of the hearthstone and, above all, for love, the purest, the profoundest and the holiest of all passions.

We shall no longer listen to priests who regard celibacy as a higher state than marriage, nor to those statesmen who look upon a barbarous code as the foundation of all law.

As long as men imagine that they have property in wives; that women can be owned, body and mind; that it is the duty of wives to obey; that the husband is the master, the source of authority—that his will is law, and that he can call on legislators and courts to protect his superior rights, that to enforce obedience the power of the State is pledged—just so long will millions of husbands be arrogant, tyrannical and cruel.

No gentleman will be content to have a slave for the mother of his children. Force has no place in the world of love. It is impossible to control likes and dislikes by law. No one ever did and no one ever can love on compulsion. Courts can not obtain jurisdiction of the heart.

The tides and currents of the soul care nothing for the creeds. People who make rules for the conduct of others generally break them themselves. It is so easy to bear with fortitude the misfortunes of others.

Every child should be well-born—well fathered and mothered. Society has as great an interest in children as in parents. The innocent should not be compelled by law to suffer for the crimes of the guilty. Wretched and weeping wives are not essential to the welfare of States and Nations.

The church cries now "whom God hath joined together let not man put asunder"; but when the people are really civilized the State will say: "whom Nature hath put asunder let not man bind and manacle together."

Robert G. Ingersoll.

REPLY TO LYMAN ABBOTT.

This unfinished article was written as a reply to the Rev. Lyman Abbott's article entitled, "Flaws in Ingersollism," which was printed in the April number of the *North American Review* for 1890.

In your Open Letter to me, published in this *Review,* you attack what you supposed to be my position, and ask several questions to which you demand answers; but in the same letter, you state that you wish no controversy with me. Is it possible that you wrote the letter to prevent a controversy? Do you attack only those with whom you wish to live in peace, and do you ask questions, coupled with a request that they remain unanswered?

In addition to this, you have taken pains to publish in your own paper, that it was no part of your design in the article in the *North American Review,* to point out errors in my statements, and that this design was distinctly disavowed in the opening paragraph of your article. You further say, that your simple object was to answer the question "What is Christianity?" May I be permitted to ask why you addressed the letter to me, and why do you now pretend that, although you did address a letter to me, I was not in your mind, and that you had no intention of pointing out any flaws in my doctrines or theories? Can you afford to occupy this position?

You also stated in your own paper, *The Christian Union,* that the title of your article had been changed by the editor of the *Review,* without your knowledge or consent; leaving it to be inferred that the title given to the article by you was perfectly consistent with your statement, that it was no part of your design in the article in the *North American Review,* to point out errors in my (Ingersoll's) statements; and that your simple object was to answer the question, What is Christianity? And yet, the title which you gave your own article was as follows: "To Robert G. Ingersoll: A Reply."

First. We are told that only twelve crimes were punished by death: idolatry, witchcraft, blasphemy, fraudulent prophesying, Sabbath-breaking, rebellion against parents, resistance to judicial officers, murder, homicide by negligence, adultery, incestuous marriages, and kidnapping. We are then told that as late as the year 1600 there were 263 crimes capital in England.

Does not the world know that all the crimes or offences punishable by death in England could be divided in the same way? For instance, treason. This covered a multitude of offences, all punishable by death. Larceny covered another multitude. Perjury—trespass, covered many others. There might still be made a smaller division, and one who had made up his mind to define the Criminal Code of England might have said that there was only one offence punishable by death—wrong-doing.

The facts with regard to the Criminal Code of England are, that up to the reign of George I. there were 167 offences punishable by death.

Between the accession of George I. and termination of the reign of George III., there were added 56 new crimes to which capital punishment was attached. So that when George IV. became king, there were 223 offences capital in England.

John Bright, commenting upon this subject, says:

"During all these years, so far as this question goes, our Government was becoming more cruel and more barbarous, and we do not find, and have not found, that in the great Church of England, with its fifteen or twenty thousand ministers, and with its more than score of Bishops in the House of Lords, there ever was a voice raised, or an organization formed, in favor of a more merciful code, or in condemnation of the enormous cruelties which our law was continually inflicting. Was not Voltaire justified in saying that the English were the only people who murdered by law?"

As a matter of fact, taking into consideration the situation of the people, the number of subjects covered by law, there were far more offences capital in the days of Moses, than in the reign of George IV. Is it possible that a minister, a theologian of the nineteenth century, imagines that he has substantiated the divine origin of the Old Testament by endeavoring to show that the government of God was not quite as bad as that of England?

Mr. Abbott also informs us that the reason Moses killed so many was, that banishment from the camp during the wandering in the Wilderness was a punishment worse than death. If so, the poor wretches should at least have been given their choice. Few, in my judgment, would have chosen death, because the history shows that a large majority were continually clamoring to be led back to Egypt. It required all the cunning and power of God to keep the fugitives from returning in a body. Many were killed by Jehovah, simply because they wished to leave the camp—because they longed passionately for banishment, and thought with joy of the flesh-pots of Egypt, preferring the slavery of Pharaoh to the liberty of Jehovah. The memory of leeks and onions was enough to set their faces toward the Nile.

Second. I am charged with saying that the Christian missionaries say to the heathen: "You must examine your religion—and not only so, but you must reject it; and unless you do reject it, and in addition to such rejection, adopt ours, you will be eternally damned." Mr. Abbott denies the truth of this statement.

Let me ask him, If the religion of Jesus Christ is preached clearly and distinctly to a heathen, and the heathen understands it, and rejects it deliberately, unequivocally, and finally, can he be saved?

This question is capable of a direct answer. The reverend gentleman now admits that an acceptance of Christianity is not essential to salvation. If the acceptance of Christianity is not essential to the salvation of the heathen who has heard Christianity preached—knows what its claims are, and the evidences that support those claims, is the acceptance of Christianity essential to the salvation of an adult intelligent citizen of the United States? Will the reverend gentleman tell us, and without circumlocution, whether the acceptance of Christianity is necessary to the salvation of anybody? If he says that it is, then he admits that I was right in my statement concerning what is said to the heathen. If he says that it is not, then I ask him, What do you do with the following passages of Scripture: "There is none other name given under heaven or among men whereby we must be saved."

"Go ye into all the world and preach the Gospel to every creature, and whosoever believeth, and is baptized, shall be saved; and whosoever believeth not shall be damned"?

I am delighted to know that millions of Pagans will be found to have entered into eternal life without any knowledge of Christ or his religion.

Another question naturally arises: If a heathen can hear and reject the Gospel, and yet be saved, what will become of the heathen who never heard of the Gospel? Are they all to be saved? If all who never heard are to be saved, is it not dangerous to hear?—Is it not cruel to preach? Why not stop preaching and let the entire world become heathen, so that after this, no soul may be lost?

Third. You say that I desire to deprive mankind of their faith in God, in Christ and in the Bible. I do not, and have not, endeavored to destroy the faith of any man in a good, in a just, in a merciful God, or in a reasonable, natural, human Christ, or in any truth that the Bible may contain. I have endeavored—and with some degree of success—to destroy the faith of man in the Jehovah of the Jews, and in the idea that Christ was in fact the God of this universe. I have also endeavored to show that there are many things in the Bible ignorant and cruel—that the book was produced by barbarians and by savages, and that its influence on the world has been bad.

And I do believe that life and property will be safer, that liberty will be surer, that homes will be sweeter, and life will be more joyous, and death less terrible, if the myth called Jehovah can be destroyed from the human mind.

It seems to me that the heart of the Christian ought to burst into an efflorescence of joy when he becomes satisfied that the Bible is only the work of man; that there is no such place as perdition—that there are no eternal flames—that men's souls are not to suffer everlasting pain—that it is all insanity and ignorance and fear and horror. I should think that every good and tender soul would be delighted to know that there is no Christ who can say to any human being—to any father, mother, or child—"Depart ye cursed into everlasting fire prepared for the devil and his angels." I do believe that he will be far happier when the Psalms of David are sung no more, and that he will be far better when no one could sing the 109th Psalm without shuddering and horror. These Psalms for the most part breathe the spirit of hatred, of revenge, and of everything fiendish in the human heart. There are some good lines, some lofty aspirations—these should be preserved; and to the extent that they do give voice to the higher and holier emotions, they should be preserved.

So I believe the world will be happier when the life of Christ, as it is written now in the New Testament, is no longer believed.

Some of the Ten Commandments will fall into oblivion, and the world will be far happier when they do. Most of these commandments are universal. They were not discovered by Jehovah—they were not original with him.

"Thou shalt not kill," is as old as life. And for this reason a large majority of people in all countries have objected to being murdered. "Thou shalt not steal," is as old as industry. There never has been a human being who was willing to work through the sun and rain and heat of summer, simply for the purpose that some one who had lived in idleness might steal the result of his labor. Consequently, in all countries where it has been necessary to work, larceny has been a crime. "Thou shalt not lie," is as old as speech. Men have desired, as a rule, to know the truth; and truth goes with courage and candor. "Thou shalt not commit adultery," is as old as love. "Honor thy father and thy mother," is as old as the family relation.

All these commandments were known among all peoples thousands and thousands of years before Moses was born. The new one, "Thou shalt worship no other Gods but me," is a bad commandment—because that God was not worthy of worship. "Thou shalt make no graven image,"—a bad commandment. It was the death of art. "Thou shalt do no work on the Sabbath-day,"—a bad commandment; the object of that being, that one-seventh of the time should be given to the worship of a monster, making a priesthood necessary, and consequently burdening industry with the idle and useless.

If Professor Clifford felt lonely at the loss of such a companion as Jehovah, it is impossible for me to sympathize with his feelings. No one wishes to destroy the hope of another life—no one wishes to blot out any good that is, or that is hoped for, or the hope of which gives consolation to the world. Neither do I agree with this gentleman when he says, "Let us have the truth, cost what it may." I say: Let us have happiness—well-being. The truth upon these matters is of but little importance compared with the happiness of mankind. Whether there is, or is not, a God, is absolutely unimportant, compared with the well-being of the race. Whether the Bible is, or is not, inspired, is not of as much consequence as human happiness.

Of course, if the Old and New Testaments are true, then human happiness becomes impossible, either in this world, or in the world to come—that is, impossible to all people who really believe that these books are true. It is often necessary to know the truth, in order to prepare ourselves to bear consequences; but in the metaphysical world, truth is of no possible importance except as it affects human happiness.

If there be a God, he certainly will hold us to no stricter responsibility about metaphysical truth than about scientific truth. It ought to be just as dangerous to make a mistake in Geology as in Theology—in Astronomy as in the question of the Atonement.

I am not endeavoring to overthrow any faith in God, but the faith in a bad God. And in order to accomplish this, I have endeavored to show that the question of whether an Infinite God exists, or not, is beyond the power of the human mind. Anything is better than to believe in the God of the Bible.

Fourth. Mr. Abbott, like the rest, appeals to names instead of to arguments. He appeals to Socrates, and yet he does not agree with Socrates. He appeals to Goethe, and yet Goethe was far from a Christian. He appeals to Isaac Newton and to Mr. Gladstone—and after mentioning these names, says, that on his side is this faith of the wisest, the best, the noblest of mankind.

Was Socrates after all greater than Epicurus—had he a subtler mind—was he any nobler in his life? Was Isaac Newton so much greater than Humboldt—than Charles Darwin, who has revolutionized the thought of the civilized world? Did he do the one-hundredth part of the good for mankind that was done by Voltaire—was he as great a metaphysician as Spinoza?

But why should we appeal to names?

In a contest between Protestantism and Catholicism are you willing to abide by the tests of names? In a contest between Christianity and Paganism, in the first century, would you have considered the question settled by names? Had Christianity then produced the equals of the great Greeks and Romans? The new can always be overwhelmed with names that were in favor of the old. Sir Isaac Newton, in his day, could have been overwhelmed by the names of the great who had preceded him. Christ was overwhelmed by this same method—Moses and the Prophets were appealed to as against this Peasant of Palestine. This is the argument of the cemetery—this is leaving the open field, and crawling behind gravestones.

Newton was understood to be, all his life, a believer in the Trinity; but he dared not say what his real thought was. After his death there was found among his papers an argument that he published against the divinity of Christ. This had been published in Holland, because he was afraid to have it published in England. How do we really know what the great men of whom you speak believed, or believe?

I do not agree with you when you say that Gladstone is the greatest statesman. He will not, in my judgment, for one moment compare with Thomas Jefferson—with Alexander Hamilton—or, to come down to later times, with Gambetta; and he is immeasurably below such a man as Abraham Lincoln. Lincoln was not a believer. Gambetta was an atheist.

And yet, these names prove nothing. Instead of citing a name, and saying that this great man—Sir Isaac Newton, for instance—believed in our doctrine, it is far better to give the reasons that Sir Isaac Newton had for his belief.

Nearly all organizations are filled with snobbishness. Each church has a list of great names, and the members feel in duty bound to stand by their great men.

Why is idolatry the worst of sins? Is it not far better to worship a God of stone than a God who threatens to punish in eternal flames the most of his children? If you simply mean by idolatry a false conception of God, you must admit that no finite mind can have a true conception of God—and you must admit that no two men can have the same false conception of God, and that, as a consequence, no two men can worship identically the same Deity. Consequently they are all idolaters.

I do not think idolatry the worst of sins. Cruelty is the worst of sins. It is far better to worship a false God, than to injure your neighbor—far better to bow before a monstrosity of stone, than to enslave your fellow-men.

Fifth. I am glad that you admit that a bad God is worse than no God. If so, the atheist is far better than the believer in Jehovah, and far better than the believer in the divinity of Jesus Christ—because I am perfectly satisfied that none but a bad God would threaten to say to any human soul, "Depart, ye cursed, into everlasting fire, prepared for the devil and his angels." So that, before any Christian can be better than an atheist, he must reform his God.

The agnostic does not simply say, "I do not know." He goes another step, and he says, with great emphasis, that you do not know. He insists that you are trading on the ignorance of others, and on the fear of others. He is not satisfied with saying that you do not know,—he demonstrates that you do not know, and he drives you from the field of fact—he drives you from the realm of reason—he drives you from the light, into the darkness of conjecture—into the world of dreams and shadows, and he compels you to say, at last, that your faith has no foundation in fact.

You say that religion tells us that "life is a battle with temptation—the result is eternal life to the victors."

But what of the victims? Did your God create these victims, knowing that they would be victims? Did he deliberately change the clay into the man—into a being with wants, surrounded by difficulties and temptations—and did he deliberately surround this being with temptations that he knew he could not withstand, with obstacles that he knew he could not overcome, and whom he knew at last would fall a victim upon the field of death? Is there no hope for this victim? No remedy for this mistake of your God? Is he to remain a victim forever? Is it not better to have no God than such a God? Could the condition of this victim be rendered worse by the death of God?

Sixth. Of course I agree with you when you say that character is worth more than condition—that life is worth more than place. But I do not agree with you when you say that being—that simple existence—is better than happiness. If a man is not happy, it is far better not to be. I utterly dissent from your philosophy of life. From my standpoint, I do not understand you when you talk about self-denial. I can imagine a being of such character, that certain things he would do for the one he loved, would by others be regarded as acts of self-denial, but they could not be so regarded by him. In these acts of so-called self-denial, he would find his highest joy.

This pretence that to do right is to carry a cross, has done an immense amount of injury to the world. Only those who do wrong carry a cross. To do wrong is the only possible self-denial.

The pulpit has always been saying that, although the virtuous and good, the kind, the tender, and the loving, may have a very bad time here, yet they will have their reward in heaven—having denied themselves the pleasures of sin, the ecstasies of crime, they will be made happy in a world hereafter; but that the wicked, who have enjoyed larceny, and rascality in all its forms, will be punished hereafter.

All this rests upon the idea that man should sacrifice himself, not for his fellow-men, but for God—that he should do something for the Almighty—that he should go hungry to increase the happiness of heaven—that he should make a journey to Our Lady of Loretto, with dried peas in his shoes; that he should refuse to eat meat on Friday;

that he should say so many prayers before retiring to rest; that he should do something that he hated to do, in order that he might win the approbation of the heavenly powers. For my part, I think it much better to feed the hungry, than to starve yourself.

You ask me, What is Christianity? You then proceed to partially answer your own question, and you pick out what you consider the best, and call that Christianity. But you have given only one side, and that side not all of it good. Why did you not give the other side of Christianity—the side that talks of eternal flames, of the worm that dieth not—the side that denounces the investigator and the thinker—the side that promises an eternal reward for credulity—the side that tells men to take no thought for the morrow but to trust absolutely in a Divine Providence?

"Within thirty years after the crucifixion of Jesus, faith in his resurrection had become the inspiration of the church." I ask you, Was there a resurrection?

What advance has been made in what you are pleased to call the doctrine of the brotherhood of man, through the instrumentality of the church? Was there as much dread of God among the Pagans as there has been among Christians?

I do not believe that the church is a conservator of civilization. It sells crime on credit. I do not believe it is an educator of good will. It has caused more war than all other causes. Neither is it a school of a nobler reverence and faith. The church has not turned the minds of men toward principles of justice, mercy and truth—it has destroyed the foundation of justice. It does not minister comfort at the coffin—it fills the mourners with fear. It has never preached a gospel of "Peace on Earth"—it has never preached "Good Will toward men."

For my part, I do not agree with you when you say that: "The most stalwart anti-Romanists can hardly question that with the Roman Catholic Church abolished by instantaneous decree, its priests banished and its churches closed, the disaster to American communities would be simply awful in its proportions, if not irretrievable in its results."

I may agree with you in this, that the most stalwart anti-Romanists would not wish to have the Roman Catholic Church abolished by tyranny, and its priests banished, and its churches closed. But if the abolition of that church could be produced by the development of the human mind; and if its priests, instead of being banished, should become good and useful citizens, and were in favor of absolute liberty of mind, then I say that there would be no disaster, but a very wide and great and splendid blessing. The church has been the Centaur—not Theseus; the church has not been Hercules, but the serpent.

So I believe that there is something far nobler than loyalty to any particular man. Loyalty to the truth as we perceive it—loyalty to our duty as we know it—loyalty to the ideals of our brain and heart—is, to my mind, far greater and far nobler than loyalty to the life of any particular man or God. There is a kind of slavery—a kind of abdication— for any man to take any other man as his absolute pattern and to hold him up as the perfection of all life, and to feel that it is his duty to grovel in the dust in his presence. It is better to feel that the springs of action are within yourself—that you are poised upon your own feet—and that you look at the world with your own eyes, and follow the path that reason shows.

I do not believe that the world could be re-organized upon the simple but radical principles of the Sermon on the Mount. Neither do I believe that this sermon was ever delivered by one man. It has in it many fragments that I imagine were dropped from many mouths. It lacks coherence—it lacks form. Some of the sayings are beautiful, sublime and tender; and others seem to be weak, contradictory and childish.

Seventh. I do not say that I do not know whether this faith is true, or not. I say distinctly and clearly, that I know it is not true. I admit that I do not know whether there is any infinite personality or not, because I do not know that my mind is an absolute standard. But according to my mind, there is no such personality; and according to my mind, it is an infinite absurdity to suppose that there is such an infinite personality. But I do know something of human nature; I do know a little of the history of mankind; and I know enough to know that what is known as the Christian faith, is not true. I am perfectly satisfied, beyond all doubt and beyond all per-adventure, that all miracles are falsehoods. I know as well as I know that I live—that others live—that what you call your faith, is not true.

I am glad, however, that you admit that the miracles of the Old Testament, or the inspiration of the Old Testament, are not essentials. I draw my conclusion from what you say: "I have not in this paper discussed the miracles, or the inspiration of the Old Testament; partly because those topics, in my opinion, occupy a subordinate position in Christian faith, and I wish to consider only essentials." At the same time, you tell us that, "On historical evidence, and after a careful study of the arguments on both sides, I regard as historical the events narrated in the four Gospels, ordinarily regarded as miracles." At the same time, you say that you fully agree with me that the order of nature has never been violated or interrupted. In other words, you must believe that all these so-called miracles were actually in accordance with the laws, or facts rather, in nature.

Eighth. You wonder that I could write the following: "To me there is nothing of any particular value in the Pentateuch. There is not, so far as I know, a line in the Book of Genesis calculated to make a human being better." You then call my attention to "The magnificent Psalm of Praise to the Creator with which Genesis opens; to the beautiful legend of the first sin and its fateful consequences; the inspiring story of Abraham—the first self-exile for conscience sake; the romantic story of Joseph the Peasant boy becoming a Prince," which you say "would have attraction for any one if he could have found a charm in, for example, the Legends of the Round Table."

The "magnificent Psalm of Praise to the Creator with which Genesis opens" is filled with magnificent mistakes, and is utterly absurd. "The beautiful legend of the first sin and its fateful consequences" is probably the most contemptible story that was ever written, and the treatment of the first pair by Jehovah is unparalleled in the cruelty of despotic governments. According to this infamous account, God cursed the mothers of the world, and added to the agonies of maternity. Not only so, but he made woman a slave, and man something, if possible, meaner—a master.

I must confess that I have very little admiration for Abraham. (Give reasons.)

So far as Joseph is concerned, let me give you the history of Joseph,— how he conspired with Pharaoh to enslave the people of Egypt.

You seem to be astonished that I am not in love with the character of Joseph, as pictured in the Bible. Let me tell you who Joseph was.

It seems, from the account, that Pharaoh had a dream. None of his wise men could give its meaning. He applied to Joseph, and Joseph, having been enlightened by Jehovah, gave the meaning of the dream to Pharaoh. He told the king that there would be in Egypt seven years of great plenty, and after these seven years of great plenty, there would be seven years of famine, and that the famine would consume the land. Thereupon Joseph gave to Pharaoh some advice. First, he was to take up a fifth part of the land of Egypt, in the seven plenteous years—he was to gather all the food of those good years, and lay up corn, and he was to keep this food in the cities. This food was to be a store to the land against the seven years of famine. And thereupon Pharaoh said unto Joseph, "Forasmuch as God hath showed thee all this, there is none so discreet and wise as thou art: thou shalt be over my house, and according unto thy word shall all my people be ruled: only in the throne will I be greater than thou. And Pharaoh said unto Joseph, See I have set thee over all the land of Egypt."

We are further informed by the holy writer, that in the seven plenteous years the earth brought forth by handfuls, and that Joseph gathered up all the food of the seven years, which were in the land of Egypt, and laid up the food in the cities, and that he gathered corn as the sand of the sea. This was done through the seven plenteous years. Then commenced the years of dearth. Then the people of Egypt became hungry, and they cried to Pharaoh for bread, and Pharaoh said unto all the Egyptians, Go unto Joseph. The famine was over all the face of the earth, and Joseph opened the storehouses, and sold unto the Egyptians, and the famine waxed sore in the land of Egypt. There was no bread in the land, and Egypt fainted by reason of the famine. And Joseph gathered up all the money that was found in the land of Egypt, by the sale of corn, and brought the money to Pharaoh's house. After a time the money failed in the land of Egypt, and the Egyptians came unto Joseph and said, "Give us bread; why should we die in thy presence? for the money faileth." And Joseph said, "Give your cattle, and I will give you for your cattle." And they brought their cattle unto Joseph, and he gave them bread in exchange for horses and flocks and herds, and he fed them with bread for all their cattle for that year. When the year was ended, they came unto him the second year, and said, "Our money is spent, our cattle are gone, naught is left but our bodies and our lands." And they said to Joseph, "Buy us, and our land, for bread, and we and our land will be servants unto Pharaoh; and give us seed that we may live and not die, that the land be not desolate." And Joseph bought all the land of Egypt for Pharaoh; for the Egyptians sold every man his field, because the famine prevailed over them. So the land became Pharaoh's. Then Joseph said to the people, "I have bought you this day, and your land; lo, here is seed for you, and ye shall sow the land." And thereupon the people said, "Thou hast saved our lives; we will be Pharaoh's servants." "And Joseph made it a law over the land of Egypt unto this day, that Pharaoh should have the fifth part, *except the land of the priests only, which became not Pharaoh's.*"

Yet I am asked, by a minister of the nineteenth century, whether it is possible that I do not admire the character of Joseph. This man received information from God—and gave that information to Pharaoh, to the end that he might impoverish and enslave a nation. This man, by means of intelligence received from Jehovah, took from the people what they had, and compelled them at last to sell themselves, their wives and their children, and to become in fact bondmen forever. Yet I am asked by the successor of Henry Ward Beecher, if I do not admire the infamous wretch who was guilty of the greatest crime recorded in the literature of the world.

So, it is difficult for me to understand why you speak of Abraham as "a self-exile for conscience sake." If the king of England had told one of his favorites that if he would go to North America he would give him a territory hundreds of miles square, and would defend him in its possession, and that he there might build up an empire, and the favorite believed the king, and went, would you call him "a self-exile for conscience sake"?

According to the story in the Bible, the Lord promised Abraham that if he would leave his country and kindred, he would make of him a great nation, would bless him, and make his name great, that he would bless them that blessed Abraham, and that he would curse him whom Abraham cursed; and further, that in him all the families of the earth should be blest. If this is true, would you call Abraham "a self-exile for conscience sake"? If Abraham had only known that the Lord was not to keep his promise, he probably would have remained where he was—the fact being, that every promise made by the Lord to Abraham, was broken.

Do you think that Abraham was "a self-exile for conscience sake" when he told Sarah, his wife, to say that she was his sister—in consequence of which she was taken into Pharaoh's house, and by reason of which Pharaoh made presents of sheep and oxen and man servants and maid servants to Abraham? What would you call such a proceeding now? What would you think of a man who was willing that his wife should become the mistress of the king, provided the king would make him presents?

Was it for conscience sake that the same subterfuge was adopted again, when Abraham said to Abimelech, the King of Gerar, She is my sister—in consequence of which Abimelech sent for Sarah and took her?

Mr. Ingersoll having been called to Montana, as counsel in a long and important law suit, never finished this article.

ANSWER TO ARCHDEACON FARRAR.

This fragment (found among Col. Ingersoll's papers) is a mere outline of a contemplated answer to Archdeacon Farrar's article in the *North American Review,* May, 1890, entitled: "A Few Words on Col. Ingersoll."

Archdeacon Farrar, in the opening of his article, in a burst of confidence, takes occasion to let the world know how perfectly angelic he intends to be. He publicly proclaims that he can criticize the arguments of one with whom he disagrees, without resorting to invective, or becoming discourteous. Does he call attention to this because most theologians are hateful and ungentlemanly? Is it a rare thing for the pious to be candid? Why should an Archdeacon be cruel, or even ill-bred? Yet, in the very beginning, the Archdeacon in effect says: Behold, I show you a mystery—a Christian who can write about an infidel, without invective and without brutality. Is it then so difficult for those who love their enemies to keep within the bounds of decency when speaking of unbelievers who have never injured them?

As a matter of fact, I was somewhat surprised when I read the proclamation to the effect that the writer was not to use invective, and was to be guilty of no discourtesy; but on reading the article, and finding that he had failed to keep his promise, I was not surprised.

It is an old habit with theologians to beat the living with the bones of the dead. The arguments that cannot be answered provoke epithet.

I

Archdeacon Farrar criticizes several of my statements: *The same rules or laws of probability must govern in religious questions as in others.*

This apparently self-evident statement seems to excite almost the ire of this Archdeacon, and for the purpose of showing that it is not true, he states, first, that "the first postulate of revelation is that it appeals to man's spirit;" second, that "the spirit is a sphere of being which transcends the spheres of the senses and the understanding;" third, that "if a man denies the existence of a spiritual intuition, he is like a blind man criticizing colors, or a deaf man criticizing harmonies;" fourth, that "revelation must be judged by its own criteria;" and fifth, that "St. Paul draws a marked distinction between the spirit of the world and the spirit which is of God," and that the same Saint said that "the natural man receiveth not the things of the spirit of God, for they are foolishness unto him, and he cannot know them, because they are spiritually discerned." Let us answer these objections in their order.

1. "The first postulate of revelation is that it appeals to man's spirit." What does the Archdeacon mean by "spirit"? A man says that he has received a revelation from God, and he wishes to convince another man that he has received a revelation—how does he proceed? Does he appeal

to the man's reason? Will he tell him the circumstances under which he received the revelation? Will he tell him why he is convinced that it was from God? Will the Archdeacon be kind enough to tell how the spirit can be approached passing by the reason, the understanding, the judgment and the intellect? If the Archdeacon replies that the revelation itself will bear the evidence within itself, what then, I ask, does he mean by the word "evidence"? Evidence about what? Is it such evidence as satisfies the intelligence, convinces the reason, and is it in conformity with the known facts of the mind?

It may be said by the Archdeacon that anything that satisfies what he is pleased to call the spirit, that furnishes what it seems by nature to require, is of supernatural origin. We hear music, and this music seems to satisfy the desire for harmony—still, no one argues, from that fact, that music is of supernatural origin. It may satisfy a want in the brain— a want unknown until the music was heard—and yet we all agree in saying that music has been naturally produced, and no one claims that Beethoven, or Wagner, was inspired.

The same may be said of things that satisfy the palate—of statues, of paintings, that reveal to him who looks, the existence of that of which before that time he had not even dreamed. Why is it that we love color— that we are pleased with harmonies, or with a succession of sounds rising and falling at measured intervals? No one would answer this question by saying that sculptors and painters and musicians were inspired; neither would they say that the first postulate of art is that it appeals to man's spirit, and for that reason the rules or laws of probability have nothing to do with the question of art.

2. That "the spirit is a sphere of being which transcends the spheres of the senses and the understanding." Let us imagine a man without senses. He cannot feel, see, hear, taste, or smell. What is he? Would it be possible for him to have an idea? Would such a man have a spirit to which revelation could appeal, or would there be locked in the dungeon of his brain a spirit, that is to say, a "sphere of being which transcends the spheres of the senses and the understanding"? Admit that in the person supposed, the machinery of life goes on—what is he more than an inanimate machine?

3. That "if a man denies the very existence of a spiritual intuition, he is like a blind man criticizing colors, or a deaf man criticizing harmonies." What do you mean by "spiritual intuition"? When did this "spiritual intuition" become the property of man—before, or after, birth? Is it of supernatural, or miraculous, origin, and is it possible that this "spiritual intuition" is independent of the man? Is it based upon experience? Was it in any way born of the senses, or of the effect of nature upon the brain—that is to say, of things seen, or heard, or touched? Is a "spiritual intuition" an entity? If man can exist without the "spiritual intuition," do you insist that the "spiritual intuition" can exist without the man?

You may remember that Mr. Locke frequently remarked: "Define your terms." It is to be regretted that in the hurry of writing your article, you forgot to give an explanation of "spiritual intuition."

I will also take the liberty of asking you how a blind man could criticize colors, and how a deaf man could criticize harmonies. Possibly you may imagine that "spiritual intuition" can take cognizance of colors, as well as of harmonies. Let me ask: Why cannot a blind man criticize colors? Let me answer: For the same reason that Archdeacon Farrar can tell us nothing about an infinite personality.

4. That "revelation must be judged by its own criteria." Suppose the Bible had taught that selfishness, larceny and murder were virtues; would you deny its inspiration? Would not your denial be based upon a conclusion that had been reached by your reason that no intelligent being could have been its author—that no good being could, by any possibility, uphold the commission of such crimes? In that case would you be guided by "spiritual intuition," or by your reason?

When we examine the claims of a history—as, for instance, a history of England, or of America, are we to decide according to "spiritual intuition," or in accordance with the laws or rules of probability? Is there a different standard for a history written in Hebrew, several thousand years ago, and one written in English in the nineteenth century? If a history should now be written in England, in which the most miraculous and impossible things should be related as facts, and if I should deny these alleged facts, would you consider that the author had overcome my denial by saying, "history must be judged by its own criteria"?

5. That "the natural man receiveth not the things of the spirit of God, for they are foolishness unto him, and he cannot know them, because they are spiritually discerned." The Archdeacon admits that the natural man cannot know the things of the spirit, because they are not naturally, but spiritually, discerned. On the next page we are told, that "the truths which Agnostics repudiate have been, and are, acknowledged by all except a fraction of the human race." It goes without saying that a large majority of the human race are natural; consequently, the statement of the Archdeacon contradicts the statement of St. Paul. The Archdeacon insists that all except a fraction of the human race acknowledge the truths which Agnostics repudiate, and they must acknowledge them because they are by them spiritually discerned; and yet, St. Paul says that this is impossible, and insists that "the natural man cannot know the things of the spirit of God, because they are spiritually discerned."

There is only one way to harmonize the statement of the Archdeacon and the Saint, and that is, by saying that nearly all of the human race are unnatural, and that only a small fraction are natural, and that the small fraction of men who are natural, are Agnostics, and only those who accept what the Archdeacon calls "truths" are unnatural to such a degree that they can discern spiritual things.

Upon this subject, the last things to which the Archdeacon appeals, are the very things that he, at first, utterly repudiated. He asks, "Are we contemptuously to reject the witness of innumerable multitudes of the good and wise, that—with a spiritual reality more convincing to them than the material evidences which converted the apostles,"—they have seen, and heard, and their hands have handled the "Word of Life"? Thus at last the Archdeacon appeals to the evidences of the senses.

The Archdeacon then proceeds to attack the following statement: *There is no subject, and can be none, concerning which any human being is under any obligation to believe without evidence.*

One would suppose that it would be impossible to formulate an objection to this statement. What is or is not evidence, depends upon the mind to which it is presented. There is no possible "insinuation" in this statement, one way or the other. There is nothing sinister in it, any more than there would be in the statement that twice five are ten. How did it happen to occur to the Archdeacon that when I spoke of believing without evidence, I referred to all people who believe in the existence of a God, and that I intended to say "that one-third of the world's inhabitants had embraced the faith of Christians without evidence"?

Certain things may convince one mind and utterly fail to convince others. Undoubtedly the persons who have believed in the dogmas of Christianity have had what was sufficient evidence for them. All I said was, that "there is no subject, and can be none, concerning which any human being is under any obligation to believe without evidence." Does the Archdeacon insist that there is an obligation resting on any human mind to believe without evidence? Is he willing to go a step further and say that there is an obligation resting upon the minds of men to believe contrary to evidence? If one is under obligation to believe without evidence, it is just as reasonable to say that he is under obligation to believe in spite of evidence. What does the word "evidence" mean? A man in whose honesty I have great confidence, tells me that he saw a dead man raised to life. I do not believe him. Why? His statement is not evidence to my mind. Why? Because it contradicts all of my experience, and, as I believe, the experience of the intelligent world.

No one pretends that "one-third of the world's inhabitants have embraced the faith of Christians without evidence"—that is, that all Christians have embraced the faith without evidence. In the olden time, when hundreds of thousands of men were given their choice between being murdered and baptized, they generally accepted baptism— probably they accepted Christianity without critically examining the evidence.

Is it historically absurd that millions of people have believed in systems of religion without evidence? Thousands of millions have believed that Mohammed was a prophet of God. And not only so, but have believed in his miraculous power. Did they believe without evidence? Is it historically absurd to say that Mohammedanism is based upon mistake? What shall we say of the followers of Buddha, who far outnumber the followers of Christ? Have they believed without evidence? And is it historically absurd to say that our ancestors of a few hundred years ago were as credulous as the disciples of Buddha? Is it not true that the same gentlemen who believed thoroughly in all the miracles of the New Testament also believed the world to be flat, and were perfectly satisfied that the sun made its daily journey around the earth? Did they have any evidence? Is it historically absurd to say that they believed without evidence?

III.

Neither is there any intelligent being who can by any possibility be flattered by the exercise of ignorant credulity.

The Archdeacon asks what I "gain by stigmatizing as ignorant credulity that inspired, inspiring, invincible conviction—the formative principle of noble efforts and self-sacrificing lives, which at this moment, as during all the long millenniums of the past, has been held not only by the ignorant and the credulous, but by those whom all the ages have regarded as the ablest, the wisest, the most learned and the most gifted of mankind?"

Does the Archdeacon deny that credulity is ignorant? In this connection, what does the word "credulity" mean? It means that condition or state of the mind in which the impossible, or the absurd, is accepted as true. Is not such credulity ignorant? Do we speak of wise credulity—of intelligent credulity? We may say theological credulity, or Christian credulity, but certainly not intelligent credulity. Is the flattery of the ignorant and credulous—the flattery being based upon that which ignorance and credulity have accepted—acceptable to any intelligent being? Is it possible that we can flatter God by pretending to believe, or by believing, that which is repugnant to reason, that which upon examination is seen to be absurd? The Archdeacon admits that God cannot possibly be so flattered. If, then, he agrees with my statement, why endeavor to controvert it?

IV.

The man who without prejudice reads and understands the Old and New Testaments will cease to be an orthodox Christian.

The Archdeacon says that he cannot pretend to imagine what my definition of an orthodox Christian is. I will use his own language to express my definition. "By an orthodox Christian I mean one who believes what is commonly called the Apostles' Creed. I also believe that the essential doctrines of the church must be judged by her universal formulae, not by the opinions of this or that theologian, however eminent, or even of any number of theologians, unless the church has stamped them with the sanction of her formal and distinct acceptance."

This is the language of the Archdeacon himself, and I accept it as a definition of orthodoxy. With this definition in mind, I say that the man who without prejudice reads and understands the Old and New Testaments will cease to be an orthodox Christian. By "prejudice," I mean the tendencies and trends given to his mind by heredity, by education, by the facts and circumstances entering into the life of man. We know how children are poisoned in the cradle, how they are deformed in the Sunday School, how they are misled by the pulpit. And we know how numberless interests unite and conspire to prevent the individual soul from examining for itself. We know that nearly all rewards are in the hands of Superstition—that she holds the sweet wreath, and that her hands lead the applause of what is called the civilized world. We know how many men give up their mental independence for the sake of pelf and power. We know the influence of mothers and fathers—of Church and State—of Faith and Fashion. All these influences produce in honest minds what may be known as prejudice,—in other minds, what may be known as hypocrisy.

It is hardly worth my while to speak of the merits of students of Holy Writ "who," the Archdeacon was polite enough to say, "know ten thousand times more of the Scriptures" than I do. This, to say the least of it, is a gratuitous assertion, and one that does not tend to throw the slightest ray of light on any matter in controversy. Neither is it true that it was my "point" to say that all people are prejudiced, merely because they believe in God; it was my point to say that no man can read the miracles of the Old Testament, without prejudice, and believe them; it was my point to say that no man can read many of the cruel and barbarous laws said to have been given by God himself, and yet believe,—unless he was prejudiced,—that these laws were divinely given.

Neither do I believe that there is now beneath the cope of heaven an intelligent man, without prejudice, who believes in the inspiration of the Bible.

V.

The intelligent man who investigates the religion of any country, without fear and without prejudice, will not and cannot be a believer.

In answering this statement the Archdeacon says: "*Argal,* every believer in any religion is either an incompetent idiot, or coward—with a dash of prejudice."

I hardly know what the gentleman means by an "incompetent idiot," as I know of no competent ones. It was not my intention to say that believers in religion are idiots or cowards. I did not mean, by using the word "fear," to say that persons actuated by fear are cowards. That was not in my mind. By "fear," I intended to convey that fear commonly called awe, or superstition,—that is to say, fear of the supernatural,—fear of the gods—fear of punishment in another world—fear of some Supreme Being; not fear of some other man—not the fear that is branded with cowardice. And, of course, the Archdeacon perfectly understood my meaning; but it was necessary to give another meaning in order to make the appearance of an answer possible.

By "prejudice," I mean that state of mind that accepts the false for the true. All prejudice is honest. And the probability is, that all men are more or less prejudiced on some subject. But on that account I do not call them "incompetent idiots, or cowards, with a dash of prejudice." I have no doubt that the Archdeacon himself believes that all Mohammedans are prejudiced, and that they are actuated more or less by fear, inculcated by their parents and by society at large. Neither have I any doubt that he regards all Catholics as prejudiced, and believes that they are governed more or less by fear. It is no answer to what I have said for the Archdeacon to say that "others have studied every form of religion with infinitely greater power than I have done." This is a personality that has nothing to do with the subject in hand. It is no argument to repeat a list of names. It is an old trick of the theologians to use names instead of arguments—to appeal to persons instead of principles—to rest their case upon the views of kings and nobles and others who pretend eminence in some department of human learning or ignorance, rather than on human knowledge.

This is the argument of the old against the new, and on this appeal the old must of necessity have the advantage. When some man announces the discovery of a new truth, or of some great fact contrary to the opinions of the learned, it is easy to overwhelm him with names. There is but one name on his side—that is to say, his own. All others who are living, and the dead, are on the other side. And if this argument is good, it ought to have ended all progress many thousands of years ago. If this argument is conclusive, the first man would have had freedom of opinion; the second man would have stood an equal chance; but if the third man differed from the other two, he would have been gone. Yet this is the argument of the church. They say to every man who advances something new: Are you greater than the dead? The man who is right is generally modest. Men in the wrong, as a rule, are arrogant; and arrogance is generally in the majority.

The Archdeacon appeals to certain names to show that I am wrong. In order for this argument to be good—that is to say, to be honest—he should agree with all the opinions of the men whose names he gives. He shows, or endeavors to show, that I am wrong, because I do not agree with St. Augustine. Does the Archdeacon agree with St. Augustine? Does he now believe that the bones of a saint were taken to Hippo—that being in the diocese of St. Augustine—and that five corpses, having been touched with these bones, were raised to life? Does he believe that a demoniac, on being touched with one of these bones, was relieved of a multitude of devils, and that these devils then and there testified to the genuineness of the bones, not only, but told the hearers that the doctrine of the Trinity was true? Does the Archdeacon agree with St. Augustine that over seventy miracles were performed with these bones, and that in a neighboring town many hundreds of miracles were performed? Does he agree with St. Augustine in his estimate of women—placing them on a par with beasts?

I admit that St. Augustine had great influence with the people of his day—but what people? I admit also that he was the founder of the first begging brotherhood—that he organized mendicancy—and that he most cheerfully lived on the labor of others.

If St. Augustine lived now he would be the inmate of an asylum. This same St. Augustine believed that the fire of hell was material—that the body itself having influenced the soul to sin, would be burned forever, and that God by a perpetual miracle would save the body from being annihilated and devoured in those eternal flames.

Let me ask the Archdeacon a question: Do you agree with St. Augustine? If you do not, do you claim to be a greater man? Is "your mole-hill higher than his Dhawalagiri"? Are you looking down upon him from the altitude of your own inferiority?

Precisely the same could be said of St. Jerome. The Archdeacon appeals to Charlemagne, one of the great generals of the world—a man who in his time shed rivers of blood, and who on one occasion massacred over four thousand helpless prisoners—a Christian gentleman who had, I think, about nine wives, and was the supposed father of some twenty children. This same Charlemagne had laws against polygamy, and yet practiced it himself. Are we under the same obligation to share his vices as his views? It is wonderful how the church has always appealed to the so-called great—how it has endeavored to get certificates from kings and queens, from successful soldiers and statesmen, to the truth of the Bible and the moral character of Christ! How the saints have crawled in the dust before the slayers of mankind! Think of proving the religion of love and forgiveness by Charlemagne and Napoleon!

An appeal is also made to Roger Bacon. Yet this man attained all his eminence by going contrary to the opinions and teachings of the church. In his time, it was matter of congratulation that you knew nothing of secular things. He was a student of Nature, an investigator, and by the very construction of his mind was opposed to the methods of Catholicism.

Copernicus was an astronomer, but he certainly did not get his astronomy from the church, nor from General Joshua, nor from the story of the Jewish king for whose benefit the sun was turned back in heaven ten degrees.

Neither did Kepler find his three laws in the Sermon on the Mount, nor were they the utterances of Jehovah on Mount Sinai. He did not make his discoveries because he was a Christian; but in spite of that fact.

As to Lord Bacon, let me ask, are you willing to accept his ideas? If not, why do you quote his name? Am I bound by the opinions of Bacon in matters of religion, and not in matters of science? Bacon denied the Copernican system, and died a believer in the Ptolemaic—died believing that the earth is stationary and that the sun and stars move around it as a center. Do you agree with Bacon? If not, do you pretend that your mind is greater? Would it be fair for a believer in Bacon to denounce you as an egotist and charge you with "obstreperousness" because you merely suggested that Mr. Bacon was a little off in his astronomical opinions? Do you not see that you have furnished the cord for me to tie your hands behind you?

I do not know how you ascertained that Shakespeare was what you call a believer. Substantially all that we know of Shakespeare is found in what we know as his "works" All else can be read in one minute. May I ask, how you know that Shakespeare was a believer? Do you prove it by the words he put in the mouths of his characters? If so, you can prove that he was anything, nothing, and everything. Have you literary bread to eat that I know not of? Whether Dante was, or was not, a Christian, I am not prepared to say. I have always admired him for one thing: he had the courage to see a pope in hell.

Probably you are not prepared to agree with Milton—especially in his opinion that marriage had better be by contract, for a limited time. And if you disagree with Milton on this point, do you thereby pretend to say that you could have written a better poem than *Paradise Lost?*

So Newton is supposed to have been a Trinitarian. And yet it is said that, after his death, there was found an article, which had been published by him in Holland, against the dogma of the Trinity.

After all, it is quite difficult to find out what the great men have believed. They have been actuated by so many unknown motives; they have wished for place; they have desired to be Archdeacons, Bishops,

Cardinals, Popes; their material interests have sometimes interfered with the expression of their thoughts. Most of the men to whom you have alluded lived at a time when the world was controlled by what may be called a Christian mob—when the expression of an honest thought would have cost the life of the one who expressed it—when the followers of Christ were ready with sword and fagot to exterminate philosophy and liberty from the world.

Is it possible that we are under any obligation to believe the Mosaic account of the Garden of Eden, or of the talking serpent, because "Whewell had an encyclopedic range of knowledge"? Must we believe that Joshua stopped the sun, because Faraday was "the most eminent man of science of his day"? Shall we believe the story of the fiery furnace, because "Mr. Spottiswoode was president of the Royal Society"—had "rare mathematical genius"—so rare that he was actually "buried in Westminster Abbey"? Shall we believe that Jonah spent three days and nights in the inside of a whale because "Professor Clark Maxwell's death was mourned by all"?

Are we under any obligation to believe that an infinite God sent two she bears to tear forty children in pieces because they laughed at a prophet without hair? Must we believe this because "Sir Gabriel Stokes is the living president of the Royal Society, and a Churchman" besides? Are we bound to believe that Daniel spent one of the happiest evenings of his life in the lion's den, because "Sir William Dawson of Canada, two years ago, presided over the British Association"? And must we believe in the ten plagues of Egypt, including the lice, because "Professor Max Müller made an eloquent plea in Westminster Abbey in favor of Christian missions"? Possibly he wanted missionaries to visit heathen lands so that they could see the difference for themselves between theory and practice, in what is known as the Christian religion.

Must we believe the miracles of the New Testament—the casting out of devils—because "Lord Tennyson and Mr. Browning stand far above all other poets of this generation in England," or because "Longfellow, Holmes, and Lowell and Whittier" occupy the same position in America? Must we admit that devils entered into swine because "Bancroft and Parkman are the leading prose writers of America"—which I take this occasion to deny?

It is to be hoped that some time the Archdeacon will read that portion of Mr. Bancroft's history in which he gives the account of how the soldiers, commonly called Hessians, were raised by the British Government during the American Revolution.

These poor wretches were sold at so much apiece. For every one that was killed, so much was paid, and for every one that was wounded a certain amount was given. Mr. Bancroft tells us that God was not satisfied with this business, and although he did not interfere in any way to save the poor soldiers, he did visit the petty tyrants who made the bargains with his wrath. I remember that as a punishment to one of these, his wife was induced to leave him; another one died a good many years afterwards; and several of them had exceedingly bad luck.

After reading this philosophic dissertation on the dealings of Providence, I doubt if the Archdeacon will still remain of the opinion that Mr. Bancroft is one of the leading prose writers of America. If the Archdeacon will read a few of the sermons of Theodore Parker, and essays of Ralph Waldo Emerson, if he will read the life of Voltaire by James Parton, he may change his opinion as to the great prose writers of America.

My argument against miracles is answered by reference to "Dr. Lightfoot, a man of such immense learning that he became the equal of his successor Dr. Westcott." And when I say that there *are errors* and imperfections in the Bible, I am told that Dr. Westcott "investigated the Christian religion and its earliest documents au fond, and was an orthodox believer." Of course the Archdeacon knows that no one now knows who wrote one of the books of the Bible. He knows that no one now lives who ever saw one of the original manuscripts, and that no one now lives who ever saw anybody who had seen anybody who had seen an original manuscript.

VI.

Is it possible for the human mind to conceive of an infinite personality?

The Archdeacon says that it is, and yet in the same article he quotes the following from Job: "Canst thou by searching find out God?" "It is as high as Heaven; what canst thou do? deeper than Hell; what canst thou know?" And immediately after making these quotations, the Archdeacon takes the ground of the agnostic, and says, "with the wise ancient Rabbis, we learn to say, *I do not know.*"

It is impossible for me to say what any other human being cannot conceive; but I am absolutely certain that my mind cannot conceive of an infinite personality—of an infinite Ego.

Man is conscious of his individuality. Man has wants. A multitude of things in nature seems to work against him; and others seem to be favorable to him. There is conflict between him and nature.

If man had no wants—if there were no conflict between him and any other being, or any other thing, he could not say "I"—that is to say, he could not be conscious of personality.

Now, it seems to me that an infinite personality is a contradiction in terms, says "I."

VII.

The same line of argument applies to the next statement that is criticized by the Archdeacon: *Can the human mind conceive a beginningless being?*

We know that there is such a thing as matter, but we do not know that there is a beginningless being. We say, or some say, that matter is eternal, because the human mind cannot conceive of its commencing. Now, if we knew of the existence of an Infinite Being, we could not conceive of his commencing. But we know of no such being. We do know of the existence of matter; and my mind is so, that I cannot conceive of that matter having been created by a beginningless being. I do not say that there is not a beginningless being, but I do not believe there is, and it is beyond my power to conceive of such a being.

The Archdeacon also says that "space is quite as impossible to conceive as God." But nobody pretends to love space—no one gives intention and will to space—no one, so far as I know, builds altars or temples to space. Now, if God is as inconceivable as space, why should we pray to God?

The Archdeacon, however, after quoting Sir William Hamilton as to the inconceivability of space as absolute or infinite, takes occasion to say that "space is an entity." May I be permitted to ask how he knows that space is an entity? As a matter of fact, the conception of infinite space is a necessity of the mind, the same as eternity is a necessity of the mind.

VIII.

The next sentence or statement to which the Archdeacon objects is as follows:

He who cannot harmonize the cruelties of the Bible with the goodness of Jehovah, cannot harmonize the cruelties of Nature with the goodness or wisdom of a supposed Deity. He will find it impossible to account for pestilence and famine, for earthquake and storm, for slavery, and for the triumph of the strong over the weak.

One objection that he urges to this statement is that St. Paul had made a stronger one in the same direction. The Archdeacon however insists that "a world without a contingency, or an agony, could have had no hero and no saint," and that "science enables us to demonstrate that much of the apparent misery and anguish is transitory and even phantasmal; that many of the seeming forces of destruction are overruled to ends of beneficence; that most of man's disease and anguish is due to his own sin and folly and willfulness."

I will not say that these things have been said before, but I will say that they have been answered before. The idea that the world is a school in which character is formed and in which men are educated is very old. If, however, the world is a school, and there is trouble and misfortune, and the object is to create character—that is to say, to produce heroes and saints—then the question arises, what becomes of those who die in infancy? They are left without the means of education. Are they to remain forever without character? Or is there some other world of suffering and sorrow?

Is it possible to form character in heaven? How did the angels become good? How do you account for the justice of God? Did he attain character through struggle and suffering?

What would you say of a school teacher who should kill one-third of the children on the morning of the first day? And what can you say of God,—if this world is a school,—who allows a large per cent, of his children to die in infancy—consequently without education—therefore, without character?

If the world is the result of infinite wisdom and goodness, why is the Christian Church engaged in endeavoring to make it better; or, rather, in an effort to change it? Why not leave it as an infinite God made it?

Is it true that most of man's diseases are due to his own sin and folly and willfulness? Is it not true that no matter how good men are they must die, and will they not die of diseases? Is it true that the wickedness of man has created the microbe? Is it possible that the sinfulness of man created the countless enemies of human life that lurk in air and water

481

and food? Certainly the wickedness of man has had very little influence on tornadoes, earthquakes and floods. Is it true that "the signature of beauty with which God has stamped the visible world—alike in the sky and on the earth—alike in the majestic phenomena of an intelligent creation and in its humblest and most microscopic production—is a perpetual proof that God is a God of love"?

Let us see. The scientists tell us that there is a little microscopic animal, one who is very particular about his food—so particular, that he prefers to all other things the optic nerve, and after he has succeeded in destroying that nerve and covering the eye with the mask of blindness, he has intelligence enough to bore his way through the bones of the nose in search of the other optic nerve. Is it not somewhat difficult to discover "the signature of beauty with which God has stamped" this animal? For my part, I see but little beauty in poisonous serpents, in man-eating sharks, in crocodiles, in alligators. It would be impossible for me to gaze with admiration upon a cancer. Think, for a moment, of a God ingenious enough and good enough to feed a cancer with the quivering flesh of a human being, and to give for the sustenance of that cancer the life of a mother.

It is well enough to speak of "the myriad voices of nature in their mirth and sweetness," and it is also well enough to think of the other side. The singing birds have a few notes of love—the rest are all of warning and of fear. Nature, apparently with infinite care, produces a living thing, and at the same time is just as diligently at work creating another living thing to devour the first, and at the same time a third to devour the second, and so on around the great circle of life and death, of agony and joy—tooth and claw, fang and tusk, hunger and rapine, massacre and murder, violence and vengeance and vice everywhere and through all time. [Here the manuscript ends, with the following notes.]

SAYINGS FROM THE INDIAN.

"The rain seems hardest when the wigwam leaks."

"When the tracks get too large and too numerous, the wise Indian says that he is hunting something else."

"A little crook in the arrow makes a great miss."

"A great chief counts scalps, not hairs."

"You cannot strengthen the bow by poisoning the arrows."

"No one saves water in a flood."

ORIGEN.

Origen considered that the punishment of the wicked consisted in separation from God. There was too much pity in his heart to believe in the flames of hell. But he was condemned as heretical by the Council of Carthage, A. D., 398, and afterwards by other councils.

ST. AUGUSTINE.

St. Augustine censures Origen for his merciful view, and says: "The church, not without reason, condemned him for this error." He also held that hell was in the centre of the earth, and that God supplied the centre with perpetual fire by a miracle.

DANTE.

Dante is a wonderful mixture of melancholy and malice, of religion and revenge, and he represents himself as so pitiless that when he found his political opponents in hell, he struck their faces and pulled the hair of the tormented.

AQUINAS.

Aquinas believed the same. He was the loving gentleman who believed in the undying worm.

IS CORPORAL PUNISHMENT DEGRADING?

This unfinished and unrevised article was found among Col. Ingersoll's papers, and is here reproduced without change.—It is a reply to the Dean of St Paul's Contribution to the *North American Review* for Dec., 1891, entitled: "Is Corporal Punishment Degrading?"

The Dean of St. Paul protests against the kindness of parents, guardians and teachers toward children, wards and pupils. He believes in the gospel of ferule and whips, and has perfect faith in the efficacy of flogging in homes and schools. He longs for the return of the good old days when fathers were severe, and children affectionate and obedient.

In America, for many years, even wife-beating has been somewhat unpopular, and the flogging of children has been considered cruel and unmanly. Wives with bruised and swollen faces, and children with lacerated backs, have excited pity for themselves rather than admiration for savage husbands and brutal fathers. It is also true that the church has far less power here than in England, and it may be that those who wander from the orthodox fold grow merciful and respect the rights even of the weakest.

But whatever the cause may be, the fact is that we, citizens of the Republic, feel that certain domestic brutalities are the children of monarchies and despotisms; that they were produced by superstition, ignorance, and savagery; and that they are not in accord with the free and superb spirit that founded and preserves the Great Republic.

Of late years, confidence in the power of kindness has greatly increased, and there is a wide-spread suspicion that cruelty and violence are not the instrumentalities of civilization.

Physicians no longer regard corporal punishment as a sure cure even for insanity—and it is generally admitted that the lash irritates rather than soothes the victim of melancholia.

Civilized men now insist that criminals cannot always be reformed even by the most ingenious instruments of torture. It is known that some convicts repay the smallest acts of kindness with the sincerest gratitude. Some of the best people go so far as to say that kindness is the sunshine in which the virtues grow. We know that for many ages governments tried to make men virtuous with dungeon and fagot and scaffold; that they tried to cure even disease of the mind with brandings and maimings and lashes on the naked flesh of men and women—and that kings endeavored to sow the seeds of patriotism—to plant and nurture them in the hearts of their subjects—with whip and chain.

In England, only a few years ago, there were hundreds of brave soldiers and daring sailors whose breasts were covered with honorable scars—witnesses of wounds received at Trafalgar and Balaklava—while on the backs of these same soldiers and sailors were the marks of

English whips. These shameless cruelties were committed in the name of discipline, and were upheld by officers, statesmen and clergymen. The same is true of nearly all civilized nations. These crimes have been excused for the reason that our ancestors were, at that time, in fact, barbarians—that they had no idea of justice, no comprehension of liberty, no conception of the rights of men, women, and children.

At that time the church was, in most countries, equal to, or superior to, the state, and was a firm believer in the civilizing influences of cruelty and torture.

According to the creeds of that day, God intended to torture the wicked forever, and the church, according to its power, did all that it could in the same direction. Learning their rights and duties from priests, fathers not only beat their children, but their wives. In those days most homes were penitentiaries, in which wives and children were the convicts and of which husbands and fathers were the wardens and turnkeys. The king imitated his supposed God, and imprisoned, flogged, branded, beheaded and burned his enemies, and the husbands and fathers imitated the king, and guardians and teachers imitated them.

Yet in spite of all the beatings and burnings, the whippings and hangings, the world was not reformed. Crimes increased, the cheeks of wives were furrowed with tears, the faces of children white with fear— fear of their own fathers; pity was almost driven from the heart of man and found refuge, for the most part, in the breasts of women, children, and dogs.

In those days, misfortunes were punished as crimes. Honest debtors were locked in loathsome dungeons, and trivial offences were punished with death. Worse than all that, thousands of men and women were destroyed, not because they were vicious, but because they were virtuous, honest and noble. Extremes beget obstructions. The victims at last became too numerous, and the result did not seem to justify the means. The good, the few, protested against the savagery of kings and fathers.

Nothing seems clearer to me than that the world has been gradually growing better for many years. Men have a clearer conception of rights and obligations—a higher philosophy—a far nobler ideal. Even kings admit that they should have some regard for the well-being of their subjects. Nations and individuals are slowly outgrowing the savagery of revenge, the desire to kill, and it is generally admitted that criminals should neither be imprisoned nor tortured for the gratification of the public. At last we are beginning to know that revenge is a mistake—that cruelty not only hardens the victim, but makes a criminal of him who inflicts it, and that mercy guided by intelligence is the highest form of justice.

The tendency of the world is toward kindness. The religious creeds are being changed or questioned, because they shock the heart of the present. All civilized churches, all humane Christians, have given up the dogma of eternal pain. This infamous doctrine has for many centuries polluted the imagination and hardened the heart. This coiled viper no longer inhabits the breast of a civilized man.

In all civilized countries slavery has been abolished, the honest debtor released, and all are allowed the liberty of speech.

Long ago flogging was abolished in our army and navy and all cruel and unusual punishments prohibited by law. In many parts of the Republic the whip has been banished from the public schools, the flogger of children is held in abhorrence, and the wife-beater is regarded as a cowardly criminal. The gospel of kindness is not only preached, but practiced. Such has been the result of this advance of civilization—of this growth of kindness—of this bursting into blossom of the flower called pity, in the heart—that we treat our horses (thanks to Henry Bergh) better than our ancestors did their slaves, their servants or their tenants. The gentlemen of to-day show more affection for their dogs than most of the kings of England exhibited toward their wives. The great tide is toward mercy; the savage creeds are being changed; heartless laws have been repealed; shackles have been broken; torture abolished, and the keepers of prisons are no longer allowed to bruise and scar the flesh of convicts. The insane are treated with kindness—asylums are in the midst of beautiful grounds, the rooms are filled with flowers, and the wandering mind is called back by the golden voice of music.

In the midst of these tendencies—of these accomplishments—in the general harmony between the minds of men, acting together, to the end that the world may be governed by kindness through education and the blessed agencies of reformation and prevention, the Dean of St. Paul raises his voice in favor of the methods and brutalities of the past.

The reverend gentleman takes the ground that the effect of flogging on the flogged is not degrading; that the effect of corporal punishment is ennobling; that it tends to make boys manly by ennobling and teaching them to bear bodily pain with fortitude. To be flogged develops character, self-reliance, courage, contempt of pain and the highest heroism. The Dean therefore takes the ground that parents should flog their children, guardians their wards, and teachers their pupils.

If the Dean is wrong he goes too far, and if he is right he does not go far enough. He does not advocate the flogging of children who obey their parents, or of pupils who violate no rule. It follows then that such children are in great danger of growing up unmanly, without the courage and fortitude to bear bodily pain. If flogging is really a blessing it should not be withheld from the good and lavished on the unworthy. The Dean should have the courage of his convictions. The teacher should not make a pretext of the misconduct of the pupil to do him a great service. He should not be guilty of calling a benefit a punishment He should not deceive the children under his care and develop their better natures under false pretences. But what is to become of the boys and girls who "behave themselves," who attend to their studies, and comply with the rules? They lose the benefits conferred on those who defy their parents and teachers, reach maturity without character, and so remain withered and worthless.

The Dean not only defends his position by an appeal to the Bible, the history of nations, but to his personal experience. In order to show the good effects of brutality and the bad consequences of kindness, he gives two instances that came under his observation. The first is that of an intelligent father who treated his sons with great kindness and yet these sons neglected their affectionate father in his old age. The second instance is that of a mother who beat her daughter. The wretched child, it seems, was sent out to gather sticks from the hedges, and when she brought home a large stick, the mother suspected that she had obtained it wrongfully and thereupon proceeded to beat the child. And yet the Dean tells us that this abused daughter treated the hyena mother with the greatest kindness, and loved her as no other daughter ever loved a mother. In order to make this case strong and convincing the Dean states that this mother was a most excellent Christian.

From these two instances the Dean infers, and by these two instances proves, that kindness breeds bad sons, and that flogging makes affectionate daughters. The Dean says to the Christian mother: "If you wish to be loved by your daughter, you must beat her." And to the Christian father he says: "If you want to be neglected in your old age by your sons, you will treat them with kindness." The Dean does not follow his logic to the end. Let me give him two instances that support his theory.

A good man married a handsome woman. He was old, rich, kind and indulgent. He allowed his wife to have her own way. He never uttered a cross or cruel word. He never thought of beating her. And yet, as the Dean would say, in consequence of his kindness, she poisoned him, got his money and married another man.

In this city, not long ago, a man, a foreigner, beat his wife according to his habit. On this particular occasion the punishment was excessive. He beat her until she became unconscious; she was taken to a hospital and the physician said that she could not live. The husband was brought to the hospital and preparations were made to take her dying statement. After being told that she was dying, she was asked if her husband had beaten her. Her face was so bruised and swollen that the lids of her eyes had to be lifted in order that she might see the wretch who had killed her. She beckoned him to her side—threw her arms about his neck—drew his face to hers—kissed him, and said: "He is not the man. He did not do it"—then—died.

According to the philosophy of the Dean, these instances show that kindness causes crime, and that wife-beating cultivates in the highest degree the affectional nature of woman.

The Dean, if consistent, is a believer in slavery, because the lash judiciously applied brings out the finer feelings of the heart. Slaves have been known to die for their masters, while under similar circumstances hired men have sought safety in flight.

We all know of many instances where the abused, the maligned, and the tortured have returned good for evil—and many instances where the loved, the honored, and the trusted have turned against their benefactors, and yet we know that cruelty and torture are not superior to love and kindness. Yet, the Dean tries to show that severity is the real mother of affection, and that kindness breeds monsters. If kindness and affection on the part of parents demoralize children, will not kindness and affection on the part of children demoralize the parents?

When the children are young and weak, the parents who are strong beat the children in order that they may be affectionate. Now, when the children get strong and the parents are old and weak, ought not the children to beat them, so that they too may become kind and loving?

If you want an affectionate son, beat him. If you desire a loving wife, beat her.

This is really the advice of the Dean of St Paul. To me it is one of the most pathetic facts in nature that wives and children love husbands and fathers who are utterly unworthy. It is enough to sadden a life to think of the affection that has been lavished upon the brutal, of the countless pearls that Love has thrown to swine.

The Dean, quoting from Hooker, insists that "the voice of man is as the sentence of God himself,"—in other words, that the general voice, practice and opinion of the human race are true.

And yet, cannibalism, slavery, polygamy, the worship of snakes and stones, the sacrifice of babes, have during vast periods of time been practiced and upheld by an overwhelming majority of mankind. Whether the "general voice" can be depended on depends much on the time, the epoch, during which the "general voice" was uttered. There was a time when the "general voice" was in accord with the appetite of man; when all nations were cannibals and lived on each other, and yet it can hardly be said that this voice and appetite were in exact accord with divine goodness. It is hardly safe to depend on the "general voice" of savages, no matter how numerous they may have been. Like most people who defend the cruel and absurd, the Dean appeals to the Bible as the supreme authority in the moral world,—and yet if the English Parliament should re-enact the Mosaic Code every member voting in the affirmative would be subjected to personal violence, and an effort to enforce that code would produce a revolution that could end only in the destruction of the government.

The morality of the Old Testament is not always of the purest; when Jehovah tried to induce Pharaoh to let the Hebrews go, he never took the ground that slavery was wrong. He did not seek to convince by argument, to soften by pity, or to persuade by kindness. He depended on miracles and plagues. He killed helpless babes and the innocent beasts of the fields. No wonder the Dean appeals to the Bible to justify the beating of children. So, too, we are told that "all sensible persons, Christian and otherwise, will admit that there are in every child born into the world tendencies to evil that need rooting out."

The Dean undoubtedly believes in the creed of the established church, and yet he does not hesitate to say that a God of infinite goodness and intelligence never created a child—never allowed one to be born into the world without planting in its little heart "tendencies to evil that need rooting out."

So, Solomon is quoted to the effect "that he that spareth his rod hateth his son." To me it has always been a matter of amazement why civilized people, living in the century of Darwin and Humboldt, should quote as authority the words of Solomon, a murderer, an ingrate, an idolater, and a polygamist—a man so steeped and sodden in ignorance that he really believed he could be happy with seven hundred wives and three hundred concubines. The Dean seems to regret that flogging is no longer practiced in the British navy, and quotes with great cheerfulness a passage from Deuteronomy to prove that forty lashes on the naked back will meet with the approval of God. He insists that St. Paul endured corporal punishment without the feeling of degradation not only, but that he remembered his sufferings with a sense of satisfaction. Does the Dean think that the satisfaction of St. Paul justified the wretches who beat and stoned him? Leaving the Hebrews, the Dean calls the Greeks as witnesses to establish the beneficence of flogging. They resorted to corporal punishment in their schools, says the Dean and then naively remarks "that Plutarch was opposed to this."

The Dean admits that in Rome it was found necessary to limit by law the punishment that a father might inflict upon his children, and yet he seems to regret that the legislature interfered. The Dean observes that "Quintillian severely censured corporal punishment" and then accounts for the weakness and folly of the censure, by saying that "Quintillian wrote in the days when the glories of Rome were departed." And then adds these curiously savage words: "It is worthy of remark that no children treated their parents with greater tenderness and reverence than did those of Rome in the days when the father possessed the unlimited power of punishment."

Not quite satisfied with the strength of his case although sustained by Moses and Solomon, St. Paul and several schoolmasters, he proceeds to show that God is thoroughly on his side, not only in theory, but in practice; "whom the Lord loveth lie chasteneth, and scourgeth every soul whom he receiveth.".

The Dean asks this question: "Which custom, kindness or severity, does experience show to be the less dangerous?" And he answers from a new heart: "I fear that I must unhesitatingly give the palm to severity."

"I have found that there have been more reverence and affection, more willingness to make sacrifices for parents, more pleasure in contributing to their pleasure or happiness in that life where the tendency has been to a severe method of treatment."

Is it possible that any good mail exists who is willing to gain the affection of his children in that way? How could such a man beat and bruise the flesh of his babes, knowing that they would give him in return obedience and love; that they would fill the evening of his days—the leafless winter of his life—with perfect peace?

Think of being fed and clothed by children you had whipped—whose flesh you had scarred! Think of feeling in the hour of death upon your withered lips, your withered cheeks, the kisses and the tears of one whom, you had beaten—upon whose flesh were still the marks of your lash!

The whip degrades; a severe father teaches his children to dissemble; their love is pretence, and their obedience a species of self-defense. Fear is the father of lies.